CLYMER®
MANUALS

HARLEY-DAVIDSON
SPORTSTER • 1959-1985

WHAT'S IN YOUR TOOLBOX?

YouTube™

More information available at Clymer.com
Phone: 805-498-6703

Haynes Publishing Group
Sparkford Nr Yeovil
Somerset BA22 7JJ England

Haynes North America, Inc
861 Lawrence Drive
Newbury Park
California 91320 USA

ISBN 10: 0-89287-126-1
ISBN-13: 978-0-89287-126-1

Printed in the U.S.A.

M419, 3S1, 14-384 **ABCDEFGHIJKLMNOPQRS**

Common spark plug conditions

NORMAL

Symptoms: Brown to grayish-tan color and slight electrode wear. Correct heat range for engine and operating conditions.
Recommendation: When new spark plugs are installed, replace with plugs of the same heat range.

WORN

Symptoms: Rounded electrodes with a small amount of deposits on the firing end. Normal color. Causes hard starting in damp or cold weather and poor fuel economy.
Recommendation: Plugs have been left in the engine too long. Replace with new plugs of the same heat range. Follow the recommended maintenance schedule.

CARBON DEPOSITS

Symptoms: Dry sooty deposits indicate a rich mixture or weak ignition. Causes misfiring, hard starting and hesitation.
Recommendation: Make sure the plug has the correct heat range. Check for a clogged air filter or problem in the fuel system or engine management system. Also check for ignition system problems.

ASH DEPOSITS

Symptoms: Light brown deposits encrusted on the side or center electrodes or both. Derived from oil and/or fuel additives. Excessive amounts may mask the spark, causing misfiring and hesitation during acceleration.
Recommendation: If excessive deposits accumulate over a short time or low mileage, install new valve guide seals to prevent seepage of oil into the combustion chambers. Also try changing gasoline brands.

OIL DEPOSITS

Symptoms: Oily coating caused by poor oil control. Oil is leaking past worn valve guides or piston rings into the combustion chamber. Causes hard starting, misfiring and hesitation.
Recommendation: Correct the mechanical condition with necessary repairs and install new plugs.

GAP BRIDGING

Symptoms: Combustion deposits lodge between the electrodes. Heavy deposits accumulate and bridge the electrode gap. The plug ceases to fire, resulting in a dead cylinder.
Recommendation: Locate the faulty plug and remove the deposits from between the electrodes.

TOO HOT

Symptoms: Blistered, white insulator, eroded electrode and absence of deposits. Results in shortened plug life.
Recommendation: Check for the correct plug heat range, over-advanced ignition timing, lean fuel mixture, intake manifold vacuum leaks, sticking valves and insufficient engine cooling.

PREIGNITION

Symptoms: Melted electrodes. Insulators are white, but may be dirty due to misfiring or flying debris in the combustion chamber. Can lead to engine damage.
Recommendation: Check for the correct plug heat range, over-advanced ignition timing, lean fuel mixture, insufficient engine cooling and lack of lubrication.

HIGH SPEED GLAZING

Symptoms: Insulator has yellowish, glazed appearance. Indicates that combustion chamber temperatures have risen suddenly during hard acceleration. Normal deposits melt to form a conductive coating. Causes misfiring at high speeds.
Recommendation: Install new plugs. Consider using a colder plug if driving habits warrant.

DETONATION

Symptoms: Insulators may be cracked or chipped. Improper gap setting techniques can also result in a fractured insulator tip. Can lead to piston damage.
Recommendation: Make sure the fuel anti-knock values meet engine requirements. Use care when setting the gaps on new plugs. Avoid lugging the engine.

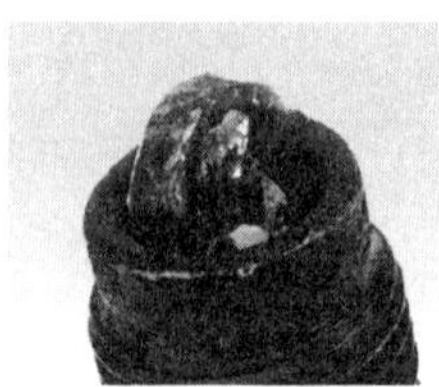

MECHANICAL DAMAGE

Symptoms: May be caused by a foreign object in the combustion chamber or the piston striking an incorrect reach (too long) plug. Causes a dead cylinder and could result in piston damage.
Recommendation: Repair the mechanical damage. Remove the foreign object from the engine and/or install the correct reach plug.

CONTENTS

QUICK REFERENCE DATA

TIRE PRESSURE[1]

	Front	Rear
1959-1969		
XLCH, 1959-1966 XLH	14	18
1967-1969 XLH	16	20
1970-1978[2]	24	30
1979-1983		
Up to 300 lb. load	24 psi	26 psi
Over 300 lb. load	25 psi	28 psi
1984-1985		
Up to 300 lb. load	24	26
Over 300 lb. load	26	32

1. Tire pressures based on 150 lb. rider weight. For each extra 50 lb., add 2 psi @ rear, 1 psi @ front.
2. Maximum tire pressure for all tires is 32 psi.

ENGINE AND TRANSMISSION OIL CAPACITIES

	Quantity
Oil tank	
1959-1978	3 quarts
1979-1981	4 quarts
1982-on	3 quarts
Transmission	1.5 pints

TUNE-UP SPECIFICATIONS

Breaker point gap	
1959-1969	
Battery ignition	0.020 in.
Magneto ignition	0.015 in.
1970	0.020 in.
1971-1978	0.018 in.
Dwell	
1959-1969	90° @ 1,000 rpm
1970-1971	90° @ 2,000 rpm
1972-1978	140° @ 2,000 rpm
Ignition timing	
1959-1969	
Advanced	
XLH, XLCH	45° BTDC
Retarded	
XLH	15° BTDC
1970-1971	
Advanced	45° BTDC
Retarded	15° BTDC
1972-1978	
Advanced	40° BTDC
Retarded	10° BTDC
1979-1985	Electronic
Compresssion	120 psi

SPARK PLUG TYPE AND GAP

	Type	Gap
1959-1969		
Average use	H-D 4	0.020 in.[1]/0.025-0.030 in.[2]
Hard use	H-D 5	0.020 in.[1]/0.025-0.030 in.[2]
1970-1978		
Average use	H-D 4	0.025-0.030 in.
Hard use	H-D 5	0.025-0.030 in.
1979	H-D 4	0.060 in.
1980-1982	H-D 4-5	0.038-0.045 in.
1980-1982	H-D 4R5[3]	0.038-0.045 in.
1983-1985	H-D 4R5[3]	0.038-0.045 in.

1. Magneto ignition.
2. Battery ignition.
3. Harley-Davidson spark plugs 4R5 are special resistor plugs to reduce radio interference originating in the motorcycle ignition system. These plugs are recommended for all 1980 and later models with electronic ignition.

FRONT FORK OIL CAPACITY*

	Quantity
1959-1967	
Wet	3 1/2 oz.
Dry	4 1/2 oz.
1968-1969	
Wet	4 1/2 oz.
Dry	5 1/2 oz.
1970-1972	
Wet	5 1/2 oz.
Dry	6 1/2 oz.
1973-1983	
Wet	5 oz.
Dry	6 oz.
1984-1985	
Wet	5.4 oz.
Dry	6.4 oz.

*Use "dry" quantity if fork has been disassembled. Otherwise, use "wet" quantity.

QUICK INDEX

CHAPTER ONE

GENERAL INFORMATION

Troubleshooting, tune-up, maintenance and repair are not difficult, if you know what tools and equipment to use and what to do. Anyone of average intelligence and with some mechanical ability can perform most of the procedures in this manual.

Due to the large number of engine and chassis combinations used over the period covered by this manual, many of the procedures provided are somewhat general in nature and may require some interpretation. Every effort has been made, however, to be as specific as possible.

It is important to note also, that because of the parts interchangeability with Harley-Davidson motorcycles, your model, if purchased second hand, may be equipped with parts different from its original equipment.

Some of the procedures require the use of special tools. Using an inferior substitute tool for a special tool is not recommended, as it can be dangerous to you and may damage the part. Where possible, we have devised suitable special tools that can be fabricated in your garage or by a machinist or purchased at motorcycle or tool stores.

MANUAL ORGANIZATION

U.S. standards are used throughout this manual. Metric to U.S. conversion is given in **Table 1**.

This chapter provides general information and discusses equipment and tools useful both for preventive maintenance and troubleshooting.

Chapter Two provides methods and suggestions for quick and accurate diagnosis and repair of problems. Troubleshooting procedures discuss typical symptoms and logical methods to pinpoint the trouble.

Chapter Three explains all periodic lubrication and routine maintenance necessary to keep your Harley-Davidson operating well. Chapter Three also includes recommended tune-up procedures, eliminating the need to constantly consult other chapters on the various assemblies.

Subsequent chapters describe specific systems such as the engine, clutch, primary drive, transmission, fuel system, exhaust system, suspension, steering and brakes. Each chapter provides disassembly, repair and assembly procedures in simple step-by-step form. If a repair is impractical for a home mechanic, it is so indicated. It is usually faster and less expensive to take such repairs to a dealer or competent repair shop. Specifications concerning a particular system are included at the end of the appropriate chapter.

NOTES, CAUTIONS AND WARNINGS

The terms NOTE, CAUTION and WARNING have specific meanings in this manual. A NOTE provides additional information to make a step or procedure easier or clearer. Disregarding a NOTE could cause inconvenience, but would not cause damage or personal injury.

A CAUTION emphasizes areas where equipment damage could occur. Disregarding a CAUTION could cause permanent mechanical damage; however, personal injury is unlikely.

A WARNING emphasizes areas where personal injury or even death could result from negligence. Mechanical damage may also occur. WARNINGS *are to be taken seriously.* In some cases, serious injury and death have resulted from disregarding similar warnings.

SAFTEY FIRST

Professional mechanics can work for years and never sustain a serious injury. If you observe a few rules of common sense and safety, you can enjoy many safe hours servicing your own machine. If you ignore these rules you can hurt yourself or damage the equipment.

1. Never use gasoline as a cleaning solvent.
2. Never smoke or use a torch in the vicinity of flammable liquids, such as cleaning solvent, in open containers.
3. If welding or brazing is required on the machine, remove the fuel tank and rear shocks to a safe distance, at least 50 feet away. Welding on a gas tank requires special safety precautions and must be performed by someone skilled in the process. Do not attempt to weld or braze a leaking gas tank.
4. Use the proper sized wrenches to avoid damage to nuts and injury to yourself.
5. When loosening a tight or stuck nut, be guided by what would happen if the wrench should slip. Be careful; protect yourself accordingly.
6. When replacing a fastener, make sure to use one with the same measurements and strength as the old one. Incorrect or mismatched fasteners can result in damage to the vehicle and possible personal injury. Beware of fastener kits that are filled with cheap and poorly made nuts, bolts, washers and cotter pins. Refer to *Fasteners* in this chapter for additional information.
7. Keep all hand and power tools in good condition. Wipe greasy and oily tools after using them. They are difficult to hold and can cause injury. Replace or repair worn or damaged tools.
8. Keep your work area clean and uncluttered.
9. Wear safety goggles during all operations involving drilling, grinding, the use of a cold chisel or anytime you feel unsure about the safety of your eyes. Safety goggles should also be worn anytime compressed air is used to clean a part.
10. Keep an approved fire extinguisher nearby. Be sure it is rated for gasoline (Class B) and electrical (Class C) fires.
11. When drying bearings or other rotating parts with compressed air, never allow the air jet to rotate the bearing or part; the air jet is capable of rotating them at speeds far in excess of those for which they were designed. The bearing or rotating part is very likely to disintegrate and cause serious injury and damage.

SERVICE HINTS

Most of the service procedures covered are straightforward and can be performed by anyone reasonably handy with tools. It is suggested, however, that you consider your own capabilities carefully before attempting any operation involving major disassembly of the engine or transmission.

1. "Front," as used in this manual, refers to the front of the motorcycle; the front of any component is the end closest to the front of the motorcycle. The "left-" and "right-hand" sides refer to the positions of parts as viewed by a rider sitting on the seat facing forward. For example, the throttle control is on the right-hand side. These rules are simple, but confusion can cause a major inconvenience during service.
2. Whenever servicing the engine or transmission, or when removing a suspension component, the bike should be secured in a safe manner. If the bike is to be parked on its sidestand, check the stand to make sure it is secure and not damaged. Block the front and rear wheels if they remain on the ground. A small hydraulic jack and a block of wood can be used to raise the chassis. If the transmission is not going to be worked on and the drive chain or drive belt is connected to the the rear wheel, shift the transmission into first gear.
3. Disconnect the negative battery cable when working on or near the electrical, clutch or starter systems and before disconnecting any wires. On most batteries, the negative terminal will be marked with a minus (-) sign and the positive terminal with a plus (+) sign.
4. When disassembling a part, it is a good practice to tag the parts for location and mark all parts which mate together. Small parts, such as bolts, can be identified by placing them in plastic sandwich bags. Seal the bags and label them with masking tape and a marking pen. When reassembly will take place immediately, an accepted practice is to place nuts and bolts in a cupcake tin or egg carton in the order of disassembly.
5. Finished surfaces should be protected from physical damage or corrosion. Keep gasoline and brake fluid off painted surfaces.
6. Use penetrating oil on frozen or tight bolts, then strike the bolt head a few times with a hammer and punch (use a screwdriver on screws). Avoid the use of heat where possible, as it can warp, melt or affect

the temper of parts. Heat also ruins finishes, especially paint and plastics.

7. Keep flames and sparks away from a charging battery or flammable liquids and do not smoke in the area. It is a good idea to have a fire extinguisher handy in the work area. Remember that many gas appliances in home garages (water heater, clothes drier, etc.) have pilot lights.

8. No parts removed or installed (other than bushings and bearings) in the procedures given in this manual should require unusual force during disassembly or assembly. If a part is difficult to remove or install, find out why before proceeding.

9. Cover all openings after removing parts to prevent dirt, small tools, etc. from falling in.

10. Read each procedure *completely* while looking at the actual parts before starting a job. Make sure you *thoroughly* understand what is to be done and then carefully follow the procedure, step by step.

11. Recommendations are occasionally made to refer service or maintenance to a Harley-Davidson dealer or a specialist in a particular field. In these cases, the work will be done more quickly and economically than if you performed the job yourself. Some operations, for example, require the use of a hydraulic press. It would be wiser to have these operations performed by a shop equipped for such work, rather than to try to do the job yourself with makeshift equipment that may damage your machine.

12. In procedural steps, the term "replace" means to discard a defective part and replace it with a new or exchange unit. "Overhaul" means to remove, disassemble, inspect, measure, repair or replace defective parts, reassemble and install major systems or parts.

13. Repairs go much faster and easier if your machine is clean before you begin work. There are many special cleaners on the market, like Bel-Ray Degreaser, for washing the engine and related parts.

Just follow the manufacturer's directions on the container for the best results. Clean all oily or greasy parts with cleaning solvent as you remove them.

WARNING

Never use gasoline as a cleaning agent. It presents an extreme fire hazard. Be sure to work in a well-ventilated area when using cleaning solvent. Keep a fire extinguisher, rated for gasoline fires, handy in any case.

14. Much of the labor charged for repairs made by dealers is for the labor hours involved during the removal, disassembly, assembly, and reinstallation of other parts in order to reach the defective part. It is frequently possible to perform the preliminary operations yourself and then take the defective unit to the dealer for repair at considerable savings.

15. If special tools are required, make arrangements to get them before you start. It is frustrating and time-consuming to get partly into a job and then be unable to complete it.

16. Make diagrams (or take a Polaroid picture) wherever similar-appearing parts are found. For instance, crankcase bolts are often not the same length. You may think you can remember where everything came from, but mistakes are costly. There is also the possibility that you may be sidetracked and not return to work for days or even weeks—in which the carefully laid out parts may have become disturbed.

17. When assembling parts, be sure all shims and washers are replaced exactly as they came out.

18. Whenever a rotating part butts against a stationary part, look for a shim or washer. Use new gaskets if there is any doubt about the condition of the old ones. A thin coat of oil on non-pressure type gaskets may help them seal more effectively.

19. If it is necessary to make a gasket and you do not have a suitable old gasket to use as a guide, apply engine oil to the gasket surface of the part. Then place the part on the new gasket material and press the part slightly. The oil will leave a very accurate outline on the gasket material that can be cut around.

20. Heavy grease can be used to hold small parts in place if they tend to fall out during assembly. However, keep grease and oil away from electrical and brake components.

21. A carburetor is best cleaned by disassembling it and soaking the parts in a commercial carburetor cleaner. Never soak gaskets and rubber parts in these cleaners. Never use wire to clean out jets and air passages unless otherwise instructed to do so in Chapter Six. They are easily damaged. Use compressed air to blow out the carburetor only if the float has been removed first.

22. Take your time and do the job right. Do not forget that a newly rebuilt engine must be broken in just like a new one.

TORQUE SPECIFICATIONS

Torque specifications throughout this manual are given in foot-pounds (ft.-lb.).

Table 2 lists general torque specifications for nuts and bolts that are not listed in the respective chapters. To use the table, first determine the size

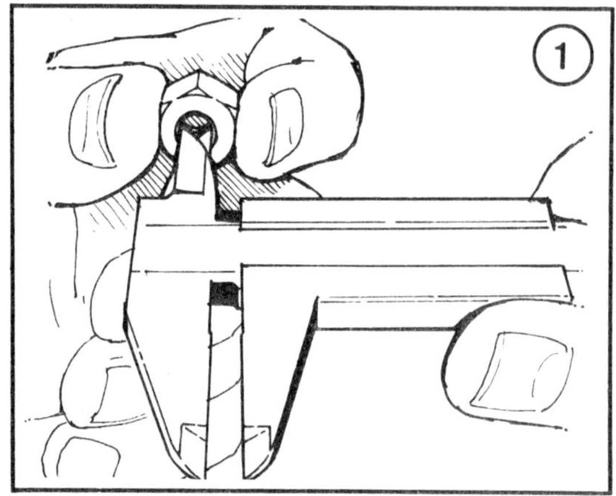

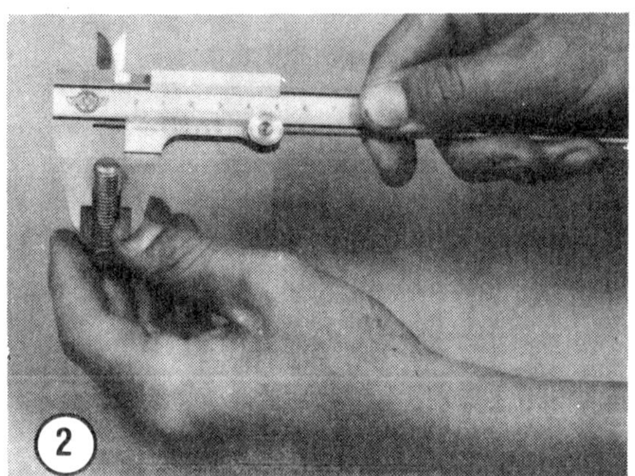

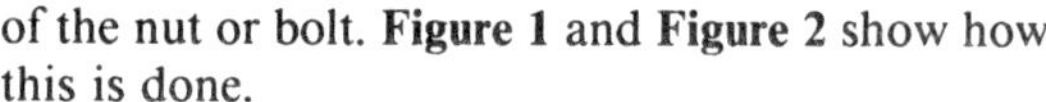

of the nut or bolt. **Figure 1** and **Figure 2** show how this is done.

FASTENERS

The materials and designs of the various fasteners used on your Harley-Davidson are not arrived at by chance or accident. Fastener design determines the type of tool required to work the fastener. Fastener material is carefully selected to decrease the possibility of physical failure.

Threads

Nuts, bolts and screws are manufactured in a wide range of thread patterns. To join a nut and bolt, the diameter of the bolt and the diameter of the hole in the nut must be the same. It is just as important that the threads on both be properly matched.

The best way to tell if the threads on 2 fasteners are matched is to turn the nut on the bolt (or the bolt into the threaded hole in a piece of equipment) with fingers only. Be sure both pieces are clean. If much force is required, check the thread condition on each fastener. If the thread condition is good but the fasteners jam, the threads are not compatible. A thread pitch gauge can also be used to determine threads per inch.

Four important specifications describe every thread:

a. Diameter.
b. Threads per inch.
c. Thread pattern.
d. Thread direction.

Figure 3 shows the first 2 specifications. Thread pattern is more subtle. Italian and British standards exist, but the most commonly used by motorcycle manufacturers are metric standard and American standard. Harley-Davidsons are manufactured with American standard fasteners.

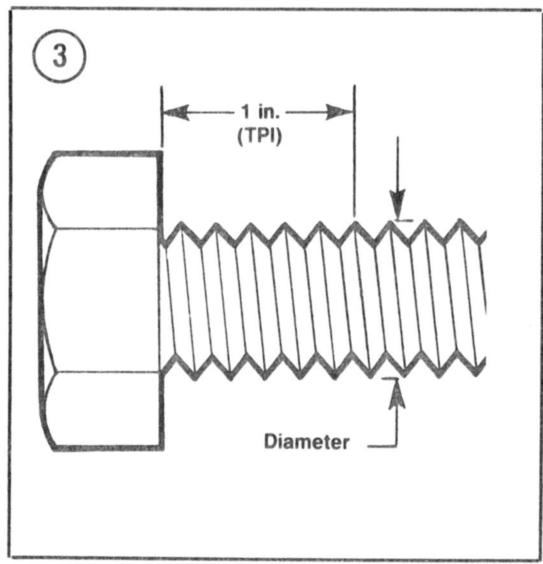

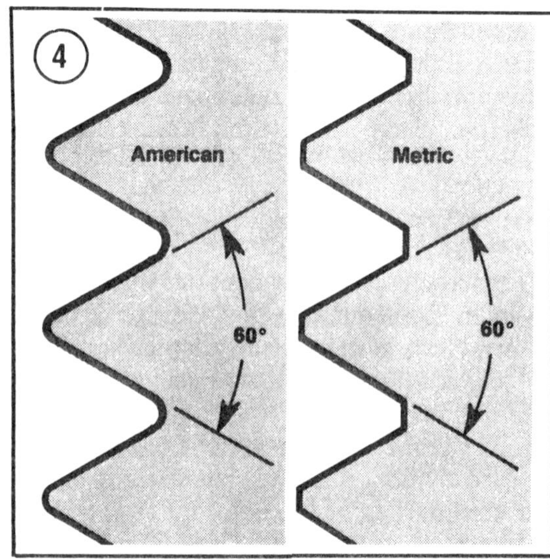

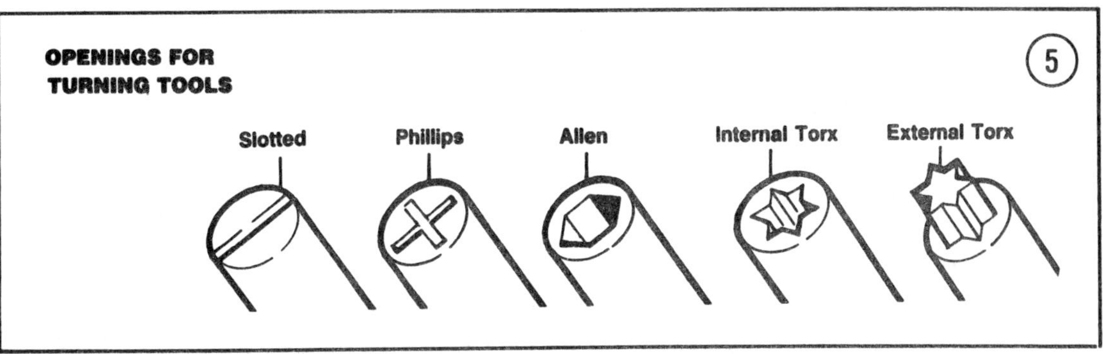

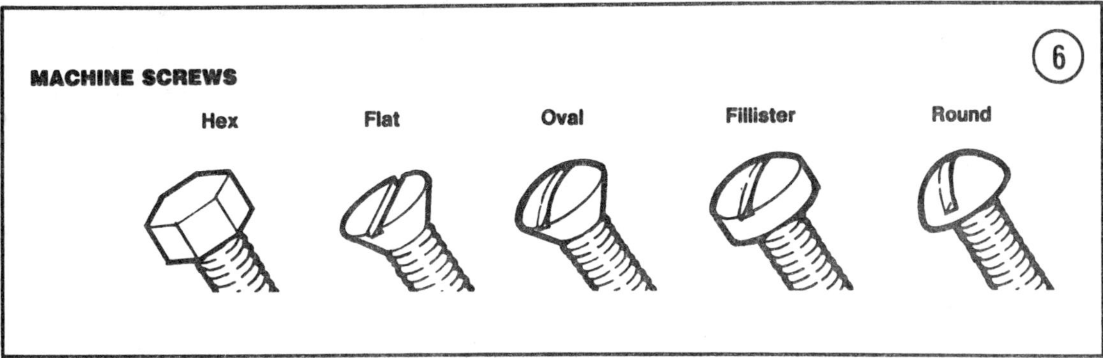

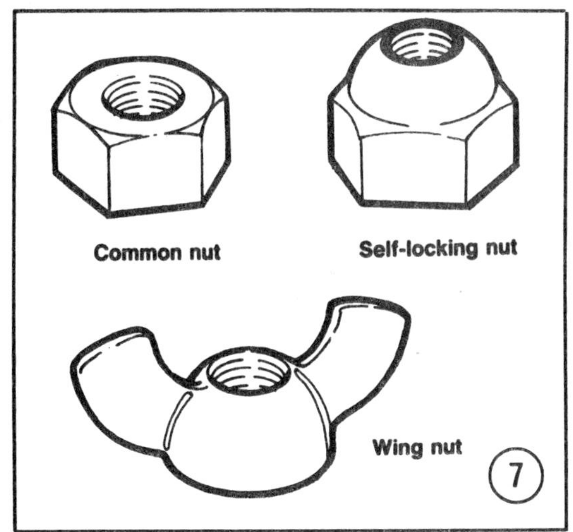

The threads are cut differently as shown in **Figure 4**.

Most threads are cut so that the fastener must be turned clockwise to tighten it. These are called right-hand threads. Some fasteners have left-hand threads; they must be turned counterclockwise to be tightened. Left-hand threads are used in locations where normal rotation of the equipment would tend to loosen a right-hand threaded fastener.

Machine Screws

There are many different types of machine screws. **Figure 5** shows a number of screw heads requiring different types of turning tools. Heads are also designed to protrude above the metal (round) or to be slightly recessed in the metal (flat). See **Figure 6**.

Bolts

Commonly called bolts, the technical name for these fasteners is cap screw. They are normally described by diameter, threads per inch and length. For example, 1/4-20×1 indicates a bolt 1/4 in. in diameter with 20 threads per inch, 1 inch long. The measurement across 2 flats on the head of the bolt indicates the proper wrench size to be used. **Figure 2** shows how to determine bolt diameter.

Nuts

Nuts are manufactured in a variety of types and sizes. Most are hexagonal (6-sided) and fit on bolts, screws and studs with the same diameter and threads per inch.

Figure 7 shows several types of nuts. The common nut is generally used with a lockwasher. Self-locking nuts have a nylon insert which prevents the nut from loosening; no lockwasher is required. Wing nuts are designed for fast removal by hand. Wing nuts are used for convenience in non-critical locations.

To indicate the size of a nut, manufacturers specify the diameter of the opening and the threads per inch. This is similar to bolt specifications, but without the length dimension. The measurement of the inside bore (**Figure 1**) indicates the proper wrench size to be used.

Self-Locking Fasteners

Several types of bolts, screws and nuts incorporate a system that develops an interference between the bolt or screw, and nut or tapped hole threads. Interference is achieved in various ways: by distorting threads, coating threads with dry adhesive or nylon, distorting the top of an all-metal nut, using a nylon insert in the center or at the top of a nut, etc.

Prevailing torque fasteners offer greater holding strength and better vibration resistance. Some prevailing torque fasteners can be reused if in good condition; others, like the nylon insert nut, form an initial locking condition when the nut is first installed; the nylon forms closely to the bolt thread pattern, thus reducing any tendency for the nut to loosen. When the nut is removed, the locking efficiency is greatly reduced. For greatest safety, it is recommended that you install new prevailing torque fasteners whenever they are removed.

Washers

There are 2 basic types of washers: flat washers and lockwashers. Flat washers are simple discs with a hole to fit a screw or bolt. Lockwashers are designed to prevent a fastener from working loose due to vibration, expansion and contraction. **Figure 8** shows several types of washers. Washers are also used in the following functions:

a. As spacers.
b. To prevent galling or damage of the equipment by the fastener.
c. To help distribute fastener load during torquing.
d. As seals.

Note that flat washers are often used between a lockwasher and a fastener to provide a smooth bearing surface. This allows the fastener to be turned easily with a tool.

Cotter Pins

Cotter pins (**Figure 9**) are used to secure special kinds of fasteners. The threaded stud must have a hole in it; the nut or nut lock piece has castellations around which the cotter pin ends wrap. Cotter pins should not be reused after removal.

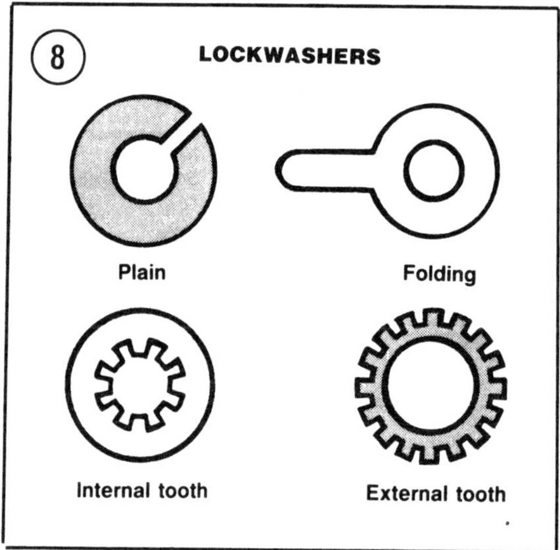

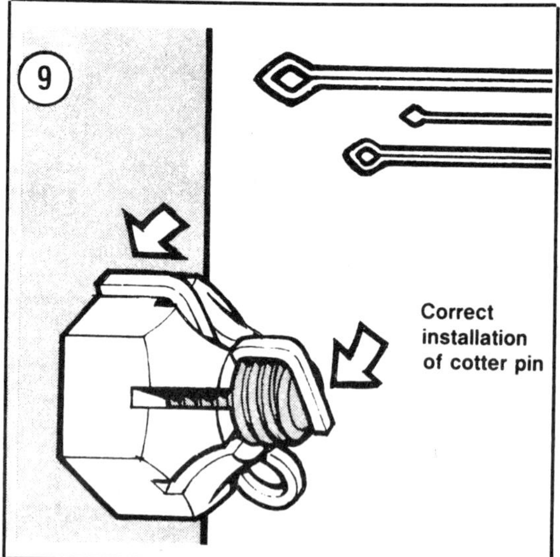

Snap Rings

Snap rings can be of internal or external design. They are used to retain items on shafts (external type) or within tubes (internal type). In some applications, snap rings of varying thicknesses are used to control the end play of parts assemblies. These are often called selective snap rings. Snap rings should be replaced during installation, as removal weakens and deforms them.

Two basic styles of snap ring are available: machined and stamped snap rings. Machined snap rings (**Figure 10**) can be installed in either direction (shaft or housing) because both faces are machined, thus creating two sharp edges. Stamped snap rings (**Figure 11**) are manufactured with one sharp edge

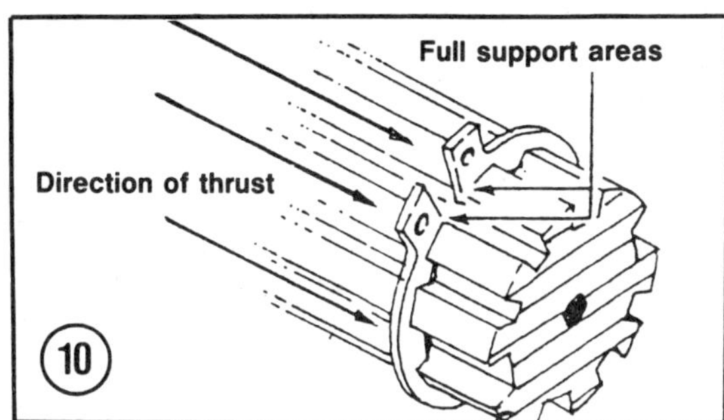

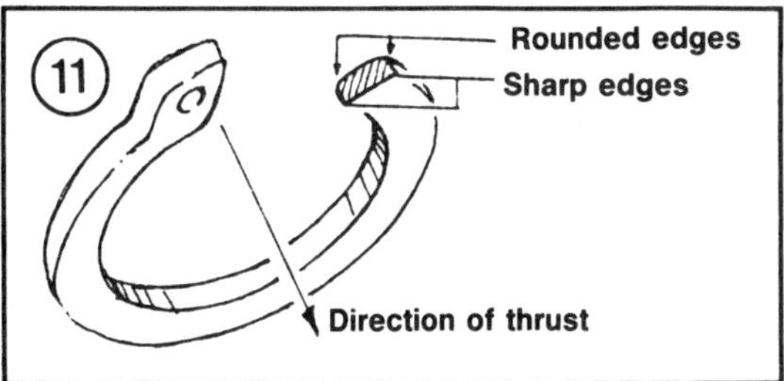

and one rounded edge. When installing stamped snap rings in a thrust situation (transmission shafts, fork tubes, etc.), the sharp edge must face away from the part producing the thrust. When installing snap rings, observe the following:

a. Compress or expand snap rings only enough to install them.
b. After the snap ring is installed, make sure it is completely seated in its groove.

LUBRICANTS

Periodic lubrication assures long life for any type of equipment. The *type* of lubricant used is just as important as the lubrication service itself, although in an emergency the wrong type of lubricant is better than none at all. The following paragraphs describe the types of lubricants most often used on motorcycle equipment. Be sure to follow the manufacturer's recommendations for lubricant types.

Generally, all liquid lubricants are called "oil." They may be mineral-based (including petroleum bases), natural-based (vegetable and animal bases), synthetic-based or emulsions (mixtures). "Grease" is an oil to which a thickening base has been added so that the end product is semi-solid. Grease is often classified by the type of thickener added; lithium soap is commonly used.

Engine Oil

Oil for motorcycle and automotive engines is graded by the American Petroleum Institute (API) and the Society of Automotive Engineers (SAE) in several categories. Oil containers display these ratings on the top or label.

API oil grade is indicated by letters; oils for gasoline engines are identified by an "S." The engines covered in this manual require SE or SF graded oil.

Viscosity is an indication of the oil's thickness. The SAE uses numbers to indicate viscosity; thin oils have low numbers while thick oils have high numbers. A "W" after the number indicates that the viscosity testing was done at low temperature to simulate cold-weather operation. Engine oils fall into the 5W-30 and 20W-50 range.

Multi-grade oils (for example 10W-40) are less viscous (thinner) at low temperatures and more viscous (thicker) at high temperatures. This allows the oil to perform efficiently across a wide range of engine operating conditions. The lower the number, the better the engine will start in cold climates. Higher numbers are usually recommended for use in hot weather conditions.

Grease

Greases are graded by the National Lubricating Grease Institute (NLGI). Greases are graded by number according to the consistency of the grease; these range from No. 000 to No. 6, with No. 6 being the most solid. A typical multipurpose grease is NLGI No. 2. For specific applications, equipment manufacturers may require grease with an additive such as molybdenum disulfide (MOS2).

PARTS REPLACEMENT

Harley-Davidson makes frequent changes during a model year, some minor, some relatively major. When you order parts from the dealer or other parts distributor, always order by engine and frame number. Write the numbers down and carry them with you. Compare new parts to old before purchasing them. If they are not alike, have the parts manager explain the difference to you.

BASIC HAND TOOLS

Many of the procedures in this manual can be carried out with simple hand tools and test equipment familiar to the average home mechanic. Keep your tools clean and in a tool box. Keep them organized with the sockets and related drives together, the open-end and combination wrenches together, etc. After using a tool, wipe off dirt and grease with a clean cloth and return the tool to its correct place.

Top quality tools are essential; they are also more economical in the long run. If you are now starting to build your tool collection, stay away from the "advertised specials" featured at some parts houses, discount stores and chain drug stores. These are usually a poor grade tool that can be sold cheaply and that is exactly what they are—*cheap*. They are usually made of inferior material and are thick, heavy and clumsy. Their rough finish makes them difficult to clean and they usually don't last very long. If it is ever your misfortune to use such tools, you will probably find out that the wrenches do not fit the heads of bolts and nuts correctly and damage the fastener.

Quality tools are made of alloy steel and are heat treated for greater strength. They are lighter and better balanced than cheap ones. Their surface is smooth, making them a pleasure to work with and easy to clean. The initial cost of good quality tools may be more but it is cheaper in the long run. Don't try to buy everything in all sizes in the beginning; do it a little at a time until you have the necessary tools. To sum up tool buying, "...the bitterness of poor quality lingers long after the sweetness of low price has faded."

The following tools are required to perform virtually any repair job. Each tool is described and

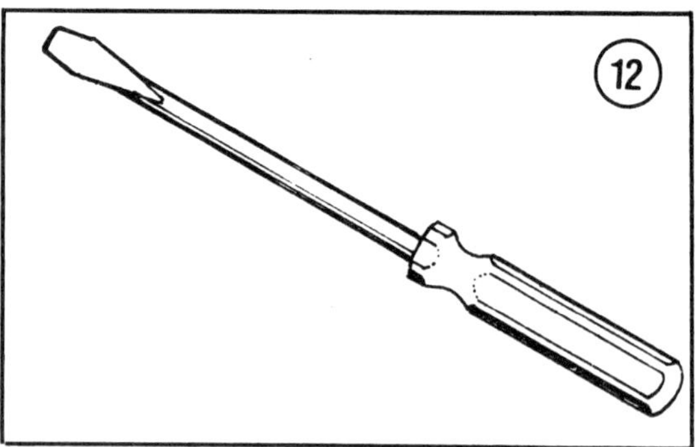

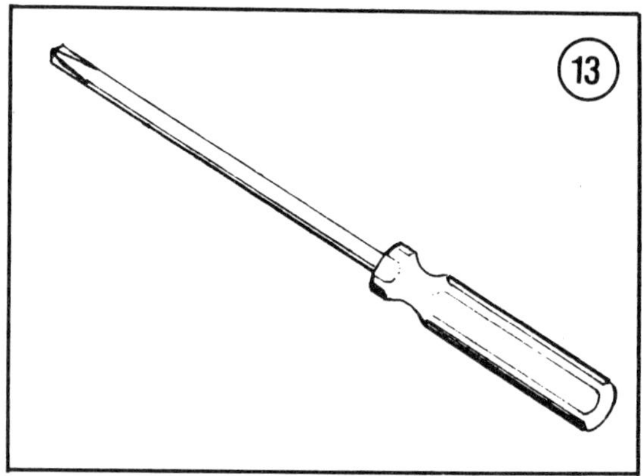

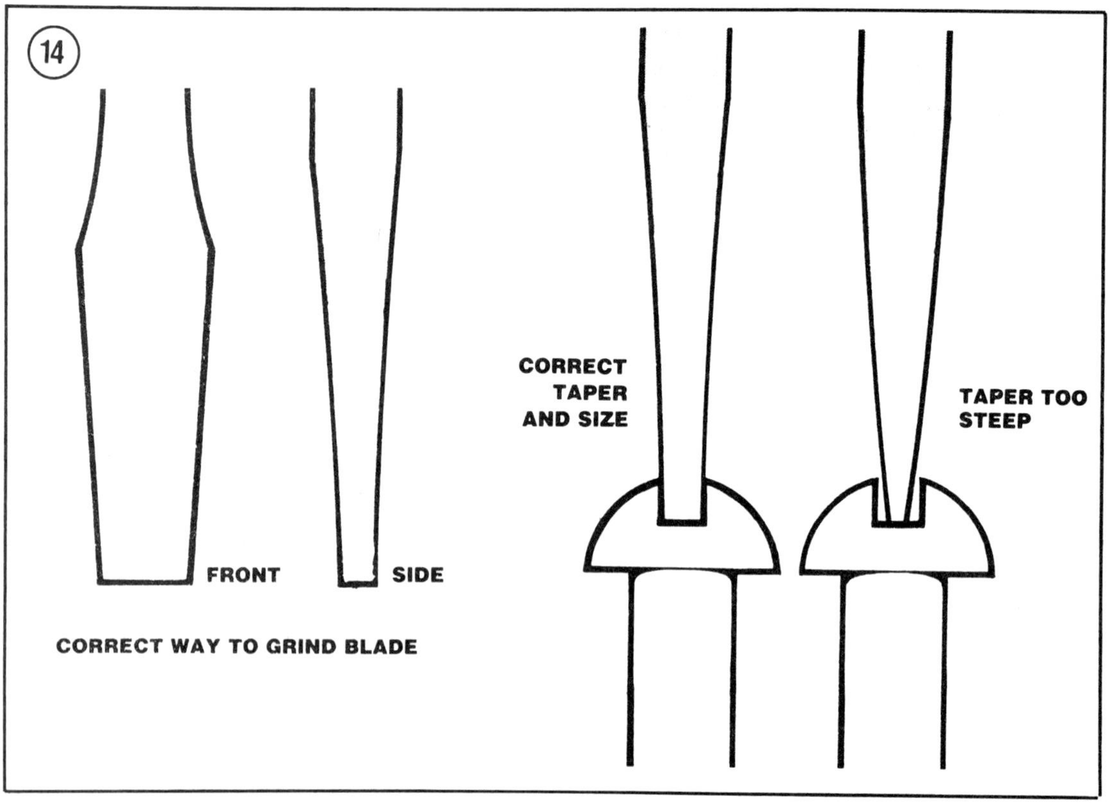

14

FRONT

SIDE

CORRECT WAY TO GRIND BLADE

CORRECT TAPER AND SIZE

TAPER TOO STEEP

the recomended size given for starting a tool collection. Additional tools and some duplicates may be added as you become familar with the vehicle. Harley-Davidson motorcycles are built with American standard fasteners—so if you are starting your collection now, buy American sizes.

Screwdrivers

The screwdriver is a very basic tool, but if used improperly it will do more damage than good. The slot on a screw has a definite dimension and shape. A screwdriver must be selected to conform with that shape. Use a small screwdriver for small screws and a large one for large screws or the screw head will be damaged.

Two basic types of screwdriver are required: common (flat-blade) screwdrivers (**Figure 12**) and Phillips screwdrivers (**Figure 13**).

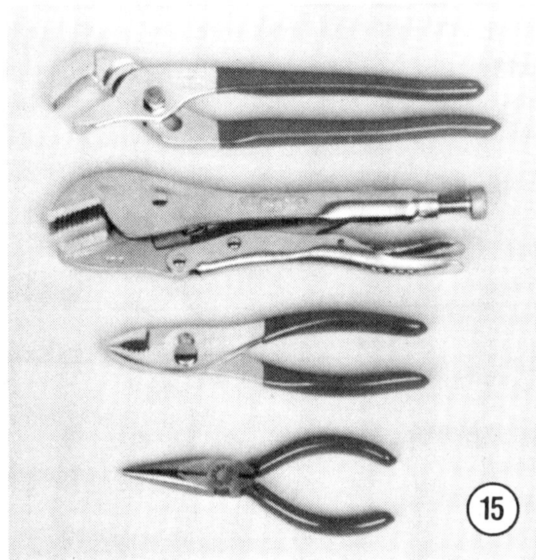

15

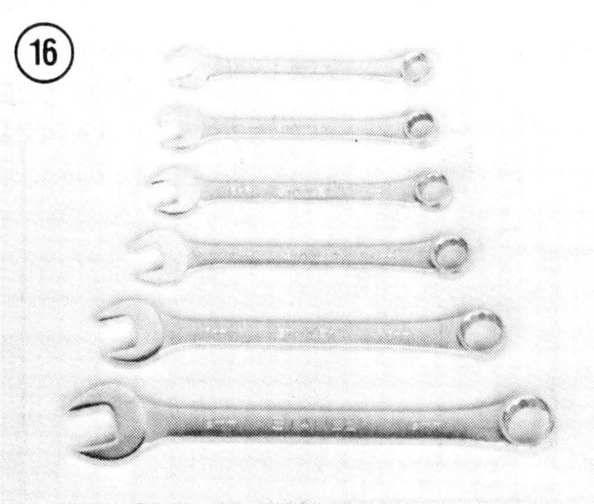

16

Screwdrivers are available in sets which often include an assortment of common and Phillips blades. If you buy them individually, buy at least the following:

a. Common screwdriver—5/16×6 in. blade.
b. Common screwdriver—3/8×12 in. blade.
c. Phillips screwdriver—size 2 tip, 6 in. blade.

Use screwdrivers only for driving screws. Never use a screwdriver for prying or chiseling metal. Do not try to remove a Phillips or Allen head screw with a common screwdriver (unless the screw has a combination head that will accept either type); you can damage the head so that the proper tool will be unable to remove it.

Keep screwdrivers in the proper condition and they will last longer and perform better. Always keep the tip of a common screwdriver in good condition. **Figure 14** shows how to grind the tip to the proper shape if it becomes damaged. Note the symmetrical sides of the tip.

Pliers

Pliers come in a wide range of types and sizes. Pliers are useful for cutting, bending and crimping. They should never be used to cut hardened objects or to turn bolts or nuts. **Figure 15** shows several pliers useful in motorcycle repairs.

Each type of pliers has a specialized function. Gas pliers are general purpose pliers and are used mainly for holding things and for bending. Vise grips are used as pliers or to hold objects very tightly, as in a vise. Needlenose pliers are used to hold or bend small objects. Channel lock pliers can be adjusted to hold various sizes of objects; the jaws remain parallel to grip around objects such as pipe or tubing. There are many more types of pliers.

Box and Open-end Wrenches

Box and open-end wrenches are available in sets or separately in a variety of sizes. The size number stamped near the end refers to the distance between 2 parallel flats on the hex head bolt or nut.

Box wrenches are usually superior to open-end wrenches (**Figure 16**). Open-end wrenches grip the nut on only 2 flats. Unless an open-end fits well, it may slip and round off the points on the nut. The box wrench grips on all 6 flats. Both 6-point and 12-point openings on box wrenches are available. The 6-point gives superior holding power; the 12-point allows a shorter swing.

Combination wrenches (**Figure 17**) which are open on one side and boxed on the other are also available. Both ends are the same size.

Adjustable Wrenches

An adjustable wrench can be adjusted to fit a variety of nuts or bolt heads (**Figure 18**). However, it can loosen and slip, causing damage to the nut and injury to your knuckles. Use an adjustable wrench only when other wrenches are not available.

Adjustable wrenches come in sizes ranging from 4-18 in. overall. A 6 or 8 in. wrench is recommended as an all-purpose wrench.

Socket Wrenches

This type is undoubtedly the fastest, safest and most convenient to use. Sockets which attach to a ratchet handle (**Figure 19**) are available with 6-point or 12-point openings and 1/4, 3/8, 1/2 and 3/4 in. drives. The drive size indicates the size of the square hole which mates with the ratchet handle. The best all-around size for motorcycle repair is 3/8 in. drive.

Torque Wrench

A torque wrench (**Figure 20**) is used with a socket to measure how tightly a nut or bolt is installed. They come in a wide price range and with either 3/8 or 1/2 in. square drive. The drive size indicates the size of the square drive which mates with the socket. Purchase one that measures 0-150 ft.-lb.

Impact Driver

This tool makes removal of tight fasteners easy and eliminates damage to bolts and screws slots. Impact drivers and interchangeable bits (**Figure 21**) are available at most large hardware and motorcycle dealers. Sockets can also be used with a hand impact driver. However, make sure the socket is designed for impact use, do not use regular hand type sockets.

Hammers

The correct hammer is necessary for repairs. Use only a hammer with a face (or head) of rubber or plastic or the soft-faced type that is filled with buckshot. These are sometimes necessary in engine teardowns. *Never* use a metal-faced hammer as severe damage will result in most cases. You can always produce the same amount of force with a soft-faced hammer.

Feeler Gauge

This tool is made with flat or wire measuring gauges; See **Figure 22**. Wire gauges are used to measure spark plug gap; flat gauges are used for all other measurements.

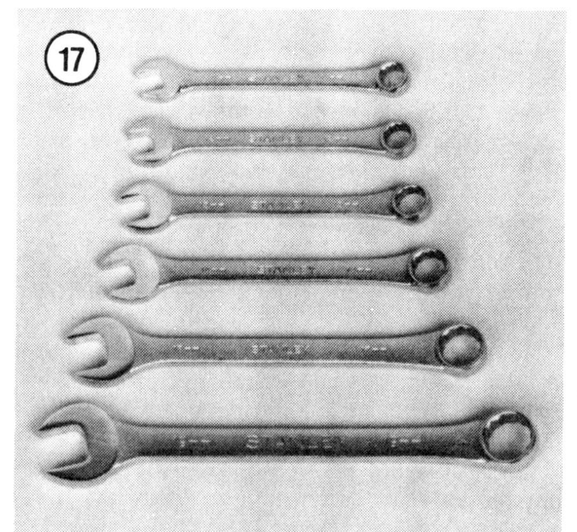

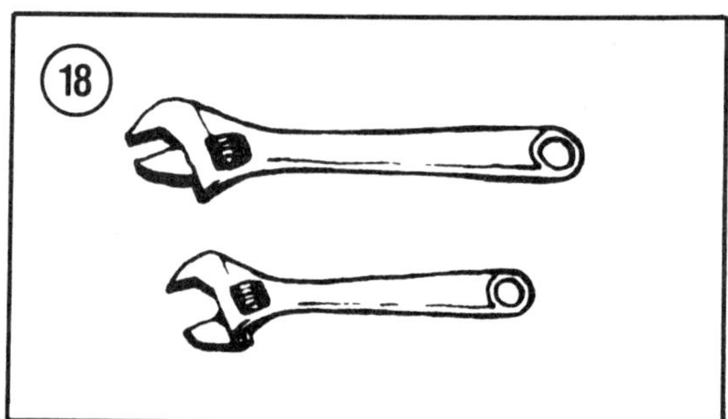

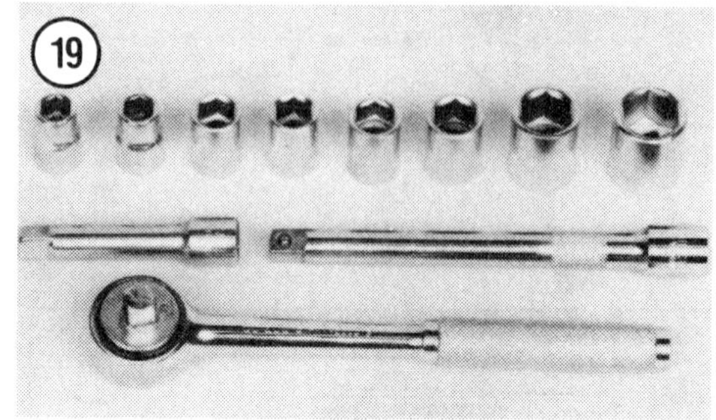

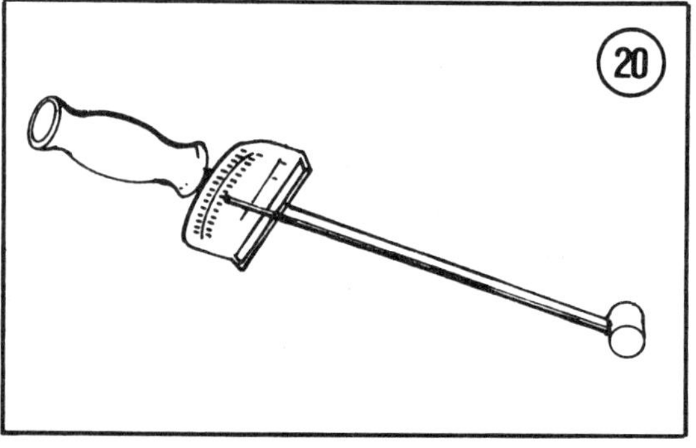

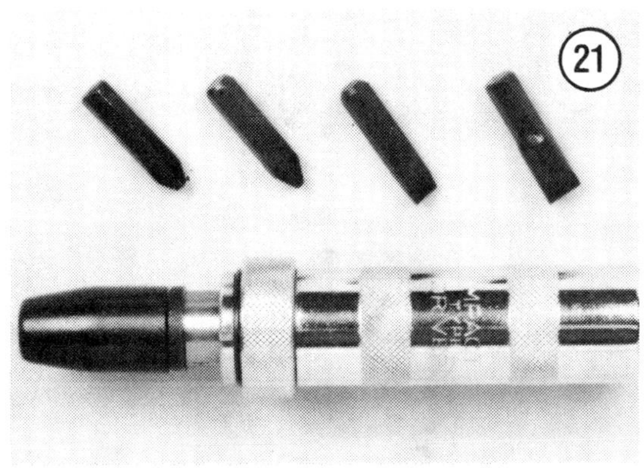

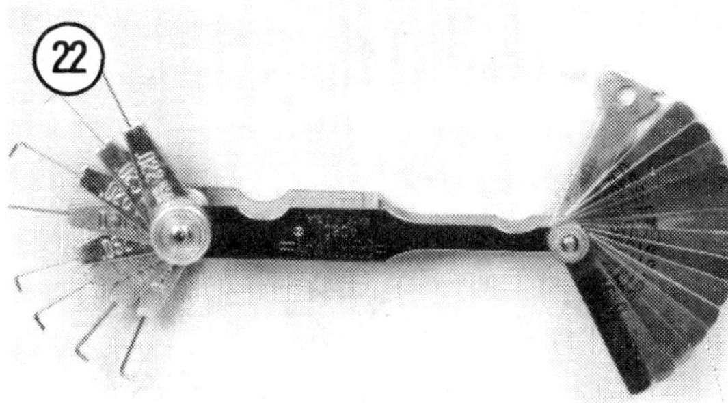

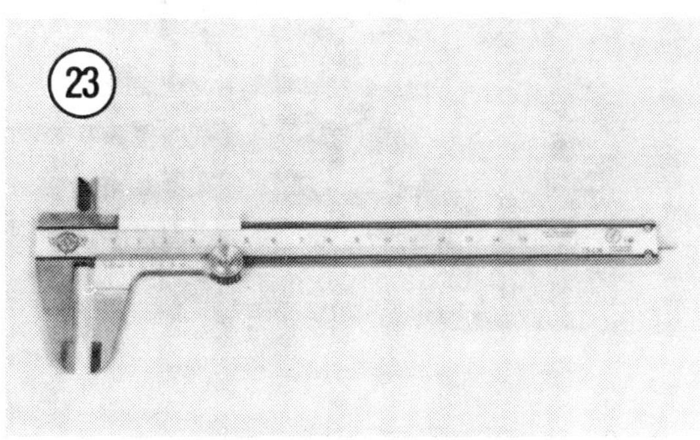

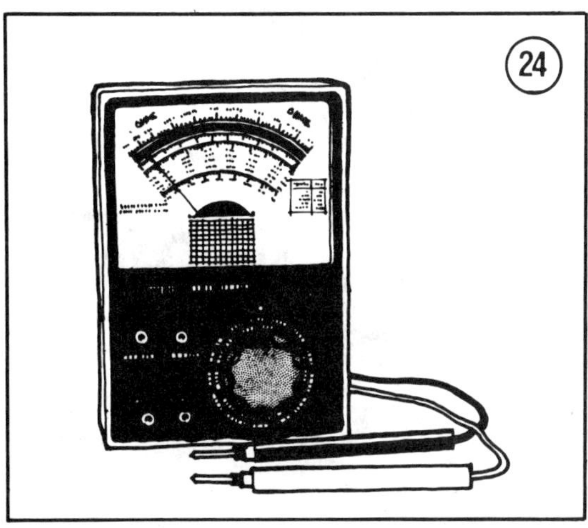

Vernier Caliper

This tool is invaluable when reading inside, outside and depth measurements to close precision. The vernier caliper can be purchased from large dealers or mail order houses. See **Figure 23**.

Other Special Tools

A few other special tools may be required for major service. These are described in the appropriate chapters and are available either from Harley-Davidson dealers or other manufacturers as indicated.

TEST EQUIPMENT

Voltmeter, Ammeter and Ohmmeter

A good voltmeter is required for testing ignition and other electrical systems. Voltmeters are available with analog meter scales or digital readouts. An instrument covering 0-20 volts is satisfactory. It should also have a 0-2 volt scale for testing points or individual contacts where voltage drops are much smaller. Accuracy should be ±1/2 volt.

An ohmmeter measures electrical resistance. This instrument is useful in checking continuity (for open and short circuits) and testing lights. A self-powered 12-volt test light can often be used in its place.

The ammeter measures electrical current. These are useful for checking battery starting and charging currents.

Some manufacturers combine the 3 instruments into 1 unit called a multimeter or VOM. See **Figure 24**.

Compression Gauge

An engine with low compression cannot be properly tuned and will not develop full power. A compression gauge measures the amount of pressure present in the engine's combustion chamber during the compression stroke. This indicates general engine condition.

The easiest type to use has screw-in adaptors that fit into the spark plug holes (**Figure 25**). Press-in rubber-tipped types (**Figure 26**) are also available.

Dial Indicator

Dial indicators (**Figure 27**) are precision tools used to check dimension variations on machined parts such as transmission shafts and axles and to check crankshaft and axle shaft end play. Dial indicators are available with various dial types for different measuring requirements.

Strobe Timing Light

This instrument is necessary for checking ignition timing. By flashing a light at the precise instant the spark plug fires, the position of the timing mark can be seen. The flashing light makes a moving mark appear to stand still opposite a stationary mark.

Suitable lights range from inexpensive neon bulb types to powerful xenon strobe lights. See **Figure 28**. A light with an inductive pickup is recommended to eliminate any possible damage to ignition wiring.

Portable Tachometer

A portable tachometer is necessary for tuning. See **Figure 29**. Ignition timing and carburetor adjustments must be performed at the specified idle speed. The best instrument for this purpose is one with a low range of 0-1,000 or 0-2,000 rpm and a high range of 0-4,000 rpm. Extended range (0-6,000 or 0-8,000 rpm) instruments lack accuracy at lower speeds. The instrument should be capable of detecting changes of 25 rpm on the low range.

Expendable Supplies

Certain expendable supplies are also required. These include grease, oil, gasket cement, shop rags and cleaning solvent. Ask your dealer for the special locking compounds, silicone lubricants and lube products which make vehicle maintenance simpler and easier. Cleaning solvent is available at some service stations.

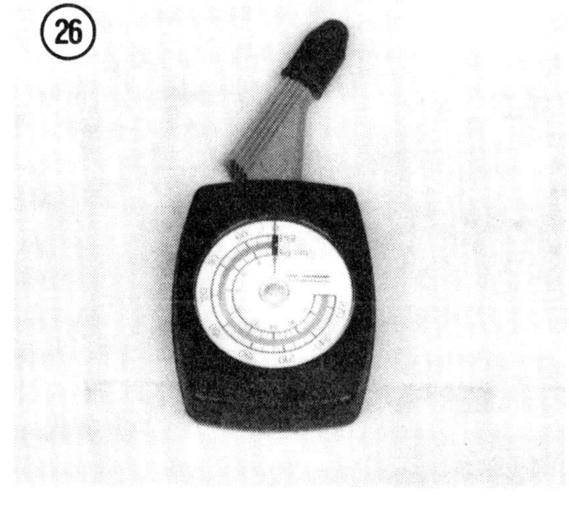

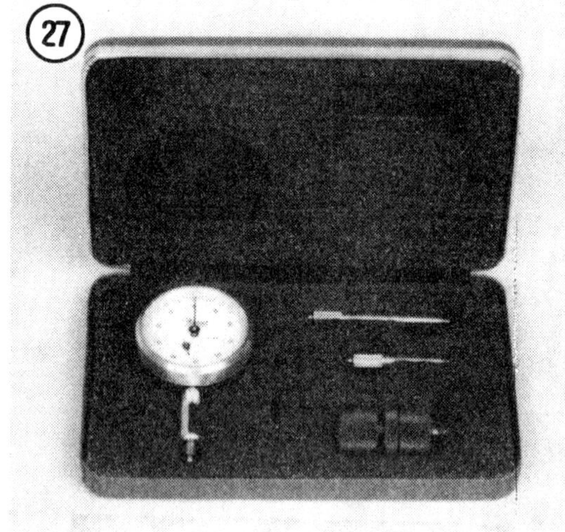

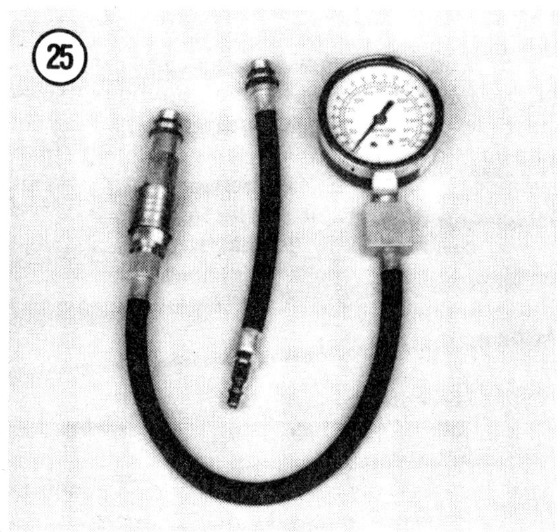

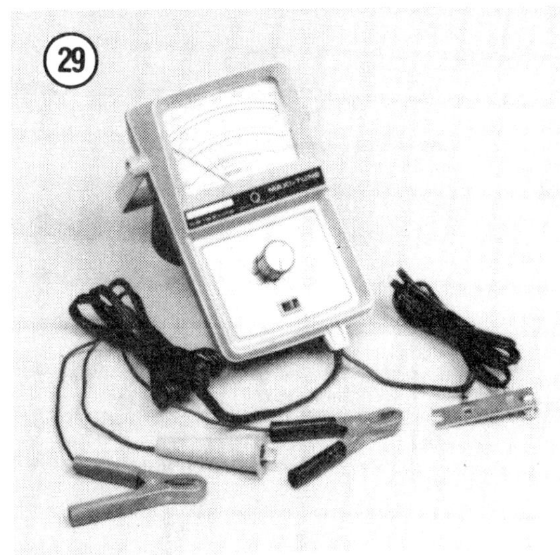

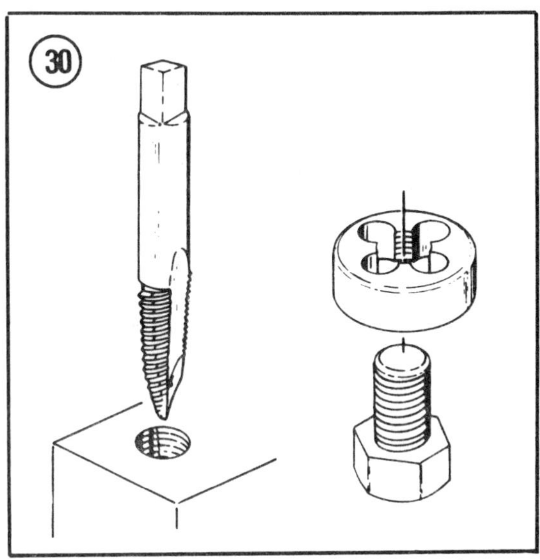

MECHANIC'S TIPS

Removing Frozen Nuts and Screws

When a fastener rusts and cannot be removed, several methods may be used to loosen it. First, apply penetrating oil such as Liquid Wrench or WD-40 (available at hardware or auto supply stores). Apply it liberally and let it penetrate for 10-15 minutes. Rap the fastener several times with a small hammer; do not hit it hard enough to cause damage. Reapply the penetrating oil if necessary.

For frozen screws, apply penetrating oil as described, then insert a screwdriver in the slot and rap the top of the screwdriver with a hammer. This loosens the rust so the screw can be removed in the normal way. If the screw head is too chewed up to use this method, grip the head with Vise-Grip pliers and twist the screw out.

Avoid applying heat unless specifically instructed, as it may melt, warp or remove the temper from parts.

Remedying Stripped Threads

Occasionally, threads are stripped through carelessness or impact damage. Often the threads can be cleaned up by running a tap (for internal threads on nuts) or die (for external threads on bolts) through the threads. See **Figure 30**. To clean or repair spark plug threads, a spark plug tap can be used (**Figure 31**).

Removing Broken Screws or Bolts

When the head breaks off a screw or bolt, several methods can be used to remove the remaining portion.

If a large portion of the remainder projects out, try gripping it with Vise Grips. If the projecting portion is too small, file it to fit a wrench or cut a slot in it to fit a screwdriver. See **Figure 32**.

If the head breaks off flush, use a screw extractor. To do this, centerpunch the exact center of the remaining porton of the screw or bolt. Drill a small hole in the screw and tap the extractor into the hole. Back the screw out with a wrench on the extractor. See **Figure 33**.

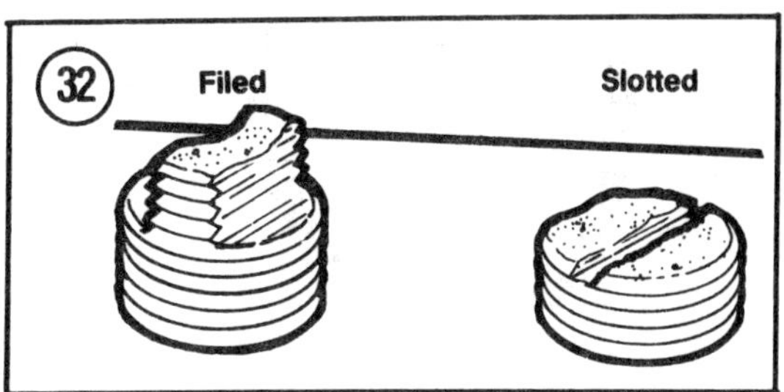

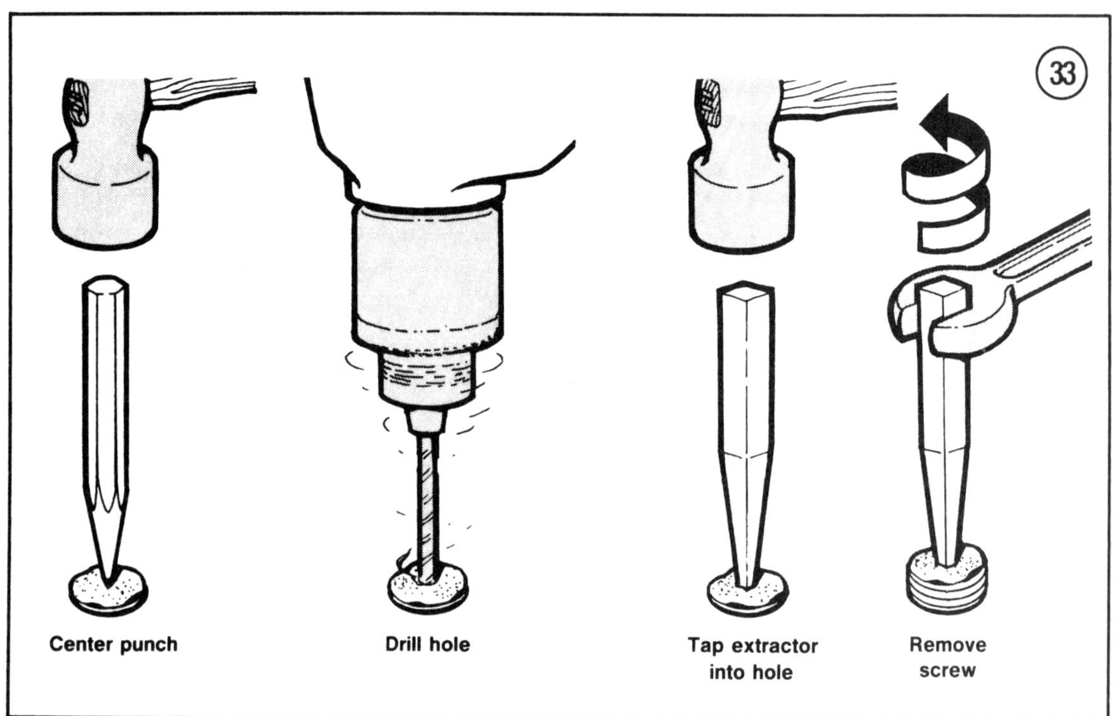
33
Center punch
Drill hole
Tap extractor into hole
Remove screw

Table 1 DECIMAL AND METRIC EQUIVALENTS

Fractions	Decimal in.	Metric mm	Fractions	Decimal in.	Metric mm
1/64	0.015625	0.39688	33/64	0.515625	13.09687
1/32	0.03125	0.79375	17/32	0.53125	13.49375
3/64	0.046875	1.19062	35/64	0.546875	13.89062
1/16	0.0625	1.58750	9/16	0.5625	14.28750
5/64	0.078125	1.98437	37/64	0.578125	14.68437
3/32	0.09375	2.38125	19/32	0.59375	15.08125
7/64	0.109375	2.77812	39/64	0.609375	15.47812
1/8	0.125	3.1750	5/8	0.625	15.87500
9/64	0.140625	3.57187	41/64	0.640625	16.27187
5/32	0.15625	3.96875	21/32	0.65625	16.66875
11/64	0.171875	4.36562	43/64	0.671875	17.06562
3/16	0.1875	4.76250	11/16	0.6875	17.46250
13/64	0.203125	5.15937	45/64	0.703125	17.85937
7/32	0.21875	5.55625	23/32	0.71875	18.25625
15/64	0.234375	5.95312	47/64	0.734375	18.65312
1/4	0.250	6.35000	3/4	0.750	19.05000
17/64	0.265625	6.74687	49/64	0.765625	19.44687
9/32	0.28125	7.14375	25/32	0.78125	19.84375
19/64	0.296875	7.54062	51/64	0.796875	20.24062
5/16	0.3125	7.93750	13/16	0.8125	20.63750
21/64	0.328125	8.33437	53/64	0.828125	21.03437
11/32	0.34375	8.73125	27/32	0.84375	21.43125
23/64	0.359375	9.12812	55/64	0.859375	21.82812
3/8	0.375	9.52500	7/8	0.875	22.22500
25/64	0.390625	9.92187	57/64	0.890625	22.62187
13/32	0.40625	10.31875	29/32	0.90625	23.01875
27/64	0.421875	10.71562	59/64	0.921875	23.41562
7/16	0.4375	11.11250	15/16	0.9375	23.81250
29/64	0.453125	11.50937	61/64	0.953125	24.20937
15/32	0.46875	11.90625	31/32	0.96875	24.60625
31/64	0.484375	12.30312	63/64	0.984375	25.00312
1/2	0.500	12.70000	1	1.00	25.40000

Table 2 GENERAL TORQUE SPECIFICATIONS

SAE 2 SAE 5 SAE 7 SAE 8

Type*	Body size or outside diameter									
	1/4	5/16	3/8	7/16	1/2	9/16	5/8	3/4	7/8	1
SAE 2	6	12	20	32	47	69	96	155	206	310
SAE 5	10	19	33	54	78	114	154	257	382	587
SAE 7	13	25	44	71	110	154	215	360	570	840
SAE 8	14	29	47	78	119	169	230	380	600	700

* Fastener strength of SAE bolts can be determined by the bolt or screw head "grade markings." Unmarked bolt-heads and cap-screws are usually considered to be mild steel. Basically, the greater the number of "grade markings," the higher the fastener quality.

CHAPTER TWO

TROUBLESHOOTING

Every motorcycle engine requires an uninterrupted supply of fuel and air, proper ignition and adequate compression. If any of these are lacking, the engine will not run.

Diagnosing mechanical problems is relatively simple if you use orderly procedures and keep a few basic principles in mind.

The troubleshooting procedures in this chapter analyze typical symptoms and show logical methods of isolating causes. These are not the only methods. There may be several ways to solve a problem, but only a systematic approach can guarantee success.

Never assume anything. Do not overlook the obvious. If you are riding along and the bike suddenly quits, check the easiest, most accessible problem spots first. Is there gasoline in the tank? Has a spark plug wire fallen off?

If nothing obvious turns up in a quick check, look a little further. Learning to recognize and describe symptoms will make repairs easier for you or a mechanic at the shop. Describe problems accurately and fully. Saying that "it won't run" isn't the same thing as saying "it quit at high speed and won't start," or that "it sat in my garage for 3 months and then wouldn't start."

Gather as many symptoms as possible to aid in diagnosis. Note whether the engine lost power gradually or all at once. Remember that the more complicated a machine is, the easier it is to

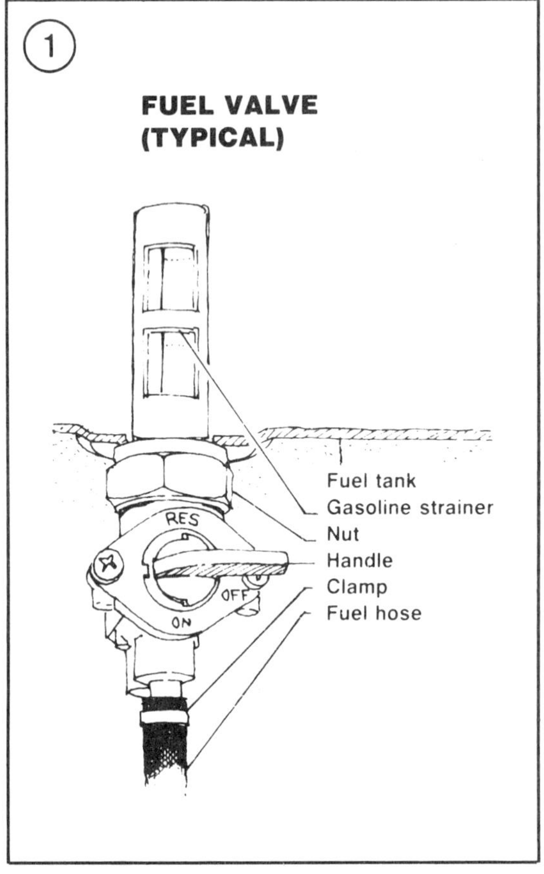

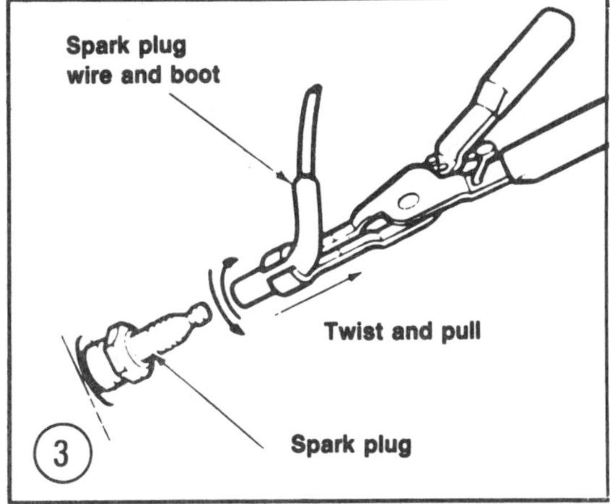

troubleshoot because symptoms point to specific problems.

After the symptoms are defined, areas which could cause problems are tested and analyzed. Guessing at the cause of a problem may provide the solution, but it can easily lead to frustration, wasted time and a series of expensive, unnecessary parts replacements.

You do not need fancy equipment or complicated test gear to determine whether repairs can be attempted at home. A few simple checks could save a large repair bill and lost time while the bike sits in a dealer's service department. On the other hand, be realistic and don't attempt repairs beyond your abilities. Service departments tend to charge heavily for putting together a disassembled engine that may have been abused. Some won't even take on such a job, so use common sense and don't get in over your head.

OPERATING REQUIREMENTS

An engine needs 3 basics to run properly: correct fuel/air mixture, compression and a spark at the correct time. If one or more are missing, the engine will not run. Four-stroke engine operating principles are described in Chapter Four under *Engine Principles*. The electrical system is the weakest link of the 3 basics. More problems result from electrical breakdowns than from any other source. Keep that in mind before you begin tampering with carburetor adjustments and the like.

If the machine has been sitting for any length of time and refuses to start, check and clean the spark plugs and then look to the gasoline delivery system. This includes the fuel tank, fuel shutoff valve and fuel line to the carburetor. Gasoline deposits may have formed and gummed up the carburetor jets and air passages. Gasoline tends to lose its potency after standing for long periods. Condensation may contaminate the fuel with water. Drain the old fuel (fuel tank, fuel lines and carburetor) and try starting with a fresh tankful.

TROUBLESHOOTING INSTRUMENTS

Chapter One lists the instruments needed and instructions on their use.

EMERGENCY TROUBLESHOOTING

When the bike is difficult to start, or won't start at all, it doesn't help to wear down the battery using the electric starter or your leg on kickstart models. Check for obvious problems even before getting out your tools. Go down the following list step by step. Do each one; you may be embarrassed to find the kill switch off, but that is better than wearing down the battery. If the bike still will not start, refer to the appropriate troubleshooting procedures which follow in this chapter.

1. Is there fuel in the tank? Open the filler cap and rock the bike. Listen for fuel sloshing around.

WARNING
Do not use an open flame to check in the tank. A serious explosion is certain to result.

2. Is the fuel supply valve in the ON position? Turn the valve to the reserve position to be sure you get the last remaining gas. See **Figure 1**.
3. Make sure the kill switch is not stuck in the OFF position and that the wire is not broken and shorting out.
4. Are the spark plug wires on tight? Push both spark plugs on (**Figure 2**) and slightly rotate them to clean the electrical connection between the plug and the connector.
5. Is the choke in the right position?

ENGINE STARTING

An engine that refuses to start or is difficult to start is very frustrating. More often than not, the problem is very minor and can be found with a simple and logical troubleshooting approach.

The following items will help isolate engine starting problems.

Engine Fails to Start

Perform the following spark test to determine if the ignition system is operating properly.

1. Remove one of the spark plugs.
2. Connect the spark plug wire and connector to the spark plug and touch the spark plug base to a good ground like the engine cylinder head. Position the spark plug so you can see the electrodes.

WARNING

*During the next step, do not hold the spark plug, wire or connector or a serious electrical shock may result. If necessary, use a pair of insulated pliers to hold the spark plug or wire (**Figure 3**). The high voltage generated by the ignition system could produce serious or fatal shocks.*

3. Crank the engine over with the starter. A fat blue spark should be evident across the spark plug electrodes.
4. If the spark is good, check for one or more of the following possible malfunctions:
   a. Obstructed fuel line or fuel filter.
   b. Leaking head gasket(s). See **Figure 4**.
   c. Low compression.
5. If the spark is not good, check for one or more of the following:
   a. Loose electrical connections.
   b. Dirty electrical connections.
   c. Loose or broken ignition coil ground wire (**Figure 5**).
   d. Broken or shorted high tension lead to the spark plug (**Figure 6**).
   e. Discharged battery.
   f. Disconnected or damaged battery connection.
   g. Oxidized breaker points (1959-1978). See **Figure 7**.

Engine is Difficult to Start

Check for one or more of the following possible malfunctions:

a. Fouled spark plug(s).
b. Improperly adjusted choke.
c. Intake manifold air leak (**Figure 8**).
d. Contaminated fuel system.
e. Improperly adjusted carburetor.

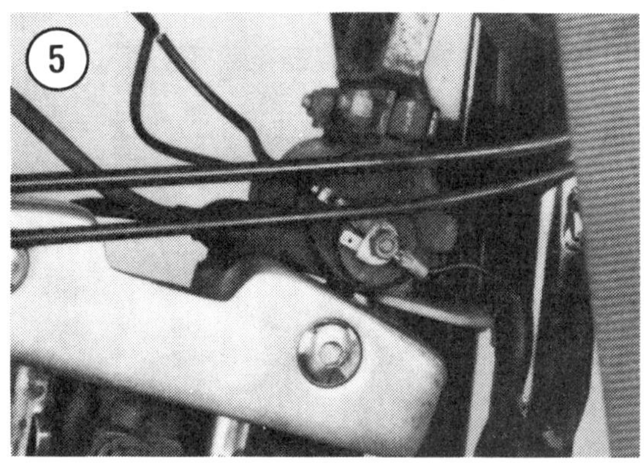

f. Weak ignition unit.
g. Weak ignition coil(s).
h. Poor compression.
i. Timing advance weight sticking in advanced position (1959-1979 models only).
j. Engine and transmission oil too heavy.

Engine Will Not Crank

Check for one or more of the following possible malfunctions:

a. Blown fuse or damaged circuit breaker.
b. Discharged battery.
c. Defective starter motor.
d. Seized piston(s).
e. Seized crankshaft bearings.
f. Broken connecting rod.

ENGINE PERFORMANCE

In the following checklist, it is assumed that the engine runs, but is not operating at peak performance. This will serve as a starting point from which to isolate a performance malfunction.

The possible causes for each malfunction are listed in a logical sequence and in order of probability.

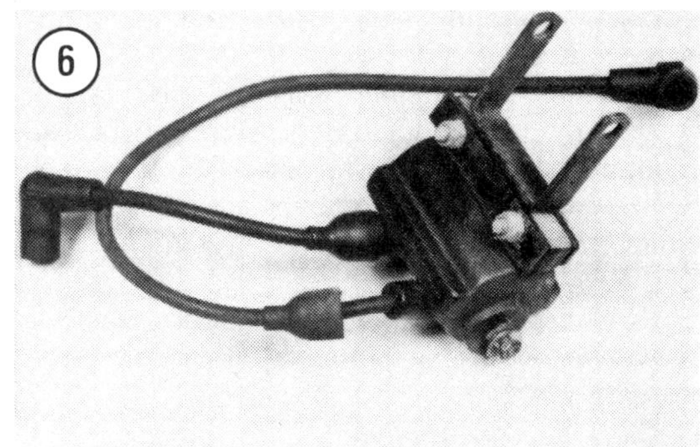

c. Incorrect ignition timing due to defective ignition component(s).
d. Weak ignition coil(s).
e. Obstructed fuel line or fuel shutoff valve.
f. Obstructed fuel filter.
g. Clogged carburetor jets.

Engine Overheating

a. Incorrect carburetor adjustment or jet selection.
b. Retarded ignition timing due to improper adjustment or defective ignition component(s).
c. 1959-1979: Overheating accompanied by low power—circuit breaker cam sticking in retarded position.
d. Improper spark plug heat range.
e. Damaged or blocked cooling fins.
f. Low oil level.
g. Oil not circulating properly.
h. Leaking valves.
i. Heavy engine carbon deposits.

Smoky Exhaust and Engine Runs Roughly

a. Clogged air filter element.
b. Carburetor adjustment incorrect—mixture too rich.
c. Choke not operating correctly.
d. Water or other contaminants in fuel.
e. Clogged fuel line.
f. Fouled spark plugs.
g. Defective ignition coil.
h. Breaker point models: points worn, dirty or out of adjustment. Loose condenser connections. Defective condenser.
i. Electronic ignition models: ignition module or sensor defective.
j. Loose or defective ignition circuit wire.
k. Short circuit from damaged wire insulation.
l. Loose battery cable connection.
m. Incorrect valve timing.
n. Intake manifold or air cleaner air leak.

Engine Loses Power At Normal Riding Speed

a. Carburetor incorrectly adjusted.
b. Overheating engine.
c. Incorrect ignition timing due to faulty ignition component(s). Circuit breaker cam sticking on 1959-1979 models.
d. Incorrectly gapped spark plugs.
e. Obstructed muffler.
f. Dragging brake(s).

Engine Will Not Idle

a. Incorrectly adjusted carburetor .
b. Fouled or improperly gapped spark plug(s).
c. Leaking head gasket(s) (**Figure 4**).
d. Obstructed fuel line or fuel shutoff valve.
e. Obstructed fuel filter.
f. Incorrect ignition timing due to defective ignition component(s).
g. Incorrect push rod clearance

Engine Misses at High Speed

a. Fouled or improperly gapped spark plugs.
b. Improper carburetor main jet selection.

Engine Lacks Acceleration

a. Carburetor mixture too lean.
b. Clogged fuel line.
c. Incorrect ignition timing due to faulty ignition component(s).
d. Dragging brake(s).

ENGINE NOISES

Often the first evidence of an internal engine problem is a strange noise. That knocking, clicking or tapping sound which you never heard before may be warning you of impending trouble.

While engine noises can indicate problems, they are difficult to interpret correctly; inexperienced mechanics can be seriously misled by them.

Professional mechanics often use a special stethoscope (which looks like a doctor's stethoscope) for isolating engine noises. You can do nearly as well with a "sounding stick" which can be an ordinary piece of doweling, a length of broom handle or a section of small hose. By placing one end in contact with the area to which you want to listen and the other end near your ear, you can hear sounds emanating from that area. The first time you do this, you may be horrified at the strange sounds coming from even a normal engine. If you can, have an experienced friend or mechanic help you sort out the noises.

Consider the following when troubleshooting engine noises:

1. *Knocking or pinging during acceleration*—Caused by using a lower octane fuel than recommended. May also be caused by poor fuel. Pinging can also be caused by a spark plug of the wrong heat range. Refer to *Correct Spark Plug Heat Range* in Chapter Three.
2. *Slapping or rattling noises at low speed or during acceleration*—May be caused by piston slap, i.e., excessive piston-cylinder wall clearance.
3. *Knocking or rapping while decelerating*—Usually caused by excessive rod bearing clearance.
4. *Persistent knocking and vibration*— Usually caused by worn main bearing(s).
5. *Rapid on-off squeal*—Compression leak around cylinder head gasket(s) (**Figure 4**) or spark plugs.
6. *Valve train noise*—Check for the following:
   a. Bent push rod(s).
   b. Push rods adjusted incorrectly.
   c. Defective tappets.
   d. Valve sticking in guide.
   e. Worn cam gears or cams.
   f. Low oil pressure.
   g. Damaged rocker arm or shaft. Rocker arm may be binding on shaft.

ENGINE LUBRICATION

An improperly operating engine lubrication system will quickly lead to engine seizure. The

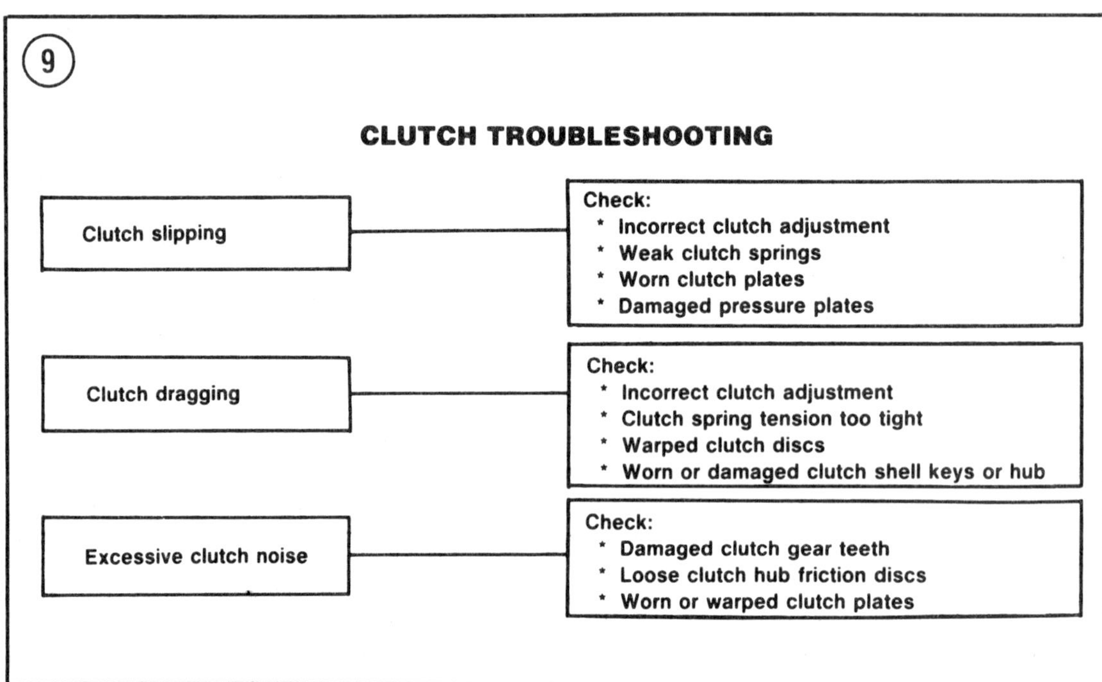

engine oil level should be checked weekly and the tank refilled, as described in Chapter Three. Oil pump service is described in Chapter Four.

Oil Consumption High or Engine Smokes Excessively

a. Worn valve guides.
b. Worn or damaged piston rings.
c. Improperly adjusted chain oiler (if so equipped).

Oil Fails to Return to Oil Tank

a. Restricted or damaged oil lines or fittings.
b. Oil pump damaged or operating incorrectly.
c. Empty oil tank.
d. Scavenger oil pump gear Woodruff key sheared.
e. Plugged or restricted oil filter (if so equipped).

Excessive Engine Oil Leaks

a. Clogged air cleaner breather hose.
b. Restricted or damaged oil tank return line.
c. Loose engine parts.
d. Damaged gasket sealing surfaces.

Excessive Oil Runoff at Crankcase Breather

a. Restricted or damaged oil lines or fittings.
b. Leaking gearcase cover gasket.
c. Oil not returning to oil tank.

CLUTCH

The three basic clutch troubles are:
a. Clutch noise.
b. Clutch slipping.
c. Improper clutch disengagement or dragging.

All clutch troubles, except adjustments, require partial clutch disassembly to identify and cure the problem. The troubleshooting chart in **Figure 9** lists clutch troubles and checks to make. Refer to Chapter Five for clutch service procedures.

TRANSMISSION

The basic transmission troubles are:
a. Excessive gear noise.
b. Difficult shifting.
c. Gears popping out of mesh.
d. Incorrect shift lever operation.

Transmission symptoms are sometimes hard to distinguish from clutch symptoms. The troubleshooting chart in **Figure 10** lists transmission troubles and checks to make. Refer to Chapter Five for transmission service procedures. Be sure that the clutch is not causing the trouble before working on the transmission.

CHARGING SYSTEM

Charging system testing procedures are described in Chapter Seven.

STARTING SYSTEM

The basic starter troubles are:
a. The starter does not spin.
b. The starter spins, but the engine does not crank.

Testing

Starting system problems are relatively easy to find. In most cases, the trouble is a loose or dirty electrical connection. Use the troubleshooting chart in **Figure 11** (1980 and earlier) or **Figure 12** (1981-1985) with the following tests.

Starter does not spin

Turn on the headlight and push the starter button. Check for one of the following conditions.

1. *Starter does not spin and headlight does not come on:* The battery is dead or there is a loose battery connection. Check the battery charge as described in Chapter Three. If the battery is okay, check the starter connections at the battery, solenoid and at the starter switch.
2. *Headlight comes on, but goes out when the starter button is pushed:* There may be a bad connection at the battery. Wiggle the battery terminals and recheck. If the starter now spins, you've found the problem. Remove and clean the battery terminal clamps. Clean the battery posts also. Reinstall the clamps and tighten securely.
3. *Headlight comes on, but dims slightly when the starter button is pushed:* The problem is probably in the starter. Remove and test the starter as described in Chapter Seven.
4. *Headlight comes on, but dims severely when the starter button is pushed:* Either the battery is run down severely or the starter or engine is partially seized. Check the battery as described in Chapter Three. Check the starter as described in Chapter Seven before checking for partial engine seizure.
5. *Headlight comes on and stays bright when the starter button is pushed:* The problem is in the starter button-to-solenoid wiring or in the starter itself. Check the starter switch, kill switch, starter relay and the solenoid switch. Check each switch

2

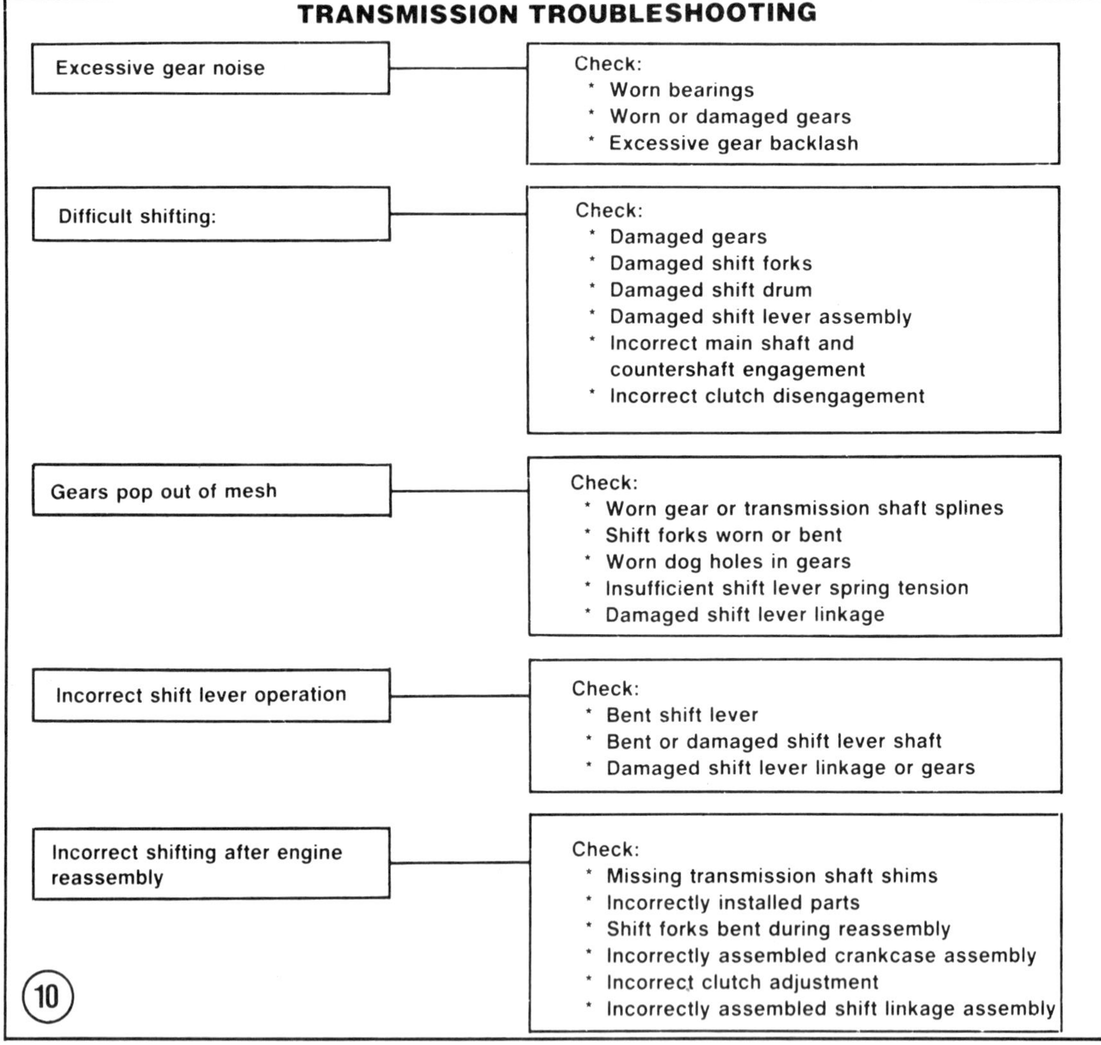

by bypassing it with a jumper wire. Check the starter as described in Chapter Seven.

Starter spins but engine does not crank

If the starter spins at normal speed but the engine fails to crank, the starter system is working correctly. The problem is in the starter drive mechanism.

NOTE

Depending upon battery condition, the battery will eventually run down as the starter button is continually pressed. Remember that if the starter cranks the engine normally, but the engine fails to start, the starter is working properly. It's time to start checking other engine systems. Don't wear the battery down.

ELECTRICAL PROBLEMS

Bulbs that continuously burn out may be caused by excessive vibration, loose connections that permit sudden current surges, or the installation of the wrong type of bulb.

Most light and ignition problems are caused by loose or corroded ground connections. Check these before replacing a bulb or electrical component.

IGNITION SYSTEM

The ignition system may be either a breaker point or breakerless type. See Chapter Seven. Most problems involving failure to start, poor driveability or rough running stem from trouble in the ignition system, particularly in breaker point systems.

2

STARTER TROUBLESHOOTING (1980 AND EARLIER)

11

Symptom	Probable Cause	Remedy
Starter does not work	Low battery Worn brushes Defective relay Defective switch Defective wiring connection Internal short circuit	Recharge battery Replace brushes Repair or replace Repair or replace Repair wire or clean connection Repair or replace defective component
Starter action is weak	Low battery Pitted relay contacts Worn brushes Defective connection Short circuit in commutator	Recharge battery Clean or replace Replace brushes Clean and tighten Replace armature
Starter runs continuously	Stuck relay	Replace relay
Starter turns; does not turn engine	Defective starter clutch	Replace starter clutch

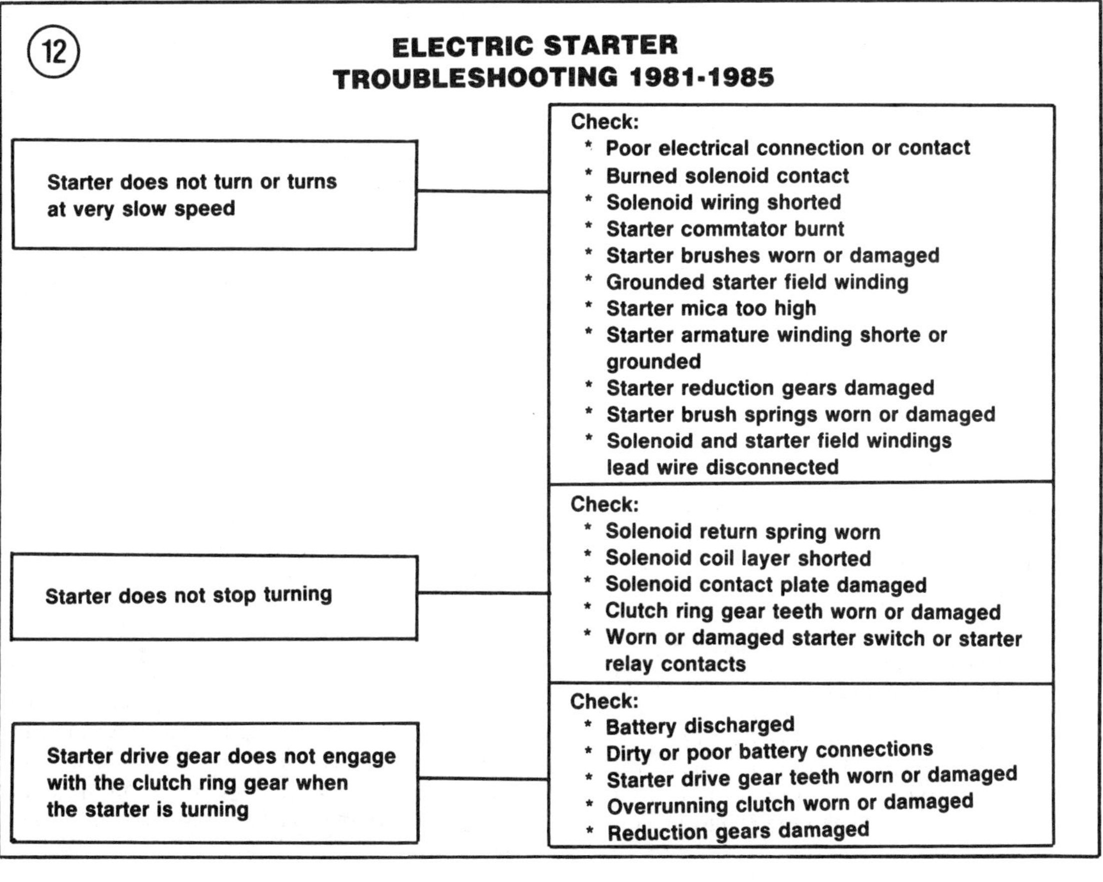

Note the following symptoms:

a. Engine misses.
b. Stumbling on acceleration (misfiring).
c. Loss of power at high speed (misfiring).
d. Hard starting (or no starting).
e. Rough idle.

Most of the symptoms can also be caused by a carburetor that is worn or improperly adjusted. However, the odds are far better that the source of the problem will be found in the ignition system rather than the fuel system.

BREAKER POINT IGNITION TROUBLESHOOTING

The following basic tests are designed to quickly pinpoint and isolate problems in the primary circuit of a breaker point ignition. It is assumed that the battery is in good condition. See Chapter Three. If the primary circuit checks out satisfactorily, refer to *Tune-up* in Chapter Three and check the circuit breaker, spark plug wires and spark plugs.

1. Remove the circuit breaker point cover.
2. Rotate the engine until the points are closed (D, **Figure 13**).
3. Disconnect the high voltage lead from one of the spark plugs.
4. Insert a metal adapter in the plug boot and hold it about 3/16 in. from a clean engine ground with insulated pliers (**Figure 14**).
5. Turn the ignition switch ON.
6. Open the points with an insulated tool made of wood. A fat, blue-white spark should jump from the spark plug lead to the cylinder. If the spark is good, the ignition system is okay. If there is no spark, or if it is thin, yellowish, or weak, continue with Step 7.
7. Turn the ignition switch OFF and close the points.
8. Connect the leads of a voltmeter to the wire on the points (A, **Figure 13**) and to a good ground. Turn the ignition switch on. If the voltmeter indicates more than 0.125 volts, the points are defective. Replace them as described in Chapter Three.
9. Connect the voltmeter between the battery terminals and note the reading. This is battery voltage. Open the points with the same tool used in Step 6. The voltmeter should indicate battery voltage. If not, consider the following troubles:

a. Shorted points.
b. Shorted condenser.
c. Open coil primary winding.

10. Disconnect the condenser and the wire from the points (A, **Figure 13**). Connect the ungrounded (positive) voltmeter lead to the wire which was connected to the points (not to the condenser wire). Connect the voltmeter negative lead to ground. If the voltmeter does not indicate battery voltage, the problem is a break or bad connection in the primary circuit or an open coil primary winding. Check the primary circuit. If the primary circuit checks out okay, replace the coil with a known good one.
11. If the voltmeter indicated battery voltage in Step 9, the coil primary circuit is okay. Connect the positive voltmeter lead to the wire which goes from the coil to the points. Block the points open as in Step 6. Connect the negative voltmeter lead to the moveable point. If the voltmeter indicates any voltage, the points are shorted and must be replaced.
12. If the checks are satisfactory, the problem is in the coil or condenser. Substitute each of these separately with a known good one to determine which is defective.

Ignition Coil

Ignition coil testing is described in Chapter Seven.

BREAKERLESS IGNITION TROUBLESHOOTING

The following tests are designed to quickly pinpoint and isolate problems in the primary circuit of the breakerless inductive discharge ignition system. The procedure requires a voltmeter, non-magnetic feeler gauge (1979) and an ignition test adapter (1980-on).

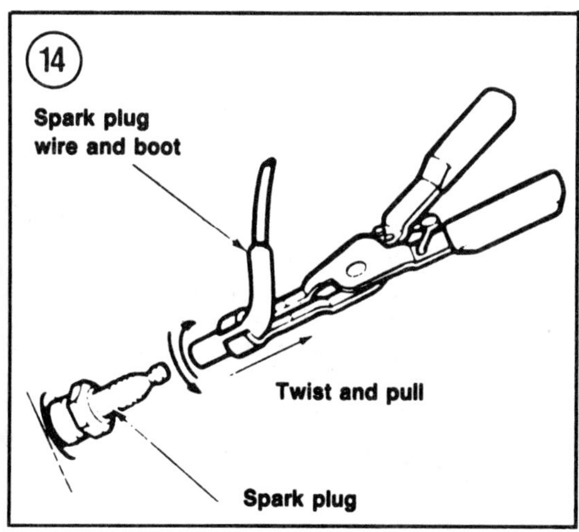

Spark Test

Perform the following spark test to determine if the ignition system is operating properly.

1. Remove one of the spark plugs.
2. Connect the spark plug wire and connector to the spark plug and touch the spark plug base to a good ground like the engine cylinder head. Position the spark plug so you can see the electrodes.

WARNING
*During the next step, do not hold the spark plug, wire or connector or a serious electrical shock may result. If necessary, use a pair of insulated pliers (**Figure 14**) to hold the spark plug or wire. The high voltage generated by the ignition system could produce serious or fatal shocks.*

3. Crank the engine over with the starter. A fat blue spark should be evident across the spark plug electrodes.
4. If a spark is obtained in Step 3, the problem is not in the breakerless ignition or coil. Check the fuel system and the opposite spark plug. On 1979 models, check the ignition advance mechanism as described in Chapter Seven. If no spark is obtained, proceed with the following tests for your model.

1979 models

1. Check the battery charge as described in Chapter Three. If battery is okay, proceed to Step 2.
2. Remove the timer case cover (2, **Figure 15**).

NOTE
*The ignition module (3, **Figure 15**) is fastened to the back of the cover.*

3. Check the control module black wire (ground) connection at the timer plate (11, **Figure 15**). Make sure the connection is tight and that the wire is not chafed or damaged.
4. Check the sensor air gap as described in Chapter Three.
5. If the air gap cannot be adjusted for both rotor lobes, the trigger rotor (7, **Figure 15**) and/or the timer mechanism shaft on the advance assembly base is bent or damaged. Replace the damaged part as described in Chapter Seven.

NOTE
After adjusting the sensor air gap, check and adjust the timing as described in Chapter Three.

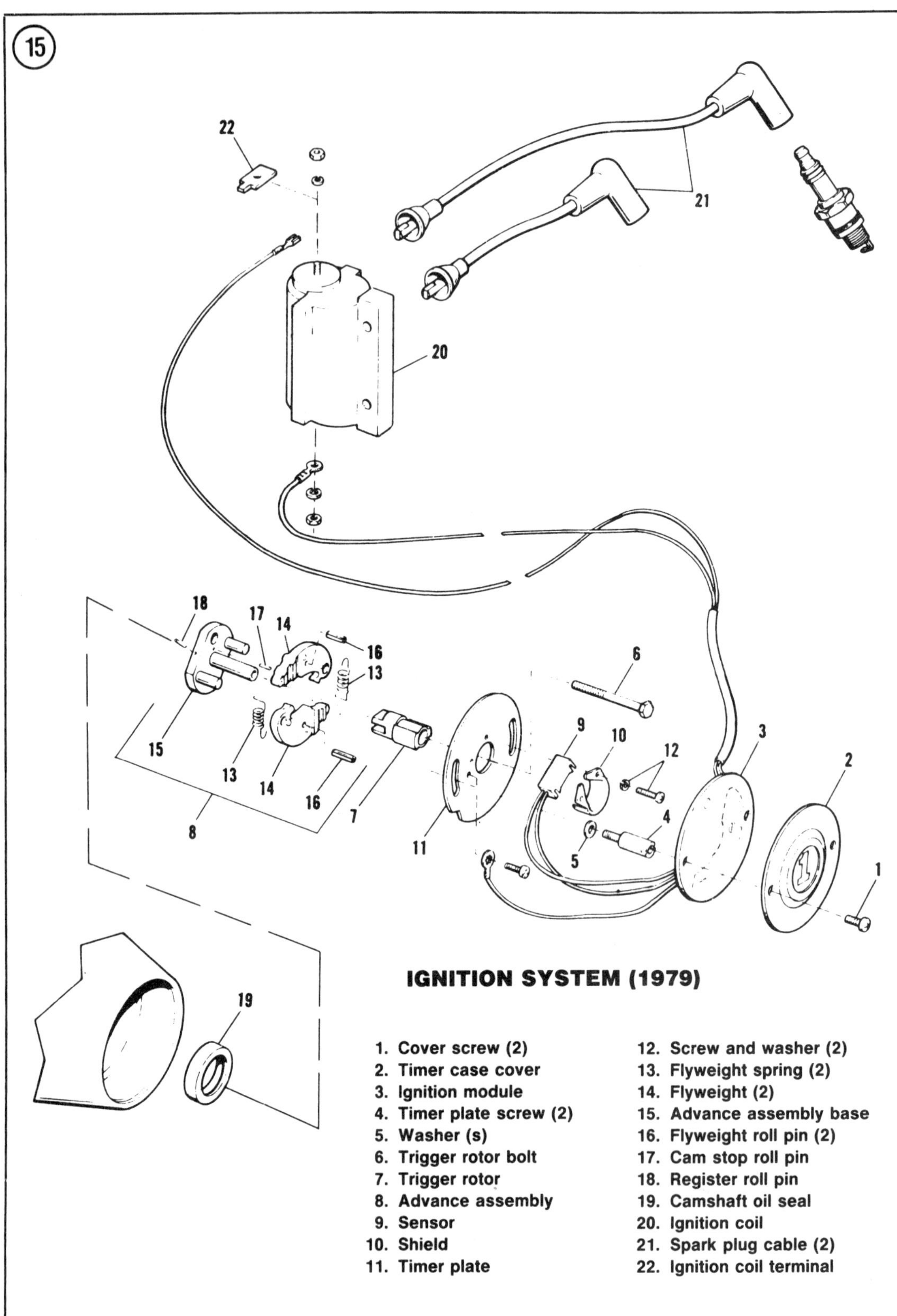

15

IGNITION SYSTEM (1979)

1. Cover screw (2)
2. Timer case cover
3. Ignition module
4. Timer plate screw (2)
5. Washer (s)
6. Trigger rotor bolt
7. Trigger rotor
8. Advance assembly
9. Sensor
10. Shield
11. Timer plate
12. Screw and washer (2)
13. Flyweight spring (2)
14. Flyweight (2)
15. Advance assembly base
16. Flyweight roll pin (2)
17. Cam stop roll pin
18. Register roll pin
19. Camshaft oil seal
20. Ignition coil
21. Spark plug cable (2)
22. Ignition coil terminal

6. Turn the engine over so that the sensor is located between the 2 trigger rotor lobes (**Figure 16**).
7. Connect a voltmeter between the ignition coil positive terminal (white wires) and a good engine ground. **Figure 17** shows the ignition circuit and wire color codes.

NOTE
The ignition and engine stop switches must be ON when performing Steps 8-11.

8. Turn the ignition and engine stop switches ON. The voltmeter should read 11.5 ±0.5 volts. Interpret results as follows:

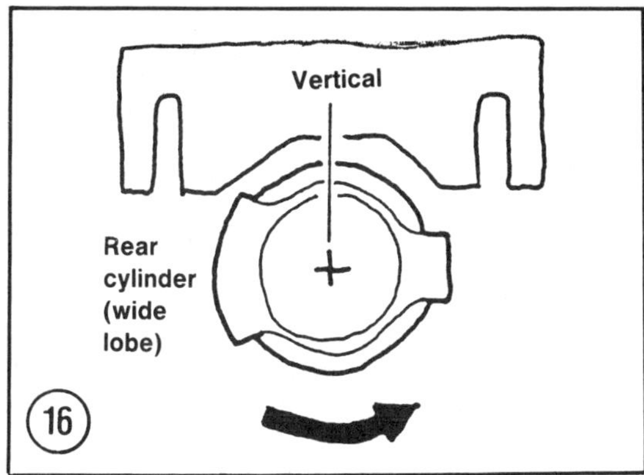

a. If the voltage is incorrect, the problem is in the battery-to-ignition coil circuit. Check the wiring connectors at the circuit breakers and at the ignition switch. See **Figure 17**.
b. If the voltage is correct, proceed to Step 9.

9. Disconnect the ignition coil negative (blue) connector (**Figure 17**). Connect a voltmeter between the coil negative terminal and a good engine ground. Turn the ignition and engine stop switches on. The voltmeter should read 11.5 ±0.5 volts. Interpret results as follows:

a. If the voltage is incorrect, the problem is in the ignition coil primary winding. Replace the ignition coil and perform the *Spark Test* as described in this chapter.
b. If the voltage is correct, proceed to Step 10.

10. Reconnect the ignition coil negative connector (blue).
11. Connect a voltmeter between the ignition coil negative terminal (**Figure 17**) and a good engine ground. The voltmeter should read 1-2 volts. Next place a screwdriver against the face of the sensor. The voltmeter should read 11.5-13 volts. Interpret results as follows:

a. If the voltage is incorrect in one or both tests, the ignition module is defective. Replace it as described in Chapter Seven.
b. If the voltage is correct, proceed to Step 12.

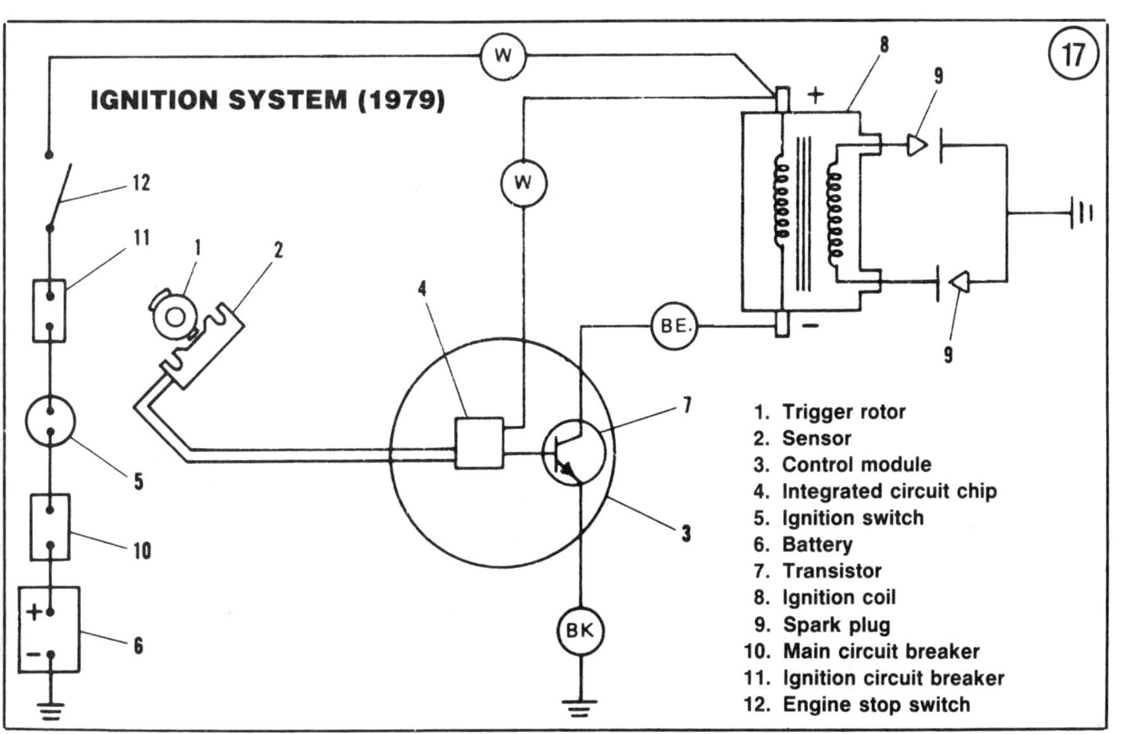

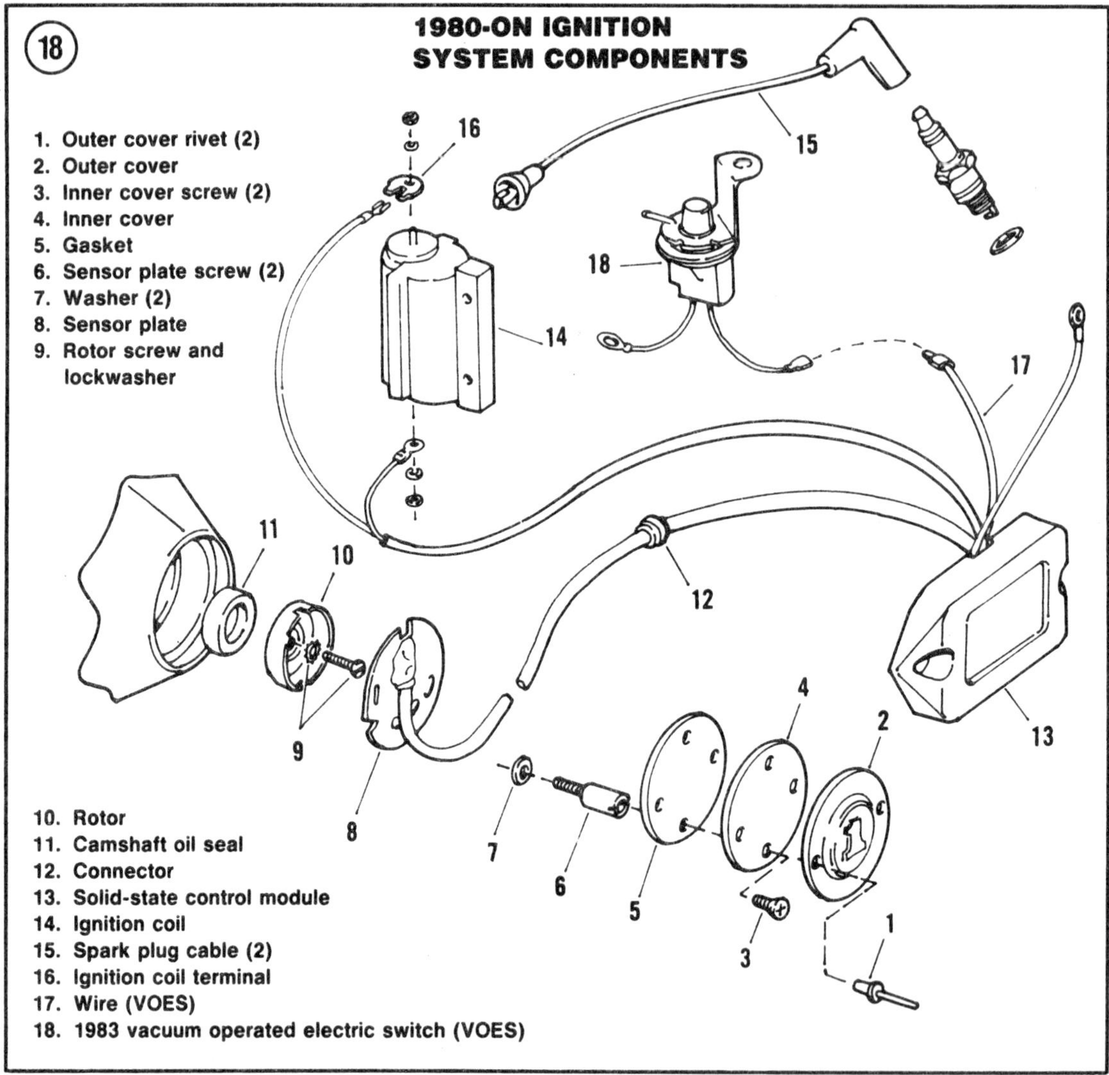

12. Disconnect one of the spark plug caps. Insert an adapter in the spark plug cap in place of the spark plug. Position the adapter so that it is approximately 3/16 in. away from the cylinder head surface. Hold the spark plug cap with insulated pliers (**Figure 14**). Place a screwdriver against the face of the sensor and at the same time watch the end of the adapter. A spark should occur each time the screwdriver touches the sensor face. If sparks do not occur, the ignition coil secondary winding is defective. Replace the ignition coil and retest.

1980-on

1. Check the battery charge as described in Chapter Three. If battery is okay, proceed to Step 2.

2. Remove the timer case outer cover (2, **Figure 18**).

3. Check that the ignition module black lead (13, **Figure 18**) is fastened securely. Check also that the battery ground lead is fastened and in good condition.

NOTE
When performing the following tests, a voltmeter with an input resistance of 20,000 ohms/volt or higher is required. A lower-resistance meter may give a faulty reading.

4. Turn the engine over so that the sensor is located between the 2 rotor lobes (**Figure 16**).

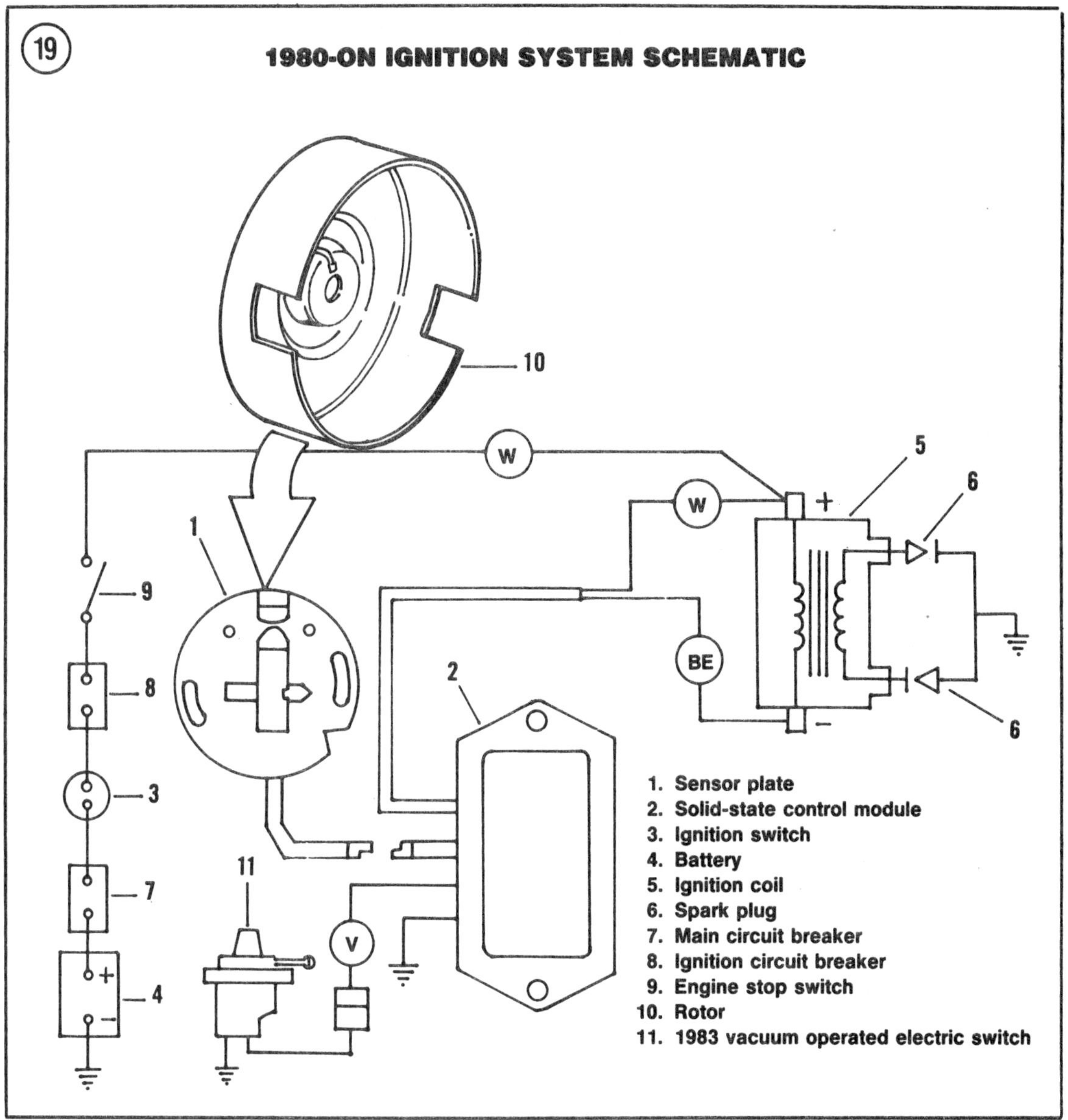

NOTE
The ignition switch and kill switch must be turned ON when performing Step 5 and step 6.

5. Connect a voltmeter between the ignition coil positive terminal (white wires) and a good engine ground. The voltmeter should read 11.5 ±0.5 volts. Interpret results as follows:
   a. If the voltage is incorrect, the problem is in the battery-to-ignition coil circuit. Check the wiring connectors at the circuit breakers (7 and 8, **Figure 19**) and at the ignition switch (3, **Figure 19**).
   b. If the voltage is correct, proceed to Step 6.

6. Disconnect the ignition coil negative (blue) connector. Connect a voltmeter between the coil negative terminal and a good engine ground. The voltmeter should read 11.5 ±0.5 volts. Interpret results as follows:
   a. If the voltage is incorrect, the problem is in the ignition coil primary winding. Replace the ignition coil and perform the *Spark Test* as described in this chapter.
   b. If the voltage is correct, check the control module and sensor beginning with Step 7.
   c. Turn the ignition switch OFF.
   d. Reconnect the ignition coil negative connector (blue).

7. Disconnect the sensor plate from the control module at the connector (12, **Figure 18**).
8. Install an ignition test adapter (HD-94465-81) and a voltmeter as shown in **Figure 20**.

NOTE
***Figure 21** shows how to make a test adapter for 1983-1985 models.*

CAUTION
When using the ignition test adapter, make sure the exposed terminal connector does not touch another connector or ground as this will damage the ignition module.

9. Turn the ignition switch and the kill switch ON and measure the voltage between the No. 1 pin (red wire) and the No. 2 pin (black wire) as shown in **Figure 20**.
10. The meter should read 4.5-5.5 volts. If it does not, the control module is defective and should be replaced as described in Chapter Seven.
11. To test the sensor operation, connect the voltmeter to the ignition test adapter as shown in **Figure 22**.
12. Turn the engine so that the rotor lobes are not aligned with the sensor (**Figure 16**). Measure the voltage reading. It should be 4.5-5.5 volts.
13. Turn the engine so that the center of the sensor is between the 2 rotor lobes (**Figure 23**). The voltmeter should read 0.1 volts.
14. If the voltage readings in Step 12 and step 13 are incorrect and the control module passes the test in Step 10, the sensor is faulty and should be replaced as described in Chapter Seven.
15. Turn the ignition switch OFF. Remove the ignition test adapter and reconnect the module connectors.

EXCESSIVE VIBRATION

This can be difficult to find without disassembling the engine. Usually this is caused by loose engine mounting hardware. High speed vibration may be due to a bent axle shaft or loose or faulty suspension components. Vibration can also be caused by the following conditions:

a. Broken frame.
b. Severely worn primary chain.
c. Tight primary chain links due to improper lubrication.
d. Improperly balanced wheels.
e. Defective or damaged wheels.
f. Defective or damaged tires.
g. Internal engine wear or damage.

CARBURETOR TROUBLESHOOTING

Troubleshooting procedures unique to HD carburetors are found in **Figure 24**. **Figure 25** lists troubleshooting procedures for Keihin carburetors. For other carburetors, use the HD carburetor

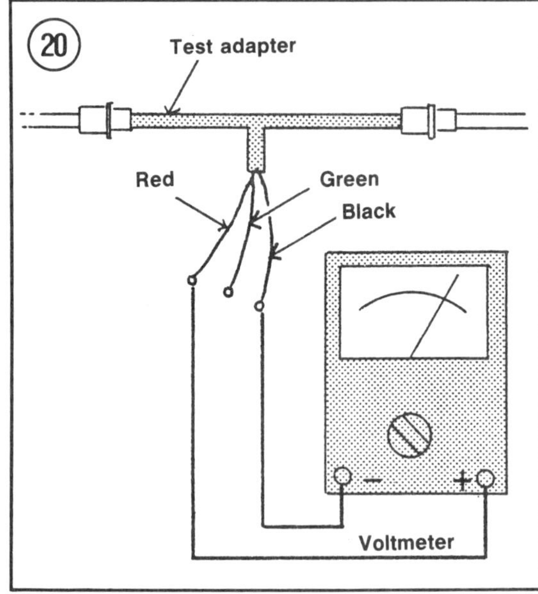

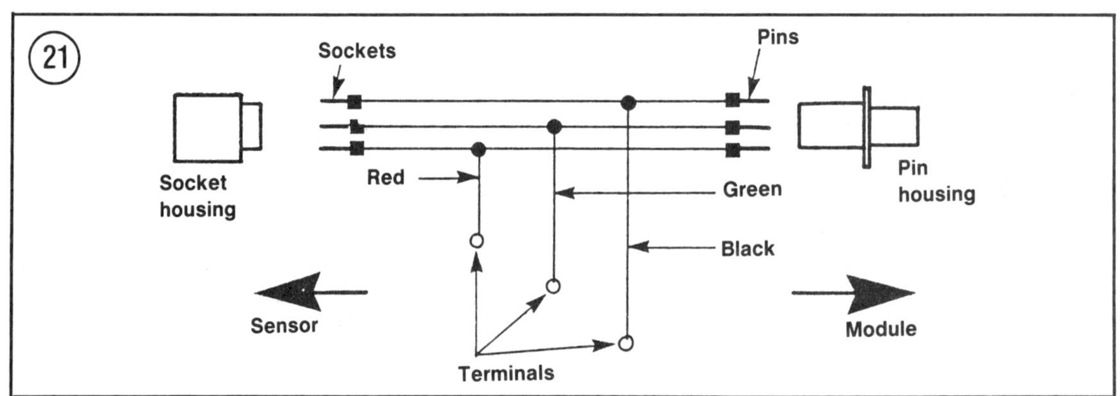

troubleshooting procedures in **Figure 24** as a basic guide.

FRONT SUSPENSION AND STEERING

Poor handling may be caused by improper pressure, a damaged or bent frame or steering components, worn wheel bearings or dragging brakes. Possible causes for suspension and steering malfunctions are listed below.

Irregular or Wobbly Steering

a. Loose wheel axle nuts.
b. Loose or worn steering head bearings.
c. Excessive wheel hub bearing play.
d. Damaged cast wheel.
e. Spoke wheel out of alignment.
f. Unbalanced wheel assembly.
g. Worn hub bearings.
h. Incorrect wheel alignment.
i. Bent or damaged steering stem or frame (at steering neck).
j. Tire incorrectly seated on rim.
k. Excessive front end loading from non-standard equipment.

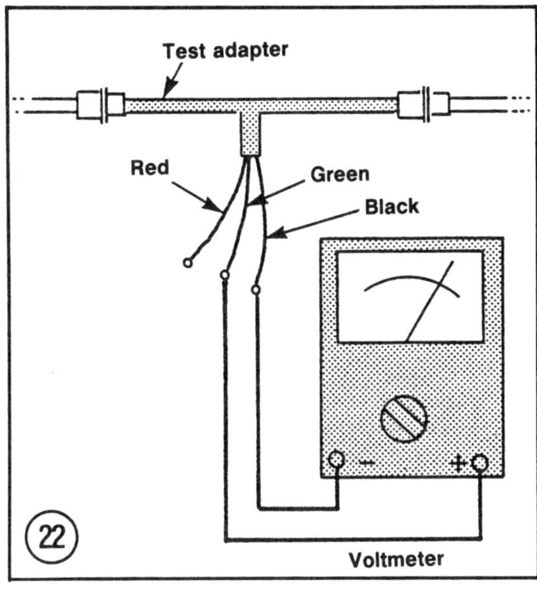

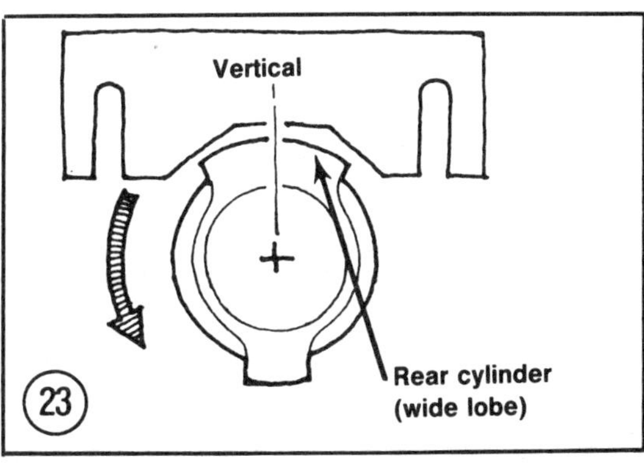

2

Stiff Steering

a. Low front tire air pressure.
b. Bent or damaged steering stem or frame (at steering neck).
c. Loose or worn steering head bearings.

Stiff or Heavy Fork Operation

a. Incorrect fork springs.
b. Incorrect fork oil viscosity.
c. Excessive amount of fork oil.
d. Bent fork tubes.

Poor Fork Operation

a. Worn or damage fork tubes.
b. Fork oil capacity low due to leaking fork seals.
c. Bent or damaged fork tubes.
d. Contaminated fork oil.
e. Incorrect fork springs.
f. Heavy front end loading from non-standard equipment.

Poor Rear Shock Absorber Operation

a. Weak or worn springs.
b. Leaking damper unit.
c. Worn or bent shock shaft.
d. Incorrect rear shock springs.
e. Incorrectly adjusted rear shocks.
f. Heavy rear end loading from non-standard equipment.
g. Incorrect loading.

BRAKE PROBLEMS

Sticking disc brakes may be caused by a stuck piston(s) in a caliper assembly, warped pad shim(s) or improper brake adjustment(rear brake only). See **Figure 26** for disc brake troubles and checks to make.

A sticking drum brake may be caused by worn or weak return springs, dry pivot and cam bushings or improper adjustment. Grabbing brakes may be caused by greasy linings which must be replaced. Brake grab may also be due to an out-of-round drum. Glazed linings will cause loss of stopping power. See **Figure 27** for drum brake troubles and checks to make.

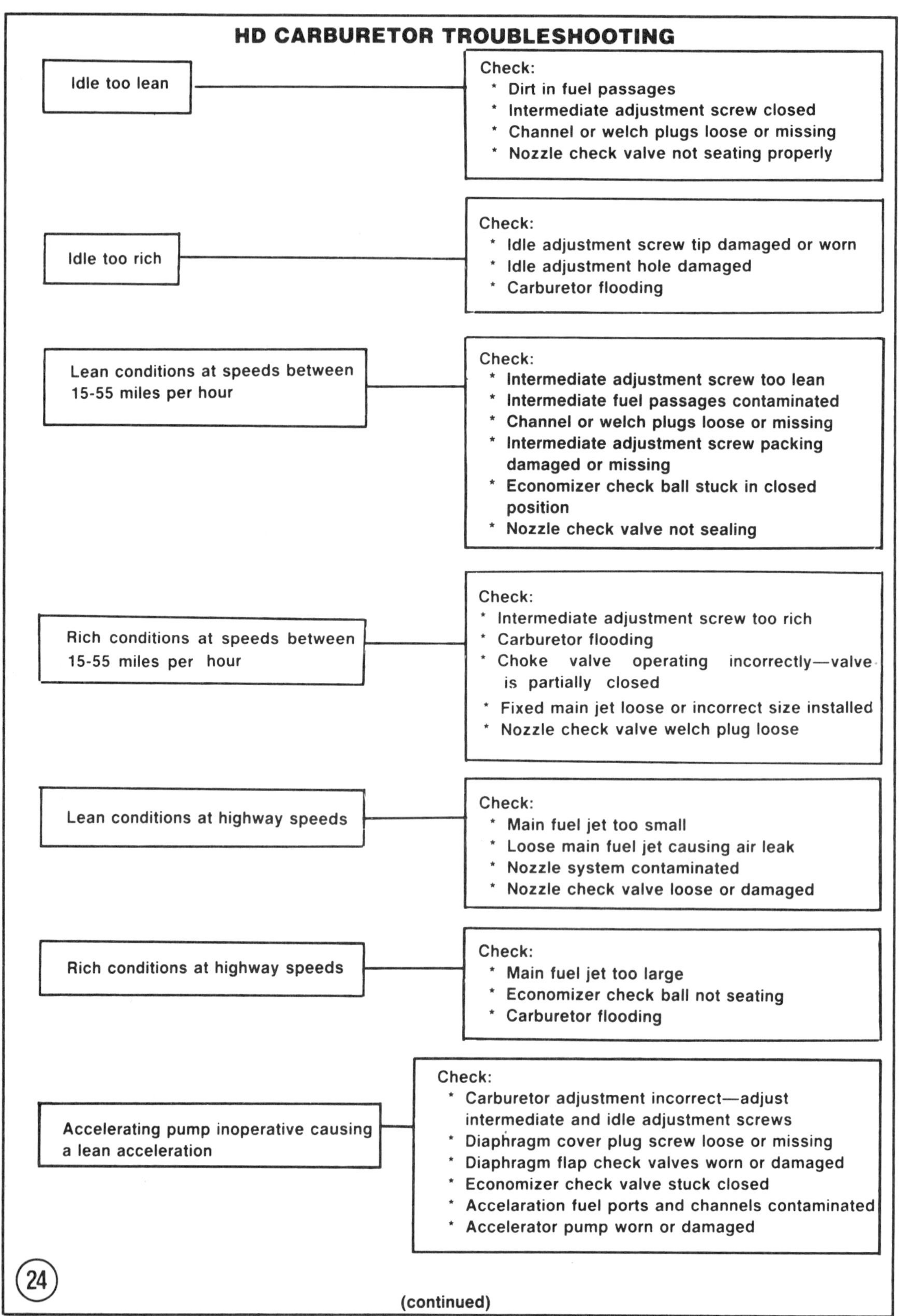
HD CARBURETOR TROUBLESHOOTING
Idle too lean
Check:
* Dirt in fuel passages
* Intermediate adjustment screw closed
* Channel or welch plugs loose or missing
* Nozzle check valve not seating properly
Idle too rich
Check:
* Idle adjustment screw tip damaged or worn
* Idle adjustment hole damaged
* Carburetor flooding
Lean conditions at speeds between 15-55 miles per hour
Check:
* Intermediate adjustment screw too lean
* Intermediate fuel passages contaminated
* Channel or welch plugs loose or missing
* Intermediate adjustment screw packing damaged or missing
* Economizer check ball stuck in closed position
* Nozzle check valve not sealing
Rich conditions at speeds between 15-55 miles per hour
Check:
* Intermediate adjustment screw too rich
* Carburetor flooding
* Choke valve operating incorrectly—valve is partially closed
* Fixed main jet loose or incorrect size installed
* Nozzle check valve welch plug loose
Lean conditions at highway speeds
Check:
* Main fuel jet too small
* Loose main fuel jet causing air leak
* Nozzle system contaminated
* Nozzle check valve loose or damaged
Rich conditions at highway speeds
Check:
* Main fuel jet too large
* Economizer check ball not seating
* Carburetor flooding
Accelerating pump inoperative causing a lean acceleration
Check:
* Carburetor adjustment incorrect—adjust intermediate and idle adjustment screws
* Diaphragm cover plug screw loose or missing
* Diaphragm flap check valves worn or damaged
* Economizer check valve stuck closed
* Accelaration fuel ports and channels contaminated
* Accelerator pump worn or damaged
24
(continued)

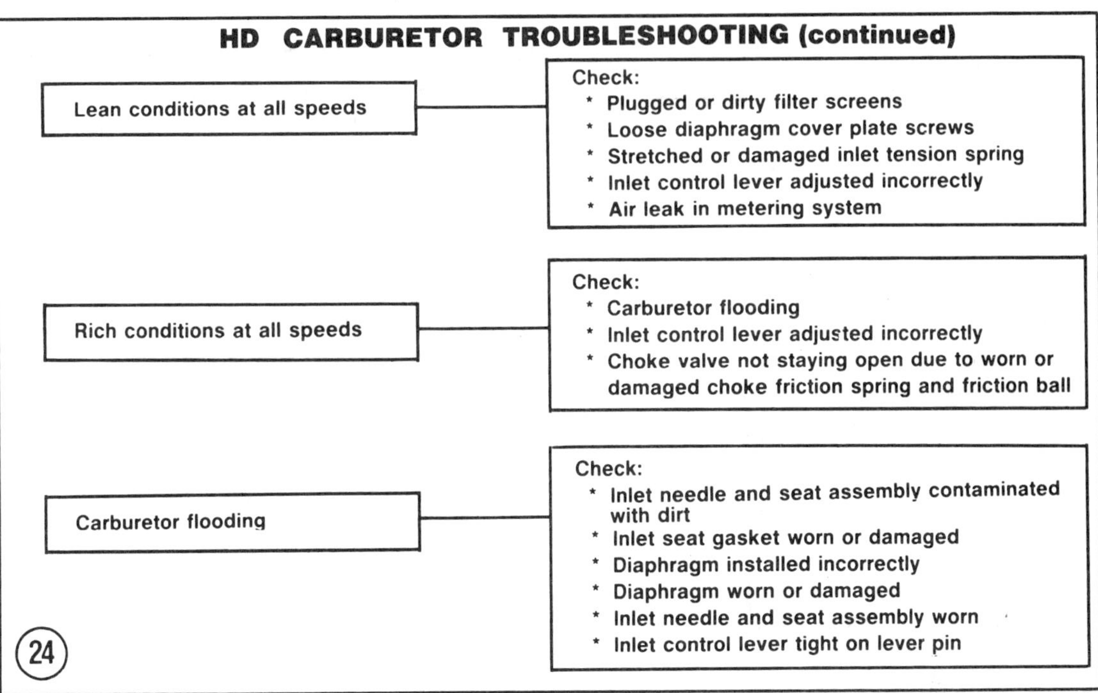

25

KEIHIN CARBURETOR TROUBLESHOOTING

Hard starting

Check:
* Choke not operating correctly
* Idle mixture misadjusted (early models with idle mixture adjustment only)
* Air leak at carburetor mounting
* Fuel overflow

Fuel overflows

Check:
* Worn float needle valve or dirty seat
* Incorrect float lever
* Damaged float bowl O-ring or loose float bowl mounting screws
* Damaged float pin or loose locking screw
* Damaged float

Poor idling

Check:
* Idle misadjusted
* Worn idle mixture screw
* Blocked jet or port in carburetor bore
* Air leak at carburetor mounting
* Accelerator pump rod too long or misadjusted

Poor acceleration

Check:
* Clogged accelerator pump
* Worn accelerator pump diaphragm
* Idle mixture misadjusted (early models with idle mixture adjustment only)
* Clogged slow jet
* Float level too high

(continued)

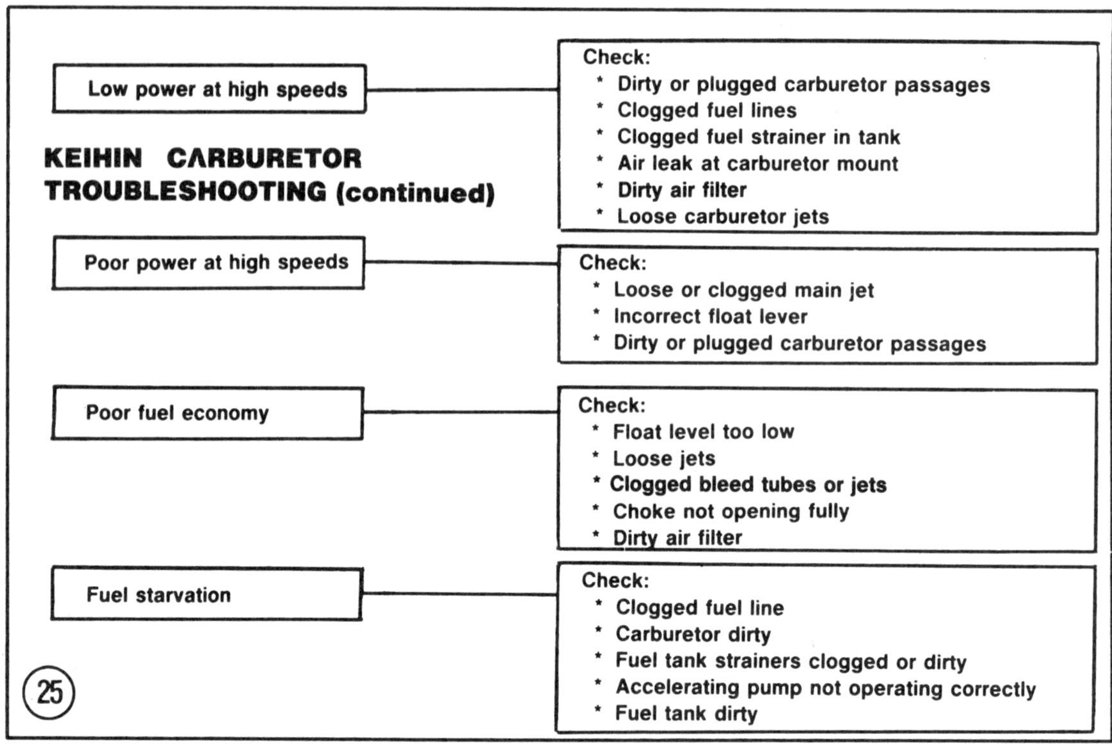

DISC BRAKE TROUBLESHOOTING

Disc brake fluid leakage

Check:
* Loose or damaged line fittings
* Worn caliper piston seals
* Scored caliper piston and/or bore
* Loose banjo bolts
* Damaged oil line washers
* Leaking master cylinder diaphragm
* Leaking master cylinder secondary seal
* Cracked master cylinder housing
* Too high brake fluid level
* Loose master cylinder cover

Brake overheating

Check:
* Warped brake disc
* Incorrect brake fluid
* Caliper piston and/or brake pads hanging up
* Riding brakes during riding

Brake chatter

Check:
* Warped brake disc
* Loose brake disc
* Incorrect caliper alignment
* Loose caliper mounting bolts
* Loose front axle nut and/or clamps
* Worn wheel bearing
* Damaged front hub
* Restricted brake hydraulic line
* Contaminated brake pads

26

(continued)

DISC BRAKE TROUBLESHOOTING (continued)

Brake locking

Check:
* Incorrect brake fluid
* Plugged passages in master cylinder
* Incorrect front brake adjustment
* Caliper piston and/or brake pads hanging up
* Warped brake disc

Insufficient brakes

Check:
* Air in brake lines
* Worn brake pads
* Low brake fluid
* Incorrect brake fluid
* Worn brake disc
* Worn caliper piston seals
* Glazed brake pads
* Leaking primary cup seal in master cylinder
* Contaminated brake pads and/or disc

Brake squeal

Check:
* Contaminated brake pads and/or disc
* Dust or dirt collected behind brake pads
* Loose parts

26

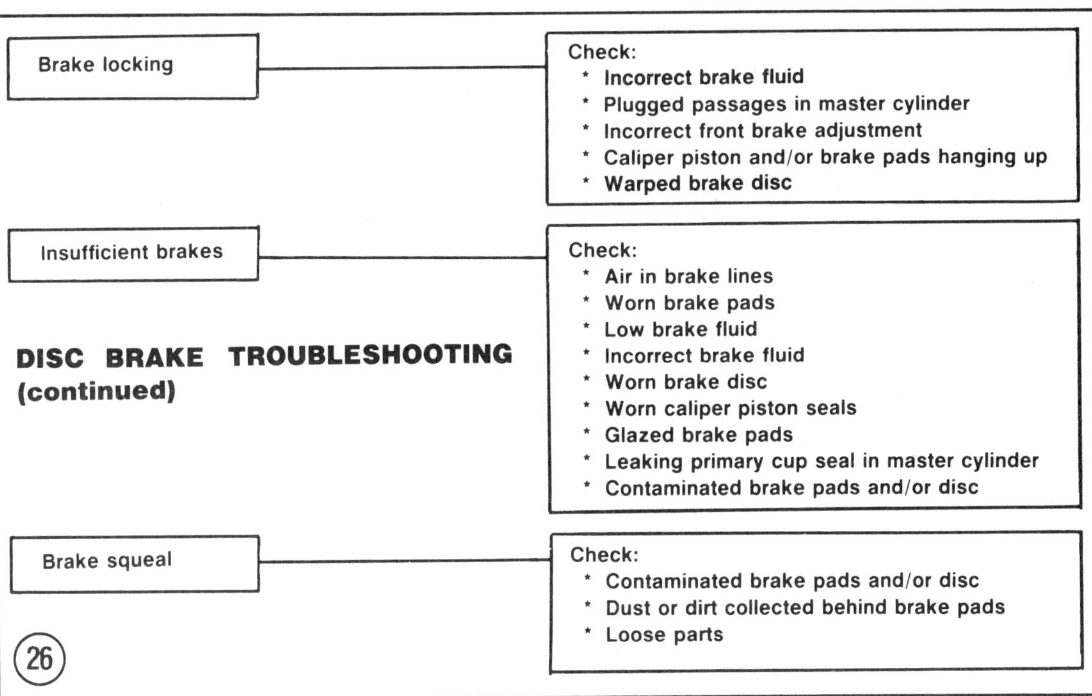

DRUM BRAKE TROUBLESHOOTING

27

Brakes do not hold

Check:
* Worn brake linings
* Glazed brake linings
* Worn brake drum
* Glazed brake drum
* Air in rear brake line
* Low rear master cylinder brake fluid
* Incorrect brake adjustment
* Worn or damaged front brake cable
* Improperly routed front brake cable
* Rear wheel cylinder defective
* Loose brake lining rivets

Brakes grab

Check:
* Worn or damaged brake return springs
* Loose brake lining rivets
* Loose brake lining
* Incorrect brake adjustment
* Brake drum out-of-round
* Loose brake drum-to-wheel mounting bolts
* Warped brake lining web
* Worn axle sleeve
* Loose or worn wheel bearings

Brakes squeal or scrape

Check:
* Worn brake linings—rivets scraping
* Brake drum out-of-round or scored
* Contaminated brake linings and drum
* Broken, loose or damaged brake component
* Loose or worn wheel bearing
* Loose brake drum-to-wheel mounting bolts

Brake chatter

Check:
* Brake drum out-of-round
* Brake linings worn unevenly
* Warped brake lining web
* Loose brake lining rivets
* Incorrect brake adjustment
* Loose or worn wheel bearing
* Worn or damaged brake return springs
* Worn cam lever bushing (1959-1971 front brake)
* Loose or damaged cam lever (1959-1971 front brake)
* Loose or worn operating shaft (1971-1972 FX)

CHAPTER THREE

PERIODIC LUBRICATION, MAINTENANCE AND TUNE-UP

Your bike can be cared for by two methods: preventive or corrective maintenance. Because a motorcycle is subjected to tremendous heat, stress and vibration (even in normal use), preventive maintenance prevents costly and unexpected corrective maintenance. A careful program of lubrication, preventive maintenance and regular tune-ups will result in longer engine and vehicle life, ensuring good performance, dependability and safety. It will also pay dividends in fewer and less expensive repair bills. Such a program is especially important if the bike is used in remote areas or on heavily traveled freeways where breakdowns are not only inconvenient but dangerous. Breakdowns are much less likely to occur if the bike has been well maintained.

Certain maintenance tasks and checks should be performed weekly. Others should be performed at certain time or mileage intervals. Still others should be done whenever certain symptoms appear. Some maintenance procedures are included under *Tune-up* at the end of this chapter. Detailed instructions will be found there. Other steps are described in the following chapters. Chapter references are included with these steps.

Scheduled maintenance requirements are provided in **Table 1** (1959-1969), **Table 2** (1970-1978) and **Table 3** (1979-1985). **Tables 1-11** are at the end of the chapter.

MAINTENANCE INTERVALS

The services and intervals shown in **Tables 1-3** are recommended by the factory. Strict adherence to these recommendations will go a long way toward insuring long service from your Harley-Davidson. If the bike is run in an area of high humidity, the lubrication service must be done more fequently to prevent possible rust damage.

For convenient maintenance of your motorcycle, most of the services shown in **Tables 1-3** are described in this chapter. Those procedures which require more than minor disassembly or adjustment are covered elsewhere in the appropriate chapter. The *Table of Contents* and *Index* can help you locate a particular service procedure.

ROUTINE CHECKS

The following simple checks should be carried out at each fuel stop.

Engine Oil Tank Level

Refer to *Periodic Lubrication* in this chapter.

General Inspection

1. Quickly examine the engine for signs of oil or fuel leakage.
2. Check the tires for imbedded stones.

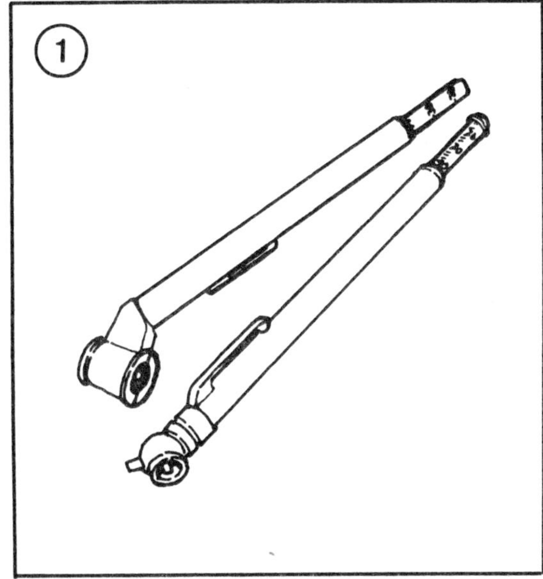

1

2

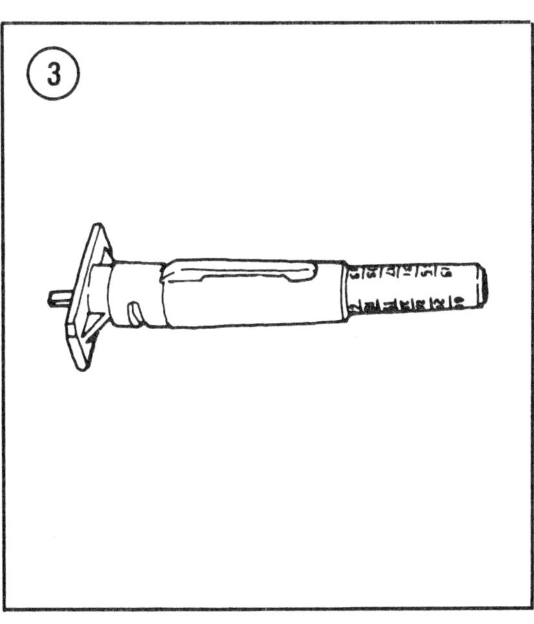

3

3. Make sure all lights work.

NOTE
At least check the brake light. It can burn out anytime. Motorists can't stop as quickly as you and need all the warning you can give.

Tire Pressure

Tire pressure must be checked with the tires cold. Correct tire pressure depends a lot on the load you are carrying. See **Table 4**.

Lights and Horn

With the engine running, check the following.

1. Pull the front brake lever and check that the brake light comes on.
2. Push the rear brake pedal and check that the brake light comes on soon after you have begun depressing the pedal.
3. With the engine running, operate all light switches and check light operation.
4. Push the horn button and note that the horn blows loudly.
5. If the horn or any light failed to work properly, refer to Chapter Seven.

TIRES

Pressure

Tire pressure should be checked and adjusted to accommodate rider and luggage weight. A simple, accurate gauge (**Figure 1**) can be purchased for a few dollars and should be carried in your motorcycle tool kit. The appropriate tire pressures are shown in **Table 4**.

NOTE
*After checking and adjusting the air pressure, make sure to reinstall the air valve cap (**Figure 2**). The cap prevents small pebbles and/or dirt from collecting in the valve stem; these could allow air leakage or result in incorrect tire pressure readings.*

Inspection

Check tire tread for excessive wear, deep cuts, imbedded objects such as stones, nails, etc. If you find a nail in a tire, mark its location with a light crayon before pulling it out. This will help to locate the hole. Refer to *Tire Changing* in Chapter Eight.

Check local traffic regulations concerning minimum tread depth. Measure with a tread depth gauge (**Figure 3**) or small ruler. Harley-Davidson recommends replacement when the tread depth is 5/16 in. or less.

3

Tread depth indicators appear across the tire when tread reaches minimum safe depth. Replace the tire at this point.

Wheel Spoke Tension

On spoked wheels, tap each spoke with a screwdriver (**Figure 4**). The higher pitch of sound it makes, the tighter the spoke. The lower the sound frequency, the looser the spoke. A "ping" is good; a "clunk" says the spoke is loose.

If one or more spokes are loose, tighten them as described in Chapter Eight.

Rim Inspection

Frequently inspect the wheel rims. If a rim has been damaged it might have been knocked out of alignment. Improper wheel alignment can cause severe vibration and result in an unsafe riding condition. If the rim portion of an alloy wheel is damaged, the wheel must be replaced as it cannot be serviced. Refer to Chapter Eight for rim service.

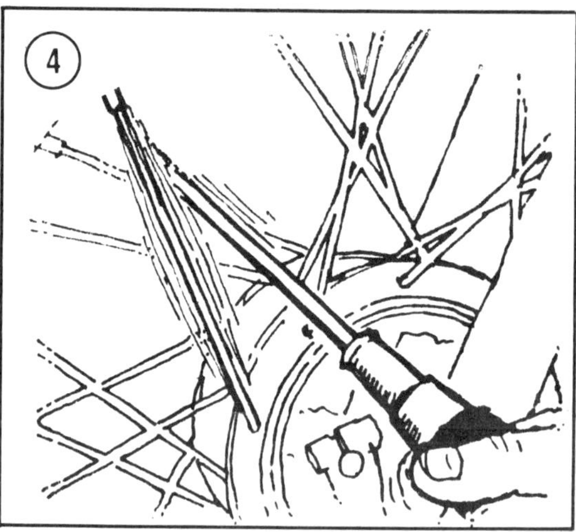

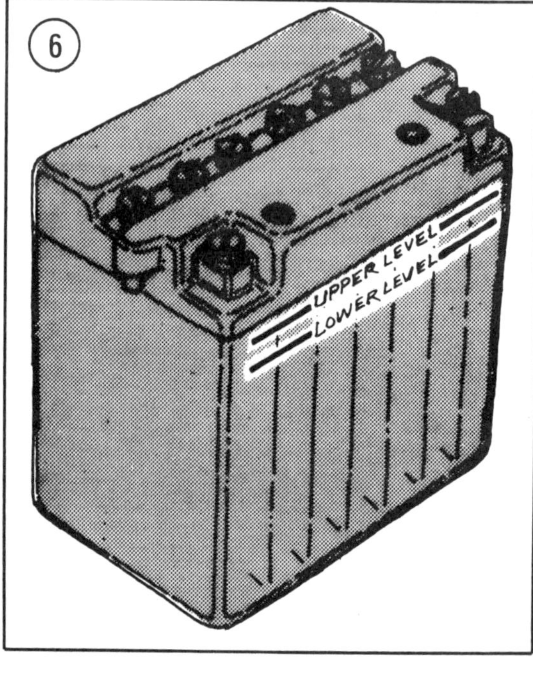

BATTERY

CAUTION

If it becomes necessary to remove the battery breather tube when performing any of the following procedures, make sure to route the tube correctly during installation to prevent acid from spilling on parts.

Checking Electrolyte Level

The battery is the heart of the electrical system. It should be checked and serviced as indicated. The majority of electrical system troubles can be attributed to neglect of this vital component.

In order to correctly service the electrolyte level it is necessary to remove the battery from the frame. The electrolyte level should be maintained between the two marks on the battery case. See **Figure 5** and **Figure 6**. If the electrolyte level is low, it's a good idea to completely remove the battery so that it can be thoroughly cleaned, serviced and checked.

NOTE

If the battery on your bike is not equipped with level marks, remove the battery and battery caps as described in this procedure. The electrolyte level should be maintained at the base of the filler hole.

1. Remove all necessary components to gain access to the battery terminals.
2. Disconnect the negative cable (**Figure 7**) from the battery.

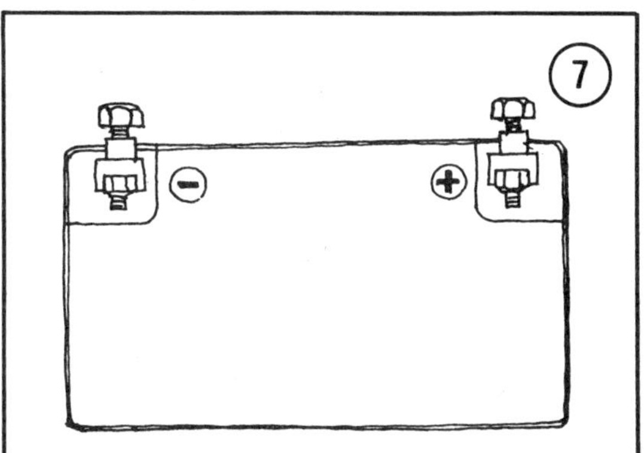

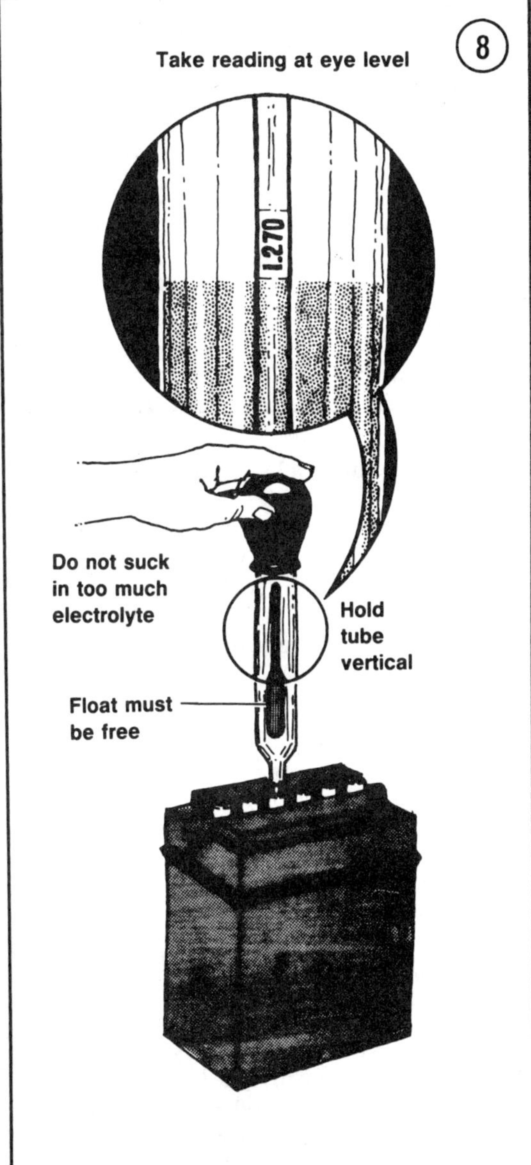

3. Disconnect the battery positive cable (**Figure 7**) from the battery.
4. Remove the battery hold-down strap. Pull the battery out slightly to provide access to the vent tube then disconnect the vent tube.
5. Slide the battery out of the box.

CAUTION
Be careful not to spill battery electrolyte on painted or polished surfaces. The liquid is highly corrosive and will damage the finish. If it is spilled, wash it off immediately with soapy water and thoroughly rinse with clean water.

6. Remove the caps from the battery cells and add distilled water to correct the level. Never add electrolyte (acid) to correct the level.
7. After the level has been corrected and the battery allowed to stand for a few minutes, check the specific gravity of the electrolyte in each cell with a hydrometer. See **Figure 8**. Follow the manufacturer's instructions for reading the instrument. See *Battery Testing* in this chapter.

Cleaning

After the battery has been removed from the bike, check it for corrosion or excessive dirt. The top of the battery in particular should be kept clean. Acid film and dirt will permit current to flow between the terminals, causing the battery to slowly discharge.

For best results when cleaning, first rinse off the top of the battery with plenty of clean water (avoid letting water enter the cells). Then carefully wash the case, both terminals and the battery box with a solution of baking soda and tap water (about 2 tablespoons of baking soda in a 1-lb. coffee can of water is a good ratio). Keep the cells sealed tight with the filler plugs so that none of the cleaning solution enters a cell as this would neutralize the cell's electrolyte and seriously damage the battery. Brush the solution on liberally with a stiff bristle parts cleaning brush. Using a strong spray from a garden hose, clean all the residue from the solution off the battery and all painted surfaces.

Testing

Hydrometer testing is the best way to check battery condition. Use a hydrometer with numbered graduations from 1.100 to 1.300 rather than one with just color-coded bands. To use the hydrometer, squeeze the rubber ball, insert the tip into the cell and release the ball. Draw enough electrolyte to float the weighted float inside the hydrometer. Note the number in line with the electrolyte surface; this is the specific gravity for this cell. Return the electrolyte to the cell from which it came. The specific gravity of the electrolyte in each battery cell is an excellent indication of that cell's condition. A fully charged cell will read 1.260-1.280, while a cell in good condition reads from 1.230-1.250 and anything below 1.140 is discharged.

NOTE
Specific gravity varies with temperature. For each 10° that electrolyte temperature exceeds 80° F, add 0.004 to the reading indicated on hydrometer. Subtract 0.004 for each 10° below 80° F.

If the cells test in the poor range, the battery requires recharging. The hydrometer is useful for checking the progress of the charging operation. **Table 5** shows approximate state of charge.

Charging

CAUTION
Always remove the battery from the motorcycle before connecting charging equipment.

WARNING
During charging, highly explosive hydrogen gas is released from the battery. The battery should be charged only in a well-ventilated area, and open flames and any other source of ignition should be kept away. Never check the charge of the battery by arcing across the terminals; the resulting spark can ignite the hydrogen gas.

1. Connect the positive (+) charger lead to the positive battery terminal and the negative (-) charger lead to the negative battery terminal.
2. Remove all vent caps from the battery, set the charger at 6 or 12 volts and switch it on. If the output of the charger is variable, it is best to select a low setting—1 1/2 to 2 amps.

NOTE
During production, 6-volt batteries were used on 1959-1966 models. Models from 1967-on use 12-volt batteries.

3. After battery has been charged for about 8 hours, turn the charger off, disconnect the leads and check the specific gravity (**Figure 8**). It should be within the limits specified in **Table 5**. If it is, and remains stable for one hour, the battery is charged.
4. To ensure good electrical contact, cables must be clean and tight on the battery's terminals. If the cable terminals are badly corroded, even after performing the above cleaning procedures, the cables should be disconnected, removed from the bike and cleaned separately with a wire brush and a baking soda solution. After cleaning, apply a very thin coating of petroleum jelly (Vaseline) to the battery terminals before reattaching the cables. After connecting the cables, apply a light coating to the connections also—this will delay future corrosion.

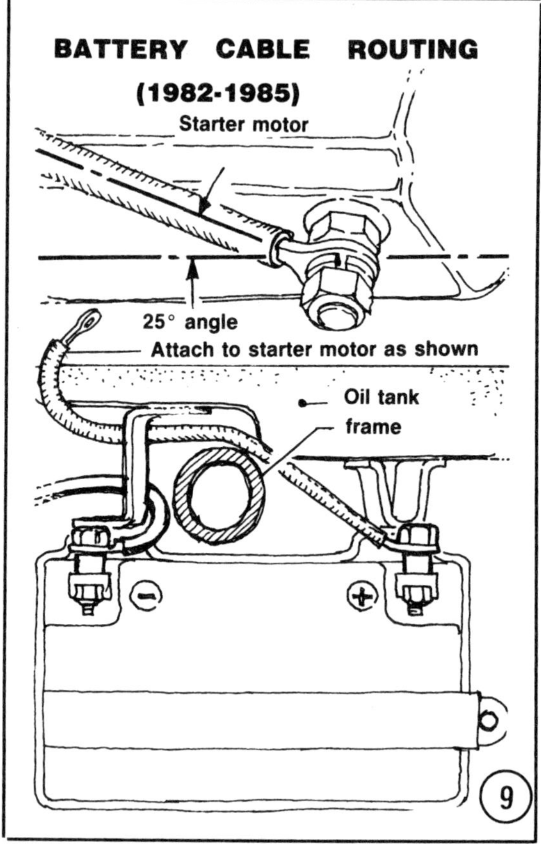

CAUTION
*When reconnecting the positive battery cable on 1982-1985 models, route the cable away from the edge of the oil tank (**Figure 9**). This surface could possibly cut the battery cable insulation and short circuit the electrical system.*

New Battery Installation

When replacing the old battery with a new one, be sure to charge it completely (specific gravity, 1.260-1.280) before installing it in the bike.

Failure to do so, or using the battery with a low electrolyte level, will permanently damage the battery.

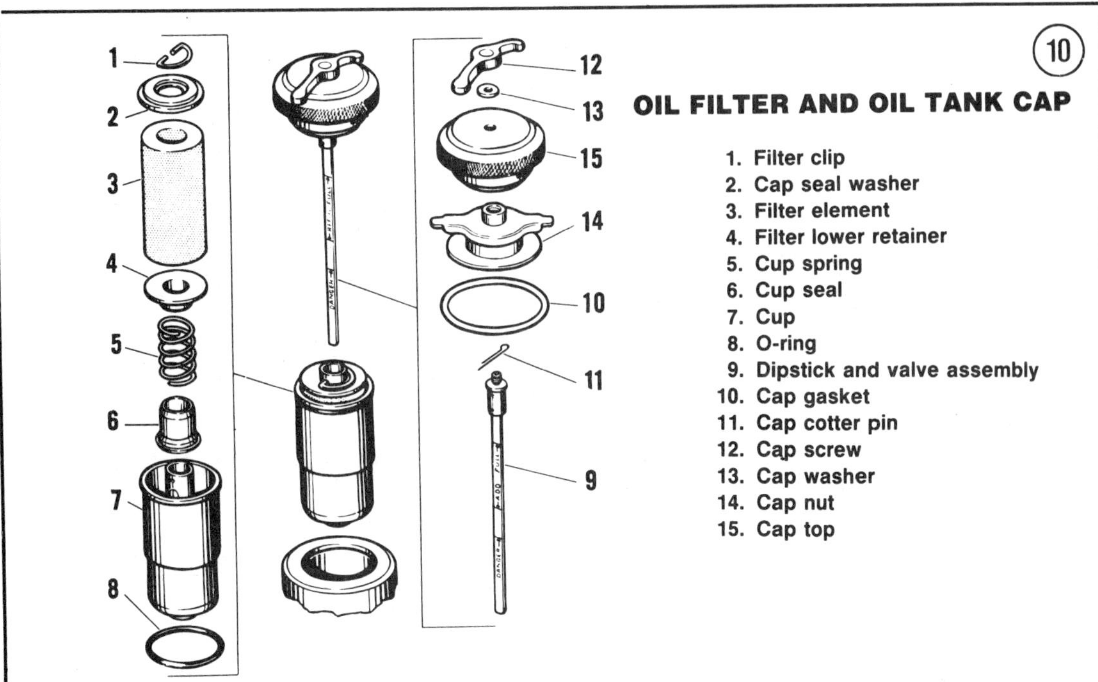

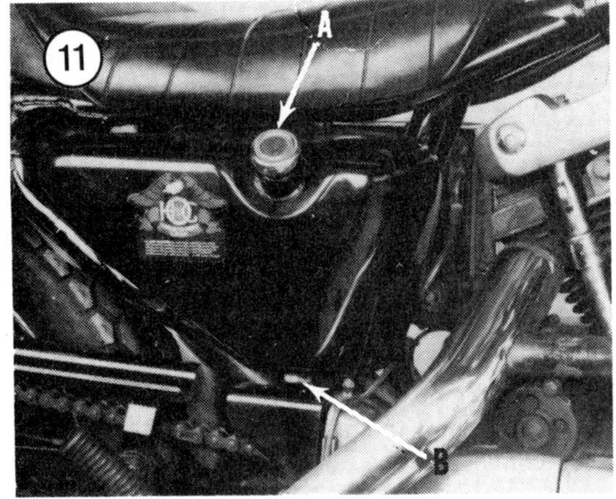

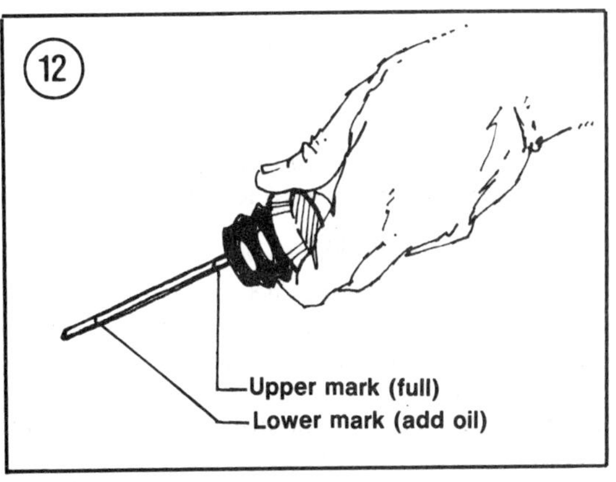

PERIODIC LUBRICATION

All lubrication checks and adjustments should be performed at the intervals specified in **Tables 1-3**.

Oil Tank Level Check

The engine oil runs cooler when the oil level is kept high in the tank.

1. Hold the bike upright.

2A. *1959-1979:* Remove the oil tank cap and dipstick. Oil level should be above "Refill" or "Add" mark (**Figure 10**). If not, add the recommended oil (**Table 6**) to bring it level with "Full" mark. Do not overfill.

2B. *1980-1985:* Remove the oil tank cap and dipstick (A, **Figure 11**). Oil level should be above lower mark on dipstick (**Figure 12**). If not, add the recommended oil (**Table 6**) to bring it level with upper dipstick mark. Do not overfill.

NOTE

On all models, 1 quart can be added when oil level is at lower dipstick mark.

3. Reinstall dipstick and oil tank cap.

Engine Oil and Filter Change

The factory-recommended oil and filter change interval is specified in **Tables 1-3**. This assumes that the motorcyle is operated in moderate climates. The time interval is more important than the mileage interval because combustion acids, formed by gasoline and water vapor, will contaminate the oil even if the motorcycle is not run for several months. If a motorcycle is operated under dusty conditions, the oil will get dirty more quickly and should be changed more frequently than recommended.

Use only a detergent oil with an API classification of SF. The classification is stamped on top of the can (**Figure 13**). Try always to use the same brand of oil. Use of oil additives is not recommended. Refer to **Table 6** for correct viscosity of oil to use under different temperatures.

To change the engine oil and filter you will need the following:

a. Drain pan.
b. Funnel.
c. Can opener or pour spout.
d. Wrench set.
e. Oil (see **Table 6** and **Table 7**).
f. Oil filter element (spin-on type).

NOTE
Never dispose of motor oil in the trash, on the ground, or down a storm drain. Many service stations accept used motor oil and waste haulers provide curbside used motor oil collection. Do not combine other fluids with motor oil to be recycled. To locate a recycler, contact the American Petroleum Institute (API) at ***www.recycleoil.org****.*

1. Place the motorcycle on its sidestand.
2. Start the engine and run it until it is at normal operating temperature, then turn it off.

NOTE
Before removing the oil tank cap, thoroughly clean off all dirt and oil around it.

3. Remove the oil tank cap and dipstick (A, **Figure 11**); this will speed up the flow of oil.
4. Place a drain pan and funnel underneath the oil tank drain plug and direct the funnel so that the oil will drain into the pan. Remove the drain plug and gasket (B, **Figure 11**).

5A. *1959-1979:* Remove and service the oil filter as follows. See **Figure 10**.

a. Remove the oil filter cup from the oil tank.
b. Remove the clip and washer and remove the oil filter.
c. Thoroughly clean the clip and washer and remove the oil filter.
d. Reinstall the oil filter into the cup.

5B. *1980-1985:* These models use an automotive type spin-on filter. Service the oil filter as follows:

13

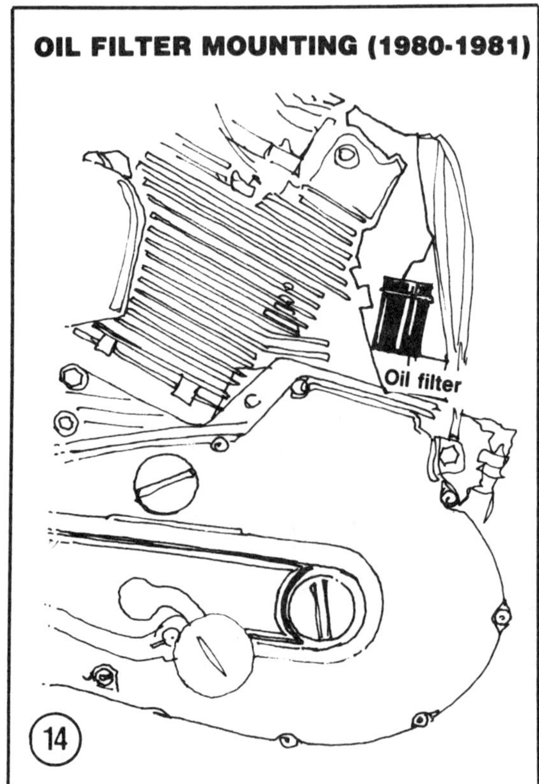

OIL FILTER MOUNTING (1980-1981)
14

a. Remove the filter with a filter wrench. On 1980-1981 models the oil filter is located between the oil tank and engine (**Figure 14**). On 1982-1985 models the oil filter is located on the lower left front engine brackete (**Figure 15**).
b. Discard the oil filter.
c. Wipe the crankcase gasket surface with a clean, lint-free cloth.
d. Coat the neoprene gasket on the new filter with clean oil (**Figure 16**).
e. Screw the filter onto the crankcase by hand until the filter gasket just touches the base, i.e.,

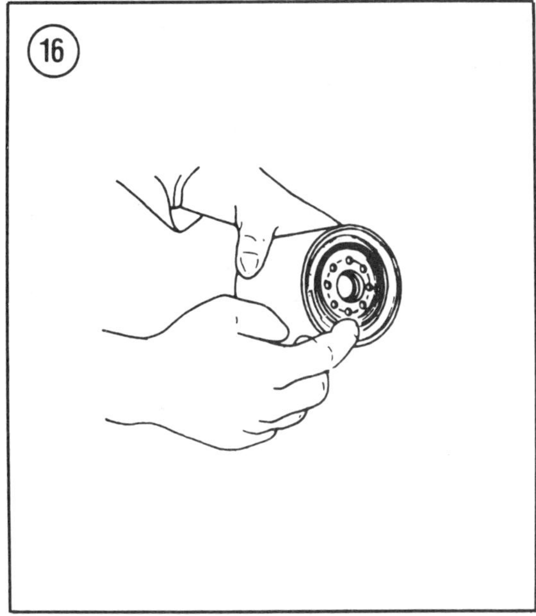

until you feel the slightest resistance when turning the filter. Then tighten the filter *by hand* 2/3 turn more.

CAUTION
Do not overtighten and do not use a filter wrench or the filter may leak.

6. At the first 500 miles, and at every second oil change, clean the oil tank as follows:
   a. Reinstall the oil tank drain plug (B, **Figure 11**) and gasket.
   b. Fill the oil tank 3/4 full with kerosene.
   c. Rock the bike from side to side to thoroughly flush the oil tank of sludge and sediment accumulation.
   d. Remove the drain plug and drain the kerosene.
   e. Reinstall the oil tank drain plug and gasket.
7. Fill the oil tank with the correct viscosity (**Table 6**) and quantity (**Table 7**) of oil.
8. Screw in the oil tank cap and dipstick securely.
9. Whenever the engine oil system is drained, air trapped in the oil lines may cause the oil pump to lose its prime. Perform the following whenever first starting the bike after changing the oil:
   a. *1959-1969 with oil pressure warning light:* Start the engine. Make sure light goes out within 1 minute. If not, perform Step "b."
   b. *1959-1969 without oil pressure warning light:* Start the engine. Then loosen the plug at the front of the oil pump and allow about 3 ounces of oil to drain out. Tighten plug.
   c. *1970-1978:* Start engine and operate at fast idle. Make sure the oil pressure warning light goes out within 1 minute. If not, loosen the plug in the fitting at the front of the oil pump (1970-1976) or loosen the pressure switch at the front of the oil pump (1977-1978) and allow about 3 ounces of oil to drain out. Tighten the plug or switch to 12-16 in.-lb.
   d. *1979-1985:* Start engine and operate at fast idle. Make sure the oil pressure warning light goes out within 1 minute. If not, loosen the oil pressure switch at the front of the oil pump (**Figure 17**) and allow about 1 ounce of oil to drain out. Tighten the switch.
   e. Add engine oil to correct the oil level in tank.

Transmission/Primary Drive Oil

The transmission and primary chain share a common oil supply. The oil should be checked and changed at the specified intervals (**Tables 1-3**).

Oil level check

1. Set the bike level with both wheels on the ground.
2. Remove the oil filler plug from the top of the primary chain cover (**Figure 18**).
3. Place a drip pan undeneath the primary chain cover.
4. Remove the oil level plug from the bottom of the cover (**Figure 19**).
5. Oil should seep out of the level hole. If it does not, slowly add the recommended oil (**Table 6**) through the filler hole (**Figure 18**) until the oil just begins to run out. Wait until the oil ceases to run out and install the level and filler plugs.

Oil change

1. Place a drip pan underneath the primary drive cover.
2. Remove the oil filler (**Figure 18**) and oil level (**Figure 19**) plugs from the primary drive cover.
3. Remove the drain plug at the bottom of the engine crankcase. **Figure 20** shows the plug on 1977-1985 models (engine removed for clarity). The transmission drain plug position on 1959-1976 models is similar. Allow the oil to drain for 10 minutes.

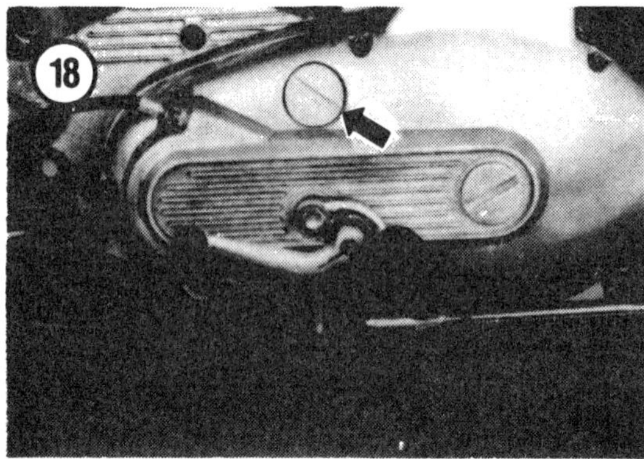

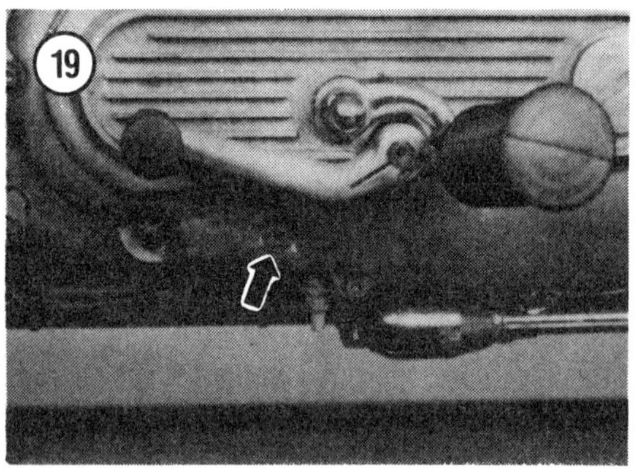

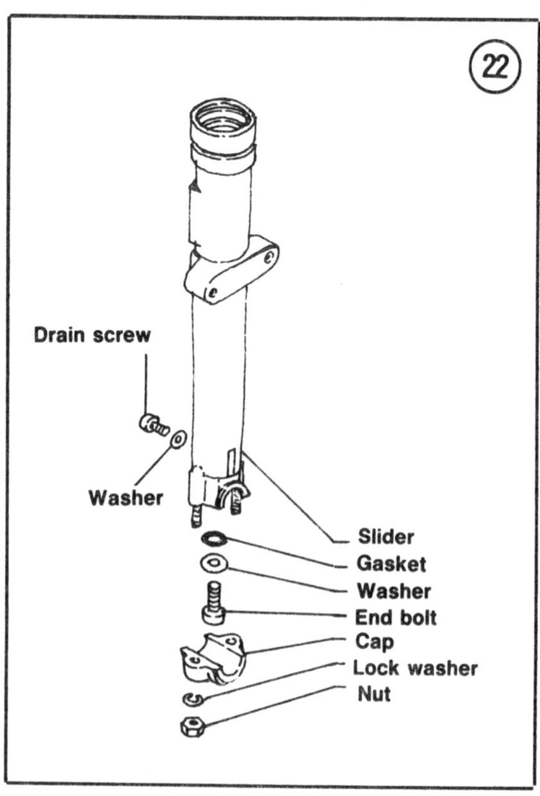

4. Clean the drain plug and install it and its gasket in the cover.
5. Refill the primary drive cover through the filler hole (**Figure 18**) with the recommended oil (**Table 6**). Continue to add oil until the oil begins to run out of the level hole (**Figure 19**). When oil ceases to run out, install the level and filler plugs.

Front Fork Oil Change

1. Remove the front wheel on 1959-1978 models as described in Chapter Eight.
2. Place a drip pan under the fork and remove the fork slider drain screw (**Figure 21**). Allow the oil to drain for at least 5 minutes.
3. *1959-1978:* Loosen the fork tube end bolt (**Figure 22**) several turns, but do not remove it.

CAUTION
Do not allow the fork oil to come in contact with any of the brake components.

4. Install the slider drain screw (**Figure 21**). On 1959-1978 models, tighten the fork tube end bolt (**Figure 22**).
5A. *1959-1978:* To facilitate filling the fork tubes, an oil filler container can be constructed with a 1-quart tin can as shown in **Figure 23**. To use the filler can, perform the following:
   a. Attach the can and hose to the front fork as shown in **Figure 24**.

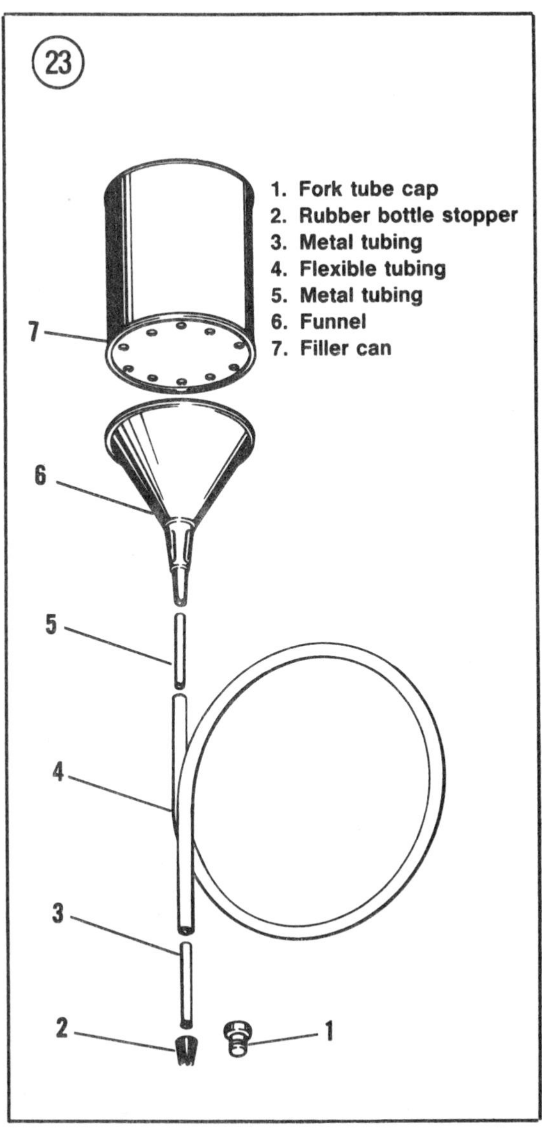

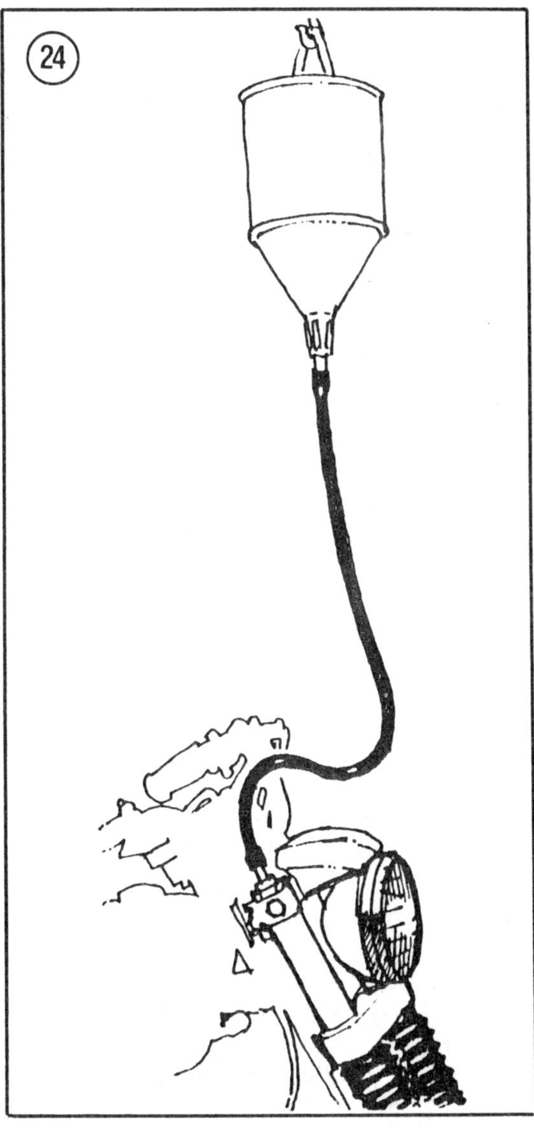

3

b. Fill the can with the correct amount (**Table 8**) and viscosity (**Table 6**) fork oil.
c. Work the fork leg up and down by hand. This action will cause oil to be sucked into the fork.

5B. *1979-1985:* Fill the fork tube with the correct amount (**Table 8**) and viscosity (**Table 6**) fork oil.

NOTE
If fork has been disassembled, refill with "dry" quantity; otherwise refill with "wet" quantity.

NOTE
In order to measure the correct amount of fluid, use a plastic baby bottle. These bottles have measurements in fluid ounces (oz.) and cubic centimeters (cc) imprinted on the side.

6. Check the condition of the fork cap O-ring (if so equipped), and replace it if necessary.
7. Install the fork cap.
8. Repeat Steps 2-7 for the opposite side.
9. Road test the bike and check for oil leaks.

Control Cables

The control cables should be lubricated at the intervals specified in **Tables 1-3**. At this time, they should also be inspected for fraying, and the cable sheath should be checked for chafing. The cables are relatively inexpensive and should be replaced when found to be faulty.

They can be lubricated with any of the popular cable lubricants and a cable lubricator or paper cone. The second method requires more time and complete lubrication of the entire cable is less certain.

NOTE
The main cause of cable breakage or cable stiffness is lack of lubrication. Maintaining the cables as described in this section will assure long service life.

Lubricator method

1. Disconnect the clutch cable from the left-hand side handlebar. Disconnect the throttle cable from the throttle grip. See Chapter Eight.
2. Attach a lubricator to the cable following the manufacturer's instructions.

NOTE
Place a shop cloth at the end of the cable(s) to catch all excess lubricant that will flow out during the next step.

3. Insert the nozzle of the lubricant can into the lubricator, press the button on the can and hold it down until the lubricant begins to flow out of the other end of the cable. See **Figure 25**.

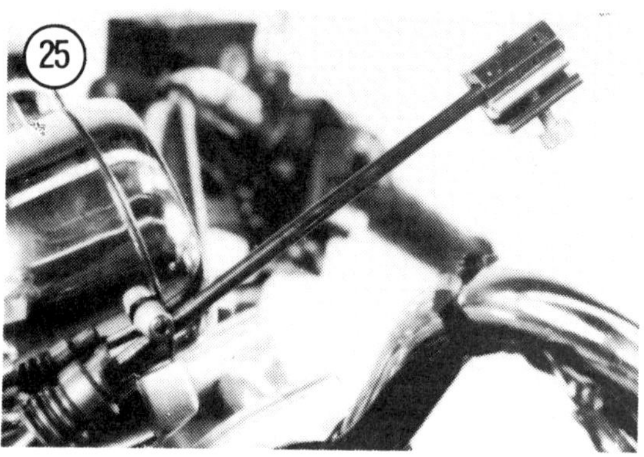

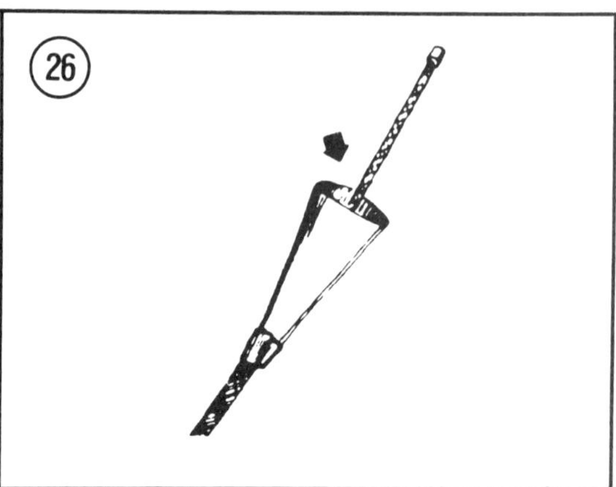

4. Remove the lubricator, reconnect and adjust the cable(s) as described in this chapter.

Oil method

1. Disconnect the cables as previously described.
2. Make a cone of stiff paper and tape it to the end of the cable sheath (**Figure 26**).
3. Hold the cable upright and pour a small amount of light oil (SAE 10W/30) into the cone. Work the cable in and out of the sheath for several minutes to help the oil work its way down to the end of the cable.
4. Remove the cone, reconnect the cable and adjust the cable(s) as described in this chapter.

Swing Arm Bearings

Repack the rear swing arm bearings with a lithium-base, waterproof wheel bearing grease.

Refer to *Swing Arm, Removal/Installation* in Chapter Nine for complete details.

Circuit Breaker Cam (1959-1979)

The circuit breaker cam (**Figure 27**) should be lightly lubricated with special breaker cam grease

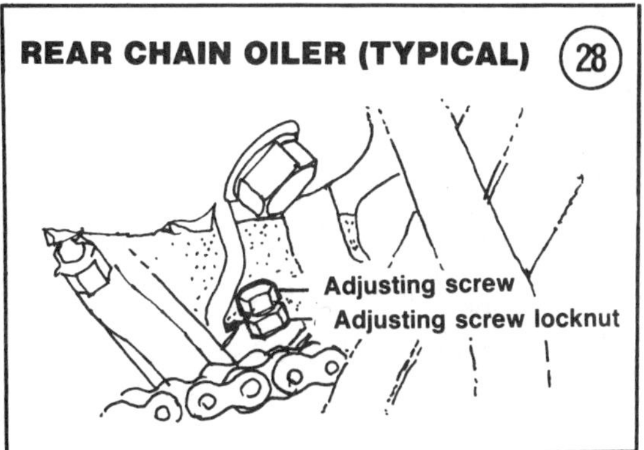

at the intervals specified in **Tables 1-3**. Refer to Chapter Seven for procedures on removing and installing the breaker cam.

Brake Cam Lubrication

Lubricate the brake cam whenever the front or rear wheel is removed (if required).

1. Remove the front or rear wheel as described in Chapter Eight or Chapter Nine.
2. Wipe away the old grease, being careful not to get any on the brake shoes.
3. Sparingly apply high-temperature grease to the camming surfaces of the camshaft, the camshaft groove, the brake shoe pivots and the ends of the springs. *Do not* get any grease on the brake shoes.

WARNING
Use only a high-temperature grease. Temperatures created by braking conditions will cause other types of grease to thin and run onto the brake shoes, causing loss of rear braking power.

4. Reassemble the wheel and install it. See Chapter Eight or Chapter Nine.

Speedometer/Tachometer Cable Lubrication

Lubricate the cables every year or whenever needle operation is erratic.

1. Remove the cable from the instrument cluster.
2. Pull the cable from the sheath.
3. If the grease is contaminated, thoroughly clean off all old grease.
4. Thoroughly coat the cable with a good grade of multi-purpose grease and reinstall into the sheath.
5. Make sure the cable is correctly seated into the drive unit. If not, it will be necessary to disconnect the cable at its lower connection and reattach.

Drive Chain Lubrication (1959-1976)

These models are equipped with an automatic drive chain oiler. Periodic chain lubrication is not required. However, inspect the drive chain every 1,000 miles for proper lubrication. If the chain is not getting sufficient lubrication or if there are signs of too much oil, adjust the rear chain oiler. At 2,000-mile intervals, the chain oil nozzle should be removed and cleaned of all oil sediment and other debris.

Refer to **Figure 28** (typical) for this procedure.

1. Back out the adjusting screw locknut (if applicable).
2. Turn adjustment screw in until it seats lightly. Count and record number of turns required.
3. Remove ajusting screw by turning it out completely.
4. Blow out the chain oiler orifice with compressed air.
5. Replace adjusting screw, then turn it in until it seats lightly.
6. Back out adjusting screw amount recorded in Step 2.
7. Oil should flow at approximately 2 to 3 drops per minute. This flow rate should occur when screw is backed out about 1/4 turn (1959-1968) or 3/4 turn (1969-1976).

Drive Chain Lubrication (1977-On)

These models are not equipped with an automatic rear chain oiler. Oil the drive chain every 300 miles or sooner if it becomes dry. A properly maintained chain will provide maximum service life and reliability.

1. Support the bike so that the rear wheel clears the ground.
2. Shift the transmission to NEUTRAL.

3

3. Oil the bottom run of the chain with a commercial chain lubricant (**Figure 29**). Concentrate on getting the lubricant down between the side plates, pins, bushings and rollers of each chain link. Rotate the wheel and oil the entire chain.

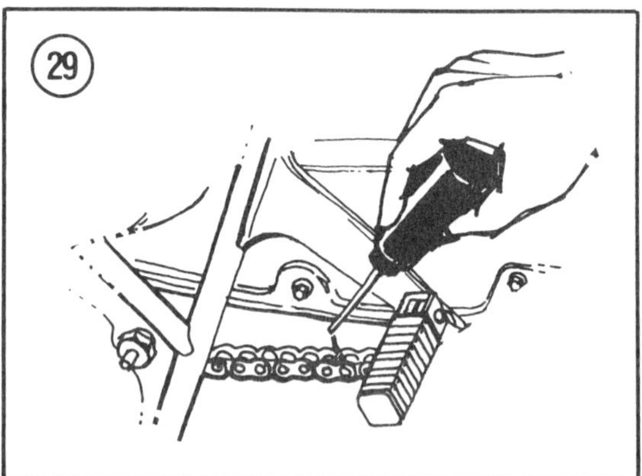

Miscellaneous Lubrication Points

Lubricate the clutch lever; front brake lever; rear brake lever (**Figure 30**); side stand (A, **Figure 31**) pivot points; and footrest pivot points (B, **Figure 31**). Use SAE 10W/30 motor oil.

PERIODIC MAINTENANCE

Maintenance schedules are listed in **Tables 1-3**.

Drive Chain Adjustment

1. Support bike so that rear wheel is off ground.

NOTE
As the drive chain stretches and wears in use, the chain will become tighter at one point. The chain must be checked and adjusted at this point.

2. Turn the rear wheel and check the chain for its tightest point. Mark this spot, and turn the wheel so that the mark is located on the chain's lower run, midway between the drive sprockets (**Figure 32**).
3. Place the rear wheel back on the ground. On 1970-1981 models, perform Step 4 with a rider mounted on the seat.
4. Push the chain up midway between the sprockets on the lower chain run and check the free play; it should be 1/2 in. See **Figure 32**.
5. If the chain adjustment is incorrect, adjust it as follows.
6. Loosen the rear axle nut (A, **Figure 33**).
7. On 1973-1978 models, loosen the anchor bolt or nut (5, **Figure 34**).
8. Loosen the axle adjuster locknut (B, **Figure 33**).
9. Turn each axle adjuster in or out as required, in equal amounts to maintain rear wheel alignment.

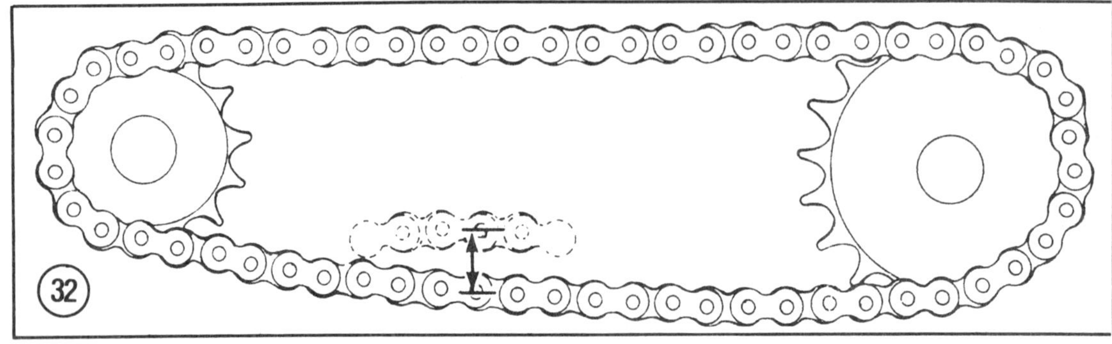

The correct amount of chain free play is described at the beginning of this procedure.

10. If you cannot adjust the drive chain within the limits of the chain adjusters, it is excessively worn and stretched and must be replaced. If the chain can be adjusted, but you feel it may be worn, pull the chain away from the rear sprocket as shown in **Figure 35**. If more than 1/2 of a sprocket tooth is exposed, the chain is worn. Always replace both sprockets when replacing the drive chain; never install a new chain over worn sprockets. Replace the drive chain as described in Chapter Nine.

WARNING
Excessive free play or a worn chain can result in chain breakage; this could cause a serious accident.

11. Sight along the top of the drive chain from the rear sprocket to see that it is correctly aligned. It should leave the top of the rear sprocket in a straight line (A, **Figure 36**). If it is cocked to one side, the rear wheel must be realigned. See Step 9.

12. Tighten the rear axle nut to 60-65 ft.-lb. On 1973-1978 models, tighten the anchor bolt or nut (5, **Figure 34**) securely.

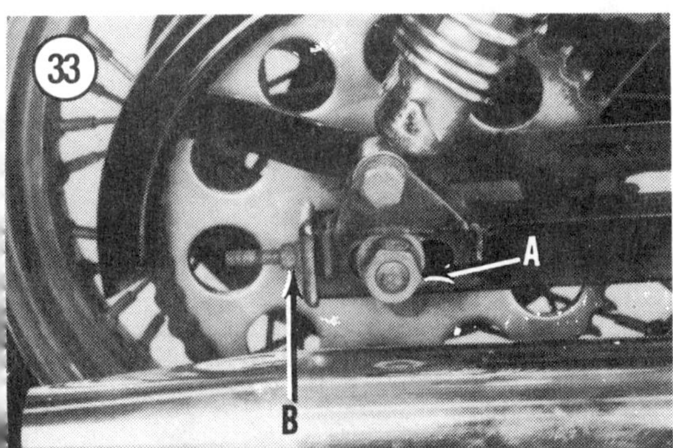

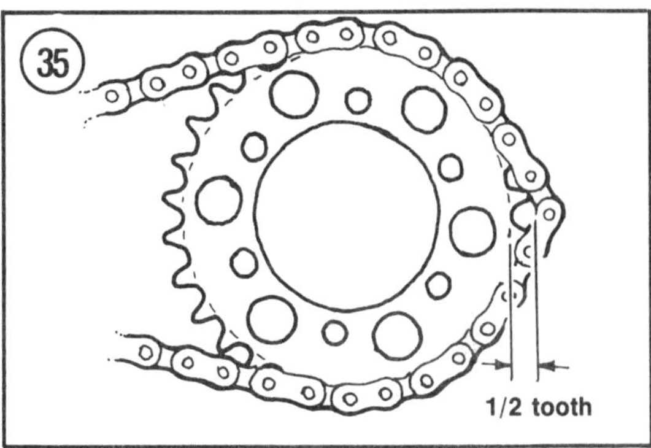

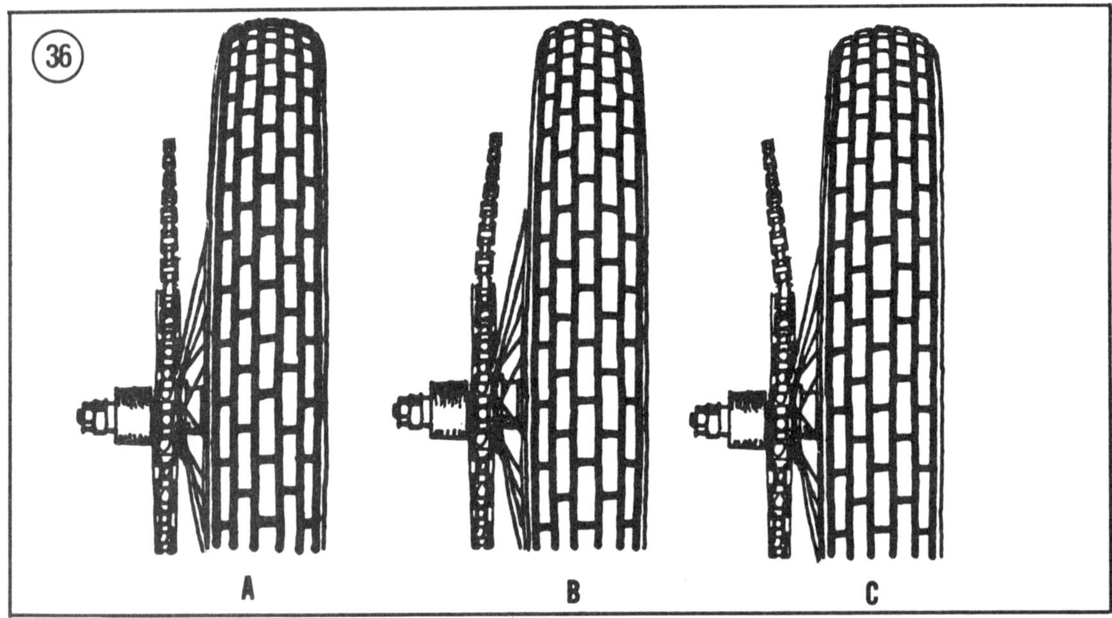

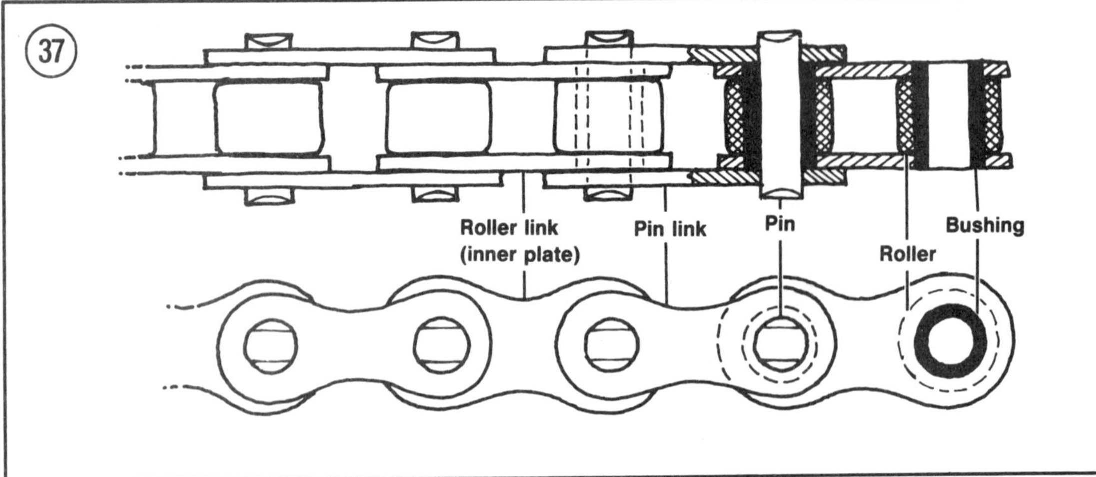

13. After the drive chain has been adjusted, the rear brake pedal free play must be adjusted as described in this chapter.

Drive Chain Cleaning, Inspection and Lubrication

The drive chain should be cleaned and inspected every 1,000 miles or more frequently if ridden in dusty conditions.

1. Remove the drive chain as described in Chapter Nine.
2. Immerse the chain in a pan of cleaning solvent and allow it to soak for about a half hour. Move it around and flex it during this period so that dirt between the pins and rollers may work its way out.
3. Scrub the rollers and side plates with a stiff brush and rinse away loosened grit. Rinse it a couple of times to make sure all dirt is washed out. Hang up the chain and allow it to dry thoroughly.
4. After cleaning the chain, examine it for the following conditions. Refer to **Figure 37**.
   a. Excessive wear.
   b. Loose pins.
   c. Damaged rollers.
   d. Damaged plates.
   e. Dry plates.

If any wear or damage is visible, replace the chain.

5. Lay the chain on a bench and push all links together so chain is shorter. Measure and record its length. See **Figure 38**.

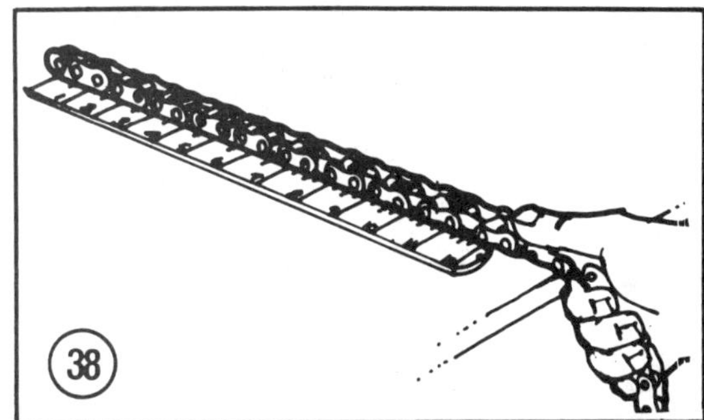

6. Stretch chain to remove all slack between links. Measure chain again.
7. If there is a one-inch or more difference between measurements obtained in Step 5 and Step 6, replace the chain.

CAUTION
*Always check both sprockets (**Figure 39** and **Figure 40**) every time the drive chain is removed. If any wear is visible on the teeth, replace the sprocket. Never install a new chain over worn sprockets or a worn chain over new sprockets.*

Disc Brake Inspection

The hydraulic brake fluid in the disc brake master cylinder(s) should be checked every month. The disc brake pads should be checked at the intervals specified in **Tables 1-3**. Inspection and replacement are described in Chapter Ten.

Disc Brake Fluid Level

1A. *Front brake:* The fluid level in the reservoir should be level with the gasket surface. To check, level the master cylinder assembly by turning the handlebar assembly to the left.
1B. *Rear brake:* The fluid level in the reservoir should be 1/8 in. below the gasket surface. To check, level the bike.
2. Wipe the master cylinder cover with a clean shop cloth.
3. Remove the cover screws and cover (**Figure 41**) and lift the diaphragm out of the housing. If necessary, correct the level by adding fresh brake fluid.

WARNING
Harley-Davidson specifies DOT 3 brake fluid for models produced prior to September, 1976 and DOT 5 for later models. Mixing the two types of brake fluids can cause brake failure. If you own a 1976 or 1977 model take your frame number to a Harley-Davidson dealer to find out your bike's production date.

CAUTION
Be careful not to spill brake fluid on painted or plated surfaces as it will destroy the surface. Wash immediately with soapy water and thoroughly rinse it off.

4. Reinstall all parts.

NOTE
*If the brake fluid was so low as to allow air in the hydraulic system, the brakes will have to be bled. Refer to **Bleeding the System** in Chapter Ten.*

3

Disc Brake Lines and Seals

Check brake lines between the master cylinder and the brake caliper. If there is any leakage, tighten the connections and bleed the brakes as described in Chapter Ten. If this does not stop the leak or if a line is obviously damaged, cracked or chafed, replace the line and seals and bleed the brake. Always replace the brake seals every two years and brake hoses every four years.

Disc Brake Pad Wear (Front and Rear)

Brake pads must be inspected for excessive or uneven wear, scoring and oil or grease on the friction surface. Because the disc brake units are not equipped with a wear indicator or inspection cover, the caliper must be partly disassembled to measure the brake pad thickness. See Chapter Ten.

Disc Brake Fluid Change

Every time you remove the reservoir cap, a small amount of dirt and moisture enters the brake fluid. The same thing happens if a leak occurs or when any part of the hydraulic system is loosened or disconnected. Dirt can clog the system and cause unnecessary wear. Water in the fluid vaporizes at high temperatures, impairing the hydraulic action and reducing brake performance.

To maintain peak braking performance, change the brake fluid as indicated in **Tables 1-3**. To change brake fluid, follow the *Bleeding the System* procedure in Chapter Ten. Continue adding new fluid to the master cylinder and bleeding at the calipers until the fluid leaving the calipers is clean and free of contaminants and air bubbles.

WARNING

Harley-Davidson specifies DOT 3 brake fluid for models produced prior to September, 1976 and DOT 5 for later models. Mixing the two types of brake fluids can cause brake failure. If you own a 1976 or 1977 model take your frame number to a Harley-Davidson dealer to find out your bike's production date.

Drum Brake Lining (Front and Rear)

The front and rear brake pads must be inspected for excessive or uneven wear, wear down to the rivet heads, scoring and oil or grease on the friction surface. Install new brake linings or replace the brake shoes and linings as described in Chapter Ten.

Front brake

Because the front drum brake units are not equipped with a wear indicator, the front wheel

43

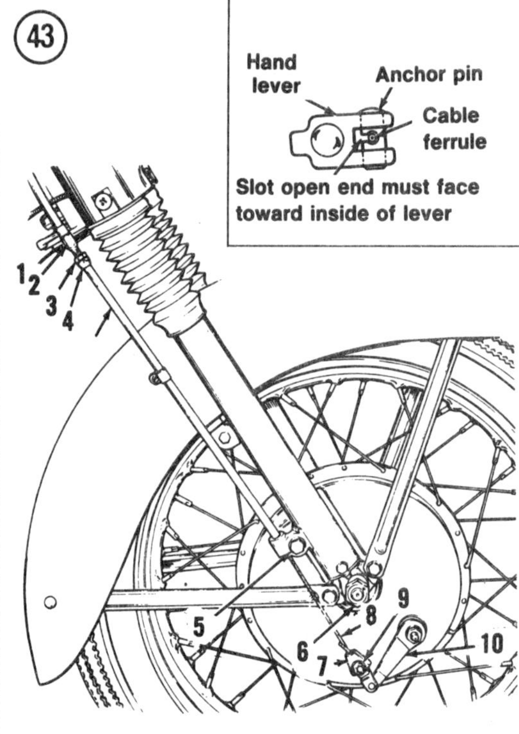

FRONT BRAKE ADJUSTMENT (1959-1972)

1. Front brake adjusting sleeve
2. Adjusting sleeve locknut
3. Adjusting sleeve nut
4. Brake cable support tube
5. Brake shoe pivot stud
6. Front wheel axle nut
7. Brake cable clevis clamp
8. Brake cable
9. Brake cable clevis clamp nut
10. Brake lever

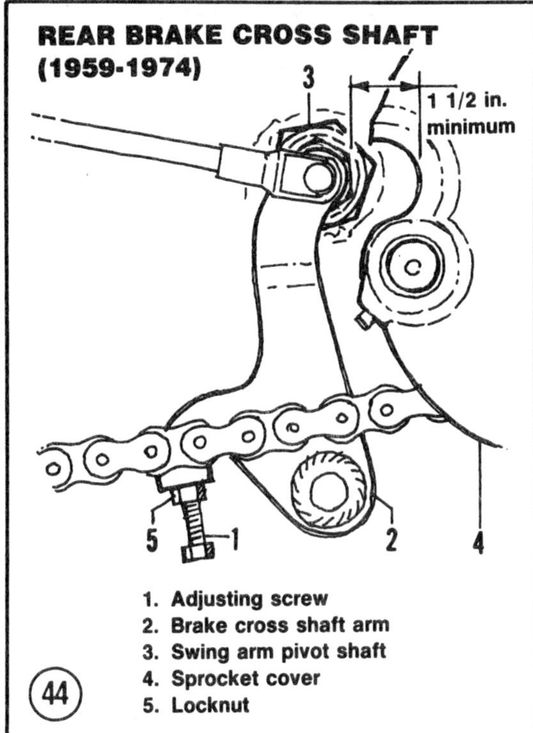

must first be removed to inspect the brake linings. See Chapter Eight.

Rear brake

On 1959-1973 models it is necessary to remove the rear wheel to inspect the brake linings. On 1974 and later models, remove the two plugs from the right-hand side of the wheel (6, **Figure 42**) and inspect the brake linings.

Front Brake Adjustment (1959-1972 Drum Brake)

The front brake on these models requires periodic adjustment. See **Figure 43**.

1. Support bike so that front wheel clears ground.
2. Loosen the adjusting sleeve locknut (2, **Figure 43**).
3. Turn the adjusting sleeve (3) nut in toward the cable support (4) to tighten brake or away from cable support to loosen brake. Hand lever should move approximately 1/4 of its total travel before brake starts to operate.
4. Tighten the adjusting sleeve locknut. Recheck the adjustment.
5. Spin the wheel to make sure the brake does not drag. If the brake drags with the proper adjustment, proceed with Step 6.
6. Referring to **Figure 43**, loosen the brake shoe pivot stud (5) and the front axle nut (6). Do not remove them.
7. Spin the wheel. While wheel is spinning, apply the front brake and stop the wheel. Hold the brake on and tighten the pivot stud (5) and the axle nut (6).
8. Recheck brake adjustment as specified in Steps 2-5.

3

Front Disc Brake Adjustment

The front disc brake does not require periodic adjustment.

Rear Brake Pedal/Cross Shaft Adjustment (1959-1974)

On these models, the rear brake lever is installed on the left-hand side of the bike. A cross-shaft connects the brake pedal with the brake arm and rod or cable. Refer to **Figure 44** when performing this procedure.

1. Measure the distance from the rear swing arm pivot bolt to the transmission sprocket cover as shown in **Figure 44**. The minimum clearance is 1 1/2 in.
2. If the specification in Step 1 is incorrect, adjust by loosening the adjusting screw locknut and turning the adjusting screw as required.
3. Tighten the locknut and recheck the adjustment.
4. Check the rear brake light switch adjustment as described in this chapter.

Rear Brake Adjustment (1959-1978 Drum Brake)

The rear brake on these models requires periodic adjustment. See **Figure 42** for this procedure.

1. Support the bike so that the rear wheel clears the ground.
2. Turn the rear brake adjustment nut on the end of the brake rod (1, **Figure 42**) until the pedal has 1 1/4 in. free play.
3. Rotate the rear wheel and check for brake drag. Also operate the pedal several times to make sure it returns to the at-rest position immediately after release. If the brake drags, proceed to Step 4.
4. Loosen the rear brake anchor bolt (4) or nut and the rear axle nut (5). Do not remove them.
5. Spin the rear wheel. While wheel is spinning, apply rear brake and tighten the anchor bolt (4) or nut and the rear axle nut (5).
6. Recheck rear brake adjustment as described in Step 2 and step 3.
7. Check the rear brake light switch adjustment as described in this chapter.

Rear Brake Pedal Adjustment (1977-1978)

The brake pedal height position on these models can be adjusted to suit rider preference. Refer to **Figure 45** for this procedure.

1. Remove the brake pedal bolt and remove the brake pedal.
2. Using a screwdriver inserted into the stop screw slot, turn the stop screw to obtain the 1/4 in. pedal dimension shown in **Figure 45**.
3. Align the brake pedal splines with the brake shaft splines and install the brake pedal at the desired position.
4. If necessary, minor changes in the brake pedal position can be made by turning the stop screw in either direction.

WARNING
When performing Step 4, do not turn the stop screw more than 3 turns in either direction. The 1/4 in. dimension obtained in Step 2 must be maintained for the rear brake to operate properly.

5. If the desired brake pedal position cannot be obtained by turning the stop screw within the limits specified in Step 4, remove the brake pedal and change its position one spline at a time.
6. Check the rear brake light switch adjustment as described in this chapter.

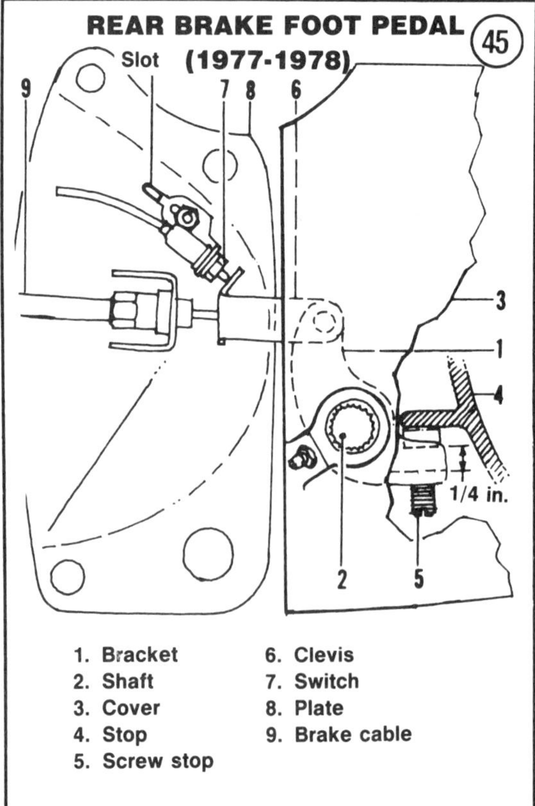

1. Bracket
2. Shaft
3. Cover
4. Stop
5. Screw stop
6. Clevis
7. Switch
8. Plate
9. Brake cable

Rear Brake Free Play Adjustment (Disc Brakes)

1. Place the motorcycle on the sidestand.
2. Check to be sure the brake pedal is in the at-rest position.
3. Operate the brake pedal by hand and check the master cylinder plunger movement. The rear brake pedal should move approximately 1/16 in. before the plunger contacts the piston in the master cylinder. If necessary, adjust as follows.
4. Loosen the locknut and turn the adjusting bolt (**Figure 46**) to achieve the correct plunger movement (1/16 in.). Tighten the locknut securely.
5. Adjust the rear brake light switch as described in this chapter.

Rear Brake Light Switch Adjustment

1. Turn the ignition switch ON.
2. Depress the brake pedal. The light should come on just as the brake begins to work.
3. If necessary, adjust the brake light switch position to make the light come on earlier. **Figure 45** shows a typical brake light switch.
4. Tighten the switch mounting bolts and recheck the adjustment.

Clutch Adjustment

1959-1970

Refer to **Figure 47** for this procedure.

1. Remove the clutch adjuster cover from the sprocket cover.
2. Loosen the clutch adjusting screw locknut (7, **Figure 47**).
3. Turn the clutch adjusting screw (8) counterclockwise.

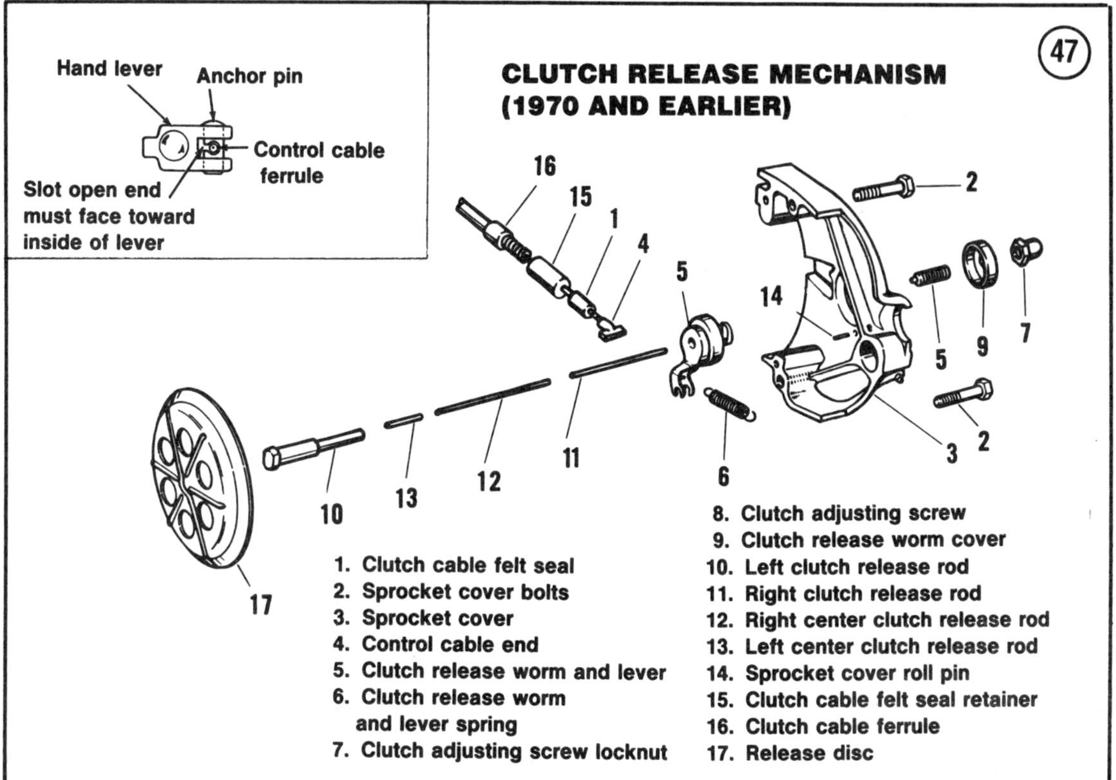

4. Check that the clutch release worm (5) inside the sprocket cover seats against the stop when the clutch hand lever is fully extended. If lever does not seat fully, clutch cable may be binding in its housing.
5. Turn the cable adjuster at the clutch hand lever so that clutch release worm does not return against its stop. This adjustment will cause the clutch hand lever to remain fully extended.
6. Turn the clutch adjusting screw (8) clockwise until the clutch hand lever moves 1/8 of its travel before the clutch starts to release. This condition can be checked by slightly increasing the tension on the clutch hand lever as it is moved to its released position.
7. Tighten the clutch adjusting screw locknut (7). Make sure that the adjusting screw setting is not disturbed when the locknut is tightened.

1971-early 1984

Refer to **Figure 48** for this procedure.
1. Remove the clutch access cover (A, **Figure 49**) from the primary chain case cover.
2. Loosen the locknut (3, **Figure 48**). Then turn the cable adjuster (2, **Figure 48**) clockwise until there is excessive free-play at the clutch lever.
3. Loosen the adjusting screw locknut (**Figure 50**) and turn the clutch release adjusting screw clockwise until it becomes harder to turn. Then turn an additional 2 turns to make sure the clutch is disengaged.
4. Turn the cable adjuster (2, **Figure 48**) counterclockwse to remove all clutch cable free play.

NOTE

Do not turn the cable adjuster so that there is excessive tension on the clutch cable.

5. With all slack removed from the clutch cable (Step 4), tighten the locknut (3, **Figure 48**).
6. Loosen the adjusting screw locknut (**Figure 50**) and turn the adjusting screw counterclockwise until it moves freely (no tension). Then turn the screw clockwise until it seats lightly. From this point, turn the screw counterclockwise 1/4-1/2 turn (1971-1978) or 1/8-1/4 turn (1979-early 1984).
7. Hold the adjusting screw in position and tighten the locknut (**Figure 50**).
8. Check the clutch lever free play. It should be 1/8 in. If not, loosen the locknut (3, **Figure 48**) and turn the cable adjuster (2, **Figure 48**) as required. Tighten the locknut.
9. Reinstall the clutch access cover (A, **Figure 48**).

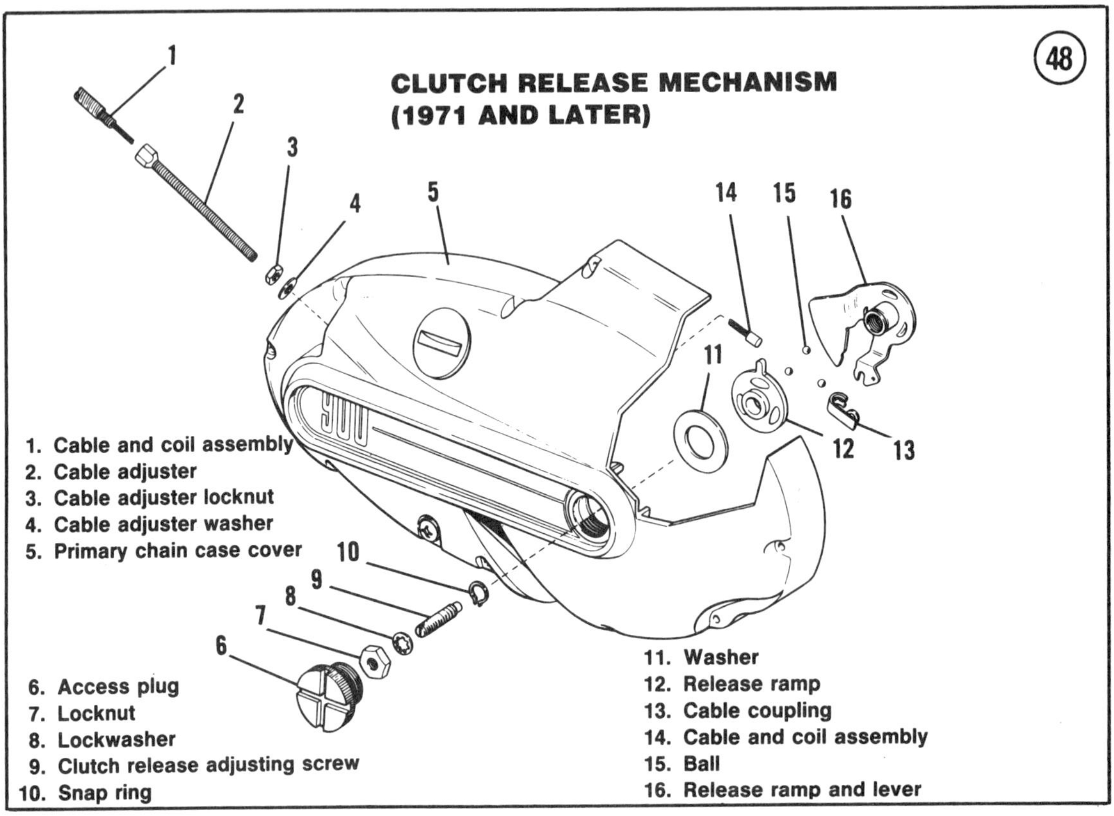

CLUTCH RELEASE MECHANISM (1971 AND LATER)

(48)

1. Cable and coil assembly
2. Cable adjuster
3. Cable adjuster locknut
4. Cable adjuster washer
5. Primary chain case cover
6. Access plug
7. Locknut
8. Lockwasher
9. Clutch release adjusting screw
10. Snap ring
11. Washer
12. Release ramp
13. Cable coupling
14. Cable and coil assembly
15. Ball
16. Release ramp and lever

Late 1984-1985

Refer to **Figure 51** for this procedure.

1. Loosen the clutch cable adjuster locknut and turn the adjuster clockwise to obtain an excessive amount of clutch lever free play at the handlebar.
2. Remove the clutch access cover (A, **Figure 49**) and remove the adjusting screw spring (14, **Figure 51**) and lockplate (13).
3. Turn the clutch adjusting screw (5) counterclockwise to remove all free play from the screw.
4. Adjust the mechanism as follows:
   a. Turn the clutch adjusting screw clockwise 1/4 turn.
   b. Install the lockplate (13) and spring (14) on the adjusting screw (5).
   c. The hex on the lockplate must match with the recess in the primary chain cover. If not, rotate the adjusting screw clockwise as necessary to obtain correct alignment.
   d. Install the clutch access cover.
   e. Turn the clutch cable adjuster counterclockwise (2) to remove all slack from the cable. Then turn the adjuster to obtain approximately 1/16 in. free play at the clutch lever.

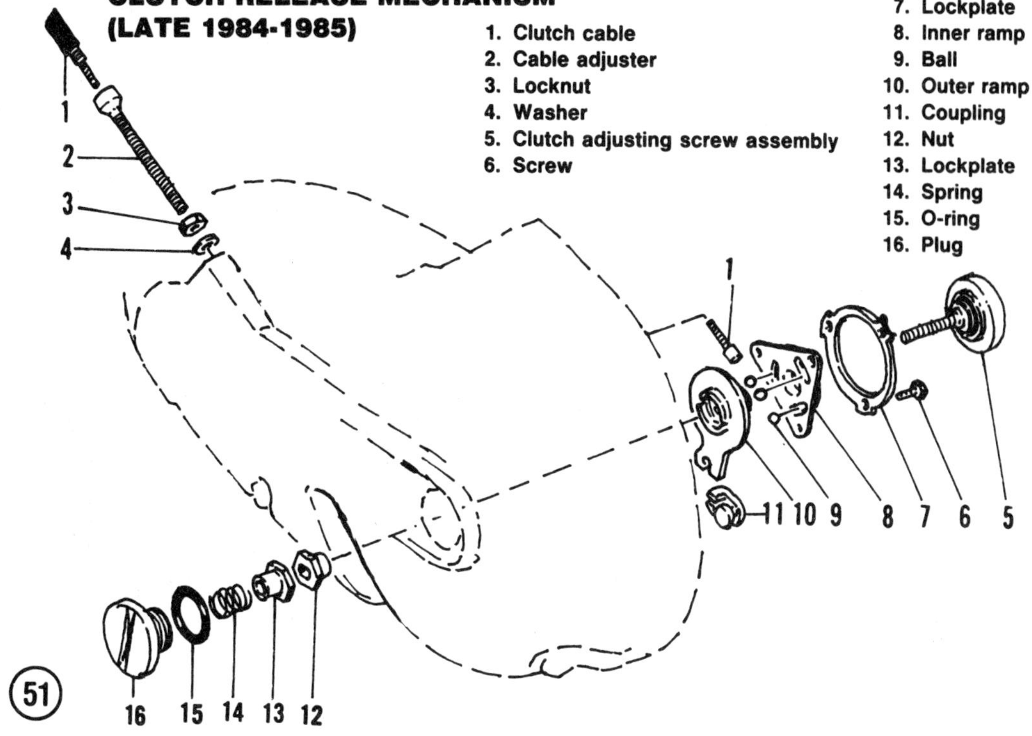

CLUTCH RELEASE MECHANISM (LATE 1984-1985)

1. Clutch cable
2. Cable adjuster
3. Locknut
4. Washer
5. Clutch adjusting screw assembly
6. Screw
7. Lockplate
8. Inner ramp
9. Ball
10. Outer ramp
11. Coupling
12. Nut
13. Lockplate
14. Spring
15. O-ring
16. Plug

(51)

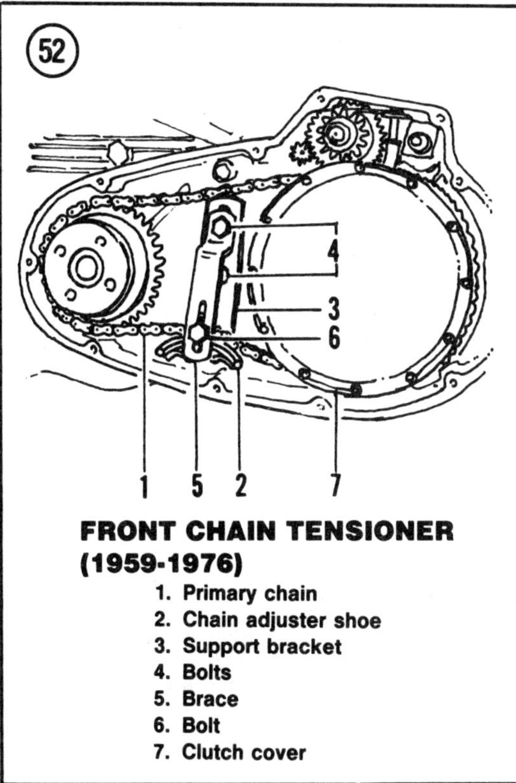

FRONT CHAIN TENSIONER (1959-1976)

1. Primary chain
2. Chain adjuster shoe
3. Support bracket
4. Bolts
5. Brace
6. Bolt
7. Clutch cover

f. Tighten the clutch cable adjuster locknut (3). Recheck the free play.

Primary Chain Adjustment

Correct chain adjustment is 5/8-7/8 in. (cold engine) or 3/8-5/8 in. (hot engine).

1959-1976

1. Remove the primary chain cover as described under *Clutch Removal* in Chapter Five.
2. Rotate primary chain until its tightest point is halfway between the sprockets on the upper chain run (**Figure 52**).
3. Lift chain up with finger to check free play. Correct chain adjustment is 5/8-7/8 in. (cold engine) or 3/8-5/8 in. (hot engine).
4. If necessary, adjust primary chain as follows.
   a. Loosen the chain adjuster shoe center bolts (**Figure 52**).
   b. Move the shoe support (3, **Figure 52**) up or down to adjust chain play.
   c. Tighten the bolts and recheck adjustment.
5. Reinstall the primary chain cover as described in Chapter Five.
6. Refill the clutch/transmission oil as described in this chapter.

1977-1985

1. Remove the access cover (B, **Figure 49**).
2. Rotate primary chain until its tightest point is halfway between the sprockets on the upper chain run (**Figure 52**).
3. Lift chain (**Figure 53**) up with finger to check free play. Correct chain adjustment is 5/8-7/8 in. (cold engine) or 3/8-5/8 in. (hot engine).
4. If necessary, adjust primary chain as follows.
   a. Loosen the chain adjuster locknut (**Figure 54**).
   b. Move the shoe support (3, **Figure 52**) up or down to adjust chain play.
   c. Tighten the chain adjuster locknut and recheck the adjustment.
5. Reinstall the access cover.

Throttle Cable(s)

Check the throttle cable(s) from grip to carburetor. Make sure they are not kinked or chafed. Replace if necessary.

Make sure that the throttle grip rotates smoothly from fully closed to fully open. Check at center, full left and full right position of steering.

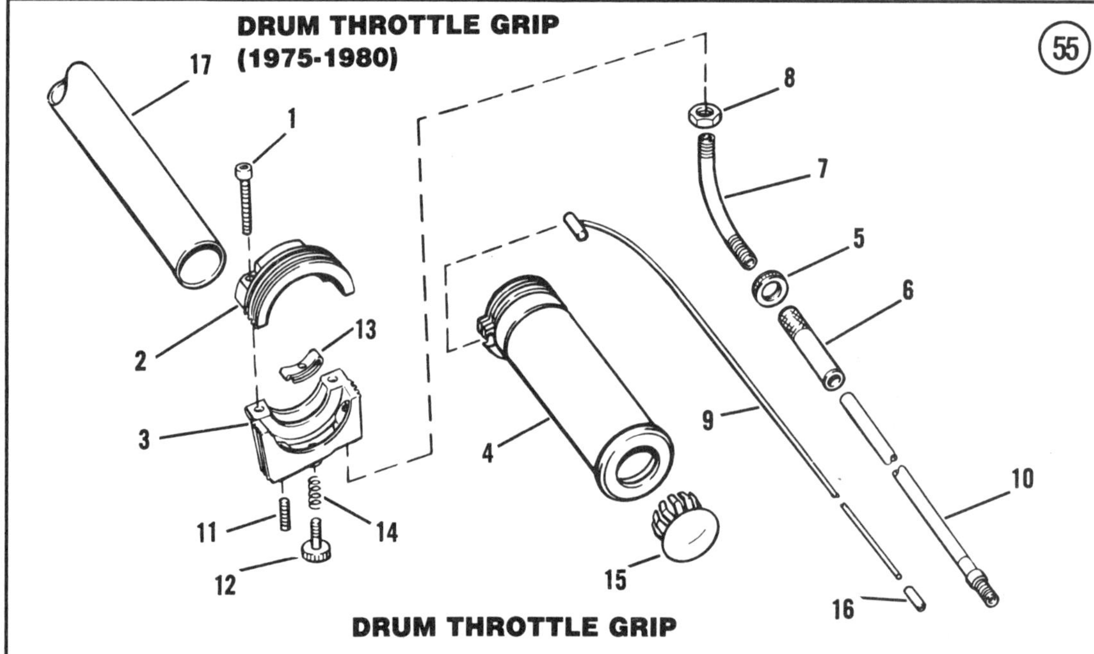

DRUM THROTTLE GRIP

1. Throttle control clamp screw
2. Upper clamp
3. Lower clamp
4. Throttle grip assembly
5. Control adjuster locknut
6. Control adjuster
7. Control elbow
8. Control elbow locknut
9. Control wire
10. Control wire casing
11. Stop screw
12. Grip friction adjusting screw
13. Grip friction spring
14. Grip friction screw spring
15. Grip plug
16. Control wire ferrule
17. Handlebar

Throttle Cable Adjustment (1959-1974)

Refer to *Handlebar, Throttle Control Assembly, Spiral Grip* in Chapter Eight for adjustment procedures.

Throttle Adjustment (1975-1980)

Refer to **Figure 55** for this procedure.

1. When the throttle grip is operated and then released, it must return to its closed or idle position. If not, loosen the adjusting screw (12, **Figure 55**) a little at a time until the grip returns correctly. If the grip is hard to turn, check the throttle cables from grip to carburetor. Make sure they are not kinked or chafed.

WARNING

The adjusting screw (12, ***Figure 55****) must not be so tight as to prevent the throttle grip from closing when it is released. This could cause a very dangerous riding condition.*

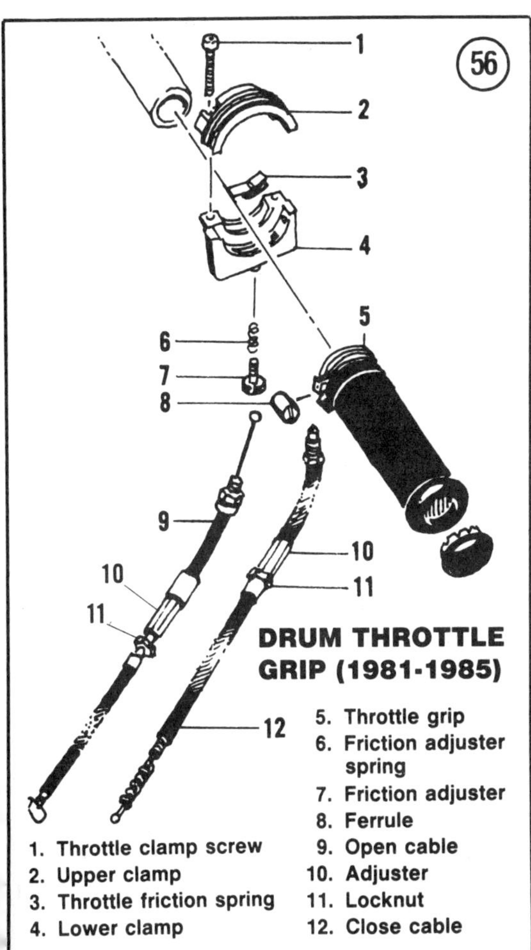

2. Support the bike so that the front wheel can be turned from side to side. Observe the throttle cable at the carburetor when turning the front wheel. The inner control wire (9) should not pull on the carburetor throttle. If it does, adjust cable free play by loosening the control adjuster locknut (5) and turning the control adjuster (6) to correct the overall cable length. Tighten the locknut and recheck the adjustment.
3. With the motorcycle's front wheel pointing straight ahead, open the throttle fully with the throttle grip and notice the carburetor lever operation. When the grip is in the fully open position, the carburetor lever should reach its fully open position. If not, adjust the grip travel limit by turning the stop screw (11).
4. Start the engine and rev it several times to be sure the engine returns fully to idle.

Throttle Adjustment (1981-1985)

Refer to **Figure 56** for this procedure.

1. Loosen both cable adjuster locknuts (11, **Figure 56**) and shorten the adjusters all the way. See **Figure 56**.
2. With the motorcycle's front wheel pointing straight ahead, open the throttle fully with the throttle grip. While the grip is fully open, lengthen the open cable adjuster until the throttle valve pulley just touches the stop boss cast into the carburetor body. If you are not sure if the throttle valve is fully open, turn the pulley by hand to see if there is more movement. Tighten the open cable adjuster locknut (**Figure 56**).
3. With the motorcycle's front wheel turned all the way to the right, lengthen the close cable adjuster until the lower end of the close cable just contacts the spring in the outer cable fitting. Tighten the locknut.
4. Start the engine and rev it several times to be sure the engine returns fully to idle. Lengthen the close cable adjuster if the engine does not return to idle.

Air Cleaner Removal/Installation

A clogged air cleaner can decrease the efficiency and life of the engine. Never run the bike without the air cleaner installed; even minute particles of dust can cause severe internal engine wear.

The service intervals specified in **Tables 1-3** should be followed if the bike is given general use. However, the air cleaner should be serviced more often if the bike is ridden in dusty areas.

3

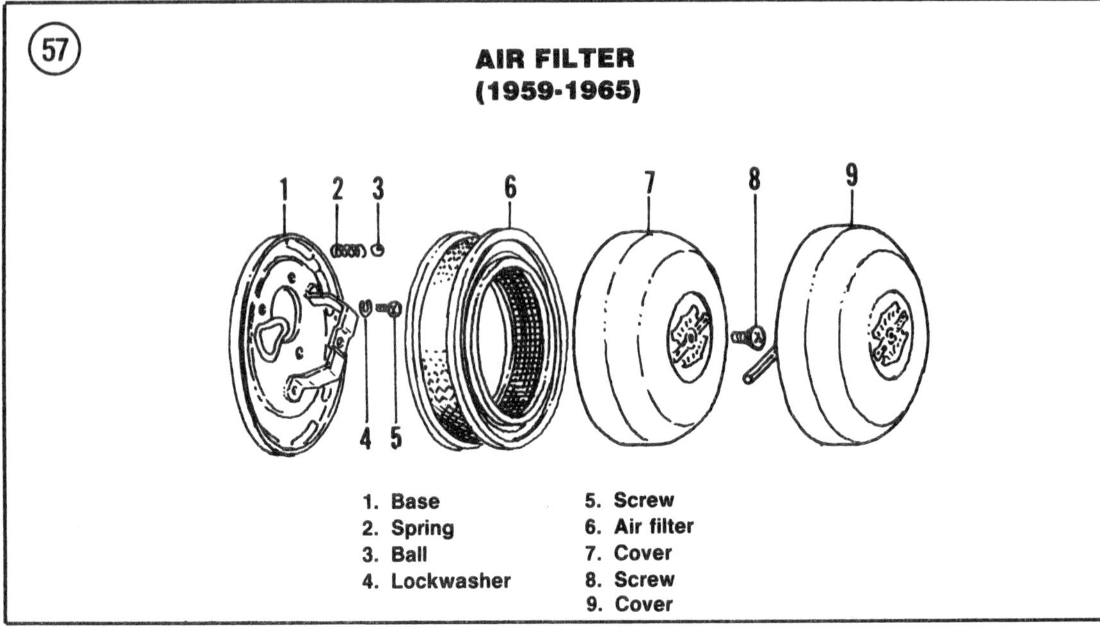

AIR FILTER (1959-1965)

1. Base
2. Spring
3. Ball
4. Lockwasher
5. Screw
6. Air filter
7. Cover
8. Screw
9. Cover

58

AIR CLEANER ASSEMBLY (1979-1982)

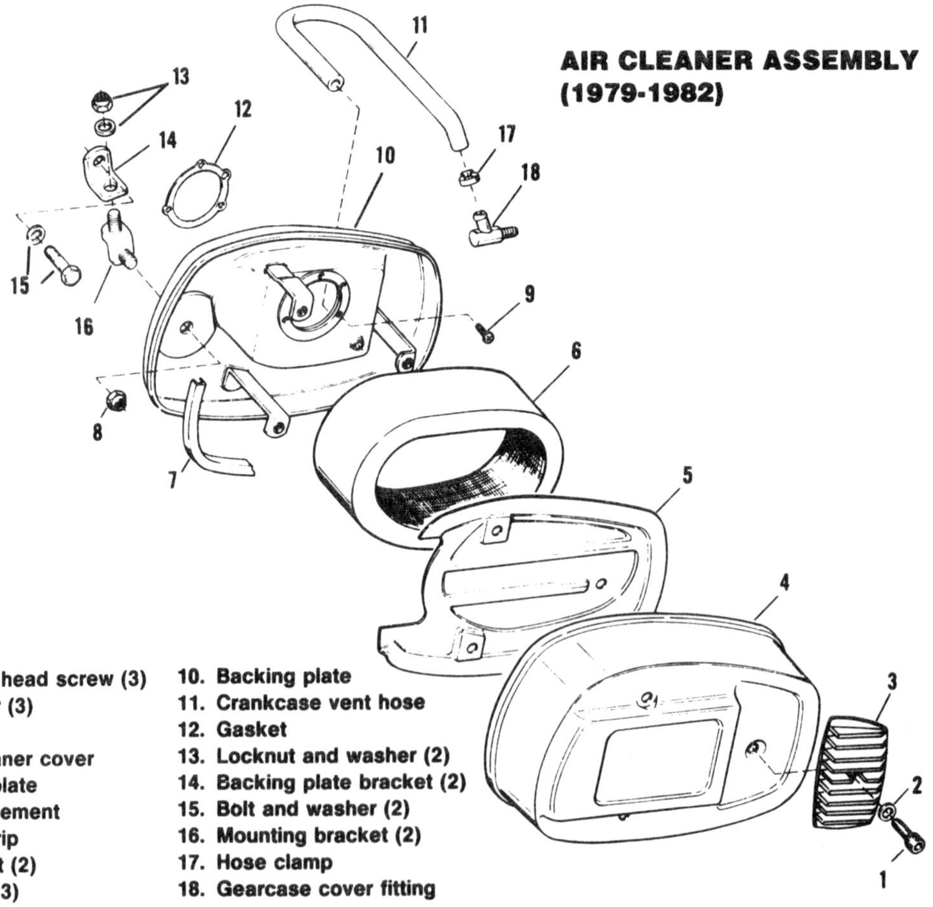

1. Socket head screw (3)
2. Washer (3)
3. Grille
4. Air cleaner cover
5. Baffle plate
6. Filter element
7. Seal strip
8. Locknut (2)
9. Screw (3)
10. Backing plate
11. Crankcase vent hose
12. Gasket
13. Locknut and washer (2)
14. Backing plate bracket (2)
15. Bolt and washer (2)
16. Mounting bracket (2)
17. Hose clamp
18. Gearcase cover fitting

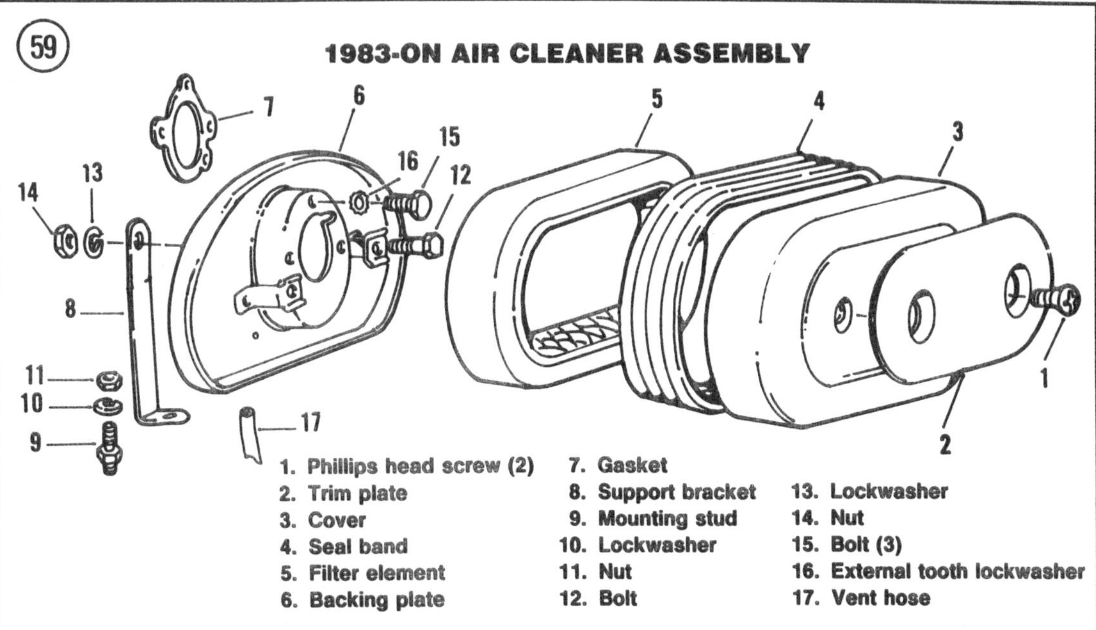

59

1983-ON AIR CLEANER ASSEMBLY

1. Phillips head screw (2)
2. Trim plate
3. Cover
4. Seal band
5. Filter element
6. Backing plate
7. Gasket
8. Support bracket
9. Mounting stud
10. Lockwasher
11. Nut
12. Bolt
13. Lockwasher
14. Nut
15. Bolt (3)
16. External tooth lockwasher
17. Vent hose

60

61

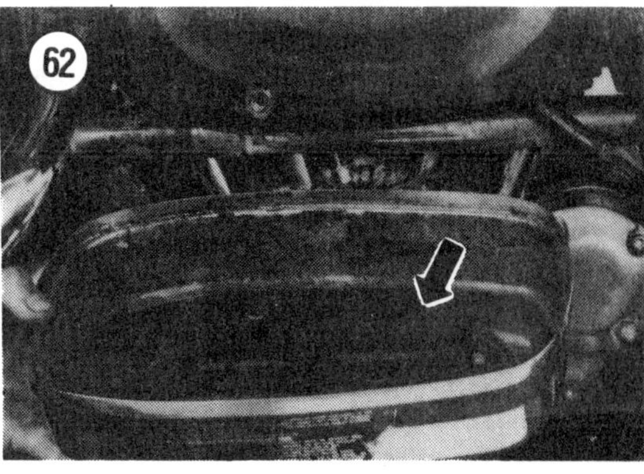

62

The air filter on all models is installed on the right-hand side of the bike. See **Figure 57**, **Figure 58** or **Figure 59** for this procedure.

1A. *1959-1965:* Remove the air filter as follows:
  a. Remove the filter cover screw and cover.
  b. Remove the air filter.
  c. Service the air filter as described in this chapter.
  d. If necessary, remove the air filter housing screws and remove the housing from the carburetor.

1B. *1966-1985:* Remove the air filter as follows:
  a. Remove the air intake grille (**Figure 60**), if so equipped.
  b. Remove the air filter cover screws and remove the cover (**Figure 61**).
  c. Remove the baffle (**Figure 62**) from inside the cover (if so equipped).

d. Remove the air filter (**Figure 63**).
e. Service the air filter as described in this chapter.
f. If necessary, remove the air filter housing screws (**Figure 64**) and remove the housing from the carburetor.

2. Installation is the reverse of these steps.

Air Filter Cleaning

Refer to **Figures 57-59** for this procedure.

1A. *Paper filter:* Tap the filter lightly to remove dirt and dust on outside of filter. If element is oily or sooted with dirt, replace it with a new filter.

1B. *Metal mesh or foam filters:* Remove wire mesh frame from inside filter. Wash filter in soap and water and allow to dry.

2. Inspect the element and make sure it is in good condition. Replace if necessary.

3A. *Paper filter:* Install paper filters dry; do not oil.

3B. *Metal mesh or foam filters:* Saturate the filter with engine oil. Work the oil over the entire filter surface with hands. Then squeeze the filter to remove all excess oil. Filter should be uniform in color to indicate that entire filter is oiled. Reinstall wire mesh frame into filter.

4. Clean out the inside of the air box with a shop rag and cleaning solvent. Remove any foreign matter that may have passed through a broken cleaner element.

NOTE
When cleaning the inside of air box, do not to allow any dirt or other debris to run into the carburetor hoses.

Fuel Shutoff Valve/Filter

Refer to Chapter Six for complete details on removal, cleaning, and installation of the fuel shutoff valve.

Fuel Line Inspection

Inspect the fuel lines from the fuel tank to the carburetor. If any are cracked or starting to deteriorate they must be replaced. Make sure the small hose clamps are in place and holding securely.

WARNING
A damaged or deteriorated fuel line presents a very dangerous fire hazard to both the rider and the bike if fuel should spill onto a hot engine or exhaust pipe.

Exhaust System

Check for leakage at all fittings (**Figure 65**). Do not forget the crossover pipe connections. Tighten all bolts and nuts; replace any gaskets as necessary.

Removal and installation procedures are described in Chapter Six.

Wheel Bearings

The wheel bearings should be cleaned and repacked at the intervals specified in **Tables 1-3**.

Refer to Chapter Eight and Chapter Nine for complete service procedures.

Steering Play

The steering head should be checked for looseness at the intervals specified in **Tables 1-3**.

1. Prop up the bike so that the front tire clears the ground.

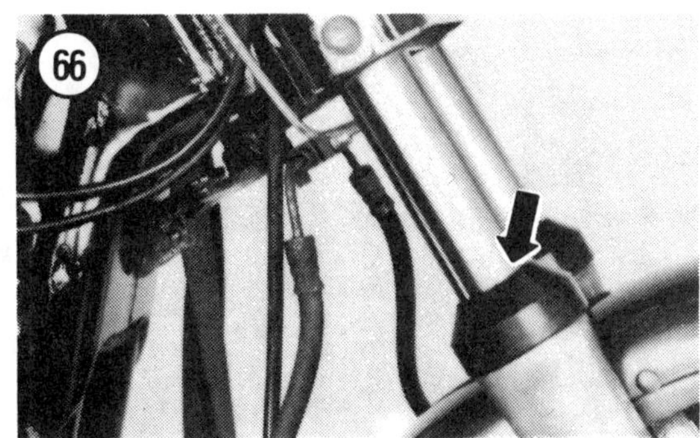

2. Center the front wheel. Push lightly against the left handlebar grip to start the wheel turning to the right, then let go. The wheel should continue turning under its own momentum until the forks hit their stop.
3. Center the wheel, and push lightly against the right handlebar grip. The wheel should continue turning under its own momentum until the forks hit their stop.
4. If, with a light push in either direction, the front wheel will turn all the way to the stop, the steering adjustment is not too tight.
5. Center the front wheel and kneel in front of it. Grasp the bottoms of the 2 front fork slider legs. Try to pull the forks toward you, and then try to push them toward the engine. If no play is felt, the steering adjustment is not too loose.
6. If the steering adjustment is too tight or too loose, readjust it as described in Chapter Eight under *Front Fork Installation*.

Steering Head Bearings

The steering head bearings should be repacked at the intervals specified in **Tables 1-3**. Refer to Chapter Eight for procedures.

Front Suspension Check

1. Apply the front brake and pump the fork up and down as vigorously as possible. Check for smooth operation and check for any oil leaks at the oil seal (**Figure 66**). If necessary, replace leaking fork oil seals as described in Chapter Eight.
2. Make sure the upper and lower fork bridge bolts are tight.
3. Check that the handlebar bolts are tight.
4. Check that the front axle cap bolts (if so equipped) are tight (**Figure 67**).

CAUTION
If any of the previously mentioned bolts and nuts are loose, refer to Chapter Eight for correct procedures and torque specifications.

Rear Suspension Check

1. Place the bike on the sidestand.
2. Push hard on the rear wheel sideways to check for side play in the rear swing arm bushings or bearings.
3. Check the tightness of the upper and lower shock absorber mounting nuts and bolts (**Figure 68**).
4. Make sure the rear axle nut is tight.
5. Check the tightness of the rear brake torque arm bolts, if so equipped.

CAUTION
If any of the previously mentioned nuts or bolts are loose, refer to Chapter Nine for correct procedures and torque specifications.

Nuts, Bolts, and Other Fasteners

Constant vibration can loosen many fasteners on a motorcycle. Check the tightness of all fasteners, especially those on:

a. Engine mounting hardware.
b. Engine crankcase covers.
c. Gearshift lever.

d. Sprocket bolts and nuts.
e. Brake pedal and lever.
f. Exhaust system.
g. Lighting equipment.

SUSPENSION ADJUSTMENT

Rear Shock Absorber Adjustment

On all models, the shock absorber spring seat (**Figure 69**) can be adjusted to suit rider preference. Rotate the cam ring at the base of the spring to compress the spring (heavy loads) or extend the spring (light loads). See **Figure 70**.

NOTE
Use a spanner wrench to adjust the spring preload. Set both shocks to the same position.

TUNE-UP

A complete tune-up restores performance and power that is lost due to normal wear and deterioration of engine parts. Because engine wear occurs over a combined period of time and mileage, the engine tune-up should be performed at the intervals specified in **Tables 1-3**. More frequent tune-ups may be required if the bike is ridden primarily in stop-and-go traffic.

Table 9 summarizes tune-up specifications.

Before starting a tune-up procedure, make sure to first have all new parts on hand.

Because different systems in an engine interact, the procedures should be done in the following order:

a. Clean or replace the air filter element.
b. Adjust pushrod clearance.
c. Check engine compression.
d. Check or replace the spark plugs.
e. Check the ignition timing.
f. Adjust carburetor idle speed.

To perform a tune-up on your Harley-Davidson, you will need the following tools:

a. Spark plug wrench.
b. Socket wrench and assorted sockets.
c. Flat feeler gauge.
d. Compression gauge.
e. Spark plug feeler gauge and gap adjusting tool.
f. Ignition timing light.

Air Cleaner

The air cleaner element should be cleaned or replaced prior to doing other tune-up procedures, as described in this chapter.

69

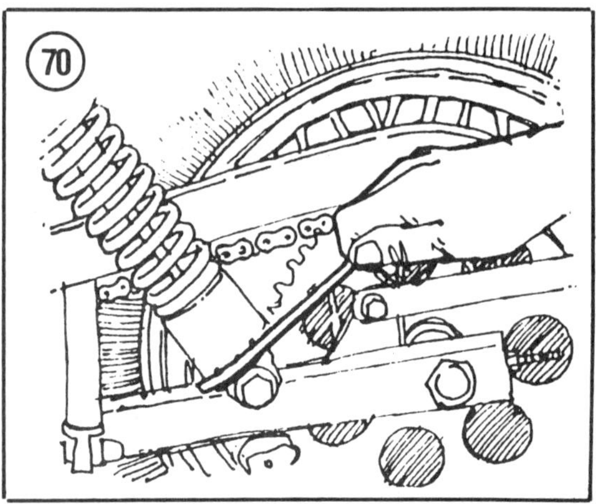
70

Pushrod Clearance

Refer to Chapter Four under *Pushrod* for complete procedures.

Compression Test

At every tune-up, check cylinder compression. Record the results and compare them at the next check. A running record will show trends in deterioration so that corrective action can be taken before complete failure.

The results, when properly interpreted, can indicate general cylinder, piston ring and valve condition.

1. Warm the engine to normal operating temperature. Ensure that the choke valve and throttle valve are completely open.
2. Remove the spark plugs.
3. Connect the compression tester to one cylinder following manufacturer's instructions (**Figure 71**).
4. Have an assistant crank the engine over until there is no further rise in pressure.
5. Remove the tester and record the reading.
6. Repeat Steps 3-5 for the other cylinder.

When interpreting the results, actual readings are not as important as the difference between the

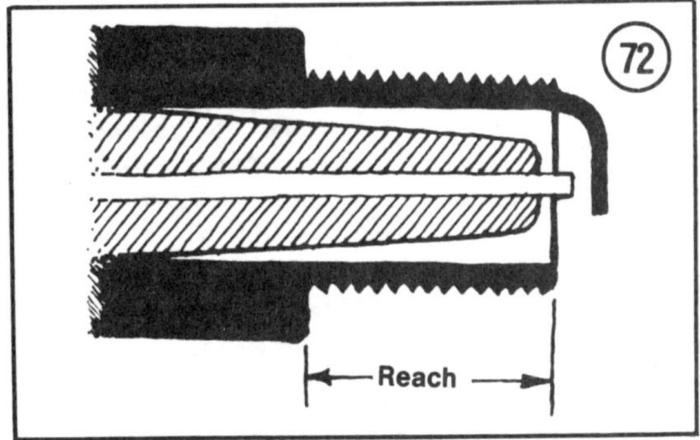

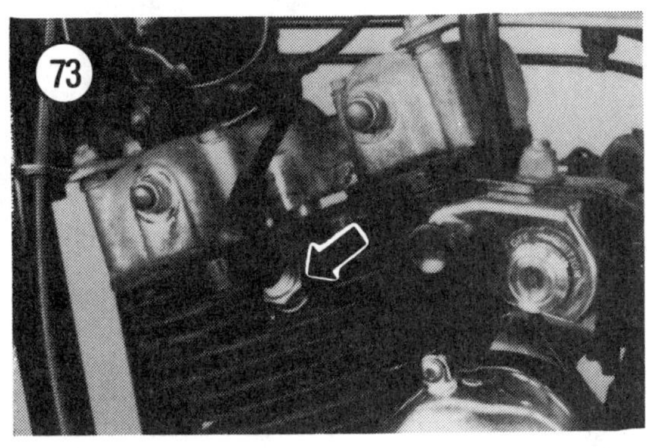

readings. Standard compression pressure is shown in **Table 9**. Pressure should not vary from cylinder to cylinder by more than 10 psi. Greater differences indicate worn or broken rings, leaky or sticky valves, blown head gasket or a combination of all.

If compression readings do not differ between cylinders by more than 10 psi, the rings and valves are in good condition.

If a low reading (10% or more) is obtained on one of the cylinders, it indicates valve or ring trouble. To determine which, pour about a teaspoon of engine oil through the spark plug hole onto the top of the piston. Turn the engine over once to clear some of the excess oil, then take another compression test and record the reading. If the compression returns to normal, the valves are good but the rings are defective on that cylinder. If compression does not increase, the valves require servicing. A valve could be hanging open but not burned or a piece of carbon could be on a valve seat.

NOTE
If the compression is low, the engine cannot be tuned to maximum performance. The worn parts must be replaced and the engine rebuilt.

Correct Spark Plug Heat Range

Spark plugs are available in various heat ranges that are hotter or colder than the spark plugs originally installed at the factory.

Select plugs in a heat range designed for the loads and temperature conditions under which the engine will operate. Using incorrect heat ranges can cause piston seizure, scored cylinder walls or damaged piston crowns.

In general, use a hotter plug for low speeds, low loads and low temperatures. Use a colder plug for high speeds, high engine loads and high temperatures.

NOTE
In areas where seasonal temperature variations are great, a "two-plug system"—a cold plug for hard summer riding and a hot plug for slower winter operation—may prevent spark plug and engine problems.

The reach (length) of a plug is also important. A longer than normal plug could interfere with the valves and pistons, causing permanent and severe damage. Refer to **Figure 72**. The standard heat range spark plugs are listed in **Table 10**.

Spark Plug Cleaning/Replacement

1. Grasp the spark plug leads as near to the plug as possible and pull them off the plugs.
2. Blow away any dirt that has accumulated in the spark plug wells (**Figure 73**).

CAUTION
The dirt could fall into the cylinders when the plugs are removed, causing serious engine damage.

3. Remove the spark plugs (**Figure 73**) with a spark plug wrench.

NOTE
If plugs are difficult to remove, apply penetrating oil such as WD-40 or

SPARK PLUG CONDITION

NORMAL
- Identified by light tan or gray deposits on the firing tip.
- Can be cleaned.

GAP BRIDGED
- Identified by deposit buildup closing gap between electrodes.
- Caused by oil or carbon fouling. If deposits are not excessive, the plug can be cleaned.

OIL FOULED
- Identified by wet black deposits on the insulator shell bore and electrodes.
- Caused by excessive oil entering combustion chamber through worn rings and pistons, excessive clearance between valve guides and stems, or worn or loose bearings. Can be cleaned. If engine is not repaired, use a hotter plug.

CARBON FOULED
- Identified by black, dry fluffy carbon deposits on insulator tips, exposed shell surfaces and electrodes.
- Caused by too cold a plug, weak ignition, dirty air cleaner, too rich a fuel mixture or excessive idling. Can be cleaned.

LEAD FOULED
- Identified by dark gray, black, yellow or tan deposits or a fused glazed coating on the insulator tip.
- Caused by highly leaded gasoline. Can be cleaned.

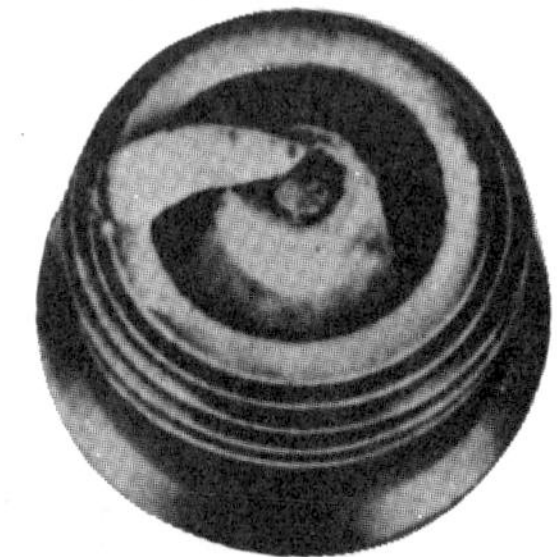

WORN
- Identified by severely eroded or worn electrodes.
- Caused by normal wear. Should be replaced.

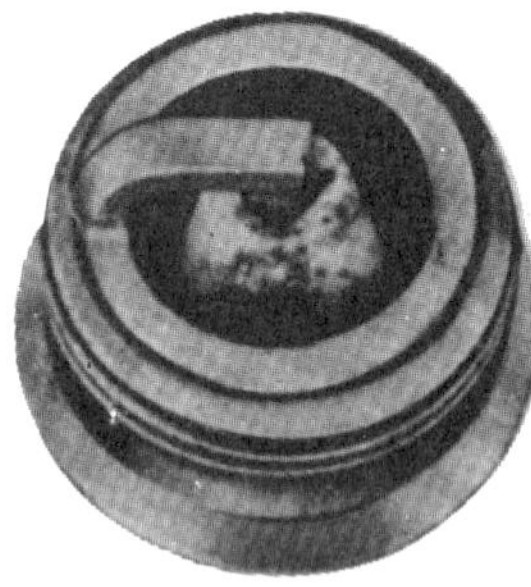

FUSED SPOT DEPOSIT
- Identified by melted or spotty deposits resembling bubbles or blisters.
- Caused by sudden acceleration. Can be cleaned.

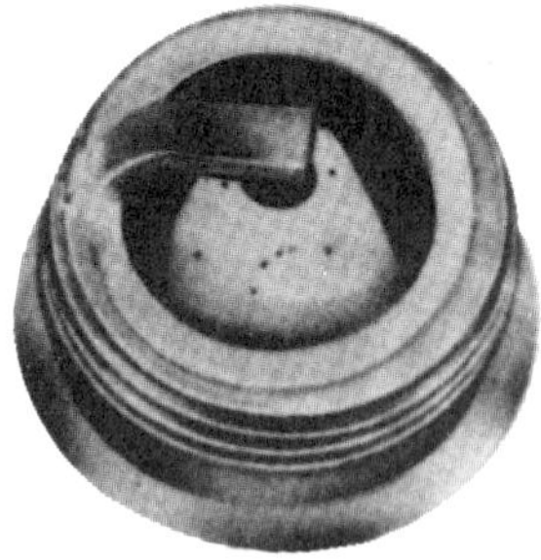

OVERHEATING
- Identified by a white or light gray insulator with small black or gray brown spots and with bluish-burnt appearance of electrodes.
- Caused by engine overheating, wrong type of fuel, loose spark plugs, too hot a plug or incorrect igntion timing. Replace the plug.

PREIGNITION
- Identified by melted electrodes and possibly blistered insulator. Metallic deposits on insulator indicate engine damage.
- Caused by wrong type of fuel, incorrect igntion timing or advance, too hot a plug, burned valves or engine overheating. Replace the plug.

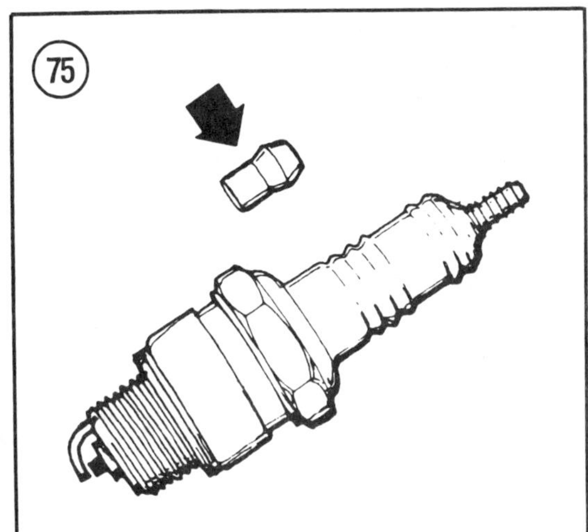

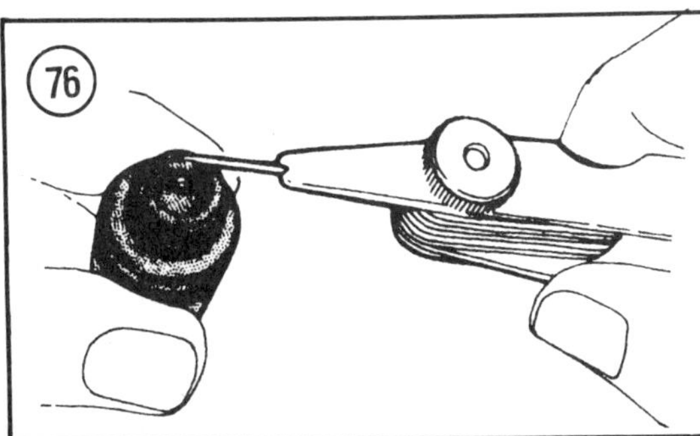

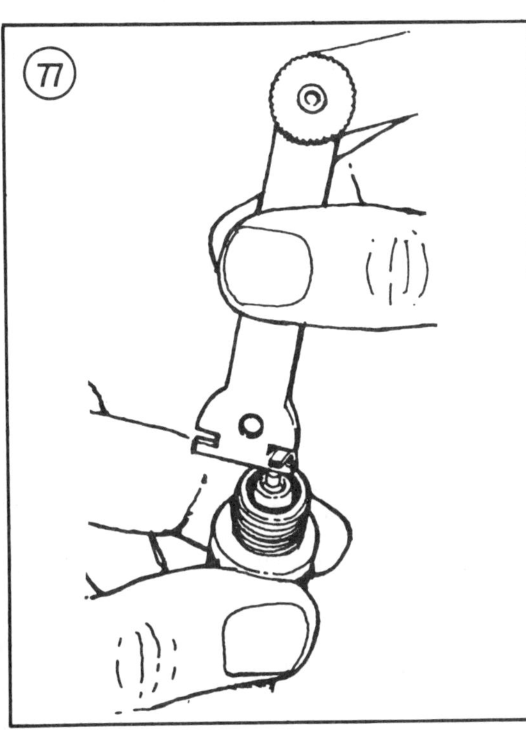

Liquid Wrench around base of plugs and let it soak in about 10-20 minutes.

4. Inspect spark plug carefully. Look for plugs with broken center porcelain, excessively eroded electrodes and excessive carbon or oil fouling (**Figure 74**). Replace such plugs.

CAUTION
Spark plug cleaning with the use of a sand-blast type device is generally not recommended. While this type of cleaning is thorough, the plug must be perfectly free of all abrasive cleaning material when done. If not, it is possible for the cleaning material to fall into the engine during operation and cause damage.

Spark Plug Gapping and Installation

New plugs should be carefully gapped to ensure a reliable, consistent spark. You must use a special spark plug gapping tool.

1. Remove the new plugs from the box. Screw in the small pieces that may be loose in each box (**Figure 75**).
2. Insert a wire gauge between the center and the side electrode of each plug (**Figure 76**). The correct gap is listed in **Table 10**. If the gap is correct, you will feel a slight drag as you pull the wire through. If there is no drag, or the gauge won't pass through, bend the side electrode *with the gapping tool* (**Figure 77**) to set the proper gap (**Table 10**).
3. Put a small drop of oil or anti-seize compound on the threads of each spark plug.
4. Screw each spark plug in by hand until it seats. Very little effort is required. If force is necessary, you have the plug cross-threaded or the spark plug threads in the cylinder head are damaged or contaminated with carbon or other debris; unscrew it and try again.
5. Tighten the spark plugs to 14 ft.-lb. If you don't have a torque wrench, an additional 1/4 to 1/2 turn is sufficient after the gasket has made contact with the head. If you are reinstalling old, regapped plugs and are reusing the old gasket, only tighten an additional 1/4 turn.

CAUTION
Do not overtighten. Besides making the plug difficult to remove, the excessive torque will squash the gasket and destroy its sealing ability.

6. Install each spark plug wire. Make sure it goes to the correct spark plug.

Reading Spark Plugs

Much information about engine and spark plug performance can be determined by careful examination of the spark plugs. This information is only valid after performing the following steps.

1. Ride bike a short distance at full throttle in third or fourth gear.
2. Turn off kill switch before closing throttle and simultaneously pull in clutch. Coast and brake to a stop. *Do not* downshift transmission while stopping.
3. Remove spark plugs and examine them. Compare them to **Figure 74**.

If the insulator tip is white or burned, the plug is too hot and should be replaced with a colder one.

A too-cold plug will have sooty deposits ranging in color from dark brown to black. Replace with a hotter plug and check for too-rich carburetion or evidence of oil blow-by at the piston rings.

If any one spark plug is found unsatisfactory, discard both plugs.

BREAKER POINT IGNITION SERVICE

The expendable ignition parts (spark plugs, breaker points and condenser) should be replaced and the ignition timing checked and adjusted if necessary as part of a tune-up. If the bike is used primarily in stop-and-go city driving or is driven extensively at low engine speeds, these components should be cleaned, adjusted or replaced at more frequent intervals.

Breaker Point Service

1. Check breaker point contact surfaces. Points with an even, overall gray color and only slight roughness or pitting need not be replaced. They can be dressed with a clean point file. Do not use sandpaper or emery cloth for dressing points and do not attempt to remove all irregularities—just remove scale or dirt.
2. Check the alignment of the points and correct as necessary. See **Figure 78**.

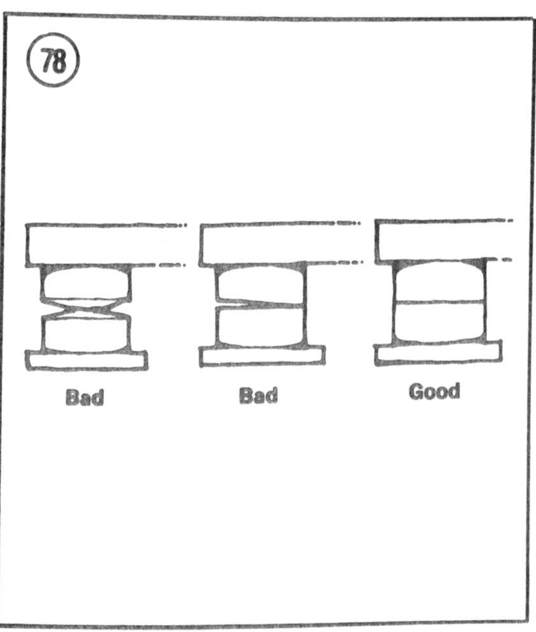

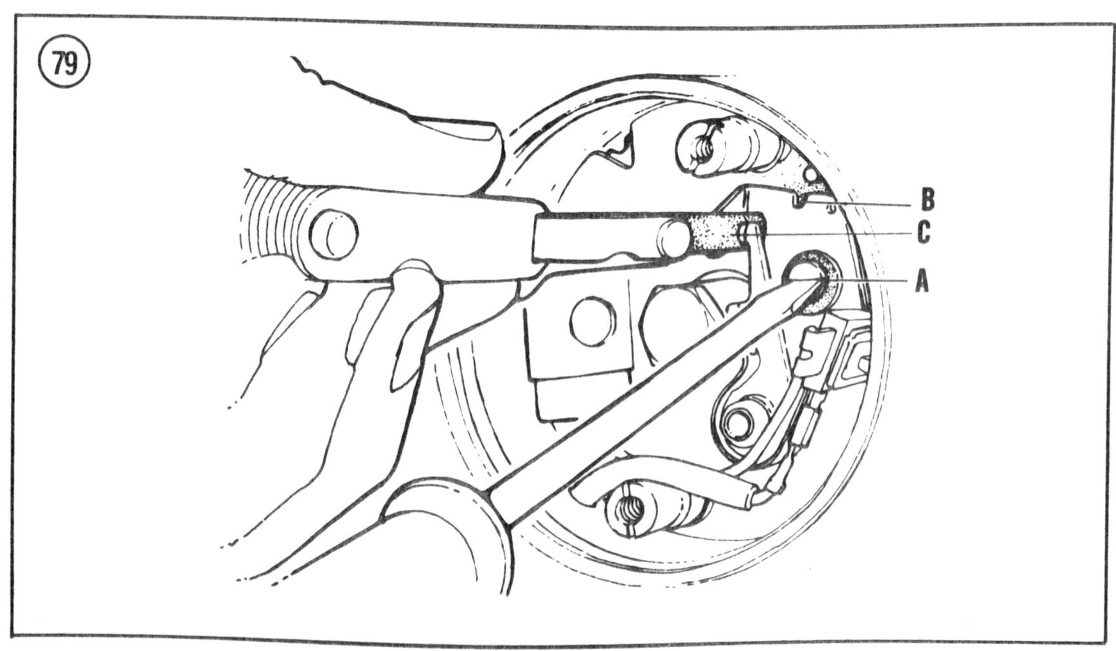

(80) SINGLE CONTACT POINT CIRCUIT BREAKER (MANUAL ADVANCE)

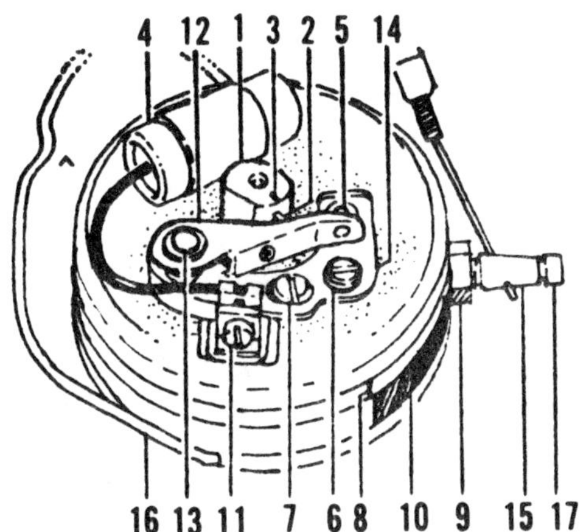

1. Breaker cam
2. Fiber cam follower
3. Cam timing mark
4. Condenser
5. Contact points
6. Lock screw
7. Adjust screw
8. Timing mark
9. Locknut
10. Stud plate (adjust)
11. Screw
12. Circuit breaker lever
13. Pivot stud
14. Support
15. Timing adjust stud
16. Cover retainer
17. Lock screw

(81) SINGLE CONTACT POINT CIRCUIT BREAKER (AUTOMATIC ADVANCE)

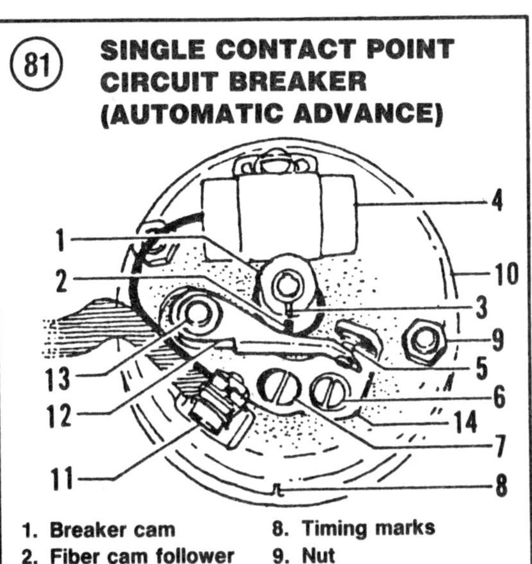

1. Breaker cam
2. Fiber cam follower
3. Cam timing mark
4. Condenser
5. Contact points
6. Lock screw
7. Adjust screw
8. Timing marks
9. Nut
10. Cover
11. Screw
12. Circuit breaker lever
13. Pivot stud
14. Support

3. Check the point gap with a feeler gauge placed between the points (C, **Figure 79**) while the breaker arm rubbing block is on the high point of the cam lobe. The correct gap is listed in **Table 9**. The gap is correct when the gauge passes between the contact points with a slight drag.
4. If the point gap requires adjustment, loosen the retaining screw. See **Figures 80-82**. Insert the screwdriver tip into the eccentric screw or into the notch beside the points (B, **Figure 79**). Twist the screwdriver (A, **Figure 79**) to open or close the point gap as required. When adjustment is correct, tighten the retaining screw. Recheck gap to make sure it did not change when the screw was tightened.
5. If points need replacing, refer to **Figure 83** (typical) and proceed as follows:
   a. Loosen the wire stud screw at the points (A) and disconnect the wires.
   b. Remove the breaker point lock screw (B) and lift the point set from the breaker plate.
   c. Remove the condenser attaching screw and condenser.
   d. Wipe the breaker plate, cam and inside of cover with a lint-free cloth to remove all dirt and grease.
   e. Lightly lubricate the cam surfaces (E) with breaker cam grease.
   f. Position the new breaker point set on the breaker plate and install the attaching screws. Position a new condenser on the breaker plate and install the attaching screw.

(82)

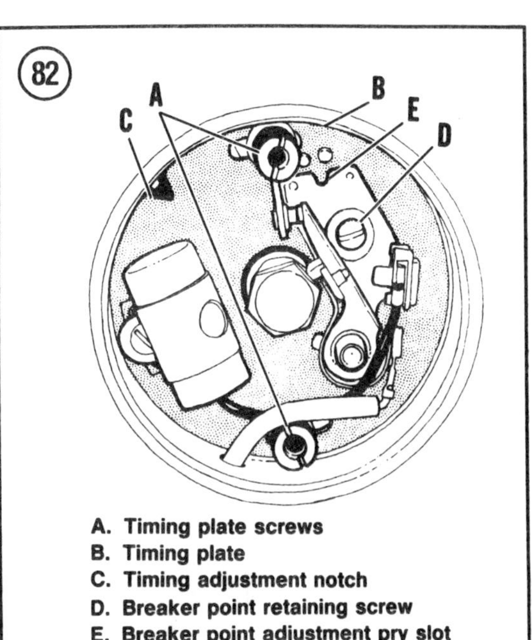

A. Timing plate screws
B. Timing plate
C. Timing adjustment notch
D. Breaker point retaining screw
E. Breaker point adjustment pry slot

g. Attach the wire leads to the breaker point set. Tighten the nut or screw securely.
6. Align points and adjust gap as described in Steps 2-5.

Ignition Timing Adjustment

Ignition timing should be checked and adjusted after point adjustment or replacement has been completed.

Refer to **Figure 80**, **Figure 81** or **Figure 82** for this procedure.

1. Remove the crankcase timing hole plug (**Figure 84**). Then install a clear plastic timing hole plug to prevent oil splash. Timing hole plugs can be purchased through a Harley-Davidson dealer.
2. Connect a timing light and tachometer according to manufacturer's instructions. Attach the timing light trigger lead to the front cylinder spark plug lead.

CAUTION

Work carefully with the tachometer and timing light wire leads. The wires can be damaged if they contact the hot exhaust pipes.

3. Start the engine and run at idle. Check the idle speed and compare to specifications in **Table 11**. If necessary, adjust idle speed as described in this chapter.
4. Point the timing light at the timing inspection hole (**Figure 84**). If the ignition is properly timed, the timing bar will be aligned as shown in **Figure 85**. If the marks are not correctly aligned, perform the following.

5A. *1959-1970:* Slightly loosen the circuit breaker clamp (**Figure 86**). Then rotate the circuit breaker housing as required until the ignition timing is correct. Tighten the clamp and recheck the timing.

5B. *1971-1978:* Remove the points cover from the right-hand side. Slightly loosen both timing plate screws (A, **Figure 82**). Then turn the timing plate (B, **Figure 82**) as required, using a screwdriver in the notch (C, **Figure 82**). Tighten the timing plate screws and recheck the timing. Reinstall the points cover.

6. Shut the engine off. Disconnect and remove all test equipment. Remove the clear plastic timing hole plug and reinstall the solid plug.

MAGNETO

The expendable ignition parts (spark plugs, breaker points and condenser) should be replaced

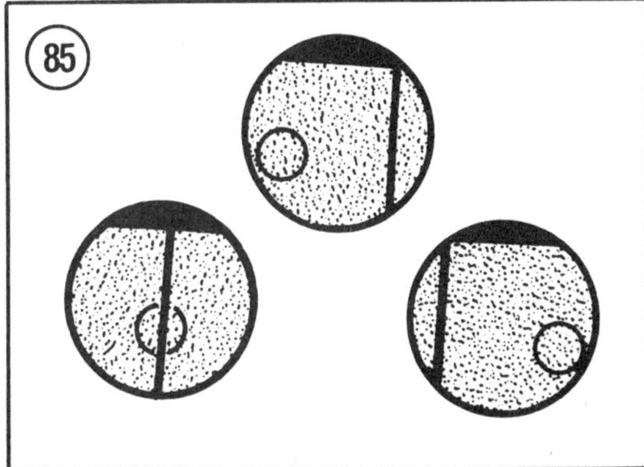

and the ignition timing checked and adjusted if necessary as part of a tune-up. If the bike is used primarily in stop-and-go city driving or is driven extensively at low engine speeds, these components should be cleaned, adjusted or replaced at more frequent intervals.

Breaker Point Service

1. Check breaker point contact surfaces. Points with an even, overall gray color and only slight roughness or pitting need not be replaced. They can be dressed with a clean point file. Do not use sandpaper or emery cloth for dressing points and do not attempt to remove all irregularities—just remove scale or dirt.
2. Check the alignment of the points and correct by bending contact plate as necessary. See **Figure 78**.
3. Check the point gap with a feeler gauge placed between the points (**Figure 79**) while the breaker arm rubbing block is on the high point of the cam lobe. The correct gap is 0.015 in. The gap is correct when the gauge passes between the contact points with a slight drag.
4. If the point gap requires adjustment, loosen the retaining screw (11, **Figure 87**). Insert the screwdriver tip into the eccentric screw or into the notch beside the points. Twist the screwdriver to open or close the point gap as required. When adjustment is correct, tighten the retaining screw. Recheck gap to make sure it did not change when the screw was tightened.
5. If points need replacing, refer to **Figure 87** and proceed as follows:
   a. Loosen the wire stud screw at the points (16, **Figure 87**) and disconnect the wires.
   b. Remove the breaker point pin and remove the circuit breaker lever from the pivot stud.
   c. Remove the pivot (10) and adjustment (11) screw. Then remove the cam wick holder and the stationary circuit breaker contact.
   d. Remove the condenser attaching screw and condenser.
   e. Wipe the breaker plate, cam and inside of cover with a lint-free cloth to remove all dirt and grease.
   f. Lightly lubricate the cam surfaces with breaker cam grease.
   g. Reverse to install the new breaker points. Position a new condenser on the breaker plate and install the attaching screw.
   h. Attach the wire leads to the breaker point set. Tighten the screw securely.
6. Align points and adjust gap as described in Steps 2-4.

Ignition Timing Adjustment

Ignition timing should be checked and adjusted after point adjustment or replacement has been completed.

Refer to **Figure 87** for this procedure.

1. Remove the crankcase timing hole plug (**Figure 84**). Then install a clear plastic timing hole plug to prevent oil splash. Timing hole plugs can be purchased through a Harley-Davidson dealer.

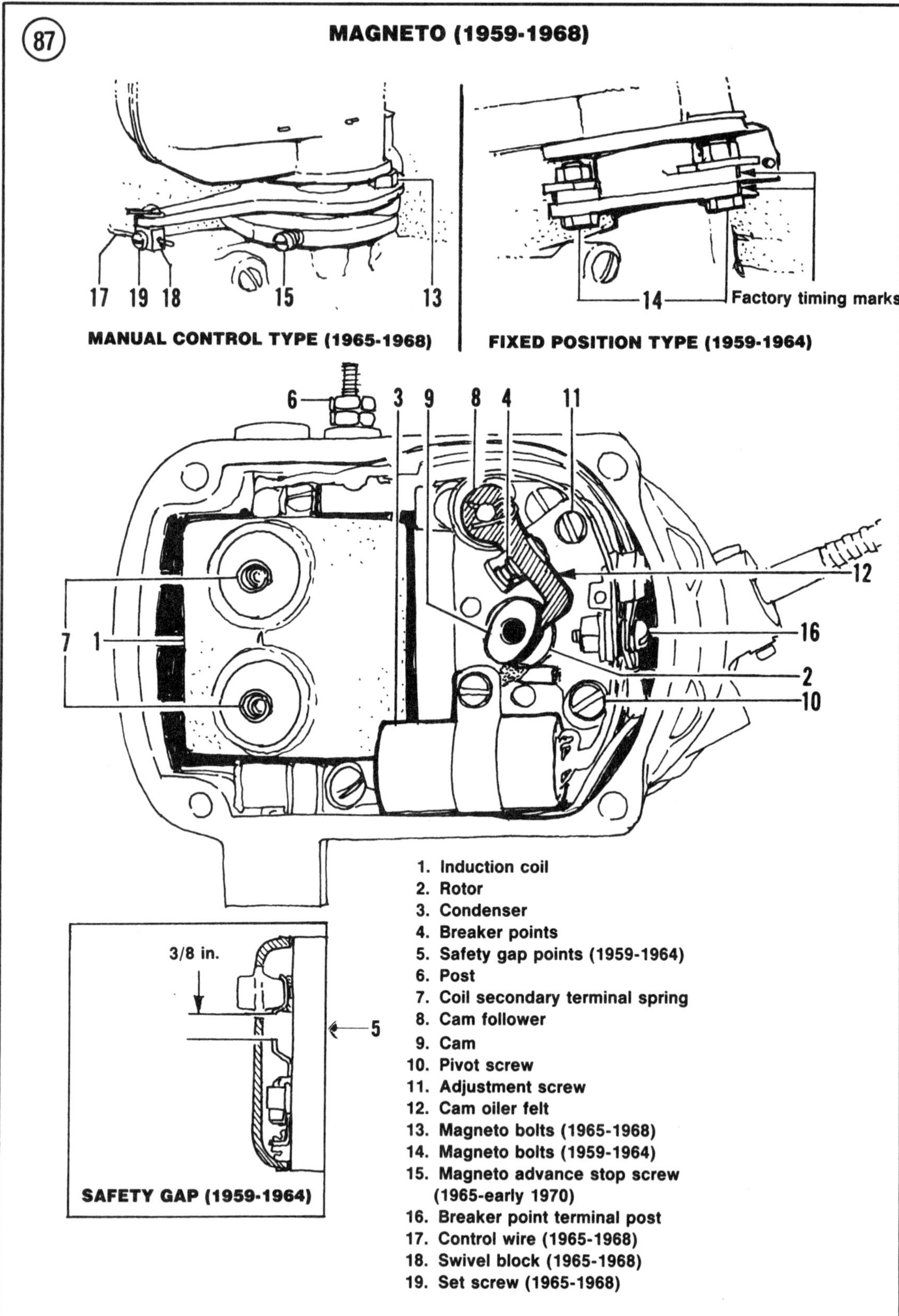
87
MAGNETO (1959-1968)
17 19 18 15 13
MANUAL CONTROL TYPE (1965-1968)
14 Factory timing marks
FIXED POSITION TYPE (1959-1964)
6 3 9 8 4 11
12
7 1
16
2
10
3/8 in.
5
SAFETY GAP (1959-1964)
1. Induction coil
2. Rotor
3. Condenser
4. Breaker points
5. Safety gap points (1959-1964)
6. Post
7. Coil secondary terminal spring
8. Cam follower
9. Cam
10. Pivot screw
11. Adjustment screw
12. Cam oiler felt
13. Magneto bolts (1965-1968)
14. Magneto bolts (1959-1964)
15. Magneto advance stop screw (1965-early 1970)
16. Breaker point terminal post
17. Control wire (1965-1968)
18. Swivel block (1965-1968)
19. Set screw (1965-1968)

2. Connect a timing light and tachometer according to manufacturer's instructions. Attach the timing light trigger lead to the front cylinder spark plug lead.

CAUTION
Work carefully with the tachometer and timing light wire leads. The wires can be damaged it they contact the hot exhaust pipes.

3. Start the engine and run at fast idle.
4. Point the timing light at the timing light inspection hole (**Figure 84**). If the ignition is properly timed, the timing bar will be aligned as shown in **Figure 85**. If the marks are not correctly aligned, perform the following.
5. Loosen the magneto clamps and turn the magneto either way as required to adjust the ignition timing.
6. Tighten the magneto clamps and recheck the ignition timing.

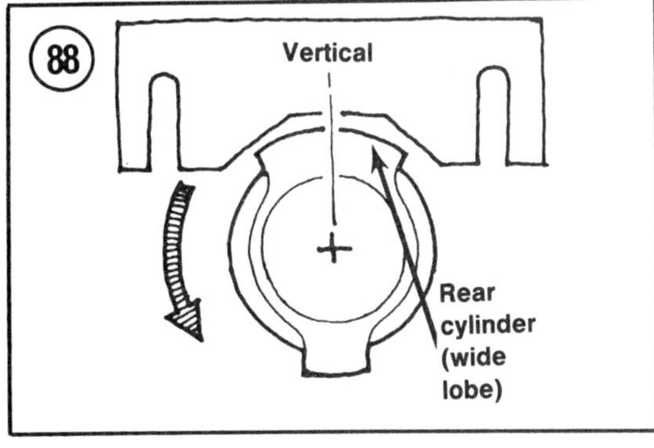

7. Shut the engine off. Disconnect and remove all test equipment. Remove the clear plastic timing hole plug and reinstall the solid plug.

BREAKERLESS IGNITION SYSTEM (1979)

Sensor Air Gap

Inspect the sensor air gap according to the maintenance schedule (**Table 3**).

1. Disconnect the spark plug leads at the spark plugs. Remove the spark plugs.
2. Remove the ignition timing cover.
3. Turn the crankshaft and center the wide rotor lobe opposite the sensor (**Figure 88**).
4. Measure the gap between the sensor and the rotor with a flat non-magnetic feeler gauge. It should be 0.004-0.006 in. If the gap is incorrect, loosen the 2 screws that attach the sensor (**Figure 89**) and move the sensor until the gap is correct. Then, holding the sensor steady, tighten the screws.

NOTE
If the engine doesn't run smoothly and spits back because of the standard lean fuel mixture, set the sensor air gap as close to 0.004 in. as possible. This will strengthen the ignition signal for better combustion.

5. Rotate the crankshaft to center the small lobe opposite the sensor. Measure the gap as before and correct it if necessary. Both gaps must be within the specified range.
6. Install the spark plugs and check the ignition timing as described in this chapter.

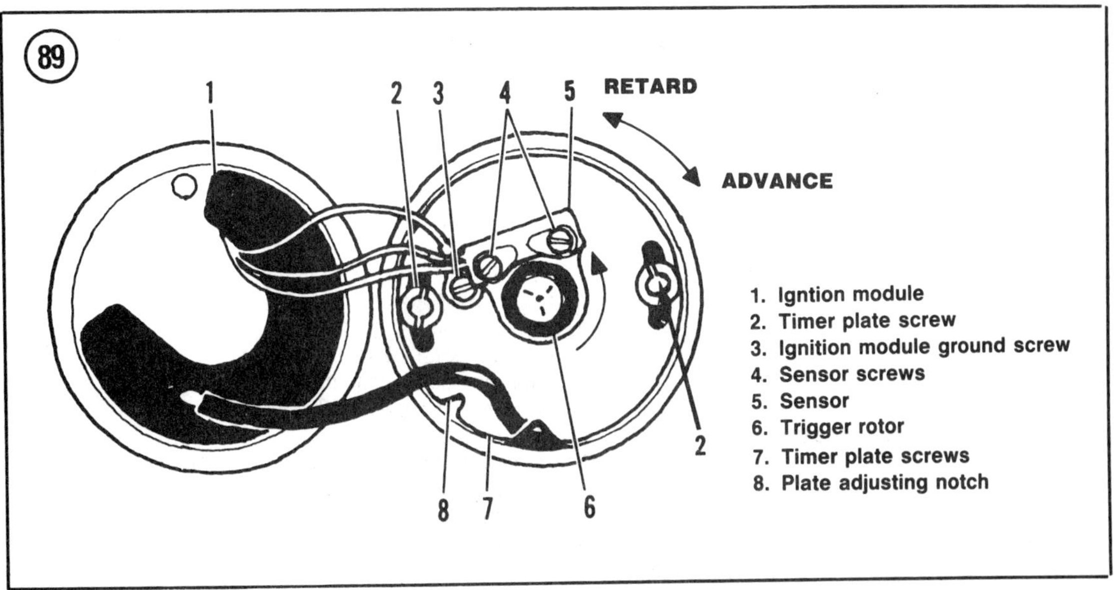

3

Ignition Timing Inspection

NOTE
Before starting this procedure, check all electrical connections related to the ignition system. Make sure all connections are tight and free of corrosion and that all ground connections are tight.

1. Check the sensor air gap as described in this chapter.
2. Remove the plug from the timing hole on the left side of the engine (**Figure 84**). A clear plastic viewing plug is available from Harley-Davidson dealers to minimize oil spray. Make sure the plug doesn't contact the flywheel.
3. Remove the timer cover.
4. Connect a portable tachometer following the manufacturer's instructions. The bike's tach is not accurate enough in the low rpm range for this adjustment.
5. Connect a timing light to the front cylinder spark plug wire following the manufacturer's instructions.

CAUTION
The use of a timing light with an inductive clamp-on pickup is recommended. If you must use another type, do not puncture the spark plug wire or cap; use an adaptor.

6. Start the engine and allow to idle at 2,000 rpm. If necessary, adjust idle as described in this chapter.
7. Aim the timing light at the timing inspection hole. At 2,000 rpm, the front cylinder's advance mark should appear in the center of the inspection window (**Figure 90**). If the mark is not in the correct position, loosen the timer plate screws (2, **Figure 89**) and turn the timer plate as required by prying the notch (8, **Figure 89**) with a screwdriver. Observe the front cylinder timing mark with the strobe light and tighten the timer plate screws when timing is correct.
8. Install the ignition timer cover and the inspection hole plug.

BREAKERLESS IGNITION SERVICE (1980-ON)

Ignition Timing Inspection and Adjustment

1. Remove the plug from the timing hole on the left side of the engine (**Figure 84**). Install a clear plastic viewing plug, available from Harley-Davidson dealers, to minimize oil spray.

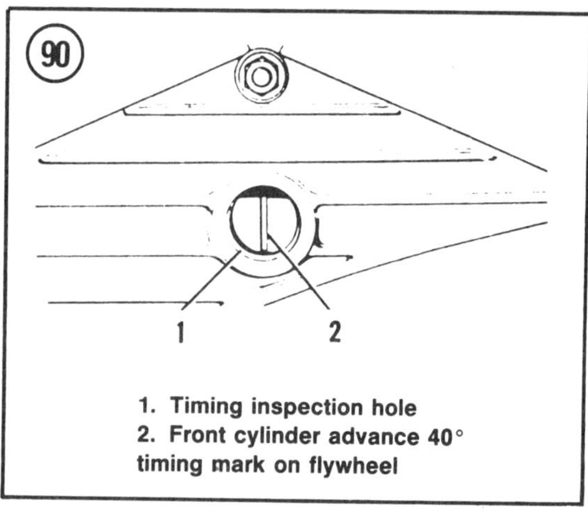

1. Timing inspection hole
2. Front cylinder advance 40° timing mark on flywheel

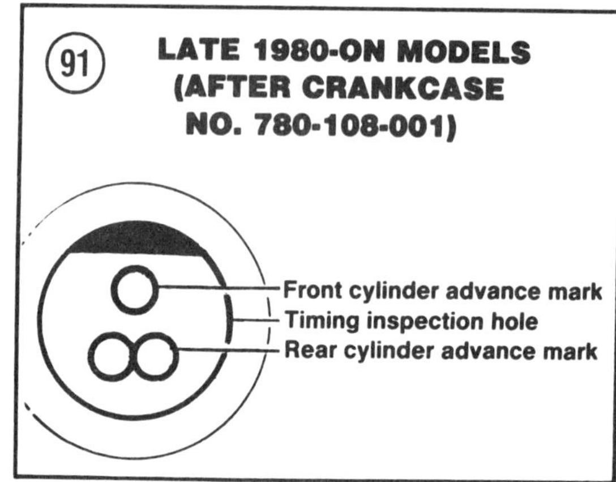

2. Connect a portable tachometer following the manufacturer's instructions. The bike's tach is not accurate enough in the low rpm range for this adjustment.
3. Connect a timing light to the front cylinder spark plug wire following the manufacturer's instructions.

CAUTION
The use of a timing light with an inductive clamp-on pickup is recommended. If you must use another type, do not puncture the spark plug wire or cap; use an adaptor.

4. Start the engine and allow to idle at 2,000 (1980-1982) or 1,300 (1983-1985) rpm. If necessary, adjust the idle as described in this chapter.
5. Aim the timing light at the timing inspection hole. With the engine idling at the rpm set in Step 4, the front cylinder's advance mark should appear in the center of the inspection window. **Figure 90** shows the advance mark for early 1980 engines up

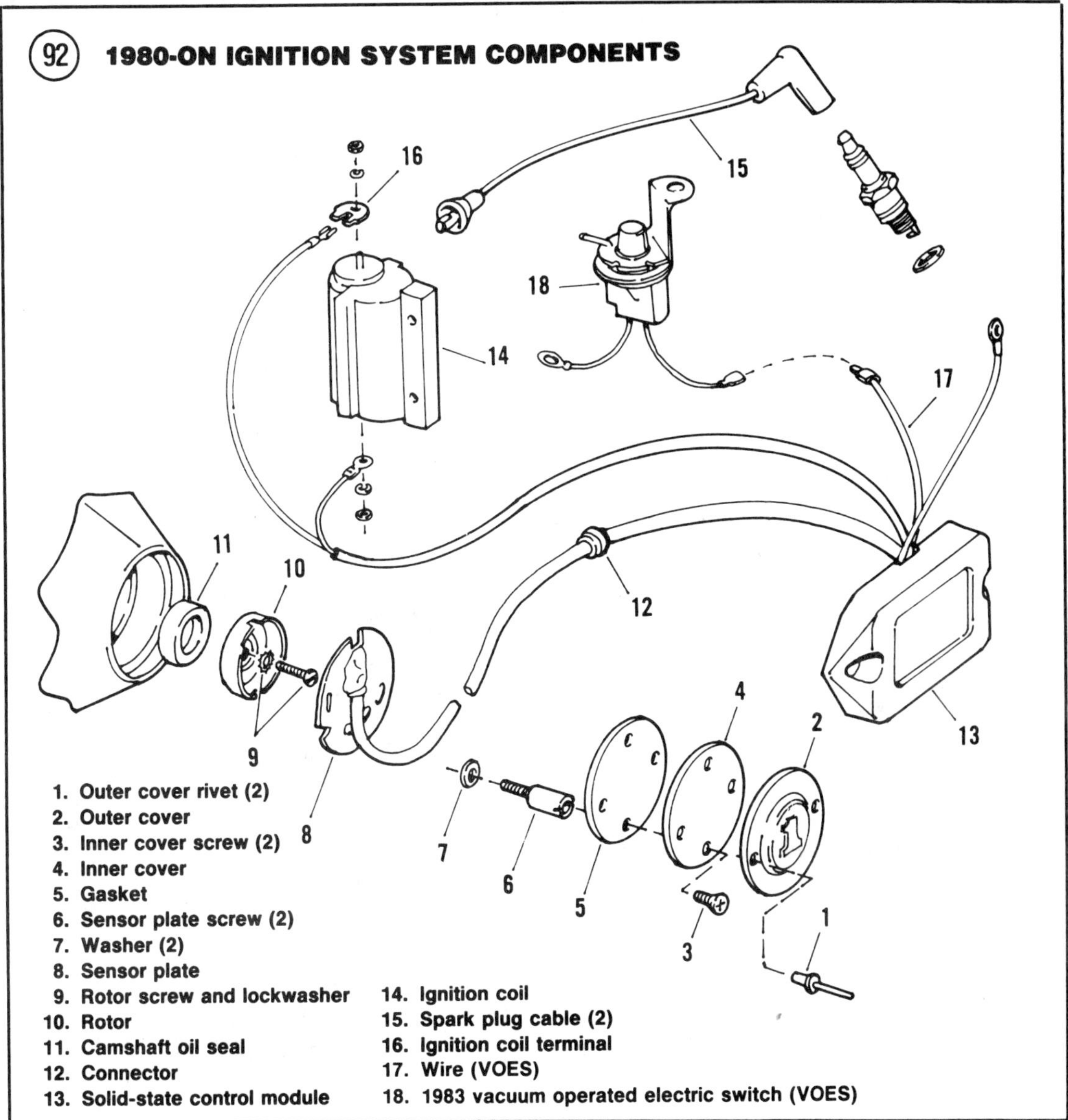

(92) **1980-ON IGNITION SYSTEM COMPONENTS**

1. Outer cover rivet (2)
2. Outer cover
3. Inner cover screw (2)
4. Inner cover
5. Gasket
6. Sensor plate screw (2)
7. Washer (2)
8. Sensor plate
9. Rotor screw and lockwasher
10. Rotor
11. Camshaft oil seal
12. Connector
13. Solid-state control module
14. Ignition coil
15. Spark plug cable (2)
16. Ignition coil terminal
17. Wire (VOES)
18. 1983 vacuum operated electric switch (VOES)

to engine number 780-108-001. **Figure 91** shows the single drilled dot that shows full advance for the front cylinder on later engines. The small dot (early 1980 models) or the "lazy figure 8" (late 1980-1985 models) drilled marks represent full advance for the rear cylinder. If the proper mark does not align, adjust the ignition timing as described in Steps 7-9.

6. If the ignition timing is correct, reinstall the timing hole plug. Then refer to Step 12.
7. Drill out the 2 pop rivets (1, **Figure 92**) with a 3/8 in. drill bit.
8. Referring to **Figure 92**, remove the outer cover (2), inner cover (4) and gasket (5).
9. Loosen the timing plate sensor plate screws (6, **Figure 92**) just enough to allow the plate to rotate. Start the engine and turn the plate as required so that the advanced mark is aligned as described in Step 5. Tighten the screws and recheck the timing.
10. Install the gasket and inner cover.
11. Install the outer cover with new rivets.

NOTE
When installing pop rivets to secure the outer cover, make sure to use the headless type shown in ***Figure 93****. The end of a normal pop rivet will break off on installation and damage the timing mechanism.*

12. *1983-1985 models:* After checking and adjusting the ignition timing, the VOES (vacuum operated electric switch) operation must be checked as described in this chapter.

CAUTION
If the VOES is defective, the ignition timing may be advanced too far and cause severe engine knocking and eventual damage.

VOES Testing/Replacement

Refer to **Figure 92** for this procedure.

1. Start engine and run at idle. Remove the VOES vacuum hose from the carburetor and temporarily plug the carburetor fitting with a piece of tape.
2. The ignition timing should retard and the engine idle speed should decrease. Reconnect the vacuum hose. The ignition timing mark should reappear and the engine speed should increase to the original level.
3. If the engine speed and ignition timing do not change as outlined when the vacuum hose is removed, check the VOES wire connected to the control module as well as the ground wire. If the wiring connections are good, the VOES or the control module is defective. Perform the following to further check the VOES:
   a. Disconnect the wires and vacuum hose from the VOES and remove the unit from the motorcycle.
   b. Connect an ohmmeter or test light between the 2 VOES wires. With no vacuum there should be no continuity.
   c. Connect a hose to the vacuum fitting on the VOES. Create suction in the hose. When a vacuum is present, continuity must be present.
   d. If the VOES does not meet these tests, replace it. If the switching action of the unit is good when removed, but defective when installed and connected to the control module, replace the ignition control module as described in Chapter Seven.

CARBURETOR ADJUSTMENTS

Model HD Carburetor Adjustment

Refer to **Figure 94** for this procedure.

1. Attach a tachometer to the engine following the manufacturer's instructions.
2. Check that the throttle lever (4) is fully closed when the throttle grip is closed.
3. Turn the low speed needle (1) clockwise until it seats lightly, then back it out 7/8 turn.
4. Turn the intermediate speed needle (2) in until it seats lightly, then back it out 7/8 turn.

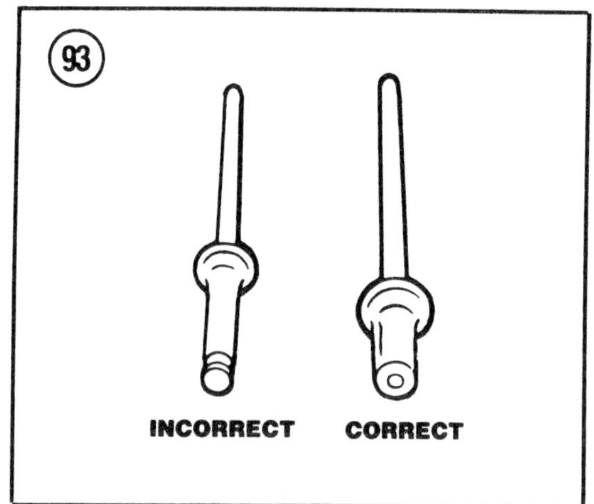

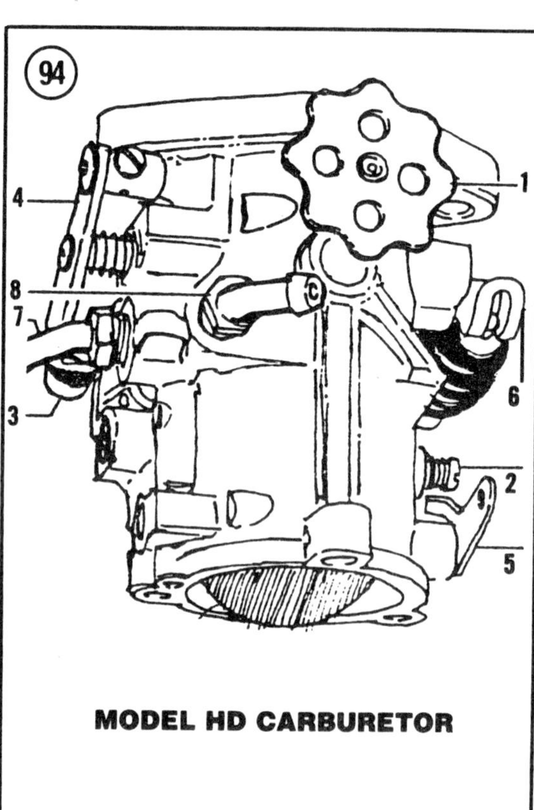

MODEL HD CARBURETOR

1. Low speed needle
2. Intermediate speed needle
3. Throttle stop screw
4. Throttle lever
5. Choke lever
6. Acclerating pump
7. Inlet fitting
8. Vent fitting

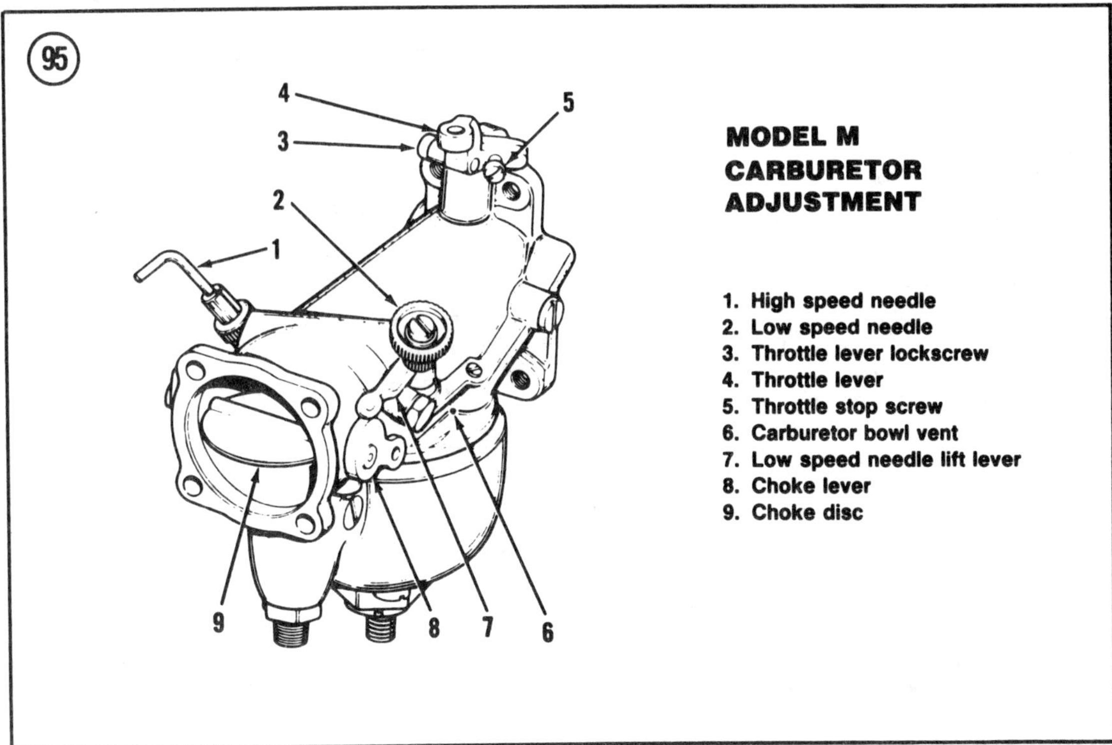

MODEL M CARBURETOR ADJUSTMENT

1. High speed needle
2. Low speed needle
3. Throttle lever lockscrew
4. Throttle lever
5. Throttle stop screw
6. Carburetor bowl vent
7. Low speed needle lift lever
8. Choke lever
9. Choke disc

5. Start the engine and run it until it reaches normal operating temperature and the choke can be turned off.
6. Slowly turn the intermediate speed needle (2) in the direction in which the highest engine speed is produced without missing or surging. Then turn the intermediate speed needle (2) counterclockwise 1/8 turn from that point.
7. Turn the throttle stop screw until the engine idles at 900-1,100 rpm.
8. Alternately adjust the low speed needle (1) and the throttle stop screw (3) to produce a smooth idle at 900-1,100 rpm.
9. Remove the tachometer.

Model M Carburetor Adjustment

Refer to **Figure 95** for this procedure.

1. Attach a tachometer to the engine following the manufacturer's instructions.
2. Turn the high speed needle (1) in until it seats lightly, then back it out 2 turns.
3. Turn the low speed needle (2) in until it seats, then back it out 5 turns.
4. Start the engine and run it until it reaches normal operating temperature and the choke can be turned off.
5. Idle the engine at 2,000 rpm to advance the ignition timing. Then turn the low speed needle (2) in one notch at a time until the engine falters and misses. Then back it out 5 to 10 notches, or until engine runs smoothly with throttle closed and ignition advanced.
6. Adjust engine idle to 900-1,100 rpm by turning the throttle stop screw (5).
7. Repeat Steps 5 and 6 as necessary. Overall engine operation will be better with idle mixture slightly rich (counterclockwise adjustment of low speed needle (2)).
8. Retard spark fully. If adjustment is correct, engine will continue to run evenly, but slower.
9. Operate the motorcycle at various road speeds, then turn the high speed needle (1) in or out as required to obtain best overall performance.

Bendix 16P12 Carburetor Adjustment

Refer to **Figure 96** for this procedure.

1. Attach a tachometer to the engine following the manufacturer's instructions.
2. Turn low speed needle (1) clockwise until it seats lightly, then back it out 1 1/2 turns.
3. Start the engine until it reaches normal operating temperature and the choke can be turned off.
4. Adjust throttle stop screw (2) so that engine runs at 700-800 rpm with throttle fully closed.

5. Adjust low speed needle (1) as required to make engine accelerate and run smoothly at idle.
6. Adjust throttle stop screw (2), if necessary, to obtain idle of 700-900 rpm.

Keihin Carburetor (Late 1976-early 1978)

Refer to **Figure 97** for this procedure.
1. Attach a tachometer to the engine following the manufacturer's instructions.
2. Turn the idle mixture screw (12) clock wise until it seats lightly. Then back it out 7/8 turn (late 1976-1977) or 1 1/2 turns (early 1978).
3. Start the engine and warm it to normal operating temperature.
4. Turn the throttle stop screw (4) and set the idle to 700-900 rpm.
5. Turn the idle mixture screw in or out as required, to get the highest and smoothest idle speed. The best performance will usually result if the mixture is slightly rich (screw turned in a little).
6. Rev the engine a couple of times and see if the idle speed is constant. Readjust the idle speed, if necessary, to 700-900 by turning the throttle stop screw (3).
7. Adjust the accelerator pump volume, if necessary, with the rocker arm adjust screw (4). The standard setting is about 1/4 in. between the tip of the screw and its stop. Backing the screw out increases fule boume. The pump stroke may also be adjusted by moving the rocker arm spring to other than the standard center notch in the rocker arm.

Keihin Carburetor (Late 1978-on)

Refer to **Figure 98**, **Figure 99** or **Figure 100** for this procedure.
1. Attach a tachometer to the engine following the manufacturer's instructions.
2. Start the engine and warm it to normal operating temperature. Check that the choke is off.
3. Set the idle speed to 900 rpm with the throttle stop screw.
4A. *Late 1978-1979:* The idle mixture screw has a limiter cap (2, **Figure 98**) on it. Turn the limiter cap out (counterclockwise) to the leanest setting that gives a smooth idle.

NOTE
The low-speed mixture screw limiter cap should not be removed unless the carburetor is being disassembled for cleaning. If the cap has been removed, turn the idle mixture screw in (clockwise) until it seats lightly, then

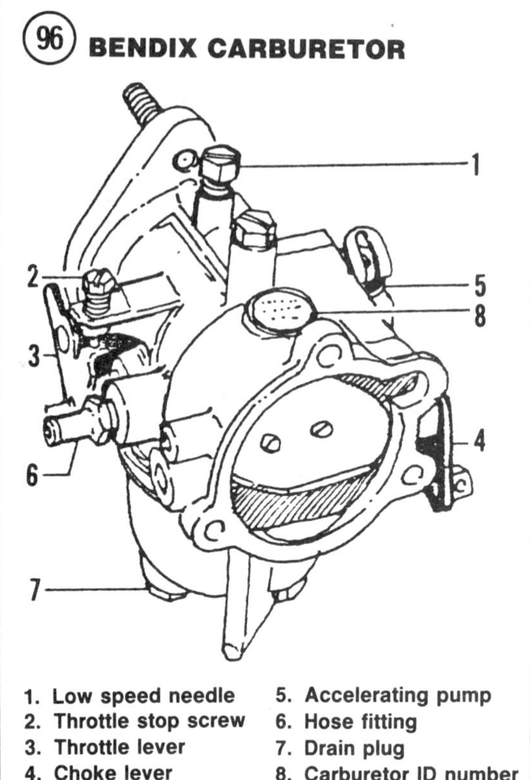

1. Low speed needle
2. Throttle stop screw
3. Throttle lever
4. Choke lever
5. Accelerating pump
6. Hose fitting
7. Drain plug
8. Carburetor ID number

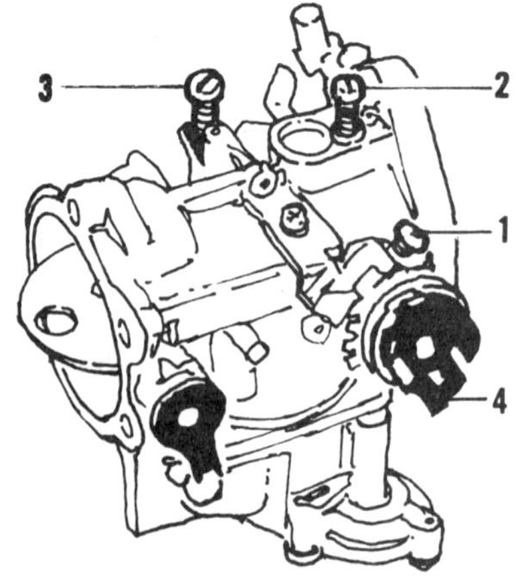

1. Pump adjust screw
2. Idle mixture screw
3. Throttle stop screw
4. Rocker arm

98

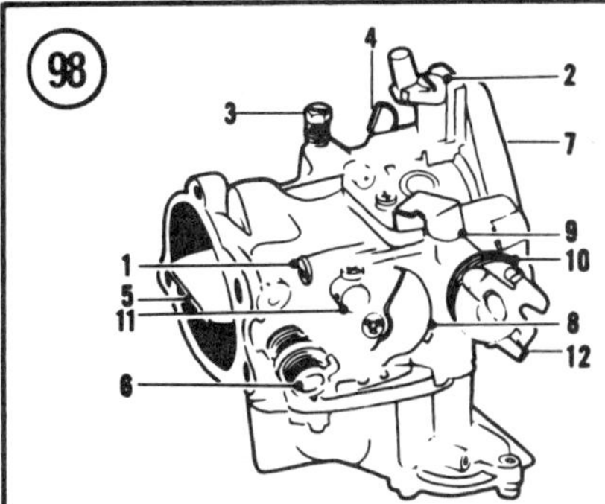

KEIHIN CARBURETOR (LATE 1978-1980)

1. Fast idle adjusting screw
2. Limiter cap (late 1978-1979)
3. Throttle stop screw
4. Throttle lever
5. Choke plate
6. Choke lever shaft
7. Mounting flange
8. Accelerating pump lever
9. Rocker arm
10. Rocker arm spring
11. Intermediate lever
12. Fast idle cam

99

KEIHIN CARBURETOR (1981-1983)

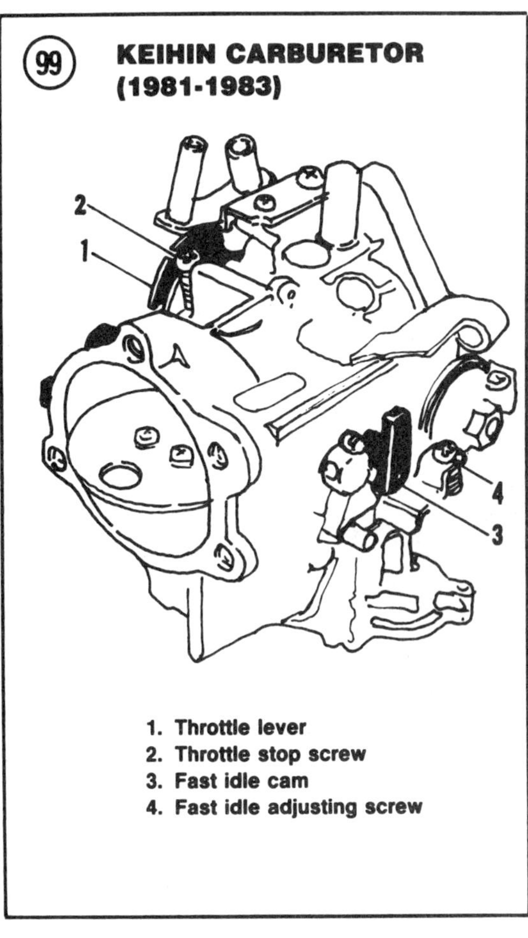

1. Throttle lever
2. Throttle stop screw
3. Fast idle cam
4. Fast idle adjusting screw

100

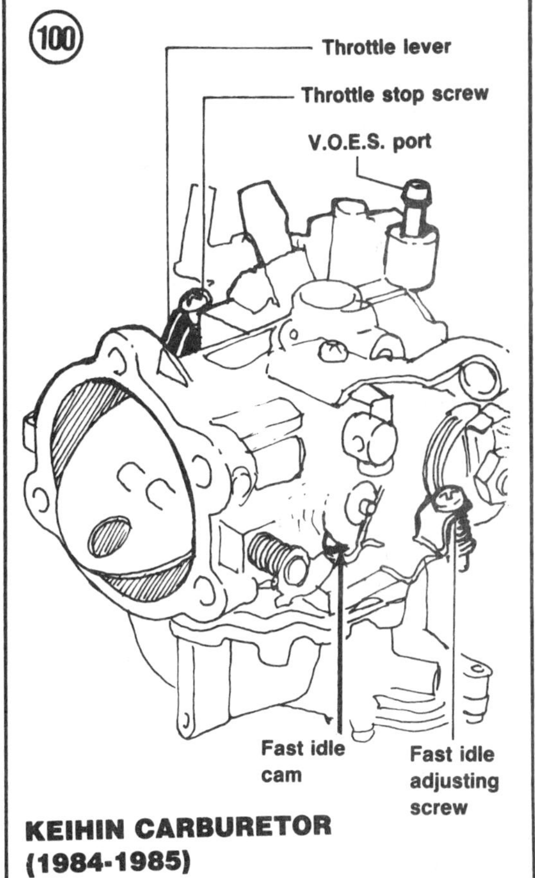

KEIHIN CARBURETOR (1984-1985)

back it out 1 1/4 turns. Install the limiter cap in its center position.

NOTE

Turning the idle mixture screw to the right (clockwise) leans the mixture. Turning it to the left (counterclockwise) enriches the mixture.

4B. *1980-1985:* The idle mixture is set and sealed at the factory. It is not intended to be adjustable.

5. Rev the engine a couple of times and see if the idle speed is constant. If necessary, readjust the idle speed to 900 rpm.

6. Pull the choke knob out to its first detent and turn the fast idle screw to set fast idle at 1,500 rpm. Push the choke knob all the way in and check that idle drops to 900 rpm.

Table 1 MAINTENANCE SCHEDULE* (1959-1969)

Weekly	• Check tire pressure • Check battery electrolyte level
Initial 300 miles	• Check engine oil level
Every 1,000 miles	• Check engine oil level • Check transmission oil level • Lubricate drive chain • Check drive chain tension and adjust if necessary • Clean air filter • Check battery electrolyte level
Every 2,000 miles	• Adjust push rod clearance • Adjust clutch • Adjust front and rear brakes • Change engine oil and filter • Adjust engine primary chain • Check ignition timing • Grease front and rear brake shafts • Grease clutch release worn • Grease shift lever • Grease seat bar roller and bolt • Grease kick starter shaft • Grease rear wheel hub bearings • Grease tachometer drive gear • Oil rear brake rod and front brake cable clevis • Oil brake and clutch levers • Lubricate all cables • Lubricate generator bearing (1959-1960)
Every 5,000 miles or 1 year	• Check front and rear fork bearing adjustment • Replace spark plugs • Change engine oil and filter • Check and adjust ignition timing • Inspect tires • Clean gas tank strainer • Check generator brushes • Check shock rubber bushings • Grease throttle and spark control spiral • Grease circuit breaker camshaft • Grease front wheel hub bearings (1959-1968) • Grease speedometer and tachometer cables
Every 10,000 miles	• Replace rear fork pivot bearings • Lubricate generator bearing (1959-1960)
Every 50,000 miles	• Inspect and repack steering head bearings

* This Harley-Davidson factory maintenance schedule should be considered a guide to general maintenance and lubrication intervals. Harder than normal use and exposure to mud, water, high humidity, etc., will naturally dictate more frequent attention to most maintenance items

Table 2 MAINTENANCE SCHEDULE* (1970-1978)

Weekly	• Check tire pressure • Check battery electrolyte level
Initial 300 miles	• Check engine oil level • Lubricate rear chain (1977-1978)
Every 1,000 miles	• Check engine oil level • Check transmission oil level • Lubricate drive chain • Check drive chain tension and adjust if necessary • Clean air filter • Check battery electrolyte level • Check oil and brake lines for leakage • Adjust clutch • Adjust brakes • Adjust front primary chain • Check fuel system lines and fittings • Grease rear brake foot lever shaft • Grease kick starter shaft • Grease speedometer drive gear • Grease circuit breaker camshaft • Oil clutch and brake hand levers • Oil rear brake rod and front brake cable clevis
Every 2,000 miles	• Check and adjust push rod clearance • Change engine oil and filter • Check carburetor adjustments • Check rear chain oiler (1970-1976) • Check ignition timing • Check brake fluid level • Inspect and regap spark plugs • Check nut and bolts for correct tightness • Grease front and rear brake shafts • Grease clutch release worn (1970) • Grease shift lever • Grease seat bar roller and bolt • Grease rear wheel hub • Oil front brake cable • Oil front brake cable clevis
Every 5,000 miles or 1 year	• Check front and rear fork bearing adjustment • Replace spark plugs • Change engine oil and filter • Check and adjust ignition timing • Inspect tires • Clean gas tank strainer • Check generator brushes • Check shock rubber bushings • Change brake fluid • Change front fork oil (1973 and later) • Grease speedometer and tachometer cables • Grease throttle control spiral • Grease circuit breaker camshaft (1979)
Every 10,000 miles	• Repace rear fork pivot bearings • Clean and repack wheel bearings
Every 50,000 miles	• Inspect and repack steering head bearings

* This Harley-Davidson factory maintenance schedule should be considered a guide to general maintenance and lubrication intervals. Harder than normal use and exposure to mud, water, high humidity, etc., will naturally dictate more frequent attention to most maintenance items.

Table 3 MAINTENANCE SCHEDULE[1] (1979-1985)

Every 300 miles	• Lubricate rear chain
Initial 500 miles, then every 2,500 miles	• Change engine oil and filter • Check and adjust push rod clearance • Inspect and clean air filter • Check and adjust rear chain • Check and adjust primary chain • Check and adjust rear brake pedal • Check brake fluid level • Check brake pad lining and disc condition • Check and adjust clutch • Clean fuel tank filter screen • Check fuel lines and fittings for leakage • Check brake lines and fittings for leakage • Oil brake and clutch levers • Oil all cables • Grease the speedometer drive gear • Check wheel spoke tightness • Check tire pressure • Check tire condition • Check and adjust carburetor • Check throttle and choke controls • Check switch operation
Initial 500 miles, then every 5,000 miles	• Change transmission oil • Check and adjust front fork bearing adjustment • Check battery electrolyte level • Clean and tighten battery connections
Every 2,500 miles	• Check ignition timing • Clean and regap spark plugs • Sensor air gap[2]
Every 5,000 miles	• Replace spark plugs • Grease throttle control grip sleeve • Check rear shock rubber bushing • Change front fork oil
Every 10,000 miles	• Check alternator • Clean and repack wheel bearings • Clean and repack rear fork bearings
Every 2 years	• Change brake fluid

1. This Harley-Davidson factory maintenance schedule should be considered a guide to general maintenance and lubrication intervals. Harder than normal use and exposure to mud, water, high humidity, etc., will naturally dictate more frequent attention to most maintenance items.
2. 1979 models.

Table 4 TIRE PRESSURE[1]

	Front	Rear
1959-1969		
XLCH, 1959-1966 XLH	14	18
1967-1969 XLH	16	20
1970-1978[2]	24	30
1979-1983		
Up to 300 lb. load	24 psi	26 psi
Over 300 lb. load	25 psi	28 psi
1984-1985		
Up to 300 lb. load	24	26
Over 300 lb. load	26	32

1. Tire pressures based on 150 lb. rider weight. For each extra 50 lb., add 2 psi @ rear, 1 psi @ front.
2. Maximum tire pressure for all tires is 32 psi.

Table 5 STATE OF CHARGE

Specific gravity	State of charge
1.110-1.130	Discharged
1.140-1.160	Almost discharged
1.170-1.190	One-quarter charged
1.200-1.220	One-half charged
1.230-1.250	Three-quarters charged
1.260-1.280	Fully charged

Table 6 RECOMMENDED LUBRICANTS[1]

Brake fluid	
Prior to Sept., 1976 production[1]	DOT 3
Sept., 1976 and later production[1]	DOT 5
Fork oil[2]	
1959-1978	HD type B
1979-1985	HD type E
Battery top up	Distilled water
Engine oil[2]	
1959-1978	
Below +40° F	HD grade 58
+40° F and up	HD grade 75
Severe engine operating conditions @ +90° F	HD grade 105
1979-1985	
Below +40° F	HD special light
40-60° F	HD medium heavy
+60° F and up	HD regular heavy
Severe engine operating conditions @ +80° F	HD extra heavy grade 60
Transmission oil[2]	HD Power Blend Super Premium oil

1. Never mix DOT 3 and DOT 5 fluids. This can cause brake failure.
2. Lubricants recommended are Harley-Davidson brands.

Table 7 ENGINE AND TRANSMISSION OIL CAPACITIES

	Quantity
Oil tank	
1959-1978	3 quarts
1979-1981	4 quarts
1982-on	3 quarts
Transmission	1.5 pints

Table 8 FRONT FORK OIL CAPACITY*

	Quantity
1959-1967	
Wet	3 1/2 oz.
Dry	4 1/2 oz.
1968-1969	
Wet	4 1/2 oz.
Dry	5 1/2 oz.
1970-1972	
Wet	5 1/2 oz.
Dry	6 1/2 oz.
1973-1983	
Wet	5 oz.
Dry	6 oz.
1984-1985	
Wet	5.4 oz.
Dry	6.4 oz.

* Use "dry" quantity if fork has been disassembled. Otherwise, use "wet" quantity.

Table 9 TUNE-UP SPECIFICATIONS

Breaker point gap	
1959-1969	
Battery ignition	0.020 in.
Magneto ignition	0.015 in.
1970	0.020 in.
1971-1978	0.018 in.
Dwell	
1959-1969	90° @ 1,000 rpm
1970-1971	90° @ 2,000 rpm
1972-1978	140° @ 2,000 rpm
Ignition timing	
1959-1969	
Advanced	
XLH, XLCH	45° BTDC
Retarded	
XLH	15° BTDC
1970-1971	
Advanced	45° BTDC
Retarded	15° BTDC
1972-1978	
Advanced	40° BTDC
Retarded	10° BTDC
1979-1985	Electronic
Compresssion	120 psi

Table 10 SPARK PLUG TYPE AND GAP

	Type	Gap
1959-1969		
Average use	H-D 4	0.020 in.[1]/0.025-0.030 in.[2]
Hard use	H-D 5	0.020 in.[1]/0.025-0.030 in.[2]
1970-1978		
Average use	H-D 4	0.025-0.030 in.
Hard use	H-D 5	0.025-0.030 in.
1979	H-D 4	0.060 in.
1980-1982	H-D 4-5	0.038-0.045 in.
1980-1982	H-D 4R5[3]	0.038-0.045 in.
1983-1985	H-D 4R5[3]	0.038-0.045 in.

1. Magneto ignition.
2. Battery ignition.
3. Harley-Davidson spark plugs 4R5 are special resistor plugs to reduce radio interference originating in the motorcycle ignition system. These plugs are recommended for all 1980 and later models with electronic ignition.

Table 11 CARBURETOR IDLE SPEED

Carburetor	Idle
HD	900-1,100 rpm
Bendix	700-900 rpm
Model M	*
Keihin	900 rpm

* Adjust until engine idles and runs smoothly.

3

CHAPTER FOUR

ENGINE

The Harley-Davidson Sportsters are equipped with air-cooled 4-cycle, V-twin engines. Valves are operated by pushrods and rocker arms.

Both cylinders fire once in 720° of crankshaft rotation. The rear cylinder fires 315° after the front cylinder. The front cylinder fires again in another 405°. Note that one cylinder is always on its exhaust stroke when the other fires on its compression stroke.

This chapter provides complete service and overhaul procedures, including information for removal, disassembly, inspection, service and reassembly of the engine. **Tables 1-3** at the end of this chapter provide complete engine specifications.

Before starting any work, read the service hints in Chapter One. You will do a better job with this information fresh in your mind.

ENGINE PRINCIPLES

Figure 1 explains how the engine works. This will be helpful when troubleshooting or repairing the engine.

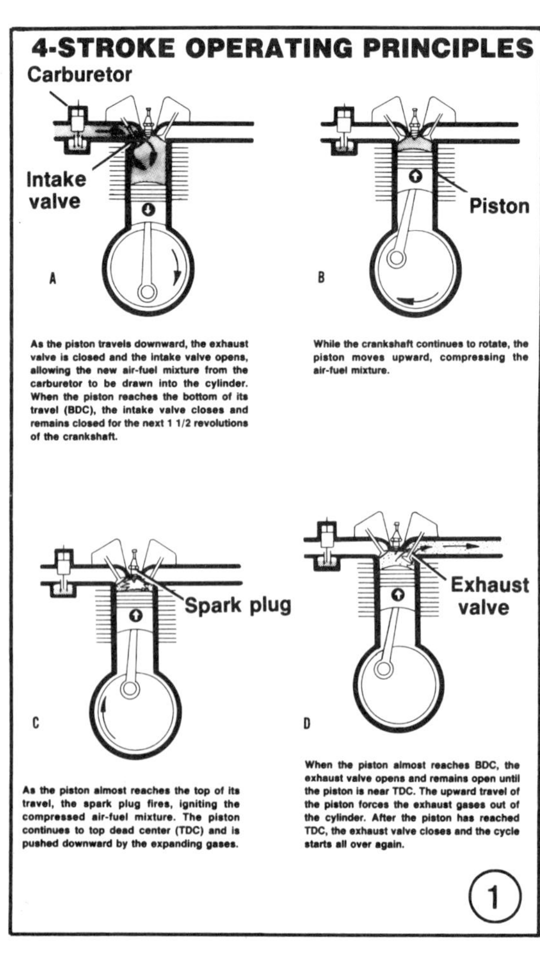

SERVICING ENGINE IN FRAME

Many components can be serviced while the engine is mounted in the frame:

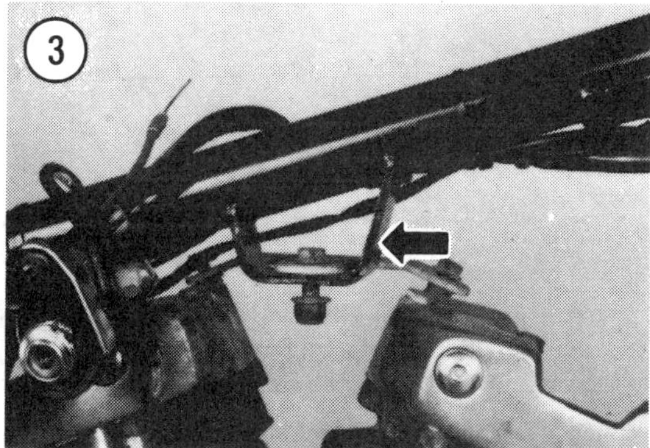

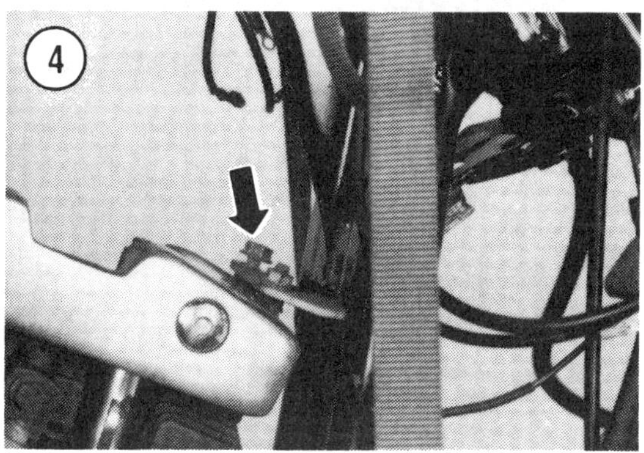

a. Cylinder head.
b. Cylinder and pistons.
c. Gearshift mechanism.
d. Clutch.
e. Camshafts.
f. Transmission.
g. Carburetor.
h. Starter motor and gears.
i. Generator or alternator.

ENGINE

Removal/Installation

1. Thoroughly clean the engine exterior of dirt, oil and foreign material, using one of the cleaners designed for the purpose.
2. Remove the fuel tank as described in Chapter Six.
3. Remove the air cleaner assembly as described in Chapter Three.
4. Disconnect the horn and ignition switch wires, then remove the horn and ignition switch bracket (**Figure 2**).
5. Remove the carburetor as described in Chapter Six.

6A. *1959-1978:* Remove the upper engine support bracket bolt. There are shims installed between the cylinder head and the frame lug. Note location and quantity of these shims; they will have to be reinstalled during engine installation.

6B. *1979-1985:* On 1983-1985 models, remove the vacuum operated electric switch (VOES) located near the rear engine support bracket. Then remove the top (**Figure 3**) and front (**Figure 4**) engine support brackets.

7. Remove the exhaust system as described in Chapter Six.
8. Drain the crankcase oil. On 1980 and later models, disconnect the oil filter line.
9. Disconnect both spark plug wires.
10. If necessary, remove the ignition coil(s) from the frame.
11. Disconnect and remove the engine oil lines (**Figure 5**).
12. Disconnect the engine oil hoses (**Figure 6**).
13. Remove the cylinder heads with the rocker arm covers attached, as described in this chapter.
14. Remove the cylinders as described in this chapter.
15. Remove the clutch as described in Chapter Five.
16. Remove the generator or alternator assembly as described in Chapter Seven.
17. Remove the engine drive sprocket as described in this chapter.

18. Remove the transmission as described in Chapter Five.
19. Remove the cams as described in this chapter.
20. Remove the starter as described in Chapter Seven.
21. Remove the battery as described in Chapter Three.
22. Remove the oil tank, if necessary.
23. Disconnect the tachometer cable, if required.
24. Take a final look all over the engine to make sure everything has been disconnected.
25. Loosen all engine mount bolts and remove them. See **Figure 7** and **Figure 8**.
26. With the help of an assistant, remove the engine from the left side of the frame.
27. Installation is the reverse of these steps, noting the following.
28. Fill the engine and transmission with the recommended type and quantity of engine oil. Refer to Chapter Three.
29. Adjust the clutch and throttle cables as described in Chapter Three.
30. Adjust the drive chain as described in Chapter Three.
31. Start the engine and check for leaks.

ROCKER ARMS AND CYLINDER HEAD

This procedure describes removal of the rocker arm covers, rocker arms and cylinder heads. The rocker arm cover and cylinder head must be removed together. The unit can be removed with the engine in the frame.

Removal/Installation

NOTE

Before performing the following steps, mark the individual parts during removal so that they can be reinstalled in their original positions.

Refer to **Figure 9** or **Figure 10** for this procedure.

1. Perform Steps 1-10 under *Engine Removal.*
2. Remove the spark plugs.
3. Disconnect the oil line nuts (**Figure 5**) at the rocker arm cover.
4. Using a screwdriver, pry the push rod cover spring keeper out of the push rod assembly (**Figure 11**). Repeat for each push rod.
5. Lift the lower push rod covers upward and secure each with a bent coat hanger as shown in **Figure 12**. Rotate the engine until both valves are closed in the cylinder head to be removed. Valve position can be determined by observing the tappet (**Figure 13**) position. If the tappets are lower in the tappet guide, the valves for that cylinder head are closed. Remove the coat hangers.
6. Referring to **Figure 14** and **Figure 15**, loosen the tappet adjuster locknuts and thread the valve adjuster screw all the way into the tappet body.

CAUTION

When performing Step 7, do not bind the push rod in the rocker arm housing as this may damage the push rod.

7. Lift the push rod assembly (**Figure 16**) out of the gear case and remove it.

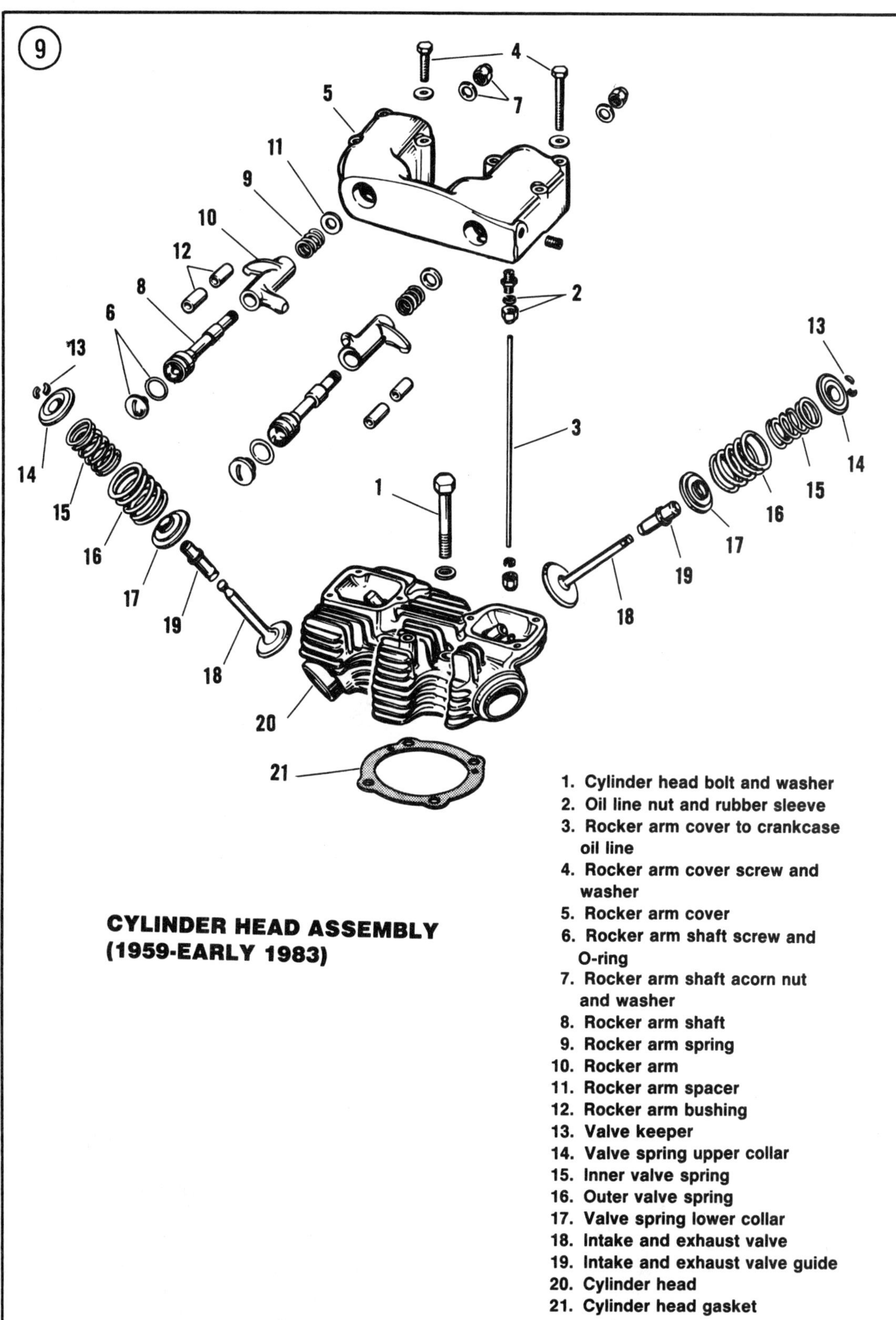

CYLINDER HEAD ASSEMBLY (1959-EARLY 1983)

1. Cylinder head bolt and washer
2. Oil line nut and rubber sleeve
3. Rocker arm cover to crankcase oil line
4. Rocker arm cover screw and washer
5. Rocker arm cover
6. Rocker arm shaft screw and O-ring
7. Rocker arm shaft acorn nut and washer
8. Rocker arm shaft
9. Rocker arm spring
10. Rocker arm
11. Rocker arm spacer
12. Rocker arm bushing
13. Valve keeper
14. Valve spring upper collar
15. Inner valve spring
16. Outer valve spring
17. Valve spring lower collar
18. Intake and exhaust valve
19. Intake and exhaust valve guide
20. Cylinder head
21. Cylinder head gasket

(10)

CYLINDER HEAD ASSEMBLY (LATE 1983-1985)

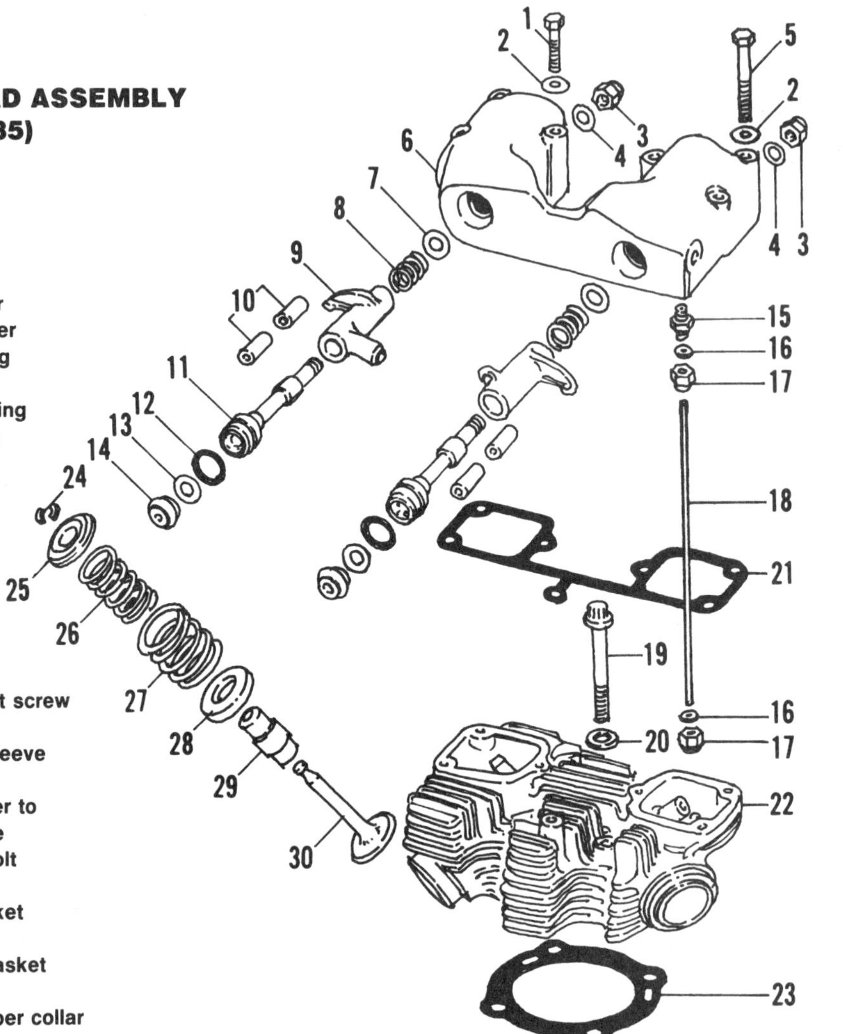

1. Bolt
2. Flat washer
3. Nut
4. Washer
5. Bolt
6. Rocker arm cover
7. Rocker arm spacer
8. Rocker arm spring
9. Rocker arm
10. Rocker arm bushing
11. Rocker arm shaft
12. O-ring
13. Shim
14. Rocker arm shaft screw
15. Oil line fitting
16. Oil line rubber sleeve
17. Oil line nut
18. Rocker arm cover to crankcase oil line
19. Cylinder head bolt
20. Washer
21. Rocker arm gasket
22. Cylinder head
23. Cylinder head gasket
24. Valve key
25. Valve spring upper collar
26. Inner valve spring
27. Outer valve spring
28. Valve spring lower collar
29. Valve guide
30. Valve

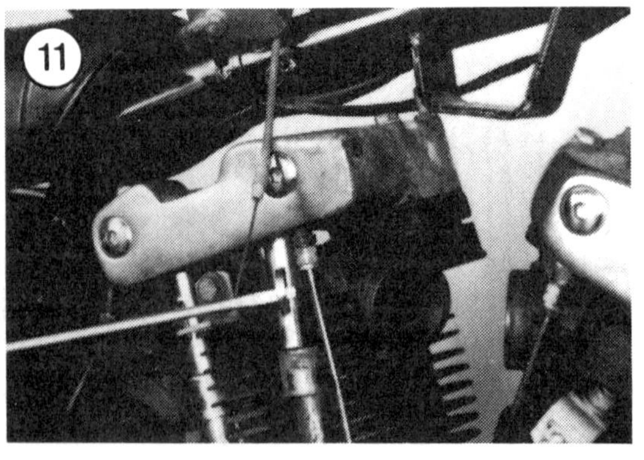

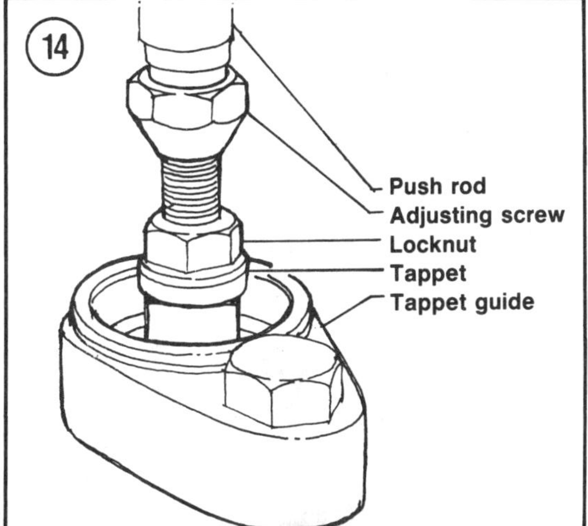

8. Remove the cylinder head bolts in a criss-cross pattern.
9. Tap the cylinder head with a rubber mallet to free it. Then remove the cylinder head and rocker arm cover as an assembly. See **Figure 17**.
10. Tag each part so that it can be reinstalled in its original position.
11. Repeat Steps 3-10 and remove the opposite cylinder head and rocker arm cover.
12. Disassemble the cylinder head/rocker arm cover assembly as described in this chapter.
13. Install by reversing these removal steps, noting the following.
14. Clean the cylinder head and cylinder mating surfaces of any gasket material.
15. *1959-1969:* Apply a light coat of oil or grease to the new cylinder head gasket.
16. Install the cylinder head gasket (**Figure 18**), making sure the oil return hole in the gasket lines up with the oil hole in the cylinder head.
17. Turn the engine over so that the tappets are in their lowest position.
18A. *1959-1978:* Install the cylinder head, push rods and push rod covers as an assembly.
18B. *1979-1985:* Perform the following:
  a. Install the push rods and push rod cover.

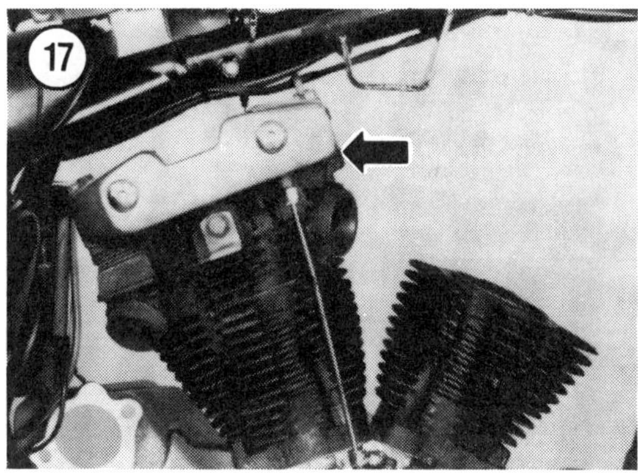

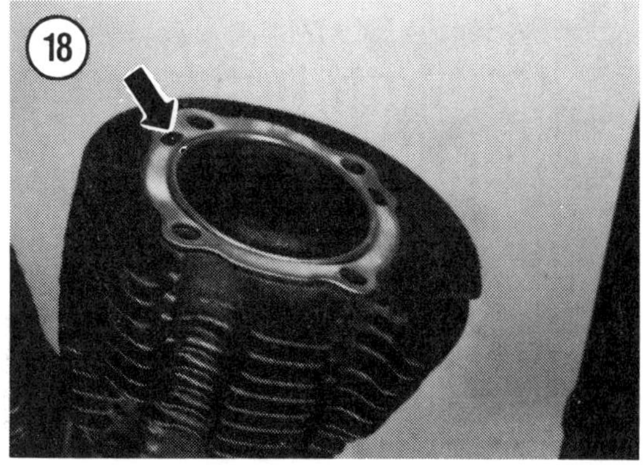

4

b. From the left side, install the cylinder head assembly over the oil lines and push rods.

NOTE

*Make sure that the push rod ends fit properly in the tappet adjuster screw sockets at the lower ends (**Figure 19**), and in the push rod sockets at the upper ends.*

19. Install each cylinder head bolt with a flat washer under its head. Do not tighten the bolts at this time.
20. Align the intake manifold with the cylinder head intake port faces.
21. Tighten each bolt in a criss-cross pattern 1/8 to 1/4 turn until all are tightened to torque specifications in **Table 2** or **Table 3**.
22. Apply Loctite Pipe Sealant With Teflon to the oil line threads. Then tighten the oil line nut (**Figure 5**) securely.
23. Adjust the tappets as described in this chapter under *Push Rods.*
24. Repeat for the other cylinder head.

Disassembly

Refer to **Figure 9** or **Figure 10** for this procedure.

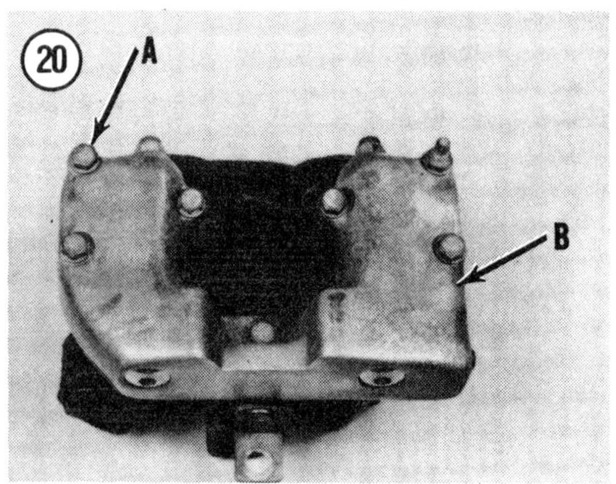

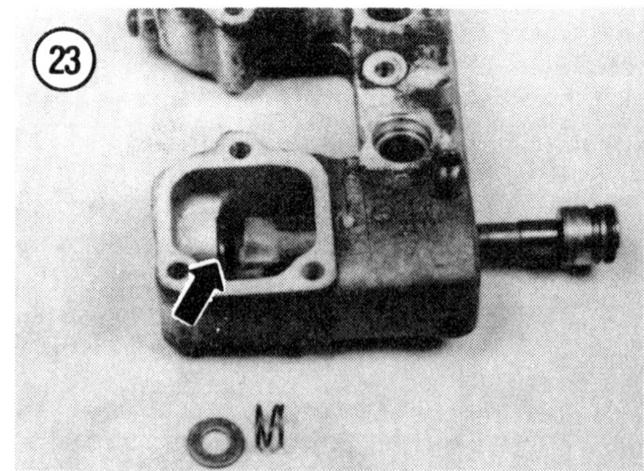

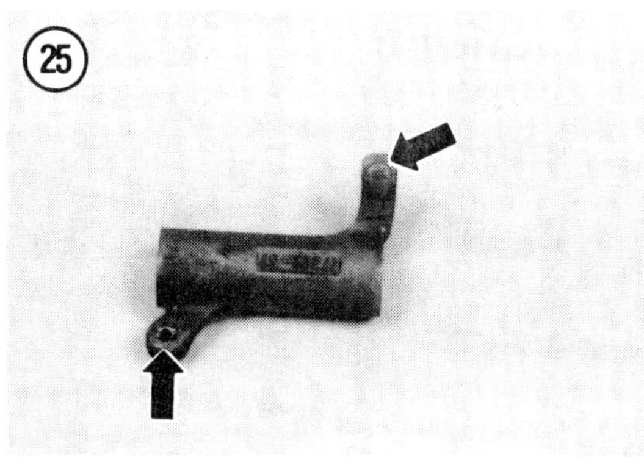

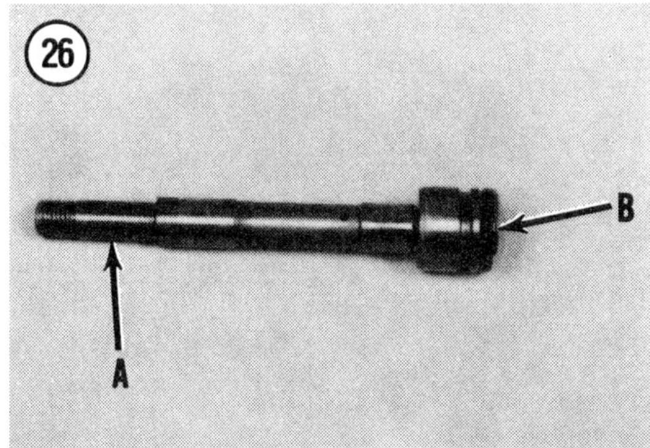

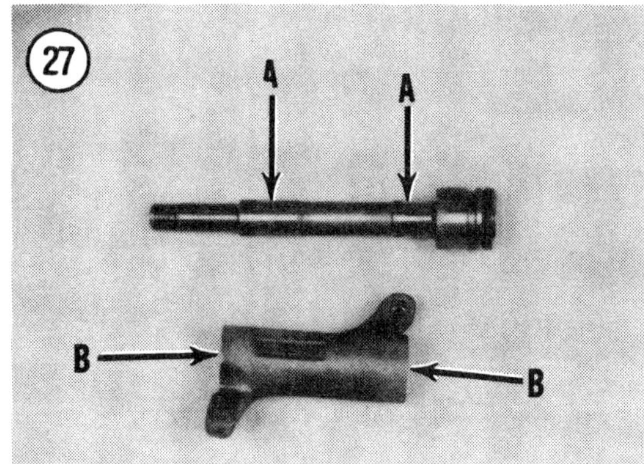

1. Remove the rocker cover screws (A, **Figure 20**) and remove the rocker cover (B, **Figure 20**).
2. Remove the rocker arm shaft acorn nut (**Figure 21**) and washer from the rocker arm cover.
3. Using a suitable size drift, tap the rocker arm shaft (**Figure 22**) from the cover and remove the following parts:
   a. Spring and spacer (**Figure 23**).
   b. Rocker arm (**Figure 24**).

Tag the rocker arm shafts and rocker arms so that if they are reused, they may be returned to their original positions.

CAUTION
Rocker arms are not interchangeable. There is an extra oil hole in the exhaust rocker arms to provide additional lubrication and cooling to the end of each exhaust valve stem.

Rocker Arm Inspection

1. Clean all parts in solvent. Blow compressed air through all oil passages to make sure they are clear.
2. Examine the rocker arm pads and ball sockets (**Figure 25**) for pitting and excessive wear; replace the rocker arms if necessary.
3. Check the rocker arm shaft (A, **Figure 26**) for cracks, deep scoring or heat discoloration. If the rocker arm shaft is in good condition, proceed to Step 4. If the rocker arm shaft is damaged, remove the rocker arm shaft screw (B, **Figure 26**) and shim and replace the rocker arm shaft.
4. Measure the rocker arm shaft outside diameter (A, **Figure 27**) where it rides in the rocker arm. Then measure the rocker arm shaft bore inside diameter (B, **Figure 27**). Replace the bushings if the clearance exceeds the specifications in **Table 1**. Rocker arm bushing replacement is described in this chapter.
5. Check the rocker arm spring (**Figure 28**) for cracks or sagging.
6. Check the rocker arm oil line fitting (**Figure 29**) for tightness.

4

Rocker Arm Bushing Replacement

Replace worn or damaged rocker arm bushings as follows.

1. Press or drive the old rocker arm bushings from the rocker arm cover. If the bushings prove difficult to remove, perform the following:
   a. Thread a 5/8-11 tap (1959-1978) or a 9/16-18 in. tap (1979-1985) into the bushing in the rocker arm (**Figure 30**).
   b. Carefully press on the tap and drive the bushing out.

CAUTION
Be very careful when driving against the tap. Taps are made of very brittle material and can break easily.

2. Using rifle cleaning brushes, clean the rocker arm bushing bore thoroughly of all foreign material. Wash the rocker arm thoroughly and dry with compressed air.
3. Press the new bushings into the rocker arm cover. Make sure the oil holes in the bushings are correctly aligned with those in the rocker arm cover and that the split portion of the bushing faces toward the top of the arm. Press the bushing flush with the edge of the arm.
4. Line ream the new bushings using Harley-Davidson tool 94804-57.

NOTE
On 1979-1985 models, replacement rocker arms are supplied with bushings correctly reamed.

Cylinder Head Inspection

1. Without removing valves, remove all carbon deposits from the combustion chambers (**Figure 31**) with a wire brush or scraper.

CAUTION
If the combustion chambers are cleaned while the valves are removed, make sure to keep the scraper or wire brush away from the valve seats to prevent damaging the seat surfaces. A damaged or even slightly scratched valve seat will cause poor valve seating.

2. Examine the spark plug threads in the cylinder head for damage. If damage is minor or if the threads are dirty or clogged with carbon, use a spark plug thread tap to clean the threads following the manufacturer's instructions. If thread damage is severe, refer further service to a Harley-Davidson dealer or competent machine shop.

30

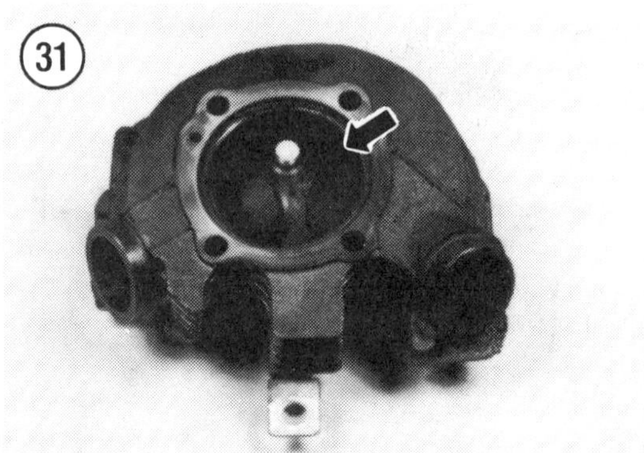
31

32

3. After all carbon is removed from combustion chambers and valve ports and the spark plug thread holes are repaired, clean the entire head in solvent.
4. Clean away all carbon on the piston crowns. Do not remove the carbon ridge at the top of the cylinder bore.
5. Check for cracks in the combustion chamber and valve ports (**Figure 32**). A cracked head must be replaced.
6. After the head has been thoroughly cleaned, place a straightedge across the gasket surface at several points (**Figure 33**). Measure warp by

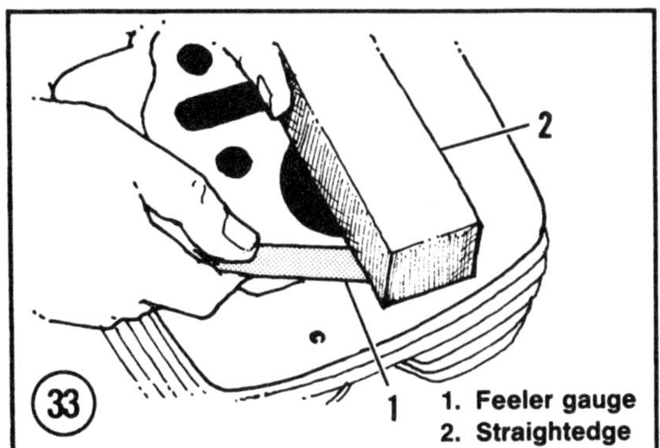

33

34

35

36

inserting a feeler gauge between the straightedge and cylinder head at each location. Maximum allowable warpage is 0.005 in. If warpage exceeds this limit, the cylinder head must be replaced.
7. Check the rocker arm cover mating surface using the procedure in Step 6. There should be no warpage.
8. Check the condition of the valves and valve guides as described under *Valves and Valve Components* in this chapter.

Assembly

1. Clean the cylinder head and rocker arm mating surfaces of any gasket residue.
2. Install the rocker arm into the cover (**Figure 24**).
3. Apply a light coat of oil to the rocker arm shaft.
4. Insert the rocker arm shaft partway into the rocker arm (**Figure 34**).
5. Install the spacer (**Figure 35**) and spring (**Figure 36**).
6. Insert the rocker arm shaft through the spring and spacer.
7. Install the rocker arm shaft acorn nut and washer. Tighten securely.

NOTE
Check the rocker arm to make sure it does not bind on the shaft.

8A. *1959-1969:* Apply a thin coat of aluminum paint to the top of the cylinder head mating surface.
8B. *1970-1985:* Install a new rocker arm gasket on the cylinder head mating surface.
9. Install the rocker arm cover (B, **Figure 20**). Install the rocker arm cover screw (A, **Figure 20**) with a flat washer under the head of each screw. Tighten the screws in a criss-cross pattern in 2 or 3 steps to specifications (**Table 2** or **Table 3**).

PUSH RODS

Removal

Refer to **Figure 37** (1959-early 1979) or **Figure 38** (late 1979-1985) for this procedure.
1. Using a screwdriver as shown in **Figure 39**, pry the spring keeper off of the push rod.
2. Lift the lower push rod cover upwards and secure with a bent coat hanger as shown in **Figure 40**.
3. Rotate the engine until the tappet (**Figure 41**) for the push rod to be removed just starts upward.
4. Loosen the push rod locknut (**Figure 42**) and turn the adjusting screw (**Figure 42**) to obtain slack in the push rod.
5. Lift the push rod assembly out of the engine.

4

6. Remove and discard the upper and lower push rod cork washers or O-rings (**Figure 43**).

NOTE
*If the cams are removed and the tappets are not to be removed, secure them in place with a rubber band or discarded O-ring as shown in **Figure 44**.*

7. Repeat Steps 1-6 to remove remaining push rods, corks or O-rings.

Disassembly/Inspection/Reassembly

1. Remove the push rod (**Figure 45**) from the push rod cover assembly.
2. Disassemble the push rod cover as follows:
   a. Remove the lower push rod cover (**Figure 46**).
   b. Remove the middle cork washer or O-ring (**Figure 47**).
   c. Remove the washer (**Figure 48**).
   d. Remove the spring (**Figure 49**).
   e. Remove the cover spring cap (**Figure 50**).

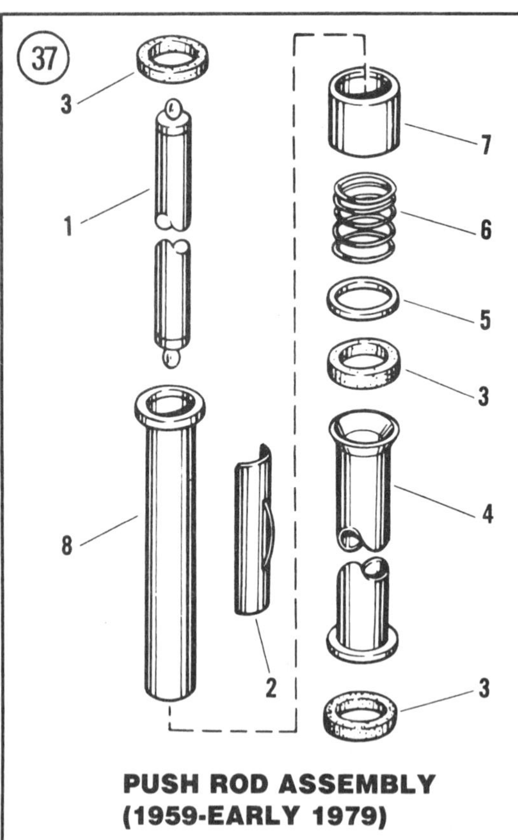

PUSH ROD ASSEMBLY (1959-EARLY 1979)

1. Push rod
2. Cover spring keeper
3. Cover cork washer
4. Lower cover
5. Cover screw washer
6. Cover spring
7. Spring retainer
8. Upper cover

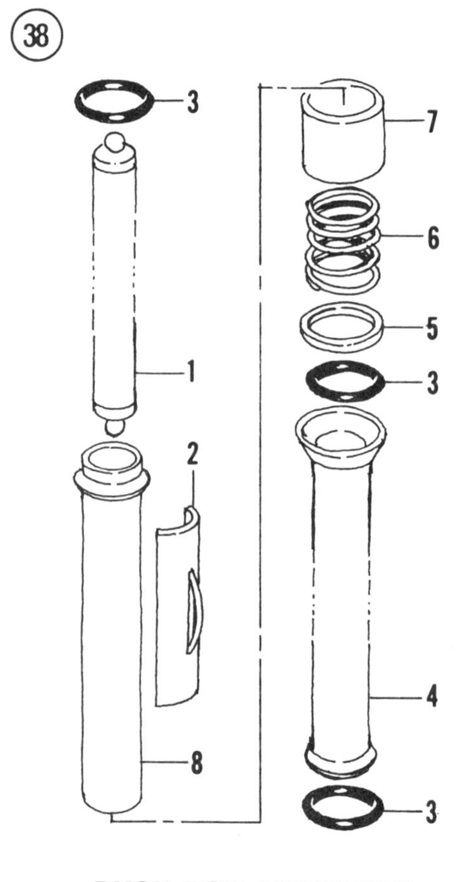

PUSH ROD ASSEMBLY (LATE 1979-1985)

1. Push rod
2. Spring keeper
3. O-ring
4. Lower cover
5. Washer
6. Spring
7. Spring retainer
8. Upper cover

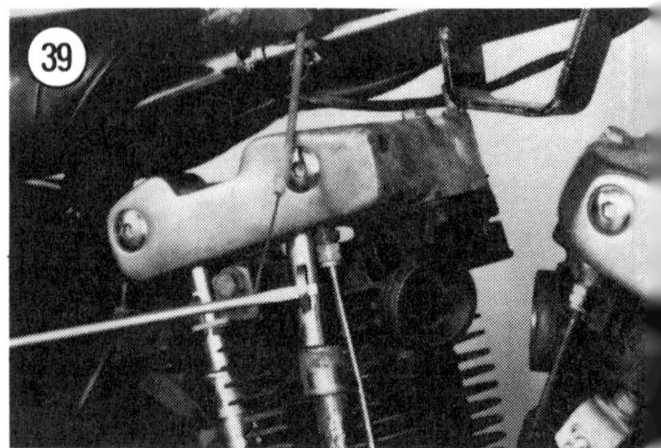

40

43

41

44

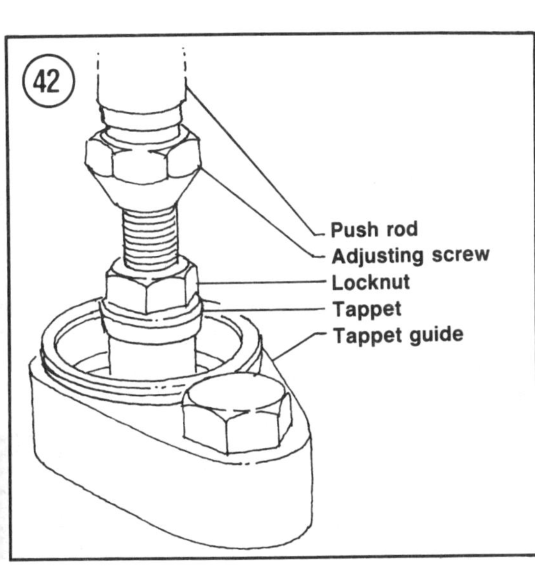
42
Push rod
Adjusting screw
Locknut
Tappet
Tappet guide

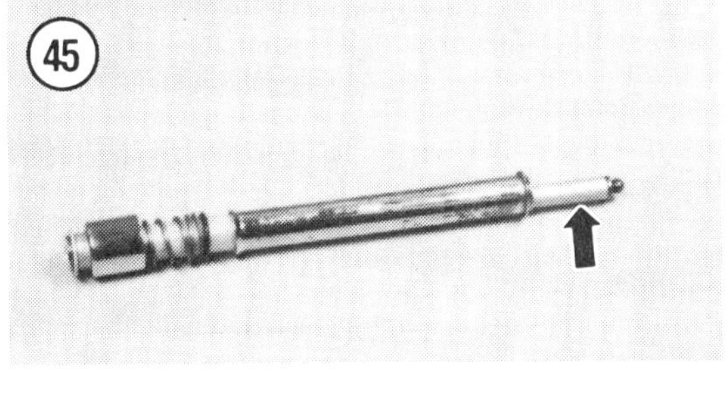
45

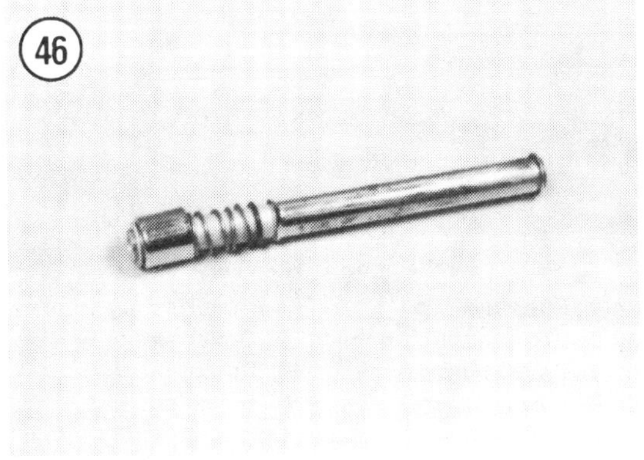
46

4

3. Clean all parts (**Figure 51**) in solvent and thoroughly dry. Discard the cork washer or O-ring.
4. Check the push rod ends for wear (**Figure 52**).
5. Roll the push rod (**Figure 53**) on a flat surface, such as a piece of glass, and check for bending and straightness. Replace the push rod if necessary.
6. Check the push rod spring (**Figure 54**) for cracks, distortion or metal flaking. Replace the spring if necessary.
7. Reverse Step 1 and Step 2 to reassemble the push rod. Install a new middle cork washer or O-ring (**Figure 47**) during reassembly. Push the lower push rod cover into the cover spring cap to seat the O-ring or cork washer.

Push Rod Installation and Adjustment

The push rods must be adjusted whenever they are removed or after assembling the engine. Before adjusting a push rod (**Figure 55**), its valve must be fully closed. Valve position can be determined by observing the corresponding push rod on the other cylinder. For example, when the rear cylinder intake valve tappet (B, **Figure 56**) is

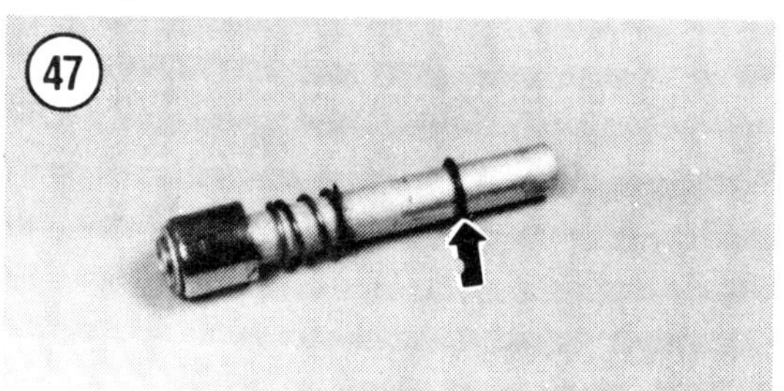
47

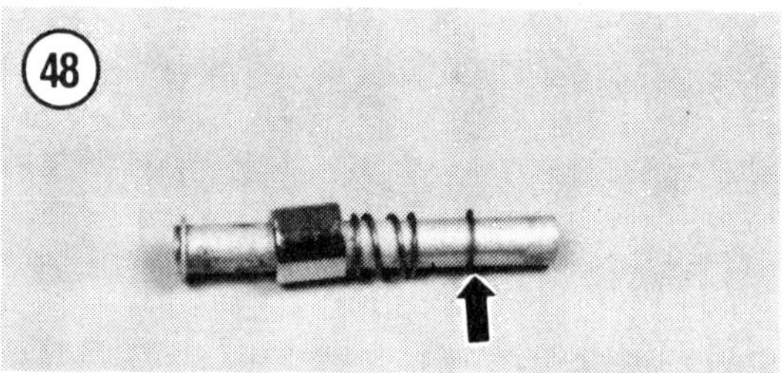
48

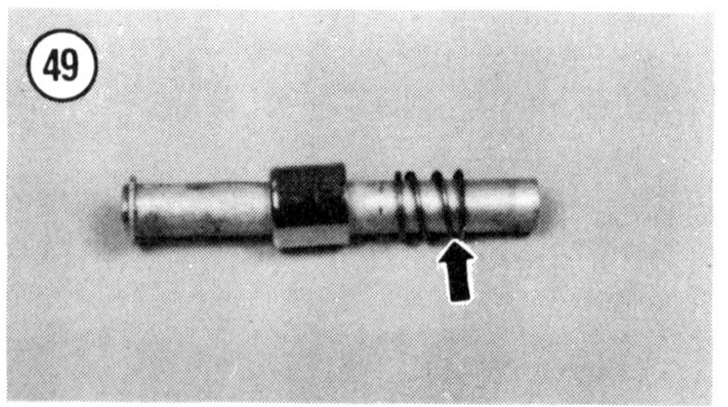
49

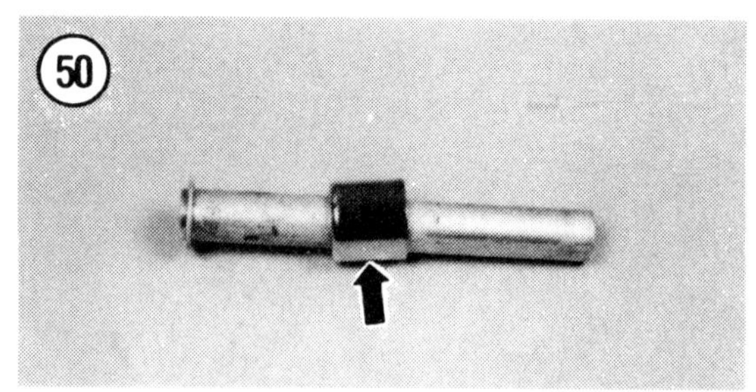
50

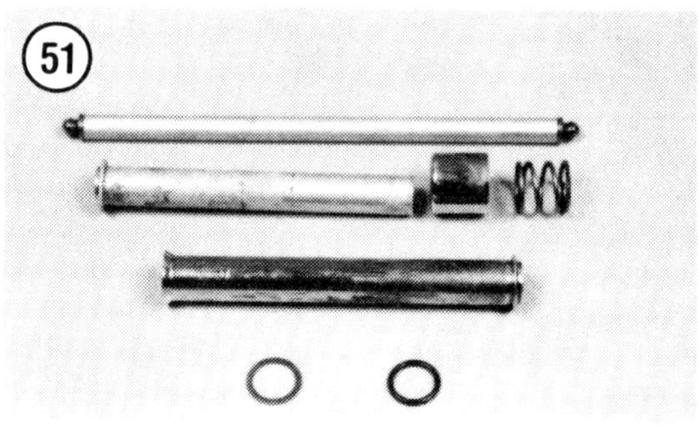
51

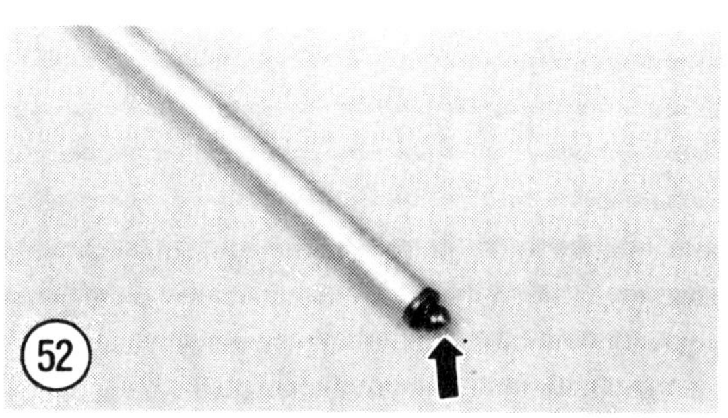
52

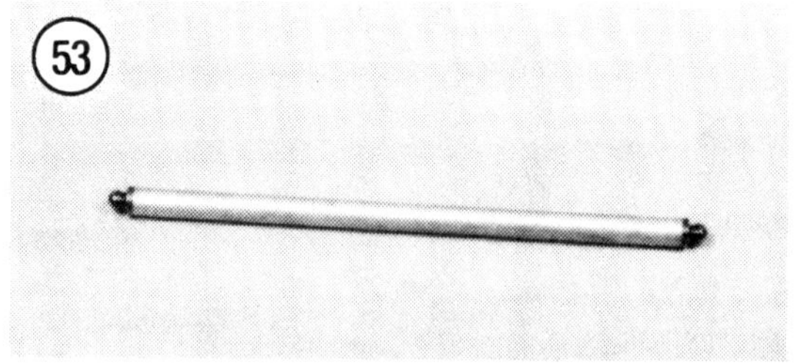
53

54

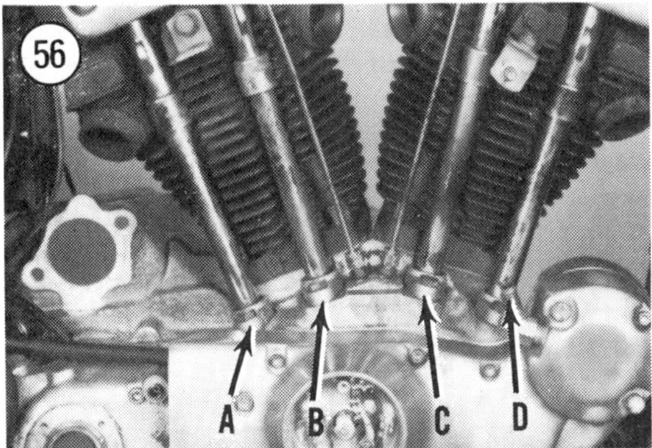

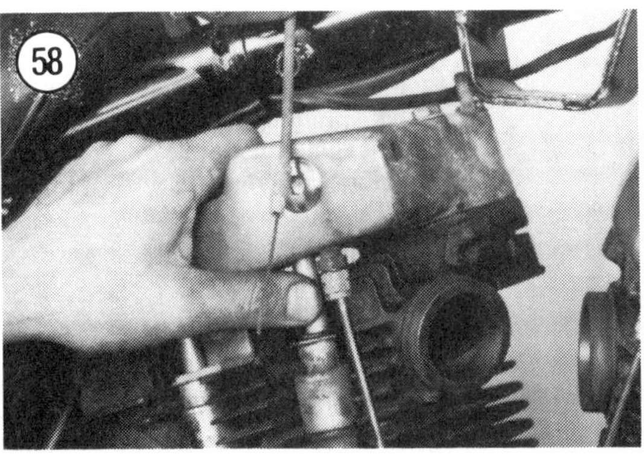

raised (fully open), the front cylinder intake valve (C, **Figure 56**) is fully closed, and the front intake push rod can be adjusted.

1. Install new upper and lower push rod cork washers or O-rings.
2. Rotate the engine until the front cylinder exhaust tappet (D, **Figure 56**) is fully raised.
3. Install the rear cylinder exhaust push rod and push rod cover (A, **Figure 56**).
4. Raise the lower push rod cover and secure it with a coat hanger as shown in **Figure 40**. This allows easy access to the push rod adjustment screw.
5. Rotate the engine until the front cylinder intake push rod tappet (C, **Figure 56**) is fully raised.
6. Install the rear cylinder intake push rod and push rod cover (B, **Figure 56**).
7. Repeat for front cylinder push rods and covers.
8. Adjust the push rods as follows.
   a. Rotate engine so that the rear cylinder exhaust push rod tappet (A, **Figure 56**) is fully raised. Then turn the front cylinder exhaust push rod adjusting screw (**Figure 42**) clockwise until the push rod's ball end is seated in the tappet with a slight amount of play.
   b. Hold the adjusting screw across its flats with a wrench. Then tighten the locknut against the adjusting screw (**Figure 57**).
   c. Recheck the adjustment. The push rod should have a slight amount of play and must turn freely by hand (**Figure 58**) without any trace of binding or dragging.
   d. Repeat for the other push rods.
9. Using a screwdriver as shown in **Figure 59**, lift the upper push rod cover up and seat it against the upper cork washer or O-ring.
10. Install the push rod retainer as shown in **Figure 60**.

4

VALVES AND VALVE COMPONENTS

Refer to **Figure 61** for this procedure. A valve spring compressor (**Figure 62**) is required to remove and install the valves.

CAUTION
All component parts of each valve assembly must be kept together. Do not mix with like components from other valves or excessive wear may result.

1. Remove the cylinder head(s) as described in this chapter.
2. Install a valve spring compressor squarely over the upper valve collar (**Figure 63**) with other end of tool placed against valve head.
3. Tighten valve spring compressor until split valve keeper separates (**Figure 63**). Lift out split keeper with needle nose pliers.
4. Gradually loosen valve spring compressor and remove from head. Lift off the upper valve collar.

CAUTION
*Remove any burrs from the valve stem grooves before removing the valve (**Figure 64**). Otherwise the valve guides will be damaged.*

5. Remove inner and outer springs.
6. Remove the valve stem seals, if so equipped.
7. Remove the valve.
8. Remove the lower spring collar.
9. Repeat Steps 2-8 and remove remaining valves.

Inspection

1. Clean valves with a wire brush and solvent.
2. Inspect the contact surface of each valve for burning (**Figure 65**). Minor roughness and pitting can be removed by lapping the valve as described in this chapter. Excessive unevenness to the contact surface is an indication that the valve is not serviceable. The contact surface of the valve may be ground on a valve grinding machine, but it is best to replace a burned or damaged valve with a new one.
3. Inspect the valve stems for wear and roughness.
4. Measure valve stems for wear using a micrometer (**Figure 66**). Record this measurement.
5. Remove all carbon and varnish from the valve guides with a stiff spiral wire brush.

NOTE
Step 6 requires special measuring equipment. If you do not have the required measuring devices, proceed to Step 8.

6. Measure each valve guide at top, center and bottom with a small hole gauge.

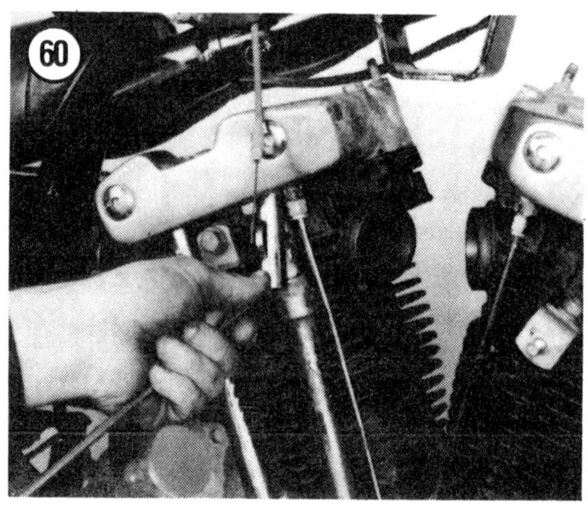

VALVE ASSEMBLY (TYPICAL)

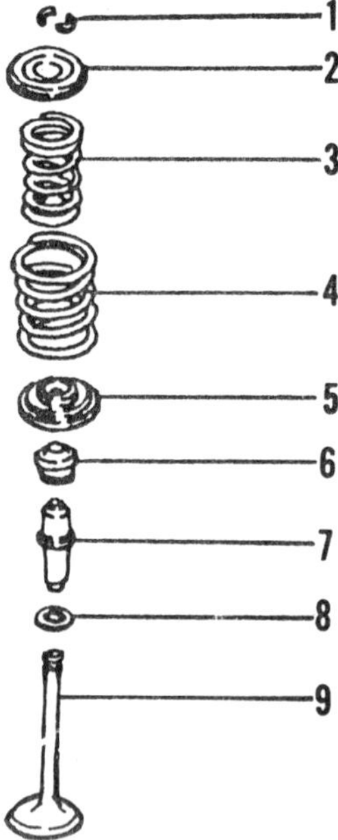

1. Valve keeper
2. Valve spring upper collar
3. Inner valve spring
4. Outer valve spring
5. Valve spring lower collar
6. Valve stem seal
7. Valve guide
8. Spring seat
9. Valve

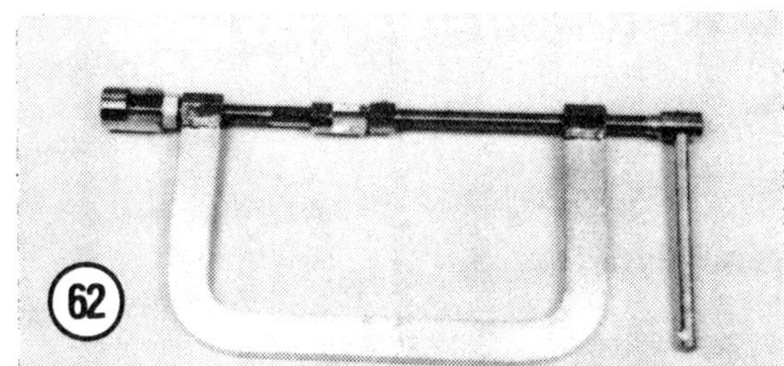

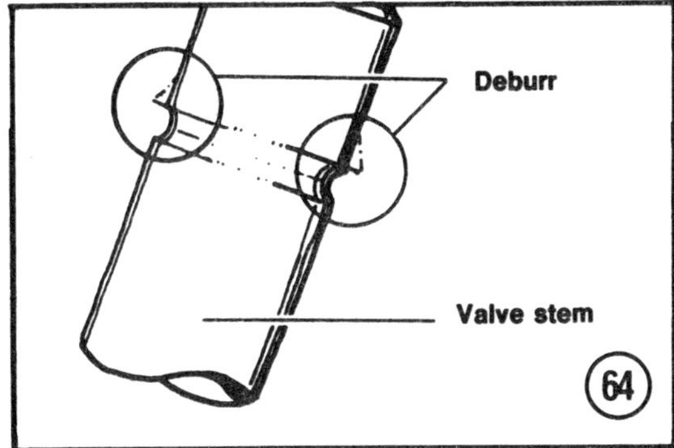

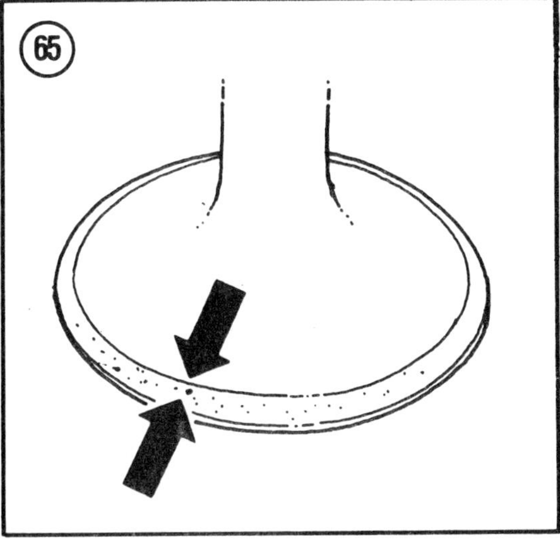

7. Subtract the measurement made in Step 4 from the measurement made in Step 6 above. The difference is the valve guide-to-valve stem clearance. See specifications in **Table 1** for correct clearance. Replace any guide or valve that is not within tolerance.

8. Insert each valve in its guide. Hold the valve just slightly off its seat and rock it sideways. If it rocks more than slightly, the guide is probably worn and should be replaced. As a final check, take the head to a dealer and have the valve guides measured.

9. Measure the valve spring heights with a vernier caliper (**Figure 67**). All should be of length specified in **Table 1** with no bends or other distortion. Replace defective springs.

10. Check the valve spring collars and split keepers. If they are in good condition, they may be reused.

11. Inspect valve seats. If worn or burned, they must be reconditioned. This should be performed by your dealer or local machine shop. Seats and valves in near-perfect condition can be reconditioned by lapping with fine carborundum paste. Lapping, however, is always inferior to precision grinding.

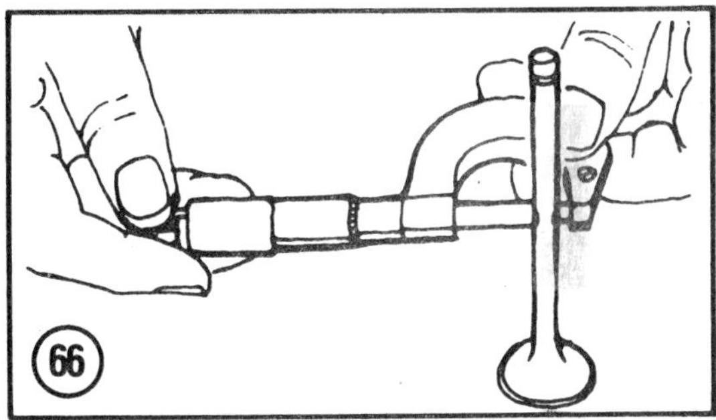

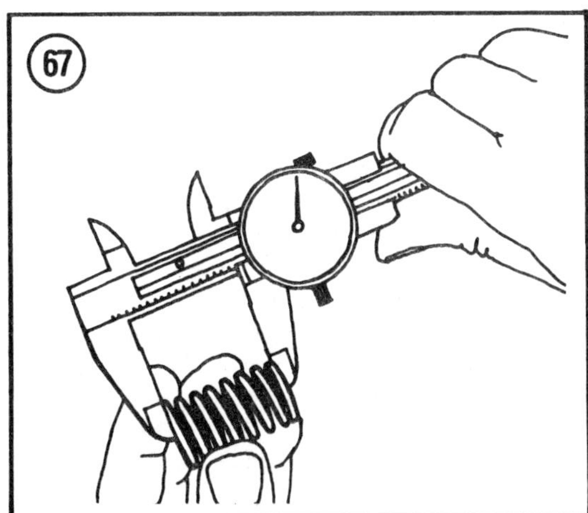

Installation

1. Coat the valve stems with oil and insert into cylinder head.
2. Install the new spring seat and a new valve stem seal (if used).
3. Install the bottom collar.
4. Install valve springs. Then install the upper valve spring collar.
5. Push down on upper valve spring collar with the valve spring compressor and install split keepers. After releasing tension from compressor, examine split keepers (**Figure 68**) and make sure they are seated correctly.

Valve Guide Replacement

When guides are worn so that there is excessive stem-to-guide clearance or valve tipping, they must be replaced. Replace all, even if only one is worn. This job should only be done by a Harley-Davidson dealer or qualified specialist as special tools are required.

Valve Seat Reconditioning

This job is best left to your dealer or local machine shop. They have the special equipment and knowledge for this exacting job. You can still save considerable money by removing the cylinder heads and taking just the heads to the shop.

Valve Lapping

Valve lapping is a simple operation which can restore the valve seal without machining if the amount of wear or distortion is not too great.
1. Smear a light coating of fine grade valve lapping compound on seating surface of valve.
2. Insert the valve into the head.
3. Wet the suction cup of the lapping stick (**Figure 69**) and stick it onto the head of the valve. Lap the valve to the seat by spinning the lapping stick in both directions. Every 5 to 10 seconds, rotate the

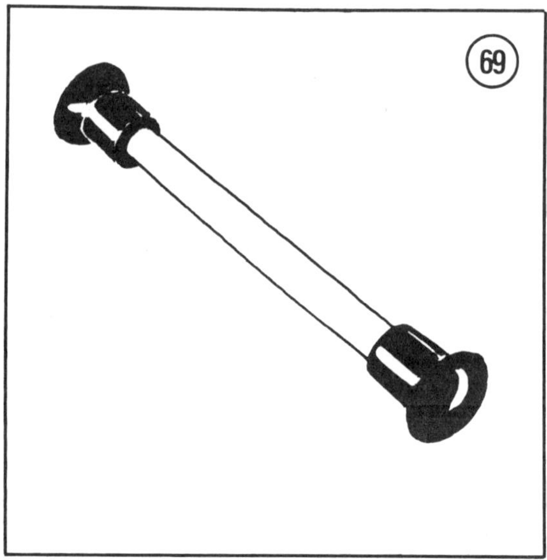

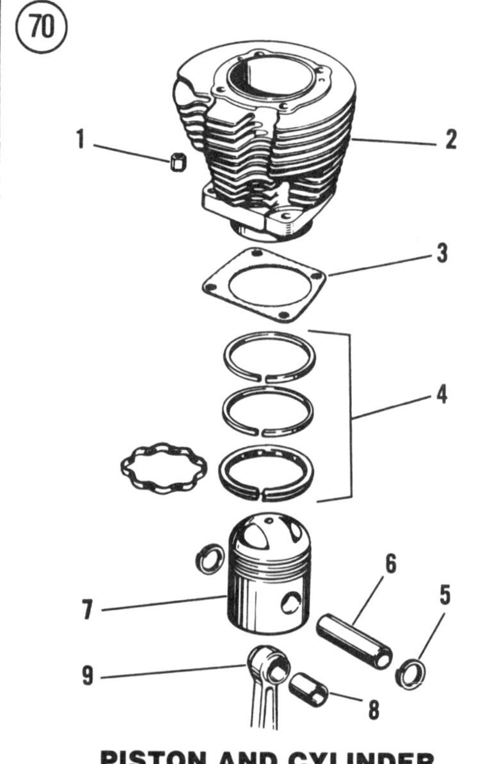

PISTON AND CYLINDER

1. Cylinder base nut
2. Cylinder
3. Cylinder base gasket
4. Piston rings
5. Piston pin lock rings
6. Piston pin
7. Piston
8. Piston pin bushing
9. Connecting rod

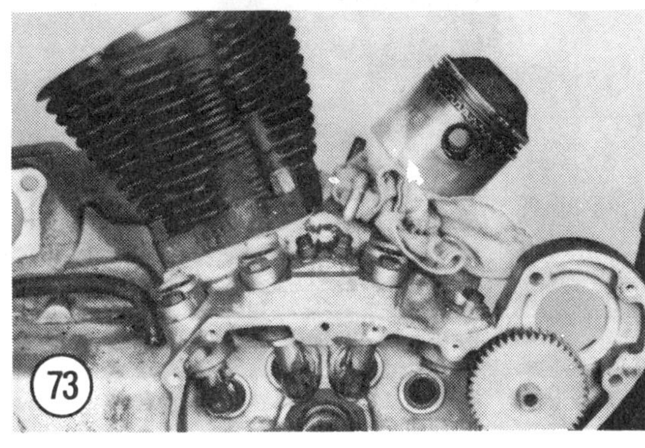

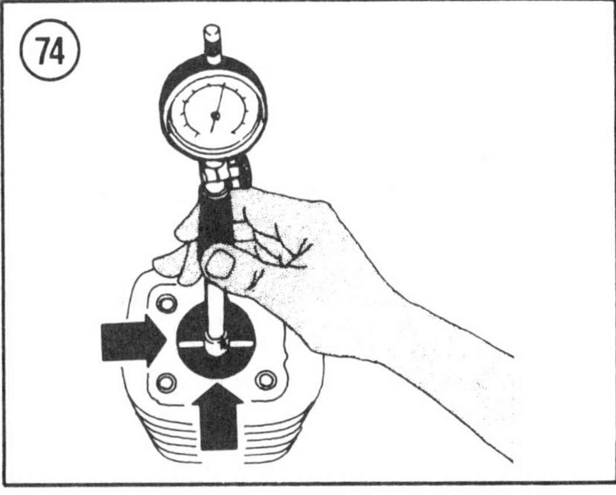

valve 180° in the valve seat; continue lapping until the contact surfaces of the valve and the valve seat are a uniform gray. Stop as soon as they are, to avoid removing too much material.

4. Thoroughly clean the valves and cylinder head in solvent to remove all grinding compound. Any compound left on the valves or the cylinder head will end up in the engine and cause rapid engine wear.

5. After the lapping has been completed and the valve assemblies have been reinstalled into the head, the valve seal should be tested. Check the seal of each valve by pouring solvent into each of the intake and exhaust ports. There should be no leakage past the seat. If leakage occurs, combustion chamber will appear wet. If fluid leaks past any of the seats, disassemble that valve assembly and repeat the lapping procedure until there is no leakage.

CYLINDER

Figure 70 is an exploded view of a typical piston and cylinder.

Removal

1. Remove the cylinder head as described in this chapter.
2. Remove all dirt and foreign material from the cylinder base.
3. Turn the engine over until the piston is at bottom dead center (BDC).
4. Remove the cylinder base nuts (**Figure 71**).
5. Loosen the cylinder by tapping around the perimeter with a rubber or plastic mallet.
6. Pull the cylinder (**Figure 72**) straight up and off the piston and cylinder studs.
7. Stuff clean shop rags into the crankcase opening to prevent objects from falling undetected into the crankcase. See **Figure 73**.
8. Repeat Steps 1-7 for the other cylinder.

Inspection

The following procedure requires the use of highly specialized and expensive measuring instruments. If such instruments are not readily available, have the measurements performed by a dealer or qualified machine shop.

1. Thoroughly clean the cylinder with solvent and dry with compressed air. Lightly oil the cylinder bore to prevent rust after performing Steps 2-4.
2. Measure the cylinder bores with a cylinder gauge (**Figure 74**) or inside micrometer at the points shown in **Figure 75**.
3. Measure in 2 axes—in line with the piston pin and at 90° to the pin. If the taper or out-of-round is

greater than specifications (**Table 1**), the cylinders must be rebored to the next oversize and new pistons and rings installed. Rebore both cylinders even though only one may be worn.

NOTE
*The new pistons should be obtained before the cylinders are bored so that the pistons can be measured; slight manufacturing tolerances must be taken into account to determine the actual size and the working clearance. The standard and service limit dimensions for piston-to-cylinder clearance are listed in **Table 1**.*

4. Check the cylinder walls for scratches; if evident, the cylinders should be rebored.

Installation

1. Clean the cylinder top and bottom machined surfaces (**Figure 76**) of all gasket residue.
2. Install a new cylinder base gasket to the crankcase. Make sure all holes align.

NOTE
If both cylinders are removed when performing Step 3, make sure to hold the opposite piston to protect it from damage when turning the engine over.

3. Turn the engine over until the piston is at top dead center (TDC).
4. Lubricate the cylinder bores and pistons liberally with engine oil.
5. Compress the rings with aircraft type hose clamps of appropriate diameter (**Figure 77**). Tighten the hose clamp just enough to compress the rings.

CAUTION
Don't tighten the clamp any more than necessary to compress the rings. If the rings can't slip through easily, the clamp may gouge the rings and piston.

6. Carefully align the cylinder over the piston and slide it down. Once the rings are positioned in the cylinder, remove the hose clamp installed in Step 5.
7. Rotate the cylinder as necessary and slide it over the crankcase studs.
8. Install the cylinder base nuts (**Figure 71**) and tighten to specifications in **Table 2** or **Table 3**.
9. Install the cylinder head as described in this chapter.

PISTONS AND PISTON RINGS

The pistons and rings may be removed with the engine in the frame by removing the cylinder head

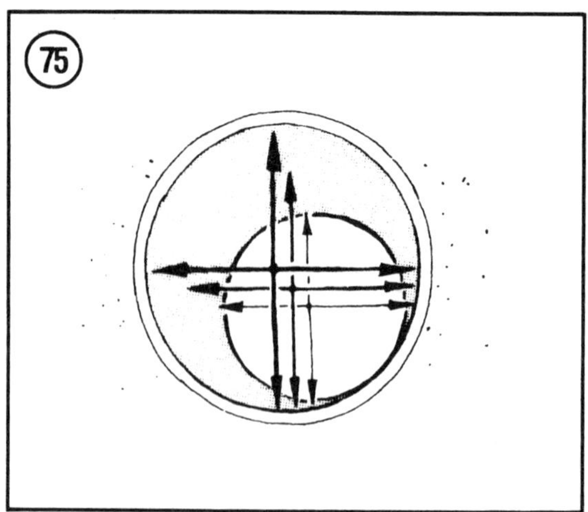

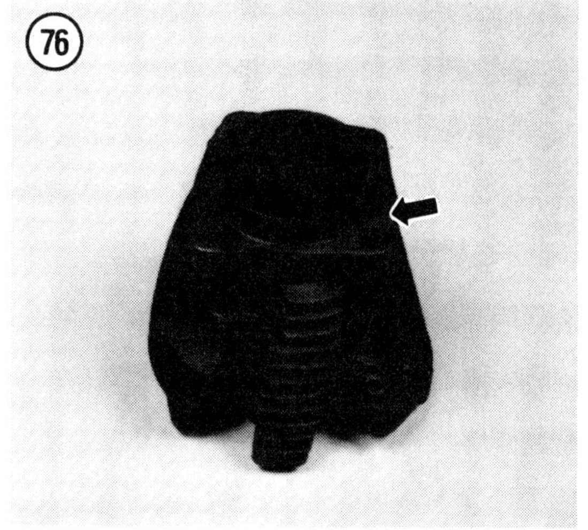

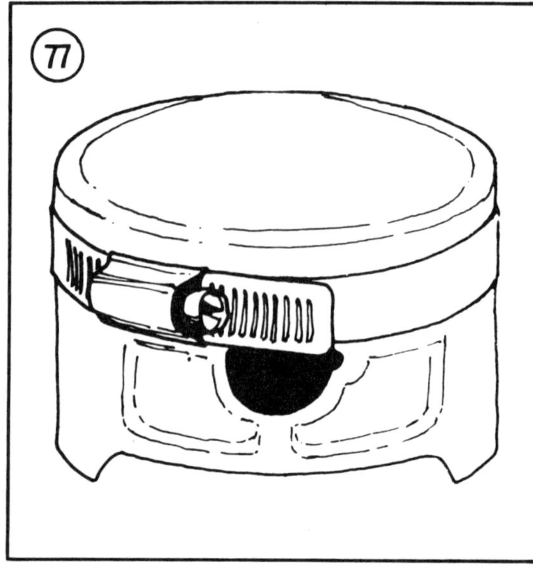

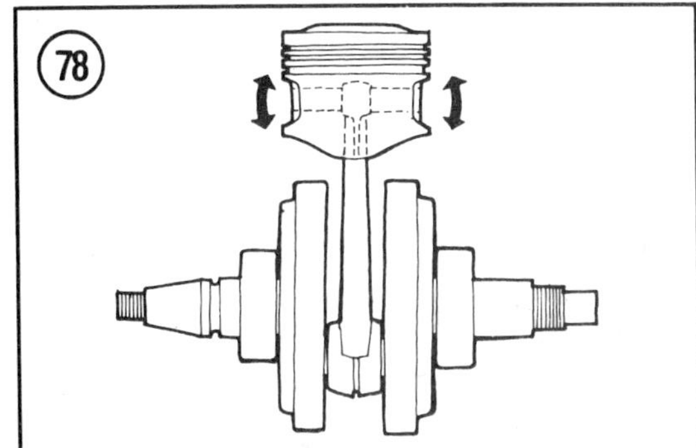

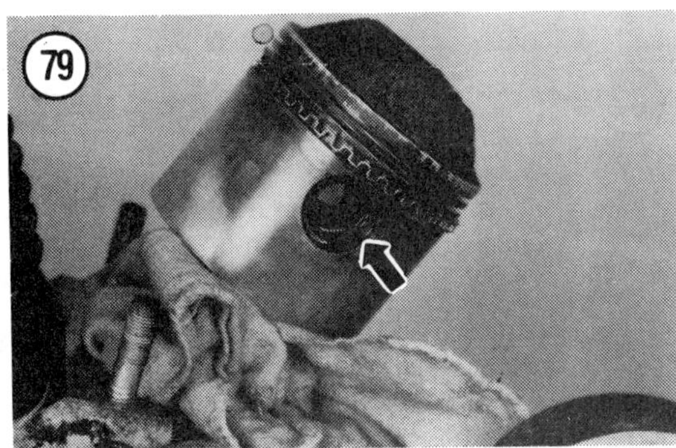

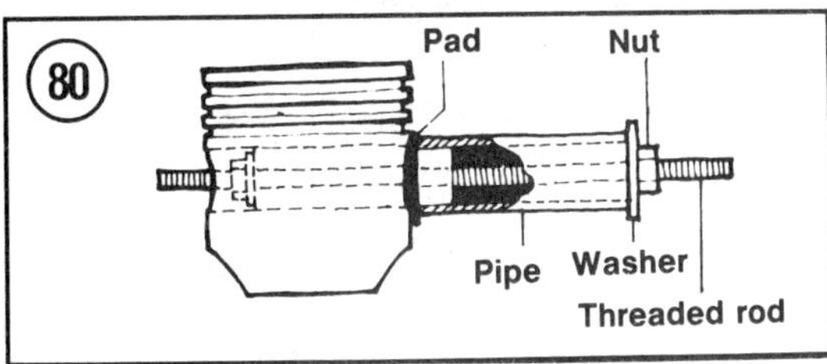

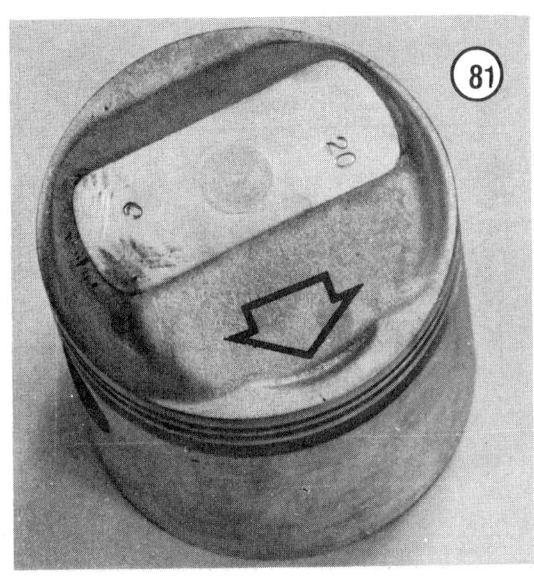

and the cylinder. Refer to **Figure 70** for this procedure.

Piston Removal/Installation

1. Remove the cylinder head and cylinder as described in this chapter.
2. Stuff the crankcase with clean shop rags to prevent objects from falling into the crankcase (**Figure 73**).
3. Lightly mark the pistons with an F (front) or R (rear) so they will be installed into the correct cylinder.
4. Remove the piston rings as described under *Piston Ring Replacement* in this chapter.
5. Before removing the piston, hold the rod tightly and rock piston as shown in **Figure 78**. Any rocking motion (do not confuse with the normal sliding motion) indicates wear on the piston pin, rod bushing, pin bore, or more likely, a combination of all three.
6. Remove the piston pin lock rings from the piston pin bores (**Figure 79**).
7. Support the piston and remove the piston pin with a piston pin remover or use a homemade tool as shown in **Figure 80**.
8. Inspect the piston as described in this chapter.
9. Coat the connecting rod bushing, piston pin and piston with assembly oil.
10. Place the piston over the connecting rod. If you are installing old parts, make sure the piston is installed on the correct rod as marked during removal. The intake valve pocket on the piston crown (**Figure 81**) must face toward the intake valve.
11. Align the piston pin with the piston and install with a piston pin installer or use the home-made tool (**Figure 80**) but eliminate the piece of pipe. Push the pin in until it is centered in the piston.
12. Install *new* piston pin lock rings in the piston bores with the sharp end facing out. Make sure the pin seats completely in the piston groove.
13. Install rings as described under *Piston Ring Replacement* in this chapter.

Piston Inspection

1. Carefully clean the carbon from the piston crown with a soft scraper (**Figure 82**). Do not remove or damage the carbon ridge around the circumference of the piston above the top ring. If the pistons, rings and cylinders are found to be dimensionally correct and can be reused, removal of the carbon ring from the top of the piston or the

4

carbon ridges from the cylinders will promote excessive oil consumption.

CAUTION
Do not wire brush piston skirts.

2. Examine each ring groove for burrs, dented edges and wide wear. Pay particular attention to the top compression ring groove, as it usually wears more than the others.
3. Measure piston-to-cylinder clearance as described under *Piston Clearance* in this chapter.
4. If damage or wear indicates piston replacement, select a new piston as described under *Piston Clearance* in this chapter.

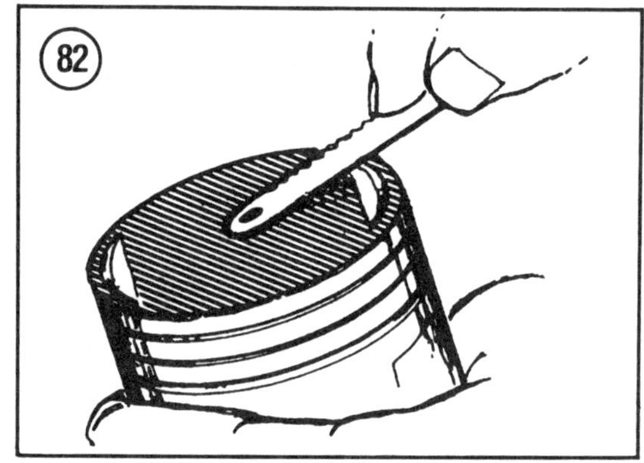
82

Piston Clearance

1. Make sure the piston and cylinder walls are clean and dry.
2. Measure the inside diameter of the cylinder bore at a point 1/2 in. (13 mm) from the upper edge with a bore gauge (**Figure 74**).
3. Measure the outside diameter of the piston at the base of the piston 90° to the piston pin axis (**Figure 83**).
4. Subtract the piston diameter from the bore diameter; the difference is the piston-to-cylinder clearance. Compare to specifications in **Table 1**. If clearance is excessive, the piston should be replaced and the cylinder rebored. Purchase the new piston first; measure its diameter and add the specified clearance to determine the proper cylinder bore diameter.

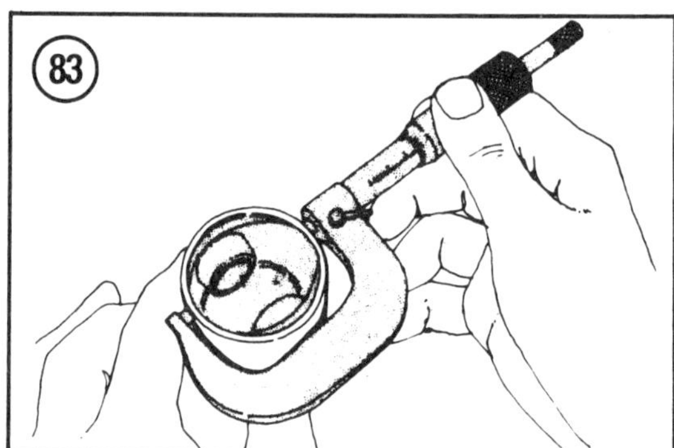
83

Piston Ring Replacement

1. Remove the old rings with a ring expander tool or by spreading the ring ends with your thumbs and lifting the rings up evenly (**Figure 84**).
2. Using a broken piston ring, remove all carbon from the piston ring grooves (**Figure 85**).
3. Inspect grooves carefully for burrs, nicks, or broken or cracked lands. Recondition or replace piston if necessary.
4. Check end gap of each ring. To check ring, insert the ring into the bottom of the cylinder bore and square it with the cylinder wall by tapping it with the piston. The ring should be pushed in about 1/2 in. Insert a feeler gauge as shown in **Figure 86**. Compare gap with **Table 1**. Replace ring if gap is too large. If the gap on the new ring is smaller than specified, hold a small file in a vise, grip the ends of the ring with your fingers and enlarge the gap (**Figure 87**).

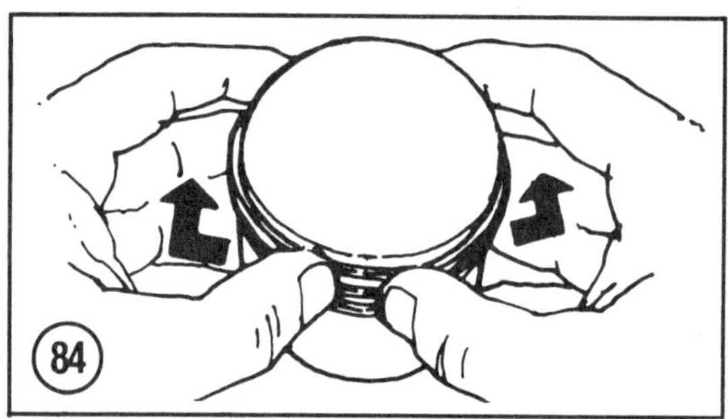
84

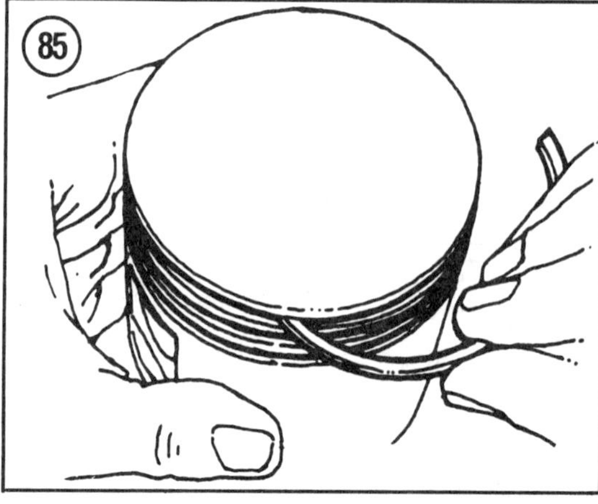
85

NOTE
The 2 oil control ring spacers are unmeasurable. If the oil control ring

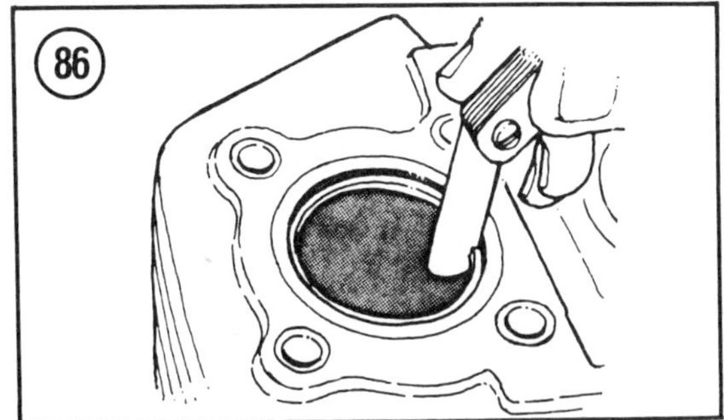

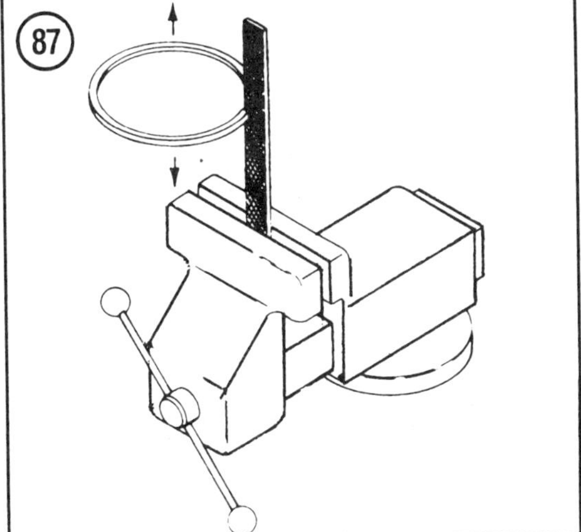

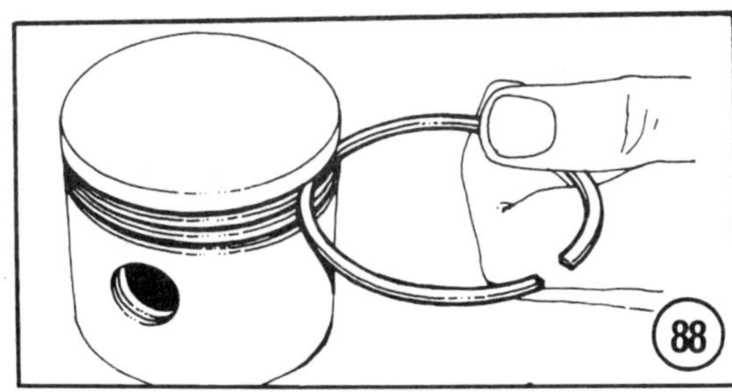

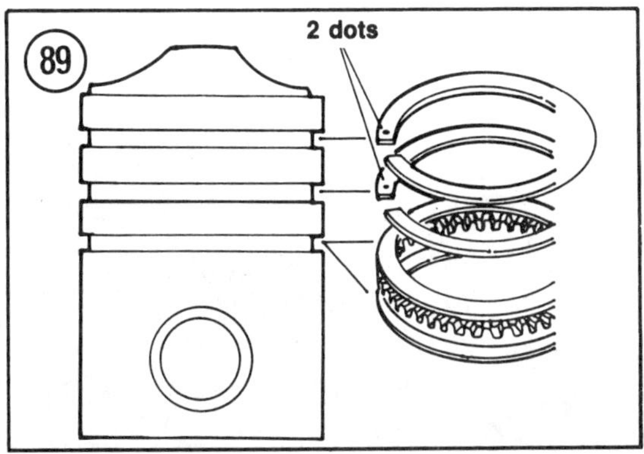

rail shows wear, the rail and spacers should be replaced as a set.

5. Roll each ring around its piston groove as shown in **Figure 88** to check for binding. Minor binding may be cleaned up with a fine-cut file.

NOTE
*Install all rings with their markings facing up (**Figure 89**).*

6. Install oil ring in oil ring groove with a ring expander tool or by spreading the ends with your thumbs.
7. Install the 2 compression rings carefully with a ring expander tool or by spreading the ends with your thumbs. Oversize compression rings are stamped with a number to indicate their size. If installing oversize compression rings, check the number to make sure the correct rings are being installed. The ring numbers should be the same as the piston oversize number.
8. Check side clearance of each ring as shown in **Figure 90**. Compare with specifications in **Table 1**.
9. Distribute ring gaps around piston as shown in **Figure 91**.

OIL PUMP (1959-1976)

Oil Pump Check Valve Removal/Installation

Refer to **Figure 92** for this procedure.

1. Clean the outside of the oil pump with solvent.
2. Disconnect the oil pressure switch wire and remove the oil pressure switch from the oil pump.
3. Remove the oil pump nipple. Then remove the check valve spring and ball.
4. Install by reversing these steps, noting the folowing:
   a. Oil all parts prior to assembly.

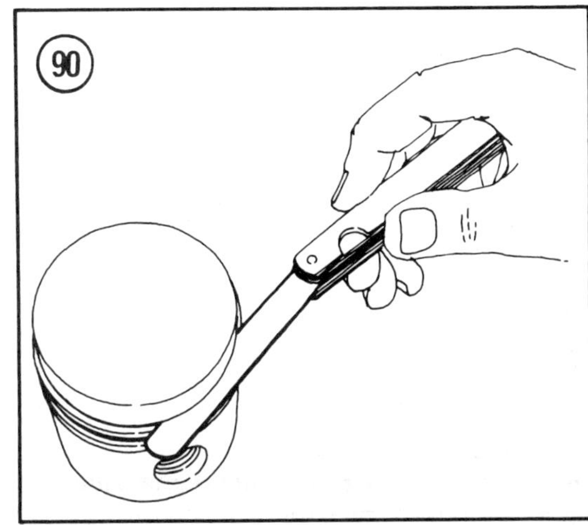

b. Make sure the check valve ball is seated correctly and that the valve action is free.

Inspection

1. Clean all parts in solvent.
2. Clean the pump nipple oil passage and spring guide with compressed air.
3. Check the spring for wear, rust or damage. Measure the spring with a caliper. If the spring length is appreciably shorter than 1 15/64 in., replace the spring.
4. Check the oil pump check valve ball for wear and rust. Replace the ball if it is not perfectly round and smooth.
5. Check the oil pump nipple for damage or wear that could bind the spring during operation. Replace the nipple if necessary.

Oil Pump Removal

NOTE
The breather valve gear and shaft (19, ***Figure 92****) are a part of the oil pump. While it is not necessary to remove the circuit breaker, gearcase cover and timing gears to remove the oil pump, these parts must be removed before the breather valve gear is installed so that the gear can be timed correctly.*

1. Remove the engine from the frame as described in this chapter.
2. Thoroughly clean the pump area with solvent.
3. Remove the oil pump mounting nuts (**Figure 93**) and pull the oil pump off of the crankcase studs. See **Figure 94**.

Disassembly

Refer to **Figure 92** for this procedure.
1. Tap the body plate (5, **Figure 92**) and remove it from the oil pump.
2. Pry the gasket (6) off of the oil pump and discard it.
3. Remove the retainer ring (7) or the half ring retainer (7A) and remove the scavenger gears (8 and 9).
4. Remove the key (10) from the breather valve gear and shaft assembly.
5. Remove the oil pump cover (11) and the breather valve gear and shaft (19) as one assembly. Discard the gasket (17).
6. Remove the pump (13) and the pump idler (14) gears from the pump cover.

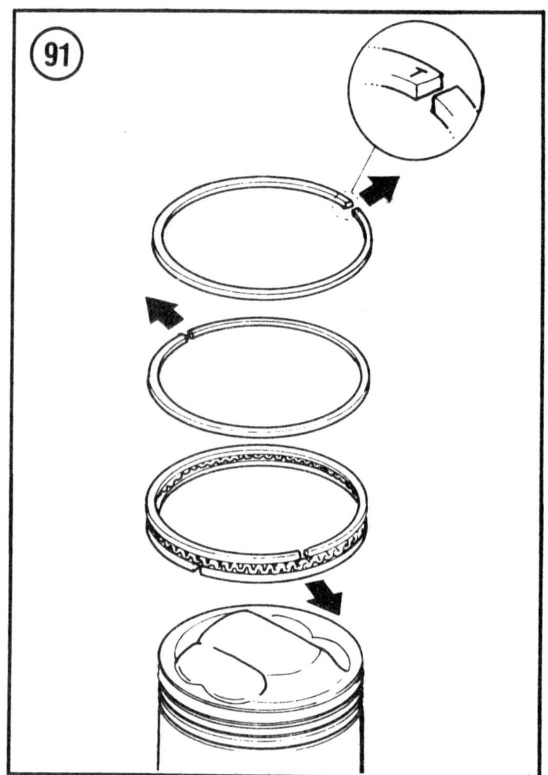

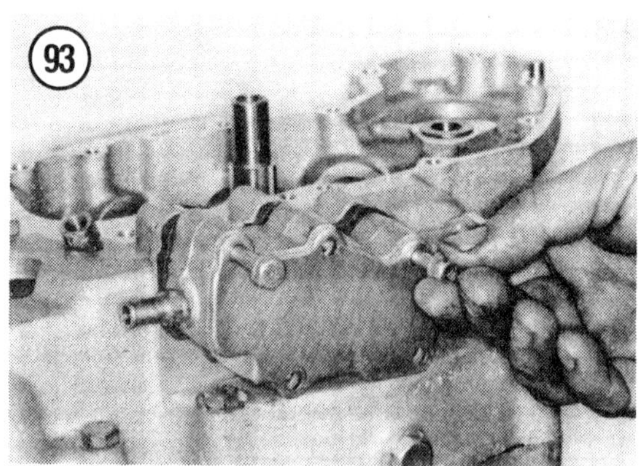

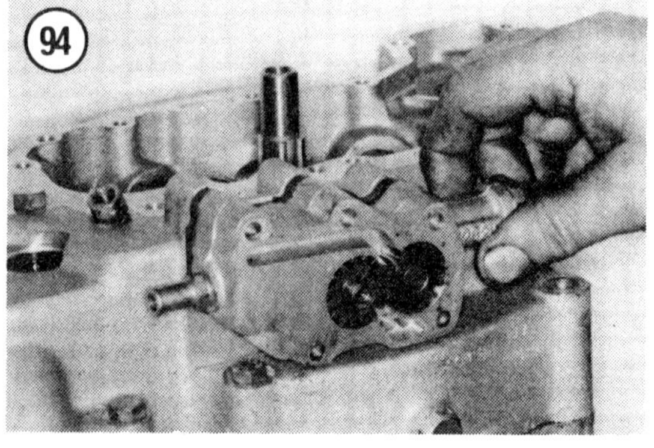

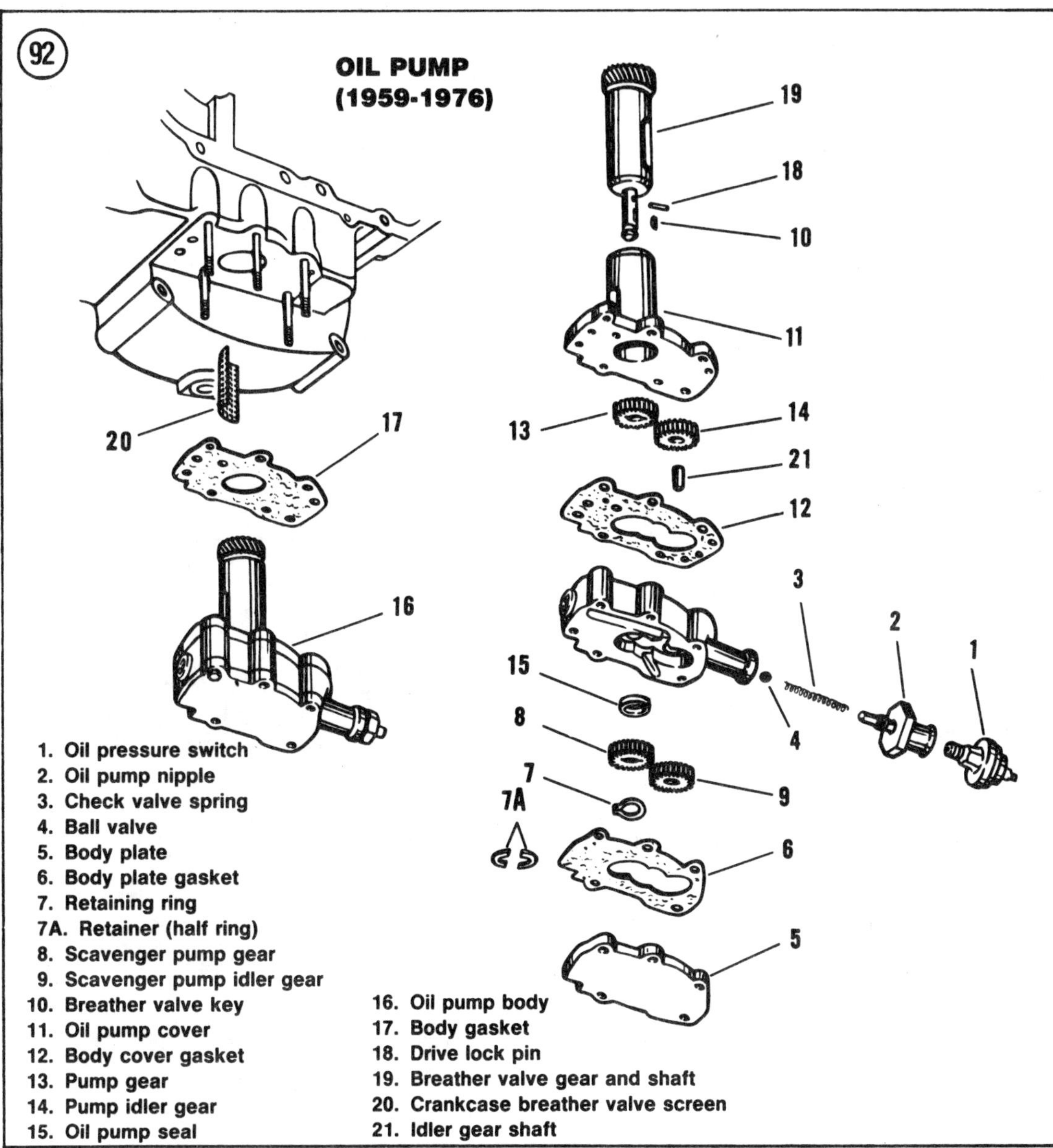

NOTE
Perform Step 7 if replacement of the breather valve gear and shaft and the oil pump cover is required.

7. Using a punch, remove the lock pin (18) from the breather valve shaft.
8. Remove the breather valve screen (20) from the crankcase.
9. Remove and discard the pump body oil seal.

Inspection

1. Clean all parts thoroughly in solvent.
2. Replace all gaskets with factory made gaskets.

CAUTION
Never use "homemade" gaskets to check and reassemble the oil pump. Factory gaskets are made to a specified thickness with holes placed accurately to pass oil through the oil pump. Gaskets of the wrong thickness can cause loss of oil pressure and severe engine damage.

3. Replace the oil pump seal.
4. Assemble the pump and pump idler gears and a *new* pump body gasket. Measure the height of the

gears in relation to the gasket surface. The gear faces should be no more than 0.0005 in. below or 0.0025 in. above the body gasket surface. If these clearances are incorrect, install a new oil pump body gasket.

5. Insert the breather valve into the oil pump cover. The breather valve should turn freely with no binding.
6. Install the breather valve key (10) onto the breather valve shaft (19) and check its fit. If the key is loose on the shaft, replace it.
7. Check all parts for wear or damage. If there is any doubt as to the condition of any part, replace it.

Assembly/Installation

1. Coat all parts with fresh engine oil prior to installation.
2. Install the breather valve screen (20) in the crankcase.
3. Install a *new* drive lock pin (18) into the breather valve shaft.
4. If the idler gear shaft (21) was removed from the pump body, install a new one by pressing it into place.
5. Install the pump (13) and pump idler (14) gears.
6. Apply a non-hardening gasket sealer to a new body cover gasket (12) and install it. Make sure to align the oil holes in the gasket with the pump body.
7. Install the oil pump breather valve gear, shaft and oil pump cover assembly on the pump body. Slide a new oil pump body seal over the breather valve shaft so that the seal's lip side faces away from the pump body. Then press the seal into the oil pump body so that it is flush with the surface.
8. Install the key (10) in the breather valve shaft.
9. Install the scavenger pump (8) and pump idler (9) gears. Secure gears with the retaining rings (7 or 7A) installed in the breather valve shaft groove.
10. Lightly coat a new body plate gasket (6) with a non-hardening gasket sealer and install it.
11. Install the oil pump body plate (5) on the oil pump.
12. Align the oil pump with the crankcase studs and install the oil pump. Install the pump attaching nuts and tighten in a crisscross pattern to 100 in.-lb.
13. Rotate the exposed oil pump gear and check that the gears turn freely with no binding or drag. If the pump does not operate freely, loosen the oil pump nuts and reposition the oil pump on the crankcase. Tighten the screws and recheck.

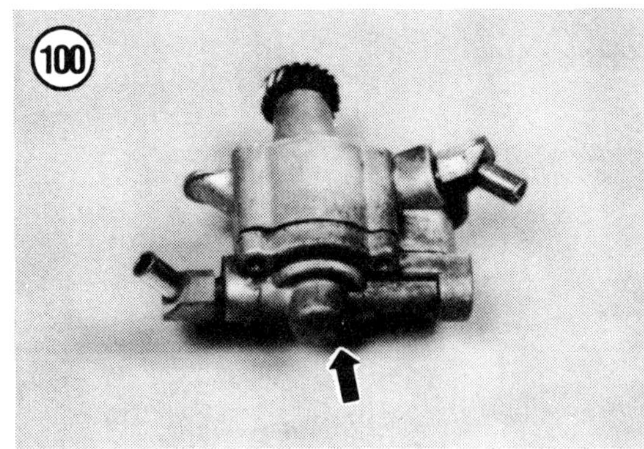

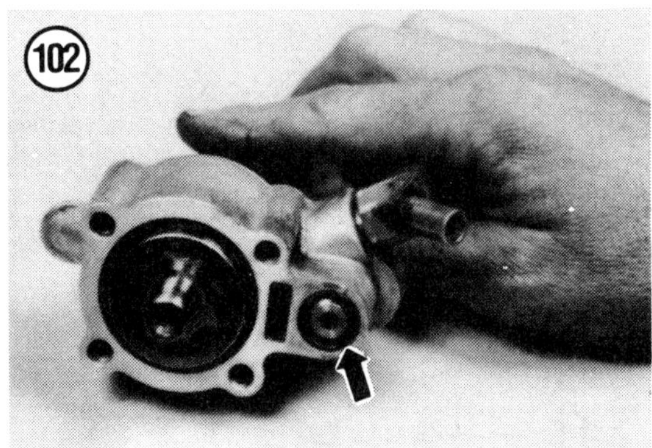

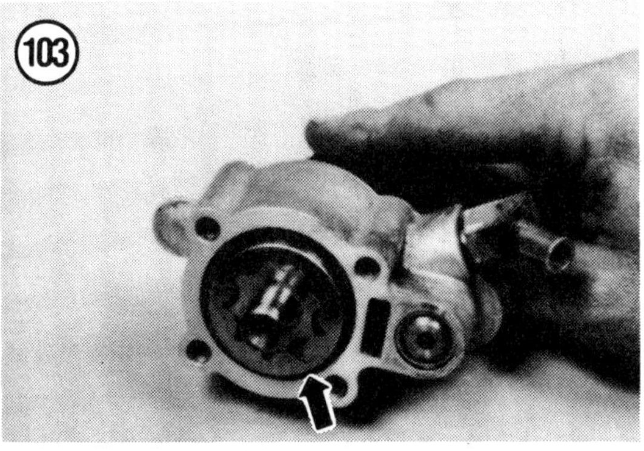

14. After completing Step 13, it is necessary to time the oil pump. Refer to *Timing Gearcase Breather Valve, 1959-1976* in this chapter.
15. Install the engine as described in this chapter.

OIL PUMP (1977-1985)

Removal/Installation

The oil pump can be removed with the engine in the frame and without removing the gearcase cover. The gearcase cover is shown removed in this procedure for clarity.

WARNING
Make certain the engine and the oil are cool before removing the oil pump; otherwise, painful burns could result from hot oil.

1. Place a drip pan underneath the engine.
2. From underneath the engine, disconnect the wire from the oil pressure switch.
3. Disconnect the oil lines from the pump (**Figure 95**) and plug the lines to keep the oil from draining.
4. Unscrew the 4 Allen bolts that attach the pump to the bottom of the crankcase and remove the pump (**Figure 96**).
5. Install by reversing these steps, noting the following.
6. Clean the crankcase oil pump machined surface (**Figure 97**) of all gasket residue.
7. Use a new gasket and coat it with Hitak or a similar gasket sealer.
8. Tighten the Allen bolts to 8 ft.-lb.
9. After installing the oil pump, prime it as described in this chapter.

Disassembly

Refer to **Figure 98** for this procedure.

1. Remove the oil pump mounting screws (**Figure 99**).
2. Remove the cover (**Figure 100**) from the pump body and remove the O-ring (**Figure 101**) from the groove in the cover.
3. Remove the O-ring (**Figure 102**) from the check valve.
4. Remove the outer (**Figure 103**) and inner (**Figure 104**) narrow gerotor set from the shaft. Pull the pin (**Figure 105**) out of the shaft with needlenose pliers.
5. Remove the outer plate (**Figure 106**), spring washer (**Figure 107**) and the inner plate (**Figure 108**).
6. Remove the retaining ring (**Figure 109**) from the gear shaft.
7. Remove the inner (**Figure 110**) and outer (**Figure 111**) wide gerotor set.

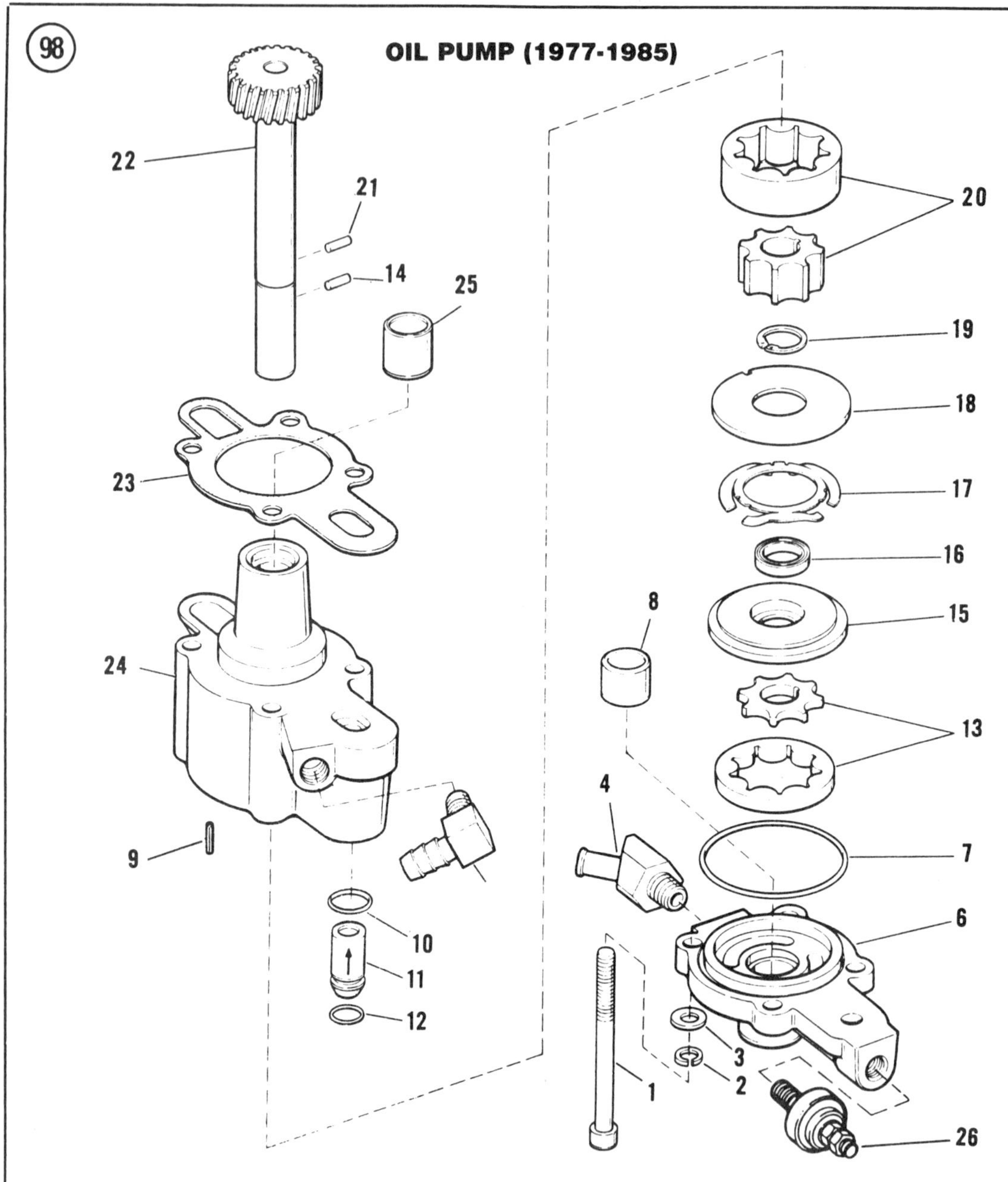

1. Screw (4)
2. Lockwasher (4)
3. Washer (4)
4. Feed fitting
5. Return fitting
6. Cover
7. O-ring
8. Bushing
9. Roll pin
10. O-ring
11. Check valve
12. O-ring
13. Gerotor set, feed (thin)
14. Gear shaft pin
15. Outer plate
16. Outer plate seal
17. Spring washer
18. Inner plate
19. Retaining ring
20. Gerotor set, return (thick)
21. Gear shaft pin
22. Gear shaft
23. Gasket
24. Body
25. Bushing
26. Oil pressure switch

104

108

105

109

106

110

107

111

8. Remove the pin (**Figure 112**) from the shaft and remove the gear shaft (**Figure 113**) from the pump body.
9. Press the check valve and O-ring (**Figure 114**) out of the pump body.

Cleaning/Inspection

1. Clean all of the parts thoroughly with solvent and blow them dry with compressed air. Blow out all of the ports and passages to ensure that no sludge or solvent remains.
2. Replace any O-rings that are deformed or damaged.
3. Replace the seal in the outer plate (**Figure 115**). Tap the new seal in so that its lip faces in the direction shown in A, **Figure 116**.
4. Inspect the check valve (**Figure 117**). It should be clean and the spring-loaded cup should move freely and return to the closed position under spring pressure. If it is not satisfactory, replace it.
5. Inspect the spring washer (**Figure 118**) for damage and replace it if any of the fingers are broken.
6. Check the gerotor sets for scoring and damage. Assemble the inner and outer rotors of each set. See **Figure 119** and **Figure 120**. Measure the assembled clearance with a flat feeler gauge as

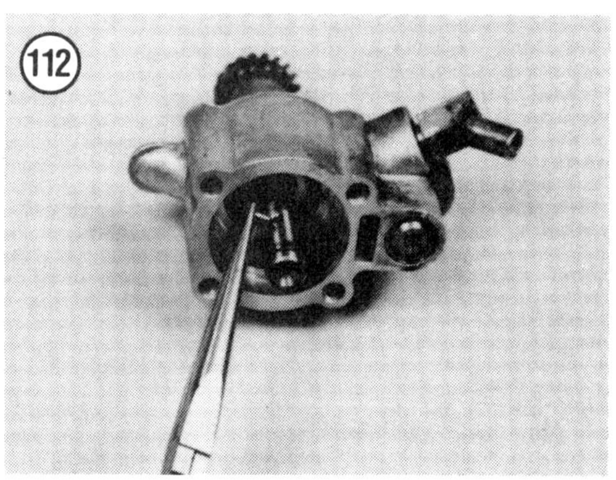

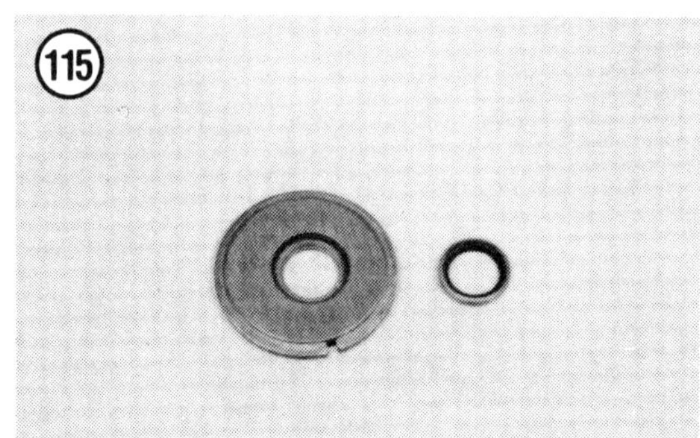

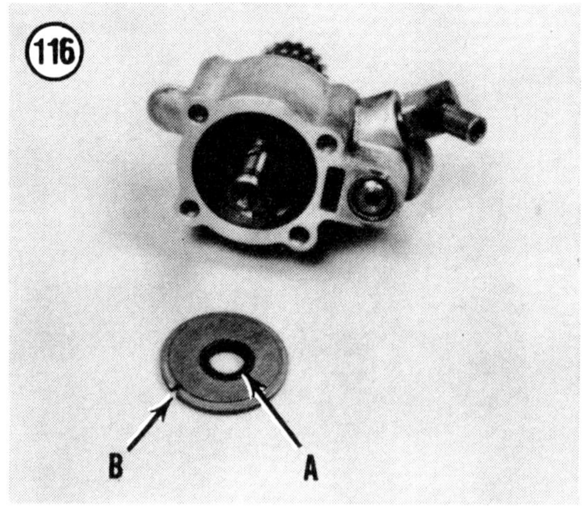

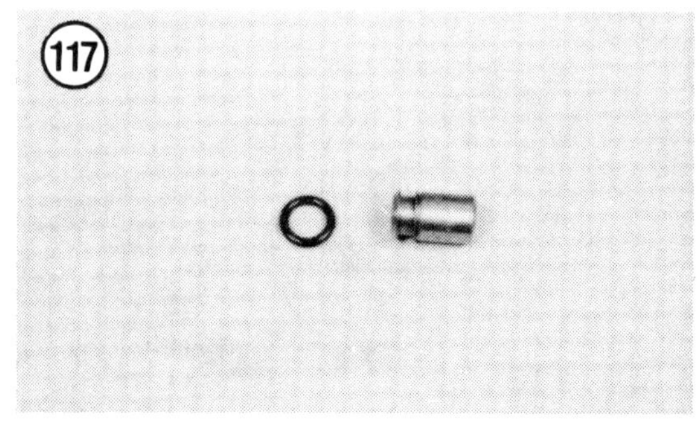

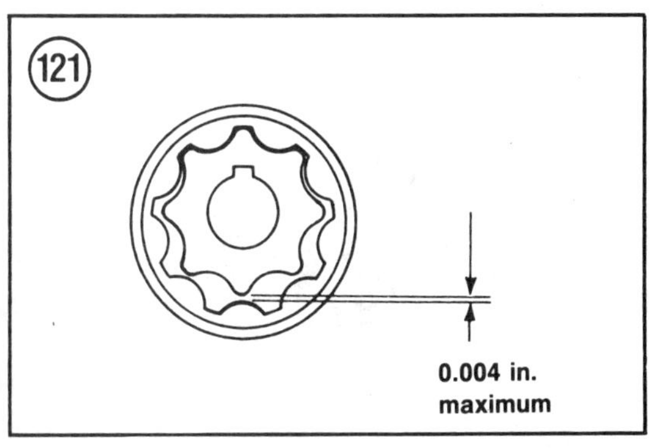

shown in **Figure 121**. If the clearance is greater than 0.004 in., replace the worn gerotor set.

7. Measure the thickness of the inner and outer feed (narrow) gerotors with a micrometer (**Figure 122**). If both pieces are not the same thickness, replace them as a set.

8. Assemble the narrow gerotor assembly into the pump body (**Figure 123**). Then measure the fit of the narrow gerotor set as shown in **Figure 124**. Place the gerotor set in the pump body cover and set a straightedge on top of it. Insert a flat feeler gauge between the straightedge and the flange of the cover. The distance should be 0.001-0.011 in. If the distance is less than 0.001 in, remove material from the cover flange by stroking it back and forth on a piece of fine-grit emery cloth (No. 280 to start and No. 400 to finish) set on a piece of glass or

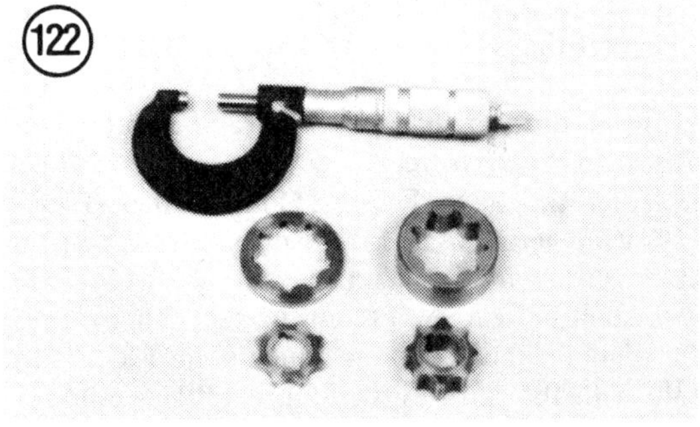

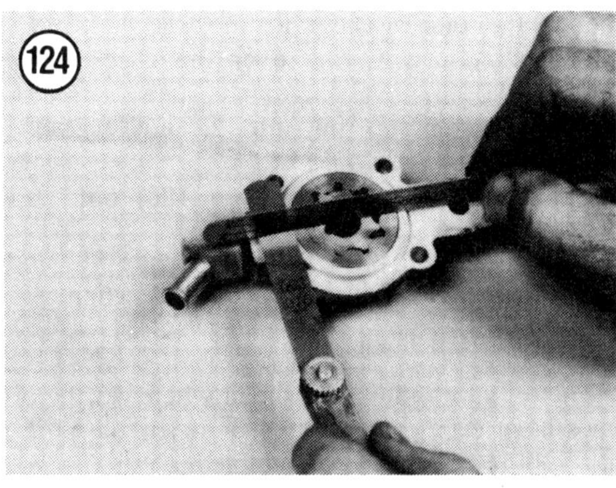

other flat, hard surface. If the distance is greater than 0.011 in., replace the cover.

9. Inspect the bushing in the body (**Figure 125**) and in the cover (8, **Figure 98**) for scoring, wear and damage. If worn, have them replaced by a Harley-Davidson dealer.

10. Inspect the drive shaft pinion gear teeth (**Figure 126**). Replace the shaft if any of the teeth are damaged or if they are severely worn.

11. Inspect the gerotor machined surfaces in the body (**Figure 127**) and cover (**Figure 128**) for scoring or cracks. Replace the oil pump if these parts are damaged.

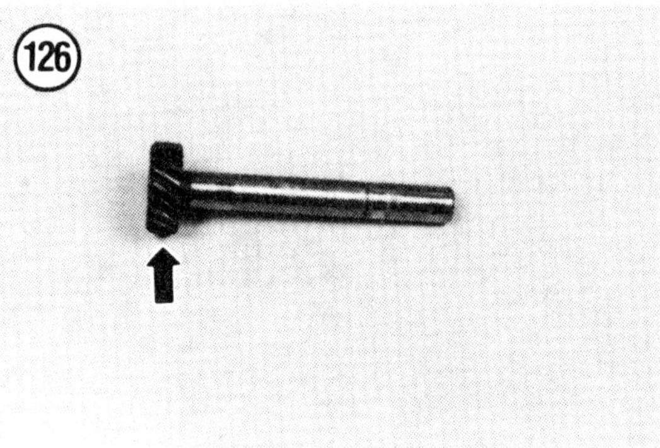

Assembly

1. Lightly oil all parts with fresh engine oil.
2. Install a new o-ring on the check valve (**Figure 117**). Then install the check valve (**Figure 114**) so that its directional arrow faces into the pump body.
3. Install the gear shaft through the body (**Figure 129**).
4. Install the gear shaft pin (**Figure 112**) in the hole closest to the drive gear.
5. Install the outer (**Figure 111**) and inner (**Figure 110**) wide gerotor set. Make sure the notch in the inner gerotor meshes with the gear shaft pin.
6. Install the gear shaft retaining ring (**Figure 109**).
7. Align the notch in the inner plate (A, **Figure 130**) with the roll pin (B, **Figure 130**) installed in the body and install the inner plate.
8. Install the spring washer (**Figure 107**) so that its fingers contact the outer plate.
9. Align the notch in the outer plate (B, **Figure 116**) with the roll pin in the body and install the outer plate. The outer plate seal lip (A, **Figure 116**) should face toward the feed gerotor set (13, **Figure 98**).
10. Install the push pin (**Figure 105**) into the gear shaft.
11. Install the thin inner gerotor (**Figure 104**) and outer geroter (**Figure 103**). Make sure the notch in the inner gerotor meshes with the gear shaft pin.
12. Install a new O-ring over the check valve (**Figure 102**).
13. Install a new O-ring into the cover groove (**Figure 101**).
14. Assemble the cover (**Figure 100**) onto the body.
15. Install the oil pump screws (**Figure 99**) and install the oil pump as described in this chapter.

Priming the Oil Pump

The oil pump must be primed whenever the oil lines have been disconnected or when the pump has been removed or disassembled.

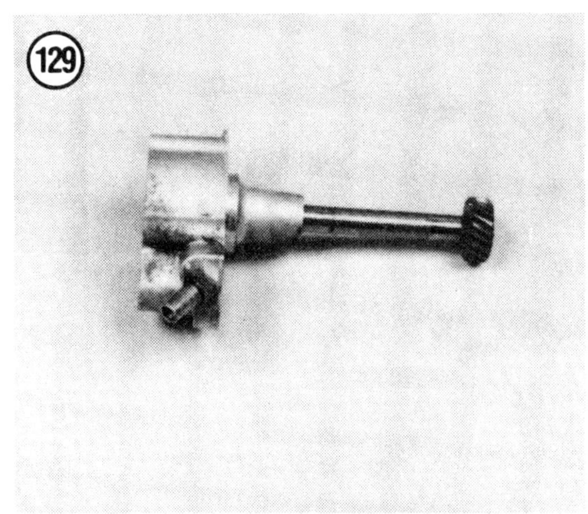
129

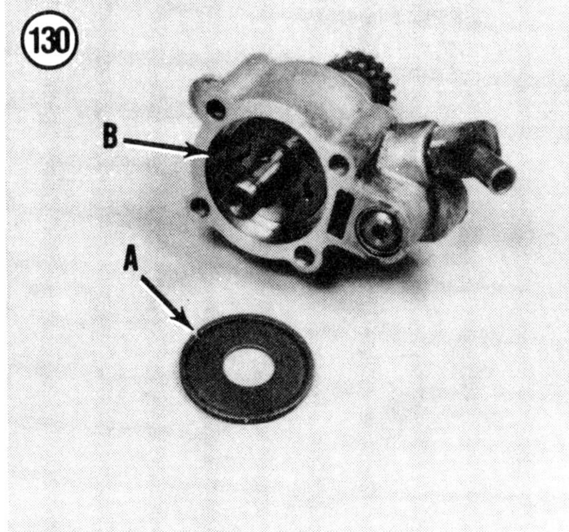

130

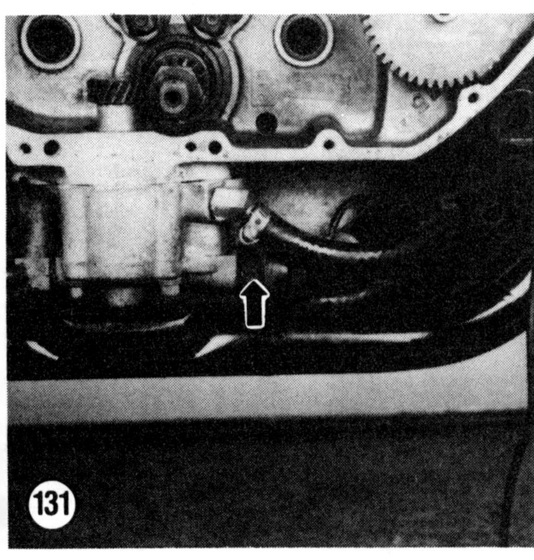
131

1. Loosen the oil pressure switch (**Figure 131**) and start the engine.

NOTE
Figure 131 *shows the engine partially disassembled for clarity. Engine disassembly is not necessary for this procedure.*

2. Allow the engine to idle and let several ounces of oil run out of the switch port to ensure that the pump is primed and that oil is circulating. Then tighten the switch and connect the wires.
3. Check the oil level in the tank as described in Chapter Three.

GEARCASE

Refer to **Figure 132** (1959-early 1984) or **Figure 133** (late 1984-1985) for this procedure.

Disassembly

1. Clean the area around the tappets and the gearcase cover.
2. Remove the exhaust pipe as described in Chapter Six.
3. Remove the footrest and brake pedal (**Figure 134**).
4. Remove the air cleaner assembly as described in Chapter Three.
5. Remove the push rods as described in this chapter.
6. Secure the tappets with rubber bands or discarded O-rings (**Figure 135**) to prevent them from falling into the gearcase when the cams are removed.

7A. *1959-1978:* Remove the circuit breaker or magneto as described in Chapter Seven.

7B. *1979-1985:* Remove the sensor plate and rotor as described in Chapter Seven.

8. Place a flat pan under gearcase cover to catch oil.
9. Remove the gearcase cover screws. Then tap the gearcase cover (**Figure 136**) with a plastic mallet and remove it. Discard the gasket.

NOTE
The gearcase cover is located by snug dowel pins and must be worked off carefully. Do not pry the gearcase cover with any metal tool. If necessary, tap the cover lightly with a soft faced hammer at the point where the cover projects beyond the crankcase.

10. *1959-early 1984:* Perform the following:
    a. If the generator is installed, remove the generator drive gear.

4

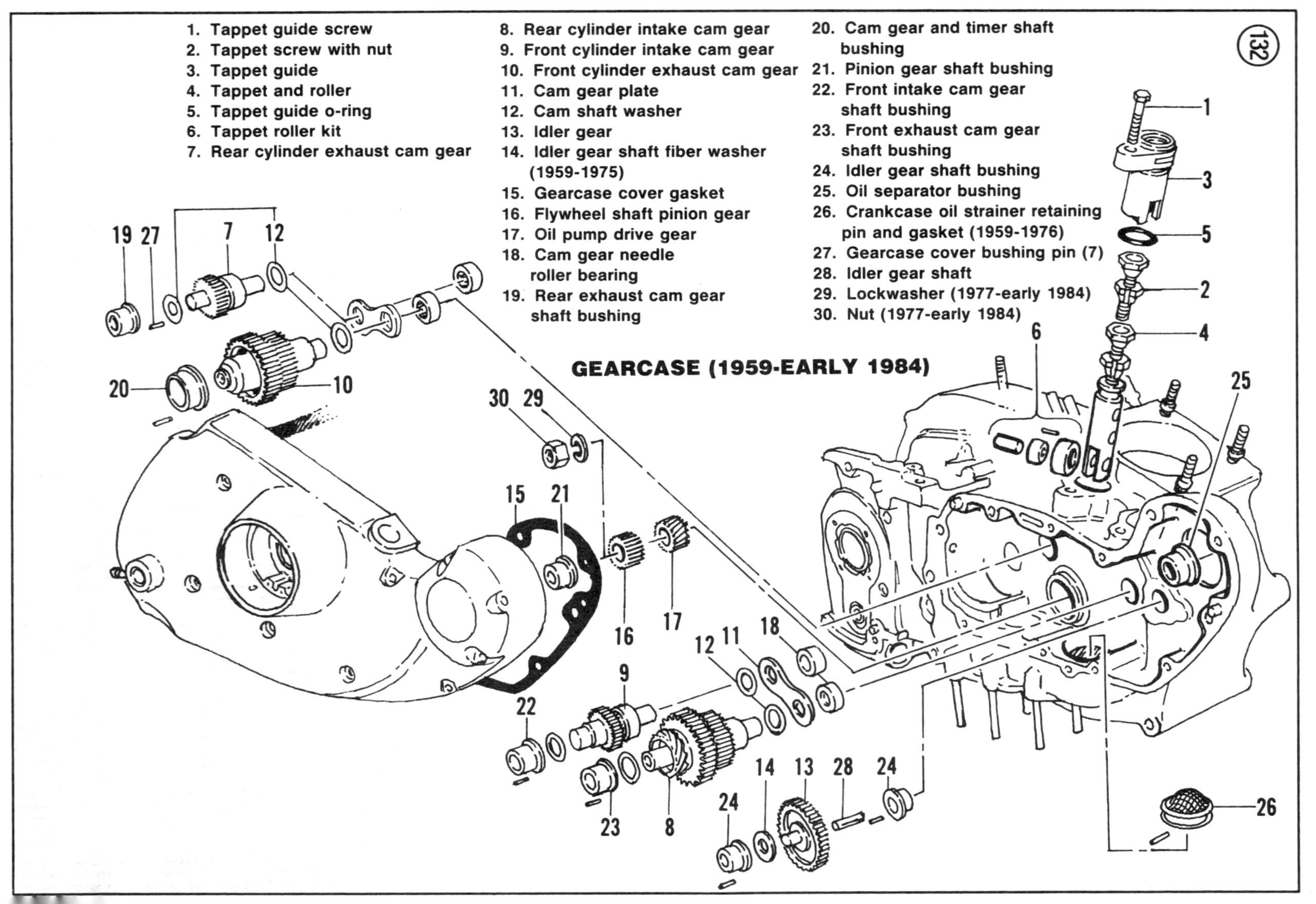
132
1. Tappet guide screw
2. Tappet screw with nut
3. Tappet guide
4. Tappet and roller
5. Tappet guide o-ring
6. Tappet roller kit
7. Rear cylinder exhaust cam gear
8. Rear cylinder intake cam gear
9. Front cylinder intake cam gear
10. Front cylinder exhaust cam gear
11. Cam gear plate
12. Cam shaft washer
13. Idler gear
14. Idler gear shaft fiber washer (1959-1975)
15. Gearcase cover gasket
16. Flywheel shaft pinion gear
17. Oil pump drive gear
18. Cam gear needle roller bearing
19. Rear exhaust cam gear shaft bushing
20. Cam gear and timer shaft bushing
21. Pinion gear shaft bushing
22. Front intake cam gear shaft bushing
23. Front exhaust cam gear shaft bushing
24. Idler gear shaft bushing
25. Oil separator bushing
26. Crankcase oil strainer retaining pin and gasket (1959-1976)
27. Gearcase cover bushing pin (7)
28. Idler gear shaft
29. Lockwasher (1977-early 1984)
30. Nut (1977-early 1984)
GEARCASE (1959-EARLY 1984)

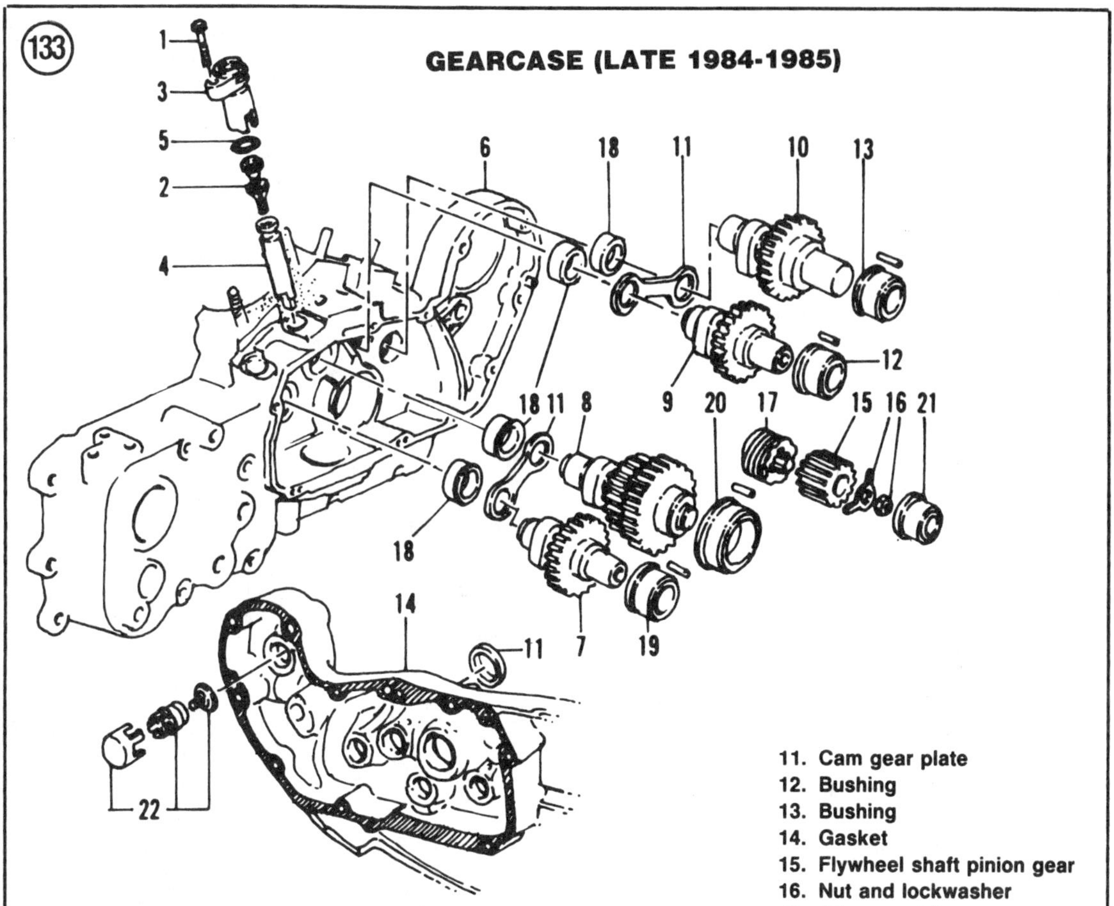

133

GEARCASE (LATE 1984-1985)

1. Screw
2. Screw
3. Tappet guide
4. Tappet and roller
5. O-ring
6. Crankcase half
7. Rear cylinder exhaust cam gear
8. Rear cylinder intake cam gear
9. Front cylinder intake cam gear
10. Front cylinder exhaust cam gear
11. Cam gear plate
12. Bushing
13. Bushing
14. Gasket
15. Flywheel shaft pinion gear
16. Nut and lockwasher
17. Oil pump drive gear
18. Roller bearing
19. Bushing
20. Bushing
21. Bushing
22. Breather assembly

b. *1959-1975:* Remove the idler shaft gear fiber washer (14, **Figure 132**).
c. Remove the idler gear (**Figure 137**).

NOTE
When performing Step 11, note whether or not the cam gears have steel washers on either end of the cam gear shafts. If so, these washers must be installed in the same position. Mark each component to ensure correct installation.

11. Remove the cams in the following order:
  a. Front exhaust cam gear (**Figure 138**).
  b. Rear intake cam gear (**Figure 139**).
  c. Front intake cam gear (**Figure 140**).
  d. Cam gear plate (**Figure 141**).
  e. Rear exhaust cam gear (A, **Figure 142**).
  f. Cam gear plate (B, **Figure 142**).

12A. *1959-1976:* Remove the pinion gear with a pinion gear puller (HD 96830-51). See **Figure 143**. Remove the oil pump drive gear (17, **Figure 132**).

12B. *1977-early 1985:* Remove the pinion gear nut and washer (**Figure 144**). Then remove the pinion and oil pump gears from the pinion shaft with a

136

137

138

139

140

141

puller (**Figure 143**). Remove the oil pump drive gear.

13. *Late 1985:* These models are equipped with a cam gear oiler. If necessary, remove it as follows. Refer to **Figure 145**.

a. Back off the cam gear oiler clamps.
b. Remove the oiler manifold screws and spacers.
c. Remove the plug from the gearcase.
d. Insert a punch (1/4 in. end diameter) through the plug hole and tap the oiler manifold out of the crankcase.

Inspection

1. Thoroughly clean gearcase compartment, cover and components with solvent. Blow out all oil passages with compressed air. Make sure that all traces of gasket compound are removed from the gasket mating surfaces.

2. On 1959-1976 models, check the pinion gear press fit on the pinion shaft. The smallest amount of play will result in noisy operation.

3. Inspect the cams as follows:

a. Check the cam gear teeth (**Figure 146**) for signs of wear or damage.

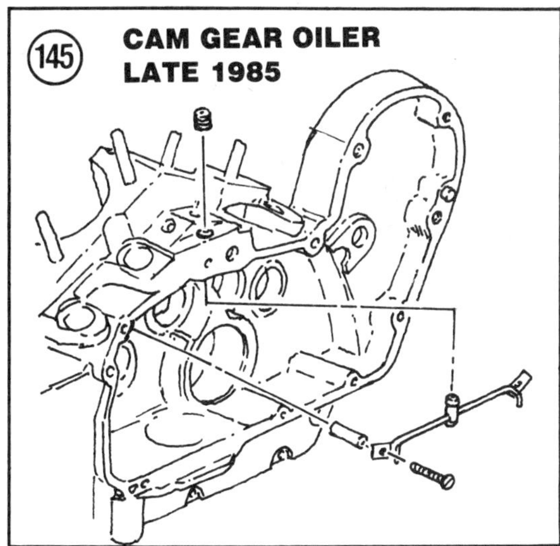

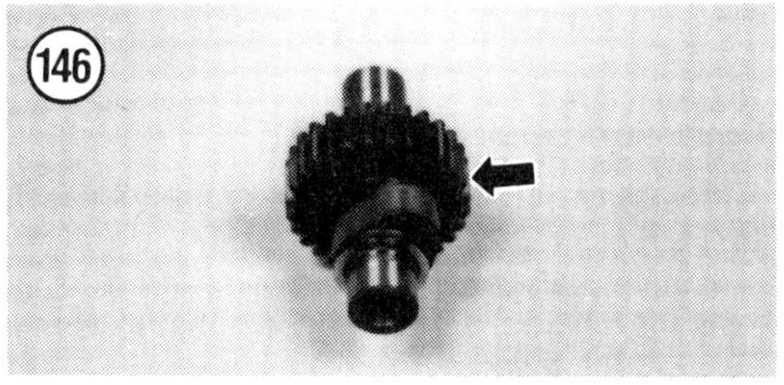

b. Check the cam gear profile (**Figure 147**) for wear, scoring or metal flaking.

c. If necessary, replace cams as described in this chapter.

4. Insert each cam gear in its respective crankcase bearing (A, **Figure 142**) and check running clearance with a dial indicator. Refer to **Table 1** for the correct clearances. If the cam gear-to-bearing clearance is excessive, the crankcase bearings will have to be replaced as described in this chapter.

5. Examine the cam gear plates (**Figure 148**) for damage or excessive wear; replace if necessary.

6. *1959-1976:* Check the crankcase oil strainer to make sure it is not plugged. Clean or replace it as required.

7. *1959-1978:* The oil separator bushing should have 1/16 in. ±1/64 in. clearance between the bushing and the generator oil slinger washer. If the clearance is excessive, install a suitable size washer between the gear and the oil slinger washer.

Gearcase Bearing and Bushing Replacement

Because of special tools and procedures, gearcase bearing replacement (**Figure 149** and **Figure 150**) should be entrusted to a qualified Harley-Davidson dealer.

Cam Gear Replacement

If replacement of one or more cam gears (**Figure 151**) is required, allow a Harley-Davidson dealer to determine the correct replacement gears. Cam gears must be correctly sized to the mating gear to ensure smooth and quiet operation.

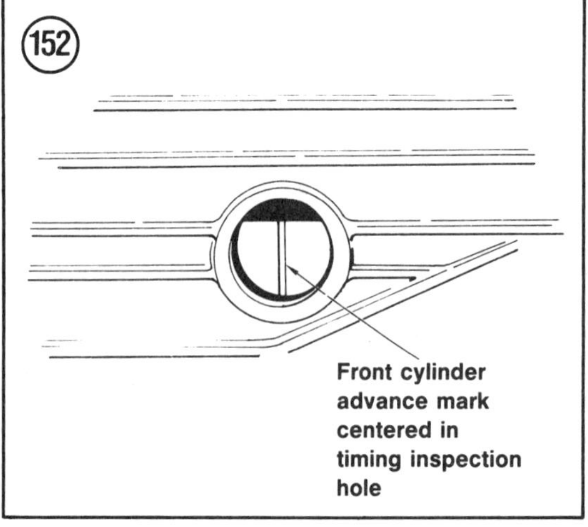

3. Next, position the spiral-cut oil pump drive gear so the marked side (D, **Figure 153**) is facing outward (away from crankcase). Slide the gear on the pinion shaft (E, **Figure 153**) so the timing hole (B, **Figure 153**) remains aligned with the notch (C) in the breather bushing.
4. Press the pinion gear (**Figure 154**) on the pinion shaft. The gear is correctly installed when its outer face is exactly 5/16 in. from the gearcase mating surface.

Timing Gearcase Breather Valve (1959-1976)

The rotary crankcase breather valve must be retimed once it is disengaged from the oil pump drive gear on the pinion shaft. Refer to **Figure 132** for this procedure.

1. Remove the plug from the timing inspection hole (**Figure 152**) located on the left side of the engine. Rotate the engine and position the flywheel timing mark in the exact center of the inspection hole as shown in **Figure 152**.

2. Position the breather sleeve gear so the timing hole (B, **Figure 153**) is aligned with the notch (C) in the breather bushing.

Assembly

1. Coat all bearings, shafts, bushings and gears with engine oil.
2. *Late 1985:* Assemble the cam gear oiler as follows:
   a. Coat the plug with teflon thread sealant and install it into the crankcase.
   b. Install the spacer and oil manifold as shown in Figure 145.

NOTE
The oiler manifold must be installed so that its ounting tabs face behind the oiler tube.

c. Apply a few drops of Loctite removable thread lock (blue color) onto the oiler manifold screws. Then install the screws through the manifold and spacers and tighten to 5 to 7 in.-lb. Do not overtighten.

d. Bend the oiler manifold locktab over the screws to lock them.

3. *1977-1985:* Assemble the pinion shaft as follows:

a. Install the oil pump gear onto the pinion shaft.

b. Align the timing marks on the pinion gear with those of the pinion shaft and install the pinion gear onto the pinion shaft. Make sure the gears are installed with their beveled edge facing toward the crankcase.

c. Install the pinion shaft lockwasher and nut (**Figure 144**) and tighten to 50 ft.-lb. Bend over the lockwasher tabs to lock the nut.

4. Install both cam gear plates (**Figure 141**) in their gearcase recesses. Position cam gear plates so that beveled side of holes faces outward toward cams.

5. Install the cam gears in the following order so that timing marks on all 4 cam gears and pinion gear align as shown in **Figure 155** (1959-early 1984) or **Figure 156** (late 1984-1985).

a. Rear exhaust cam gear (A, **Figure 142**).

b. Front intake cam gear (**Figure 140**).

c. Rear intake cam gear (**Figure 139**).

d. Front exhaust cam gear (**Figure 138**).

NOTE

On some early 1980 models, between engine case numbers 780-213-041 and 780-211-001, the exhaust cam gear was incorrectly marked at the factory. If you have an engine within this number range, the original exhaust cam gear may be one tooth away from correct timing, even when installed according to the procedure described by the factory; see your Harley-Davidson dealer to check and confirm correct cam gear installation.

NOTE

On late 1984-1985 models, the front exhaust cam gear has a dimple timing mark; all other gears use a straight line timing mark.

156

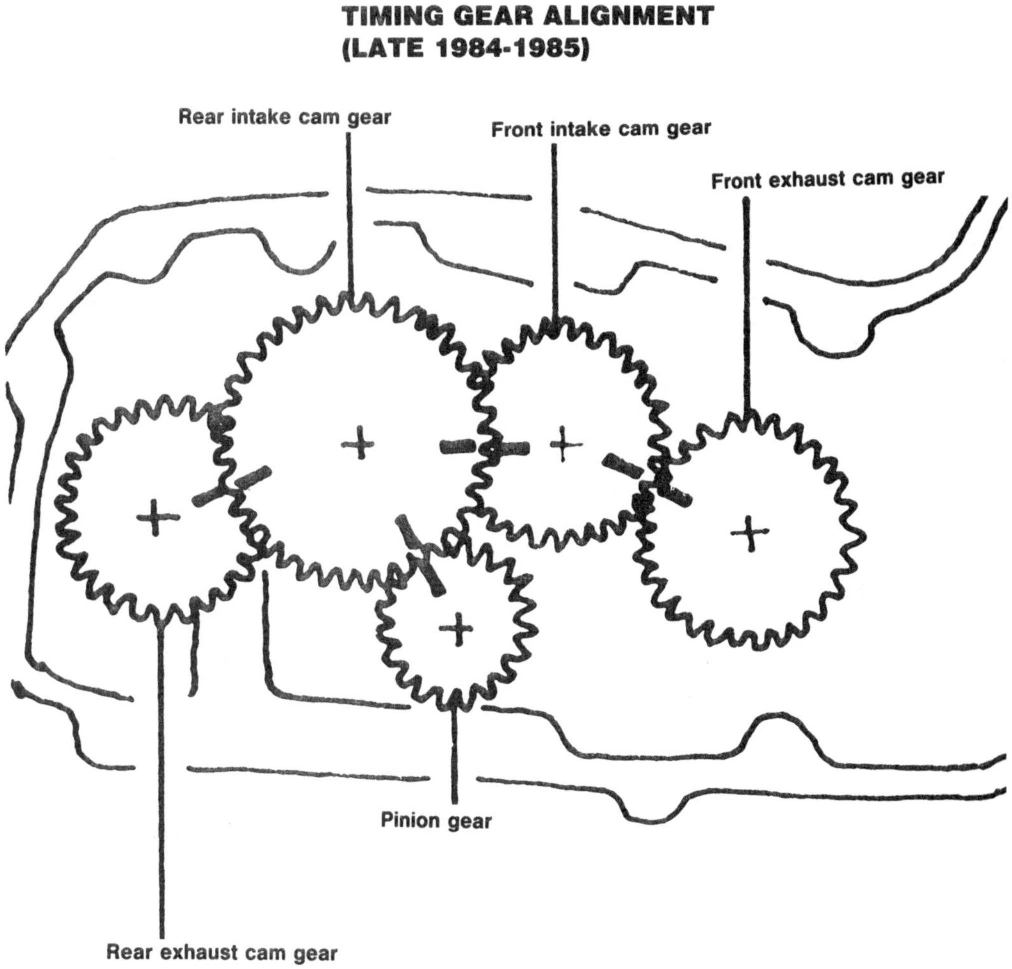

TIMING GEAR ALIGNMENT (LATE 1984-1985)

Rear intake cam gear

Front intake cam gear

Front exhaust cam gear

Pinion gear

Rear exhaust cam gear

5. Measure the cam gear end play as described under *Cam Gear End Play* in this chapter. The end play should be as follows:
   a. Rear intake gear: 0.004 in.
   b. All other gears: 0.005 in.

If end play exceeds these specifications, add shims as required to produce the correct end play.

6. Install the gearcase cover with a new gasket. Tighten all cover screws to 80-110 in.-lb.
7. Reverse Steps 1-6 to complete installation.

Cam Gear End Play

Cam gears are numbered 1 through 4, beginning with rear cylinder exhaust valve cam and numbering from rear to front. See **Figure 157**. Before final assembly of gearcase components, end play of cam gears must be checked and adjusted.

1. Remove the tappets as described in this chapter.
2. Temporarily install both cam gear plates in the gearcase compartment. Position cam gear plates so that beveled side of holes faces outward toward cams.
3. Install each cam gear.
4. Assemble gearcase cover with a new dry gasket and tighten securely. It is not necessary to install generator bolts (if so equipped).
5. Turn engine over until the number one (rear cylinder exhaust) cam lobe is pointing upward.
6. Using a long screwdriver through tappet hole, pry the number one cam gear toward the gearcase cover. Measure clearance, using a feeler gauge, between camshaft shoulder and the gear plate. If end-play exceeds specifications (**Table 1**), add shims as required to produce the correct end play.
7. Repeat Step 6 for each cam gear.

TAPPETS AND GUIDES

Tappets rarely require removal, except for unusual wear or when checking the cam gear end play.

Removal

Tag all parts to that they can be returned to their original positions.

1. Remove all dirt from the tappet area.
2. Remove the push rods as described in this chapter.

3A. *1959-1976:* The tappet guides are pressed into the crankcase. To remove, use the tappet guide puller (HD 95724-57) as follows:

 a. Make sure the cam gears are installed in the crankcase before attempting tappet guide removal.
 b. Remove the tappet adjusting screw (**Figure 158**).
 c. Remove the tappet guide screw.
 d. Using the tappet guide puller (**Figure 159**), remove the tappet guide(s).

3B. *1977-1985:* Remove the tappet guide bolts and remove the tappet guide and tappet (**Figure 160**). If the tappet is tight in the guide, tap it lightly with a rubber faced hammer and remove it.

CAUTION
Do not pry the tappet guide out of the crankcase.

Disasembly/Inspection

1. Check the tappet rollers (**Figure 161**) for pitting, scoring, galling or excessive wear. If the rollers are worn excessively, check the mating cam lobes (**Figure 147**) for the same wear conditions. The cam lobes can be observed through the tappet guide hole in the crankcase. Replace the cam, if necessary, as described in this chapter.
2. Check the roller end clearance by grasping the tappet assembly in one hand and attempting to move the roller back and forth. **Table 1** lists wear specifications. If the end clearance is excessive, Harley-Davidson recommends to replace the tappet assembly. However, factory tappet roller kits are available that allow replacement of the roller. If the roller is replaced, it must fit the needle bearing with 0.0005 to 0.0010 in. radial clearance,

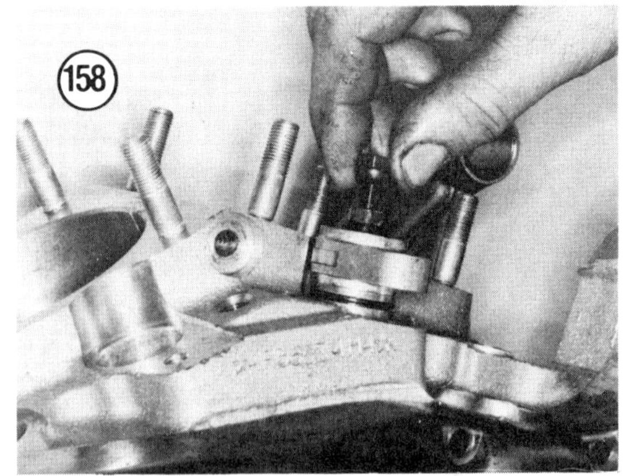
158

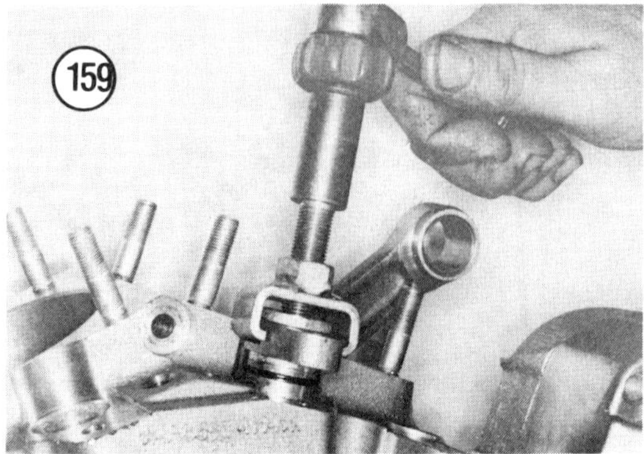
159

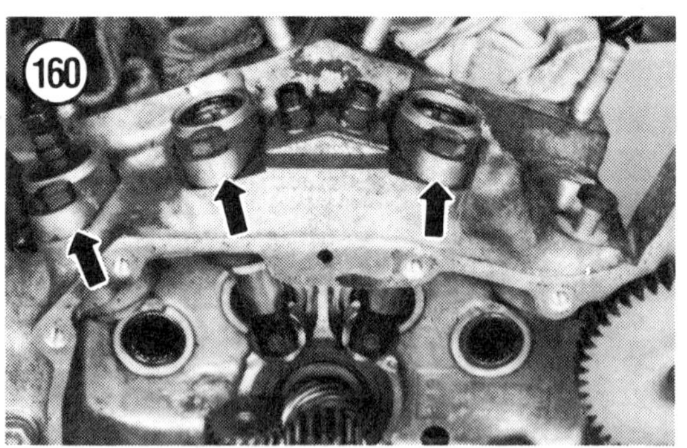
160

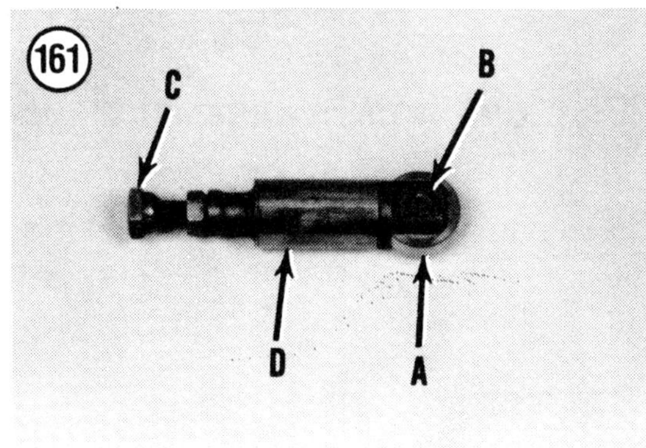

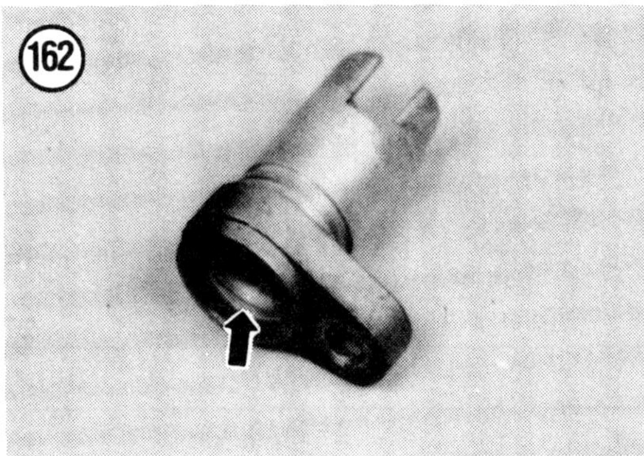

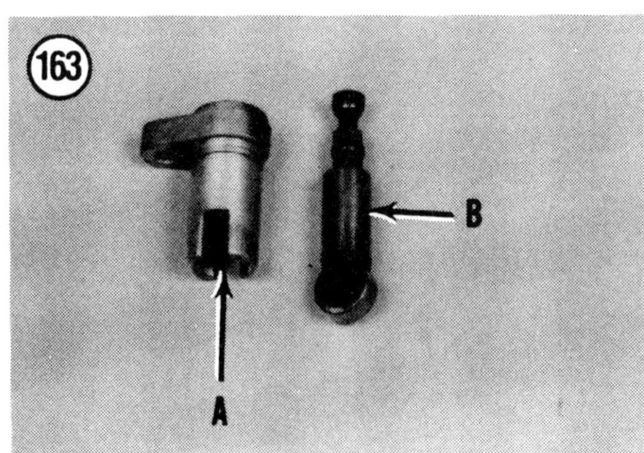

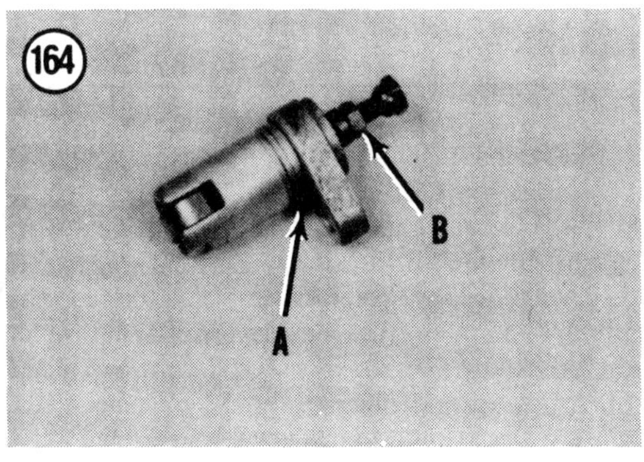

and approximately 0.008-0.010 in. end play after installation. To install, remove the rivet (B, **Figure 161**) and disassemble. Reassemble using a new rivet.

3. Replace the tappet adjusting screw (C, **Figure 161**) if damaged, pitted or worn egg-shaped.
4. Check the tappet inside bore (**Figure 162**) for wear and damage.

NOTE
Steps 5-7 require expensive measuring equipment. If you do not have access to such equipment, have a Harley-Davidson dealer or machine shop perform the measurement for you.

5. Measure the tappet guide inside diameter (A, **Figure 163**) with a bore gauge or telescoping gauge. Record the measurement.
6. Measure the tappet outside diameter (B, **Figure 163**) with a micrometer.
7. The difference in the measurements taken in Step 4 and Step 5 is the tappet guide clearance. Replace the tappet or guide if the clearance is excessive.

Assembly/Installation

1. If removed, thread the tappet adjusting screw (C, **Figure 161**) onto the tappet.
2. Coat the tappet, tappet guide and needle bearing with engine oil.
3. Install a new O-ring onto the tappet guide. Make sure the O-ring seats completely in the tappet guide groove (A, **Figure 164**).
4. Insert the tappet into the guide (B, **Figure 164**).

CAUTION
If the tappet is not installed correctly, the roller and cam may be damaged when the assembly is installed in Step 5.

5. Perform the following:
   a. Align the tappet guide with the crankcase holes.
   b. Align the tappet in the guide so that the tappet roller is crosswise to the guide and cam (A, **Figure 164**).

NOTE
On models in which a puller was required to remove the tappet guide, the guide will have to be pressed into the crankcase with a block of wood and hammer.

   c. Install the tappet guide (**Figure 160**) and tappet.

4

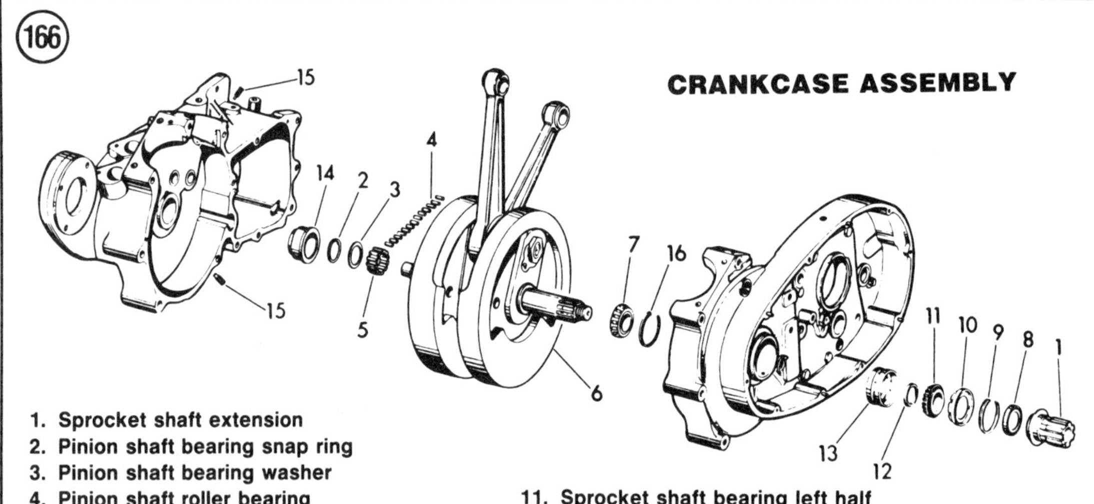

1. Sprocket shaft extension
2. Pinion shaft bearing snap ring
3. Pinion shaft bearing washer
4. Pinion shaft roller bearing
5. Pinion shaft roller bearing retainer
6. Connecting rod and flywheel assembly
7. Sprocket shaft bearing right half
8. Sprocket shaft oil seal
9. Sprocket shaft bearing spring ring (outer)
10. Sprocket shaft bearing spacer
11. Sprocket shaft bearing left half
12. Sprocket shaft bearing spacer
13. Sprocket shaft bearing outer race
14. Pinion shaft bushing
15. Pinion shaft bearing bushing screw
16. Sprocket shaft bearing spring ring (inner)

d. Install the tappet bolts and tighten to 8-14 ft.-lb.

6. Install and adjust the push rods as described under *Push Rods* in this chapter.

CRANKCASE

Crankcases must be disassembled to service the crankshaft, connecting rod bearings, pinion shaft bearings and sprocket shaft bearings. This section describes basic checks and procedures that can be performed in the home shop. Bearing and crankshaft service should be referred to a Harley-Davidson shop equipped to handle such repairs.

Flywheel End Play Check

Flywheel end play should be measured before completely disassembling the crankcase.

NOTE
*Do not remove the sprocket shaft extension or the clutch engine sprocket (**Figure 165**) when performing Step 1. These parts must be installed to preload the bearing races.*

1. Remove the following components as described in this chapter:
   a. Cylinder heads.
   b. Cylinders.
   c. Oil pump.

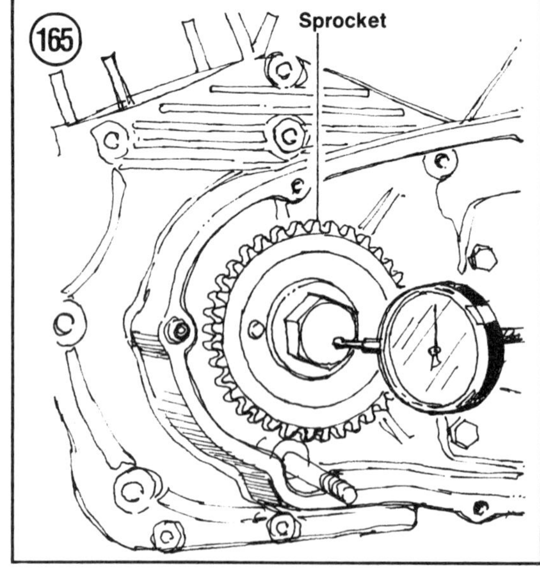

   d. Gearcase cover.
   e. Cam gears.

2. Attach a dial indicator so that the probe touches against the end of the gear shaft (**Figure 165**).

3. Using a large screwdriver, pry the flywheel upward and note the end play registering on the dial indicator. If end play exceeds limit in **Table 1**, the sprocket shaft bearing must be replaced by a Harley-Davidson dealer.

(167)

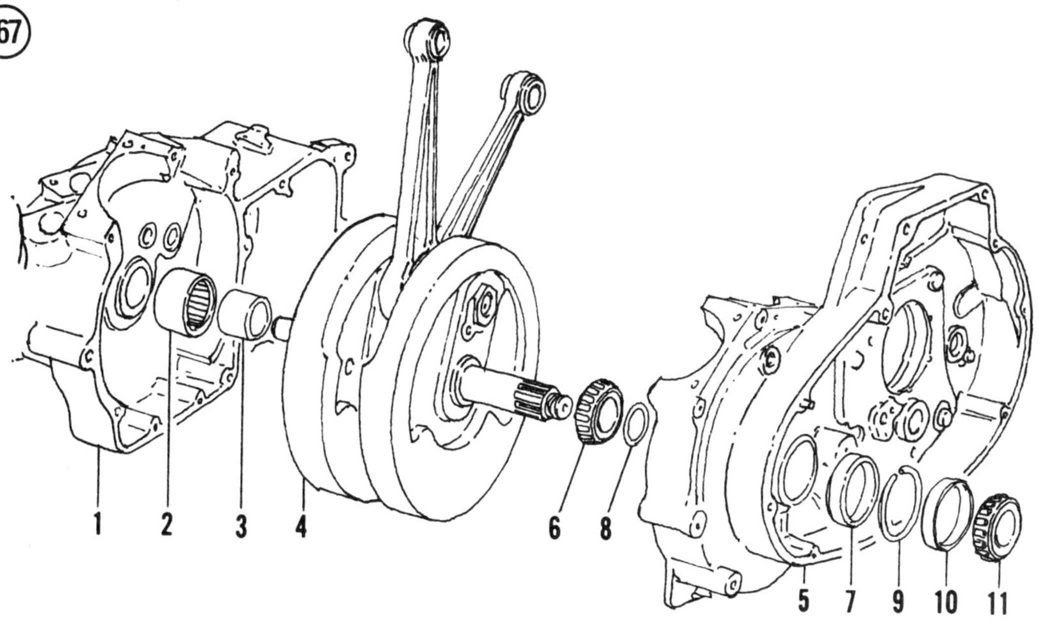

CRANKCASE (1979-1985)

1. Right crankcase half
2. Pinion bearing
3. Pinion race (1979-early 1981)
4. Crankshaft assembly
5. Left crankcase half
6. Right-hand sprocket bearing
7. Right-hand outer sprocket race
8. Spacer
9. Lock ring
10. Left-hand outer sprocket race
11. Left-hand bearing

Disassembly

Refer to **Figure 166** (1959-1978) or **Figure 167** (1979-1985) for this procedure.

1. Remove the engine from the frame as described in this chapter.
2. Disassemble and remove the gearcase assembly as described in this chapter.
3. Remove the oil pump as described in this chapter.
4. Check the flywheel end play as described in this chapter.
5. *1959-1978:* Remove the sprocket shaft extension (1, **Figure 166**) with Harley-Davidson tool No. 96015-56. See **Figure 168**. If equipped

with a solid sprocket, remove it with a universal type claw puller.

6. Referring to **Figures 169-172**, perform the following:

a. Remove the rear engine mount (**Figure 173**).
b. Remove the front (**Figure 174**) and rear (**Figure 175**) crankcase bolts.

7. Lay the crankcase assembly on wood blocks so that the right-hand side (**Figure 176**) faces up.

8. Tap the crankcase with a plastic mallet and remove the right-hand crankcase half.

NOTE
*Further disassembly of the crankcase/flywheel assembly is not recommended. A hydraulic press is required to separate the crankshaft (**Figure 177**) from the left-hand crankcase half. Furthermore, additional equipment is required to properly install and line ream new bearings.*

9. Check connecting rod side play with a feeler gauge as shown in **Figure 178**. If the side play is not

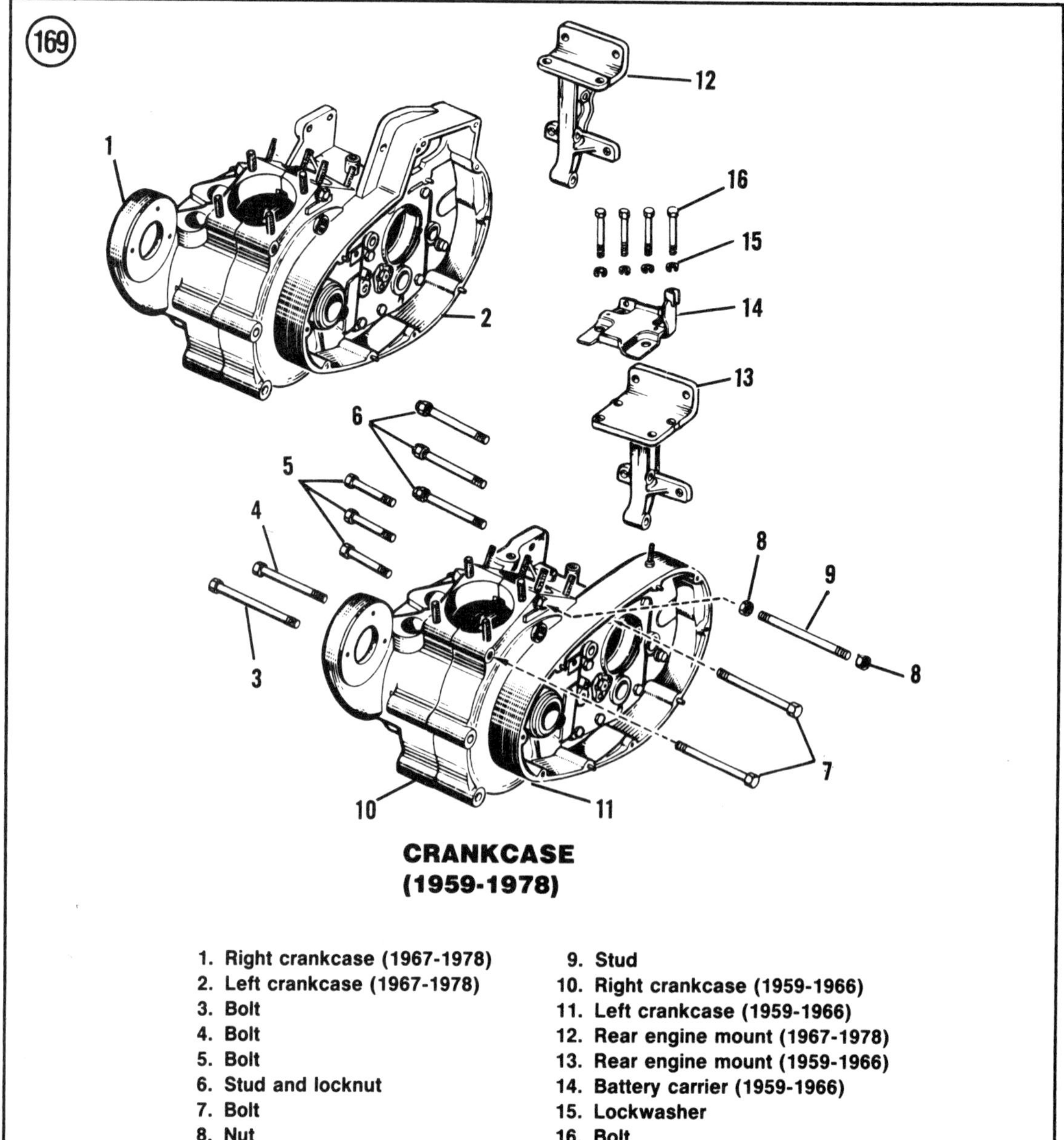

CRANKCASE (1959-1978)

1. Right crankcase (1967-1978)
2. Left crankcase (1967-1978)
3. Bolt
4. Bolt
5. Bolt
6. Stud and locknut
7. Bolt
8. Nut
9. Stud
10. Right crankcase (1959-1966)
11. Left crankcase (1959-1966)
12. Rear engine mount (1967-1978)
13. Rear engine mount (1959-1966)
14. Battery carrier (1959-1966)
15. Lockwasher
16. Bolt

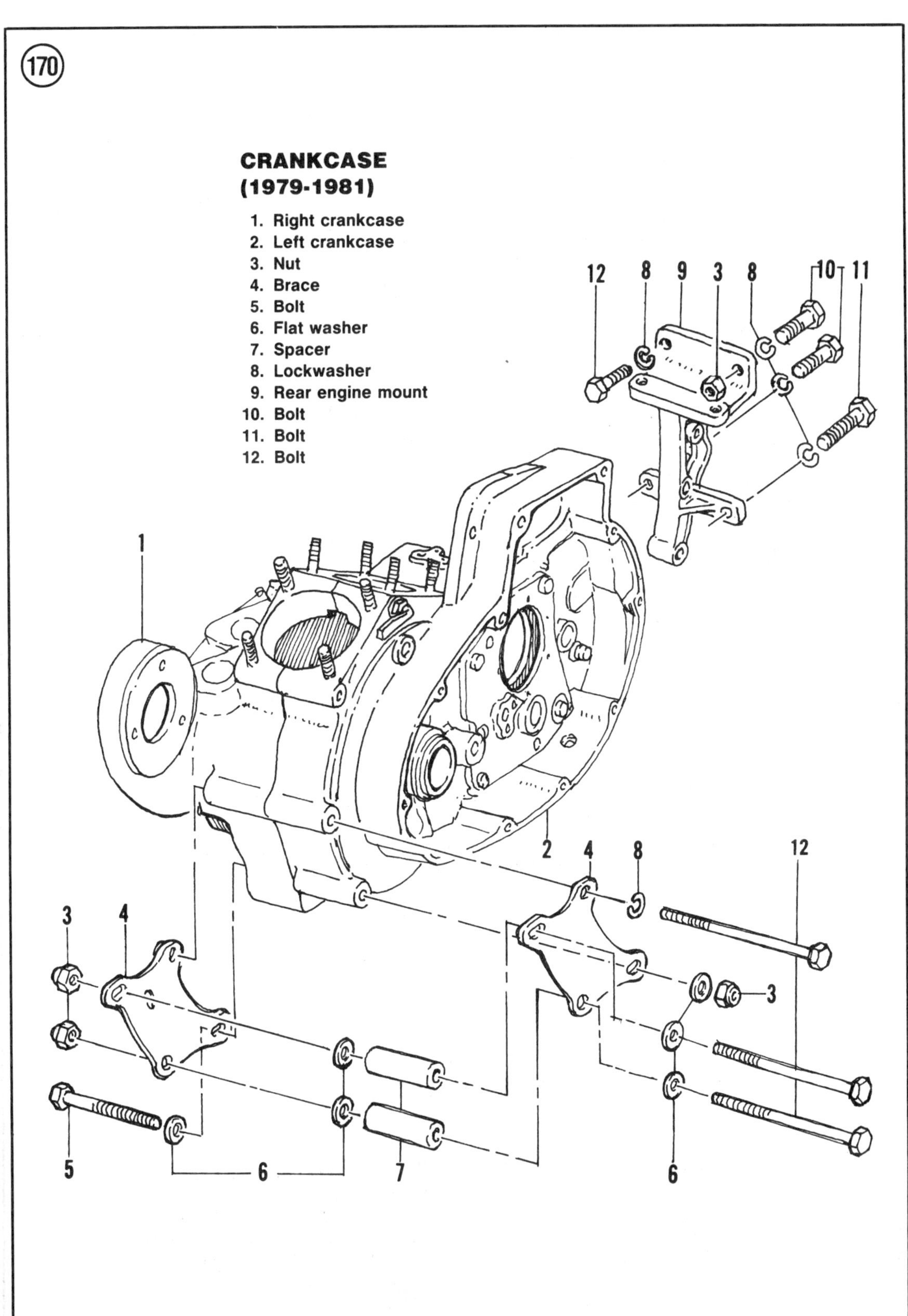
170
CRANKCASE
(1979-1981)
1. Right crankcase
2. Left crankcase
3. Nut
4. Brace
5. Bolt
6. Flat washer
7. Spacer
8. Lockwasher
9. Rear engine mount
10. Bolt
11. Bolt
12. Bolt
12
8
9
3
8
10
11
1
2
4
8
12
3
4
3
5
6
7
6

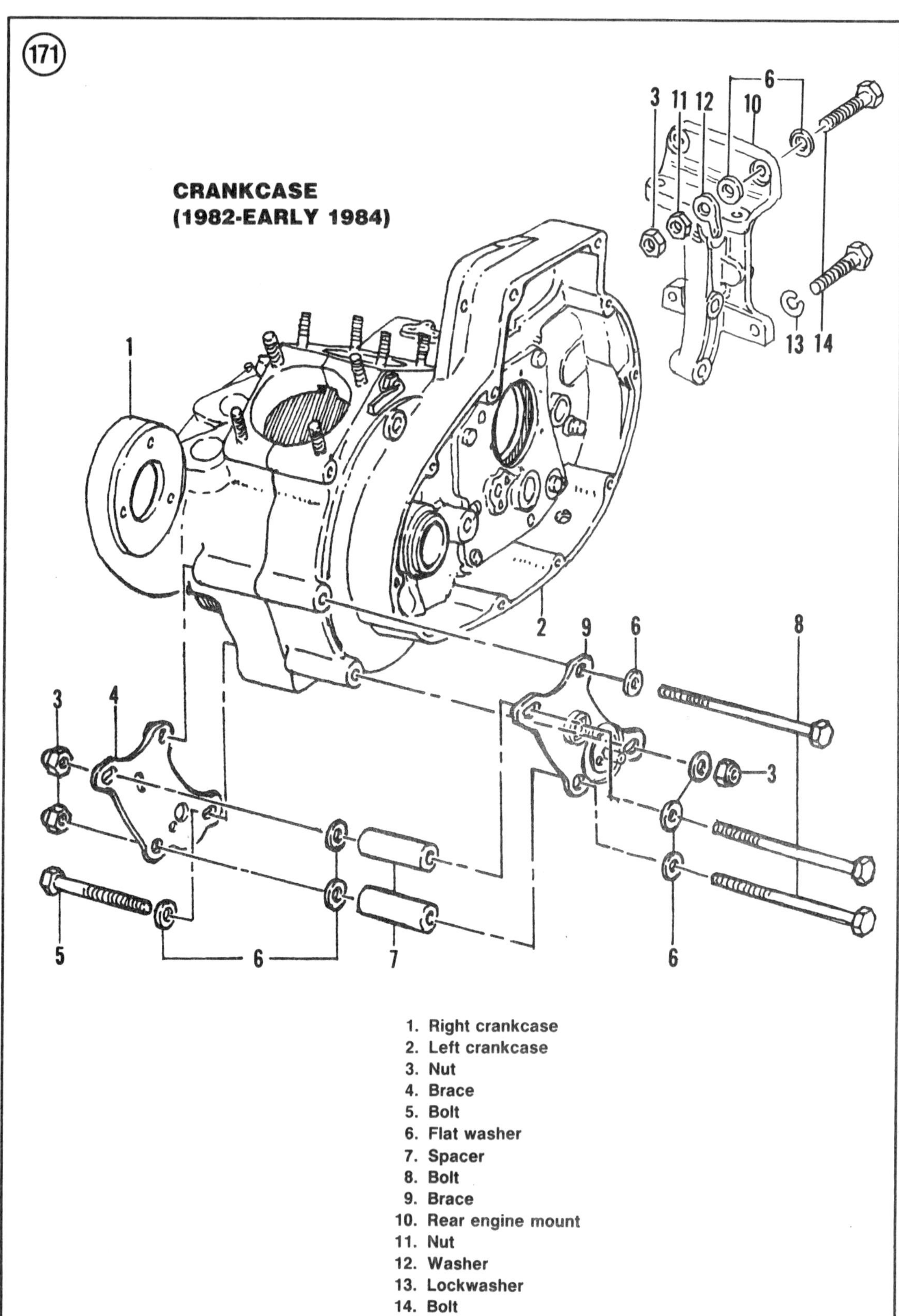
171
CRANKCASE
(1982-EARLY 1984)
1. Right crankcase
2. Left crankcase
3. Nut
4. Brace
5. Bolt
6. Flat washer
7. Spacer
8. Bolt
9. Brace
10. Rear engine mount
11. Nut
12. Washer
13. Lockwasher
14. Bolt

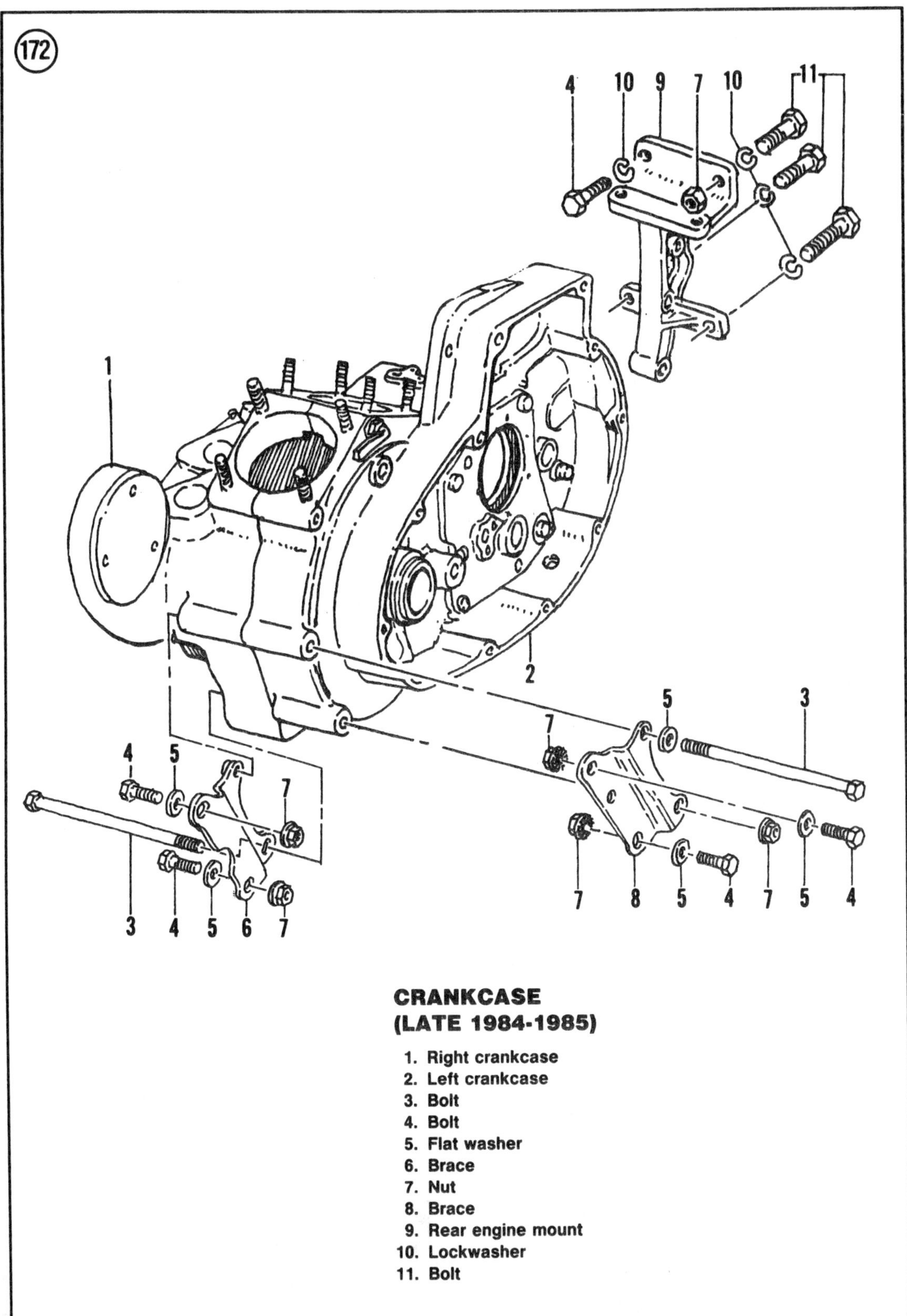

CRANKCASE (LATE 1984-1985)

1. Right crankcase
2. Left crankcase
3. Bolt
4. Bolt
5. Flat washer
6. Brace
7. Nut
8. Brace
9. Rear engine mount
10. Lockwasher
11. Bolt

within the specifications in **Table 1**, refer service to a Harley-Davidson dealer.

10. Refer crankcases to a Harley-Davidson dealer for inspection and repair.

11. Installation is the reverse of these steps, noting the following:

 a. If the crankshaft was removed, have it pressed into the left-hand crankcase by a Harley-Davidson dealer.
 b. Make sure rods are aligned as shown in **Figure 179** before assembling the right-hand crankcase.
 c. If the bearings and lock rings were removed, install them in the order shown in **Figure 166** or **Figure 167**.
 d. Coat the crankcase mating surfaces with Harley-Davidson Crankcase Sealant or RTV silicone sealant.
 e. Align the crankcase halves and install the right-hand crankcase (**Figure 176**).
 f. Install the crankcase bolts. Tighten bolts in a crisscross pattern until all are snug. Then tighten the bolts securely.
 g. On 1959-1977 models, install the sprocket shaft extension with the same tool used during removal.

173

174

175

176

177

178

179

180

DRIVE SPROCKET

Removal/Installation

1. Remove the sprocket cover (**Figure 180**).
2. Pry back the drive sprocket nut lockwasher tab.
3. Apply the rear brake and remove the sprocket nut (**Figure 181**). On late 1984-1985 models, remove the drive sprocket lock screw (**Figure 182**) before removing the sprocket nut.
4. Loosen the rear axle nut and loosen the chain adjusters.
5. Attach a puller onto the drive sprocket (**Figure 183**) and remove the sprocket.
6. Check the mainshaft oil seal (**Figure 184**). If leaking, replace it as described in this chapter.
7. Inspect the drive sprocket and drive chain as described in Chapter Three.
8. Installation is the reverse of these steps, noting the following.

9A. *1959-early 1984:* After tightening the sprocket nut, lock the nut with the lockwasher tab.

9B. *Late 1984-1985:* Install the lock screw after tightening the sprocket nut. Install the lock screw so that it rests against the flat side of the nut.

NOTE

On late 1984-1985 models, the drive sprocket nut may require additional

181

183

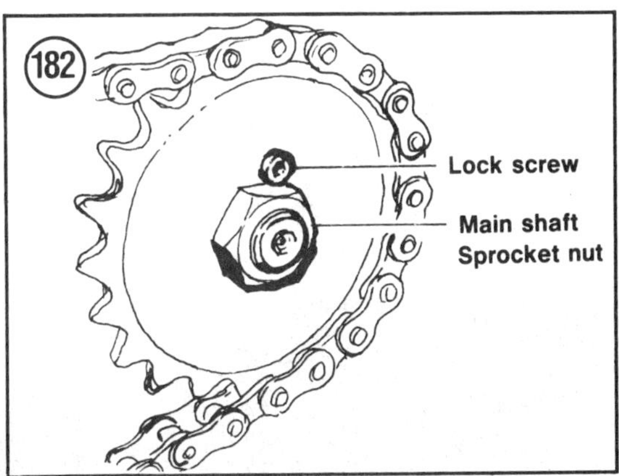

182

184

tightening so that the lock screw can be installed in one of the 3 sprocket lock screw holes. When tightening the nut, do not exceed 90 ft.-lb.

10. Adjust the drive chain as described in Chapter Three.

ENGINE SEALS

Replacement

Mainshaft oil seal—1959-early 1984

The mainshaft oil seal (**Figure 184**) can be replaced with the engine in the frame.

1. Remove the mainshaft oil seal housing (**Figure 184**).
2. Clean the crankcase mating surface (**Figure 185**) of all gasket residue.
3. Remove the old seal from the seal housing (**Figure 186**) or install a new housing and seal.
4. Installation is the reverse of these steps. Install a new seal housing gasket (**Figure 186**).

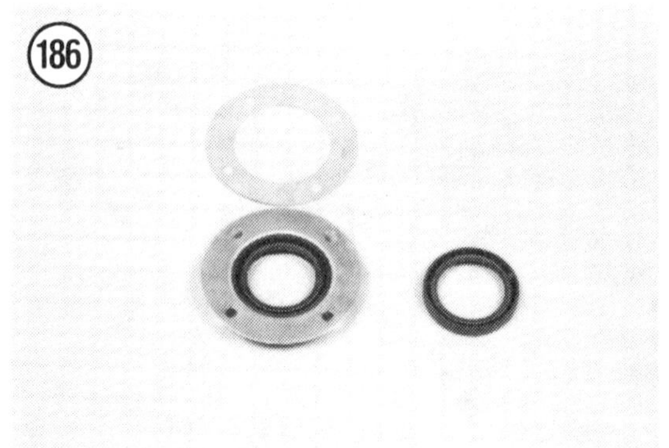

Mainshaft oil seal—late 1984-1985

The mainshaft oil seal can be replaced with the engine in the frame.

1. Remove the transmission as described in Chapter Five.
2. Carefully pry the old seal out of the crankcase.
3. Clean the mainshaft seal area thoroughly.
4. Install a new seal by driving it into the crankcase with a socket placed on the outside of the seal. Drive the seal in squarely.

Crankcase oil seal

The crankcase oil seal (**Figure 187**) can be replaced with the engine in the frame.

1. Remove the clutch as described in Chapter Five.
2. *1959-1976:* Remove the spring ring (9, **Figure 166**).
3. Carefully pry the old seal out of the crankcase (**Figure 188**).
4. Clean the crankcase seal area thoroughly.
5. Install a new seal by driving it into the crankcase with a socket placed on the outside of the seal (**Figure 189**). Drive the seal in squarely.
6. *1959-1976:* Install the spring ring (9, **Figure 166**).

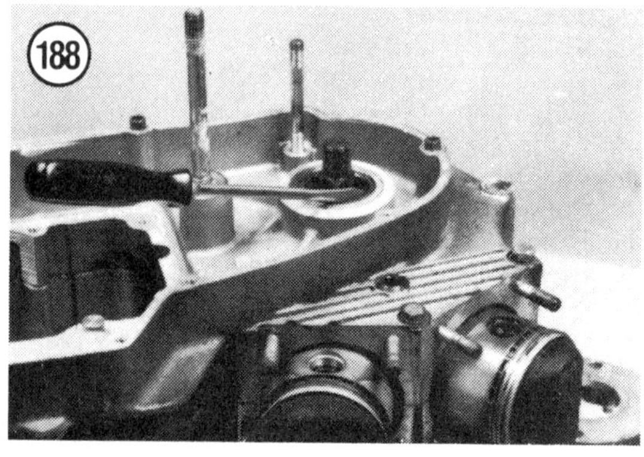

Gearcase cover seal

If necessary, replace the gearcase cover seal (**Figure 190**) by prying it out of the cover with a screwdriver. Install the new seal by driving it into the cover with a suitable size socket placed on the outside of the seal. Drive the seal in squarely.

STARTER DRIVE SHAFT AND HOUSING (1967-1980)

Removal/Disassembly

Refer to **Figure 191** for this procedure.

1. Remove the solenoid as described in Chapter Seven.
2. Remove the clutch as described in Chapter Five.
3. Rotate the shifter lever (25, **Figure 191**) and disengage it from the shifter collar (21).
4. Pull the pinion gear and shaft assembly (14) from the starter shaft housing.
5. Remove the drive gear (23) from the drive shaft (22).
6. If necessary, disassemble the pinion gear and shaft assembly (14) as follows:
   a. Remove the thrust washer (15).

NOTE
The pinion shaft nut (16) uses left-hand threads (tightens counterclockwise).

   b. Secure the pinion shaft nut (16) in a vise. Then turn the pinion shaft counterclockwise to

STARTER SHAFT, HOUSING AND SOLENOID (1967-1980) (191)

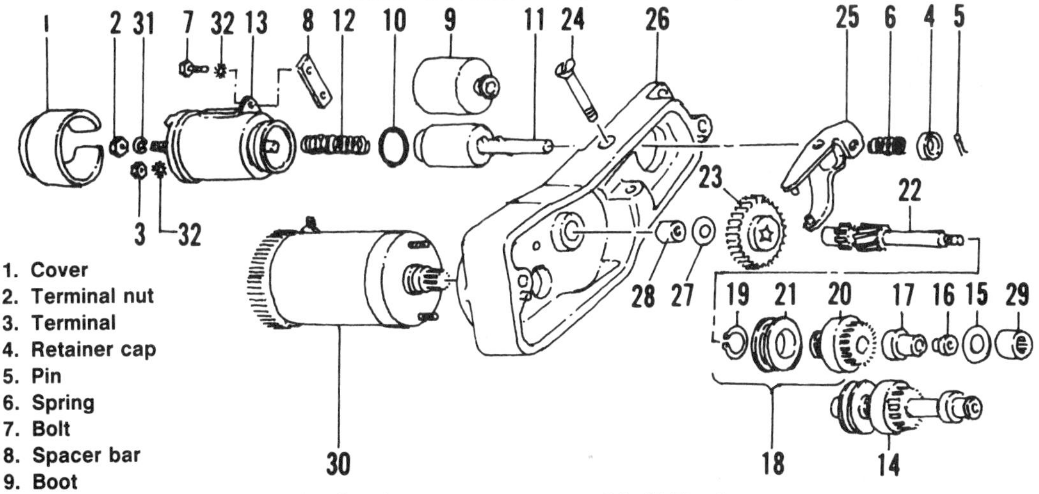

1. Cover
2. Terminal nut
3. Terminal
4. Retainer cap
5. Pin
6. Spring
7. Bolt
8. Spacer bar
9. Boot
10. Gasket
11. Plunger
12. Plunger spring
13. Solenoid
14. Pinion gear and shaft
15. Thrust washer
16. Pinion shaft nut
17. Bearing race
18. Pinion and shifter collar
19. Lock ring
20. Pinion gear
21. Shifter collar
22. Shaft
23. Drive gear
24. Shifter lever screw
25. Shifter lever
26. Starter shaft housing
27. Flat washer
28. Needle bearing
29. Needle bearing
30. Starter
31. Lockwasher
32. Lockwasher

b. ... remove the pinion shaft nut from the drive shaft.
c. Remove the bearing race (17) from the drive shaft.
d. Remove the pinion and shifter collar assembly (18) off of the drive shaft.
e. Remove the lock ring (19). Then separate the pinion gear (20) from the shifter collar (21).

NOTE
It is necessary to remove the starter housing (26) or the battery and carrier to gain access to the shifter lever screw (24) in order to remove the shifter lever.

7. Remove the bolts securing the starter shaft housing (26) to the engine and remove it and the starter as an assembly.
8. Remove the shifter lever screw (24) and remove the shifter lever (25) from the housing.
9. Assemble and install in the reverse order, noting the following.
10. The pinion gear (20) and drive shaft (22) should be assembled with no lubrication on the worm threads.
11. Apply Loctite Stud N' Bearing Mount onto the pinion shaft nut (16) before reassembly. Tighten the nut securely.

Inspection

1. Inspect all parts for wear and damage. Replace parts as necessary.
2. Inspect the starter housing needle bearings. If the bearings are worn or damaged have them replaced by a Harley-Davidson dealer or machine shop, as a press is required.

Table 1 ENGINE SPECIFICATIONS

General	
Type	Air cooled, 4-stroke, OHV, V-twin
Number of cylinders	2
Bore and stroke	
1959-1971	3.000×3.8125 in.
1972-1985	3.188×3.8125 in.
Displacement	
1959-1971	53.9 cu. in.
1972-1985	60.9 cu. in.
Compression ratio	
1959-1969	
XL	7.5:1
XLCH, XLH	9.0:1
1970-1981	9.0:1
1982	8.0:1
1983-1985	8.8:1
Lubrication	Force feed oiling system
Cylinder	
Cylinder taper	0.008 in.
Out-of-round	0.002 in.
Valves	
Fit in guide	
Exhaust	0.0025-0.0045 in.
Intake	0.0015-0.0035 in.
Valve spring free length	
1959-early 1983	
Outer	1 1/2 in.
Inner	1 23/64 in.
Late 1983-1985	
Outer	1 9/16 in.
Inner	1 11/32 in.

(continued)

Table 1 ENGINE SPECIFICATIONS (continued)

Rocker arm	
Fit in bushing	
1959-1969	0.0005-0.002 in.
1970-1978	0.001-0.0025 in.
1979-1985	0.0005-0.0025 in.
Piston	
Clearance	
1959-1969	0.0025-0.003 in.
1970-1985	0.003-0.004 in.
Wear limit (all)	0.006 in.
Piston pin fit	Light hand press @ 70°
Piston rings	
End gap	
1959-1969	0.010-0.020 in.
1970-1978	0.015-0.025 in.
1979-1982	0.010-0.031 in.
1983-1985	
1st	0.008-0.022 in.
2nd	0.008-0.030 in.
Side clearance	
1959-1969	
Compression	0.0025-0.004 in.
Oil	0.003-0.005 in.
1970-1978	0.0035-0.005 in.
1979-1985	
Compression	0.004-0.006 in.
Oil	0.003-0.006 in.
Connecting rod	
End play	
1959-1969	0.006-0.010 in.
1970-1978	0.005-0.015 in.
1979-1985	0.005-0.030 in.
Fit on crank	
1959-1969	0.0008-0.001 in.
1970-1978	0.0005-0.0015 in.
1979-1985	0.001-0.007 in.
Tappets	
Guide fit	
1959-1978	0.0005-0.001 in. (press)
1979-1985	0.001-0.002 in.
Roller fit	
1959-1978	0.0005-0.001 in.
1979-1985	0.0005-0.0012 in.
Roller end clearance	
1959-1978	0.008-0.010 in.
1979-1985	0.008-0.012 in.
Tappet clearance	Free (no lash) with engine cold
Gearcase	
Intermediate gear shaft in bushing	
1959-1978	0.0005-0.001 in.
1979-1985	0.0005-0.003 in.
Cam gear shaft in bushing	
1959-1978	0.0005-0.002 in.
1979-1985	0.0005-0.003 in.
Cam gear shaft in needle bearing	
1959-1969	0.0005-0.0025 in.
1970-1985	0.0005-0.003 in.

(continued)

4

Table 1 ENGINE SPECIFICATIONS (continued)

Cam gear end play	
1959-1969	0.001-0.006 in.
1970-1976	0.001-0.005 in.
1977-1978	
Rear intake	0.004-0.010 in.
All others	0.005-0.012 in.
1979-1985	
Rear intake	0.004 in.
All others	minimum 0.005 in.
Cam gear backlash	
1959-1969	Not specified
1970-1985	0.000-0.0005 in.
Flywheel	
Flywheel runout (maximum)	
1959-1969	0.002 in.
1970-1978	0.003 in.
1979-1985	0.006 in.
End play (maximum)	0.001 in.
Mainsháft runout (maximum)	
1959-1969	0.001 in.
1970-1985	0.002 in.
Sprocket Shaft Bearing	
Cup fit in crankcase	
1959-1978	0.0005-0.0025 in.
1979-1985	0.0004-0.0024 in.
Cone fit on shaft	
1959-1969	0.0002-0.0012 in.
1970-1985	0.0002-0.0015 in.
End play	
1959-1969	0.001-0.010 in.
1970-1978	0.001-0.007 in.
Pinion gear shaft bearing	
Shaft fit in roller bearing	
1959-1969	0.0008-0.001 in.
1970-1985	0.0005-0.0015 in.
Shaft fit in cover bushing	
1959-1969	0.0005-0.0012 in.
1970-1985	0.0005-0.0015 in.

Table 2 TIGHTENING TORQUES (1959-1978)

Item	ft.-lb.
Cylinder head	65
Cylinder base nuts	30
Rocker arm cover	20
Tappet adjusting locknut	8-10
Rear motor mount bolt/nut	16-24

Table 3 TIGHTENING TORQUES (1979-1984)

Item	ft.-lb.
Gear shaft nut	100-120
Sprocket shaft nut	100-120
Cylinder head bolts	55-65
Cylinder base nuts	25-35
Rocker arm cover screw	14-19
Tappet adjusting locknut	6-11
Rear motor mount bolt and nut	16-24
Oil pump mounting screws	90-110 in.-lb.

CHAPTER FIVE

CLUTCH, PRIMARY DRIVE, TRANSMISSION AND KICKSTARTER

This chapter describes service procedures for the clutch, primary drive, kickstarter and transmission. **Tables 1-9** are at the end of the chapter.

CLUTCH

Clutch Removal (1959-1970)

Refer to **Figure 1** for this procedure.

1. On electric start models, disconnect the battery negative cable to prevent accidental starter operation.
2. Remove the left footpeg.
3. Disconnect the stoplight switch and remove the rear brake lever.
4. Place an oil drain pan underneath the chain cover. Remove the chain cover and its gasket and allow the oil to drain in the pan.
5. Remove the clutch cover screws and retainers. Then remove the clutch cover and its gasket.
6. Remove the 7/16 in. nuts (5, **Figure 1**) and the 1/2 in. nuts (6, **Figure 1**).
7. Remove the spring tension adjusting plate (4).
8. Remove the springs (3), backing plate cups (2) and the releasing disc (1).
9. Remove one friction plate (12) and one driven plate (11). Then continue and remove all plates. Stack plates in order of removal.
10. Remove the backing plate (28).
11. Remove the front chain adjuster brace and the 3 chain adjuster screws (1, **Figure 2**).
12. Install a suitable tool between the clutch sprocket and the engine sprocket to prevent these sprockets from turning. A wooden wedge works well. See 5, **Figure 2**.
13. Pry back the locking tabs on the clutch hub nut lockwasher (25, **Figure 1**).
14. Remove the left clutch release rod through the clutch nut. See 10, **Figure 3**.
15. Secure the clutch hub (24, **Figure 1**) with a special tool like the "Grabbit." See **Figure 4**.
16. Remove the clutch hub nut (26 or 27, **Figure 1**) and lockwasher (25).
17. Pry the oil seal (22 or 23) from the clutch housing with a screwdriver.
18. Remove the clutch hub, using Harley-Davidson puller No. 95960-52 (**Figure 5**).
19. On 1967 XLH models, remove the O-ring from the groove in the end of the mainshaft.
20. Remove the compensating sprocket shaft nut with Harley-Davidson wrench No. 94557-55 (**Figure 5**).
21. Remove the compensating sprocket, primary chain and clutch shell as a unit.
22. On 1959-1966 models, pry out the O-ring (34, **Figure 1**) from the clutch gear extension. Remove the gear extension (35) by tapping the side of the extension.

Clutch Inspection (1959-1970)

1. Clean all clutch parts in a non-oil based solvent and thoroughly dry with compressed air.

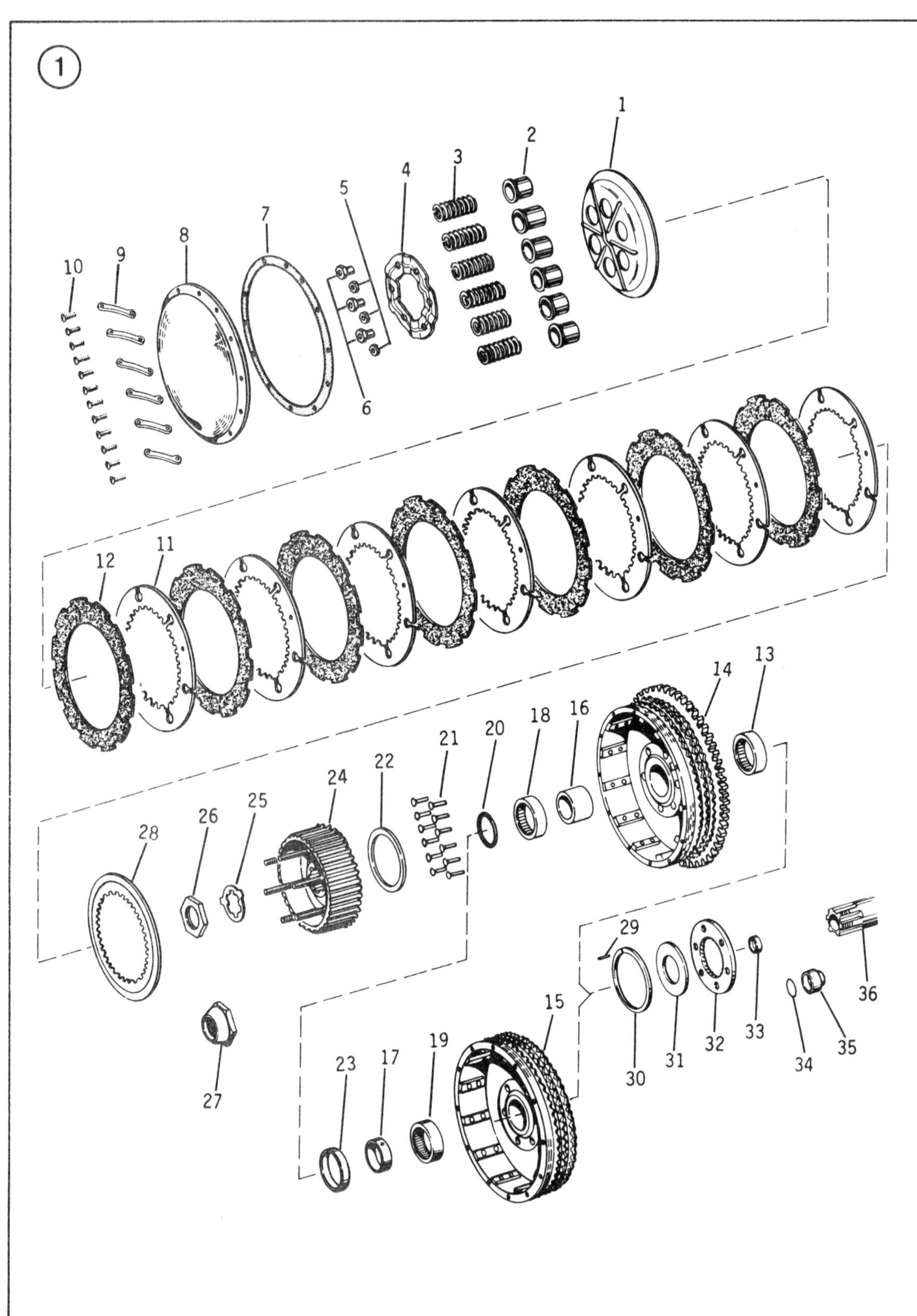
1
1
2
3
4
5
6
7
8
9
10
11
12
13
14
15
16
17
18
19
20
21
22
23
24
25
26
27
28
29
30
31
32
33
34
35
36

CLUTCH ASSEMBLY (1970 AND EARLIER)

1. Releasing disc
2. Backing plate cups
3. Clutch springs
4. Pressure plate
5. Short hub stud nuts
6. Long hub stud nuts
7. Clutch cover gasket
8. Clutch cover
9. Clutch cover screw retainers
10. Clutch cover screws
11. Driven plates
12. Friction drive plates
13. Needle bearing (two on 1967-1970 XLH)
14. Clutch shell (1967-1970 XLH)
15. Clutch shell (1967 XLCH, all 1966 and earlier)
16. Clutch hub spacer (1967-1970 XLH)
17. Clutch hub spacer
18. Needle bearing (two on 1967-1970 XLH)
19. Needle bearing (1967 and all 1966 and earlier)
20. Clutch hub O-ring (1967-1970 XLH)
21. Sprocket rivets
22. Clutch hub oil seal (1967-1970 XLH)
23. Clutch hub oil seal (1967 XLCH and all 1966 and earlier)
24. Clutch hub assembly
25. Hub nut lockwasher
26. Hub nut (1967-1970 XLH)
27. Hub nut (1967 XLCH and all 1966 and earlier)
28. Backing plate
29. Sprocket hub washer pin
30. Sprocket hub washer
31. Sprocket bearing washer
32. Starter clutch
33. Clutch gear (push rod) oil seal
34. Clutch gear extension o-ring (1967 XLCH and 1966 and earlier)
35. Clutch gear extension
36. Clutch gear

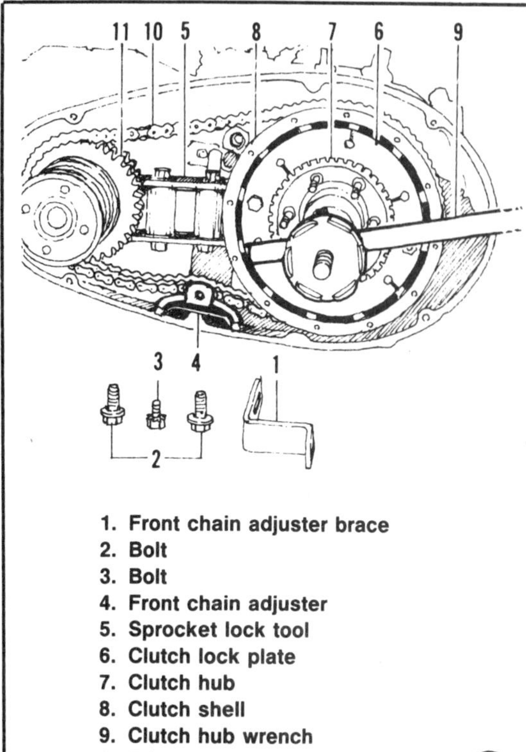

1. Front chain adjuster brace
2. Bolt
3. Bolt
4. Front chain adjuster
5. Sprocket lock tool
6. Clutch lock plate
7. Clutch hub
8. Clutch shell
9. Clutch hub wrench
10. Primary chain
11. Compensating sprocket

(2)

2. Measure the free length of each clutch spring as shown in **Figure 6**. Replace any springs that are too short (**Table 1**).
3. Inspect friction plates for wear, deep grooves or oil soaking. Plates which show one or more of these conditions should be replaced. Replace all friction discs if any one is found too thin. Plates that are in good condition can be sanded with a medium grade emery cloth.
4. Check the metal driven plates for warpage as shown in **Figure 7**. If any plate is warped excessively, replace the entire set of plates. Plates that have turned blue from heat, but are otherwise smooth and in good condition, can be reused after cleaning thoroughly.
5. Check the release disc for wear, grooving or scoring. Replace if necessary.
6. Check the clutch hub spacer for appreciable play in the bearing. Replace the bearing if necessary.
7. Check the teeth on the clutch shell. Check also for worn or loose keys and rivets. If the clutch shell is damaged, it should be replaced. However, if the only apparent damage is a loose rivet, a new rivet can be installed. Set rivets until they are flush to 0.010 in. (maximum) above starter face or 0.080 in.

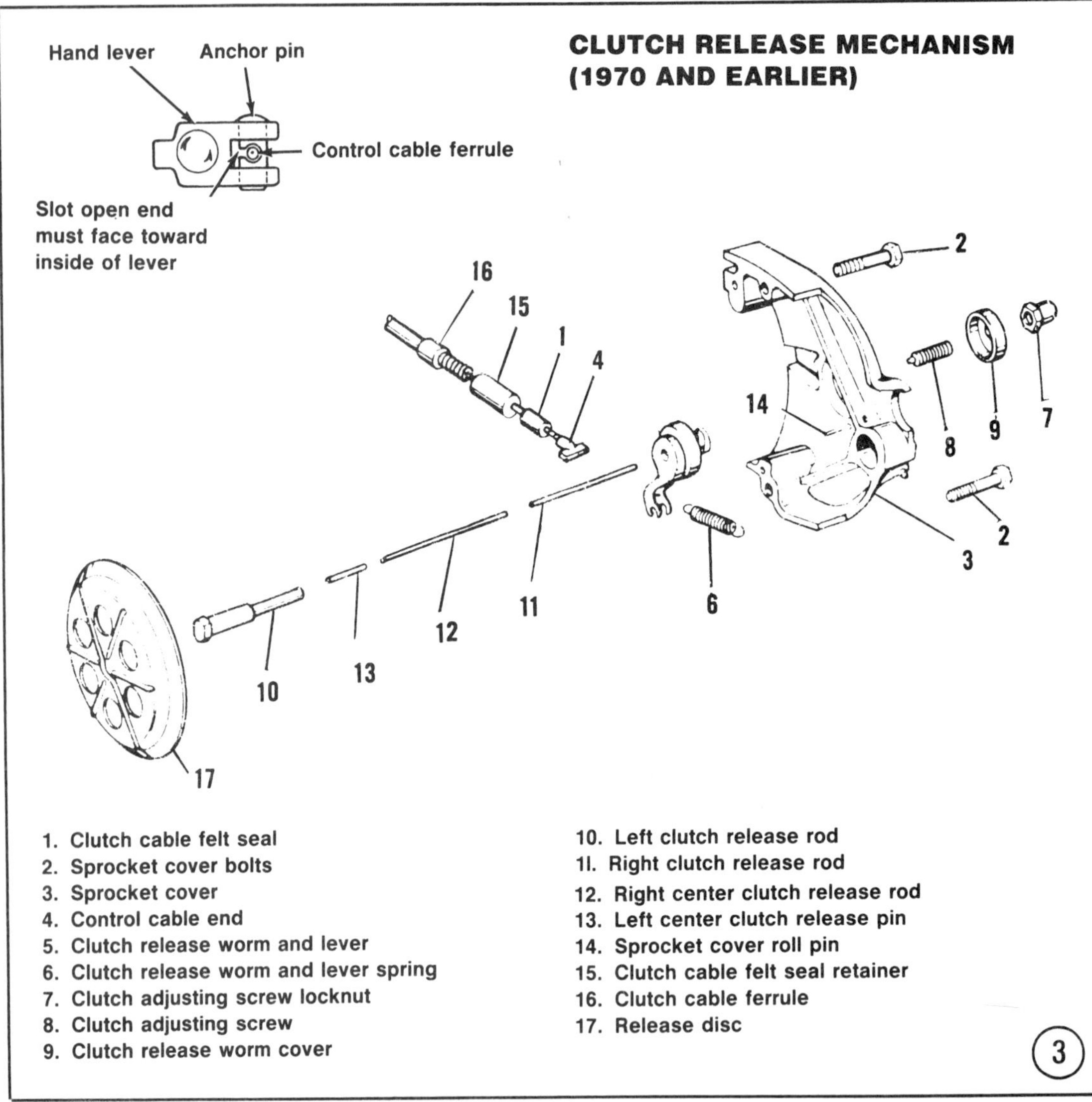

between rivet head and bottom of sprocket tooth for rivets which secure keys. Seal rivets on both sides after installation, using a solvent-proof sealer.

8. Inspect starter clutch teeth for wear or damage. If worn or damaged, replace as described under *Clutch Sprocket Needle Bearing and Starter Clutch Replacement* in this chapter.

Compensating Sprocket Inspection (1959-1970)

1. Clean all parts in non oil-based solvent such as lacquer thinner, then blow dry. Do not use an oil-based solvent to clean these parts.
2. Check the sprocket teeth, shaft splines and the cam surfaces for wear. Replace any worn or damaged part.

NOTE
The sprocket shaft extension and the sprocket sliding cam are available only as a matched set.

3. Check the spring tension. If the spring is worn or damaged, the cam action will be very rough.

Clutch Installation (1959-1970)

Refer to **Figure 1** for this procedure.

1. Make sure all parts are clean, dry and free of oil.
2. On 1959-1966 models, press the clutch gear extension (35) into the end of the main shaft. Apply aluminum paint (used as a sealer) to the extension before installation.
3. Install a new oil seal in the end of the extension (33).

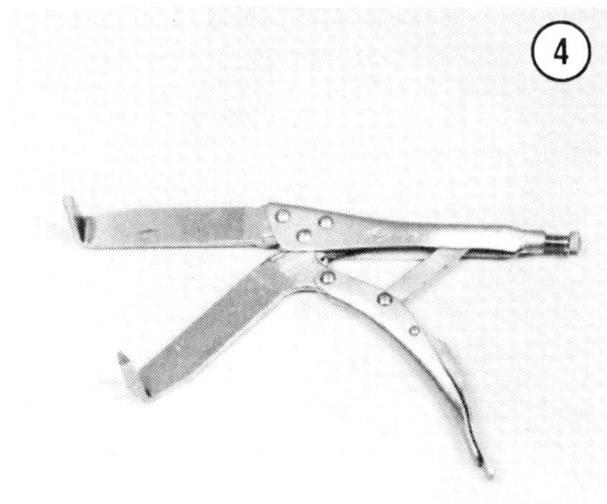

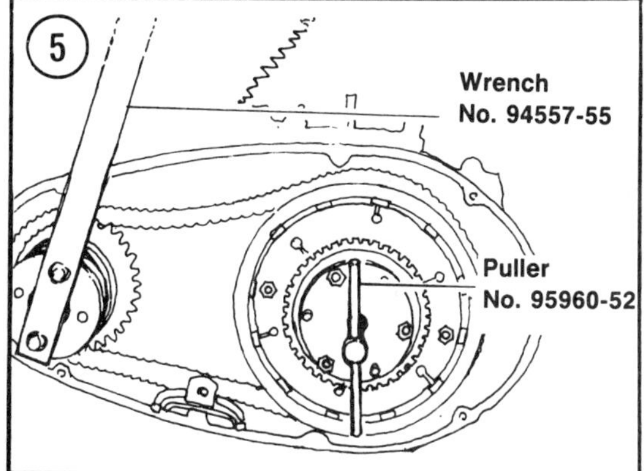

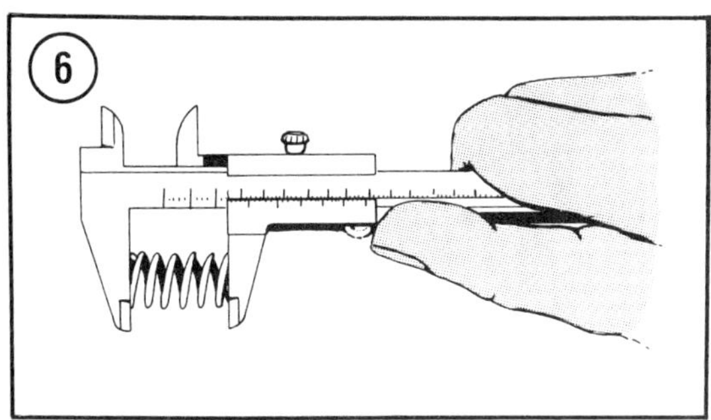

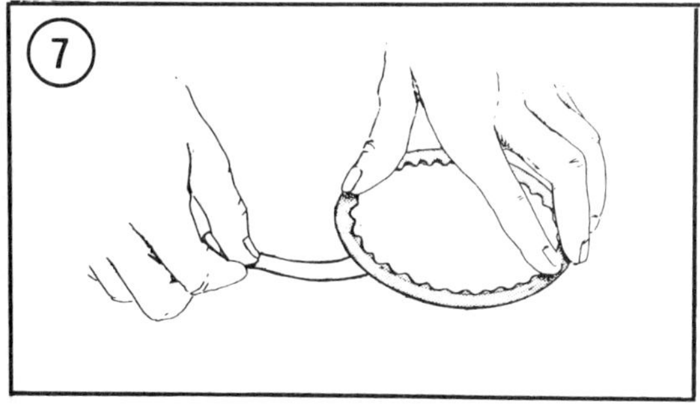

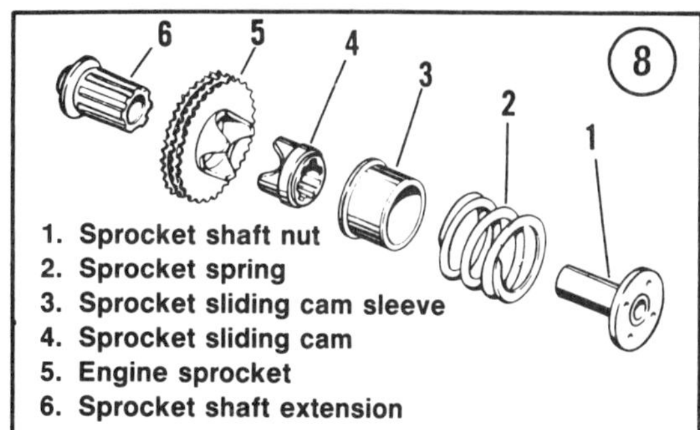

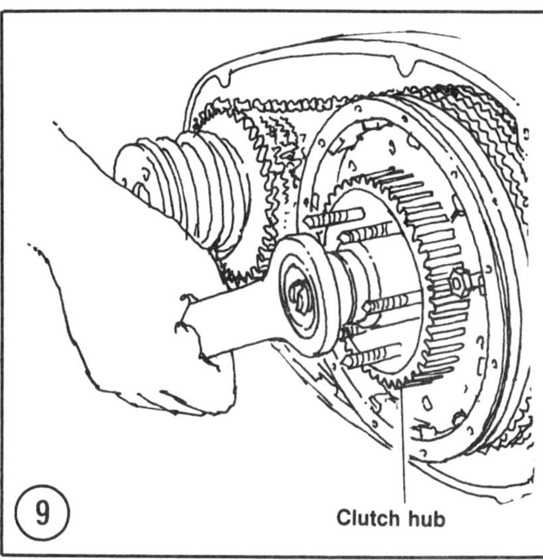

4. Insert the left clutch release rod (10, **Figure 3**) into the main shaft.
5. Apply a light coat of grease to the compensating sprocket shaft extension (**Figure 8**) and to the clutch shell roller bearing(s).
6. Install the clutch hub spacer (16 or 17) into the clutch shell.
7. Install a new O-ring on the main shaft.
8. Install the primary drive chain over the clutch shell sprocket and the compensating sprocket. Then install the parts as one assembly. Make sure the chain adjuster is positioned behind the chain.
9. Assemble the compensating sprocket assembly in the order shown in **Figure 8**. Tighten the sprocket with the same tool used to remove the sprocket during disassembly (**Figure 5**).
10. Install the clutch hub using the Harley-Davidson clutch hub tool (part number 97170-55A). See **Figure 9**.
11. Lock the clutch and engine sprockets as during disassembly (**Figure 2**).
12. Secure the clutch hub with the same tool used during disassembly (**Figure 2** and **Figure 4**).

13. Install a new clutch hub lockwasher. Install and tighten the clutch hub nut to 150 ft.-lb. Bend the lockwasher tabs against the hub nut to lock it. Check that the clutch hub spins freely on the main shaft.

CAUTION
If the starter clutch, clutch gear or clutch shell were replaced, it is necessary to check the clearance between the starter clutch gear and the starter clutch. See ***Kickstarter, Starter Clutch Gear/Starter Clutch Clearance*** *in this chapter.*

14. Adjust the primary chain tension as described in Chapter Three.
15. Install the backing plate (28).
16. Install a driven plate (11), then a friction plate (12). Continue to install all plates in order (**Figure 1**).
17. Install the release disc (1) onto the clutch hub. Make sure the clutch hub studs are centered with the clutch spring cup holes in the pressure plate. This alignment is easily made by aligning the largest depression on the pressure plate rim with the notched tooth in the clutch hub.
18. Install the backing plate cups (2) and springs (3). Install the pressure plate with the raised surface facing outward.
19. Install the three 1/2 in. nuts on their respective studs. Tighten these nuts in a crisscross pattern until the spring tension adjusting plate is pulled over the remaining 3 studs enough to allow the smaller nuts to be installed.
20. Tighten the 6 nuts in a crisscross pattern until the inside of the spring tension adjusting plate is 3/16 in. from the outside surface at each spring cup flange. Do not decrease the spring tension measurement to less than 7/64 in. or the clutch will not release.
21. Install the clutch cover with a new gasket. Install the gasket (without sealer) so that the gasket's graphite side faces the cover.

CAUTION
Do not hit the clutch cover hard with a hammer during installation. This may distort the cover and cause oil leakage.

22. Install the clutch cover retainers and screws. Lightly stake each retainer to its screw.
23. Install the primary chain cover using a new gasket. Coat both sides of the gasket with sealer.
24. Install the rear brake pedal, stoplight switch and footpeg.
25. Refill the primary case with the correct type and quantity oil. See Chapter Three.

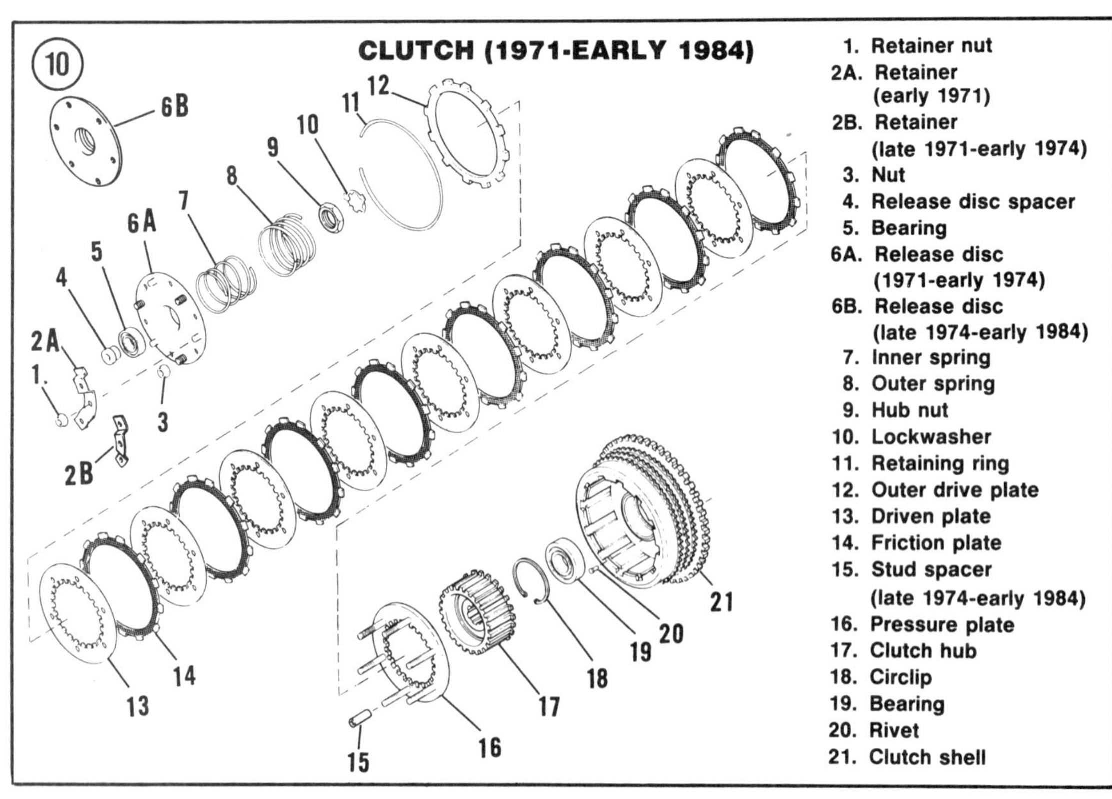

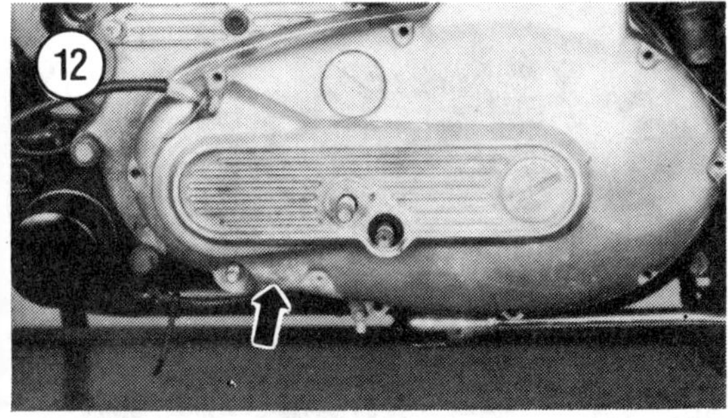

Clutch Sprocket Needle Bearing and Starter Clutch Replacement (1959-1970)

A hydraulic or arbor press is required for this procedure.

1. Remove the oil seal from the front of the clutch shell.
2. Remove the rivets from the clutch shell. Then remove the following parts in order:
   a. Starter clutch.
   b. Sprocket bearing washer.
   c. Sprocket hub washer.
3. Press the needle bearing(s) and pin out of the clutch shell.

NOTE
1967 XLH models use 2 clutch shell needle bearings.

4. Clean the clutch shell bearing bore with solvent before installing new bearing(s).
5. On models with one bearing, press the bearing in from the inside to a depth of 0.025-0.029 in. measured from the clutch shell inner face to the edge of the bearing. Press on printed side of bearing only. The sprocket hub washer pin should extend 0.08 in. from the top of the pin to the sprocket shell.
6. On models with 2 bearings, press in first bearing until its inner face is 0.010-0.015 in. from the clutch shell. Then from the starter clutch side, press second bearing until it is flush against first bearing.
7. Place clutch shell on workbench so that gear end faces up. Install washer on roll pin.
8. Install one or more bearing washers in the clutch shell. (These washers are available in thickness increments of 0.002 in.) Then install the starter clutch on the clutch shell back plate. With the back plate held down (under pressure), measure clearance between the variable washer and the starter clutch. Select washer to obtain a clearance of 0.001-0.004 in.

NOTE
When determining washer thickness, note that pull of rivets will take up approximately 0.001 in.

9. Install new rivets from inside the clutch shell. Peen rivets until they are flush to 0.010 in. (maximum) above starter clutch face. Seal both sides of rivets with a solvent-proof sealer.

Clutch Removal (1971-early 1984)

Refer to **Figure 10** for this procedure.

1. Disconnect the battery negative cable to prevent accidental starter operation.
2. Remove the left footpeg and the gearshift lever. See **Figure 11**.
3. Place a drain pan underneath the chain cover.
4. Remove the chain case drain plug (if so equipped) to drain the chain case oil. If bike is not equipped with a drain plug, allow oil to drain when the chain case cover is removed in Step 5.
5. Remove the chain case cover (**Figure 12**) and its gasket.
6. Install a spring compression tool (H-D 97178-71) onto the crankcase as shown in **Figure 13**. Compress the releasing disc to remove tension from nuts. Remove the nuts (**Figure 14**).
7. Remove the release disc (**Figure 15**).
8. Remove the inner and outer springs (**Figure 16**) and remove the compression tool.

5

9. Remove the retaining ring (**Figure 17**) from the clutch shell.

10. Remove the outer drive plate (**Figure 18**).

11. Remove one driven plate (**Figure 19**) and one friction plate (**Figure 20**). Continue until all plates are removed in order.

12. Remove the pressure plate (**Figure 21**). On 1974 and later models, stud spacers (**Figure 22**) are used on the pressure plate. Remove and store these parts until reassembly.

13. *1971-1978:* Remove the front chain adjuster brace and the 3 chain adjuster screws.

14. Install a suitable tool between the clutch sprocket and the engine sprocket to prevent these sprockets from turning. A wooden wedge works well.

15. Pry back the locking tabs on the clutch hub lockwasher (**Figure 23**).

16. Secure the clutch hub with a special tool like the "Grabbit." See **Figure 4**.

17. Remove the clutch hub nut (**Figure 23**) and lockwasher.

18. Remove the clutch hub (**Figure 24**) using a suitable puller (**Figure 25**).

19A. *1971-1976:* Remove the compensating sprocket shaft nut (**Figure 8**) using

Harley-Davidson tool No. 94557-55. See **Figure 5**. Then remove the compensating sprocket, primary chain and clutch shell as a unit.

19B. *1977-early 1984*: Remove the engine sprocket nut (**Figure 26**). Then remove the engine sprocket, primary chain and clutch shell as a unit. See **Figure 27**. Account for any shims or spacers.

NOTE

*If the engine sprocket is tight, it will be necessary to attach a puller to the sprocket tapped holes (**Figure 28**) and pull the sprocket off.*

Clutch Inspection (1971-early 1984)

1. Clean all clutch parts in a non-oil based solvent such as lacquer thinner and thoroughly dry with compressed air.
2. Measure the free length of each clutch spring as shown in **Figure 29**. Replace any springs that are too short (**Table 1**).

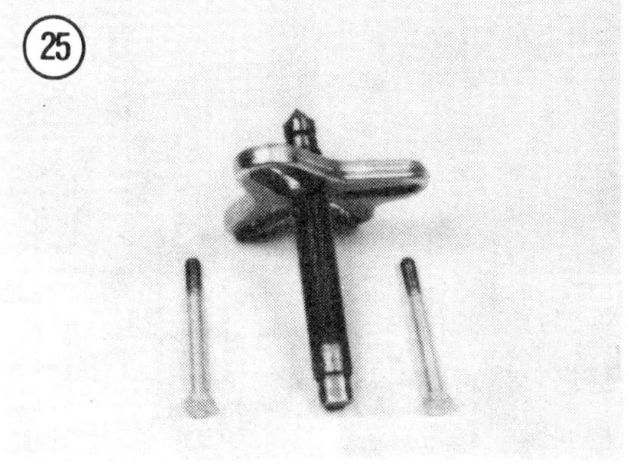

5

3. Inspect friction plates (A, **Figure 30**) for wear, deep grooves or oil soaking. Plates which show one or more of these conditions should be replaced. Replace all friction plates if any one is found too thin. Plates that are in good condition can be sanded with medium grade sandpaper.
4. Check the metal driven plates (B, **Figure 30**) for warpage as shown in **Figure 7**. If any plate is warped excessively, replace the entire set of plates. Plates that have turned blue from heat, but are otherwise smooth and in good condition, can be reused after cleaning thoroughly.
5. Check the bearing (**Figure 31**) in the clutch shell. If any roughness or excessive play is detected, have the bearing pressed out by a dealer or machine shop and a new bearing installed.
6. Check the clutch shell for worn splines (A, **Figure 32**), loose rivets, worn sprocket teeth (B, **Figure 32**) or damaged ring gear teeth. See **Figure 33** and **Figure 34**. If damage or wear is detected, replace the clutch shell.
7. Check the engine sprocket (**Figure 8** or **Figure 35**) for worn sprocket teeth and splines. Replace the sprocket if necessary.
8. Inspect the primary chain (**Figure 36**) for loose plate rivets or signs of wear or damage. Replace the chain if necessary.

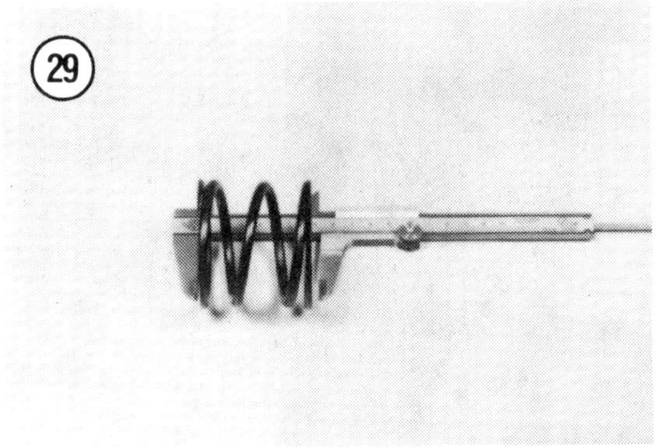

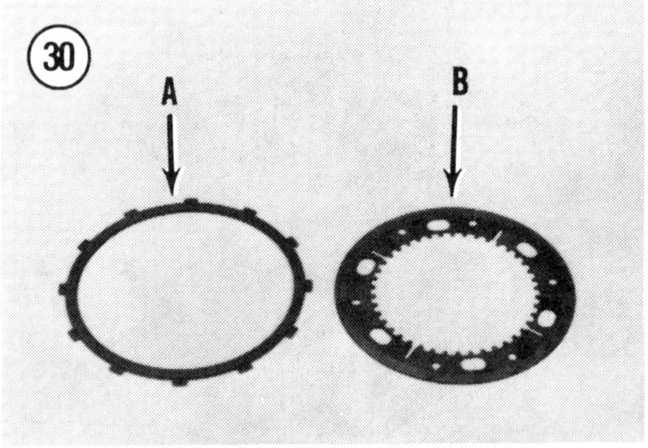

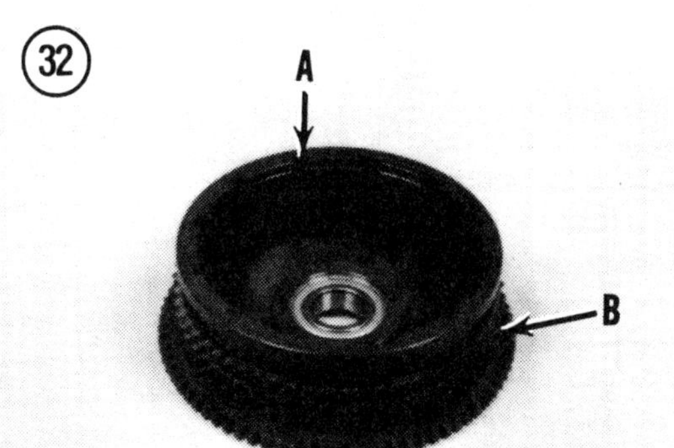

NOTE

*If any component in Steps 7-9 was replaced because of teeth or chain wear, replace all 3 components (**Figure 37**) to prevent premature wear to the new part.*

9. Examine the releasing disc bearing (**Figure 38**) as described in Step 6. If necessary, have the bearing replaced by a dealer or machine shop with access to a press.
10. Check the outer drive plate retaining ring (**Figure 39**) for cracks, scoring or excessive wear. Replace the ring if necessary.
11. Inspect the clutch hub splines (**Figure 40**) for wear or damage.
12. Inspect the pressure plate (**Figure 41**) studs for damage or looseness. Check the inner splines for wear or damage.

5

Compensating Sprocket Inspection (1971-1976)

1. Clean all parts in non-oil based solvent such as lacquer thinner, then blow dry. Do not use an oil-based solvent to clean these parts.

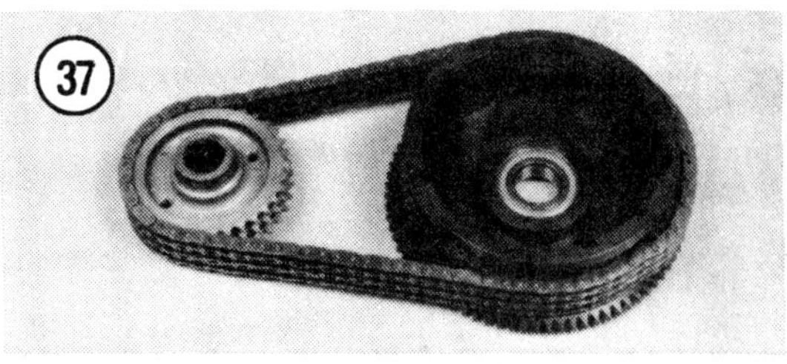

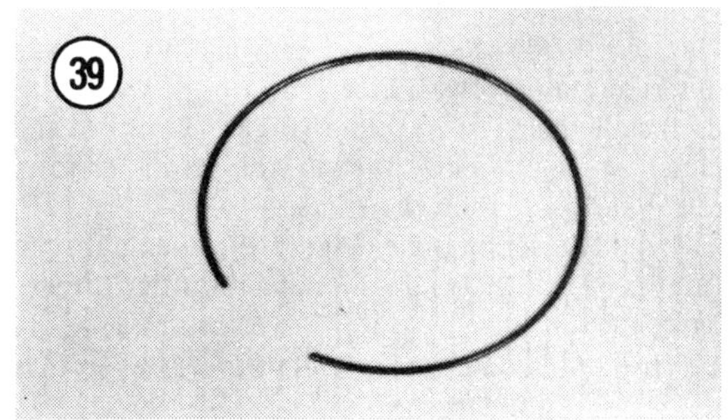

2. Check the sprocket teeth, shaft splines and the cam surfaces for wear. Replace any worn or damaged part.

NOTE
The sprocket shaft extension and the sprocket sliding cam are available only as a matched set.

3. Check the spring tension. If the spring is worn or damaged, the cam action will be very rough.

Clutch Installation (1971-early 1984)

Refer to **Figure 10** for this procedure.

NOTE
When performing this procedure, use the same tools and procedures to secure the clutch components as used during removal.

1. Make sure all parts are clean.
2. Install the primary drive chain over the clutch shell sprocket and the compensating sprocket or engine sprocket (**Figure 37**). Then install the parts as one unit. Make sure the chain adjuster is positioned behind the chain (**Figure 42**).
3. *1971-1976:* Assemble the compensating sprocket in the order shown in **Figure 8**.
4. *1977-early 1984:* Tighten the engine sprocket nut (**Figure 26**).
5. Install the clutch hub (**Figure 24**).
6. Install a new clutch hub lockwasher. Install and tighten the clutch hub nut to 150 ft.-lb. Bend the lockwasher tabs against the hub nut to lock it. Check that the clutch hub spins freely on the main shaft.

CAUTION
*If the starter clutch, clutch gear or clutch shell was replaced on kickstarter models, it is necessary to check the clearance between teeth on the starter ratchet gear and starter ratchet. See **Kickstarter, Starter Clutch Gear/ Starter Clutch Clearance** in this chapter.*

7. *1971-1978:* Adjust the primary chain tension as described in Chapter Three.
8. Install the pressure plate (**Figure 21**) over the clutch hub splines. Install the stud spacers (1974-early 1984) on the studs.
9. Install a friction plate (**Figure 20**), then a driven (**Figure 19**) plate. Install all plates in order (**Figure 10**).
10. Install the outer drive plate (**Figure 18**) so that the friction side faces in.

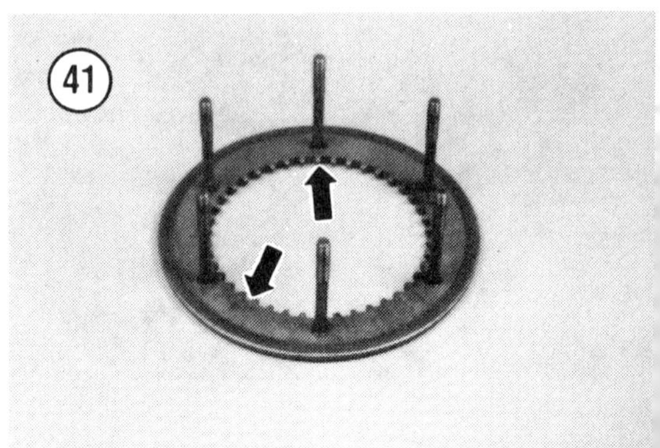

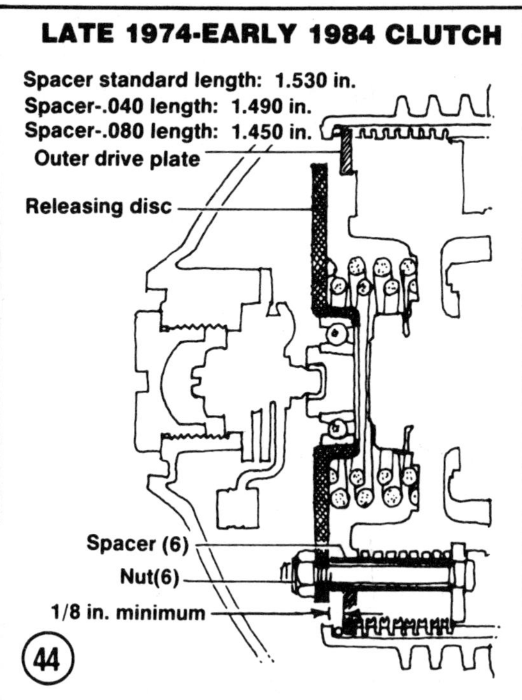

1. Install the retaining ring (**Figure 17**) in the lutch shell. Make sure the ring seats completely in he groove.
2. Install the clutch spring compressor tool used luring disassembly. Install the inner and outer lutch springs (**Figure 16**) and the release disc Figure 15) under the tool screw.
3. Compress the tool so that the pressure plate tuds enter the holes in the releasing disc enough so hat the nuts can be threaded on the studs. After tarting all of the nuts (**Figure 14**), remove the ompression tool.
4. Adjust the spring tension as follows:
   a. *1971-early 1974:* Tighten each pressure plate nut (**Figure 43**) 1/2 turn at at time until the releasing disc outer surface is 11/32 in. from the outer drive plate surface. When tightening the nuts, make sure that the specified dimension is not less than 5/16 in., or the clutch may not release.
   b. *Late 1974-early 1984:* Tighten the 6 releasing disc nuts evenly until they bottom out. There should be 1/8 in. minimum clearance between the drive plate outer surface and the releasing disc inner surface (**Figure 44**).

NOTE
*To compensate for wear, the stock spacer sleeves can be replaced with shorter sleeves. See **Figure 44**.*

15. Install the primary chain cover using a new gasket.
16. *1979-early 1984:* Adjust the primary chain as described in Chapter Three.
17. Adjust the clutch release mechanism as described in Chapter Three.
18. Install the rear brake pedal, stoplight switch and footpeg.
19. Refill the primary case with the correct type and quantity of oil. See Chapter Three.

Clutch Removal/Installation (Late 1984-1985)

NOTE
*This procedure describes removal of the complete clutch assembly only. If the clutch must be disassembled to gain access to the clutch plates, refer to **Clutch Disassembly/Inspection/Assembly, Late 1984-1985** in this section for further details.*

Refer to **Figure 45** for this procedure.

1. Disconnect the negative battery cable.
2. Place a drain pan under the primary cover and remove the oil filler plug and the drain plug. Allow the oil to drain.
3. Remove the gearshift pedal and the left footpeg.
4. Loosen the locknut (**Figure 46**) and unscrew the adjuster to loosen the primary drive chain.
5. Remove the clutch access plug (1, **Figure 45**) and remove the adjusting screw spring (3) and lockplate (4).
6. Remove the primary chain cover (**Figure 47**) and gasket.
7. Remove the clutch adjusting screw circlip (6) and remove the guide (8) and adjusting screw assembly (10).
8. Remove the engine sprocket nut (**Figure 48**).

CAUTION
Do not attempt to disassemble the clutch assembly after removing it from the bike. The clutch must be disassembled while mounted on the engine.

NOTE
*If complete disassembly of the clutch is required, refer to **Clutch Disassembly/Inspection/Assembly, Late 1984-1985**.*

9. Remove the clutch circlip (24) and spacer (23). Then remove the clutch assembly, primary chain and engine sprocket as an assembly. See **Figure 49**.

NOTE
*If necessary, use a puller as shown in **Figure 50** to loosen the engine sprocket.*

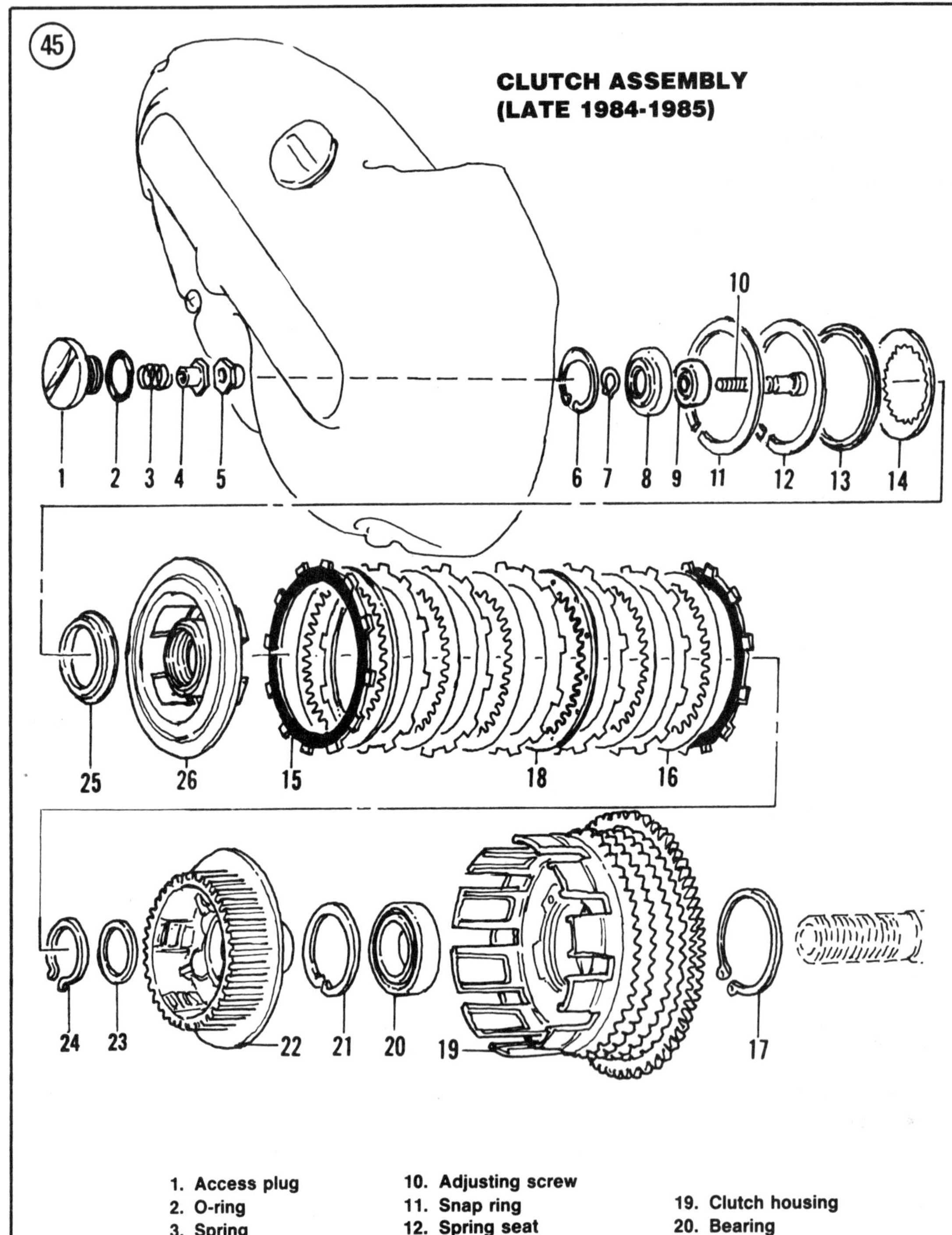

1. Access plug
2. O-ring
3. Spring
4. Lockplate
5. Nut
6. Circlip
7. Circlip
8. Guide
9. Bearing
10. Adjusting screw
11. Snap ring
12. Spring seat
13. Spring seat
14. Clutch spring
15. Friction plate
16. Drive plate
17. Circlip
18. Spring plate
19. Clutch housing
20. Bearing
21. Circlip
22. Clutch boss
23. Spacer
24. Circlip
25. Inner clutch spring seat
26. Pressure plate

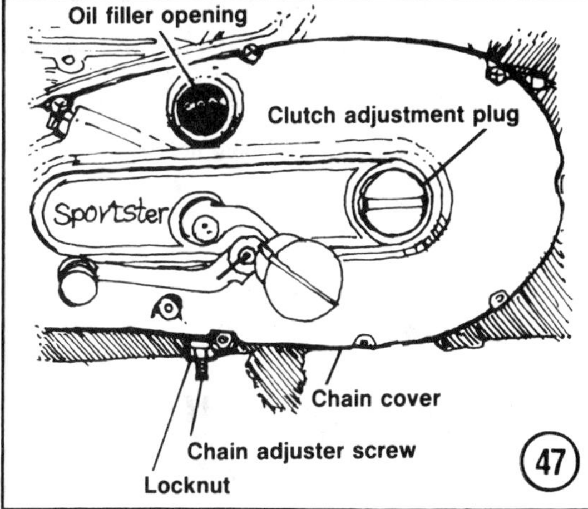

10. Installation is the reverse of steps 1-9 noting the following:
   a. Install a new clutch adjuster screw circlip.
   b. Tighten the engine sprocket nut to 150-165 ft.-lb.
   c. Adjust the clutch as described in Chapter Three.
   d. Adjust the primary chain as described in Chapter Three.

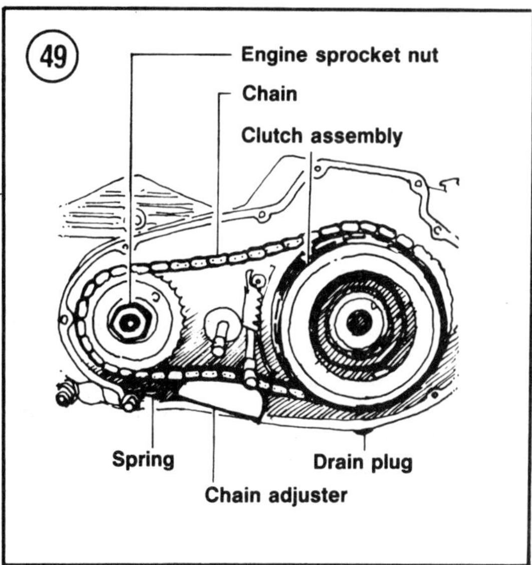

   e. Refill the primary case and transmission with oil as described in Chapter Three.

Clutch Disassembly/Inspection/ Assembly (Late 1984-1985)

1. Perform Steps 1-6 under *Clutch Removal/Installation, Late 1984-1985.*

WARNING
Do not attempt to disassemble the clutch assembly without the use of the special Harley-Davidson tool described in Step 2. The snap ring is held under considerable pressure and will fly off if pressure is not first removed.

2. Referring to **Figure 51**, install the Harley-Davidson spring compression tool (HD-34761) onto the clutch assembly. Secure the compression tool with a nut threaded on the adjusting screw. Tighten the nut securely.
3. Turn the adjusting screw counterclockwise until the compression tool releases the pressure on the snap ring (**Figure 51**). Remove the snap ring. Now turn the adjusting screw clockwise and remove the nut and compression tool.
4. Refer tp **Figure 45**. Disassemble the clutch housing by removing the following parts in order:
   a. Adjusting screw assembly (7-10).
   b. Outer clutch spring seats (12 and 13).
   c. Clutch spring (14).
   d. Inner clutch spring seat (25).
   e. Pressure plate (26).
5. Remove the clutch plates in the order shown in **Figure 45**.

5

6. Remove the clutch circlip (21). Then remove the clutch housing, primary chain and engine sprocket as an assembly.

NOTE
If necessary, use a puller as shown in ***Figure 50*** *to loosen the engine sprocket.*

7. Remove the circlip (17) and separate the clutch boss from the clutch housing.
8. Inspect the clutch components as described under *Clutch Inspection, 1971-early 1984* in this chapter. Refer to **Table 2** for clutch specifications.
9. Installation is the reverse of disassembly, noting the following.
10. Install a new clutch adjuster screw retaining ring.
11. Tighten the engine sprocket nut to 150-165 ft.-lb.
12. Assemble the clutch plates by installing a friction plate, then a drive plate and then alternating until all plates are installed. The spring plate (18, **Figure 45**) is installed between the third and fourth friction plates from the clutch housing.
13. Install the pressure plate (26) in the clutch housing. Then slip the inner spring seat (25) over the pressure plate hub with the concave side facing toward the pressure plate.
14. Place the clutch spring (14) onto the clutch boss (22).
15. Install the U-shaped outer spring seat (13) and the flat spring seat (12) in the pressure plate (26).
16. Install the adjusting screw assembly and secure it with the circlip.
17. Install the Harley-Davidson spring compression tool (HD-34761) onto the clutch assembly. Secure the compression tool with a nut threaded on the adjusting screw. Tighten the nut securely. See **Figure 51.**
18. Turn the adjusting screw counterclockwise until the clutch spring is fully compressed. Then install a new snap ring (11). Make sure the snap ring is seated completely in the groove before removing the nut and compression tool.
19. Adjust the clutch as described in Chapter Three.
20. Adjust the primary chain as described in Chapter Three.
21. Refill the primary case and transmission with oil as described in Chapter Three.

PRIMARY CHAIN

Removal/Installation

Remove the primary chain as described under clutch removal for your model in this chapter.

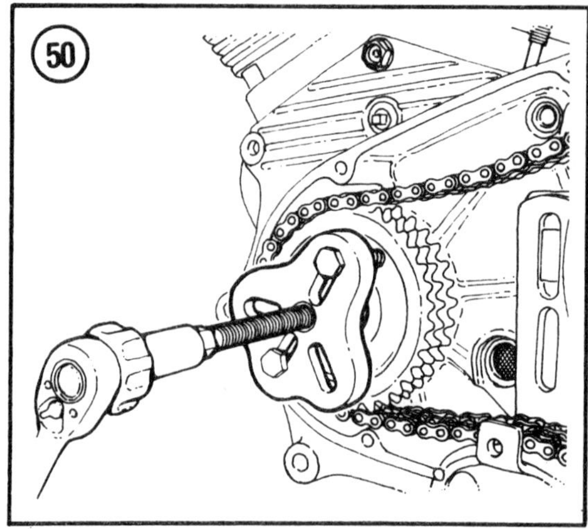

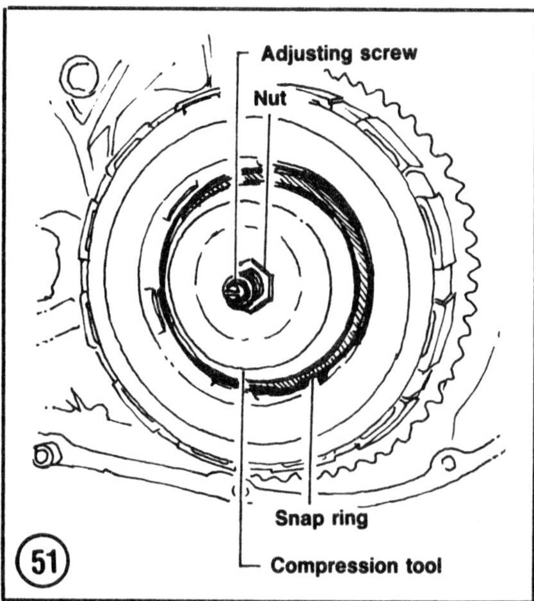

Adjustment

Refer to Chapter Three for complete adjustment procedures.

KICKSTARTER

Refer to **Figure 52** for this procedure.

Service Notes

A clicking noise from the kickstarter gears with the engine running and the kickstarter pedal upright indicates an immediate service problem. This noise is usually caused by the starter clutch gear teeth (3, **Figure 52**) making partial contact with the starter clutch (2) teeth. This condition can be caused by a loose starter shaft nut (6), excessive

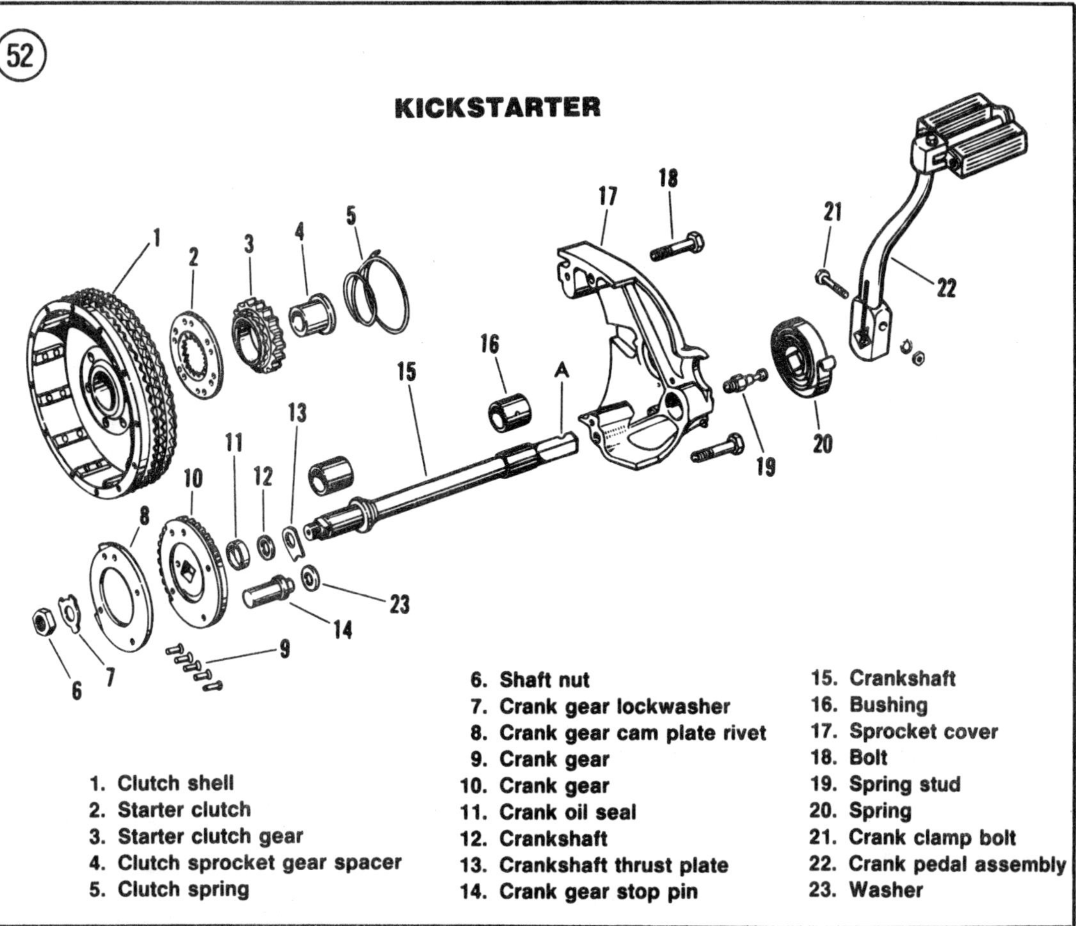

1. Clutch shell
2. Starter clutch
3. Starter clutch gear
4. Clutch sprocket gear spacer
5. Clutch spring
6. Shaft nut
7. Crank gear lockwasher
8. Crank gear cam plate rivet
9. Crank gear
10. Crank gear
11. Crank oil seal
12. Crankshaft
13. Crankshaft thrust plate
14. Crank gear stop pin
15. Crankshaft
16. Bushing
17. Sprocket cover
18. Bolt
19. Spring stud
20. Spring
21. Crank clamp bolt
22. Crank pedal assembly
23. Washer

kickstarter shaft (15) end-play or a loose starter crank gear cam plate (8).

If the kickstarter crank (22) slips or only partially engages when cranking the engine, check for a badly worn starter clutch (2 and 3), damaged or weak clutch spring (5) or the clutch gear (3) binding on the clutch sprocket gear spacer (4).

Removal

1. Remove the kickstarter pedal (22, **Figure 52**).
2. Remove the right-hand footpeg.
3. Remove the rear brake master cylinder (if so equipped) as described in Chapter Ten. Do not disconnect the hydraulic line.
4. Loosen the exhaust pipe and muffler.
5. Remove the sprocket cover.
6. Remove the clutch as described in this chapter.
7. Rotate the crank gear (10) to free the starter clutch gear (3), spacer (4) and spring (5).
8. Remove the shaft nut (6) and its lockwasher.
9. Tap the end of the kickstarter shaft to loosen the crank gear (10). Remove the crank gear.
10. Remove the kickstarter shaft (15), oil seal (11), thrust plate (13) and shims (12) (if used).

Inspection

1. Clean all parts in solvent and allow to dry.
2. Inspect for badly worn or damaged teeth on the starter ratchet gear and the starter clutch. Replace if there is any doubt about gear tooth condition. Replace the starter clutch if necessary.
3. Examine the bushing face on the starter ratchet gear for burrs or other damage which could affect free movement of the clutch sprocket spacer. Check for binding between these parts by assembling gear on spacer.
4. Check the ratchet spring for fatigue or breakage. Replace the spring if its free length is less than 1 in.
5. Check that the kickstarter shaft is not bent or badly worn, particularly on the thrust plate and shaft collar surfaces.

5

NOTE
Step 6 describes how to measure the kickstarter shaft end play.

6. Install the kickstarter shaft into the left-hand crankcase. Then assemble the shim, oil seal and crank gear on end of shaft. Secure these parts with the kickstarter shaft lockwasher and nut. Measure the kickstarter shaft end play with a dial indicator. If the end play is not within the specified limits of 0.001-0.007 in., it is necessary to install a 0.007 in. shim between the crankcase and the thrust plate as indicated in **Figure 53**.
7. Check the crank gear for wear or damage; replace if necessary.
8. Examine ears on the cam plate for bending or wear. Check cam plate rivets for looseness. Cam plate rivets may be replaced, provided gear is in good condition. Install new rivets from the gear side.
9. Check the kickstarter shaft oil seal for wear or damage; replace if necessary.
10. Replace the kickstarter shaft lockwasher if worn or damaged.
11. If the kickstarter shaft is not worn, but shows significant looseness in the transmission cover and left crankcase bushings, the bushings should be replaced by a Harley-Davidson dealer or machine shop. Bronze bushings are pressed into the transmission cover and the left crankcase.
12. Check the stop pin (14, **Figure 52**) and washer for damage. If replacement is required, the engine must be removed from the frame, and the crankcases separated, as described in Chapter Four.

NOTE
The stop pin is a press fit. If replacement is necessary, you can save considerable expense by removing the engine and splitting the crankcases as described in Chapter Four. Then refer stop pin replacement to a Harley-Davidson dealer or machine shop.

Installation

1. Install the oil seal (11) into the left-hand crankcase.
2. Slip the thrust plate (13) onto the kickstarter shaft. Turn the thrust plate so that the flat side faces upward as positioned on bike.
3. Install the kickstarter shaft into the left crankcase. Engage the notch on the thrust plate (13)

53

with the stop pin washer (23). If necessary, apply grease to the thrust plate to hold it in position.

4. Turn the kickstarter shaft in the crankcase until the notch (A, **Figure 52**) is positioned at the top (12 o'clock position).

5. Install the crank gear (10) onto the end of the kickstarter shaft. When installing gear, the cam plate (8) recessed portion must face downward (**Figure 54**) with the slot end against the stop pin (11).

NOTE

When installing the cam gear, make sure the thrust plate (13) does not disengage from its position on the stop pin washer (23).

6. Install the lockwasher (7) onto the end of the kickstarter shaft. Engage prong on lockwasher with hole on face of crank gear. Install the shaft nut (6) with the flat side facing toward the lockwasher. Tighten nut to 55-65 ft.-lb.

7. Install the starter clutch gear (3) over the spacer (4) with grooved side of gear bushing against spacer collar lip.

8. Install the ratchet spring (5) so that the small spring end fits into groove in the clutch gear bushing.

54

55

9. Install the starter clutch gear assembly over the clutch gear, compressing spring (5), and at the same time, turn the crank gear (10) to permit meshing of gear teeth.

10. Return crank gear to its installed position (**Figure 54**), with the starter clutch gear held against the cam plate by spring tension.

11. Operate the kickstarter shaft and make sure there is play between the starter clutch gear and the crank gear throughout the entire engagement range.

12. Install the clutch assembly as described in this chapter.

13. Install the transmission sprocket cover.

14. Install the exhaust pipe and muffler.

15. Install the rear master cylinder (if so equipped) as described in Chapter Ten.

16. Install the kickstarter shaft.

5

Starter Clutch Gear/Starter Clutch Clearance

If the starter clutch gear, starter clutch, clutch gear or clutch sprocket hub is replaced, it is necessary to check the clearance between the starter clutch and the starter clutch gear. Refer to **Figure 52** for this procedure.

1. Measure the distance from top of the starter clutch gear teeth to the end of the clutch sprocket spacer.

2. On the clutch sprocket assembly, measure the distance between the clutch sprocket thrust washer to the top of the starter teeth.

3. Subtract the measurement obtained in Step 2 from that obtained in Step 1 to obtain the clearance.

4. If clearance is less than 0.040 in., install a suitable length clutch sprocket gear spacer (4, **Figure 52**). Long and short spacers are available from Harley-Davidson dealers.

TRANSMISSION

Transmission specifications are found in **Tables 3-9** (end of chapter).

Access Cover/Transmission Removal

1. Drain the engine oil as described in Chapter Three.

2. Remove the clutch as described in this chapter.

3. Remove the drive sprocket as described in Chapter Four.

4. Remove the kickstarter assembly as described in this chapter.

5. Remove the transmission access cover bolts. See **Figure 55** (1959-early 1984) or **Figure 56** (late 1984-1985).

6. Remove the access cover (**Figure 57**) with the transmission and shift mechanism assembly attached. See **Figure 58**.
7. Remove the shift lever (**Figure 59**).
8. *1959-early 1984:* Remove the 23 roller bearings (**Figure 60**) from the right-hand crankcase.

Transmission Disassembly

Refer to **Figure 61** (1959-early 1984) or **Figure 62** (late 1984-1985) for this procedure.
1. Remove the main shaft thrust washer (**Figure 63**).
2. Remove the main shaft first gear (**Figure 64**).
3. Pull the main shaft and third gear from the access cover (**Figure 65**).
4. Refer to **Figure 66**. Remove the retaining ring and washer (A), then slide third gear (B) off of the main shaft.
5. Remove the following from the countershaft:
   a. First gear washer (**Figure 67**).
   b. First gear (**Figure 68**).
   c. Second gear washer (**Figure 69**).
6. Remove the shift fork shaft (**Figure 70**).
7. Remove the shift fork (**Figure 71**) from the countershaft third gear.
8. Remove the finger rollers (**Figure 72**) from the shift fork.
9. Remove countershaft third gear (**Figure 73**).
10. Remove main shaft second gear (**Figure 74**).
11. Remove the shift fork shaft (**Figure 75**). Then remove the finger rollers (**Figure 72**) from the shift fork.
12. Pull the countershaft (**Figure 76**) from the access cover.

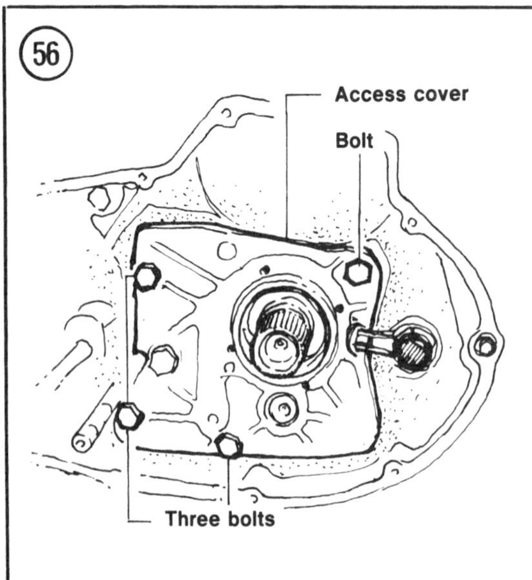

TRANSMISSION (1959-EARLY 1984) (61)

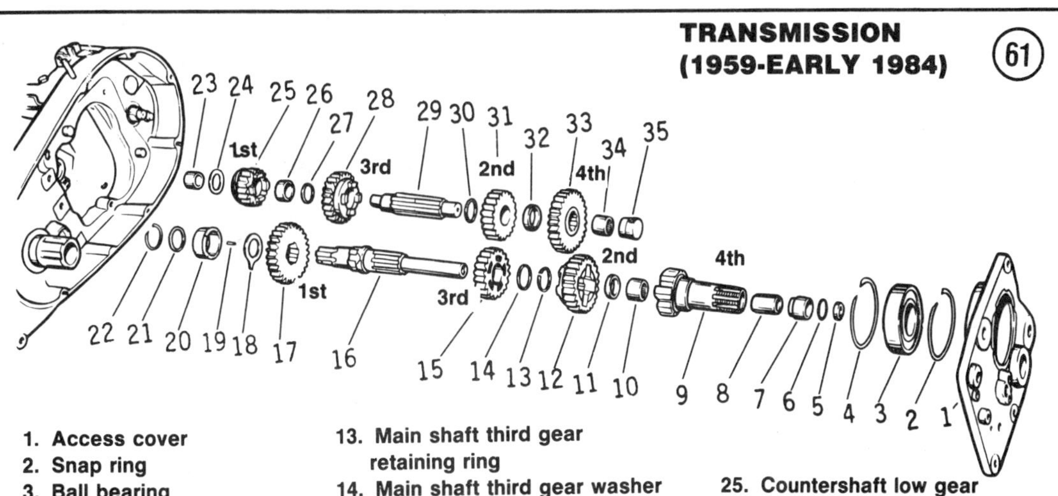

1. Access cover
2. Snap ring
3. Ball bearing
4. Snap ring
5. Clutch gear oil seal (1959-1970)
6. Clutch hub nut o-ring (1959-1970)
7. Clutch gear oil seal
8. Clutch gear bushing
9. Clutch gear
10. Clutch gear needle bearing
11. Main shaft thrust washer
12. Main shaft second gear
13. Main shaft third gear retaining ring
14. Main shaft third gear washer
15. Main shaft third gear
16. Main shaft
17. Main shaft low gear
18. Main shaft thrust washer
19. Main shaft rollers
20. Main shaft roller bearing race
21. Main shaft roller bearing washer
22. Main shaft roller bearing retaining ring
23. Countershaft bearing
24. Countershaft low gear washer
25. Countershaft low gear
26. Countershaft low gear bushing
27. Countershaft low gear washer
28. Countershaft third gear
29. Countershaft
30. Countershaft second gear thrust washer
31. Countershaft second gear
32. Countershaft gear spacer
33. Countershaft fourth gear
34. Countershaft bearing
35. Oil plug

TRANSMISSION (LATE 1984-1985) (62)

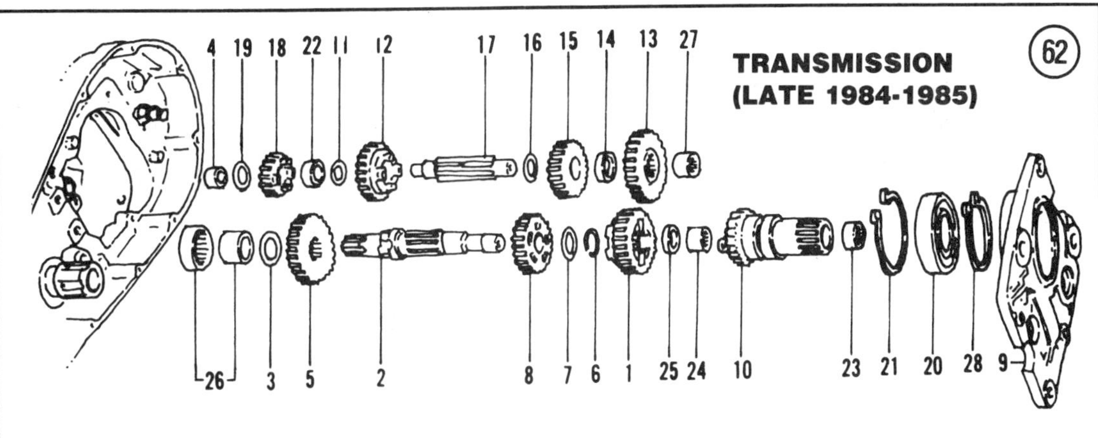

1. Main shaft 2nd gear
2. Main shaft
3. Thrust washer
4. Bearing
5. Main shaft 1st gear
6. Circlip
7. Washer
8. Mainshaft 3rd gear
9. Access cover
10. Clutch gear
11. Thrust washer
12. Countershaft 3rd gear
13. Countershaft 4th gear
14. Spacer
15. Countershaft 2nd gear
16. Thrust washer
17. Countershaft
18. Countershaft 1st gear
19. Washer
20. Bearing
21. Snap ring
22. Bearing
23. Bearing
24. Bearing
25. Thrust washer
26. Bearing
27. Bearing
28. Snap ring

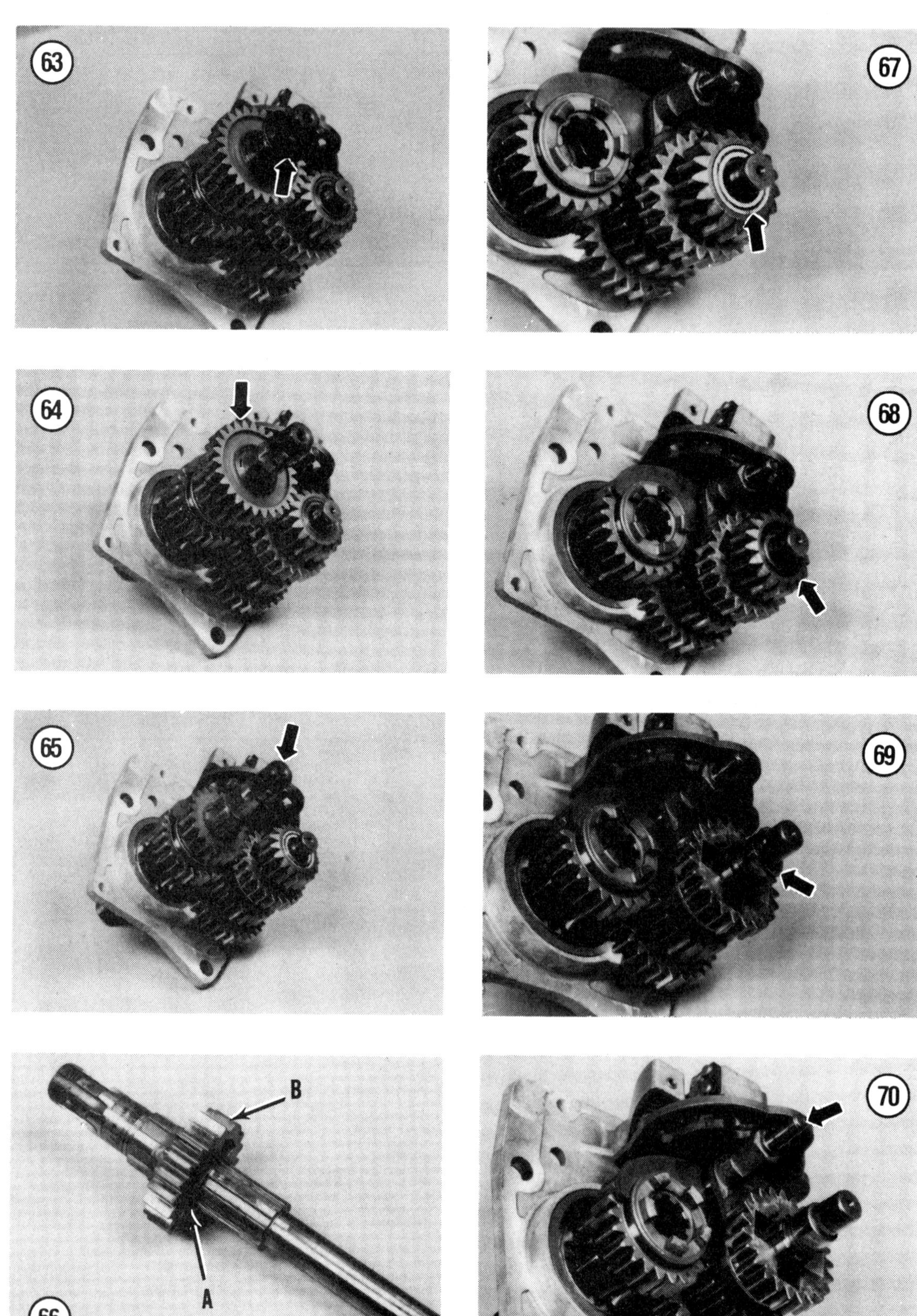
63
67
64
68
65
69
B
A
66
70

71

72

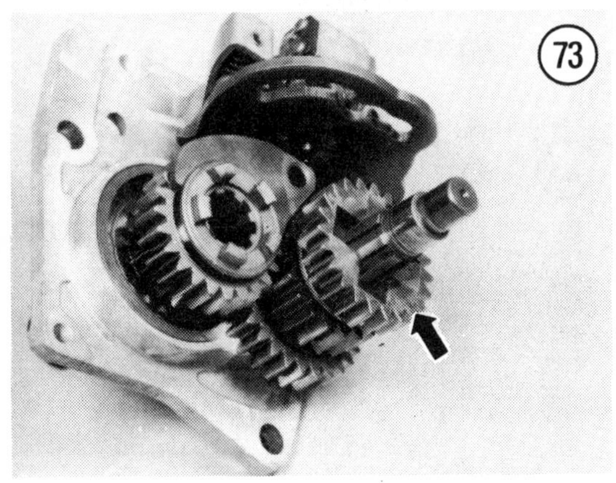
73

74

13. Remove the following from the countershaft:
   a. Fourth gear (**Figure 77**).
   b. Spacer (**Figure 78**).
   c. Second gear (**Figure 79**).
   d. Thrust washer (**Figure 80**).
14. Remove the clutch gear from the access cover as follows:
   a. Remove the snap ring (**Figure 81**).
   b. Tap the clutch gear, shaft and bearing (**Figure 82**) out of the access cover. See **Figure 83**.

Transmission Inspection

1. Examine gears (**Figure 84**) for worn or chipped teeth, pitting, scoring or other damage.
2. Examine dog clutches (**Figure 85**) for chips and rounded edges or wear.
3. Check shafts (**Figure 86**) for worn splines and worn or damaged retaining grooves.
4. Slip gears on shafts. There should be free movement without appreciable play. Replace worn parts.
5. Replace worn or damaged thrust washers.
6. Mount main shaft and countershaft in a suitable centering device. Rotate each shaft and measure bend with a dial indicator. Replace either shaft if it is bent more than 0.003 in.

75

76

77

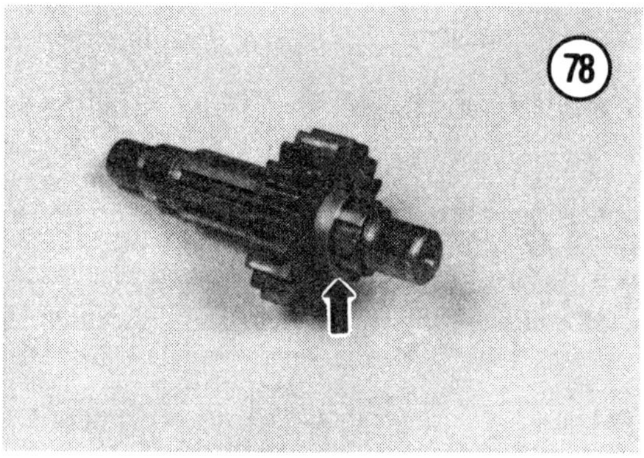

78

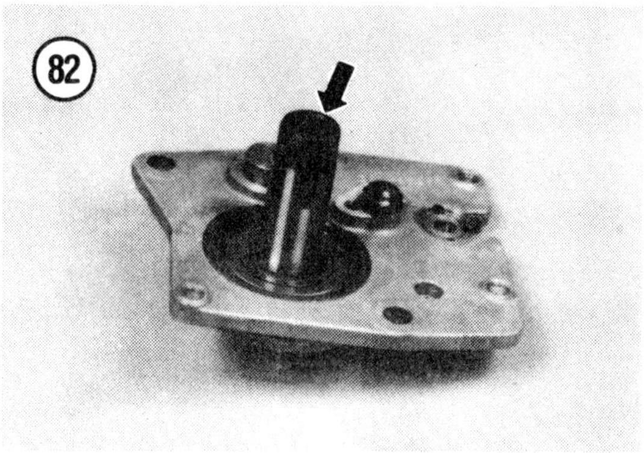

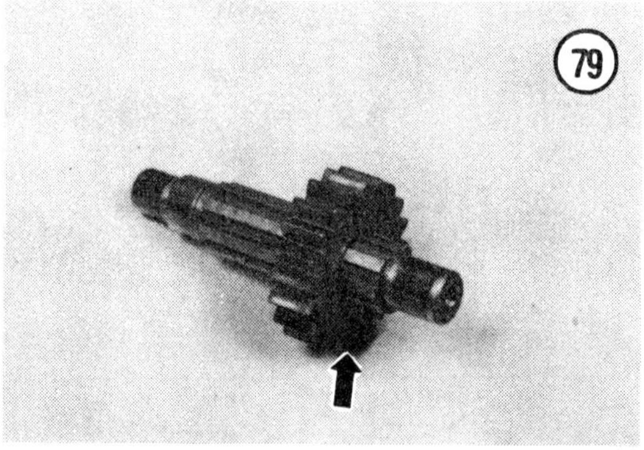

79

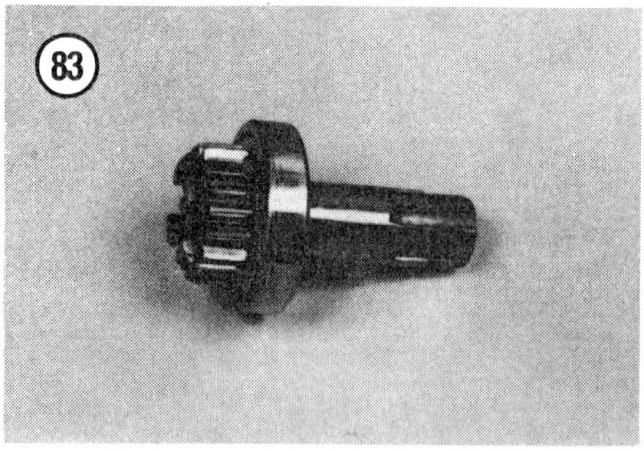

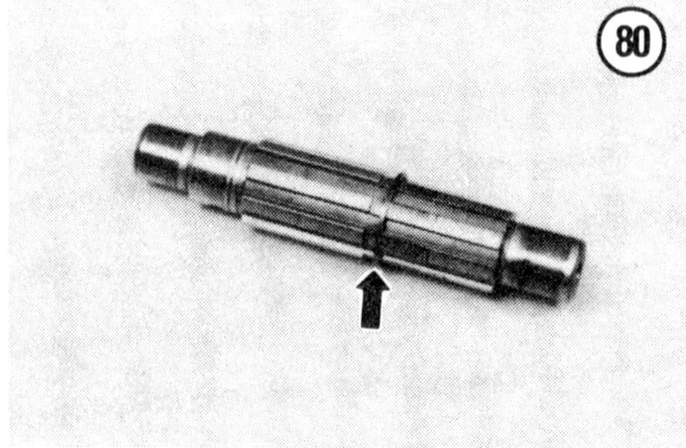
80

81

82

83

84

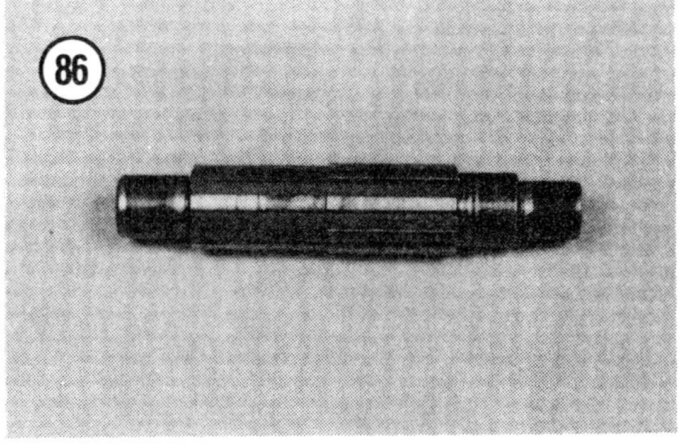

7. Check the clutch gear ball and needle bearings (**Figure 87**) for wear or roughness. If necessary, have the bearings replaced by a Harley-Davidson dealer or machine shop, as a press is required.
8. Check the clutch gear ball bearing surface in the access cover (**Figure 88**) for wear or damage. Replace the access cover if necessary.
9. Check the needle bearing (A, **Figure 89**) in the access cover for wear or roughness. If necessary, have the bearing replaced by a Harley-Davidson dealer or machine shop, as a press is required.

NOTE
*On 1959-early 1984 models, if the inner snap ring (B, **Figure 89**) is removed from the access cover, it must be installed in its original position. Do not interchange it with the outer snap ring shown in **Figure 89**. These snap rings are not interchangeable.*

10. Check the shift fork shaft for cracks, deep scoring or wear. Check the shaft for bending by rolling it on a piece of glass or other flat surface. If the shaft clicks when rolled, it is bent and should be replaced.
11. Check the shift forks (**Figure 90**) for cracks, deep scoring or excessive wear.

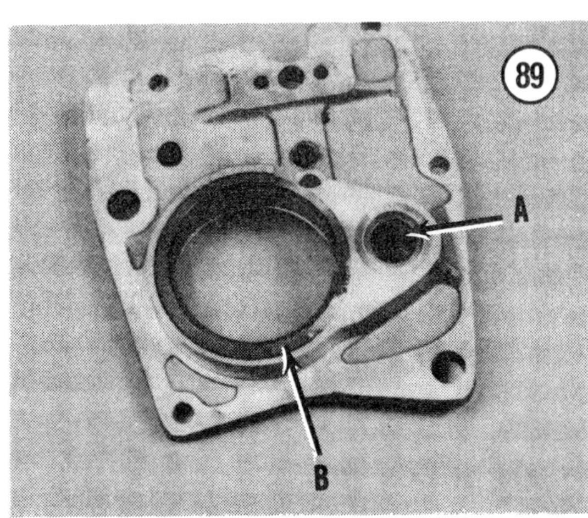

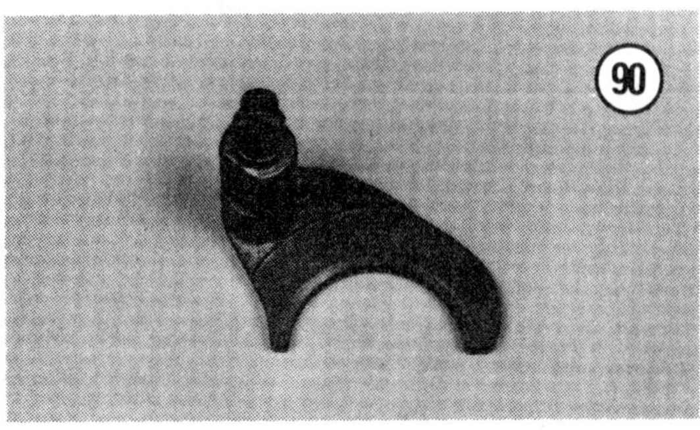

5

12. The length of the shift forks varies. If replacing a shift fork, be sure to replace it with one of the same length (**Figure 91**).

Transmission Assembly

Refer to **Figure 61** (1959-early 1984) or **Figure 62** (late 1984-1985) for this procedure.

CAUTION
Always install new retaining rings and circlips when reassembling the transmission and gear shifter assemblies.

1. Tap the clutch gear ball bearing in the access cover until its shoulder seats against the inner bearing race (**Figure 92**). Secure the bearing with the outer snap ring (**Figure 93**).

NOTE
*On late 1984-1985 models, install the snap ring (21, **Figure 62**) so that the flat side faces toward the bearing.*

2. Assemble the following components on the countershaft in the following order:
   a. Thrust washer (**Figure 80**).
   b. Second gear (**Figure 79**).
   c. Spacer (**Figure 78**).
3. Install the drive gear onto the countershaft so that the recess portion (**Figure 94**) faces toward the spacer. See **Figure 77**.
4. Check that countershaft second gear turns freely on countershaft.
5. Install the countershaft assembly (**Figure 76**) into the access cover.
6. Install the finger roller (**Figure 95**) on each shift fork.
7. Install the mainshaft second gear with its shift fork (**Figure 96**). Position the shift fork with the finger roller stud facing toward the transmission access cover. Make sure shift fork finger engages the gear slot.
8. Install the countershaft third gear with its shift fork (**Figure 97**). Engage the shift fork finger roller into the gear slot.
9. Install the shift fork shaft (**Figure 70**).

NOTE
Make sure the shift forks engage the shifter cam after installing the shift fork shaft.

10. Install the variable washer (**Figure 69**) onto the countershaft.
11. Install the countershaft first gear (**Figure 68**) and the washer (**Figure 67**).
12. Install the main shaft third gear, washer and retaining ring as shown in **Figure 66**.

91

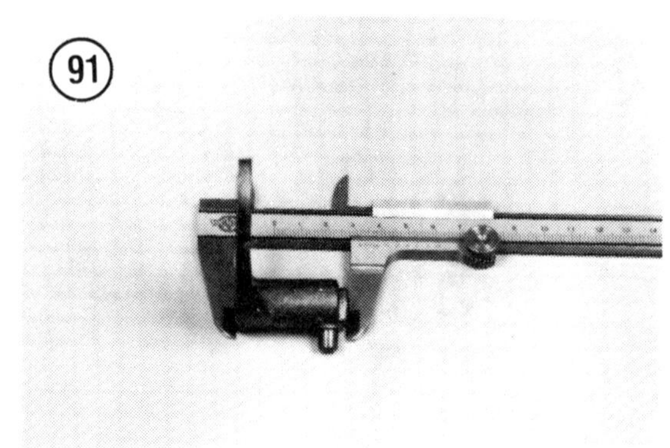

92

93

94

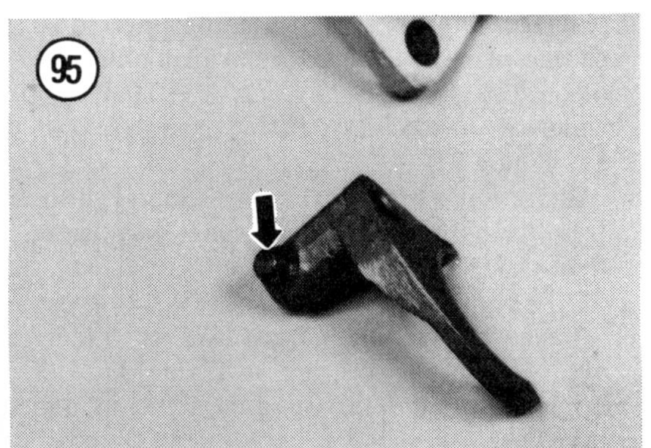

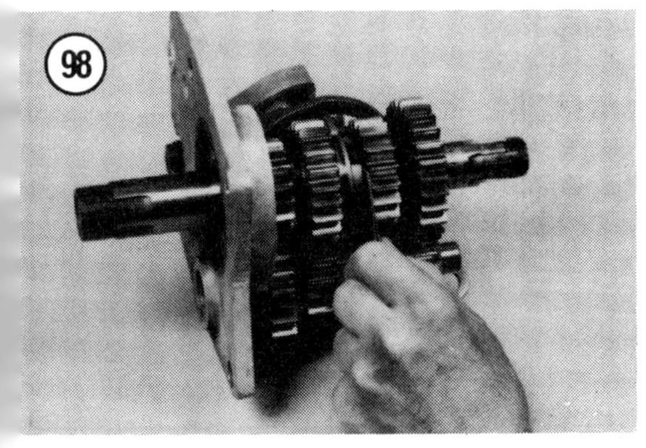

13. Install the main shaft assembly (**Figure 66**) into the main shaft second gear and clutch gear. See **Figure 65**.
14. Install the main shaft first gear (**Figure 64**) and washer (**Figure 63**).

NOTE
On 1959-early 1983 models, the tab on the main shaft thrust washer must be installed so that it faces downward. See 18, ***Figure 61****.*

15. Perform the *Transmission Gear Spacing Check* as described in this chapter.

Transmission Gear Spacing Check

Transmission gear spacing is checked with a feeler gauge as shown in **Figure 98**. **Figure 99** identifies the main shaft (A) and countershaft (B).

1959-1978

1. With the countershaft second gear and its washer installed on the countershaft, check the clearance between the countershaft first and third gear dog clutch faces. The correct clearance is 0.038-0.058 in. If the clearance is incorrect, install a new washer of a different thickness. Countershaft first gear washers are available in thicknesses of 0.065, 0.075, 0.085 and 0.100 in.
2. With all the transmission components assembled into the access cover except the main shaft thrust washer and countershaft first gear washer(s), shift the transmission through all gears several times. Then shift into NEUTRAL and check the clearance between the countershaft second and third gear dog clutches. If the clearance is not 0.038-0.058 in., the shift forks are probably bent.
3. Check the clearance between the clutch gear and main shaft second gear dog clutches and between the

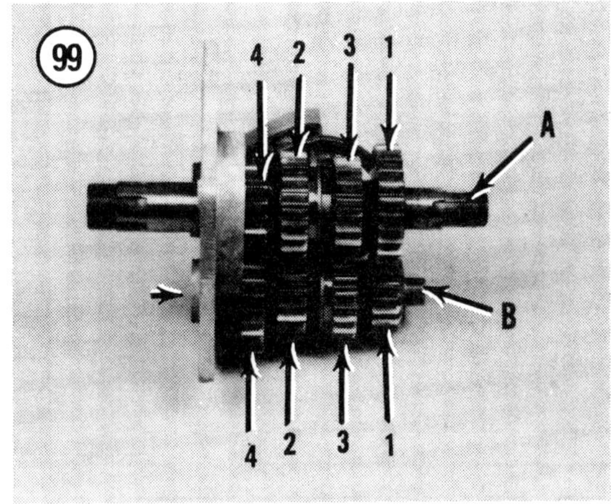

5

countershaft second and third gear dog clutches. If clearance in both instances is not 0.043-0.083 in., the shift forks are probably worn or bent.

4. Shift forks (**Figure 91**) are available in 0.020 in. oversize and undersize for use when the correct clearance (Step 2 and Step 3) cannot be obtained.

5. Pawl carrier support shims are available to space the countershaft third gear and the main shaft second gear away from the transmission access cover if required.

6. As a final check, assemble the transmission but do not install it in the crankcase. Shift the transmission through all gears and check the gear tooth engagement. Each gear must engage its mating gear by at least 50%, except first gear which must have at least 25% engagement. If the gears do not engage as specified, inspect the cam, pawl carrier, pawl carrier springs, pawl carrier support and the transmission access cover as described in this chapter; replace parts as necessary.

1979-1985

1. Measure the clearance between each gear with a feeler gauge at the points indicated in **Figure 100**. The correct clearance for both the countershaft and main shaft is 0.028-0.058 in.

2. If the clearance is not within the specifications listed in Step 1, adjust gear spacing by performing the following:

a. Change shift fork size to move individual sliding gears. Shift forks are available in sizes of +0.005 in., +0.010 in., +0.020 in., standard, -0.005 in., -0.010 in. and -0.020 in. See **Figure 91**.

b. Add or replace the pawl carrier support shims to move both shift forks an equal distance in the same direction. Refer to *Shifter Mechanism* in this chapter.

c. Change the variable thrust washer (**Figure 69**). Thrust washers are available in four thicknesses (0.065 in., 0.075 in., 0.085 in. and 0.100 in.).

d. Replacement of the variable thrust washer can be performed together with the replacement of the shift forks and pawl shims to obtain correct countershaft third gear spacing.

NOTE

*If the variable thrust washer is changed, the countershaft end play should be checked and readjusted as required. See **Main Shaft and Countershaft End Play** in this chapter.*

3. Perform the *Gear Engagement Check* in this chapter after establishing the correct gear spacing for the main shaft and countershaft assemblies.

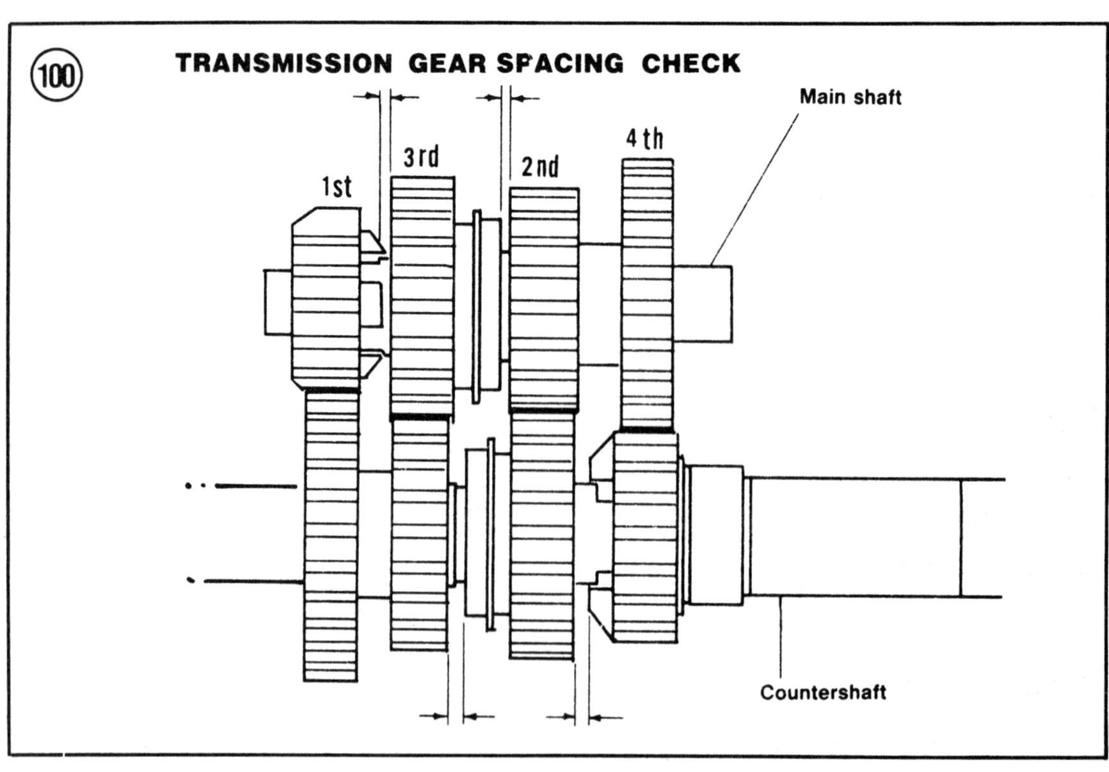

Gear Engagement Check (1979-1985)

Perform this procedure with the transmission assembly installed in the access cover.

1. Referring to **Figure 101**, slowly rotate the pawl carrier until it contacts the lifter arm. Hold the shifter cam with your opposite hand to prevent the cam follower from completing any gear shifts.

NOTE

If hand pressure is released from the shifter cam, the gears will be drawn into complete engagement; thus all inspection procedures will be performed incorrectly.

2. While holding the shift cam as described in Step 1, shift the transmission manually into first gear. Then check the gear dog-to-gear pocket engagement. Correct engagement should be approximately 25 per cent.
3. Repeat Step 2 and shift the transmission into second, third and fourth gears. Correct engagement in each gear should be approximately 50%.

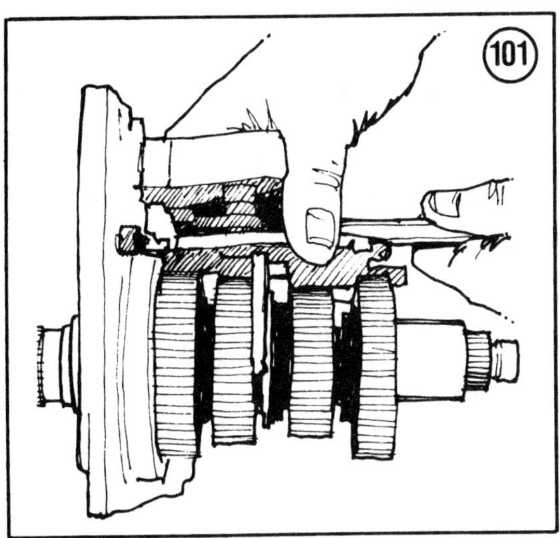

4. If engagement is less than specified in Step 2 and Step 3, either file or replace the shifter mechanism lifter arms to alter gear engagement. See *Shifter Mechanism* in this chapter.

Main Shaft and Countershaft End Play

1. Select thinnest available countershaft first gear washer (24, **Figure 61**) and main shaft thrust washer (18, **Figure 61**). Install them in their respective positions. Note that ear on main shaft thrust washer is to be placed downward (1959-early 1984 models).

NOTE

*On 1959-early 1984 models, the main shaft needle bearings will have to be installed when performing the next step. See **Transmission Installation**.*

2. Temporarily install assembled transmission access cover and transmission. Carefully align cover with dowel pins and tap into position. Install all transmission cap screws.

NOTE

On 1959-early 1984 models, the clutch must be temporarily installed when performing Step 3.

NOTE

On late 1984-1985 models, refer to Chapter Seven and install the stator spacer ring. Then install the stator on the access cover and secure it with the old Torx screws. Tighten screws securely.

3. Using a dial indicator, measure main shaft end play, gauging from sprocket end of shaft. Press the clutch gear so that the main shaft ball bearing seats against the main shaft ball bearing snap ring in the access cover. Move main shaft from side to side while holding clutch gear in. If end play is not within specifications (**Tables 6-9**), install a main shaft thrust washer of suitable size. Main shaft thrust washers come in various thicknesses.
4. Bend a discarded spoke or other suitable wire, then wedge into hole in end of countershaft. Push and pull countershaft and measure end play with a dial indicator. If end play is not within specifications (**Tables 6-9**), install a countershaft thrust washer of suitable size. Countershaft thrust washers come in various thicknesses.

Transmission Installation

1. *1959-early 1984:* Assemble the main shaft needle bearings as follows:
   a. Clean the roller bearing race in the crankcase (**Figure 102**) with solvent and allow to dry.

5

b. Pack the roller bearing race with grease (**Figure 103**).

c. Install the 23 roller bearings around the race as shown in **Figure 104**.

2. Install the shift shaft into the crankcase so that the shift lever arm is centered as shown in **Figure 105**.

NOTE

*Using a grease pencil, mark the shift shaft at the 12 o'clock position as shown in **Figure 106**. By marking the shaft, you can tell if the shift lever arm position changes when installing the transmission.*

3. Install the transmission access cover assembly (**Figure 107**). Then rotate the countershaft slowly to check that the gear shifter lever arm is engaged with the shifter pawl.

To do so, lightly rotate the shift lever shaft. A noticeable resistance to movement indicates proper engagement.

4. *Late 1984-1985:* Install the alternator as described in Chapter Seven.

CAUTION

On late 1984-1985 models, do not use the old stator Torx screws. New Torx screws have a pellet formed locking compound on their threads. When new Torx screws are installed, the pellet breaks and releases the locking compound on the bolt threads. The locking compound on the old bolts cannot be reused; if installed, the old bolts may loosen and back out during engine operation.

5. Install the clutch as described in this chapter.

6. Install the drive sprocket as described in Chapter Four.

7. Install the rear chain. Adjust it as described in Chapter Three.

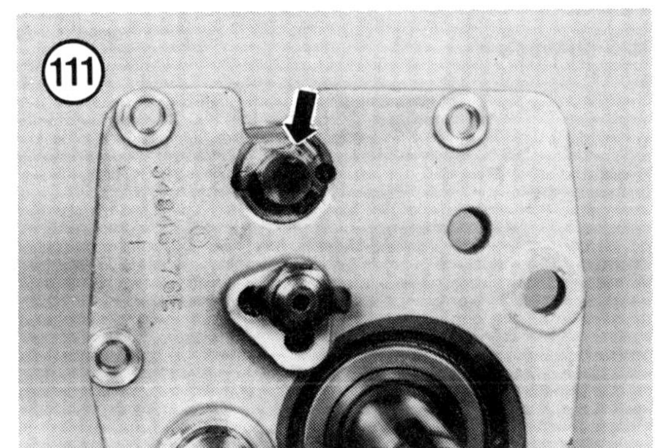

8. Refill the transmission oil as described in Chapter Three.

SHIFTER MECHANISM

Shifter Mechanism Disassembly

Refer to **Figure 108** (1959-1978), **Figure 109** (1979-early 1984) or **Figure 110** (late 1984-1985) for this procedure.

NOTE
Take careful note of location and orientation of each component as it is removed.

1. Remove the transmission and shift forks from the access cover as described in this chapter.

NOTE
*It is not necessary to remove the clutch gear (**Figure 92**) from the access cover when removing the shifter mechanism.*

2. Remove the cam cap screw (**Figure 111**) from the front of the access cover and remove the pawl carrier support (**Figure 112**).
3. Remove the pawl carrier shim, if used.
4. *1959-early 1984:* Remove the cam follower (**Figure 113**) and spring (**Figure 114**).
5. Remove the snap ring (**Figure 115**) and thrust washer (**Figure 116**) from the outside of the pawl carrier support.

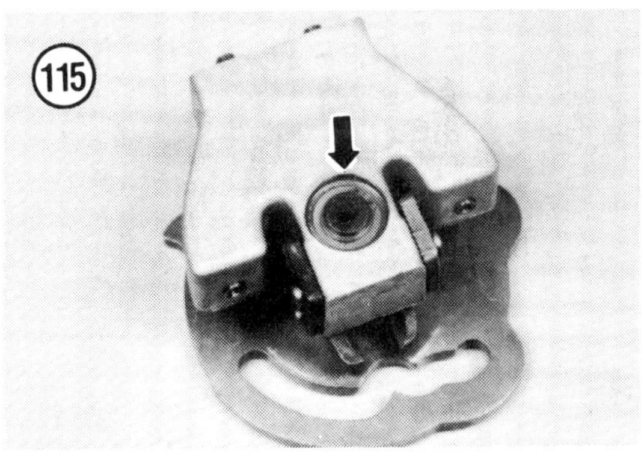

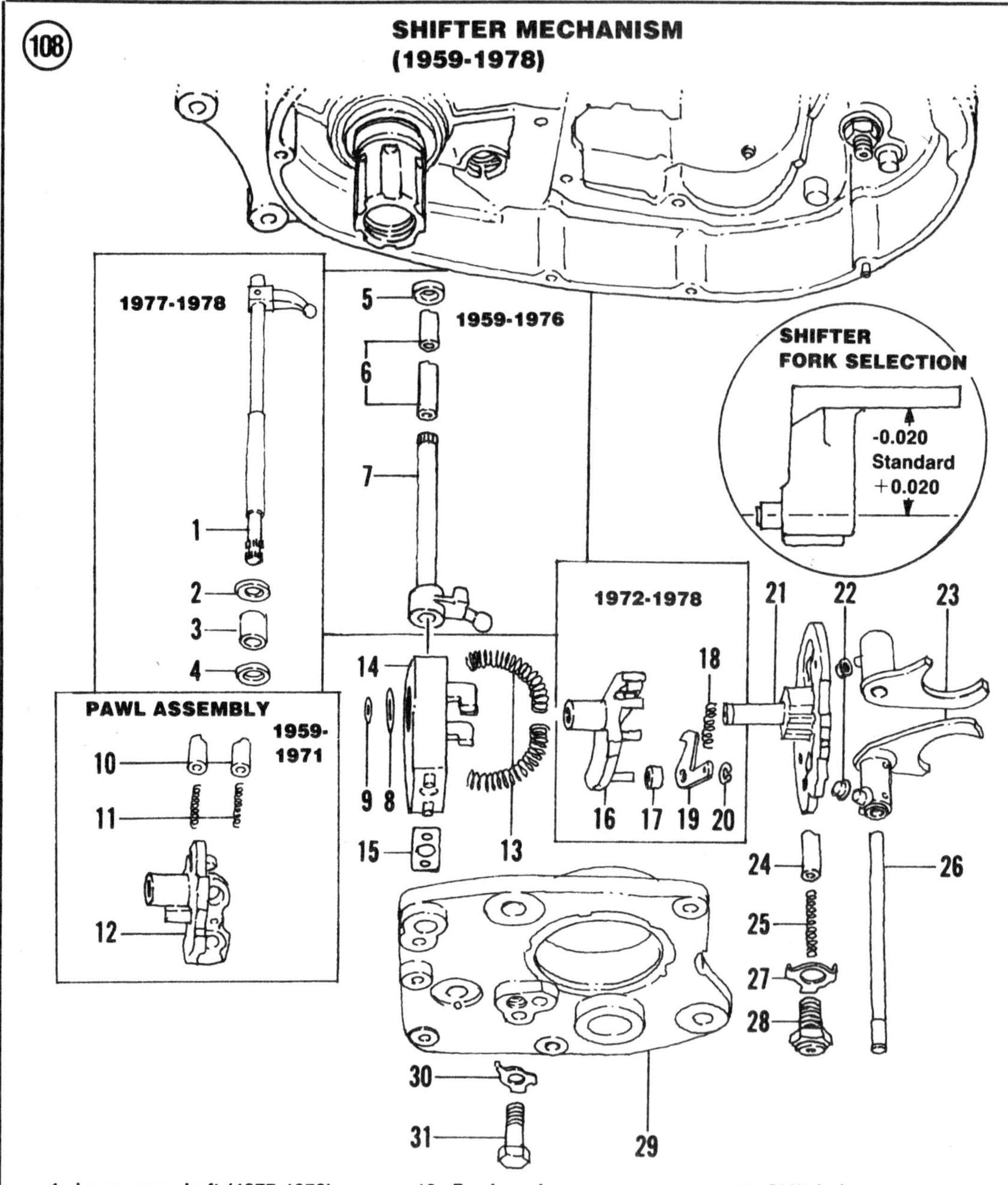

1. Lever arm shaft (1977-1978)
2. Thrust washer
3. Bushing
4. Seal
5. Oil seal
6. Bushing
7. Lever arm shaft
8. Thrust washer
9. Retaining ring
10. Pawl
11. Pawl springs
12. Pawl carrier
13. Pawl carrier
14. Pawl carrier support
15. Shim (if necessary)
16. Pawl carrier
17. Pawl spacer
18. Pawl spring
19. Pawl
20. Retaining ring
21. Gear shifter cam
22. Finger roller
23. Shift forks
24. Cam follower
25. Cam follower spring
26. Fork shaft
27. Lockwasher
28. Cam follower retainer
29. Access cover
30. Lockwasher
31. Screw

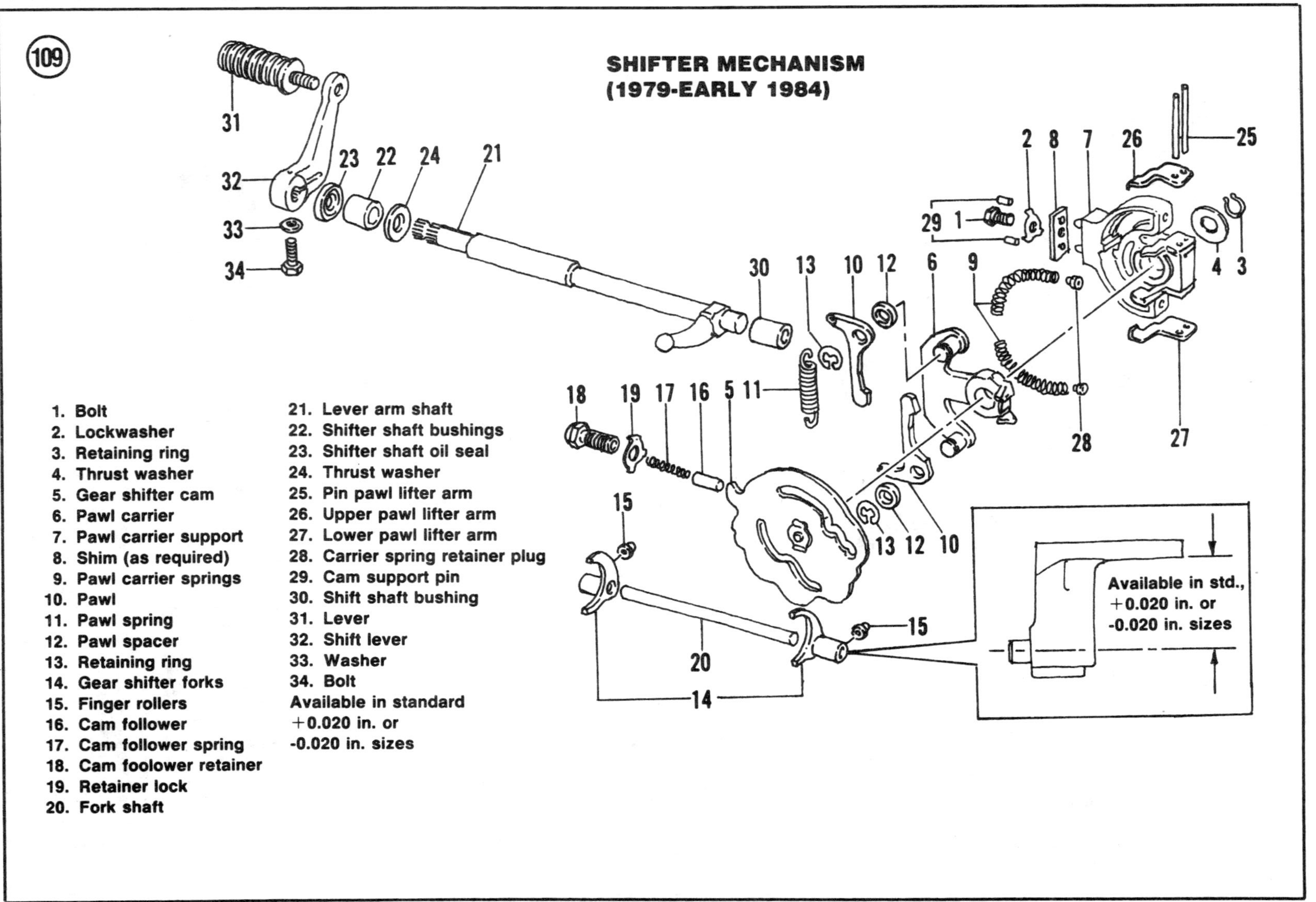
109
SHIFTER MECHANISM
(1979-EARLY 1984)
Available in std.,
+0.020 in. or
-0.020 in. sizes
1. Bolt
2. Lockwasher
3. Retaining ring
4. Thrust washer
5. Gear shifter cam
6. Pawl carrier
7. Pawl carrier support
8. Shim (as required)
9. Pawl carrier springs
10. Pawl
11. Pawl spring
12. Pawl spacer
13. Retaining ring
14. Gear shifter forks
15. Finger rollers
16. Cam follower
17. Cam follower spring
18. Cam foolower retainer
19. Retainer lock
20. Fork shaft
21. Lever arm shaft
22. Shifter shaft bushings
23. Shifter shaft oil seal
24. Thrust washer
25. Pin pawl lifter arm
26. Upper pawl lifter arm
27. Lower pawl lifter arm
28. Carrier spring retainer plug
29. Cam support pin
30. Shift shaft bushing
31. Lever
32. Shift lever
33. Washer
34. Bolt
Available in standard
+0.020 in. or
-0.020 in. sizes

5

(110)

SHIFTER MECHANISM (LATE 1984-1985)

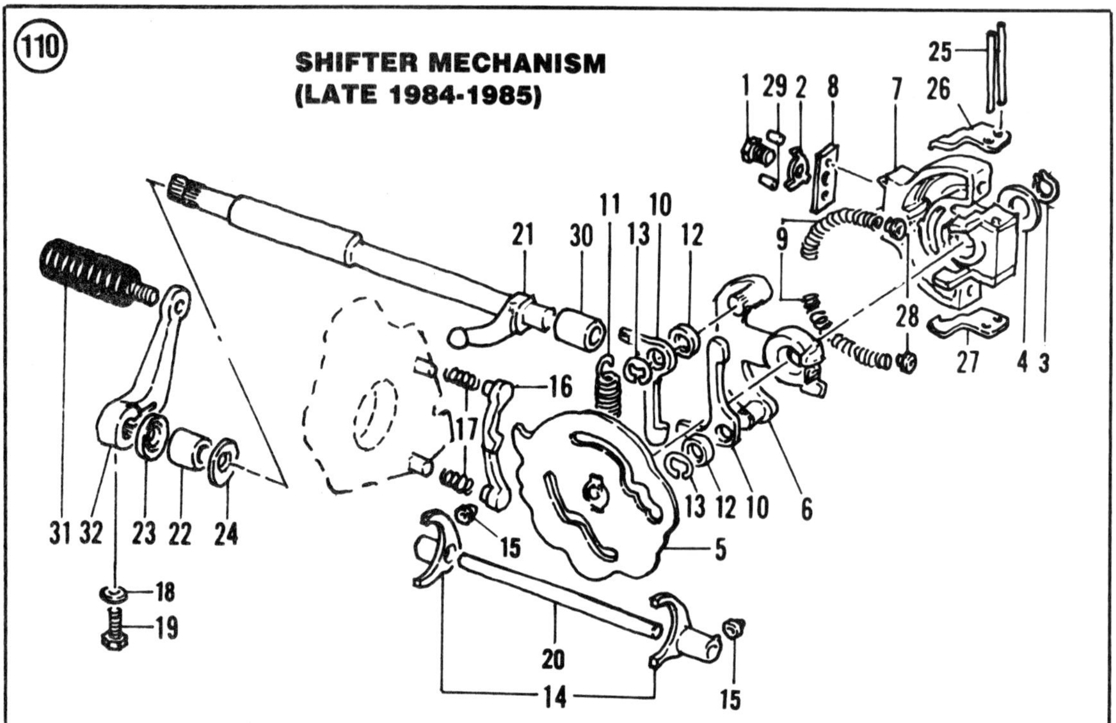

1. Bolt
2. Lockwasher
3. Circlip
4. Thrust washer
5. Gear shifter cam
6. Pawl carrier
7. Pawl carrier support
8. Shim
9. Pawl carrier springs
10. Pawl
11. Pawl spring
12. Pawl spacer
13. Circlip
14. Shift forks
15. Finger rollers
16. Cam follower
17. Cam follower spring
18. Washer
19. Bolt
20. Fork shaft
21. Lever arm shaft
22. Shifter shaft bushings
23. Shifter shaft oil seal
24. Thrust washer
25. Pin pawl lifter arm
26. Upper pawl lifter arm
27. Lower pawl lifter arm
28. Carrier spring retainer plug
29. Cam support pin
30. Shift shaft bushing
31. Lever
32. Shift lever

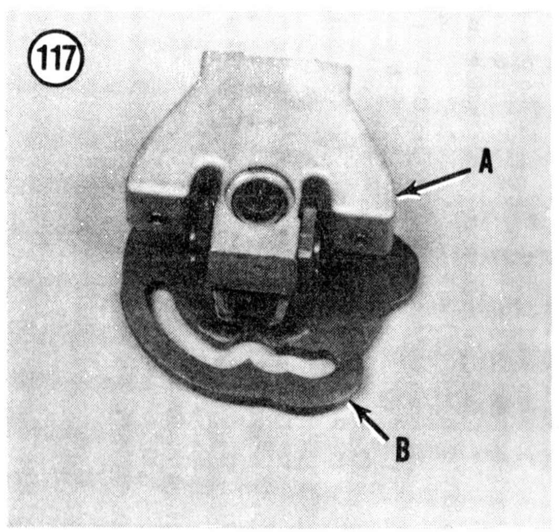

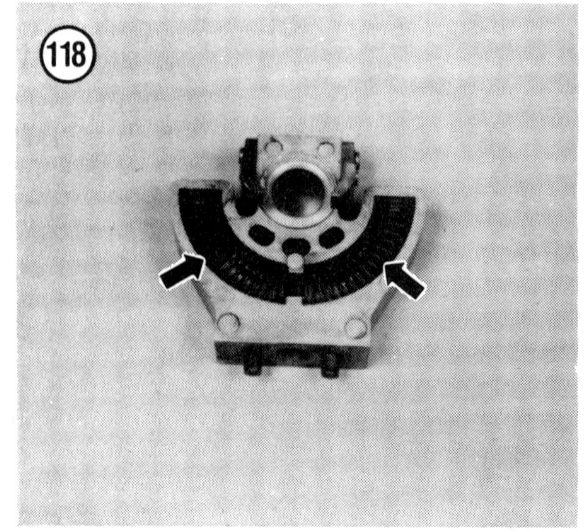

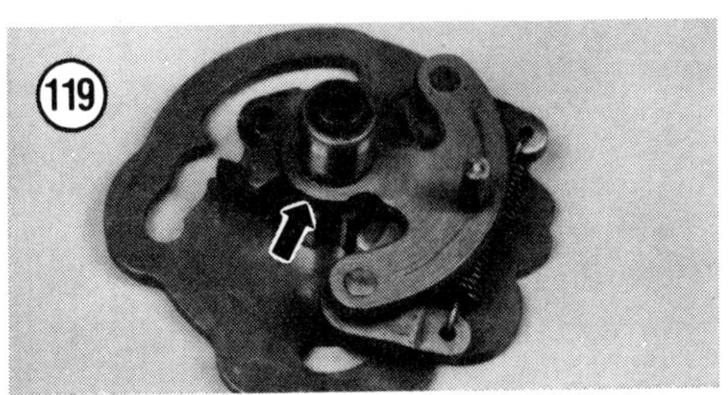
119

120

121

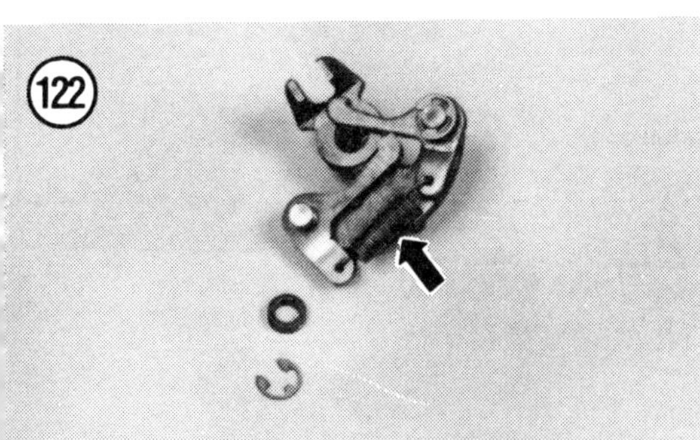
122

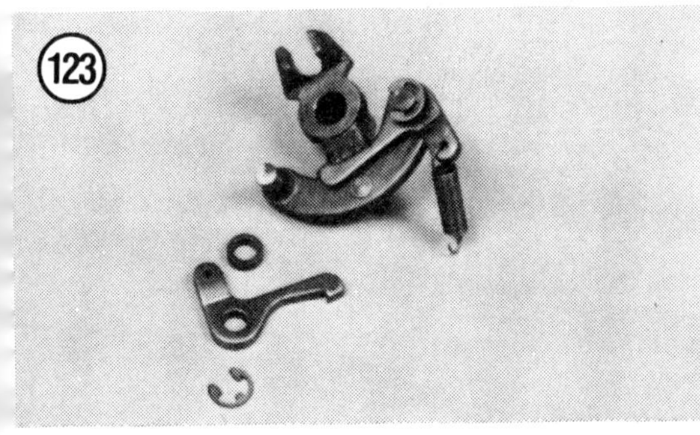
123

6. Lift the pawl carrier support (A, **Figure 117**) off of the shifter cam (B, **Figure 117**).
7. Remove the pawl carrier springs (**Figure 118**).
8. Remove the retainer plugs from the end of the pawl carrier springs (if so equipped). See **Figure 109** or **Figure 110**.
9. Disassemble the pawl carrier as follows:
   a. Lift the pawl carrier (**Figure 119**) off of the shifter cam.
   b. Remove the circlip (**Figure 120**) and remove the pawl spacer (**Figure 121**).
   c. Disconnect the pawl spring (**Figure 122**) and remove the pawl (**Figure 123**).
   d. Repeat for the opposite pawl.
10. Inspect the shifter mechanism as described in this chapter.
11. Assembly is the reverse of disassembly, noting the following.
12. Insert the pawl carrier springs (**Figure 119**) into the pawl carrier support.
13A. *1959-1971:* Install the pawl carrier in the pawl carrier support. Insert pawls and springs into their sockets with the top ratchet engaging grooves facing each other. Hold pawls in place, then assemble cam, pawl, carrier support and pawl carrier together with any shims. Install the washer and a new retaining ring. Hold down each pawl in turn, then operate cam to be sure pawls operate freely and engage cam ratchet correctly.
13B. *1972-1985:* Install pawls on pawl carrier, using spacers so that spring hook holes will align. Note that one spacer will be underneath pawl and other spacer will be on outside of pawl. Install pawl spring and retaining ring (1972-1978 models). Retract one pawl at a time, then install shifter cam into pawl carrier. Install assembly into pawl carrier support so that ear of pawl is between ends of pawl carrier springs. Install new retaining ring and washer. Be sure that pawls engage cam ratchet.

Shifter Mechanism Inspection

1. Thoroughly clean all parts in solvent, then blow dry.

NOTE
When parts have been disassembled and cleaned, visually inspect them for any signs of wear, cracks, breakage or other damage. If there is any doubt as to the condition of any part, replace it with a new one.

2. Discard old shifter cam retaining ring.
3. Carefully examine shifter cam for worn or grooved cam slots (A, **Figure 124**). Excessive wear will result in difficult shifting.

4. Check the shifter cam gear (B, **Figure 124**) for wear or damage.
5. *1959-1971:* Insert pawl springs in their respective holes and check operation. Pawls must move freely in carrier. Replace pawl springs if appreciably shorter than 1 7/32 in.
6. *1972-1985:* Examine pawl carrier (**Figure 125**) for wear or other damage. Replace pawl spring if it is appreciably longer than 1 3/4 in. between hooks.
7. Examine shifter pawls (**Figure 126**) for grooves, cracks, wear or breakage. Replace parts as necessary.
8. Examine pawl carrier springs (**Figure 127**) for fatigue or breakage. Replace them if they are appreciably shorter than 2 25/32 in. (1959-1978) or 2 21/32 in. (1979-1985). See **Figure 128**.

NOTE
When reassembling pawl carrier, do not use 14-coil cadmium springs; 16-coil cadmium plated springs are okay. Black phosphated springs of either 14 or 16 coils may also be used.

9. Check pawl carrier support (**Figure 129**) for breakage or minute surface cracks.
10. Check cam follower (**Figure 130**) for wear, especially on its thrust face.
11. Measure free length of cam follower spring. Replace if appreciably less than 1 19/32 in.
12. Install the cam follower and spring into the cam follower retainer. Slide the cam follower back and forth and check for free movement; replace damaged parts as required.
13. Check the shifter lever arm for bending or wear.
14. Loosely assemble shifter cam, pawl carrier, pawl carrier support and any shims that were installed. After assembly, check bearing action for appreciable play. Replace any worn or pitted parts.

Pawl Carrier Support Lifter Arm Replacement

On 1979 and later models, the pawl carrier support lifter arms (**Figure 131**) can be either filed (to reduce their height) or replaced to allow changes in transmission gear engagements. See *Gear Engagement Check* in this chapter. To replace a lifter arm, perform the following:

a. Grind the head of the pawl lifter pin (**Figure 131**) off.
b. Remove the lifter arm and pin.
c. Install a new pin and lifter arm.
d. Peen the head of the pin to lock the lifter arm in position.
e. Repeat for the opposite lifter arm and pin.

124

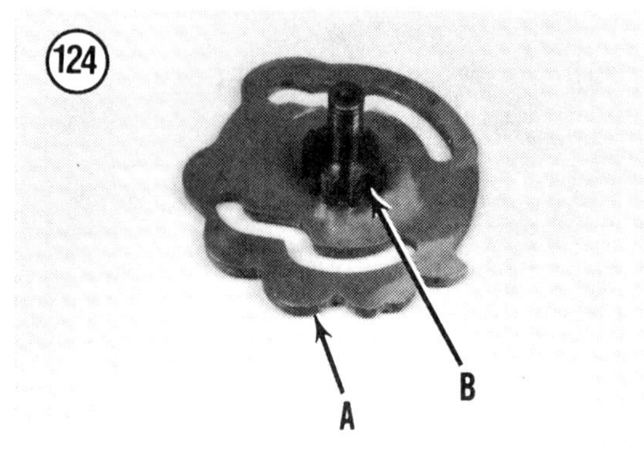

125

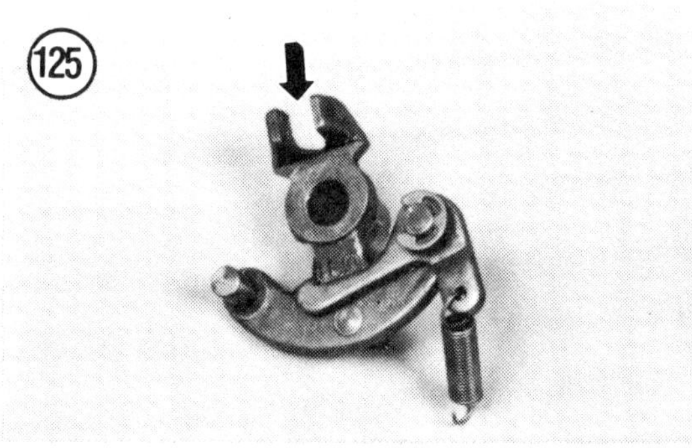

126

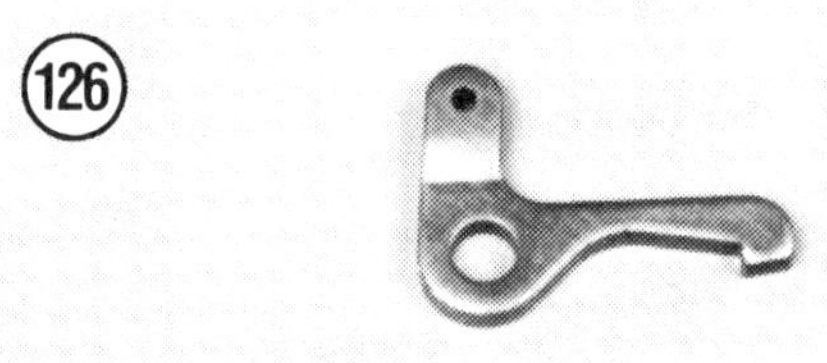

127

128

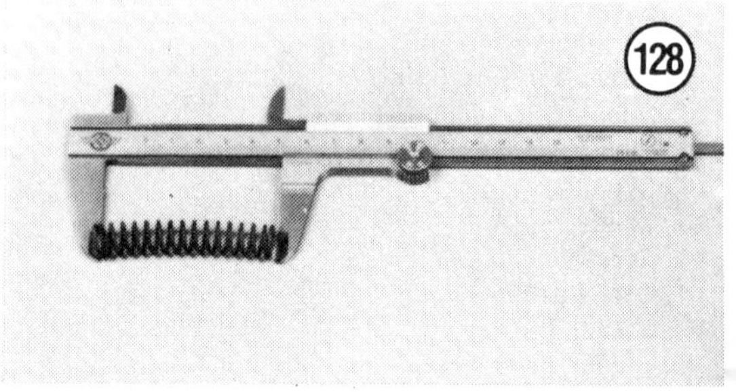

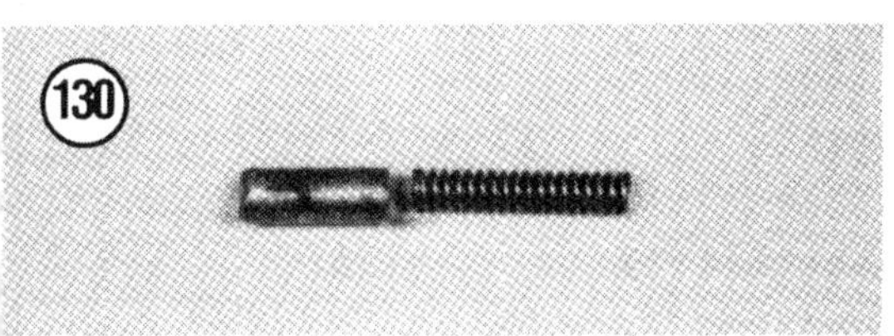

SHIFTER LINKAGE (1975-1976)

Refer to **Figure 132** for this procedure.

Removal/Adjustment/Installation

1. Remove the right-hand side exhaust assembly. See Chapter Six.
2. Remove the right-hand footrest with the brake mechanism attached.
3. Remove the sprocket cover from the right-hand side.
4. Mark the shift pedal position where it engages with the cross shaft and arm splines. These marks will be used for reassembly.
5. Remove the shift pedal nuts and bolts and remove the shift pedal.
6. From the right-hand side of the motorcycle, remove the circlip (5, **Figure 132**) and disconnect the pivot end from the cross arm.

NOTE
Count the number turns when removing the pivot end in Step 7. This will ease reassembly and adjustment.

7. Loosen the locknut (8) and unscrew the pivot end (7) from the end of the shifter link.
8. Check all parts for wear and damage and replace as needed.
9. Install by reversing Steps 1-7.

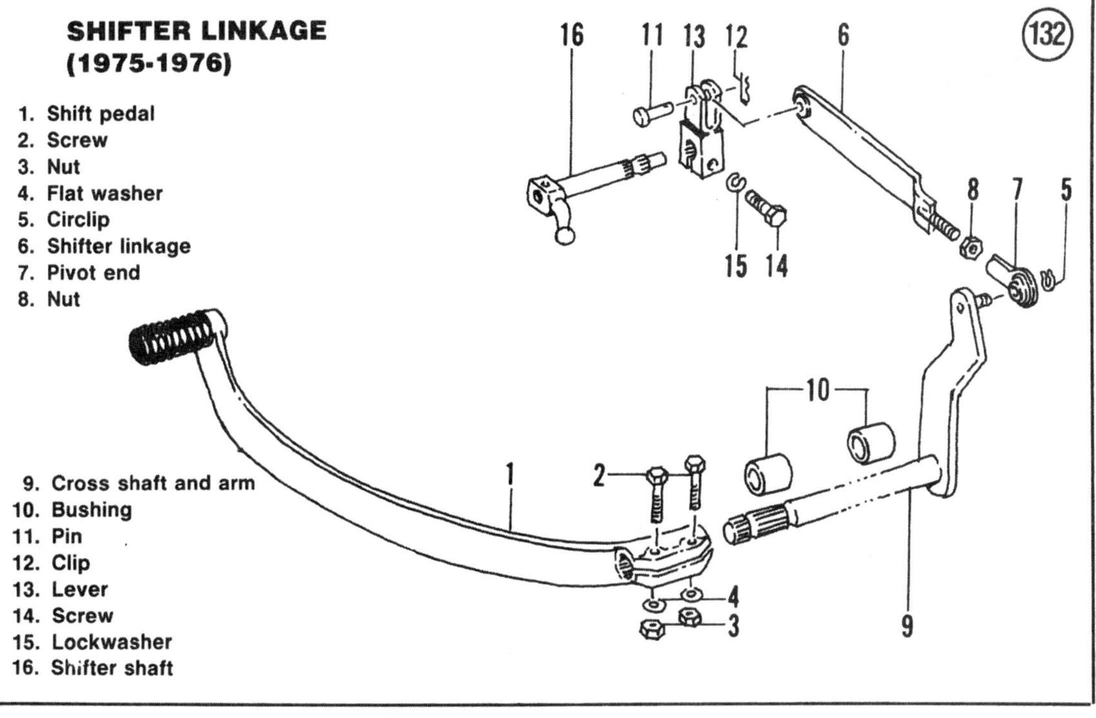

Table 1 CLUTCH SPECIFICATIONS (1959-EARLY 1984)

Clutch spring free length	
1959-1969	1 5/8 in.
1970	1 3/4 in.
1971-1978	2 1/2 in.
1979-early 1984	2 11/32 in.

Table 2 CLUTCH SPECIFICATIONS (LATE 1984-1985)

Item	in.
Clutch plate stack	0.025
Friction plate	0.0025
Intermediate plate	0.001

Table 3 CLUTCH/TRANSMISSION TIGHTENING TORQUES (1959-1978)

	ft.-lb.
Clutch hub nut	
1959-1969	120
1970-1978	150
Pinion gear nut	
1977-1978	50
Gear shaft nut	100-120
Sprocket shaft nut	100-120
Gear cover screws	100 in.-lb.

Table 4 CLUTCH/TRANSMISSION TIGHTENING TORQUES (1979-EARLY 1984)

	ft.-lb.
Drain plug	14-21
Clutch hub nut	110-150
Mainshaft nut	35-65
Transmission access cover	13-15
Chain tensioner stud nut	8-12
Primary chain case screws	80-110 in.-lb.

Table 5 CLUTCH/TRANSMISSION TIGHTENING TORQUES (LATE 1984-1985)

Item	ft.-lb.
Mainshaft nut	35-65
Mainshaft nut lock screw	50-60 in.-lb.
Access cover screws	13-15
Drain plug	14-21
Stator Torx screws	20-35 in.-lb.
Chain tensioner stud nut	8-12

Table 6 TRANSMISSION SPECIFICATIONS (1959-1969)

Mainshaft	
End play	0.004-0.009 in.
Third gear	
Fit on shaft	0.002-0.003 in.
End play	0.15-0.025 in.

(continued)

Table 6 TRANSMISSION SPECIFICATIONS (1959-1969) (continued)

Countershaft	
End play	0.004-0.009 in.
First gear end play	0.004-0.009 in.
Drive gear end play	0.004-0.009 in.
Clearnace between clutch faces	
Between first and third gears	0.038-0.058 in.
Between second and third gears	0.038-0.058 in.

Table 7 TRANSMISSION SPECIFICATIONS (1970-1978)

Mainshaft	
End play	0.003-0.009 in.
Third gear end play	0.012-0.030 in.
Countershaft	
End play	0.004-0.009 in.
First gear end play	0.004-0.009 in.
Drive gear end play	0.004-0.009 in.
Clearance between clutch faces	
1970-1976 shifter shaft end play	0.010-0.030 in.
Countershaft first and third gear	0.038-0.058 in.
Countershaft second and third gear	0.038-0.058 in.
Mainshaft third gear and second gear	0.043-0.083 in.
Mainshaft clutch gear and second gear	0.043-0.083 in.

Table 8 TRANSMISSION SPECIFICATIONS (1979-EARLY 1984)

Mainshaft	
End play	
Without axial play	0.003 in.
With axial play	0.020 in.
Third gear end play	0.012-0.030 in.
Countershaft	
End play	0.004-0.015 in.
Clearance between clutch faces	
Countershaft first and third gear	0.028-0.058 in.
Countershaft second and third gear	0.028-0.058 in.
Mainshaft third gear and second gear	0.028-0.058 in.
Mainshaft clutch gear and second gear	0.028-0.058 in.

Table 9 TRANSMISSION SPECIFICATIONS (LATE 1984-1985)

Mainshaft	
End play	
With axial play	0.020 in.
Without axial play	0.009 in.
Third gear	
End play	0.012-0.030 in.
Clearance between clutch faces	
Mainshaft clutch gear and second gear	0.028-0.058 in.
Mainshaft third gear and second gear	0.028-0.058 in.
Countershaft	
End play	0.004-0.015 in.
First gear end play	0.004-0.009 in.
Drive gear end play	0.004-0.009 in.
Clearance between clutch faces	
Countershaft first and third gear	0.028-0.058 in.
Countershaft second and third gear	0.028-0.058 in.

5

CHAPTER SIX

FUEL, EXHAUST AND EMISSION CONTROL SYSTEMS

The fuel system consists of the fuel tank, shutoff valve and filter, carburetor and air cleaner.

This chapter includes service procedures for all parts of the fuel, exhaust and emission control systems.

AIR CLEANER

The air cleaner must be cleaned or replaced at the intervals specified in Chapter Three (or more frequently in dusty areas).

Service to the air cleaner element is described in Chapter Three.

CARBURETORS

Service

Major carburetor service (removal and cleaning) should be performed when poor engine performance and/or hesitation is observed. Carburetor jetting changes should be attempted only if you're experienced in this type of "tuning" work; a bad guess could result in costly engine damage or, at best, poor performance.

NOTE
When tuning late model engines, check with local authorities for regulations concerning emissions.

If after servicing the carburetors and making adjustments as described in this chapter, the motorcycle does not perform correctly (and assuming that other factors affecting performance are correct, such as ignition timing and condition, engine tuning, etc.), the motorcycle should be checked by a dealer or a qualified performance tuning specialist.

Removal/Installation

1. Remove the air cleaner as described in Chapter Three.
2. Disconnect the fuel line at the carburetor (**Figure 1**).

NOTE
Some factory installed hose clamps must be cut off with pliers and cannot be reused. Use a reusable type of hose clamp during installation so that the fuel line can be removed more easily when performing necessary service or roadside troubleshooting.

3. Disconnect the throttle cable(s) at the carburetor. See A, **Figure 2**.
4. Loosen the choke cable (B, **Figure 2**) set screw at the carburetor and slide it out of its holder.
5. Disconnect the vacuum line at the carburetor (if so equipped).
6. Remove the carburetor mounting nuts and washers and remove the carburetor.

NOTE
Drain most of the gasoline from the carburetor assembly and place it in a

clean heavy-duty plastic bag to keep it clean until it is worked on or reinstalled.

NOTE

If the carburetor is going to be removed for any length of time, cover the exposed manifold with shop rags or tape. This will prevent the engine from damage from small objects dropped undetected into the manifold.

7. While the carburetor is removed, examine the intake manifolds on the cylinder head for any cracks or damage that would allow unfiltered air to enter the engine. Any damaged parts should be replaced.
8. Install by reversing these removal steps. Install a new manifold gasket. Adjust the throttle cable as described in Chapter Three.

Disassembly/Assembly (HD Carburetor 1959-1971)

Refer to **Figure 3** for this procedure.

1. Remove the idle (**Figure 4**) and intermediate (35, **Figure 3**) adjusting screws.
2. Remove the throttle valve screws and pull the throttle valve (47) out of its shaft.

3. Remove the accelerating pump lever screw (3). Then pull the throttle shaft out of the carburetor housing. Remove the spring (46), washers (45) and dust seals (44).
4. Remove the accelerating pump plunger assembly (1).
5. Remove the diaphragm cover (18).
6. Remove the diaphragm (17) and gasket (21). Separate the gasket from the diaphragm.
7. Remove the plug screw (19) from the diaphragm cover.
8. Remove the following parts in order:
   a. Inlet control lever screw (31).
   b. Inlet control lever pin (30).
   c. Inlet control lever (29).
   d. Inlet control lever tension spring (34).
9. Using a 3/8 in. socket, remove the inlet needle and seat assembly (32).
10. Remove the inlet needle seat gasket (33) with a piece of wire.
11. Remove the main jet plug screw (40) from the side of the carburetor.
12. Remove the main jet (39) and its gasket.
13. Welch plugs (6, 7 and 8) are used to block the main nozzle, idle port and the economizer check ball. To remove any welch plug, perform the following:
    a. Drill a 1/8 in. diameter hole off center through the welch plug only. Do not drill deeper than the welch plug.
    b. Pry out the welch plug with a small punch. Make sure the casting surrounding the edges is not damaged.

NOTE

The sides of the choke shutter plates are tapered 15° to conform to the throttle bore. Note the top and bottom positions of the choke valves before removal.

14. Remove the lower choke shutter plate (15).
15. Slide the choke shaft (13) out of the carburetor. This in turn releases the upper choke shutter plate (11) together with its spring (12), choke friction ball (9) and the friction ball spring (10).
16. Remove the choke shaft dust seal (14).
17. Clean and inspect the carburetor parts as described in this chapter.
18. Assembly is the reverse of these steps, noting the following.
19. Install new welch plugs by seating them with a flat end punch.
20. The inlet control lever tension spring (34) should seat into the body casting counterbore and locate on the inlet control lever protrusion. Adjust the inlet control lever (29) so that it is flush with

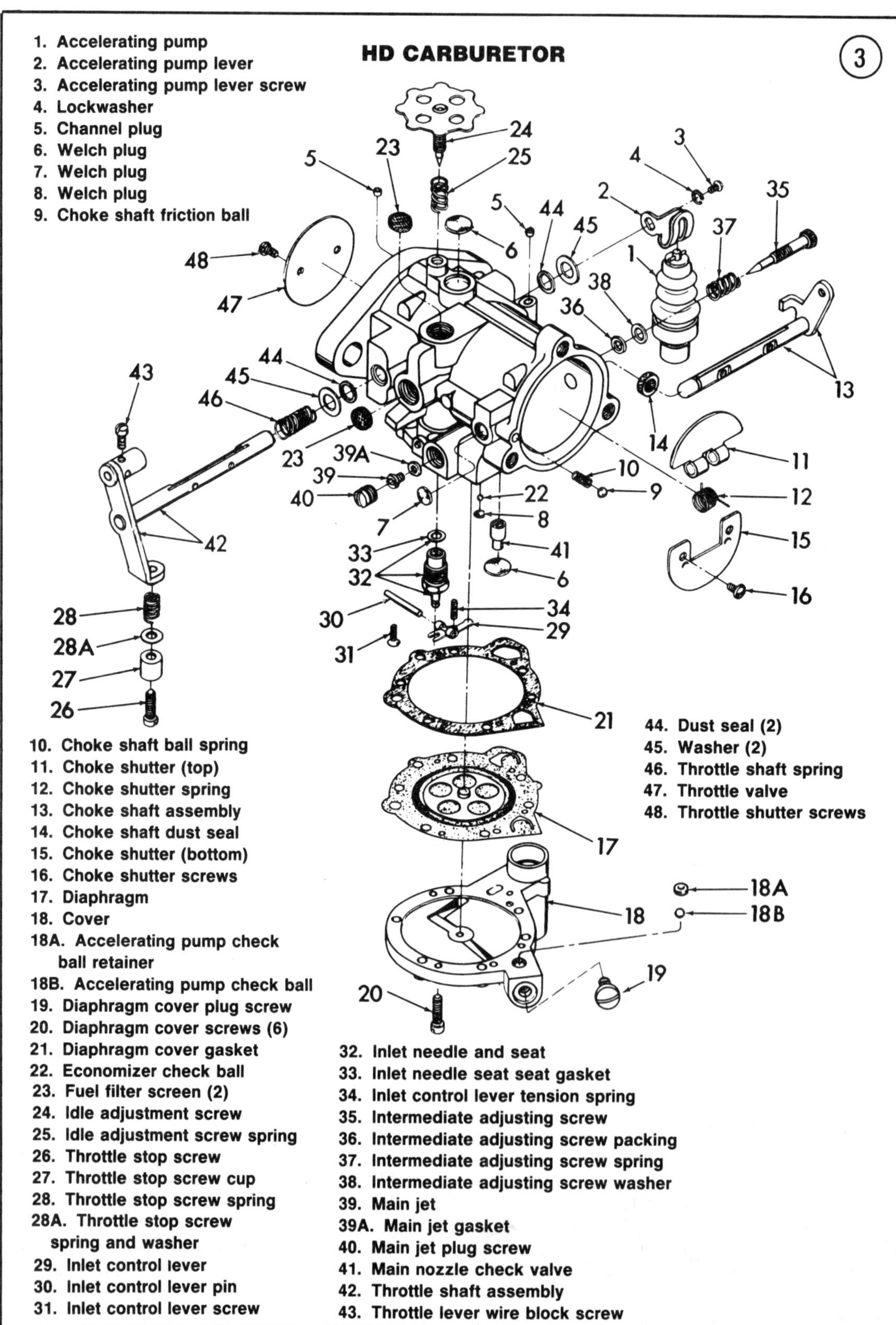
HD CARBURETOR
3
1. Accelerating pump
2. Accelerating pump lever
3. Accelerating pump lever screw
4. Lockwasher
5. Channel plug
6. Welch plug
7. Welch plug
8. Welch plug
9. Choke shaft friction ball
10. Choke shaft ball spring
11. Choke shutter (top)
12. Choke shutter spring
13. Choke shaft assembly
14. Choke shaft dust seal
15. Choke shutter (bottom)
16. Choke shutter screws
17. Diaphragm
18. Cover
18A. Accelerating pump check ball retainer
18B. Accelerating pump check ball
19. Diaphragm cover plug screw
20. Diaphragm cover screws (6)
21. Diaphragm cover gasket
22. Economizer check ball
23. Fuel filter screen (2)
24. Idle adjustment screw
25. Idle adjustment screw spring
26. Throttle stop screw
27. Throttle stop screw cup
28. Throttle stop screw spring
28A. Throttle stop screw spring and washer
29. Inlet control lever
30. Inlet control lever pin
31. Inlet control lever screw
32. Inlet needle and seat
33. Inlet needle seat seat gasket
34. Inlet control lever tension spring
35. Intermediate adjusting screw
36. Intermediate adjusting screw packing
37. Intermediate adjusting screw spring
38. Intermediate adjusting screw washer
39. Main jet
39A. Main jet gasket
40. Main jet plug screw
41. Main nozzle check valve
42. Throttle shaft assembly
43. Throttle lever wire block screw
44. Dust seal (2)
45. Washer (2)
46. Throttle shaft spring
47. Throttle valve
48. Throttle shutter screws

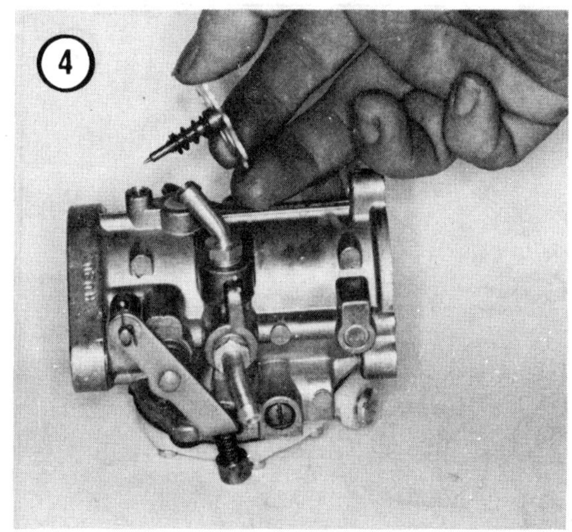

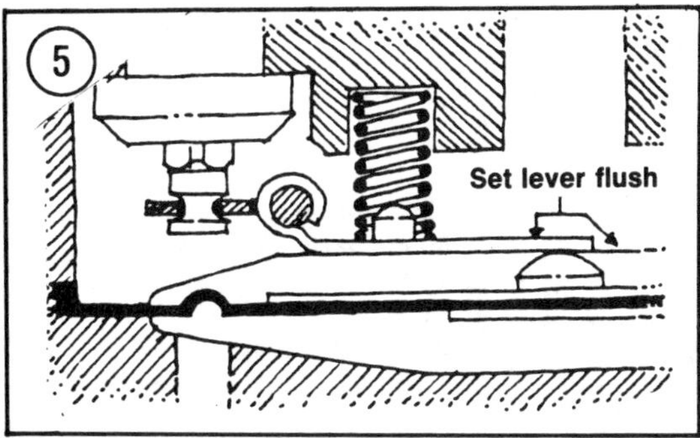

the metering chamber floor by bending the diaphragm lever end as required. See **Figure 5**.

21. Tighten the inlet seat assembly to 40-45 in.-lb. and the accelerating pump channel plug to 23-28 in.-lb.

22. Adjust the carburetor as described in Chapter Three.

Disassembly/Assembly (Model M Carburetor)

Model M carburetors were used on 1965 and earlier models. Refer to **Figure 6** for this procedure.

1. Remove the carburetor as described in this chapter.
2. Remove the float bowl locknut (1, **Figure 6**). Then remove the gasket (2), spring (3) and main nozzle (4).
3. Slightly twist the float bowl (5) and remove it and its gasket.
4. Remove the float valve seat (7) and gasket (8).
5. Unscrew the float lever pin (9) at the float bowl. Then remove the float (10), lever (11) and float valve (12) from the float bowl.
6. Loosen the throttle stop lockscrew (13). Then slide the throttle lever (14) off of the throttle shaft with the throttle lever arm (15) and throttle shaft spring (16).

NOTE
Make sure to use the correct size screwdriver in Step 7 to prevent damaging the throttle shaft screws.

7. Remove the throttle shaft screws (17). Then slip the throttle disc (18) from slot in shaft (19).
8. Slide the throttle shaft (19) out of the carburetor housing.
9. Remove the low speed needle valve (20).
10. Remove the high speed needle valve (21).
11. Remove the needle valve lever screw (22). Then remove the needle valve lever (23), lever spring (24) and lever spring collar (25).
12. Remove the air intake shaft nut and washer (26). Then remove the air intake shaft stop (27), ball (28) and spring (29).
13. Remove the air intake disc screws (30) and disc (31). Then pull the air intake shaft (32) out of the carburetor housing.
14. Remove the idle hole body plug (33).
15. Remove the idle passage plug screws (34).
16. Remove the fixed jet (35).
17. Clean and inspect the carburetor as described in this chapter.
18. Slide the throttle shaft (19) into the carburetor housing. Check shaft play in bushings by twisting sideways. A dial indicator can be used if available. If clearance exceeds 0.003 in. or if noticeable play exists, replace bushings as follows:
    a. Carefully drive the old bushings (36) out with a small drift pin.
    b. Clean the bushing bore with solvent.
    c. Press in new bushings.
    d. Line ream new bushings with a 0.250 drill installed in a drill press.

CAUTION
During the next step, do not attempt to line ream new bushings with a hand drill. Secure carburetor in a drill press.

19. Check the carburetor venturi (37) for a loose fit in the carburetor housing. Also check for a pitted or damaged intake surface. Replace if necessary.
20. Check float valve (12) and float valve seat (7) seal as follows:
    a. Assemble the float bowl by installing the following parts: Float valve (12), float lever (11), float (10), float lever pin (9), valve seat gasket and valve seat (7).

6

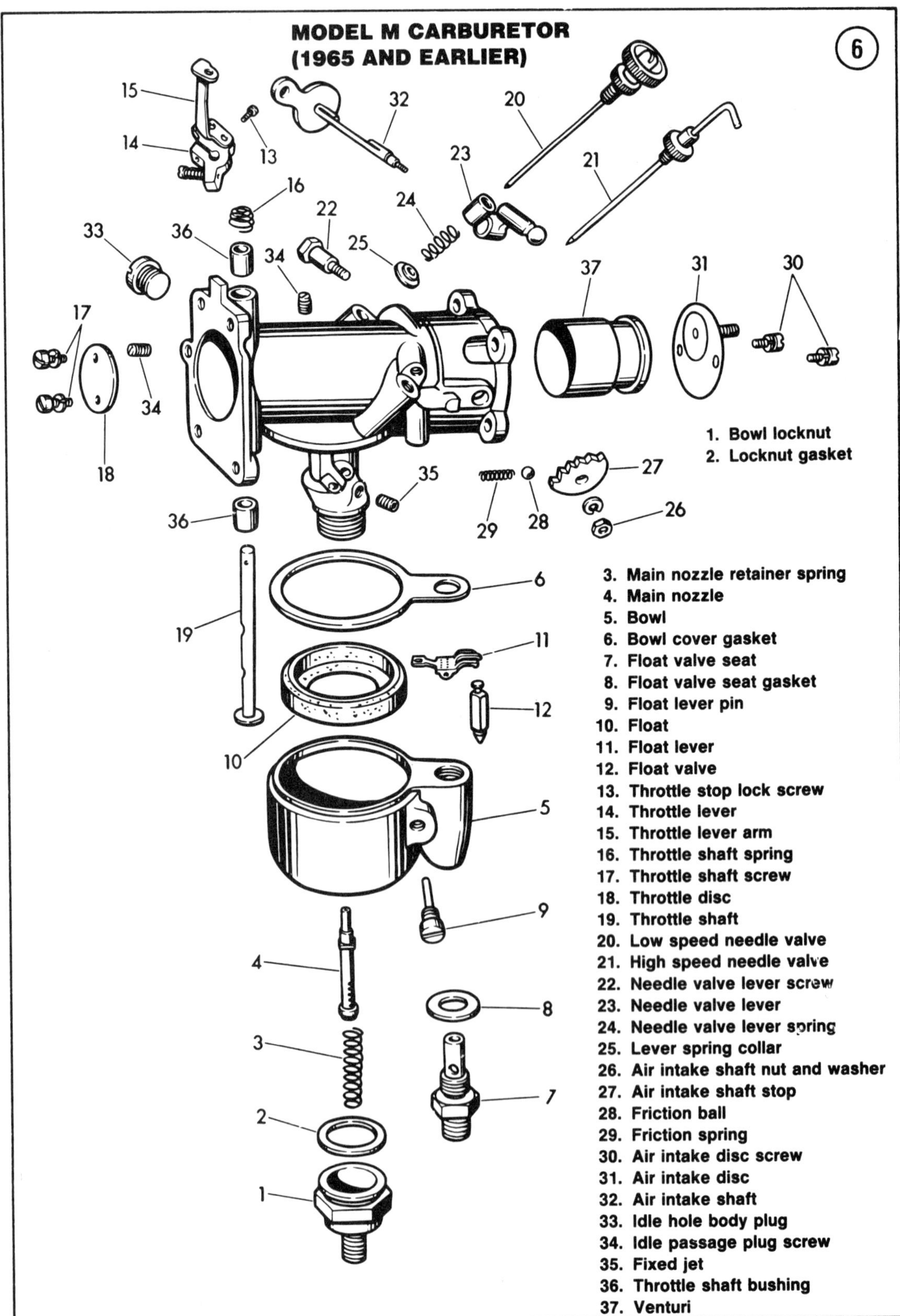
MODEL M CARBURETOR
(1965 AND EARLIER)
6
1. Bowl locknut
2. Locknut gasket
3. Main nozzle retainer spring
4. Main nozzle
5. Bowl
6. Bowl cover gasket
7. Float valve seat
8. Float valve seat gasket
9. Float lever pin
10. Float
11. Float lever
12. Float valve
13. Throttle stop lock screw
14. Throttle lever
15. Throttle lever arm
16. Throttle shaft spring
17. Throttle shaft screw
18. Throttle disc
19. Throttle shaft
20. Low speed needle valve
21. High speed needle valve
22. Needle valve lever screw
23. Needle valve lever
24. Needle valve lever spring
25. Lever spring collar
26. Air intake shaft nut and washer
27. Air intake shaft stop
28. Friction ball
29. Friction spring
30. Air intake disc screw
31. Air intake disc
32. Air intake shaft
33. Idle hole body plug
34. Idle passage plug screw
35. Fixed jet
36. Throttle shaft bushing
37. Venturi

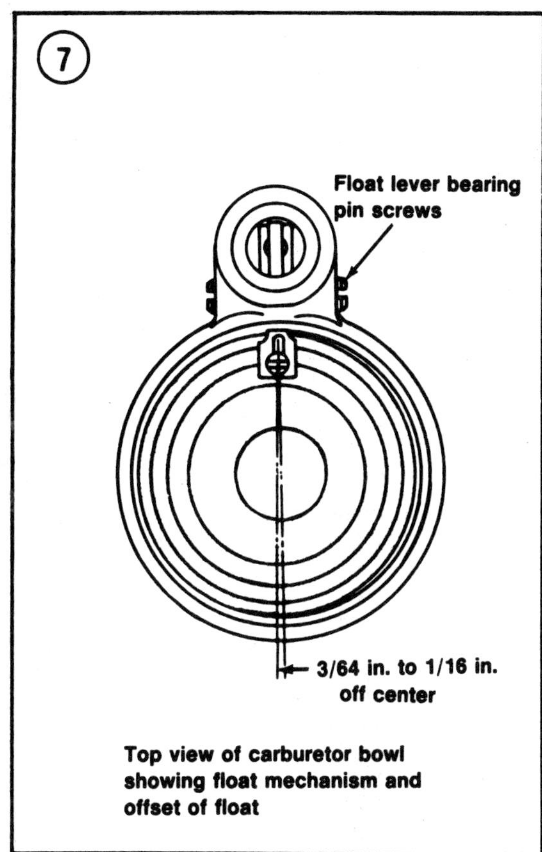

Top view of carburetor bowl showing float mechanism and offset of float

b. Turn the float bowl upside down so that the float valve closes.
c. Suck on the float valve seat. If the valve leaks, replace the float valve and seat.

21. Check the float for damage. If necessary, replace by performing the following. Refer to **Figure** 7.
   a. Cut the cement seal from around the screw that secures the float to the float lever.
   b. Remove the float screw and discard the float.
   c. Install the new float.
   d. Install the float screw but do not tighten it at this time.
   e. Position the float bowl as it would ride on the carburetor. Turn bowl so that the fuel inlet faces away from you.
   f. Pull the float toward you to the limit of the float lever. Then pull the float approximately 1/16 in. to the left of the center line as shown in **Figure** 7. This provides adequate clearance in the float bowl.
   g. Tighten the float screw.
   h. Seal the screw to the float with any cement that is not attacked by gasoline. Thick shellac also works well.

22. After assembling the float for the final time, check the float level as described in this chapter.
23. Assembly is the reverse of disassembly, noting the following.
24. Install the venturi (37) so that the small end faces toward the air intake (rear).
25. Install the throttle shaft (19) so that the counterbored screw head notches face to the left side of the carburetor when viewing the carburetor from the throttle shaft end.
26. Make sure that the throttle disc (18) seals all around the carburetor throat. To align the disc, install the disc and screws finger tight. Operate the throttle shaft several times and check the disc positioning in the carburetor throat. Tighten the screws securely when the disc is positioned correctly.

NOTE
If the throttle shaft binds after installing the disc, loosen the disc screws and reposition the disc. Tighten the screws after realignment.

27. Position the throttle disc and the throttle lever in their wide open positions before tightening the throttle stop lock screw.
28. Throttle lever and shaft should operate with a slight drag. If operation is too loose, loosen the throttle stop lock screw (13). Then compress parts on throttle shaft with fingers while retightening screw.
29. Adjust the carburetor as described in Chapter Three.

Disassembly/Assembly (Bendix Carburetor, 1972-early 1976)

The Bendix Model 16P12 carburetors are installed on 1972-early 1976 models. Refer to **Figure 8** for this procedure.

1. Remove the pump lever screw (1, **Figure 8**).
2. Remove the accelerating pump (3) as an assembly.
3. Remove idle tube (4) and its gasket (5).
4. Remove the jet and tube assembly (6) from the bottom of the float bowl. It may be necessary to give this assembly a firm tug to pull it from its bore. After pulling it out, remove its fiber washer (7) and O-ring (8).
5. Tap the float bowl (9) and remove it.
6. Carefully remove the float pivot pin (11).
7. Remove float (12), float valve (14) and float spring (13) as an assembly.
8. Remove float bowl gasket (15).
9. Remove the idle mixture needle (16) and its spring (17).

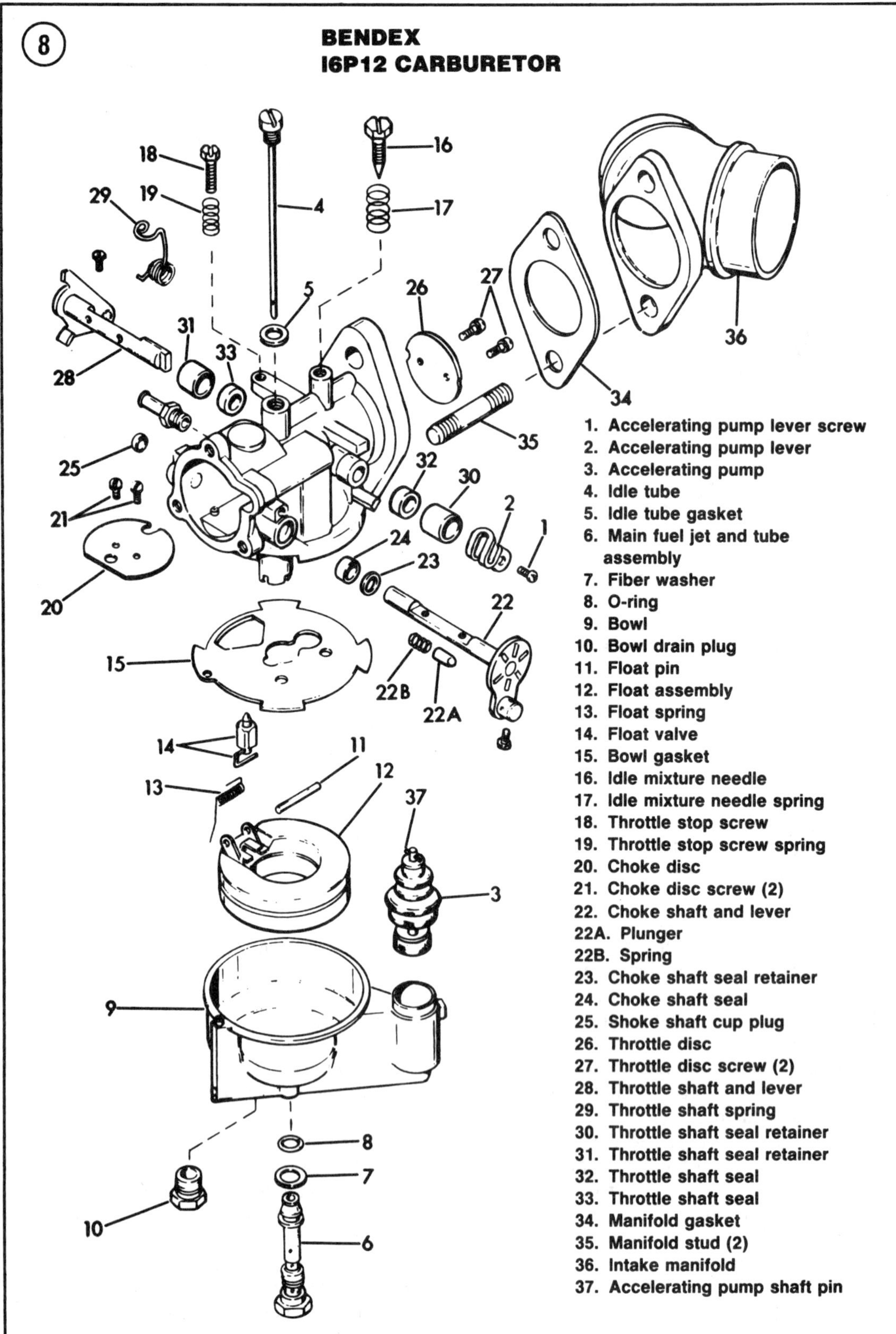
8
BENDEX
I6P12 CARBURETOR
1. Accelerating pump lever screw
2. Accelerating pump lever
3. Accelerating pump
4. Idle tube
5. Idle tube gasket
6. Main fuel jet and tube assembly
7. Fiber washer
8. O-ring
9. Bowl
10. Bowl drain plug
11. Float pin
12. Float assembly
13. Float spring
14. Float valve
15. Bowl gasket
16. Idle mixture needle
17. Idle mixture needle spring
18. Throttle stop screw
19. Throttle stop screw spring
20. Choke disc
21. Choke disc screw (2)
22. Choke shaft and lever
22A. Plunger
22B. Spring
23. Choke shaft seal retainer
24. Choke shaft seal
25. Shoke shaft cup plug
26. Throttle disc
27. Throttle disc screw (2)
28. Throttle shaft and lever
29. Throttle shaft spring
30. Throttle shaft seal retainer
31. Throttle shaft seal retainer
32. Throttle shaft seal
33. Throttle shaft seal
34. Manifold gasket
35. Manifold stud (2)
36. Intake manifold
37. Accelerating pump shaft pin

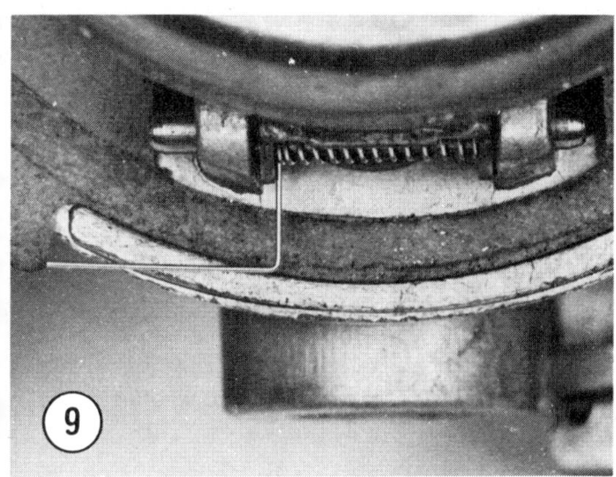

10. Remove the throttle stop screw (18) and its spring (19).

NOTE

The following steps are required only if removal of the choke and/or throttle plates is necessary.

11. Remove the choke disc screws (21). Then slide the choke disc (20) from the choke shaft (22). Remove the choke shaft, together with the plunger (22A) and spring (22B).
12. Remove the seal retainer (23) and seal (24) from inside the choke shaft opening (if replacement is required).
13. Remove the throttle disc screws (27). Then slide the disc (26) from the throttle shaft. Remove the throttle shaft, together with its lever (28).
14. Remove the throttle shaft seal retainers (30) and seals (if replacement is required).
15. Clean and inspect the carburetor as described in this chapter.
16. Assembly is the reverse of these steps, noting the following.
17. Make sure that the float needle clip is attached to the float tang.
18. Make sure that the float spring is installed as shown in **Figure 9**. When installing the float bowl, bend the end of the spring up so that it rests against the inside of the float bowl.
19. Check and adjust float level, if necessary, before installing float bowl. See *Float Level Measurement* in this chapter.
20. Adjust the carburetor as described in Chapter Three.

Disassembly/Assembly (Keihin, Late 1976-1978)

Refer to **Figure 10** for this procedure.

1. Disassemble the accelerating pump as follows:
   a. Remove accelerating pump housing (33) at the bottom of the float bowl (29).
   b. Remove the spring (32), diaphragm (31) and 2 O-rings (30).
2. Remove the float bowl (29).
3. Remove the float pin screw (6) and withdraw the float pin (5) and float (23).
4. Detach the fuel valve (21) from the float.
5. Remove the O-ring (28) from slot in float chamber wall.
6. Remove the rod (7) and boot (8) from the float bowl.
7. Remove the slow jet plug (27) and remove the slow jet (25).
8. Remove the main jet (26) and the main nozzle (24).
9. Remove the O-ring (20) from the slot in the intake mounting flange.
10. Remove the throttle lever nut (19) and washer (18). Then remove the throttle lever (17) and its spring (16).
11. If necessary, remove the 2 brackets (2 and 15) at the top of the carburetor housing.
12. The throttle and choke (40) disc assemblies are matched to the individual carburetor during manufacturing. If these parts are damaged, the carburetor must be replaced.
13. Clean and inspect the carburetor in this chapter.
14. Assembly is the reverse of these steps, noting the following.
15. Check and adjust the float level before installing the float bowl. See *Float Level Measurement* in this chapter.
16. Adjust the carburetor as described in Chapter Three.

Disassembly/Assembly (Keihin 1979-on)

Refer to **Figure 11** (1979-1980) or **Figure 12** (1981-1985) for this procedure.

1. Remove the accelerating pump housing (**Figure 13**) at the bottom of the float bowl. Then remove the spring (**Figure 14**) and diaphragm (**Figure 15**).
2. Remove the O-ring from the accelerating pump housing (**Figure 16**).
3. Remove the float bowl (**Figure 17**).
4. Remove the rubber boot (**Figure 18**) and accelerator pump rod (**Figure 19**) from the float bowl.
5. Remove the float pin screw (**Figure 20**) and withdraw the float pin and float (**Figure 21**) as an assembly.
6. Detach the fuel valve from the float (**Figure 22**).
7. Remove the low speed plug (**Figure 23**) and remove the low speed jet (**Figure 24**).
8. Remove the main jet (**Figure 25**).

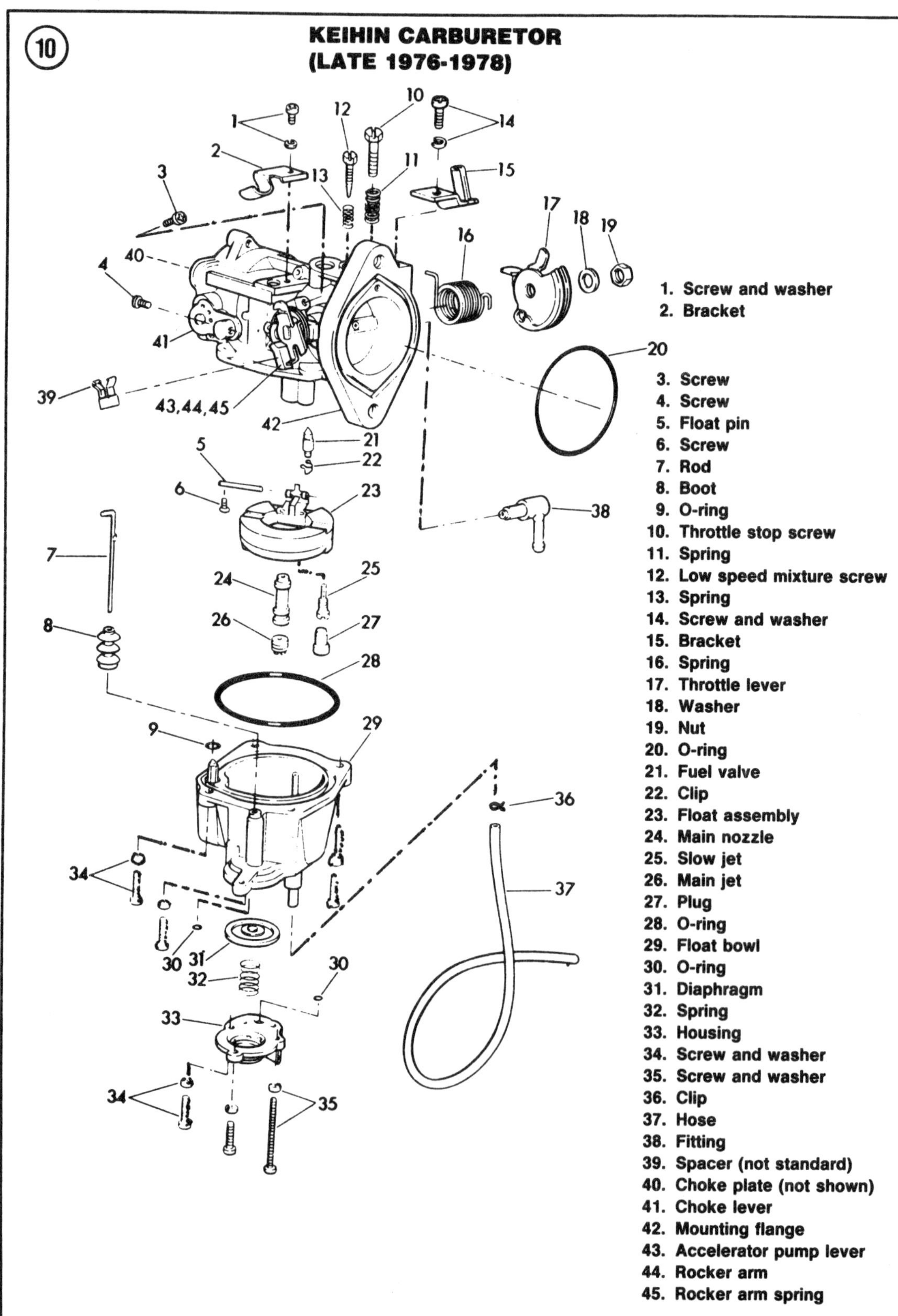

10
KEIHIN CARBURETOR
(LATE 1976-1978)
1. Screw and washer
2. Bracket
3. Screw
4. Screw
5. Float pin
6. Screw
7. Rod
8. Boot
9. O-ring
10. Throttle stop screw
11. Spring
12. Low speed mixture screw
13. Spring
14. Screw and washer
15. Bracket
16. Spring
17. Throttle lever
18. Washer
19. Nut
20. O-ring
21. Fuel valve
22. Clip
23. Float assembly
24. Main nozzle
25. Slow jet
26. Main jet
27. Plug
28. O-ring
29. Float bowl
30. O-ring
31. Diaphragm
32. Spring
33. Housing
34. Screw and washer
35. Screw and washer
36. Clip
37. Hose
38. Fitting
39. Spacer (not standard)
40. Choke plate (not shown)
41. Choke lever
42. Mounting flange
43. Accelerator pump lever
44. Rocker arm
45. Rocker arm spring

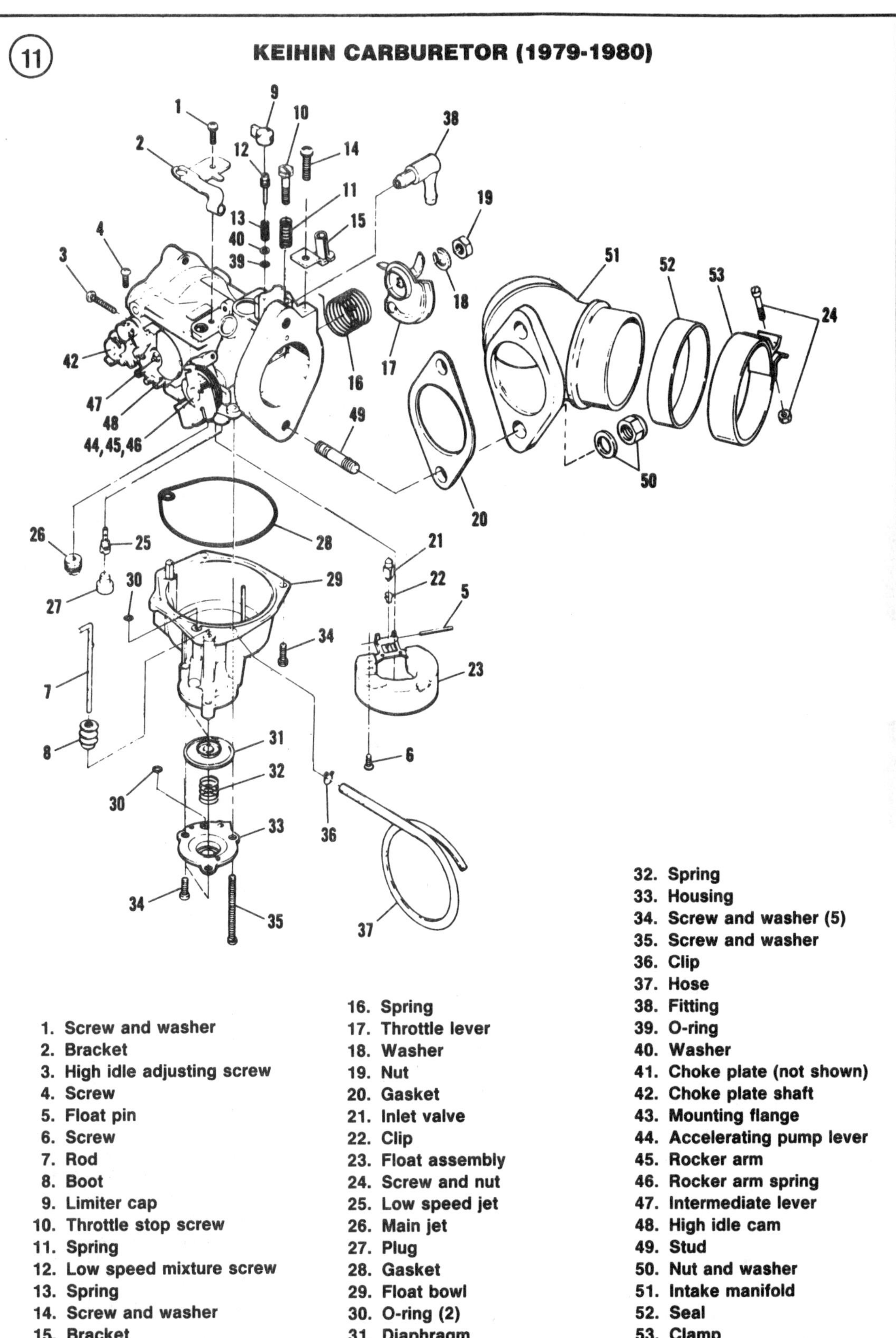
11
KEIHIN CARBURETOR (1979-1980)
1. Screw and washer
2. Bracket
3. High idle adjusting screw
4. Screw
5. Float pin
6. Screw
7. Rod
8. Boot
9. Limiter cap
10. Throttle stop screw
11. Spring
12. Low speed mixture screw
13. Spring
14. Screw and washer
15. Bracket
16. Spring
17. Throttle lever
18. Washer
19. Nut
20. Gasket
21. Inlet valve
22. Clip
23. Float assembly
24. Screw and nut
25. Low speed jet
26. Main jet
27. Plug
28. Gasket
29. Float bowl
30. O-ring (2)
31. Diaphragm
32. Spring
33. Housing
34. Screw and washer (5)
35. Screw and washer
36. Clip
37. Hose
38. Fitting
39. O-ring
40. Washer
41. Choke plate (not shown)
42. Choke plate shaft
43. Mounting flange
44. Accelerating pump lever
45. Rocker arm
46. Rocker arm spring
47. Intermediate lever
48. High idle cam
49. Stud
50. Nut and washer
51. Intake manifold
52. Seal
53. Clamp

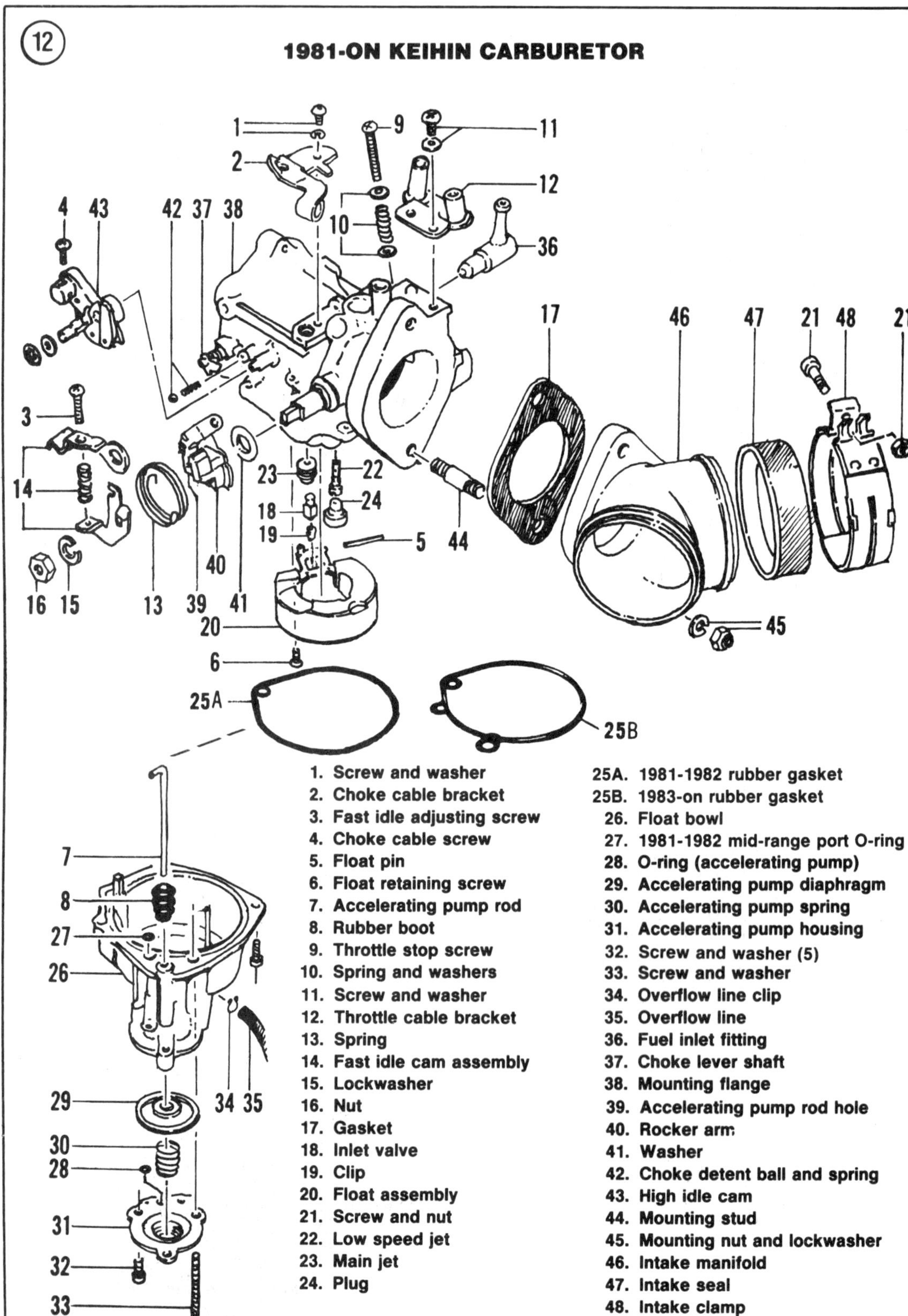
12
1981-ON KEIHIN CARBURETOR
1. Screw and washer
2. Choke cable bracket
3. Fast idle adjusting screw
4. Choke cable screw
5. Float pin
6. Float retaining screw
7. Accelerating pump rod
8. Rubber boot
9. Throttle stop screw
10. Spring and washers
11. Screw and washer
12. Throttle cable bracket
13. Spring
14. Fast idle cam assembly
15. Lockwasher
16. Nut
17. Gasket
18. Inlet valve
19. Clip
20. Float assembly
21. Screw and nut
22. Low speed jet
23. Main jet
24. Plug
25A. 1981-1982 rubber gasket
25B. 1983-on rubber gasket
26. Float bowl
27. 1981-1982 mid-range port O-ring
28. O-ring (accelerating pump)
29. Accelerating pump diaphragm
30. Accelerating pump spring
31. Accelerating pump housing
32. Screw and washer (5)
33. Screw and washer
34. Overflow line clip
35. Overflow line
36. Fuel inlet fitting
37. Choke lever shaft
38. Mounting flange
39. Accelerating pump rod hole
40. Rocker arm
41. Washer
42. Choke detent ball and spring
43. High idle cam
44. Mounting stud
45. Mounting nut and lockwasher
46. Intake manifold
47. Intake seal
48. Intake clamp

13

17

14

18

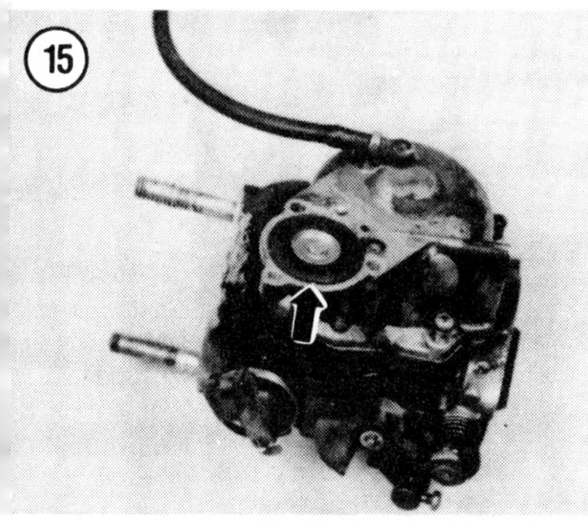
15

19

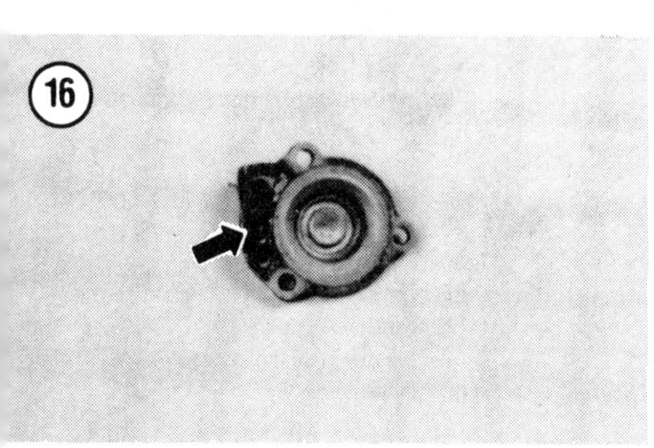
16

20

9. Remove the main nozzle (**Figure 26**).
10. Remove the nut (A, **Figure 27**) and washer from the throttle shaft. Then remove the throttle lever (B, **Figure 27**) or high idle cam and its spring.
11. If necessary, remove the bracket at the top of the carburetor housing (C, **Figure 27**).
12. The throttle (**Figure 28**) and choke (**Figure 29**) valve assemblies are matched to the individual carburetor during manufacturing. If these parts are damaged, the carburetor must be replaced. Do not remove them.
13. Remove the O-ring (**Figure 30**) and the overflow tube (**Figure 31**) from the float bowl.
14. Assembly is the reverse of these steps, noting the following.
15. Check and adjust the float level before installing the float bowl. See *Float Level Measurement* in this chapter.
16. Adjust the carburetor as described in Chapter Three.

Inspection/Cleaning (All Models)

1. Clean all metal parts in a good grade of carburtor cleaner. This solution is available at most automotive or motorcycle supply stores, in a small, resealable tank with a dip basket. If it is

21

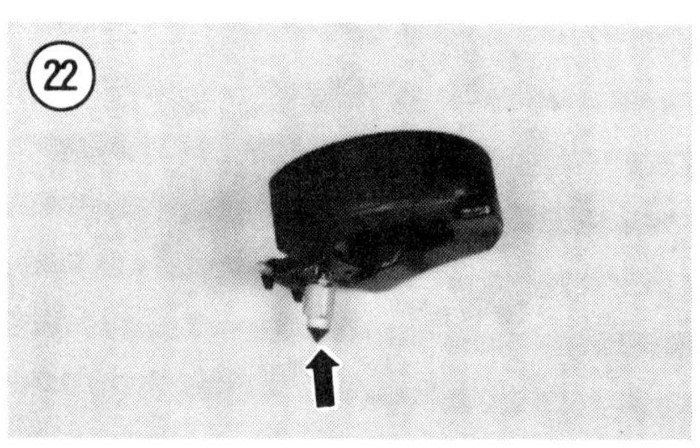
22

23

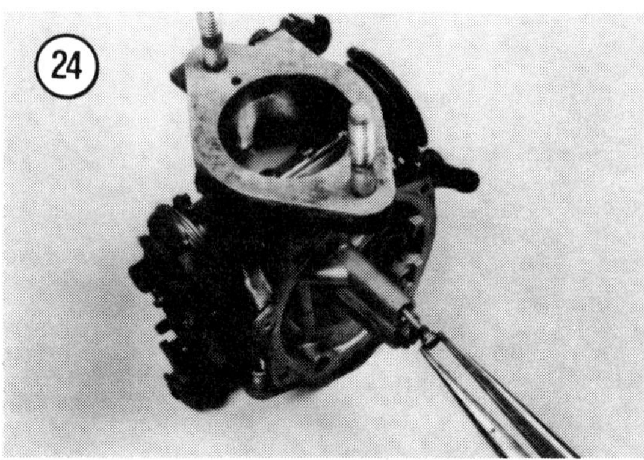
24

25

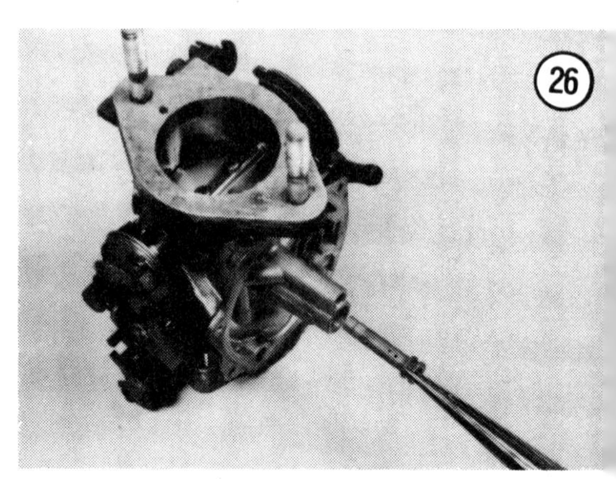
26

tightly sealed when not in use, the solution will last for several cleanings. Follow the manufacturer's instructions for correct soaking time.

CAUTION
*Do not clean rubber or other non-metal parts (**Figure 32**) in carburetor cleaner as the chemical will destroy these parts.*

2. Remove all parts from the cleaner and blow dry with compressed air. Blow out the jets with compressed air. *Do not* use a drill or piece of wire to clean them as minor gouges in a jet can alter the flow rate and upset the air/fuel mixture.
3. If the floats (**Figure 33**) are suspected of leaking, put them in a small container of a water and push them down. If the floats sink or if bubbles appear indicating a leak, the floats must be replaced.
4. Check the float needle (**Figure 34**) and seat contact areas closely. Both contact surfaces should appear smooth without any gouging or other apparant damage. Replace both needle and seat as a set if any one part is worn or damaged.
5. Inspect the accelerating pump diaphragm for holes and cracks. Replace if necessary.
6. Replace the accelerating pump rod on Keihin carburetors if bent or worn.
7. Replace all worn O-rings and gaskets.

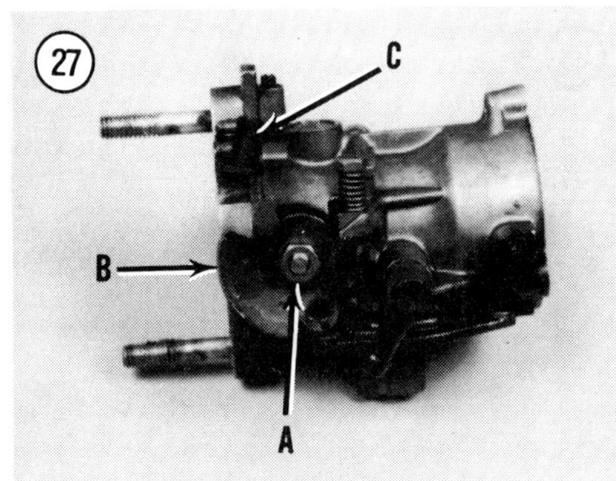

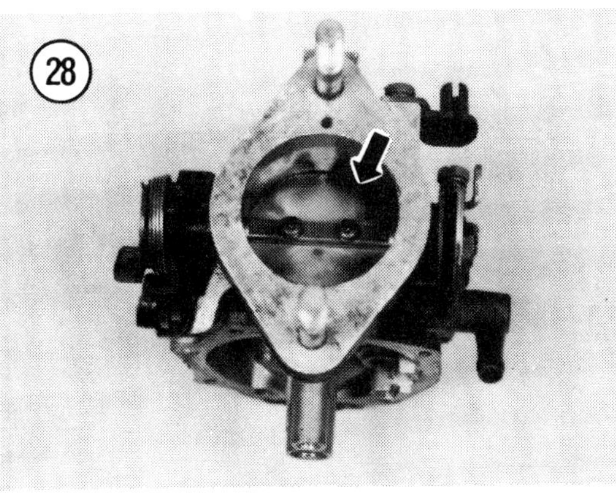

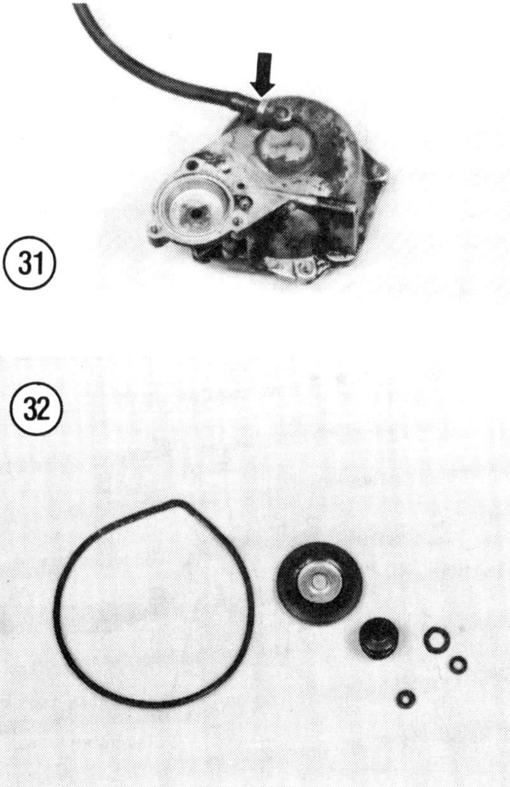

Float Level Measurement

Model M carburetors

1. Remove the carburetor as described in this chapter.
2. Remove the float bowl.
3. Turn the float bowl upside down.

NOTE
The float bowl must be assembled to perform this check.

4. Refer to **Figure 35**. Measure the distance from the lip of the float bowl to the top of the float at a point directly opposite the float lever. Correct height measurement is 1/4 in.
5. If the float height is incorrect, remove the float as described in this chapter.

CAUTION
Any attempt to adjust the float while it is installed will damage the float lever prongs.

6. To adjust, bend the float lever as required. Reinstall the float and recheck the measurement.
7. Repeat Step 6 until the correct height measurement is obtained.
8. Reinstall the float bowl as described in this chapter.

Bendix carburetors, 1972-early 1976

1. Remove the carburetor as described in this chapter.
2. Remove the float bowl.

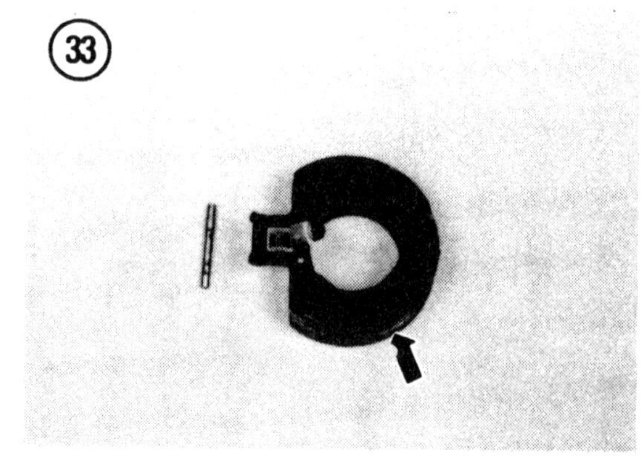

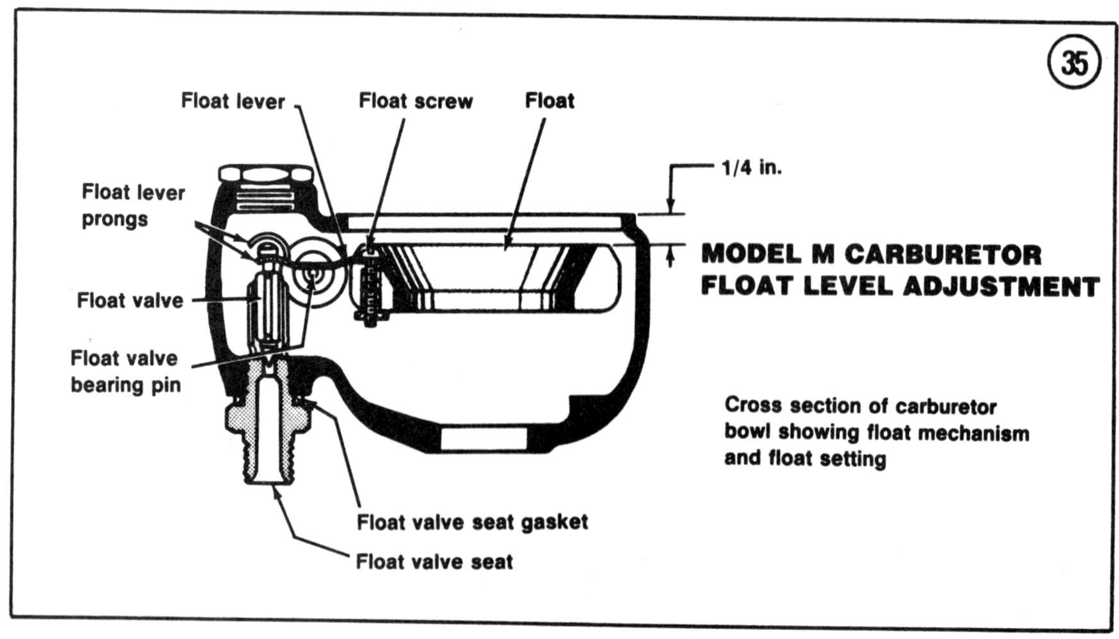

MODEL M CARBURETOR FLOAT LEVEL ADJUSTMENT

Cross section of carburetor bowl showing float mechanism and float setting

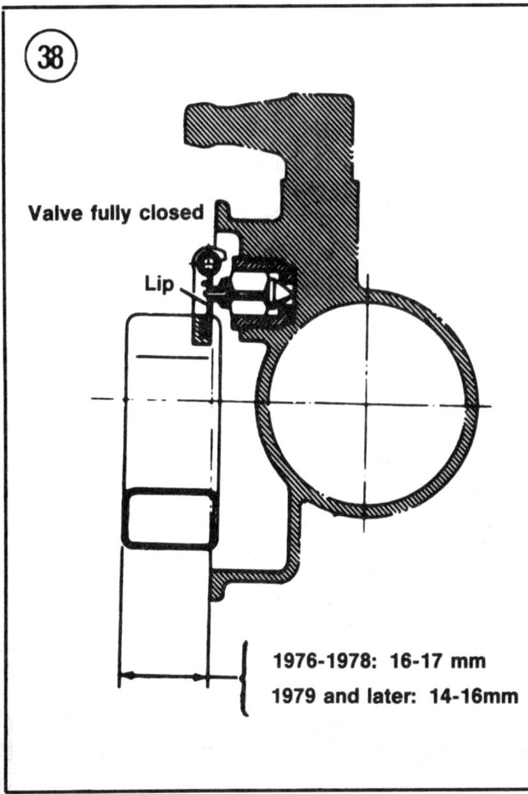

3. Turn the carburetor over so that the float is at the top.
4. In this position, the bottom float surface must be 3/16 in. from the carburetor gasket surface (**Figure 36**). A 3/16 in. drill bit may be used as a guage.
5. To adjust, bend the float tang (**Figure 37**) as required, using long-nose pliers.
6. Reinstall the float bowl and install the carburetor.

Keihin carburetors, 1976-1985

1. Remove the carburetor as described in this chapter.
2. Remove the float bowl.
3. *Valve fully closed position:* Turn the carburetor to position the float bowl as indicated in **Figure 38**. Measure the float height from the float bowl gasket surface to the top float surface. Bend the float tang (**Figure 39**) to adjust.
4. Reinstall the float bowl and install the carburetor.

Rejetting Carburetors

Do not try to solve a poor running engine problem by rejetting the carburetors if all of the following conditions hold true.

1. The engine has held a good tune in the past with the standard jetting.
2. The engine has not been modified (this includes the addition of accessory exhaust systems).
3. The motorcycle is being operated in the same geographical region under the same general climatic conditions as in the past.
4. The motorcycle was and is being ridden at average highway speeds.

If those conditions all hold true, the chances are that the problem is due to a malfunction in the

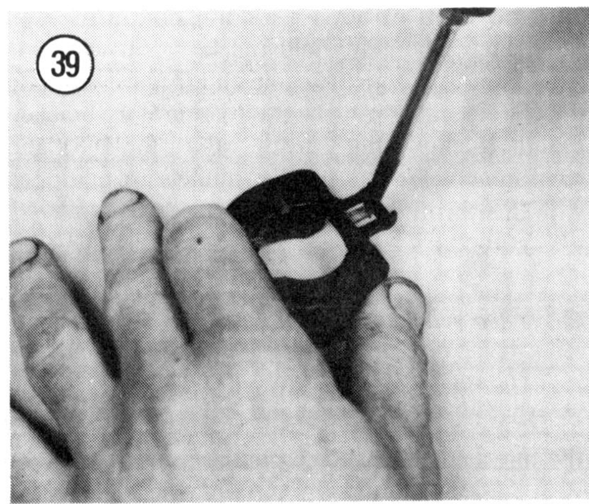

carburetor or in another components that needs to be adjusted or repaired. Changing carburetor jet size probably won't solve the problem. Rejetting the carburetors may be necessary if nay of the following conditions hold true.

1. A non-standard type of air filter element is being used.
2. A non-standard exhaust system is installed on the motorcycle.
3. Any of the top end components in the engine (pistons, cam, valves, compression ratio, etc.) have been modified.

NOTE
When installing accessory engine equipment, manufacturers often enclose guidelines on rejetting the carburetor.

4. The motorcycle is in use at considerably higher or lower altitudes or in a considerably hotter or colder climate than in the past.
5. The motorcycle is being operated at considerably higher speeds than before and changing to colder spark plugs does not solve the problem.
6. Someone has previously changed the carburetor jetting.
7. The motorcycle has never held a satisfactory engine tune.

NOTE
If it is necessary to rejet the carburetors, check with a dealer or motorcycle performance tuner for recommendations as to the size of jets to install for your specific situation.

THROTTLE CABLE REPLACEMENT

1. Remove the seat and fuel tank.
2. Disconnect the throttle cable at the handlebar as described in Chapter Eight.
3. Remove any carburetor holding bolt or bracket.
4. At the carburetor, hold the lever up with one hand and disengage the cable end (**Figure 40**). Slip the cable out through the carburetor bracket. **Figure 41** shows the throttle cables for 1981 and later models. 1980 and earlier models are equipped with one throttle cable.

NOTE
The piece of string attached in the next step will be used to pull the new throttle cable back through the frame so it will be routed in the exact same position.

5. Tie a piece of heavy string or cord to the end of the throttle cable at the carburetor. Wrap this end with masking or duct tape. Do not use an excessive amount of tape as it will be pulled through the frame loop during removal. Tie the other end of the string to the frame.
6. Carefully pull the cable (and attached string) out through the frame loop, past the electrical harness and from behind the headlight housing. Make sure the attached string follows the same path as the cable through the frame.
7. Remove the tape and untie the string from the old cable.
8. Tie the string to the new throttle cable and wrap it with tape.
9. Carefully pull the string back through the frame, routing the new cable through the same path as the old cable.

40

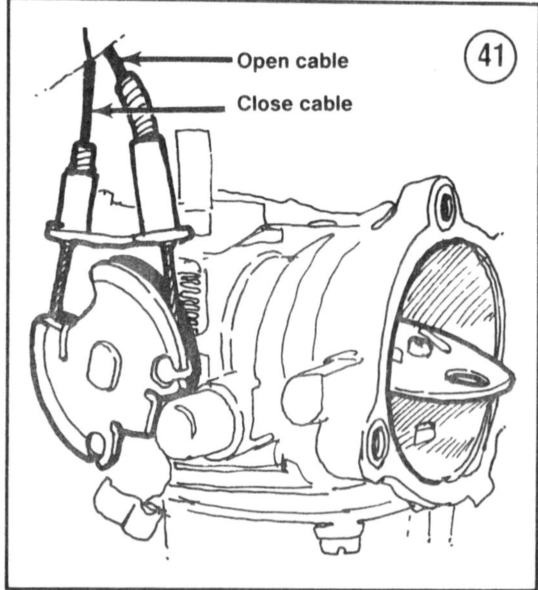

41

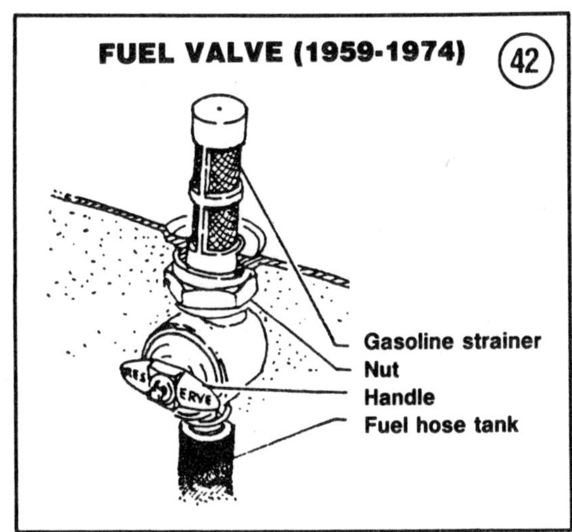

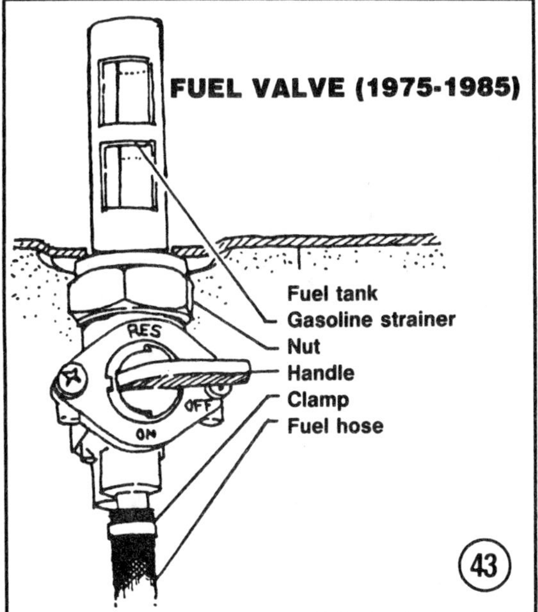

10. Remove the tape and untie the string from the cable and the frame.
11. Lubricate the new cable as described under *Control Cables* in Chapter Three.
12. Slip the cable in through the carburetor bracket. Then, while holding the lever up with one hand, engage the cable at the carburetor lever.
13. Attach the throttle cable to the throttle/switch housing and install the housing as described in Chapter Eight.
14. Operate the throttle grip and make sure the carburetor throttle linkage is operating correctly and with no binding. If operation is incorrect or there is binding, carefully check that the cables are attached correctly and there are no tight bends in the cables.
15. Adjust the throttle cable as described in Chapter Three.
16. Install all throttle attaching bolts or brackets.
17. Install the fuel tank and seat.
18. Start the engine and turn the handlebar from side-to-side. Do not operate the throttle. If the engine speed increases as the handlebar assembly is turned, the throttle cable is routed incorrectly. Remove the seat and fuel tank and recheck the cable routing. Do not ride the motorcycle until this unsafe condition has been corrected.

FUEL SHUTOFF VALVE

Removal/Installation and Filter Cleaning

Refer to **Figure 42** or **Figure 43** for this procedure.

1. Turn the valve to the OFF position.
2. Disconnect the fuel line at the shutoff valve.
3. Drain the fuel into a gasoline approved storage can or tank.
4. Remove the fuel tank.
5. Set the fuel tank on a protective pad or blanket and position it so fuel will not spill out when the shutoff valve is removed.
6. Loosen the nut and remove the fuel shutoff valve.
7. Clean the filter with a medium soft toothbrush and carefully blow out with compressed air.
8. Inspect the condition of the gasket; replace if necessary.
9. Reassemble the valve and turn the tank as it sits on the bike. Check the area around the valve carefully to make sure no fuel is leaking.
10. Install the fuel tank.

FUEL TANK

Removal/Installation

1. Disconnect the battery negative lead.
2. Disconnect the fuel line at the fuel shutoff valve. Drain the fuel into a gasoline approved tank or can, if necessary.
3. Remove the mounting bolts at the front of the fuel tank.
4. Remove the rear mounting bolts and spacers.
5. Disconnect the upper vent line.
6. Remove the fuel tank.

WARNING
Whenever removing the tank, make sure to store it in a safe place—away from open flame or objects that could fall and damage the tank.

7. Install by reversing these removal steps. Check all hose connectons for leaks.

Fuel Tank Repairs

Motorcycle fuel tanks are relatively maintenance free. However, a major cause of fuel tank leakage occurs when the fuel tank is not mounted securely and it is allowed to "vibrate" during riding. When installing the tank, make sure the rubber dampers at the front and rear of the tank are in position and that the tank is mounted securely at the front back with the proper fasteners.

If your fuel tank leaks, refer service to a qualified dealer or welding shop equipped to repair fuel tanks.

EXHAUST SYSTEM

Removal/Installation

1. Place the bike on the sidestand.
2. Remove all exhaust pipe shields.
3. Loosen and remove the rear muffler clamps and brackets.
4. Remove the mufflers (**Figure 44**).
5. Loosen the exhaust pipes (**Figure 45**) at the cylinder head and remove them.
6. Install by reversing these removal steps, noting the following.
7. Install all parts and secure fasteners finger-tight only. Then tighten the exhaust flange bolts securely and work back to the muffler. This will minimize exhaust leak at the cylinder heads.

Exhaust System Care

The appearance of the exhaust system greatly enhances any motorcycle. And, more imporant, the exhaust system is a vital key to the motorcycle's operation and performance. As the owner, you should periodically inspect, clean and polish the exhaust system. Special chemical cleaners and preservatives compounded for exhaust systems are available at most motorcycle shops.

Severe dents which cause gas flow restrictions require the replacement of the damaged part.

Problems occuring within the exhaust pipes are normally due to rust from the collection of water in the pipe. Periodically, or whenever the exhaust pipes are removed, turn the pipes to remove any trapped water.

EMISSION CONTROL (1985 CALIFORNIA MODELS)

All 1985 models sold in California are equipped with an evaporative emission control system to meet the CARB regulations in effect at the time of the model's manufacture.

Inspection/Replacement

Maintenance to the evaporative emission control system consists of periodic inspection of the hoses for proper routing and a check of the canister mounting brackets.

When removal or replacement of an emission part is required, refer to **Figures 46-48**. Route and connect all hoses as shown in the appropriate diagram.

(46)

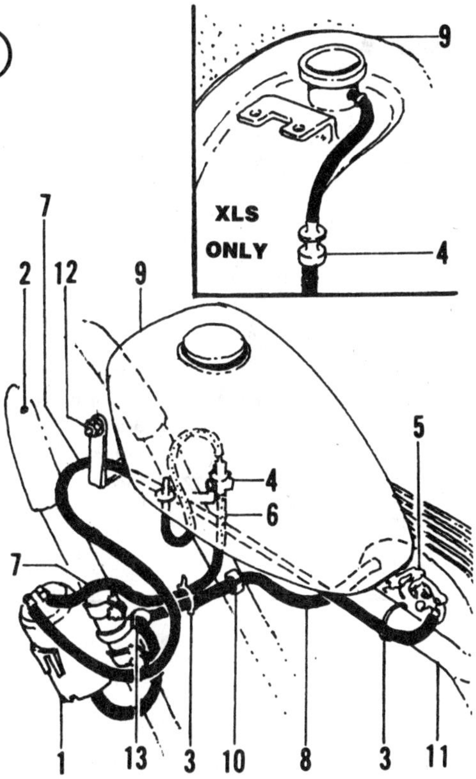

XLS ONLY

EVAPORATIVE EMISSION CONTROL SYSTEM (1985 CALIFORNIA)

1. Canister
2. Frame tube
3. Clamp
4. Vapor valve
5. Fuel valve
6. Hose
7. Hose
8. Hose
9. Fuel tank
10. Clamp
11. Frame backbone
12. Nut
13. Clamp

(47)

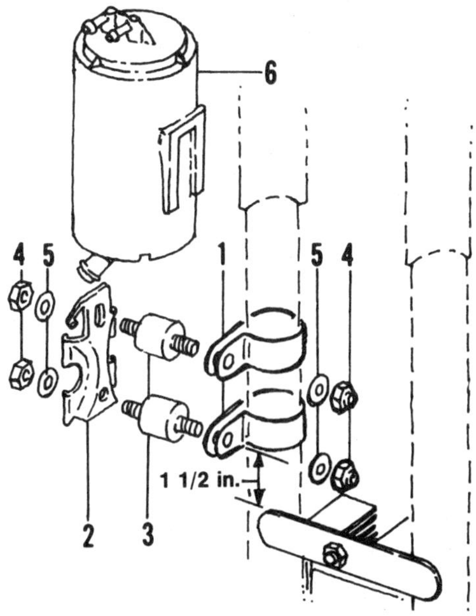

1 1/2 in.

CARBON CANISTER ASSEMBLY (1985 CALIFORNIA)

1. Clamp
2. Bracket
3. Rubber mount
4. Nut
5. Flat washer
6. Carbon canister

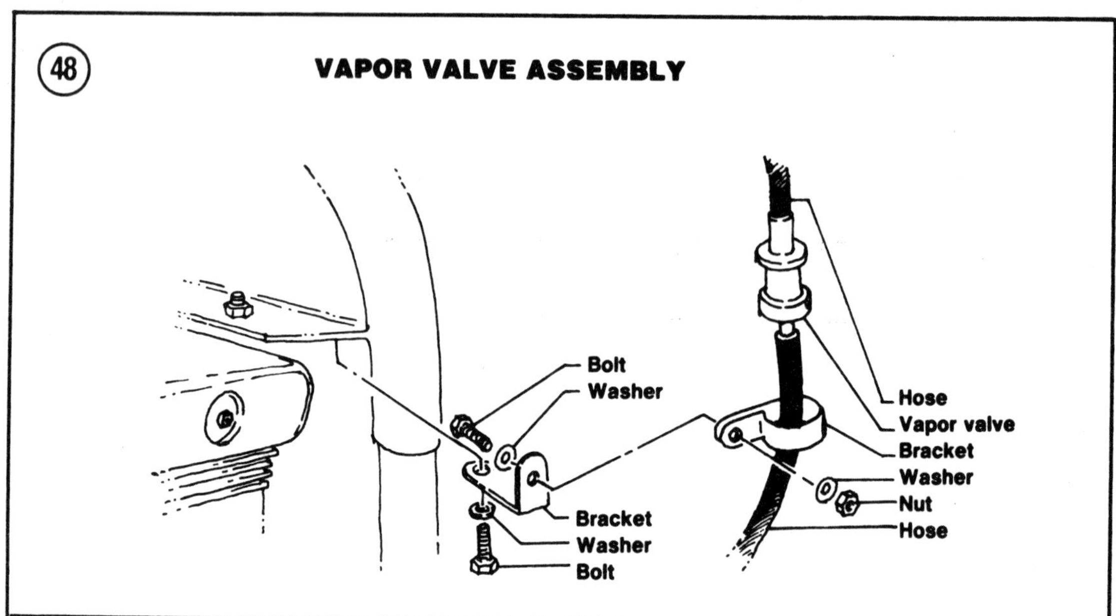
48
VAPOR VALVE ASSEMBLY
Bolt
Washer
Bracket
Washer
Bolt
Hose
Vapor valve
Bracket
Washer
Nut
Hose

CHAPTER SEVEN

ELECTRICAL SYSTEM

7

This chapter covers the following systems:

a. Charging.
b. Ignition.
c. Starting.
d. Lighting.
e. Directional signal.
f. Horn.

Refer to Chapter Three for routine ignition system maintenance. Electrical system specifications are found in **Table 1**. **Tables 1-4** are at the end of the chapter.

CHARGING SYSTEM (1959-EARLY 1984)

The charging system consists of the battery, generator and a solid state rectifier/voltage regulator.

The generator produces an alternating current (AC) which the rectifier converts to direct current (DC). The regulator maintains the voltage to the battery and load (lights, ignition, etc.) at a constant voltage regardless of variations in engine speed and load.

Charging System Test

Whenever the charging system is suspected of trouble, make sure the battery is fully charged before going any further. Clean and test the battery as described in Chapter Three. If the battery is in good condition, test the charging system as follows.

CAUTION
It is important to read this procedure thoroughly before attempting to check the charging system to prevent component damage.

1. Disconnect the generator "F" terminal wire (**Figure 1**).

NOTE
***Figure 2** shows typical generator terminal markings.*

2. Connect a jumper wire from the generator "F" terminal to a good ground on the engine (**Figure 3**).
3. Remove the wire(s) from the generator "A" terminal.
4. Connect the positive lead of a DC ammeter to the generator "A" terminal as shown in **Figure 3**.
5. Start the engine and run it at 2,000 rpm.

6. Momentarily connect the ammeter negative terminal to the positive battery terminal. The charging amperage should be 15 amps or more for a 6-volt system or 10 amps or more for a 12-volt system. If the charging amperage is not within specifications, check the generator as described in this chapter. If the charging amperage is within specifications, the problem is in the regulator or wiring. Test the separate charging system components as described in this chapter.

CAUTION
Do not run the engine with the generator field grounded any longer than necessary. Do not run the engine with no load on the generator (ammeter negative lead not connected to battery) any longer than necessary.

CAUTION
Disconnect the ammeter from the battery before turning the engine off.

7. Polarize the generator after servicing it or the regulator, or after disconnecting any charging system wiring. See *Polarizing Generator* in this chapter.

Polarizing Generator

After any charging system wiring or component has been disconnected, the generator must be polarized before starting the engine. Failure to polarize the generator may result in burned or stuck voltage regulator contacts and possible damage to the wiring and the generator windings.

NOTE
Make sure the battery is in good condition before performing the following procedures.

1959-1977

After all wiring is connected, momentarily connect a heavy jumper wire between BAT and GEN terminals on the regulator (**Figure 4**). Remove the jumper wire.

1978-early 1984

1. *Generator on bench:* Connect the battery positive cable to the generator armature terminal. Then momentarily connect the battery negative terminal to the generator field terminal. See **Figure 5**.
2. *Generator on motorcycle and connected to regulator:* Connect one end of a jumper wire to the generator armature terminal. Momentarily touch the other end of the jumper wire to the battery positive terminal. Remove the jumper wire.

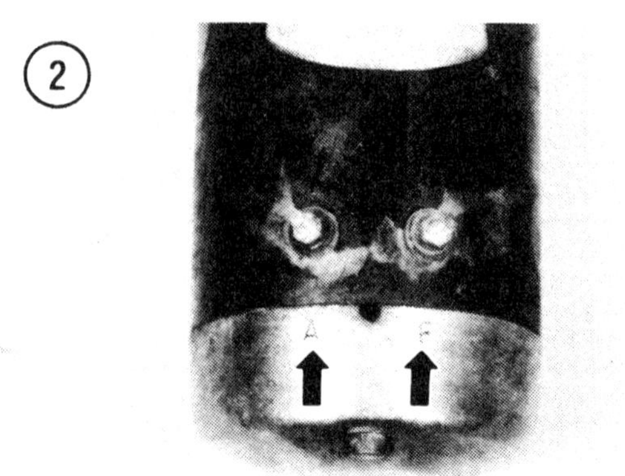

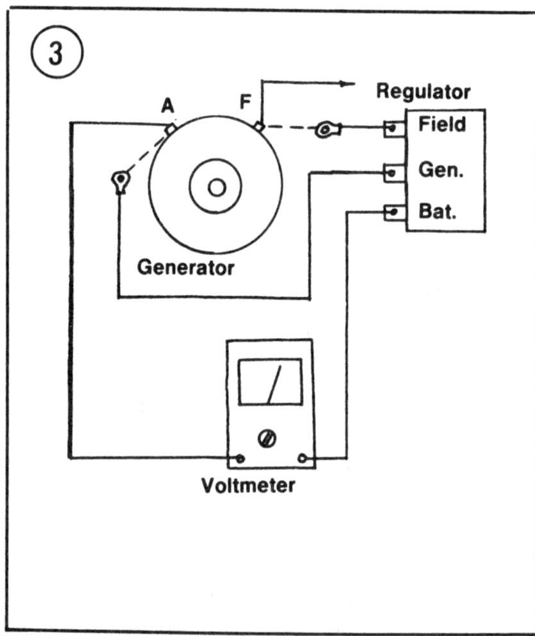

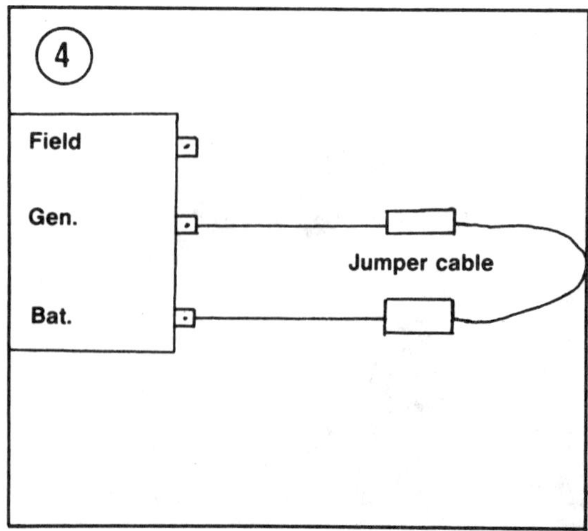

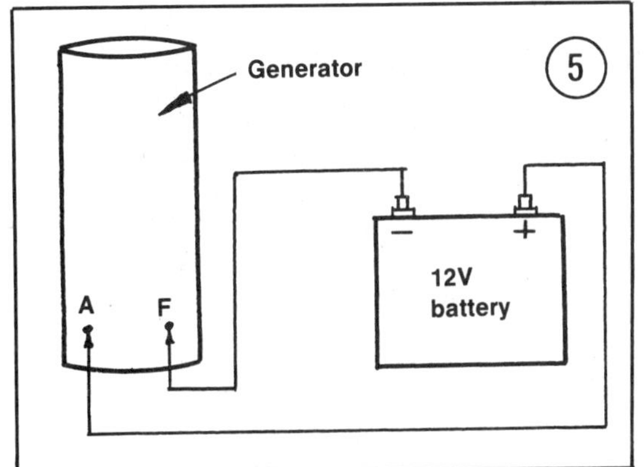

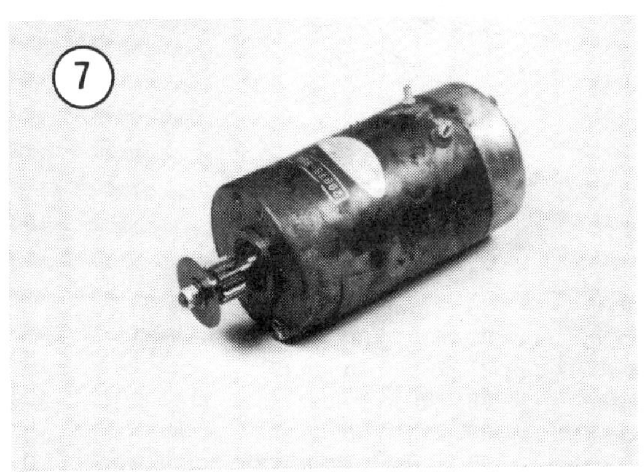

Generator

Removal/Installation

1. Disconnect and tag wires at generator (**Figure 1**).
2. Remove the 2 screws securing the generator to the gearcase (**Figure 6**).
3. *1959-1969:* Remove the regulator from the generator.
4. Remove the generator from the left side of the motorcycle with the drive gear attached (**Figure 7**).
5. Installation is the reverse of these steps.

Brush Inspection/Replacement

The overhaul of a generator is best left to an expert. This procedure shows how to replace defective generator brushes. Refer to **Figure 8** (1959-1981) or **Figure 9** (1982-early 1984) for this procedure.

1. Remove the commutator end cover nuts, washers and screws.
2. Gently tap the commutator end cover (**Figure 10**) off of the frame and armature shaft.
3. Remove the brush holder mounting plate from the frame.
4. Disconnect the black brush wires and the generator positive brush cable from the brush holder terminals.
5. Remove the brushes from the brush holders.
6. Clean the brush holders with contact cleaner.
7. Measure the longest side of each brush with a caliper (**Figure 11**). Replace the brushes if they measure 1/2 in. or less.
8. Reverse Steps 1-5 to install the brushes.

Generator Bench Testing

Generator bench testing is best left to a Harley-Davidson dealer or to an electronic repair shop specializing in motorcycles because of the specialized tools required to accurately check this component.

Voltage Regulator Testing (1959-1978)

There are 4 basic regulator tests to be performed:

a. Generating system test, which determines whether the generator or regulator is faulty.
b. Cutout relay closing voltage.
c. Voltage regulator setting.
d. Current regulator setting.

Before testing the regulator, operate the motorcycle for at least 15 minutes so that the regulator is at normal operating temperature. The regulator cover and gasket must be in place.

NOTE
Before making any voltage regulator test, be sure that the battery is in good condition and is at or near full charge. See Chapter Three for battery testing.

Delco-Remy Voltage Regulators

Generating system test

Refer to **Figure 12** for this procedure.

1. Turn the engine off.
2. Disconnect the regulator BAT terminal battery wire. Connect this wire to the negative terminal of

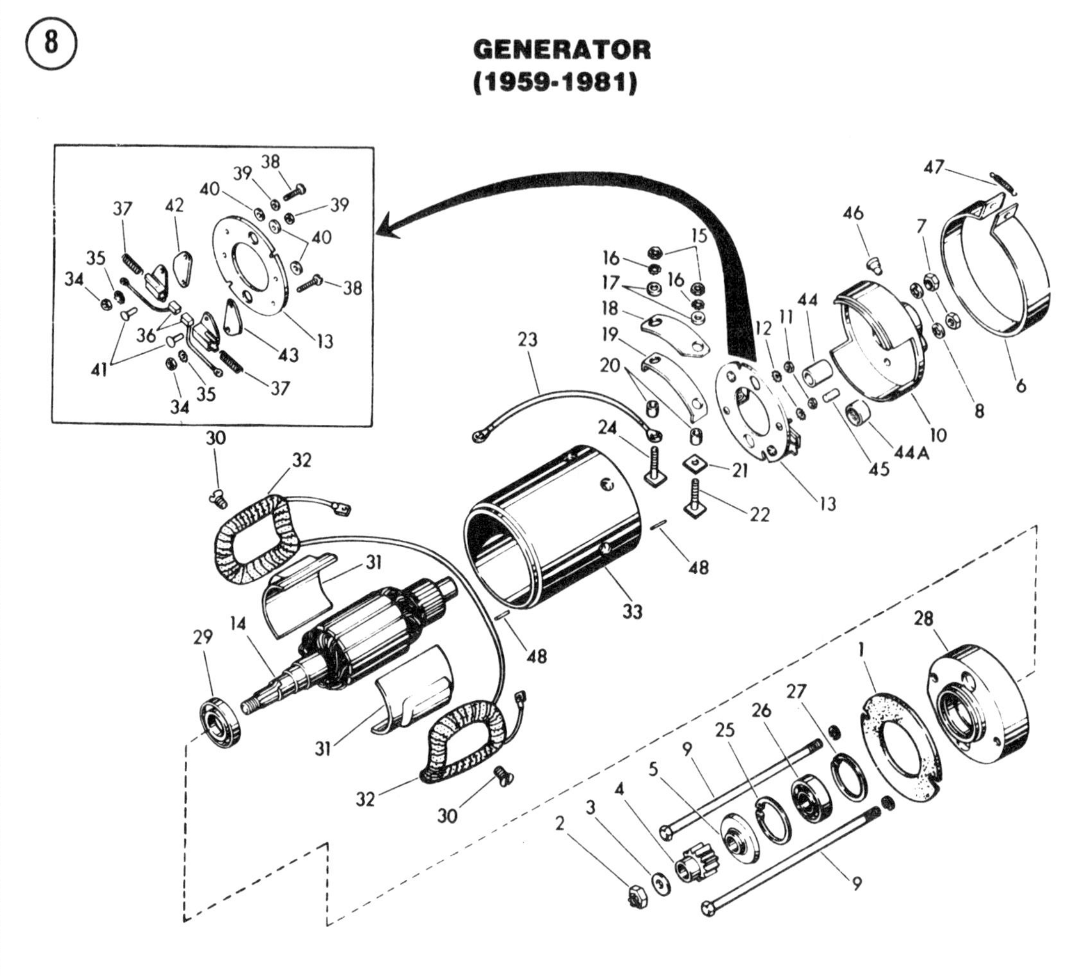

1. Mounting gasket
2. Gear shaft nut
3. Gear shaft washer
4. Drive gear
5. Drive end oil deflector
6. Brush cover strap
7. Commutator end cover nut (2)
8. Commutator end cover washer (2)
9. Frame screw (2)
10. Commutator end cover
11. Brush cable nut (2)
12. Brush cable washer (2)
13. Brush holder mounting plate
14. Armature
15. Terminal screw nut (2)
16. Terminal screw lockwasher (2)
17. Insulating washer
18. Terminal insulator
19. Terminal bolt clip
20. Terminal screw bushing
21. Bracket insulator
22. Terminal screw (2)
23. Positive brush cable
24. Terminal screw
25. Bearing retainer
26. Armature bearing
27. Bearing retainer
28. Drive end plate
29. Armature oil seal
30. Pole shoe screw (2)
31. Pole shoe (2)
32. Field coil (2)
33. Frame
34. Terminal screw nut (2)
35. Terminal screw lockwasher
36. Brush (2)
37. Brush spring (2)
38. Brush holder plate screw (2)
39. Brush holder plate screw washer (2)
40. Brush holder plate screw washer (3)
41. Brush holder plate rivet (2)
42. Brush holder insulation
43. Brush holder spacer
44. End cover spacer
44A. End cover bearing
45. Gererator oil wick
46. Commutator end cover oil cup
47. Brush cover strap spring
48. End locating pin (2)

9

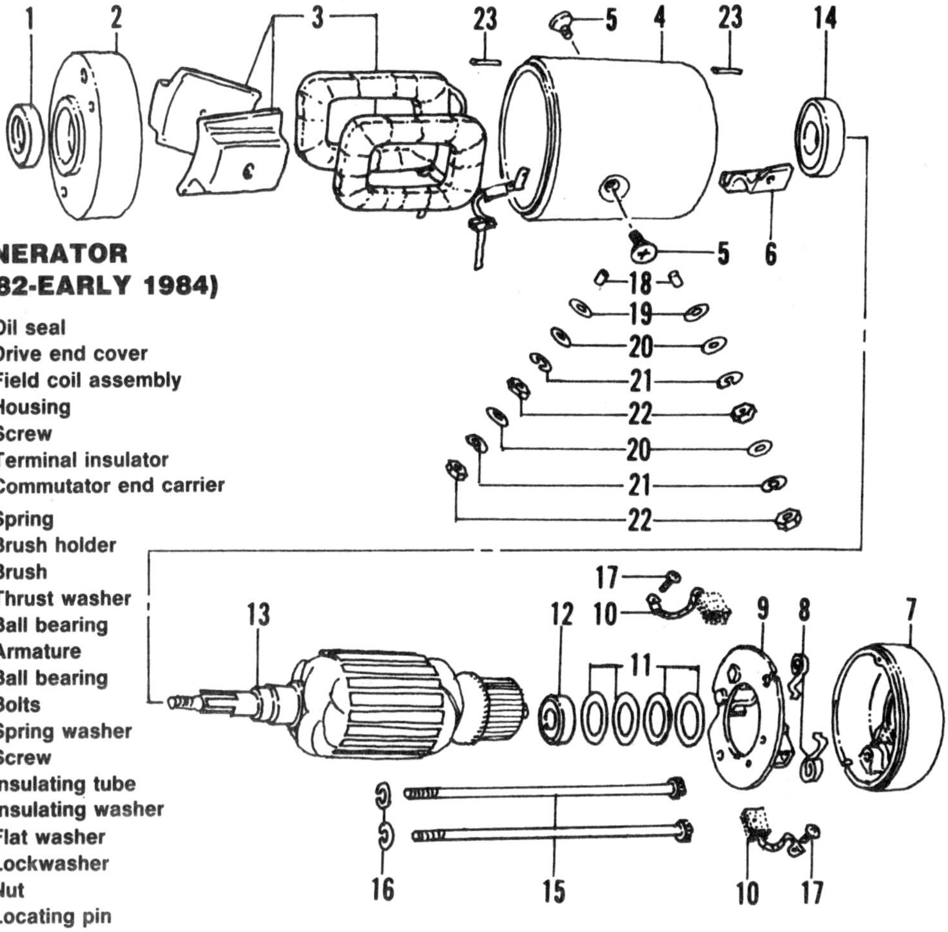

GENERATOR (1982-EARLY 1984)

1. Oil seal
2. Drive end cover
3. Field coil assembly
4. Housing
5. Screw
6. Terminal insulator
7. Commutator end carrier
8. Spring
9. Brush holder
10. Brush
11. Thrust washer
12. Ball bearing
13. Armature
14. Ball bearing
15. Bolts
16. Spring washer
17. Screw
18. Insulating tube
19. Insulating washer
20. Flat washer
21. Lockwasher
22. Nut
23. Locating pin

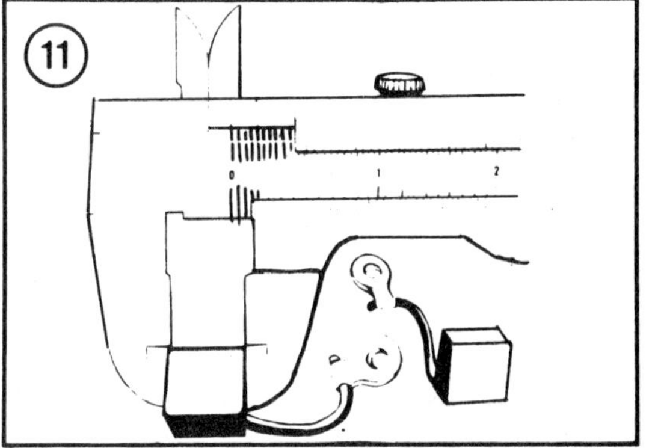

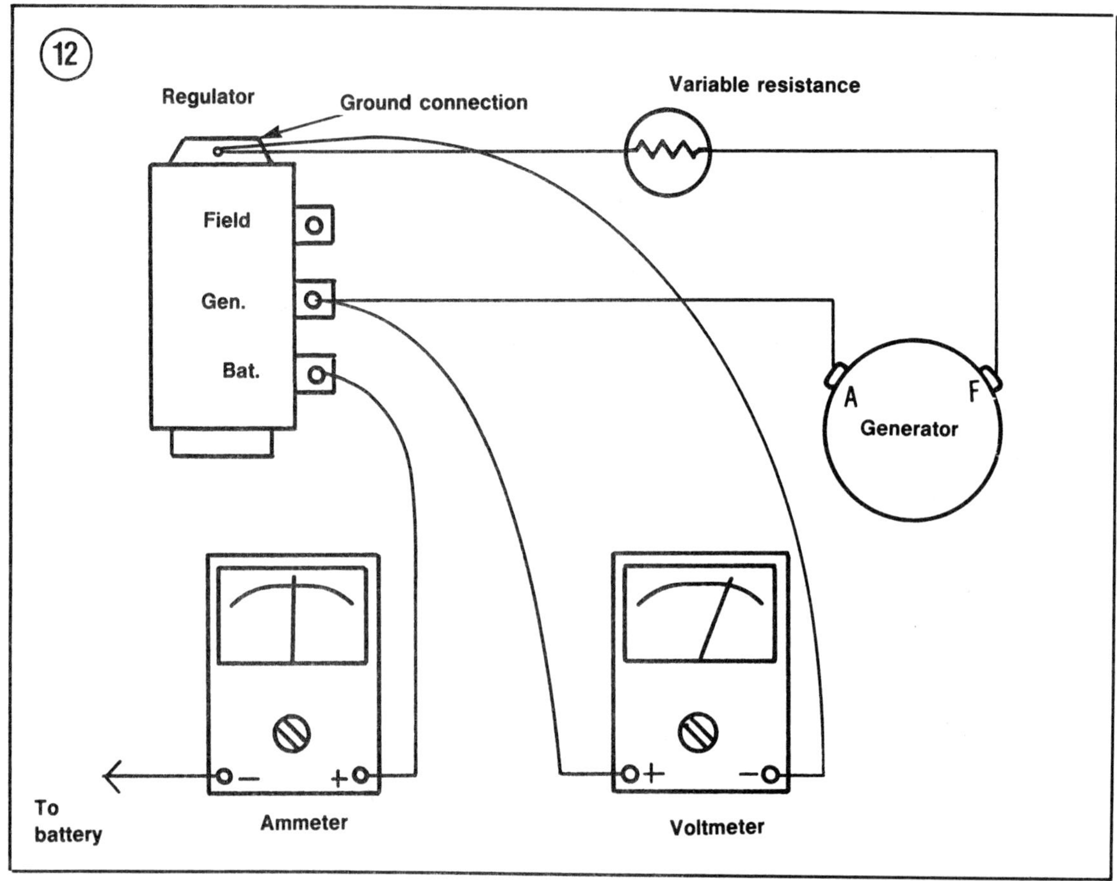

a 0-30 DC ammeter. Connect the positive ammeter wire to the BAT regulator terminal.

3. Connect the positive terminal of a 0-20 DC voltmeter to the regulator GEN teminal. Connect the negative voltmeter terminal to a good ground.

4. Disconnect the regulator "F" terminal wire. Connect this wire to one terminal of a field control rheostat. Connect the other rheostat terminal to a good ground. Set the field control rheostat to the OPEN position.

5. Start the engine and idle it at 2,000 rpm.

6. Slowly turn the field control rheostat toward the DIRECT position until the ammeter indicates 15 amps (6-volt) or 10 amps (12-volt). Interpret results as follows:

   a. If generator output is correct as listed above, the regulator is faulty.

   b. If there is no ammeter reading, or if the reading is low—below 15 amps (6-volt) or below 10 amps (12-volt)—observe the voltmeter reading. If the voltmeter reads 6 volts or less on 6-volt systems, or 12 volts or less on 12-volt systems, the generator is faulty and requires repair.

   c. If the ammeter reading is low, but the voltmeter reads 7.5 volts or more (6-volt) or 15 volts or more (12-volt), the cut-out relay in the voltage regulator is defective.

7. If the voltage regulator is defective, perform the following test procedures.

Cutout relay closing voltage

With the engine turned off, make the same testing connections as specified in *Generating system test*. See **Figure 12**.

1. Turn the field control rheostat to the OPEN position.

2. Start the engine and idle it at approximately 1,500 rpm.

3. Slowly turn the field control rheostat toward the DIRECT position and observe the voltmeter reading. It should increase slowly and then "kick" suddenly. The cutout relay closing voltage is that indicated on the voltmeter just before it "kicks." Cutout relay closing voltage should be 5.9-6.7 volts for 6-volt sytems, or 11.8-13.0 volts for 12-volt systems.

4. If the cutout relay closing voltage is not within the specifications in Step 3, have a

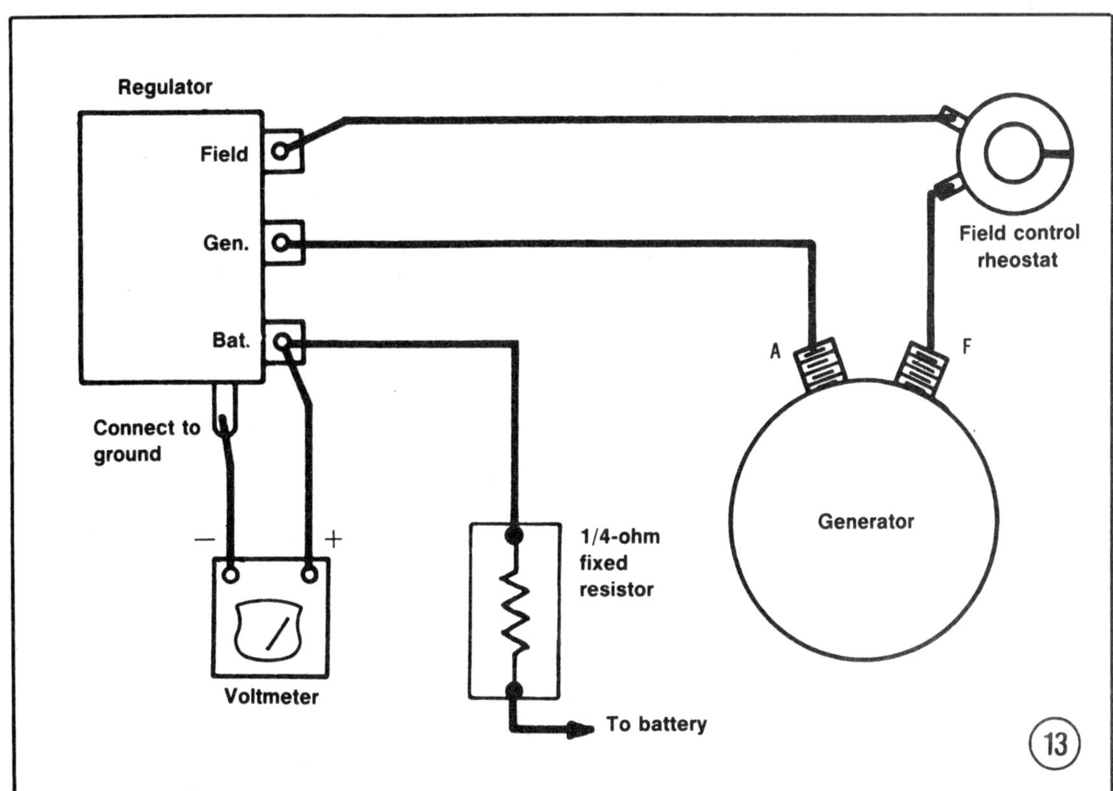

Harley-Davidson dealer adjust the cutout relay. If the relay still does not test correctly, replace it with a new unit.

Voltage regulator setting

Refer to **Figure 13** for this procedure.

1. Turn the engine off.
2. Write down the motorcycle's voltage regulator part number.
3. Disconnect wire to battery at voltage regulator BAT terminal and connect it to one terminal of a 1/4-ohm, 100-watt resistor. Connect the other resistor terminal to the voltage regulator BAT terminal.
4. Connect the positive terminal of a 0-20 DC voltmeter to the voltage regulator BAT teminal. Connect the negative voltmeter terminal to a good ground.
5. Disconnect the generator wire from the voltage regulator "F" teminal and connect it to one terminal of a field control rheostat. Connect the other field control rheostat terminal to the voltage regulator "F" terminal. Turn the field control rheostat control to DIRECT.

6A. *6-volt models:* Start the engine and idle it at 2,000 rpm. Turn the field control rheostat to OPEN, then to DIRECT position. Observe the voltmeter reading and compare it (and the part number recorded in Step 2) with **Table 2**. If the regulated voltage is incorrect, have a Harley-Davidson dealer adjust the voltage regulator. If adjustment does not correct the voltage reading, replace the voltage regulator.

6B. *12-volt systems:* Start the engine and idle it at 2,000 rpm. Turn the field control rheostat to OPEN, then to DIRECT position. Observe the voltmeter reading. The voltmeter reading is the regulated voltage of the upper regulator contacts. Maintain engine speed and slowly turn the field control rheostat toward the OPEN position until the voltmeter reading drops slightly and stabilizes. The voltmeter reading at this point is the regulated voltage of the lower regulator contacts. The lower regulator contact voltage must be 0.1-0.3 volts less than that of the upper contacts. If the regulated voltage is incorrect, have a Harley-Davidson dealer adjust the voltage regulator. If adjustment does not correct the voltage reading, replace the voltage regulator.

Current regulator setting

This test is performed only on motorcycles with 3-unit voltage regulators. See **Figure 14**.

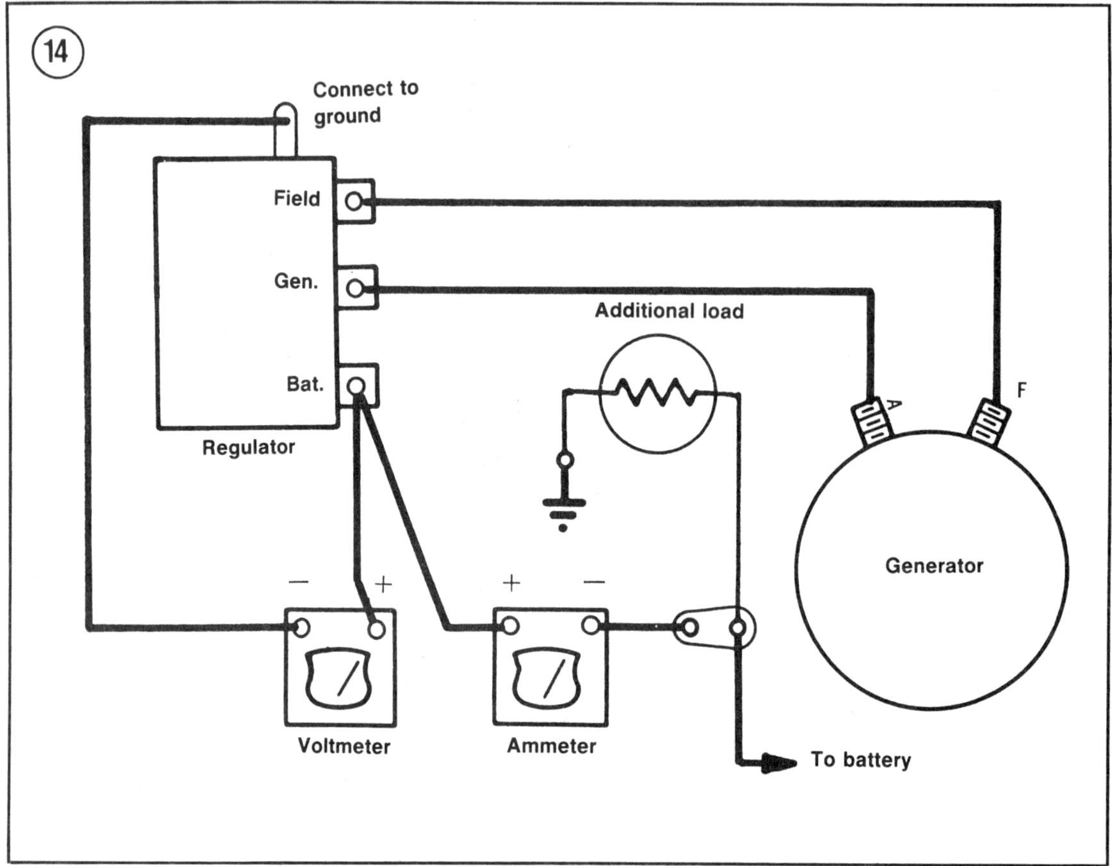

1. Disconnect the voltage regulator BAT terminal wire. Connect this wire to the negative lead of a 0-30 DC ammeter. Connect the positive ammeter lead to the voltage regulator BAT terminal.
2. Connect the positive lead of a 0-20 DC voltmeter to the voltage regulator BAT terminal. Connect the negative voltmeter lead to a good ground.
3. Start the engine and idle it at 2,000 rpm. Turn on the headlight and connect an additional load, such as an adjustable carbon pile, across the battery until the voltmeter indicates one volt less than the regulated voltage.
4. Observe the ammeter reading. If it is not within the specifications listed in **Table 3**, have a Harley-Davidson dealer adjust the voltage regulator. If adjustment does not correct the voltage reading, replace the voltage regulator.

Generating system without battery

Refer to **Figure 15** for this procedure.
1. Turn the engine off.
2. Disconnect the voltage regulator "F" terminal lead.
3. Connect a 0-20 DC ammeter and a 1 1/2 ohm resistor (rated at 100 watts or more) in series between the voltage regulator GEN teminal and one voltage regulator mounting bolt. Do not disconnect the generator armature lead from the GEN terminal. Be sure the ammeter positive terminal is connected to the GEN terminal.
4. Start the engine and run it at a slightly faster than normal idle speed. If the ammeter indicates any current flow, the generator field is grounded internally or in the wiring harness. If no current is indicated, proceed to Step 5.
5. With the engine running as in Step 4, momentarily touch the generator field lead to its regulator terminal. If the ammeter suddenly indicates current flow, the generator output is okay. Proceed to Step 6. If the ammeter does not indicate a sudden current flow, the generator is faulty and requires disassembly and inspection of the internal components.
6. Turn the engine off.
7. Refer to **Figure 16**. Disconnect the red wire from the voltage regulator BAT terminal. Connect a 1 1/2 ohm resistor (rated at 100 watts or more)

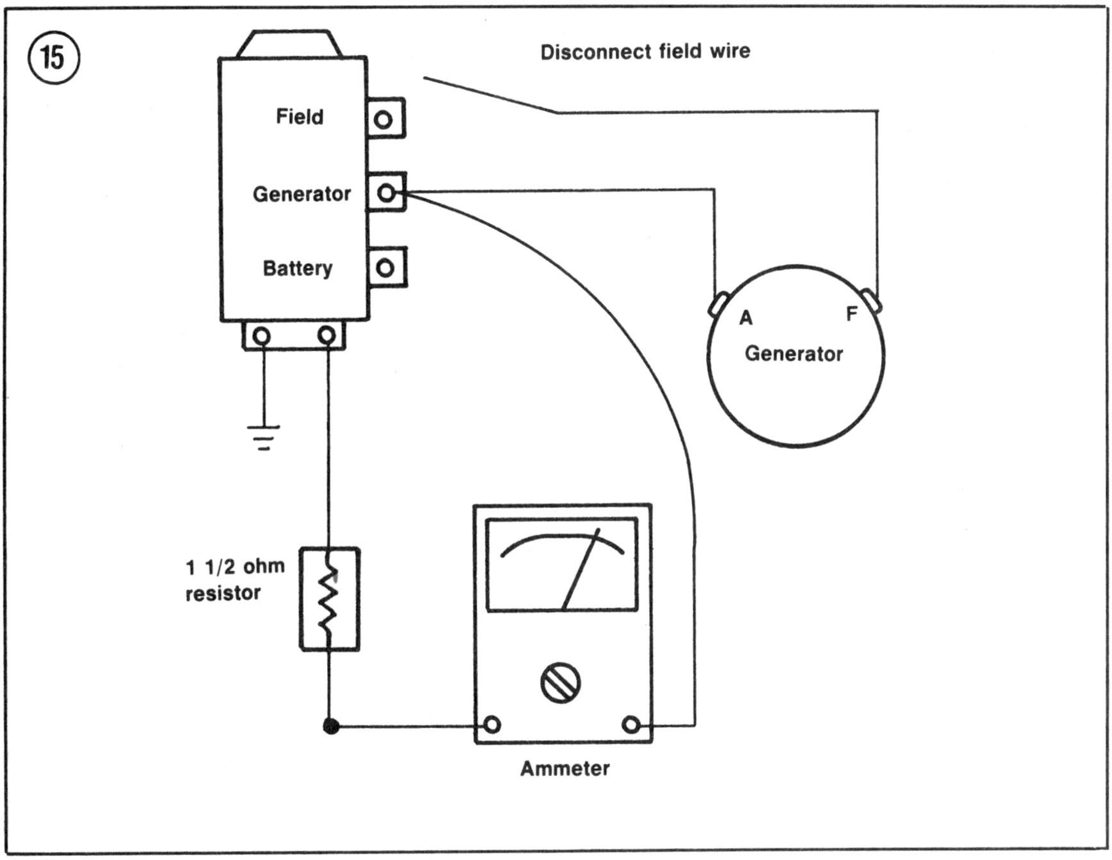

15
Disconnect field wire
Field
Generator
Battery
A
F
Generator
1 1/2 ohm
resistor
Ammeter

16
Field
Generator
Battery
A
F
Generator
+
−
Voltmeter
1/4 ohm resistor

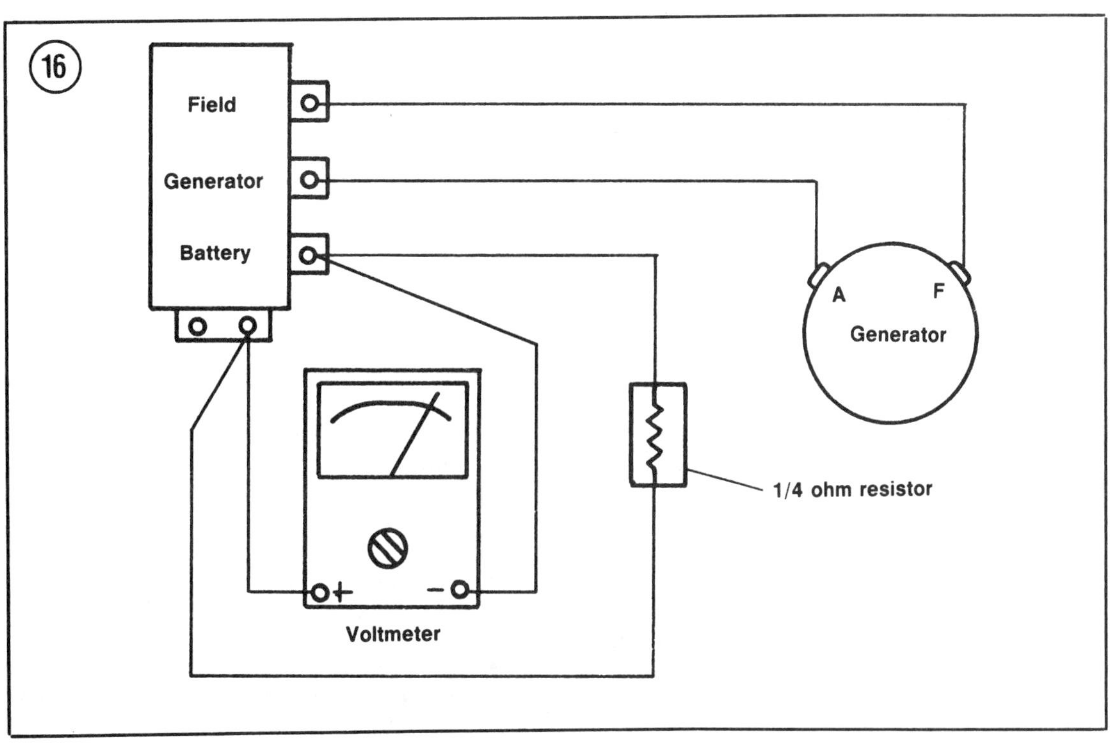

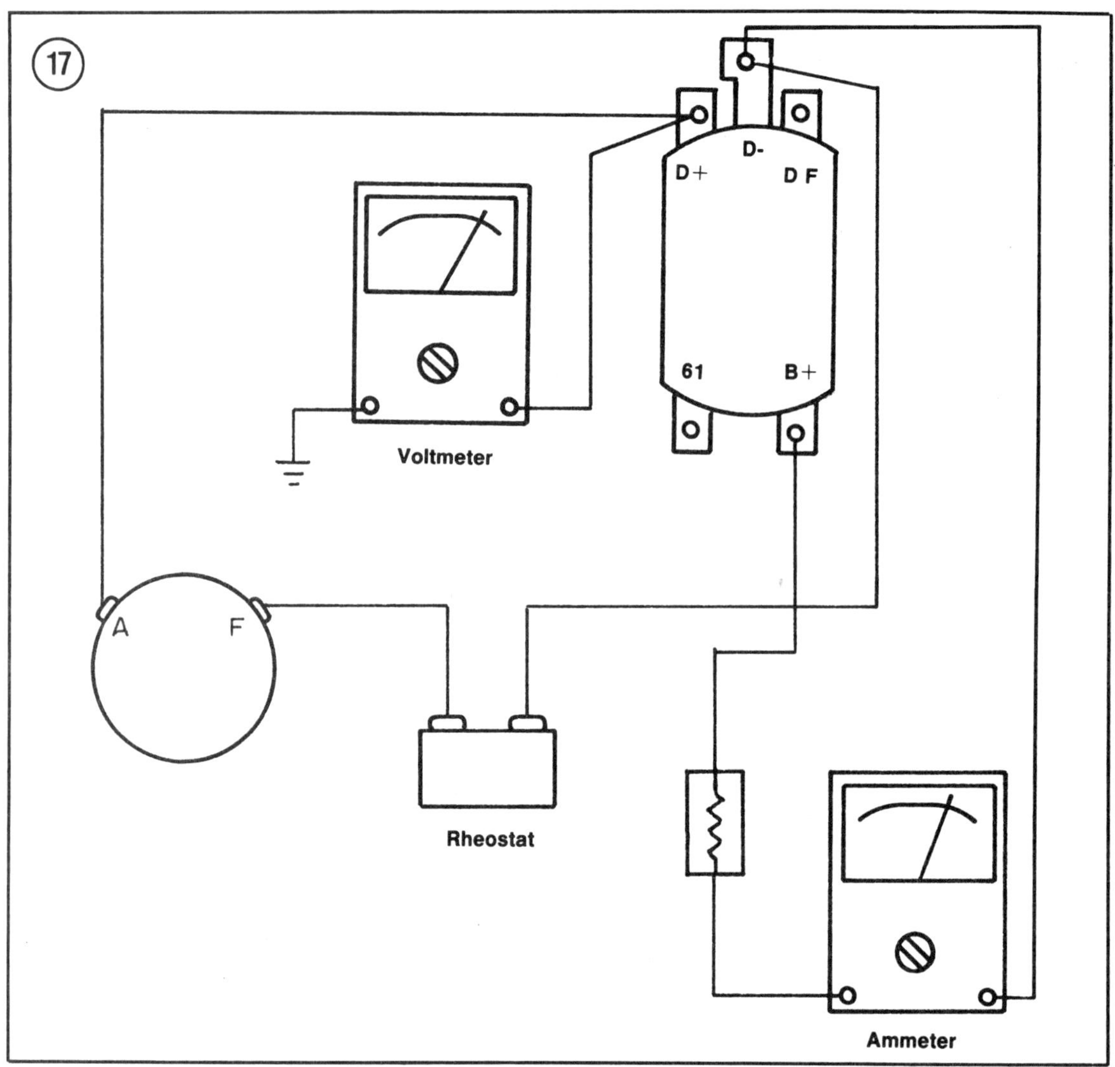

between the voltage regulator BAT terminal and one mounting bolt. Also connect the positive terminal of a DC voltmeter to the same points, with the voltmeter positive terminal connected to the voltage regulator BAT teminal.

8. Start the engine and run at a fast idle. If the voltmeter reads 5 volts or more, the voltage regulator cutout relay is okay. Proceed to Step 9. If not, replace or repair the voltage regulator.

NOTE
At low engine speeds, voltmeter indication may fluctuate between 0 and about 5 volts; this condition is normal.

9. With the voltage regulator at operating temperature and its cover in place, increase engine speed to approximately 2,700 rpm. If the voltmeter reads approximately 6.5-6.8 volts, the voltage regulator is okay. If the readings are different, replace the voltage regulator.

Bosch Voltage Regulators

The following test procedures apply to models using Bosch voltage regulators with and without batteries. Bosch voltage regulators are sealed units which must be replaced in the event of malfunction.

Generating system test

Refer to **Figure 17** for this procedure.

1. Disconnect the wire(s) from the voltage regulator B+ terminal. On XLH models, connect these wires together.
2. Connect one terminal of a 1 1/2 ohm resistor (rated at 100 watts or more) to the voltage

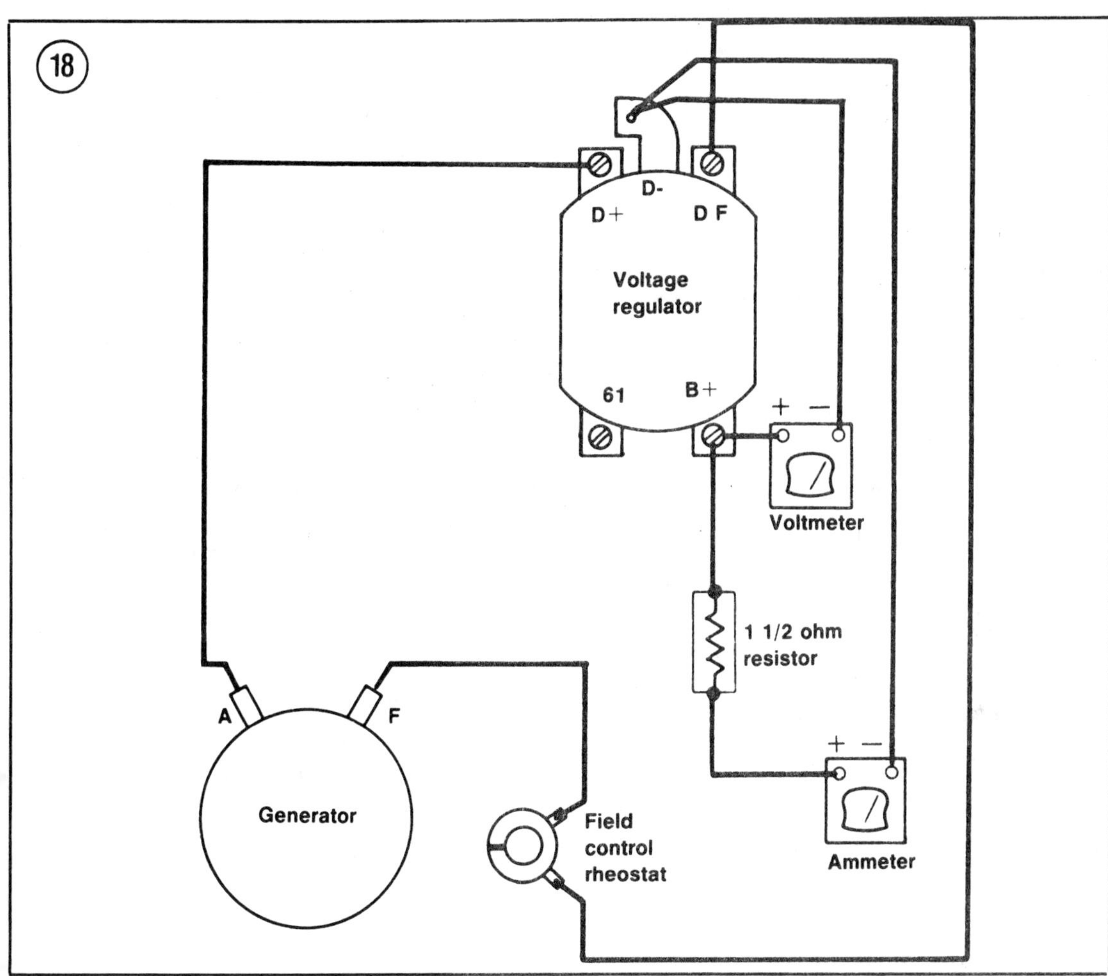

regulator B+ terminal. Connect the remaining resistor terminal to the positive terminal of a 0-20 DC ammeter. Connect the negative ammeter terminal to a good ground.

3. Connect the positive terminal of a 0-20 DC voltmeter to the voltage regulator D+ terminal. Connect the negative voltmeter terminal to a good ground.

4. Disconnect the generator field wire from the voltage regulator DF terminal. Connect the lead which was removed to one terminal of a field control rheostat. Connect the other field control rheostat terminal to ground. Turn field control rheostat to the OPEN position.

5. Start the engine and idle it at 2,700 rpm.

6. Slowly turn the field control rheostat toward the DIRECT position until the ammeter indicates 10 amps, then immediately return the rheostat to the OPEN position. If the generator output current is not 10 amps or more, or the output voltage 12 volts or more, the generator must be repaired. If the ammeter indicated 10 amps during this test, the generator is okay. Any generating system failure is in the voltage regulator or connecting wiring.

Cutout relay closing voltage

1. Refer **Figure 17** and to Steps 1-4 under *Generating system test* for test connections.

2. Set the field control rheostat to the OPEN position.

3. Start the engine and idle it at 2,000 rpm.

4. Slowly turn the field control rheostat toward the DIRECT position and read the voltmeter. Note the higest voltage reading before its pointer "kicks." It should be within 12.4-13.1 volts. If the voltage is incorrect, replace the voltage regulator.

Voltage regulator setting under load

Refer to **Figure 18** for this procedure.

1. Test connections are the same for this test as for the *Cutout relay closing voltage*, except that the

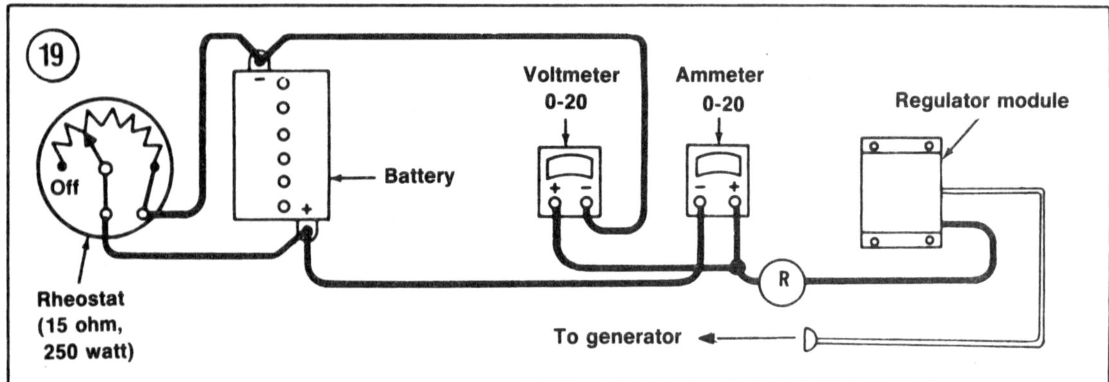

positive voltmeter terminal is connected to the regulator B+ terminal instead of the D+ terminal.
2. Set the field control rheostat to the DIRECT position.
3. Start the engine and idle it at 2,700 rpm.
4. Observe the voltmeter reading. If it does not indicate 12.7-14.5 volts, replace the voltage regulator.

Voltage regulator setting, no load

1. Remove the 1 1/2 ohm load resistor used in the previous tests by removing the ammeter connection of the voltage regulator B+ teminal. Test connections are otherwise identical to those used in the *Voltage regulator setting under load* test.
2. Set the field control rheostat to the DIRECT position.
3. Start the engine and idle it at 2,700 rpm.
4. Observe the voltmeter reading. If it does not indicate 13.8-15.4 volts, replace the voltage regulator.

Voltage Regulator Testing (1979-early 1984)

Voltage regulator test

Refer to **Figure 19** for this procedure.
1. Connect a voltmeter, ammeter and rheostat or carbon pile as shown in **Figure 19**.
2. Start the engine and run it at 2,000 rpm.
3. Adjust the rheostat so that the ammeter reads 2-7 amps.
4. Check that the voltmeter reads within the limits shown in **Figure 20**. Interpret results as follows:
   a. If the voltage is within the acceptable limits, the regulator is okay. Test the generator output.
   b. If the voltage is higher than specified, check for an accidental ground in the generator field circuit or in the green wire from the regulator to the generator field terminal. If there is no accidental ground, the regulator is faulty; install a new regulator.
   c. If the voltage is lower than specified, the regulator may be faulty or the generator may be faulty. Perform the *Generator output test*. If the generator output is okay, the regulator is faulty. Replace the voltage regulator.

Generator output test

Refer to **Figure 19** for this procedure.
1. Connect a voltmeter, ammeter and rheostat or carbon pile as shown in **Figure 19**.
2. Start the engine and run it at 2,000 rpm.
3. Adjust the rheostat so that the voltmeter reads 12.5 volts.
4. Check that the ammeter reads between 10 and 11 amps.

CAUTION
During the next step, do not ground the "F" terminal for more than 10 seconds or the regulator and generator may be damaged.

5. If the ammeter indicates no generator output current, polarize the generator as described in this chapter and repeat this test. If the ammeter still indicates no generator output, temporarily ground the generator "F" terminal while the engine is running at 2,000 rpm. When the "F" terminal is grounded, the generator output should be at least 18 amps. Interpret results as follows:
   a. If the output is adequate with the "F" terminal grounded, but the regulating voltage was low, the regulator is faulty; replace the voltage regulator.
   b. If the output is less than specified with the "F" terminal grounded, inspect and repair the generator as described in this chapter.
   c. If there is no output with the "F" terminal grounded, the regulator may be faulty. Install a

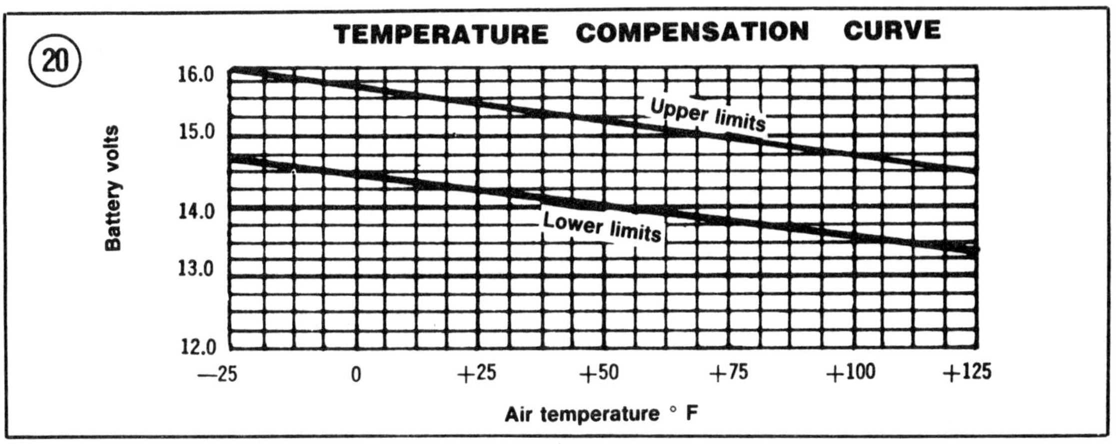

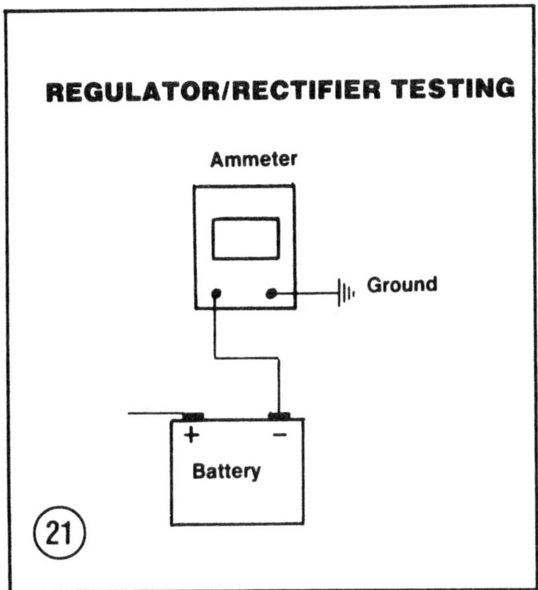

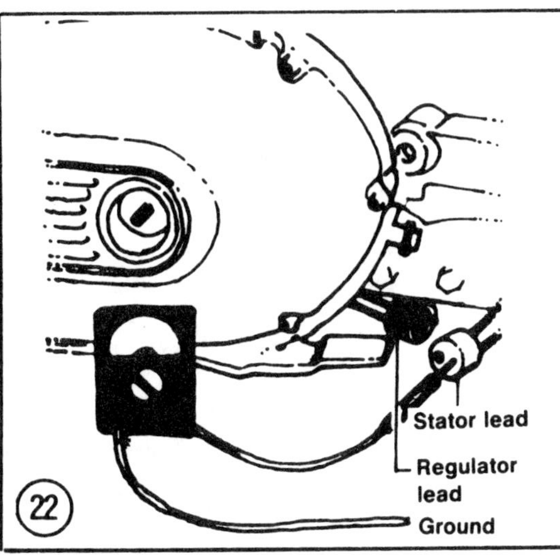

new regulator and repeat this test. If there is still no output, inspect and repair the generator as described in this chapter.

7

CHARGING SYSTEM (LATE 1984-1985)

The charging system consists of the battery, alternator and a voltage regulator.

Troubleshooting Charging System

Output test

1. Start the engine and run it at 2,000 rpm. Turn on all electrical accessores and switch the headlight beam to HIGH.
2. Referring to **Figure 21**, connect an ammeter between the battery negative terminal and ground. Then disconnect the battery ground wire.

CAUTION
Do not disconnect the battery ground wire before connecting the ammeter or attempt to start the engine with the ammeter connected or damage to electrical components may result.

3. Check that the ammeter reads 3.5 amps or more. If the reading is less than 3.5 amps, the electrical problem may be in the charging system. Perform the following checks.

Stator check

1. With ignition turned off, disconnect the regulator/rectifier connector below the crankcase on the left side.
2. See **Figure 22**. Connect an ohmmeter between the stator pin and ground. Set the ohmmeter to the R×1 scale. The ohmmeter should read infinity (no continuity). If the reading is incorrect, the stator is grounded and must be replaced.

3. See **Figure 23**. Connect the ohmmeter leads between both stator pins. Set the ohmmeter to the R×1 scale. The ohmmeter should read 0.2-0.4 ohms. If no needle movement occurs, or if the resistance is higher than specified, the stator must be replaced.
4. If the stator is okay, perform the *Rotor Test* in this section.

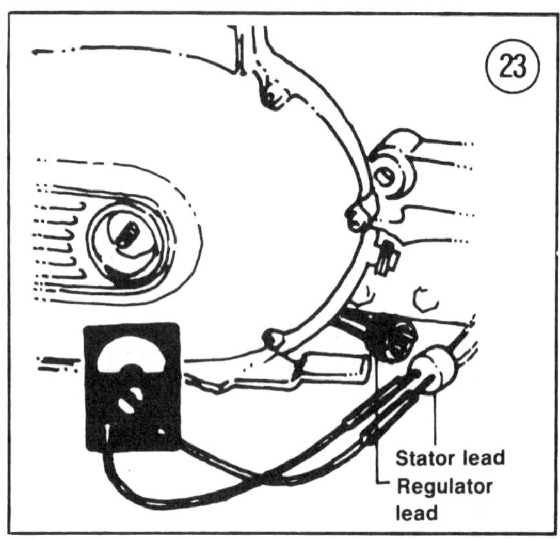

Rotor test

1. See **Figure 23**. Disconnect the regulator/rectifier connector below the crankcase on the left side.
2. Connect an AC voltmeter across both stator pins.
3. Start the engine and run it at 3,000 rpm. If the AC voltmeter does not read 60 volts or more, the rotor must be replaced.
4. If the stator and rotor test okay, replace the regulator/rectifier assembly.

Rotor
Removal/Installation

1. Remove the clutch as described in Chapter Five.

CAUTION
Do not disassemble the clutch assembly.

2. Turn the clutch assembly upside down and place it on the workbench.
3. Referring to **Figure 24**, remove the rotor circlip. Then remove the rotor/clutch shell assembly from the clutch hub.

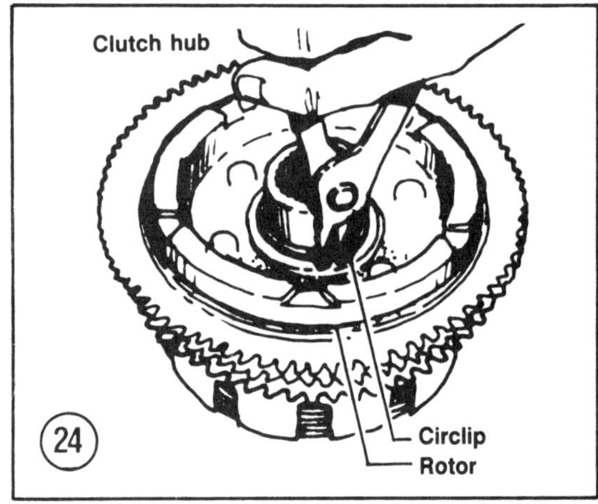

NOTE
Because a portion of the clutch shell operates as the alternator rotor, removal of the clutch shell may prove difficult due to the pull of the rotor magnets.

4. If necessary, replace the rotor/clutch shell as a single unit.
5. Install the new rotor/clutch shell assembly. Secure it with a new circlip.
6. Install the clutch as described in Chapter Five.

Stator Removal/Installation

1. Disconnect the stator electrical connector below the crankcase on the left side.
2. Remove the clutch as described in Chapter Five.

CAUTION
Do not disassemble the clutch.

3. See **Figure 25**. Remove the 4 Torx screws securing the stator to the stator support (late

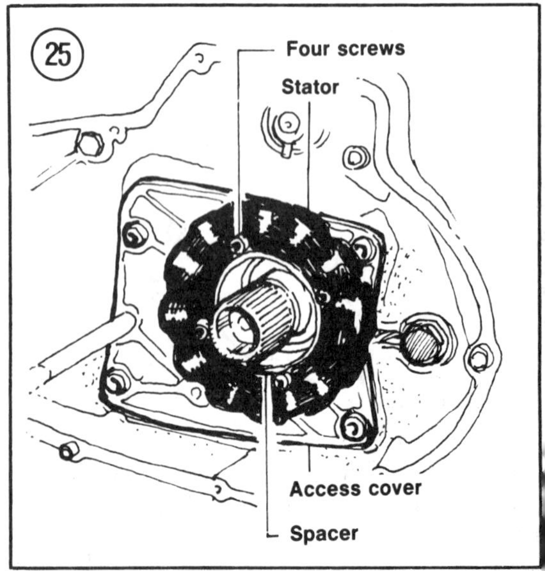

1984-early 1985) or to the access cover (late 1985). Discard the Torx screws.

4. Remove the stator by prying the stator wire grommet out of the crankcase and remove the wire/connector together with the stator.

5. *Late 1984-early 1985:* Remove the stator support plate screws and remove the support.

6. Installation is the reverse of these steps, noting the following:

   a. When routing the new stator wire and connector, route it downward between the frame and rear engine gap. Press the grommet fully into the crankcase opening.

   b. On late 1984-early 1985 models, install the stator support against the clutch gear bearing on the stator.

   c. Install new Torx screws and tighten to 20-35 in.-lb.

CAUTION
Do not use the old stator Torx screws. New Torx screws have a pellet formed locking compound on their threads. When new Torx screws are installed, the pellet breaks and releases the locking compound on the bolt threads. The locking compound on the old bolts cannot be reused; if installed, the old bolts may loosen and back out during engine operation.

   d. Install the clutch assembly as described in Chapter Five.

Voltage Regulator Removal/Installation

The regulator cannot be rebuilt; if damaged it must be replaced.

1. Remove the seat.
2. Remove the cable straps securing the regulator wires to the left frame side member.
3. Disconnect the regulator lead below the crankcase on the left side.
4. Disconnect the regulator lead from the main circuit breaker.
5. Remove the regulator mounting bolts and remove the regulator.
6. Install a new regulator by reversing Steps 1-5.

MAGNETO IGNITION SYSTEM (1959-1968)

The magneto ignition system consists of an induction coil, rotor, condenser, circuit beaker and circuit breaker cam. A kill switch is attached to the right handlebar. On 1959-1964 models, the magneto is mounted in a fixed position that produces advanced spark timing only. On 1965-1968 models, the magneto is mounted on a movable plate to allow ignition timing retard when starting the engine. The magneto is controlled manually by turning the left handlebar grip. **Figure 26** is an exploded diagram of the magneto system. Refer to it when performing procedures in this section.

Troubleshooting

Ignition troubleshooting procedures are described in Chapter Two.

Magneto Removal/Installation

1. Remove the carburetor as described in Chapter Six.
2. Disconnect the spark plug cables at the magneto.
3. Disconnect the ground wire at the magneto.
4. If a tachometer drive assembly is used, remove it as follows:
   a. Remove the tachometer drive retaining pin clip (62, **Figure 26**) and remove the pin (63).
   b. Remove the tachometer drive cable (64) and thrust washer (66).
5. On 1965 and later models, remove the control wire set screw and slide the control wire out of the bracket. See **Figure 27**.
6. Remove the mounting nuts and bolts.
7. Lift the magneto assembly away from the gearcase.
8. Disassemble, inspect and reassemble the magneto assembly as described in this chapter.
9. Remove both spark plugs.
10. Remove the timing inspection plug from the left side of the engine.
11. Telescope front cylinder intake valve pushrod cover (**Figure 28**) so that pushrod operation can be observed.
12. Turn engine until front piston is on its compression stroke, then continue turning slowly until timing mark is centered in the inspection hole. Refer to ignition timing adjustment in Chapter Three.
13. Install the magneto into the gearcase cover. On 1959-1964 models, make sure that the timing marks on the magneto base align with those on the mounting plate (**Figure 27**).
14. The narrow cam lobe should be located counterclockwise from the cam follower and should just be opening. If this condition does not exist, turn the magneto on its base.
15. If the points cannot be opened by turning the magneto housing, lift the magneto from the

7

MAGNETO (1959-1968)

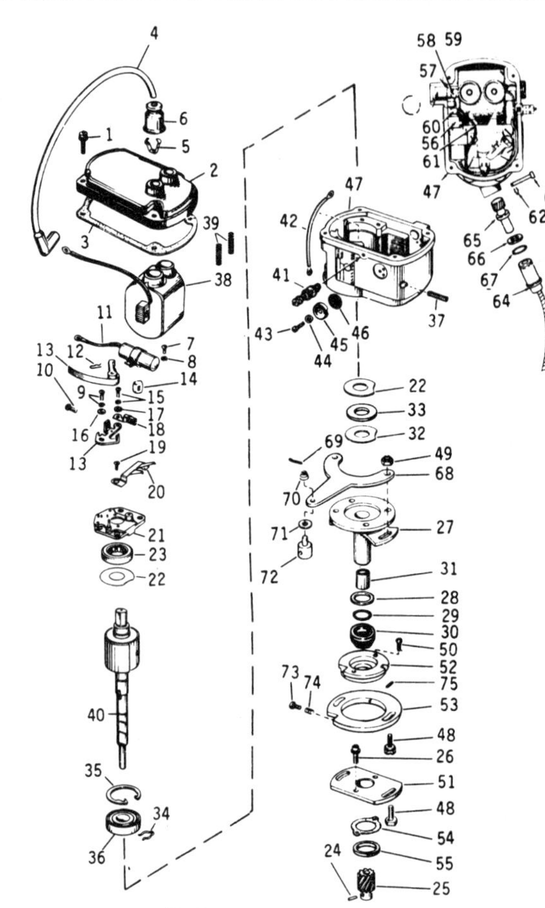

1. End cap screw
2. End cap
3. End cap gasket
4. Spark plug cable
5. Terminal
6. Cable protector
7. Screw
8. Washer
9. Screw
10. Screw
11. Condenser
12. Snap ring
13. Breaker points
14. Wick
15. Screw and washer
16. Washer
17. Washer
18. Wick
19. Screw
20. Safety gap (to late 1964)
21. Bearing support
22. Washer
23. Bearing
24. Pin
25. Drive gear
26. Screw
27. Drive housing
28. O-ring washer (late 1965-1968)
29. O-ring (late 1965-early 1968)
30. Seal (late 1968)
31. Bushing
32. Washer
33. Seal
34. Snap ring
35. Snap ring
36. Bearing
37. Set screw
38. Coil
39. Terminal spring
40. Rotor
41. Terminal
42. Wire
43. Screw
44. Vent cover screw
45. Vent cover
46. Vent screen
47. Housing
48. Bolt
49. Nut
50. Adapter screw
51. Adapter (1964 and earlier)
52. Inner adapter plate (1965)
53. Outer adapter plate (1965)
54. Gasket (early 1965)
55. Oil seal ring
56. Insulator
57. Retainer clip
58. Spring
59. Ball
60. Terminal screw
61. Thrust washer
62. Clip
63. Pin
64. Tachometer cable
65. Tachometer drive gear
66. Thrust washer
67. O-ring
68. Control arm
69. Cotter pin (1965)
70. Spring (1965)
71. Washer
72. Swivel block (1965)
73. Set screw (1965-early 1967)
74. Spring (1965-early 1967)
75. Roll pin (late 1967)

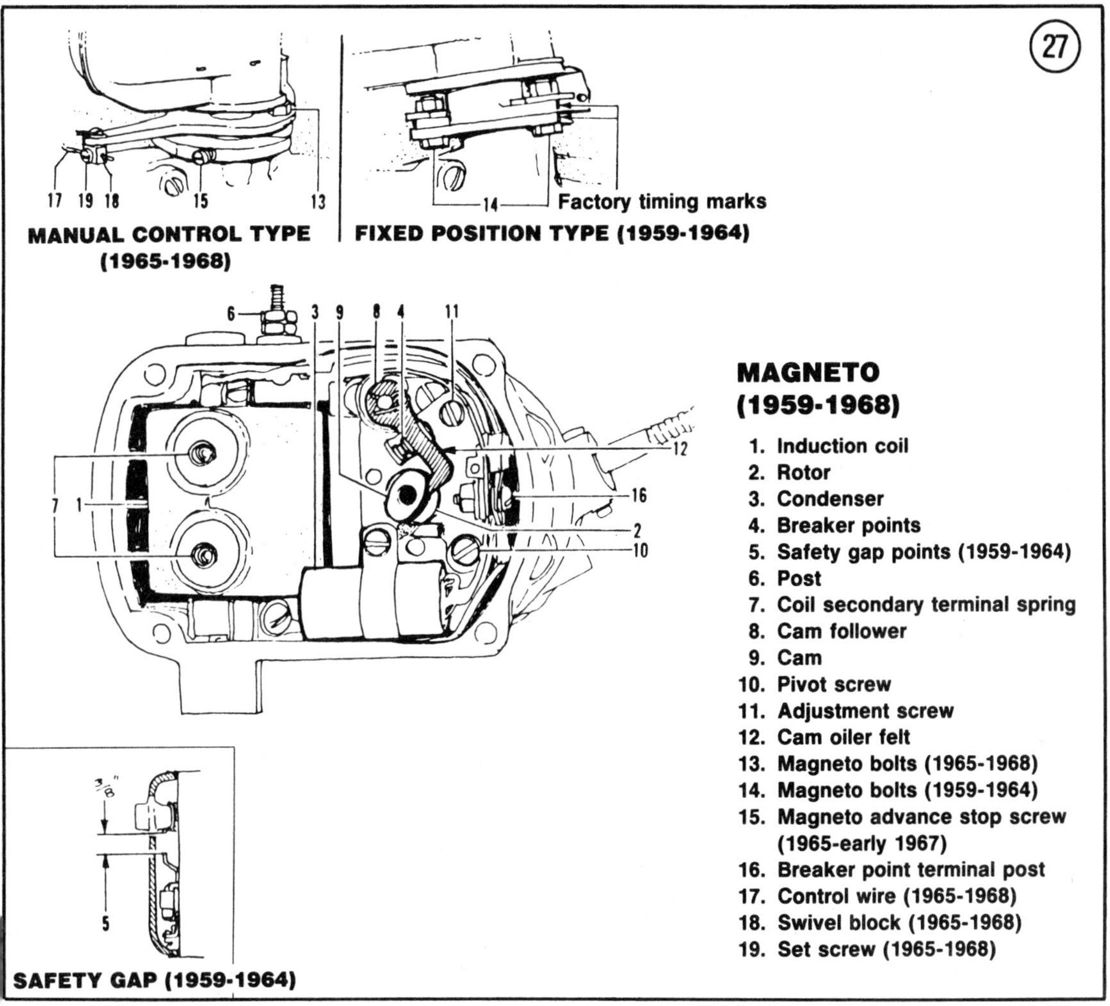
27
17 19 18 15 13
MANUAL CONTROL TYPE (1965-1968)
14 Factory timing marks
FIXED POSITION TYPE (1959-1964)
6 3 9 8 4 11
12
7 1
16
2
10
3/8"
5
SAFETY GAP (1959-1964)
MAGNETO (1959-1968)
1. Induction coil
2. Rotor
3. Condenser
4. Breaker points
5. Safety gap points (1959-1964)
6. Post
7. Coil secondary terminal spring
8. Cam follower
9. Cam
10. Pivot screw
11. Adjustment screw
12. Cam oiler felt
13. Magneto bolts (1965-1968)
14. Magneto bolts (1959-1964)
15. Magneto advance stop screw (1965-early 1967)
16. Breaker point terminal post
17. Control wire (1965-1968)
18. Swivel block (1965-1968)
19. Set screw (1965-1968)

28

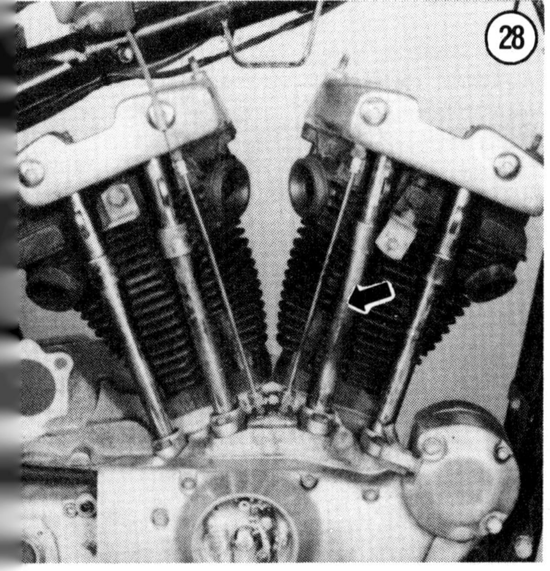

gearcase, then turn its rotor by approximately the same amount as the cam appeared to be out of position. Repeat as necessary.

16. On models with manual ignition timing retard, install the magneto control arm on the drive housing before installing the mounting bolts and nuts.
17. Install the tachometer drive assembly (if necessary).
18. Connect the ground wire at the magneto terminal.
19. Connect the spark plug cables at the magneto.
20. Install the spark plug wire and reconnect the cables.
21. Install the carburetor as described in Chapter Six.
22. Adjust the ignition timing as described in Chapter Three.
23. *1965-1968:* Install the control wire through the swivel blocks. Then turn the handlebar grip to the

full retard position and then turn to the full advance position. Make sure that the magneto returns to the fully advanced position against the screw stop. Readjust the control wire if necessary. See **Figure 27**.

Disassembly/Inspection/Assembly

Refer to **Figure 26** for this procedure.

1. Remove the end cap screws and remove the end cap (2, **Figure 26**).
2. Remove the spark plug cables from the end cap.
3. Remove the condenser (11) and its bracket.
4. If necessary, remove the ignition coil (38).
5. Remove the snap clip (12) and remove the movable breaker contact (13).
6. Remove the fixed breaker contact and its bracket (13).
7. Remove the bearing support plate screws.
8. *1959-late 1964:* Remove the safety cap from the bearing support plate.
9. Pry the rotor drive and grease retainer washer from the bottom of the bearing support plate. Then remove the rotor cam end bearing (23).
10. File the end of the rotor drive gear pin (24). Then drive it out with a punch.
11. Slide the rotor drive gear (25) off of the rotor shaft.
12. Remove the drive housing screws. Then slide the drive housing (27) off of the rotor shaft.
13. Remove the drive housing O-ring or seal.
14. Remove the following from the lower housing:
    a. Rotor drive end seal outer washer (32).
    b. Rotor drive end seal (33).
    c. Washer (22).
15. Remove the rotor shaft snap ring (34).
16. Slide the rotor out of the housing (40).
17. Remove the rotor drive end bearing snap ring (35). Then remove the rotor drive end bearing (36).
18. Remove the coil bridge set screws (37) from the housing and remove the coil assembly (38).
19. Remove the primary ground switch terminal (41) and cable (42) from the housing.
20. Remove the vent cover screw (43), washer (44), covers (45) and vent screen (46) from the housing.
21. Check all parts for wear or damage.
22. Check the drive housing bushing for wear or damage. Install the rotor into the drive housing and attempt to move the rotor sideways against the bushing. If the play is excessive, have a Harley-Davidson dealer replace the bushing.
23. Installation is the reverse of these steps. When installing the rotor, do not tap it into place. Doing so may cause it to lose its magnetism.
24. Adjust the ignition timing as described in Chapter Three.

BATTERY IGNITION

Most 1959-1978 models are equipped with a battery ignition system. Refer to **Figure 29** for a diagram of the ignition circuit.

The breaker cam rotates at 1/2 crankshaft speed. There are 2 lobes on the cam; the narrow lobe times the front cylinder; the wide lobe times the rear cylinder. A single coil fires both spark plugs simultaneously, but one spark always occurs in a cylinder which on its exhaust stroke.

When the breaker points are closed, current flows from the battery through the primary winding of the ignition coil, thereby building a magnetic field around the coil. As the points open, the magnetic field collapses. When the field collapses, a very high voltage (up to approximately 15,000 volts) is induced in the secondary windings of the ignition coil. This high voltage is sufficient to jump the gap at each spark plug.

The condenser assists the coil in producing high voltage, and also serves to protect the points. Inductance of the ignition coil primary tends to keep a surge of current flowing through the circuit even after the points have started to open. The condenser stores this surge and thus prevents arcing at the points.

Models from 1959-1970 were equipped with either manual advance or automatic advance circuit breakers. See **Figure 30**. On 1971-1978

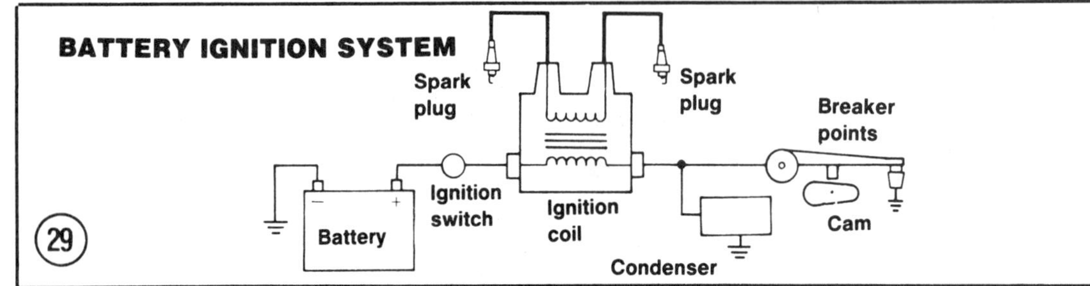

(30)

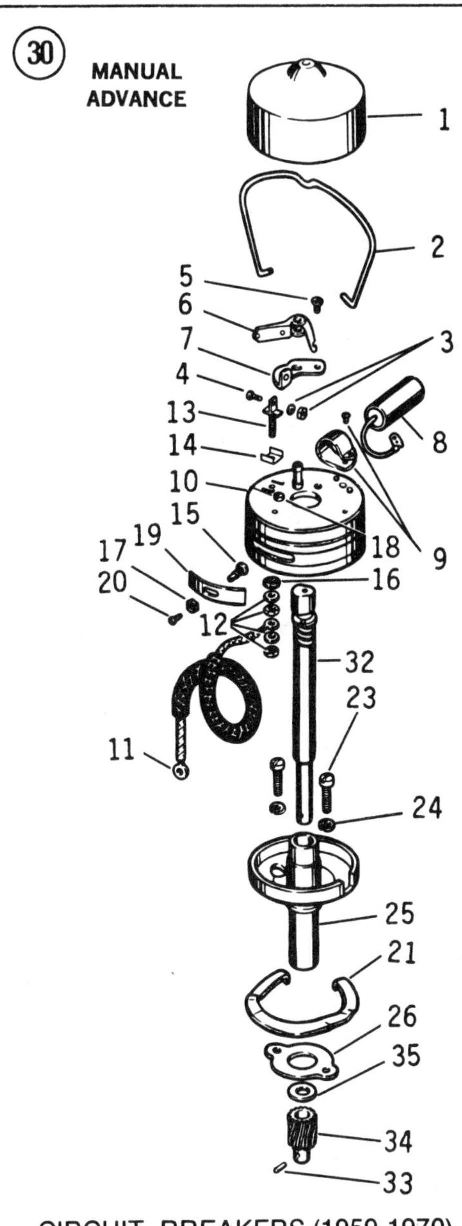

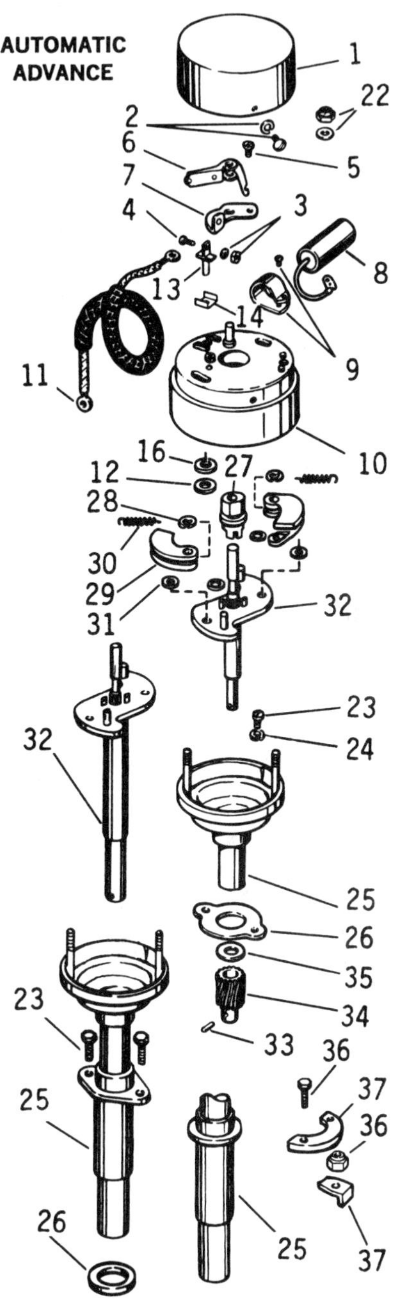

CIRCUIT BREAKERS (1959-1970)

1. Cover
2. Cover retainer or retainer screw
3. Nut and lockwasher
4. Wire stud screw
5. Screw
6. Contact point
7. Contact point
8. Condenser
9. Bracket and screw
10. Base
11. Cable
12. Stud nut and washer
13. Stud
14. Insulator
15. Locknut
16. Fiber washer
17. Locknut
18. Eccentric screw
19. Plate
20. Screw
21. Base retainer
22. Nut and washer
23. Crankcase screw
24. Lockwasher
25. Stem
26. Gasket or O-ring
27. Cam
28. Clip
29. Flyweight
30. Spring
31. Washer
32. Camshaft
33. Gear pin
34. Gear
35. Shaft washer
36. Clamp nut or bolt
37. Stem clamp

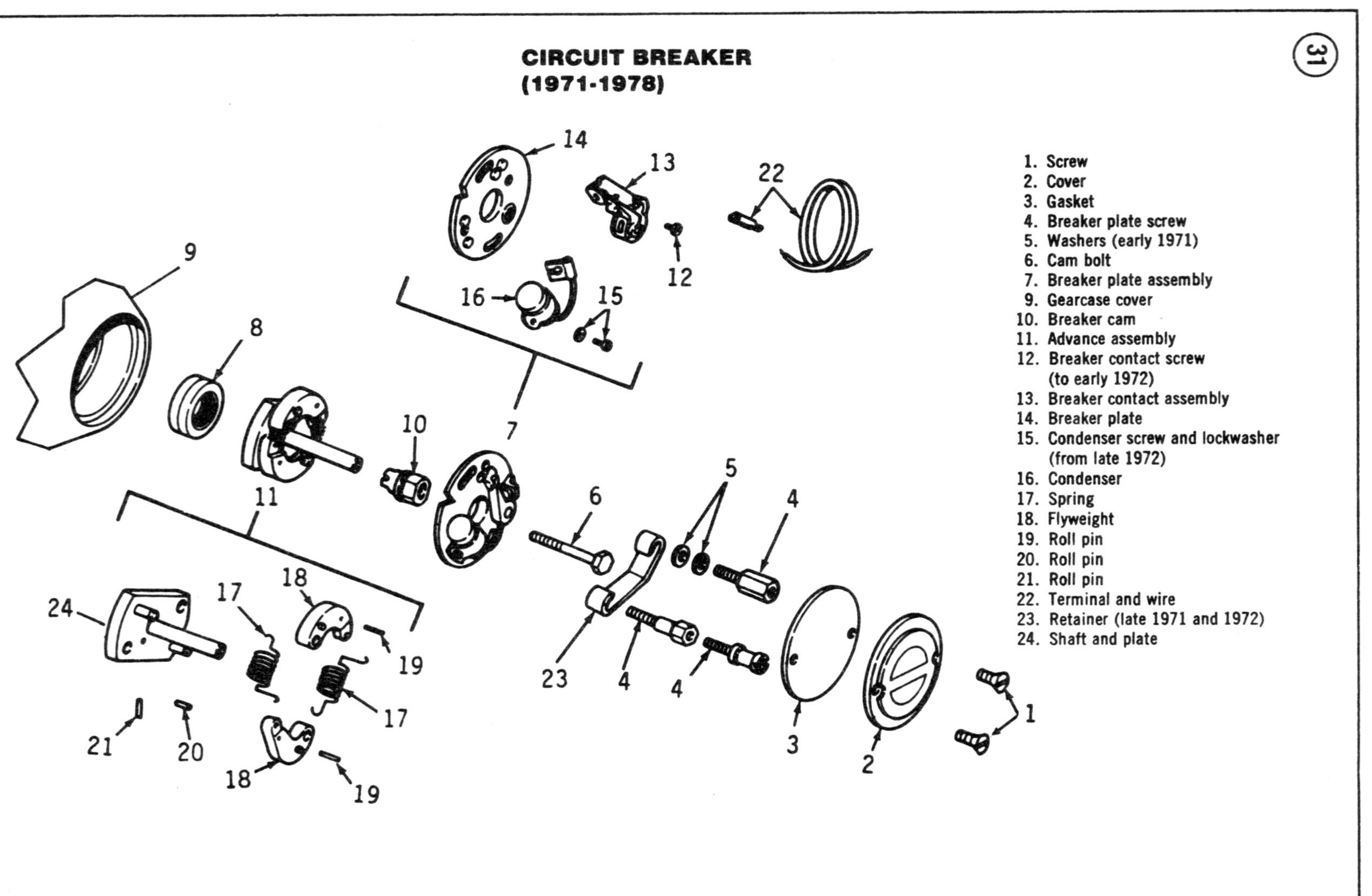
31
CIRCUIT BREAKER
(1971-1978)
1. Screw
2. Cover
3. Gasket
4. Breaker plate screw
5. Washers (early 1971)
6. Cam bolt
7. Breaker plate assembly
9. Gearcase cover
10. Breaker cam
11. Advance assembly
12. Breaker contact screw (to early 1972)
13. Breaker contact assembly
14. Breaker plate
15. Condenser screw and lockwasher (from late 1972)
16. Condenser
17. Spring
18. Flyweight
19. Roll pin
20. Roll pin
21. Roll pin
22. Terminal and wire
23. Retainer (late 1971 and 1972)
24. Shaft and plate

SINGLE CONTACT POINT CIRCUIT BREAKER (MANUAL ADVANCE) (32)

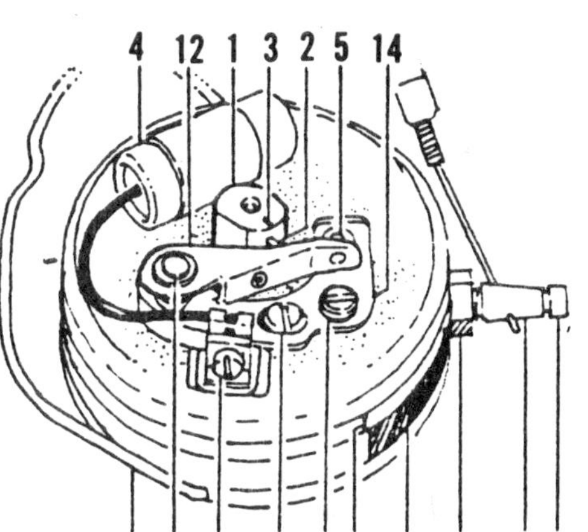

1. Breaker cam
2. Fiber cam follower
3. Cam timing mark
4. Condenser
5. Contact points
6. Lock screw
7. Adjust screw
8. Timing mark
9. Locknut
10. Stud plate (adjust)
11. Screw
12. Circuit breaker lever
13. Pivot stud
14. Support
15. Timing adjust stud
16. Cover retainer
17. Lock screw

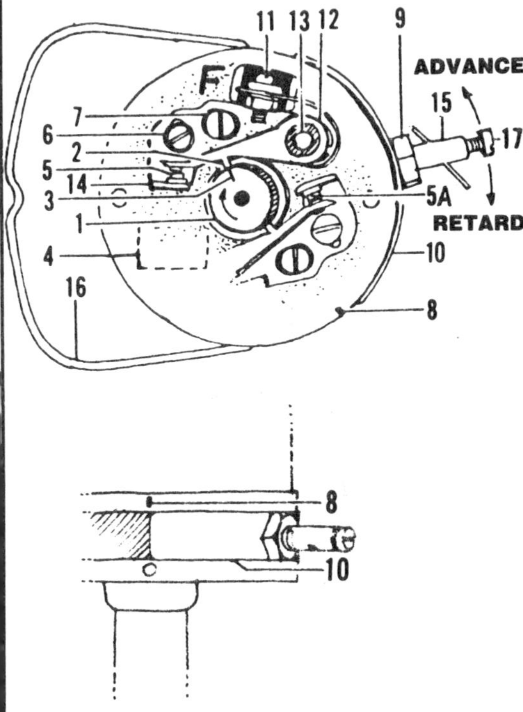

models, the circuit breaker was incorporated into the right gearcase cover (**Figure 31**). Refer to the appropriate illustration during all service procedures.

Removal (1959-1964)

1. Thoroughly clean the circuit breaker area.
2. On manual advance models, disconnect the advance cable from the adjusting stud (**Figure 32**).
3. Remove the cover.
4. Remove the base and retainer.
5. Remove the 2 mounting screws and lift the shaft and housing from the gear case cover.

Installation (1959-1964)

1. Remove the spark plugs.
2. Remove the timing inspection plug from the left side of the engine.
3. Telescope front cylinder intake valve pushrod cover (closest to carburetor) so that pushrod operation can be observed. See **Figure 28**.
4. Turn engine clockwise until the front piston is on the compression stroke, then continue turning slowly until advanced timing mark on flywheel is centered in the inspection hole (**Figure 33**). The cylinder is on its compression stroke just after its intake valve closes.
5. Install a new stem gasket or O-ring.

NOTE
Use gasket sealing compound on new stem gaskets.

6. Insert the shaft and stem assembly into the gearcase cover, making sure that the cable is inserted through the stem flange hole. Before engaging the drive gear, turn the circuit breaker camshaft approximately 60° from position where

(33)

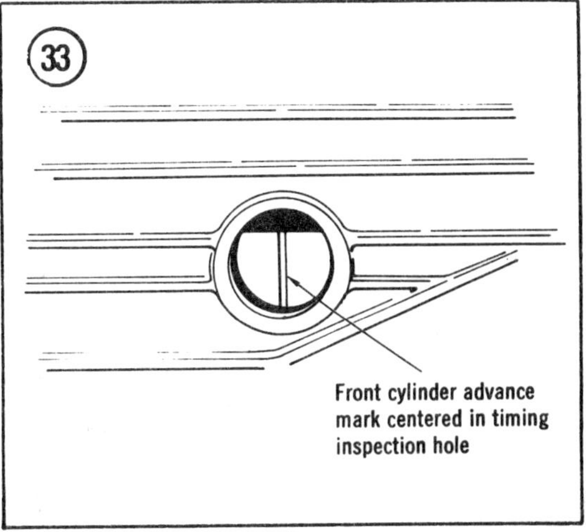

Front cylinder advance mark centered in timing inspection hole

mark on cam aligns with the fiber rubbing block on the movable breaker contact. See **Figure 32** or **Figure 34**.
7. Install both crankcase screws snugly, but do not tighten them at this point.
8. Temporarily position the circuit breaker assembly into the gear case so that the adjusting stud points toward the front the of bike and the stem housing screw holes line up with the mounting holes in the crankcase. Then move the circuit breaker base counterclockwise to the fully advanced position.
9. Notice how closely the circuit breaker cam lobe mark aligns with the breaker lever rubbing block. If it does not align, lift the circuit breaker assembly from the gearcase. Turn the shaft gear one tooth, then check alignment. Repeat until the cam mark aligns closely with the rubbing block.
10. Tighten both crankcase screws.
11. Wrap the cable clockwise around the camshaft. Then install the base retainer over the wire with the retainer end facing down toward the front cylinder.
12. Install the cover retainer, if removed.
13. Adjust the ignition timing as described in Chapter Three.

Removal (1965-1970)

1. Thoroughly clean circuit breaker area with compressed air.
2. On early models, remove the nuts and washers securing the base to the stem.
3. Remove the base. Then remove screws and washers securing the shaft and housing assembly to the gear case cover.
4. Lift the shaft and housing from the gear case cover. On 1966-1967 models with automatic advance, remove the bolts and clamp to free the circuit breaker assembly from the crankcase.

Installation (1965-1970)

1. Remove the spark plugs.
2. Remove the timing inspection plug from the left side of the engine.
3. Telescope front cylinder intake valve pushrod cover (closest to carburetor) so that pushrod operation can be observed. See **Figure 28**.
4. Turn engine clockwise until the front piston is on the compression stroke, then continue turning slowly until advanced timing mark on flywheel is centered in the inspection hole (**Figure 33**). The cylinder is on its compression stroke just after its intake valve closes.

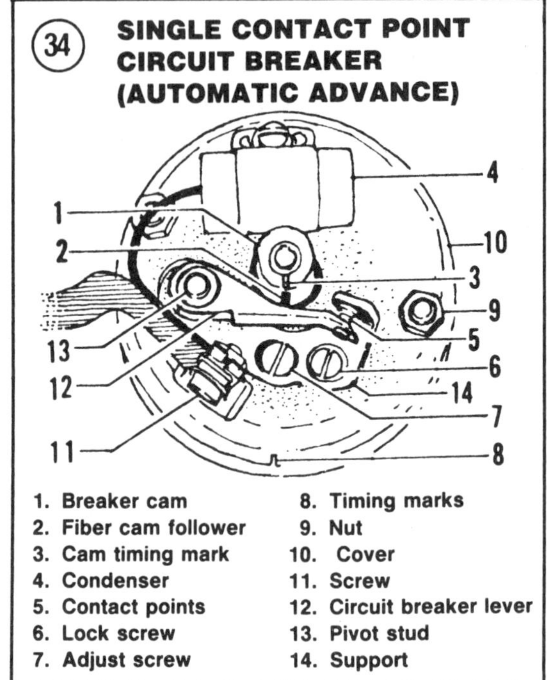

1. Breaker cam
2. Fiber cam follower
3. Cam timing mark
4. Condenser
5. Contact points
6. Lock screw
7. Adjust screw
8. Timing marks
9. Nut
10. Cover
11. Screw
12. Circuit breaker lever
13. Pivot stud
14. Support

5. Install a new gasket (26, **Figure 30**) using gasket sealing compound.
6. Insert shaft (32) and stem (25) assembly into the gearcase cover, making sure that cable (11) is inserted into hole of stem flange. Position stem (25) so that timing marks on base (**Figure 34**) face away from engine. Before engaging drive gear, turn shaft counterclockwise approximately 60° from position where mark on cam aligns with fiber rubbing block on movable breaker contact.
7. Install both crankcase screws (23) snugly, but do not tighten them.
8. Observe how closely the mark on the cam aligns with the rubbing block. If it does not align closely, lift the circuit breaker assembly and turn the shaft gear one tooth, then reinstall. Check the alignment once again.
9. Repeat Step 8 until the cam mark aligns closely with the rubbing block.
10. Tighten both crankcase screws (23).
11. Position base assembly (10) on shaft (32) so that timing marks align, then tighten nuts (23) Make sure the cam mark and the rubbing block are in correct alignment after tightening the clamp.
12. Adjust the ignition timing as described in Chapter Three.

Installation (1966-1970)

Refer to **Figure 30** for this procedure.
1. Remove the spark plugs.

2. Remove the timing inspection plug from the left side of the engine.
3. Telescope front cylinder intake valve pushrod cover (closest to carburetor) so that pushrod operation can be observed (**Figure 28**).
4. Turn engine clockwise until the front piston is on the compression stroke, then continue turning slowly until advanced timing mark on flywheel is centered in the inspection hole (**Figure 33**). The cylinder is on its compression stroke just after its intake valve closes.
5. Install the breaker base on the stem and shaft assembly. Install the washers and nuts and tighten securely.
6. Install a new stem O-ring (26, **Figure 30**).
7. Turn the shaft gear to approximately align the cam mark with the cam follower as shown in **Figure 32** or **Figure 34**. Then install the circuit breaker assembly into the gear case with the wire facing toward the rear of the engine.

NOTE
Positioning the wire toward the rear of the engine will position the circuit breaker points to the outside of the engine, thus allowing access to the adjusting screws when the cover is removed.

8. With the flywheel timing mark in the center of the timing hole (**Figure 33**), observe how closely the mark on the cam aligns with the rubbing block. If it does not align closely, lift the circuit breaker assembly and turn the shaft gear one tooth, then reinstall. Check the alignment once again.
9. Repeat Step 8 until the cam mark aligns closely with the rubbing block.
10. Install the stem clamp and tighten the clamp bolts securely. Make sure the cam mark and the rubbing block are in correct alignment after tightening the clamp.
11. Adjust the ignition timing as described in Chapter Three.

Circuit Breaker Disassembly/ Reassembly (1959-1970)

Refer to **Figure 30** to disassemble and reassemble the circuit breaker assemblies. Observe the following.

1. Clean all metal parts in solvent and allow to thoroughly dry.
2. Make sure the base plate is cleaned of all dirt or grease before installing the contact breakers.
3. Check the gear (37, **Figure 30**) for worn, chipped or broken teeth. Replace the gear if it shows these conditions.
3. Check the pin hole in the gear (37). If the hole is enlarged or distorted, check the mating hole in the end of the camshaft (32). Replace both parts if necessary. Replace the pin if it shows signs of wear.
4. On automatic advance units, check the flyweight springs (29) for sagging or breakage. Check the flyweight pivot posts on the camshaft (32) for looseness. Check the flyweight (29) pivot holes. Replace worn or damaged parts.
5. Replace all O-rings and gaskets during reassembly.

Removal/Installation (1971-1978)

Refer to **Figure 31** for this procedure.

1. Remove the circuit breaker cover (**Figure 35**) and gasket.
2. Remove the circuit breaker plate screws (**Figure 36**) and remove the plate assembly (**Figure 37**).
3. Remove the wire terminal from the circuit breaker contact terminal post (**Figure 38**).
4. Remove the circuit breaker cam bolt (A, **Figure 39**).
5. Remove the breaker cam from the advance assembly.
6. Pull the advance assembly out of the gearcase cover (B, **Figure 39**).
7. Installation is the reverse of these steps, noting the following.

7

8. The advance assembly must be installed so that the pin in the back of the plate (**Figure 40**) engages with the slot on the end of the crankshaft (**Figure 41**).

> *NOTE*
> *If the breaker cam (10, **Figure 31**) was removed from the advance assembly, refer to **Disassembly/Inspection/Reassembly** in this chapter for correct installation. The breaker cam can be installed backwards.*

9. Adjust the ignition timing as described in Chapter Three.

Disassembly/Inspection/Reassembly

1. Pull back on the flyweights (A, **Figure 42**) and pull the breaker cam (B, **Figure 42**) off of the advance assembly. See **Figure 43**.
2. Disconnect the flyweight springs from the flyweights (**Figure 44**).
3. Slip the flyweights off of the advance assembly pivots. See **Figure 45**.
4. Inspect the condenser and breaker contact points as described in Chapter Three.
5. Inspect the flyweights and springs (**Figure 46**) for wear or damage. Check also that the springs are not stretched or distorted.

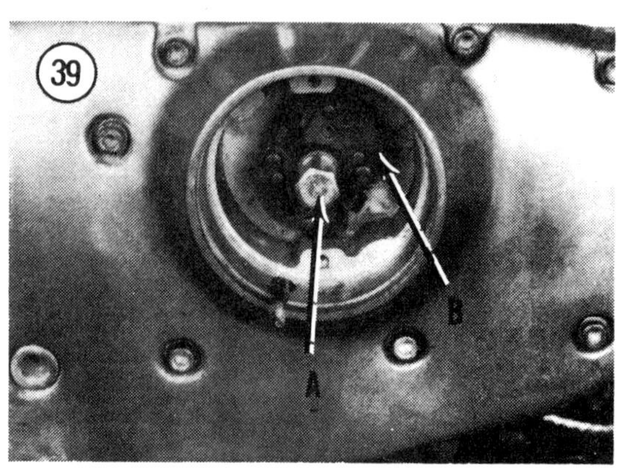

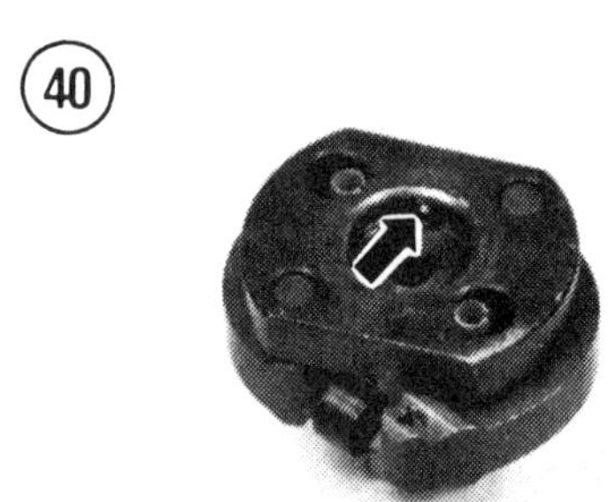

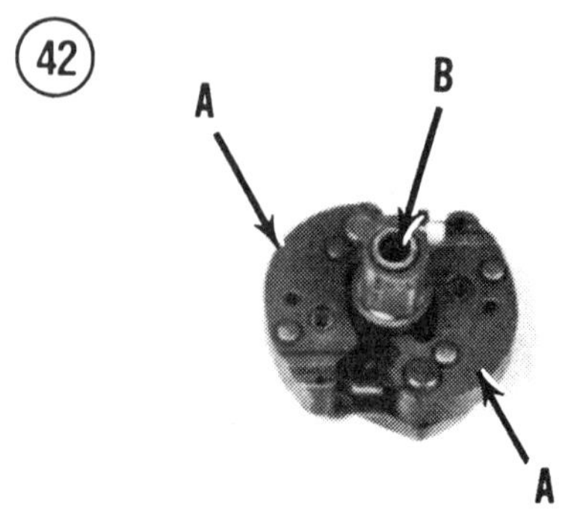

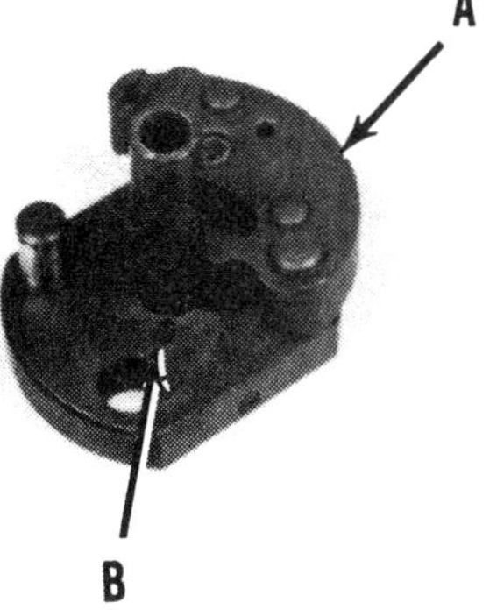

6. Check the flyweight pivots on the advance plate for wear or looseness. Replace the advance plate if necessary.
7. Check the rotor for excessive wear at the slots at the base of the cam (A, **Figure 47**). Check the cam surface (B, **Figure 47**) for pitting, deep scoring or excessive wear. Replace the cam if necessary.
8. Assembly is the reverse of these steps, noting the following.
9. When installing the cam onto the advance assembly, align flat surface on cam (**Figure 48**) with the roll pin installed in the assembly plate (B, **Figure 45**). See **Figure 49**.

NOTE
***Figure 49** shows the cam installed with one flyweight removed for clarity.*

10. Make sure tab on flyweights engage slots in cam as shown in **Figure 50**.

IGNITION SYSTEM (1979)

A breakerless electronic ignition system is installed on 1979 models. Refer to **Figure 51** and **Figure 52** for diagrams of the ignition circuit.

This system differs from breaker point systems in that the mechanical points are replaced by an

7

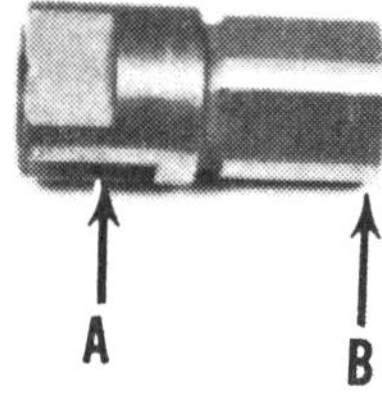

electronic ignition on the camshaft. The timer consists of a rotor and sensor. The sensor feeds signals to a control module mounted on the back of the timer inner cover. The timer rotor is mounted on a mechanical flywheel centrifugal advance, just as a point cam would be in a breaker point ignition system.

The rotor has 2 lobes—a small one that fires the front cylinder and a large lobe that fires the rear cylinder. When the ignition switch and kill switch are ON, current flows from the battery to the control module where an oscillator produces a signal that flows through the sensor, creating a magnetic field around it. Current also flows through the ignition coil primary winding. When the leading edge of a rotor lobe enters the magnetic field, it slightly weakens the field. The control module detects the weakened field and stops current flow through the ignition coil primary winding.

From this point on, the system operates like a breaker point ignition system. The sudden stoppage of current flow in the ignition coil primary winding causes a rapid collapse of the coil's magnetic field, inducing a high voltage current in the ignition coil secondary winding and firing the spark plug.

The electronic ignition sytem eliminates breaker point maintenance, but regular inspection of the

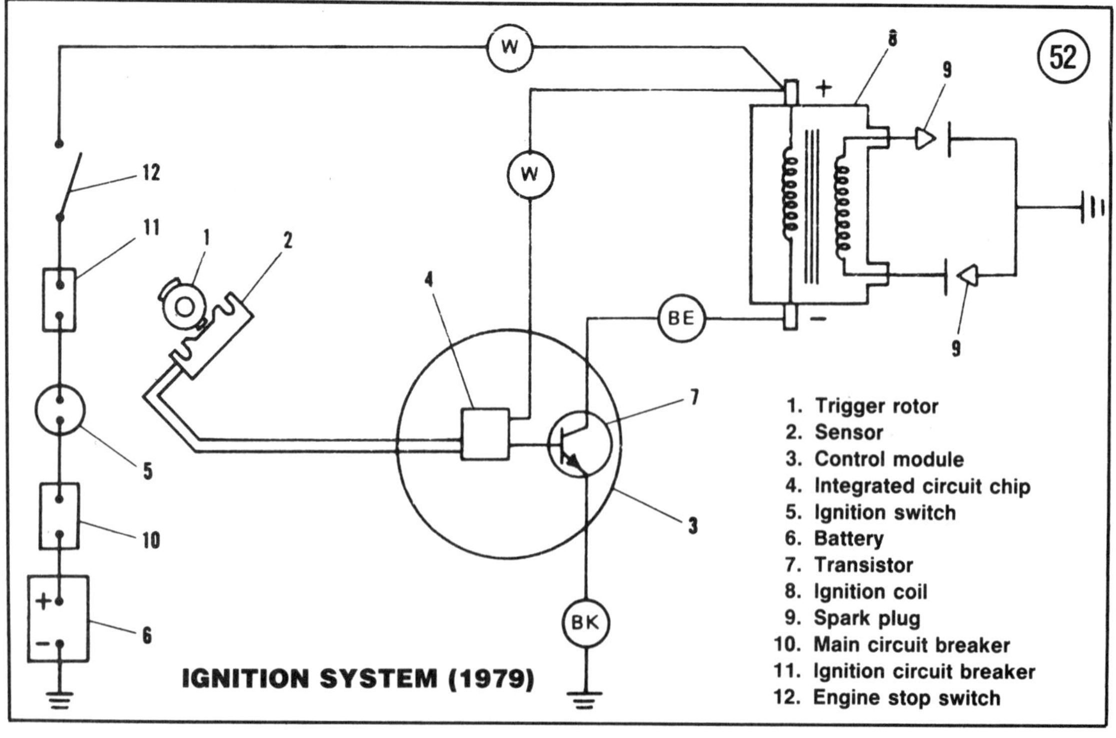

IGNITION SYSTEM (1979)

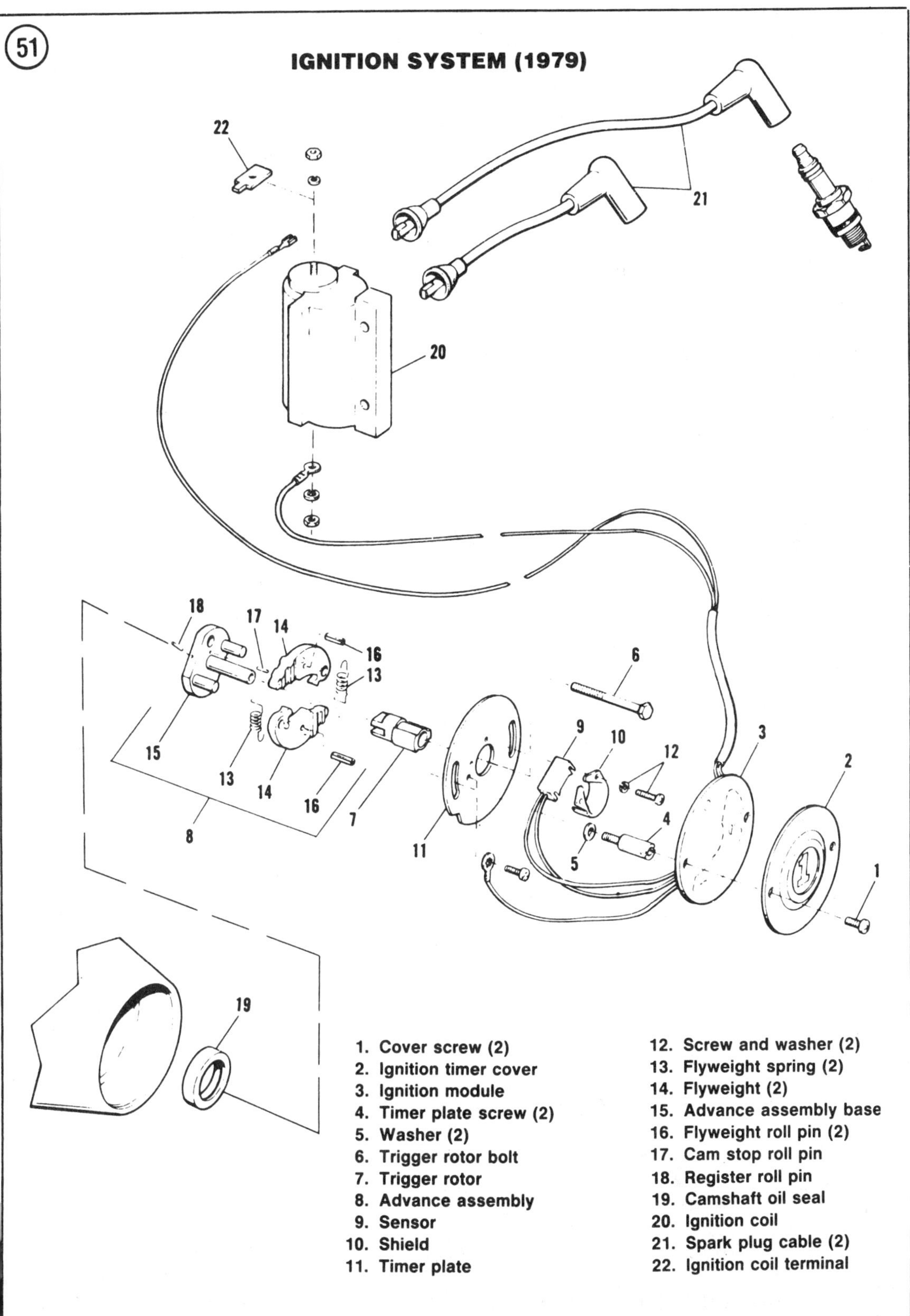
51
IGNITION SYSTEM (1979)
1. Cover screw (2)
2. Ignition timer cover
3. Ignition module
4. Timer plate screw (2)
5. Washer (2)
6. Trigger rotor bolt
7. Trigger rotor
8. Advance assembly
9. Sensor
10. Shield
11. Timer plate
12. Screw and washer (2)
13. Flyweight spring (2)
14. Flyweight (2)
15. Advance assembly base
16. Flyweight roll pin (2)
17. Cam stop roll pin
18. Register roll pin
19. Camshaft oil seal
20. Ignition coil
21. Spark plug cable (2)
22. Ignition coil terminal

sensor air gap (the gap between the rotor lobes and the sensor) and of the mechanical advance operation is required.

Sensor Air Gap

Inspect the sensor air gap according to the maintenance schedule in Chapter Three. Refer to **Figure 51** for this procedure.

1. Remove the spark plug leads at the plugs and remove the spark plugs.
2. Remove the ignition timing cover.
3. Turn the crankshaft and center the wide rotor lobe in the sensor (**Figure 53**).
4. Measure the gap between the sensor and the rotor. It should be 0.004-0.006 in. If the gap is incorrect, loosen the 2 screws (**Figure 54**) that attach the sensor and move the sensor until the gap is correct. Then, holding the sensor steady, tighten the screws.

NOTE
If the engine doesn't run smoothly and spits back because of the lean fuel mixture, set the sensor air gap as close to 0.004 in. as possible. This adjustment will strengthen the ignition signals for better combustion.

5. Rotate the crankshaft to center the small lobe in the sensor. Measure the gap as before (Step 4) and correct it if necessary. Both gaps must be within the specified tolerance.
6. Install the spark plugs.
7. Check the ignition timing as described in Chapter Three.

Ignition Removal/Installation

Refer to **Figure 51** for this procedure.

1. Remove the ignition cover and the timing module (2 and 3, **Figure 51**).
2. Remove the 2 timer plate screws (4) and washers.
3. Unscrew the trigger rotor bolt (6).
4. Remove the advance assembly (8).
5. To disassemble the sensor and shield from the timing plate, remove the screws that hold them in place.
6. To disassemble the advance mechanism, refer to *Circuit Breaker Disassembly/Inspection/Reassembly* for 1971-1978 models in this chapter.
7. Installation is the reverse of these steps, noting the following.
8. Lubricate the advance mechanism pivots with WD-40 or Loctite Anti-Seize.
9. The advance assembly must be installed so that the pin in the back of the plate (**Figure 40**) engages

53

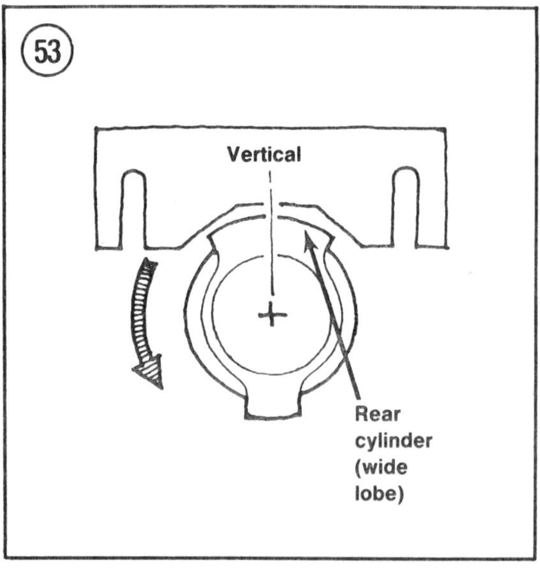

54

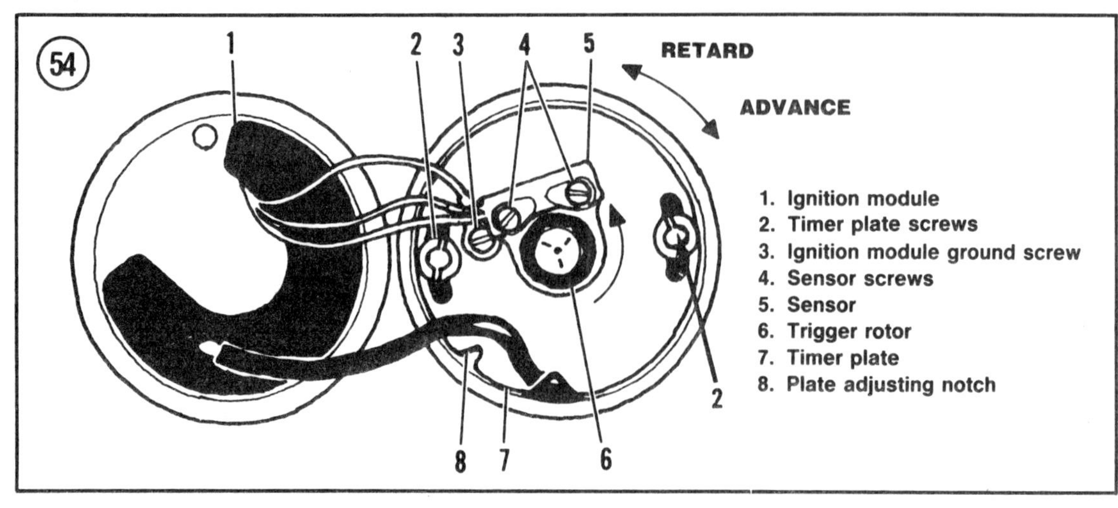

with the slot on the end of the crankshaft (**Figure 41**).

NOTE
If the breaker cam (8, ***Figure 51****) was removed from the advance assembly, refer to* ***Circuit Breaker Disassembly/Inspection/Reassembly*** *for 1971-1978 models in this chapter. The breaker cam can be installed backwards.*

10. Adjust the ignition timing as described in Chapter Three.
11. Check the sensor air gap as described in this chapter.
12. Check the ignition timing as described in Chapter Three.

IGNITION SYSTEM (1980-ON)

In 1980, a Magnavox electronic ignition was introduced. This system has a full electronic advance that replaced the mechanical advance on 1979 models. The inductive pickup unit is driven by the engine and generates pulses which are routed to the solid-state ignition control module. This control module computes the ignition timing advance and ignition coil dwell time, eliminating the need for mechanical advance and routine ignition service. Refer to **Figure 55** and **Figure 56** for diagrams of the ignition circuit.

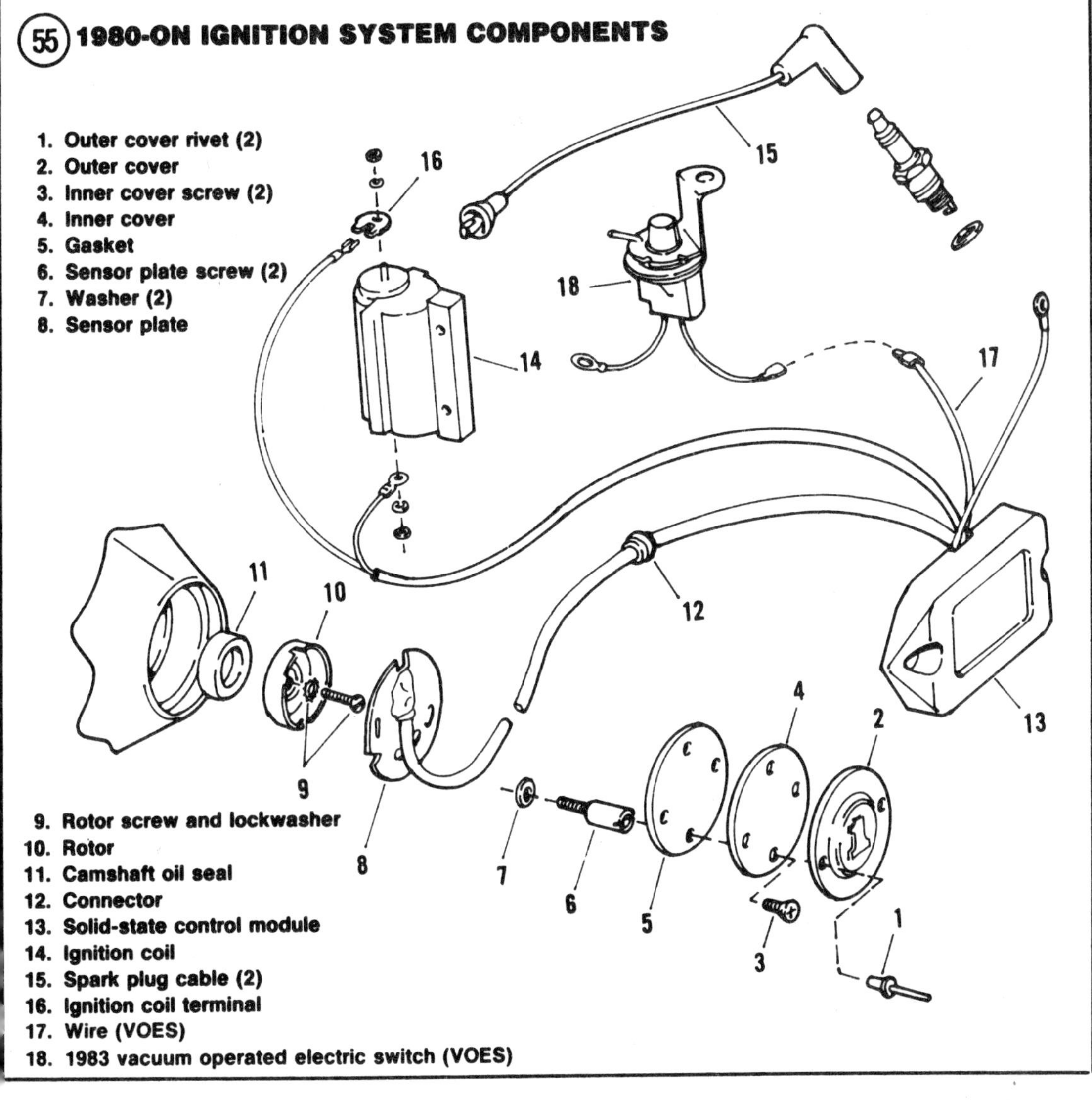

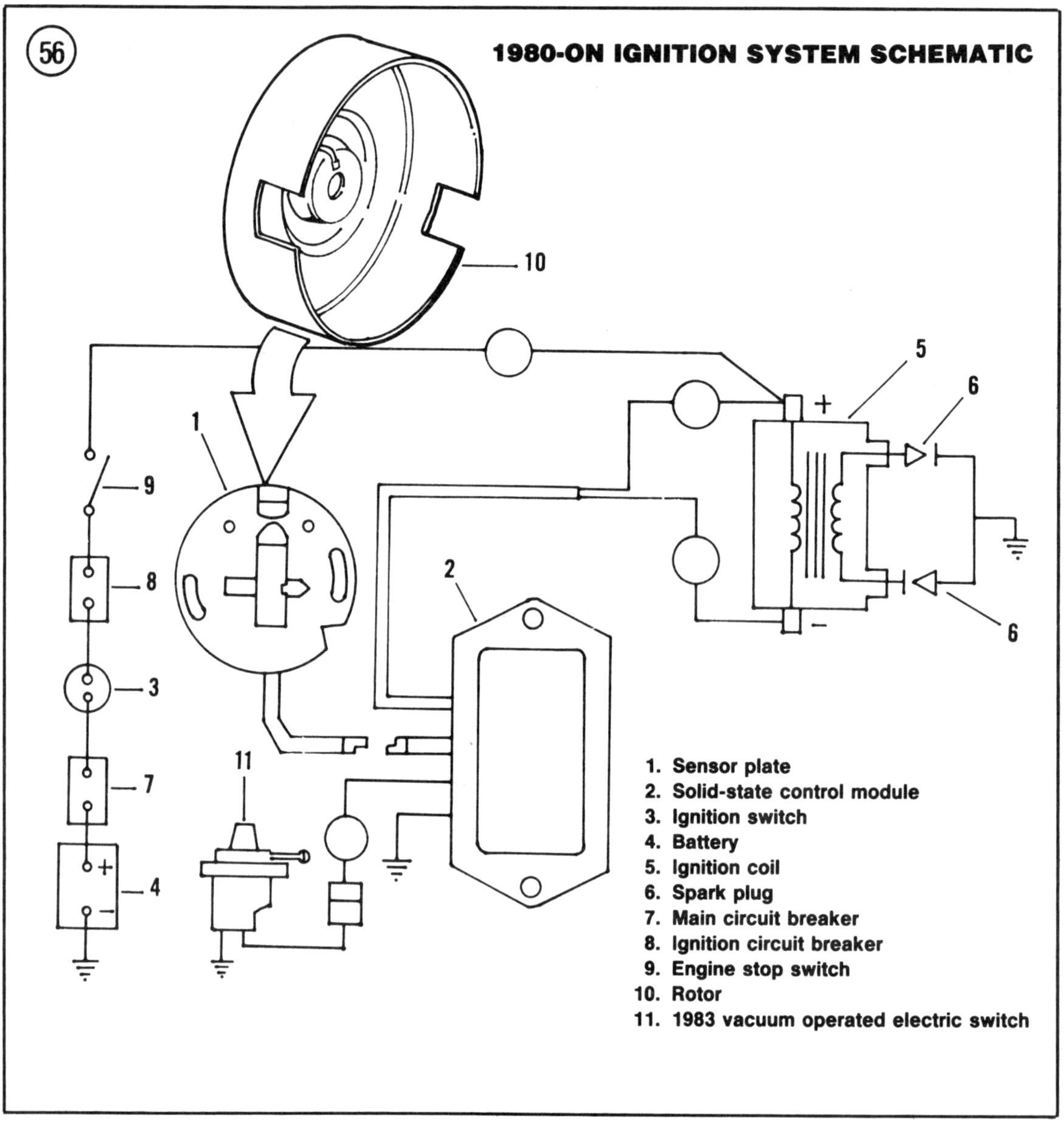

56
1980-ON IGNITION SYSTEM SCHEMATIC
10
5
6
+
1
9
2
−
6
8
3
11
7
4
+
−
1. Sensor plate
2. Solid-state control module
3. Ignition switch
4. Battery
5. Ignition coil
6. Spark plug
7. Main circuit breaker
8. Ignition circuit breaker
9. Engine stop switch
10. Rotor
11. 1983 vacuum operated electric switch

In 1983, a vacuum operated electric switch (VOES) was added to the ignition system. The switch is open when the engine is in low vacuum situations such as accleration and high load. The switch is closed when engine vacuum is high as during a low engine load condition. The VOES allows the ignition system to follow 2 spark advance curves. A maximum spark curve can be used during a high-vacuum condition to provide improved fuel economy and performance. During heavy engine load and acceleration (low vacuum) conditions, the spark can be retarded to minimize ignition knock and still maintain performance. The VOES is installed above the intake manifold.

57
Vertical
Vertical
Front
cylinder
(narrow
lobe)

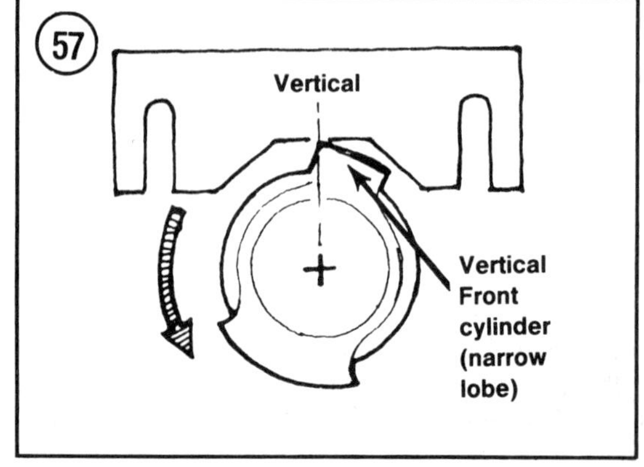

On 1980 and 1981 models, the solid-state ignition control module is mounted on the bottom of the battery carrier/oil tank. On 1982 and later models, the control module is located behind the side cover, mounted to the frame next to the battery.

NOTE
On 1980-early 1981 models, the control module shuts off current to the ignition coil 4 seconds after the ignition switch is turned ON. If the engine is not started within that time, the module must be reset by turning the ignition switch OFF and ON again. Later ignition modules allow 6 seconds for the engine to be started.

The timing sensor is triggered by the leading and trailing edges of the 2 rotor lobes shown in **Figure 57**. As rpm increases, the control module "steps" the timing in 3 stages of advance. See **Table 4**.

Troubleshooting

Refer to Chapter Two for complete troubleshooting procedures.

Ignition Component Removal

Refer to **Figure 55** for this procedure.

1. Disconnect the negative battery lead.
2. Drill out the outer cover rivets with a 3/8 in. drill bit.
3. Remove the inner cover and its gasket.
4. Remove the screws securing the sensor plate to the crankcase.
5. Disconnect the sensor wire connector at the crankcase. Then remove the connector from the wires. Withdraw the wires through the crankcase hole one wire at a time. Remove the sensor plate and wires.
6. Remove the rotor screw and rotor.

7. Disconnect the ignition module wires at the ignition coil.
8. Remove the ignition module as follows:
   a. *1980-1981:* Remove the mounting bolts and screw securing the ignition module to the battery case and remove the ignition module.
   b. *1982-1985:* Remove the ignition module side cover next to the battery. Then remove the mounting bolts and screw securing the ignition module to the frame and remove the ignition module.

Inspection

1. If necessary, follow the procedures in Chapter Two to check the electrical system.
2. Check the ignition compartment for oil leakage. If present, remove the crankcase seal (**Figure 58**) by prying it out with a screwdriver or seal remover. Install a new seal by tapping it in place with a suitable size drift placed on the outside of the seal. Drive the seal in until it seats in the crankcase.

NOTE
If the crankcase seal is not installed all the way in, it may leak.

Installation

1. Install the ignition module. Make sure the ground wire is secured tightly.
2. Connect the ignition module wires to the ignition coil as shown in **Figure 55**.
3. Install the rotor. Apply Loctite Lock 'n Seal to the rotor bolt and install it. Tighten the bolt to 75-80 in.-lb.
4. Install the sensor plate. Tighten the screws securely.
5. Check the ignition timing as described in Chapter Three.
6. Install the inner cover and its gasket. Tighten the screws securely.

NOTE
Make sure to use special timing cover rivets in Step 7. These rivets have no rivet ends to fall into the timing compartment and damage the ignition components.

7. Rivet the outer cover to the inner cover. Use only timing cover rivets (part number 8699) to secure the outer cover. See **Figure 59**.

7

IGNITION COIL

Testing

If the coil condition is doubtful, there are several checks which can be made. Disconnect the coil secondary and primary wires before testing.

1. Set an ohmmeter on R×1. Measure the coil primary resistance between both coil primary terminals (**Figure 60**). Resistance should be within the specifications in **Table 1**.
2. Set the ohmmeter on R×100. Measure the coil secondary resistance between both high voltage terminals (**Figure 61**). Resistance should be within the specifications in **Table 1**.
3. Replace the coil if it does not test within specifications in Step 1 or Step 2.

Removal/Installation (Magneto Models)

Ignition coil removal and installation for these models is described under *Magneto Disassembly/Inspection/Reassembly* in this chapter.

Removal/Installation (All Other Models)

1. Remove the coil cover (if so equipped).
2. Disconnect the spark plug wire (**Figure 62**).
3. Disconnect all wiring at the ignition coil (**Figure 63**).

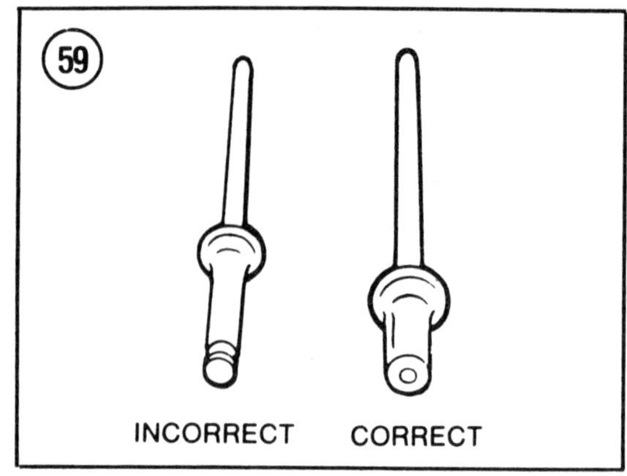

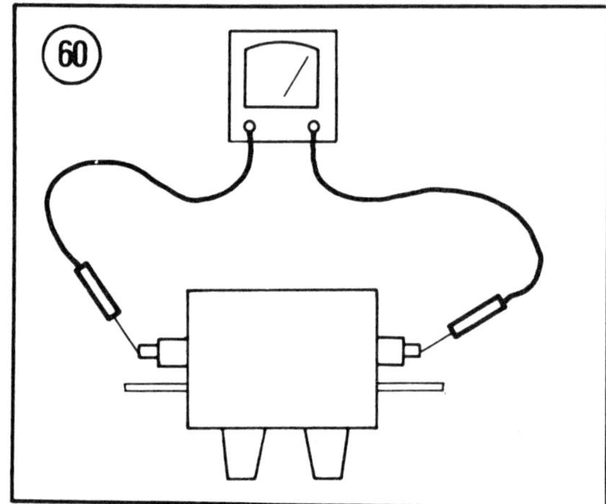

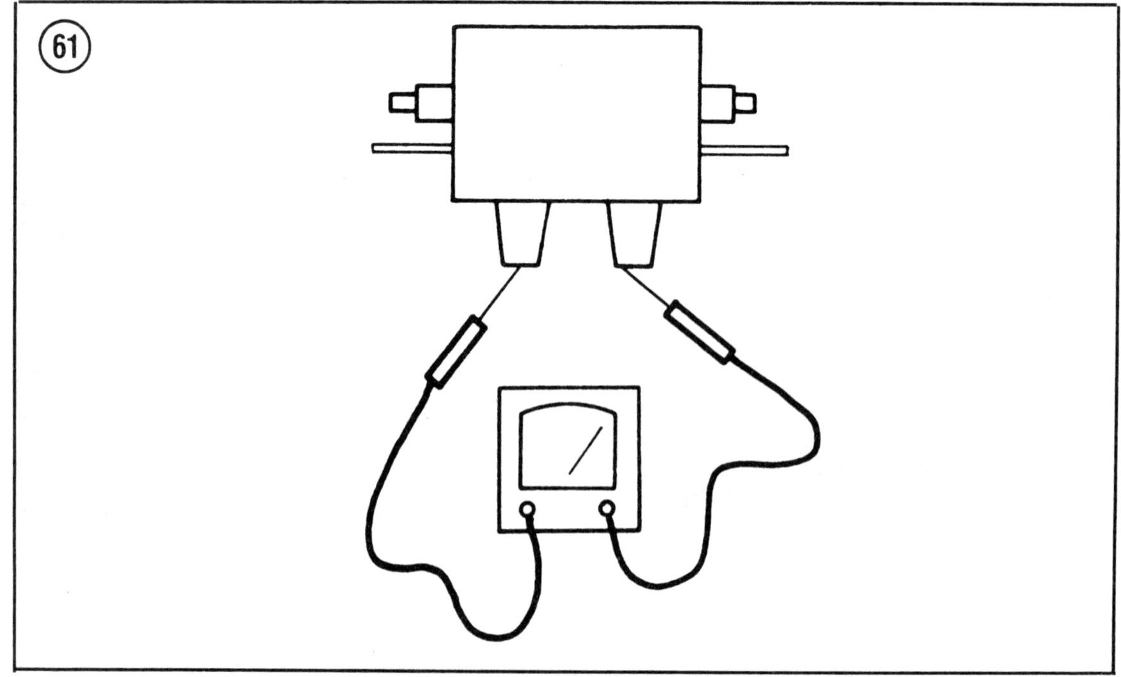

4. Remove the coil mounting bolts and remove the coil.
5. Installation is the reverse of these steps.

CAUTION
*When replacing an ignition coil on 1980 and later models, make sure the coil is marked ELECTRONIC ADVANCE (**Figure 64**). Installing an older type ignition coil could damage electronic ignition components. All 1979 models may use an old style coil.*

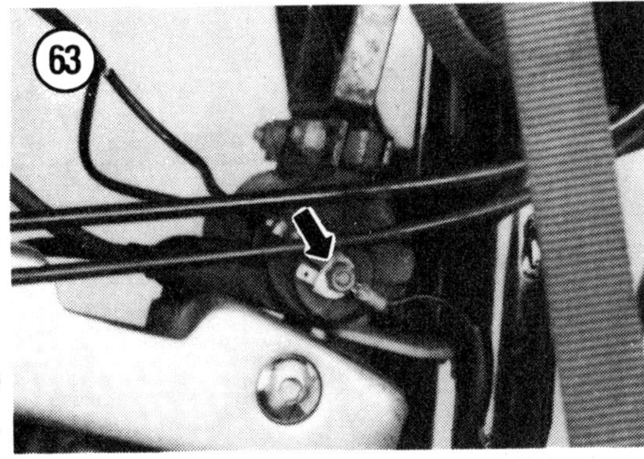

Spark Plug Cable Replacement

Magneto equipped models

Spark plug cable removal and installation for these models is described under *Magneto Disassembly/Inspection/Reassembly* in this chapter.

1959-1963

Refer to **Figure 65** for this procedure.

1. Before attempting to remove old cables, purchase new cables from a Harley-Davidson dealer. Then trim cable ends (if necessary) so that they will slip easily into holes in coil.
2. Remove the circuit breaker points cover. Rotate crankshaft so that the ignition points are closed. Then warm the ignition coil by turning the ignition switch ON.
3. Turn the ignition switch OFF when the coil is warm to the touch.
4. Clip off the old spark plug cable at the spark plug end. Then unscrew the cable packing nut (4, **Figure 65**) and slide it off of the cable along with the washer. Install the packing nut, washer and a new cable packing washer onto the new cable. Dip the coil end of a new cable in very light machine oil to ease assembly.

NOTE
Make sure the cable packing nut, washer and packing washer are facing

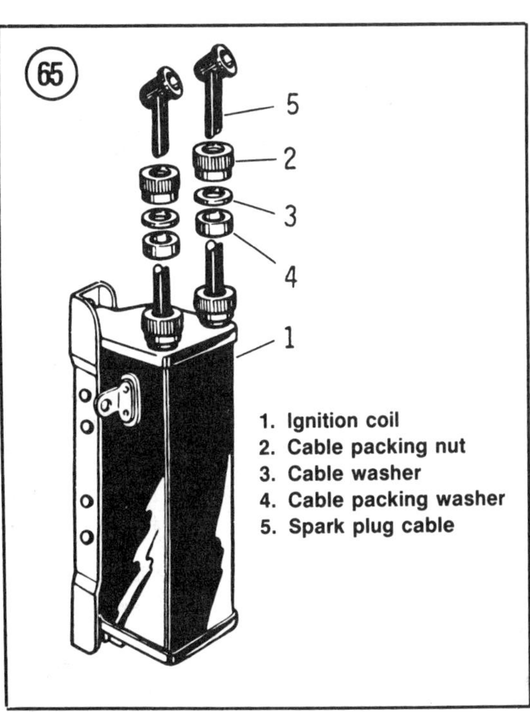

7

*in the correct direction on the cable before beginning Step 4. See **Figure 65**.*

5. Quickly pull one of the old cables out of the coil and insert the new cable. Make sure the new cable bottoms into the coil.
6. Slide the packing washer into position. Then position the washer and cable nut and tighten the nut securely.
7. Repeat Steps 3-6 to install the opposite cable.
8. If the coil sealing compound becomes too hot and softens to the extent that it prevents new cables from being fully inserted, perform the following:
   a. Allow the coil to cool.
   b. Select a piece of tubing with an outside diameter slightly larger than that of the coil wire.
   c. Using a razor blade, cut teeth into one end of the tubing (similar to that of a saw blade).
   d. Insert the tubing (teeth end first) into the coil. Make sure the tubing seats in the coil. Cut the tubing flush with the top of the coil.
   e. Install the new coil wire into the tubing installed in step "d".

Install the coil packing washer and washer, then tighten the packing nut.

1964-on

To replace the coil wire on these models, grasp the cable boot (**Figure 66**) and slide it up the wire (**Figure 67**). Then grasp the coil wire at the coil and pull it out (**Figure 68**).

Reverse to install. Replace the cable boot if worn or damaged. When reinstalling a coil wire, make sure the boot is secured to the coil to prevent moisture and dirt from entering.

NOTE
*If replacing the coil on 1964 and later models, remove the coil mount bracket (**Figure 69**) if so equipped.*

STARTER

Troubleshooting

Starter troubleshooting procedures is described in Chapter Two.

Removal/Installation (1967-1980)

Refer to **Figure 70** for this procedure.

1. Disconnect the battery negative lead.
2. Disconnect the electric starter cable at the starter.
3. Remove the clamp bolt and lockwasher from the crankcase.

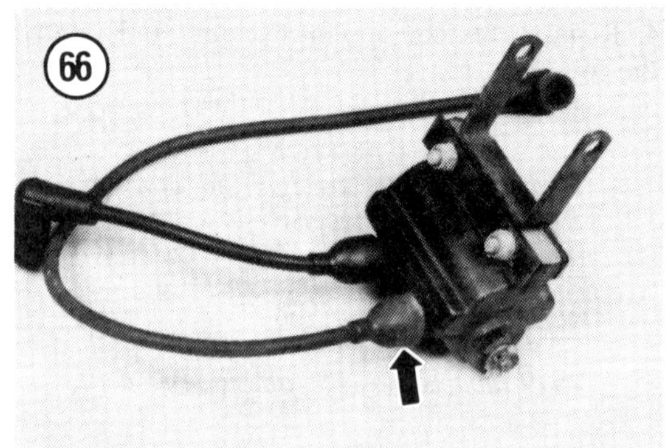
66

67

68

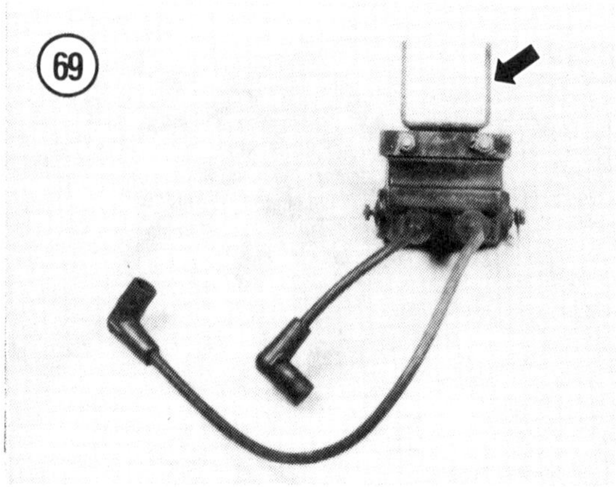
69

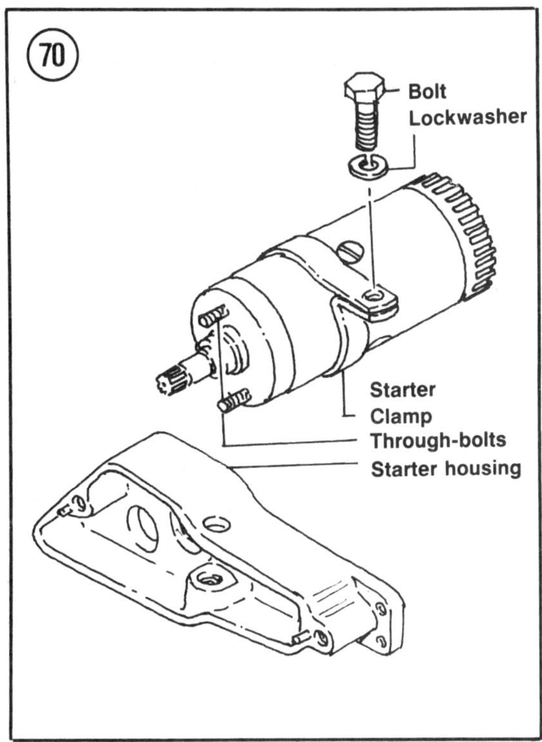

4. Remove the starter through-bolts.
5. Grasp the front and rear starter end covers (to prevent the starter from coming apart) and remove the starter.
6. Installation is the reverse of these steps.

Removal/Installation (1981-on)

1. Disconnect the battery negative lead.
2. Remove the rear exhaust pipe.
3. Remove the primary chain cover as described under *Clutch Removal* in Chapter Five.
4. See **Figure 71**. Disconnect the battery positive cable (A) and the solenoid wire (B) at the starter.
5. Remove the 2 starter mounting bolts (**Figure 72**).
6. Remove the starter (C, **Figure 71**) from the right-hand side.
7. Installation is the reverse of these steps. The long starter mounting bolt goes to the rear.

Disassembly/Assembly

1967-1980 Prestolite starters

Refer to **Figure 73** for this procedure.

1. Clean all grease, dirt and carbon from the case and end covers.
2. Remove the end cover assembly (20, **Figure 73**) if so equipped.
3. Remove the starter bolts (12).
4. Remove the commutator end cover (13).

NOTE
When removing the commutator end cover, it may be necessary to hold the brush plate in place.

5. Remove the armature (19) and drive end cover (with bearing) (15) as an assembly.
6. Inspect the starter as described in this chapter.
7. Installation is the reverse of these steps, noting the following:
   a. If the brushes and springs have been released from their holders, hold them in place with wire clips while installing the armature (**Figure 74**).
   b. Align the notch in the brush holder with the terminal insulator (**Figure 75**).
   c. The starter frame drive end cover is notched to fit with the drive end cover (**Figure 76**).
   d. The 2 ridges fixed on the commutator end cover must align with the terminal (**Figure 76**).

1974-early 1976 Hitachi starters

Refer to **Figure 77** for this procedure.

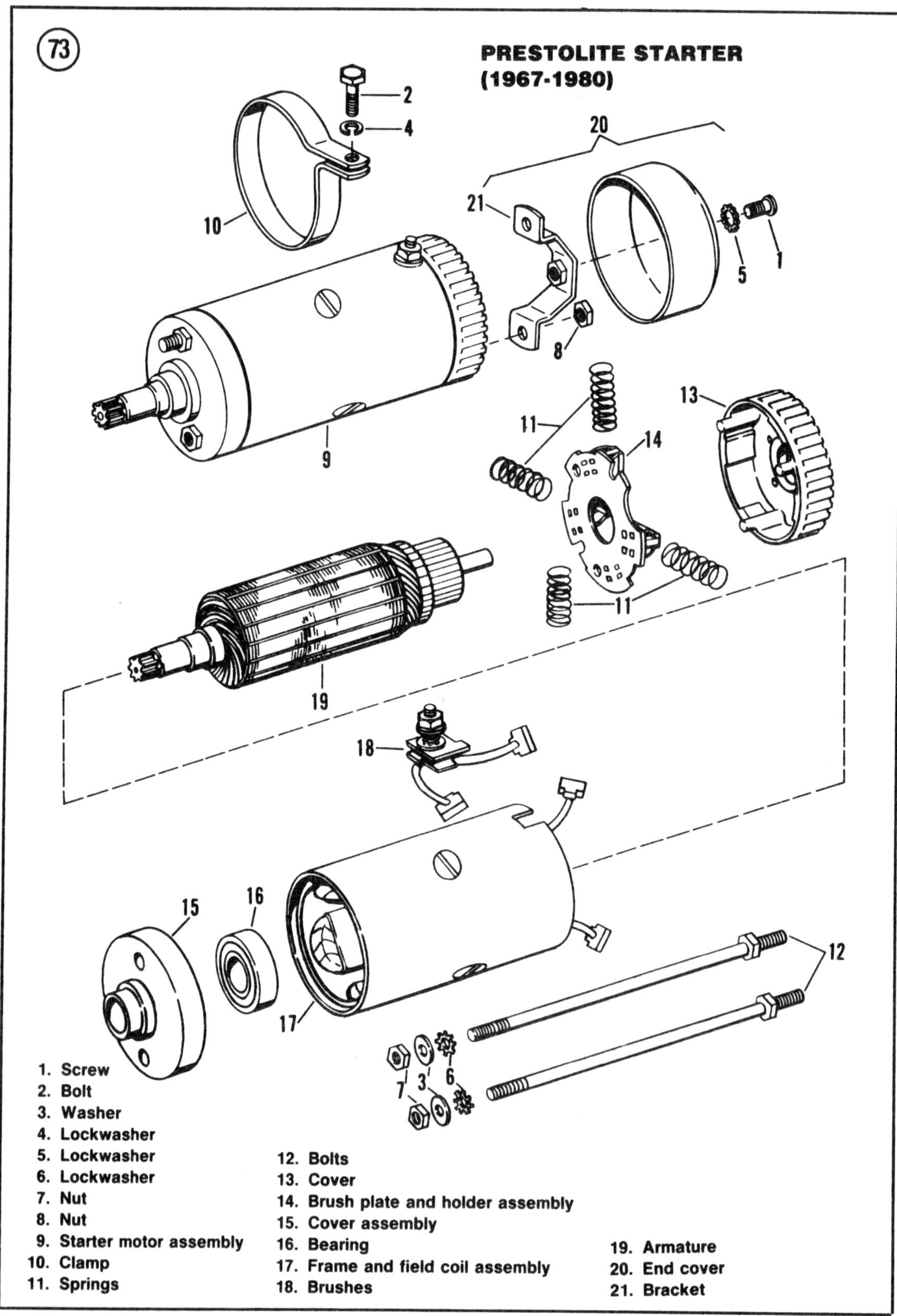
73
PRESTOLITE STARTER
(1967-1980)
1
2
3
4
5
6
7
8
9
10
11
12
13
14
15
16
17
18
19
20
21
1. Screw
2. Bolt
3. Washer
4. Lockwasher
5. Lockwasher
6. Lockwasher
7. Nut
8. Nut
9. Starter motor assembly
10. Clamp
11. Springs
12. Bolts
13. Cover
14. Brush plate and holder assembly
15. Cover assembly
16. Bearing
17. Frame and field coil assembly
18. Brushes
19. Armature
20. End cover
21. Bracket

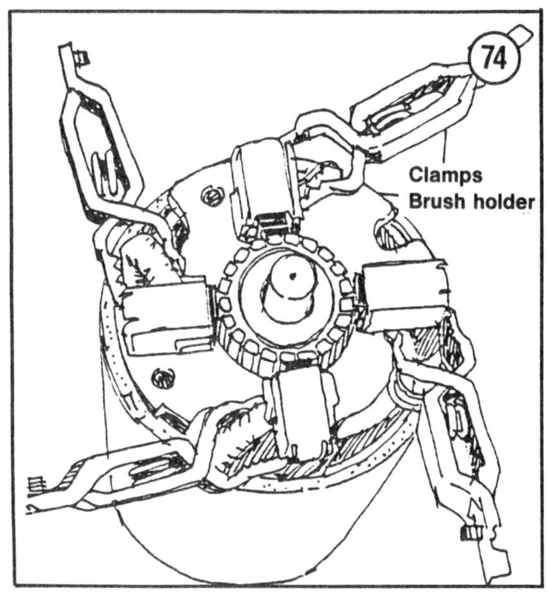

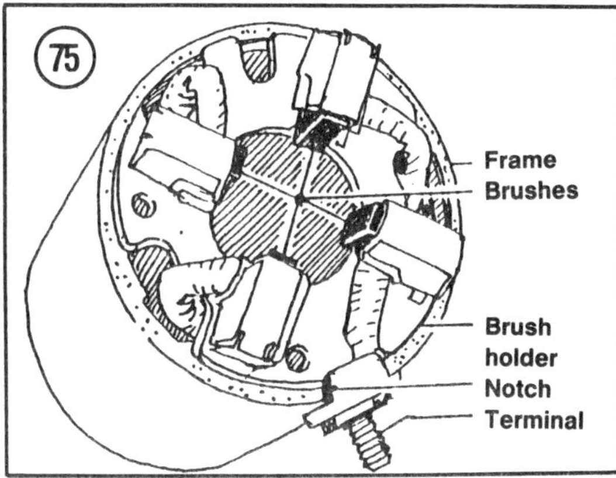

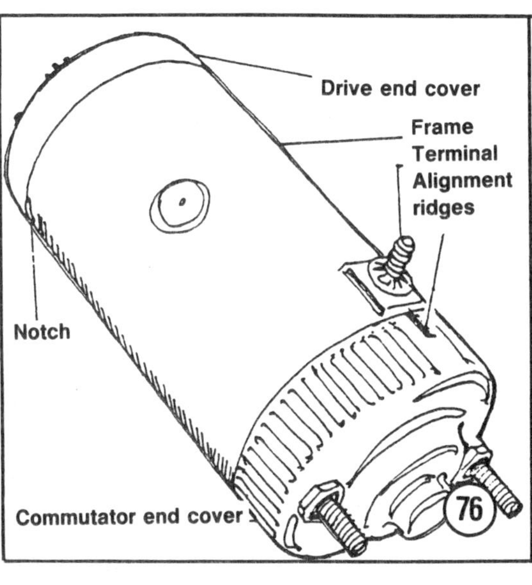

1. Clean all grease, dirt and carbon from the case and end covers.
2. Remove the end cover kit (11, **Figure 77**).
3. Remove the terminal nut and washers.
4. Remove the through-bolts (14) and washers.
5. Remove the commutator end cover screws (23) and washers.
6. Tap the commutator end cover (16) with a hammer to open a gap between the cover and the frame. Then use a screwdriver placed in the gap and push the commutator end cover away from the frame and remove it.

NOTE
Make sure the terminal and insulator remain in the frame when removing the commutator end cover.

7. Lift the brushes (20) away from the commutator.
8. Remove the front cover (15), armature (with ball bearing) (21) and washers (22).
9. Inspect the starter as described in this chapter.
10. Installation is the reverse of these steps, noting the following:
   a. Align the notch in the front cover with the projected part of the frame.
   b. Once the brushes are installed in the brush holder and the rear cover is installed, align and tighten the brush holder onto the rear cover from the outside.

7

1981-1985

Refer to **Figure 78** for this procedure.

1. Clean all grease, dirt and carbon from the case and end covers.
2. Disconnect the field wire.
3. Remove the end cover screws (2, **Figure 78**) and end cover (3).
4. Using a piece of wire, lift the brush springs and pull the brushes out of the holder.
5. Remove the brush holder (4).
6. Remove the armature (6) and field frame (7).
7. Inspect the starter as described in this chapter.
8. Installation is the reverse of these steps. Lubricate the armature bearings and the felt washer with high temperature grease.

Inspection

1. Measure the length of each brush (**Figure 79**) with a vernier caliper. If the length is less than specified in **Table 1**, it must be replaced. Replace the brushes as a set even though only one may be worn to this dimension.
2. Inspect the condition of the commutator. The mica in a good commutator is below the surface of

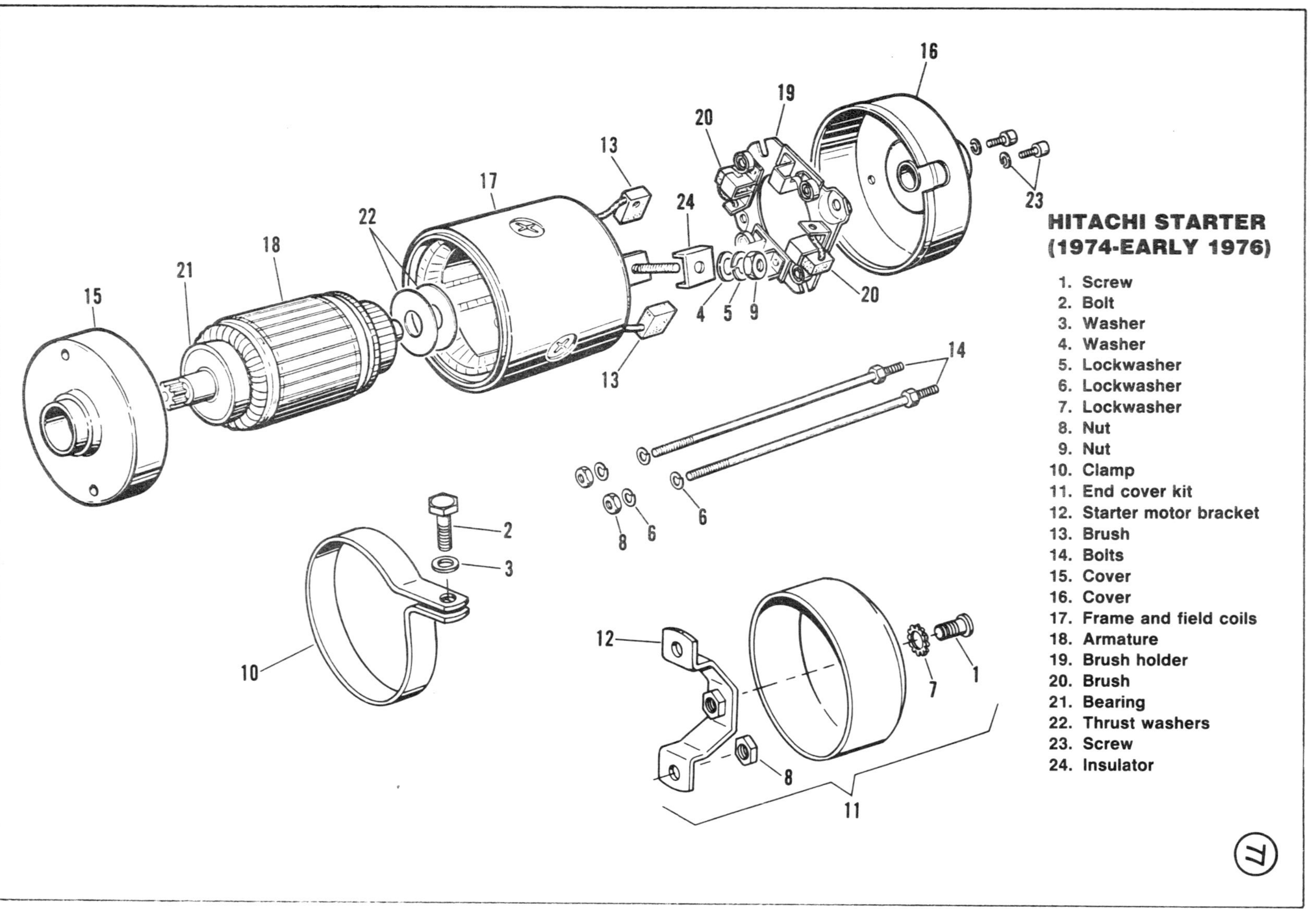
HITACHI STARTER
(1974-EARLY 1976)
1. Screw
2. Bolt
3. Washer
4. Washer
5. Lockwasher
6. Lockwasher
7. Lockwasher
8. Nut
9. Nut
10. Clamp
11. End cover kit
12. Starter motor bracket
13. Brush
14. Bolts
15. Cover
16. Cover
17. Frame and field coils
18. Armature
19. Brush holder
20. Brush
21. Bearing
22. Thrust washers
23. Screw
24. Insulator
77

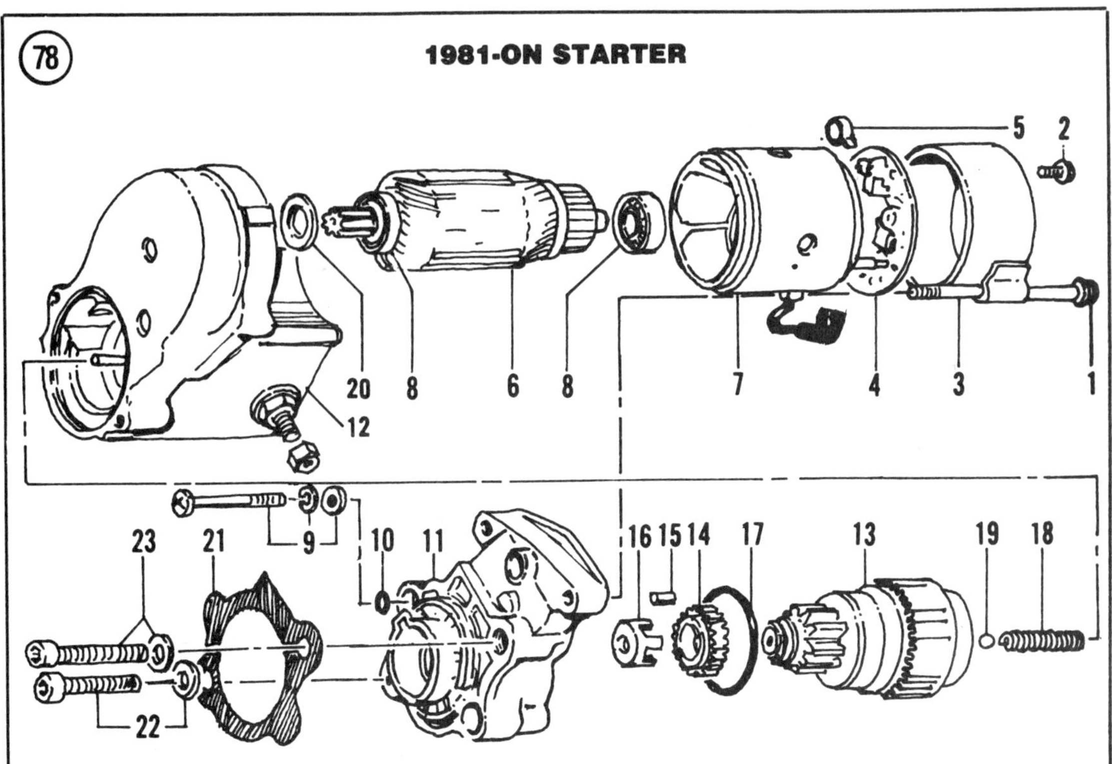

(78) **1981-ON STARTER**

1. Through-bolt
2. End cover screw (2)
3. End cover
4. Brush holder
5. Brush spring (4)
6. Armature
7. Field frame
8. Armature bearings
9. Drive housing mounting bolt, washer and lockwasher (2)
10. O-ring(2)
11. Drive housing
12. Solenoid housing
13. Drive assembly/overrunning clutch
14. Idler gear
15. Idler gear roller (5)
16. Idler gear bearing cage
17. O-ring
18. Return spring
19. Ball
20. Felt washer
21. Gasket
22. Front (short) mounting bolt and washer
23. Rear (long) mounting bolt and washer

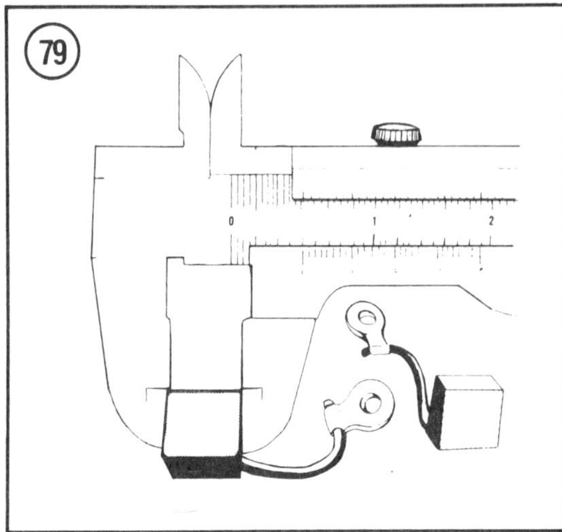

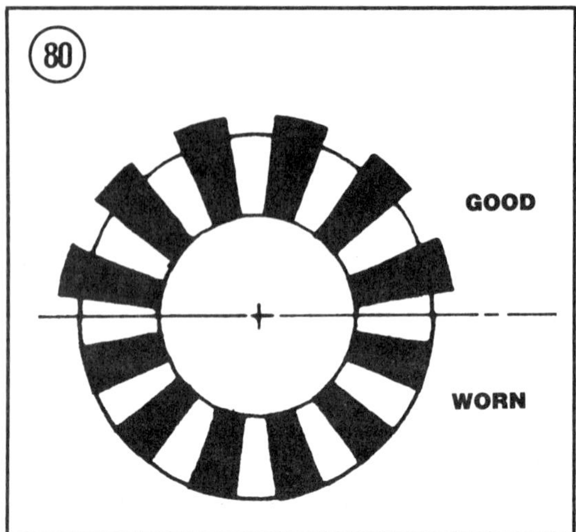

the copper bars. On a worn commutator the mica and copper bars may be worn to the same level. See **Figure 80**. If necessary, have the commutator serviced by a dealer or motorcycle or automotive electrical repair shop.

3. Inspect the commutator copper bars for discoloration. Discolored pairs of bars indicate grounded armature coils.

NOTE
Step 4 and Step 5 apply to 1981 and later models only. Because of the internal wiring connections to the earlier model starters, there is no satisfactory field test for shorted or grounded field coils.

4. Use an ohmmeter and check for continuity between the commutator bars (**Figure 81**); there should be continuity between pairs of bars. Also check continuity between the commutator bars and the shaft (**Figure 82**); there should be no continuity. If the unit fails either of these tests the armature is faulty and must be replaced.

5. Use an ohmmeter and inspect the field coil by checking continuity between the starter cable terminal and the starter case; there should be no continuity. Also check continuity between the starter cable terminal and each brush wire terminal; there should be continuity. If the unit fails either of these tests the case/field coil assembly must be replaced.

6. Connect one probe of an ohmmeter to the brush holder plate and the other probe to each of the positive (insulated) brush holders; there should be no continuity. If the unit fails at either brush holder, the brush holder assembly should be replaced.

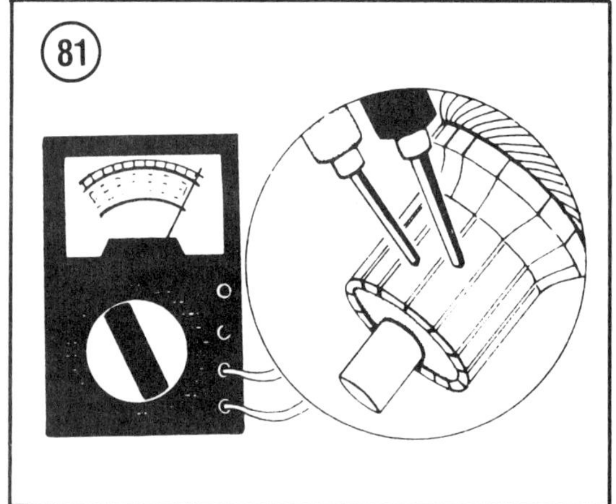

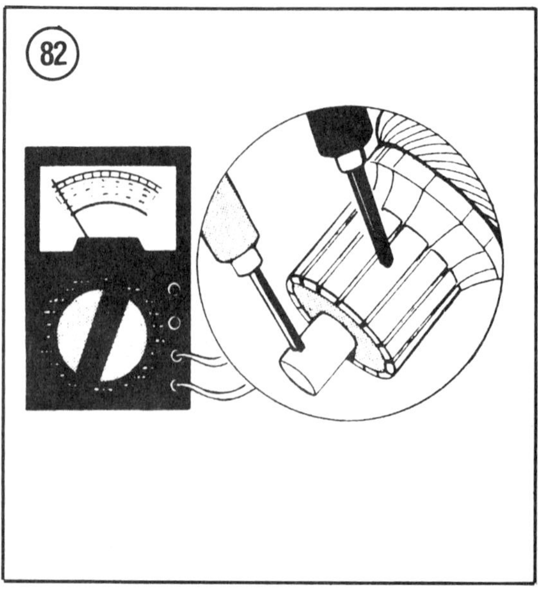

STARTER SOLENOID (1970-1980)

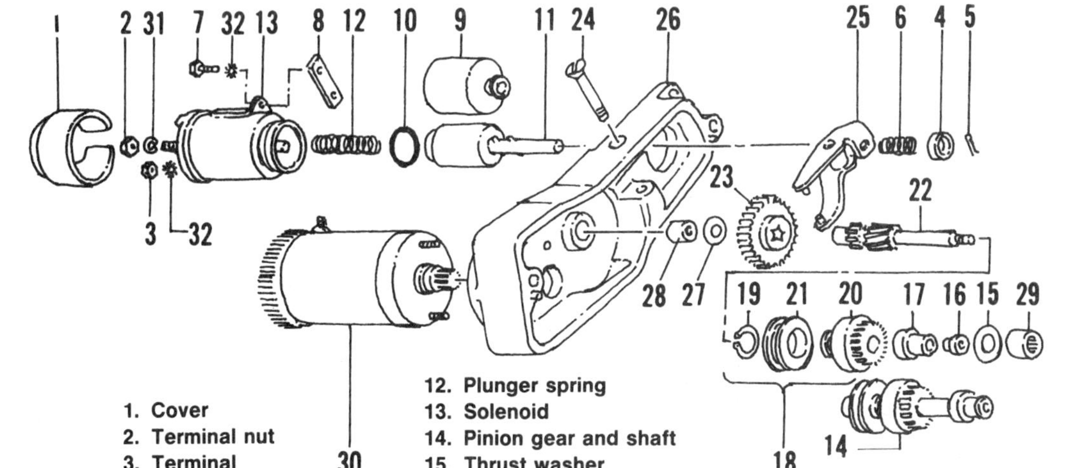

1. Cover
2. Terminal nut
3. Terminal
4. Retainer cap
5. Pin
6. Spring
7. Bolt
8. Spacer bar
9. Boot
10. Gasket
11. Plunger
12. Plunger spring
13. Solenoid
14. Pinion gear and shaft
15. Thrust washer
16. Pinion shaft nut
17. Bearing race
18. Pinion and shifter collar
19. Lock ring
20. Pinion gear
21. Shifter collar
22. Shaft
23. Drive gear
24. Shifter lever screw
25. Shifter lever
26. Starter shaft housing
27. Flat washer
28. Needle bearing
29. Needle bearing
30. Starter
31. Lockwasher
32. Lockwasher

(83)

(84)

STARTER SOLENOID

Removal/Installation (1970-1980)

Refer to **Figure 83** for this procedure.

1. Disconnect the battery negative lead.
2. Remove the solenoid cover.
3. Label and then disconnect the wires from the starter solenoid.
4. Remove the solenoid mounting bolts. Then remove the solenoid, spacer, spring and felt washer.
5. Installation is the reverse of these steps.

Removal/Installation (1981-on)

Refer to **Figure 78** for ths procedure.

1. Remove the starter as described in this chapter.
2. Disconnect the starter-to-solenoid wire (**Figure 84**).
3. Disassemble the starter as described in this chapter.
4. Remove the bolts and separate the solenoid housing from the drive housing.
5. Remove the drive, idler gear and idler gear bearing from the drive housing.
6. Installation is the reverse of these steps.

LIGHTING SYSTEM

Headlight Replacement

Refer to **Figure 85** or **Figure 86** for this procedure.

1. Remove the top plug, if so equipped.
2. Using a socket, loosen the headlight mounting nut located underneath the headlight housing.
3. Tilt the headlight backwards slightly and remove the lower mounting screw.
4. Lift and swing the headlight assembly up and remove the headlight.
5. Disconnect the connector from the headlight prongs.

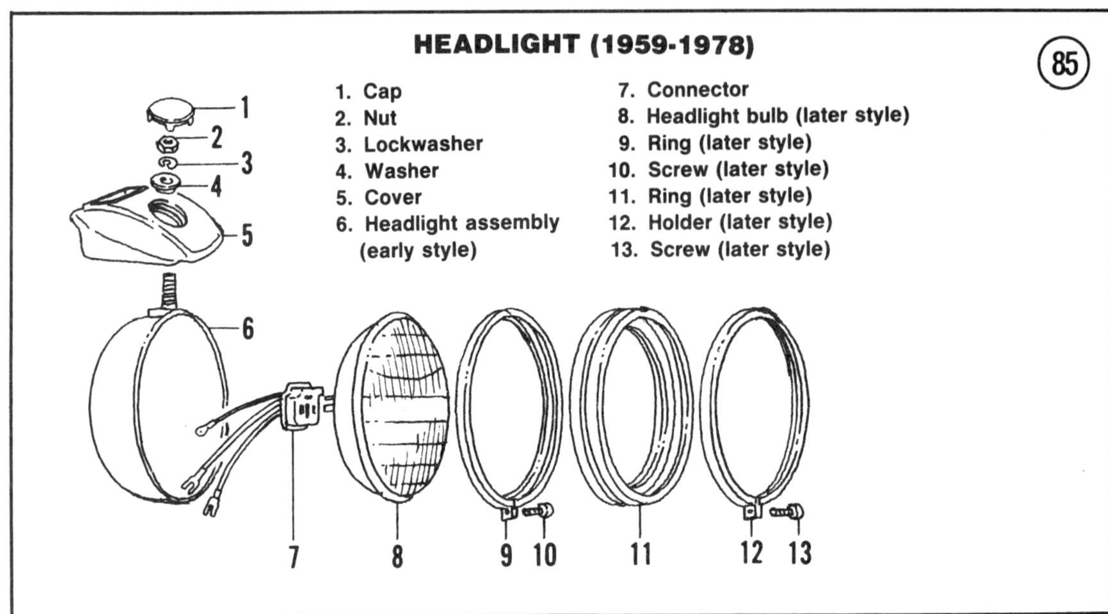

6. Pry the retaining rings away from the headlight and remove the headlight.
7. Install by reversing these removal steps.
8. Adjust the headlight as described in this chapter.

Headlight Adjustment

Adjust the headlight horizontally and vertically according to Department of Motor Vehicles regulations in your area.

1. Draw a horizontal line on a wall the same height as the center of the headlight. Place the motorcycle on a level surface approximately 25 feet from the wall (test pattern). Have a rider sit on the seat and make sure the tires are inflated to the correct pressure when performing this adjustment.
2. Aim the headlight at the wall and turn on the headlight. Switch the headlight to the high beam.
3. The top of the main beam should be even with, but not higher than the horizontal line. If the beam is incorrect, adjust as follows.
4. Loosen the headlight mounting bolts and turn the headlight assembly to adjust the beam to the conditions described in Step 3. In addition, turn the headlight to the left or right as required so that the light beam shines straight ahead.
5. Tighten the headlight mounting bolts.
6. Recheck the adjustment.

Taillight/Brake Light Replacement

1. Remove the rear lens.
2. Push in on the bulb and remove it.
3. Replace the bulb and install the lens.

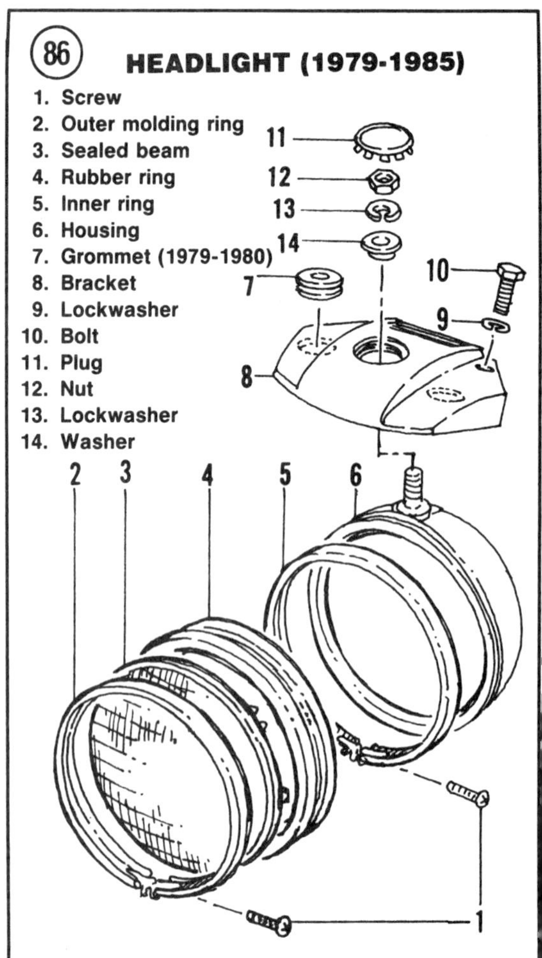

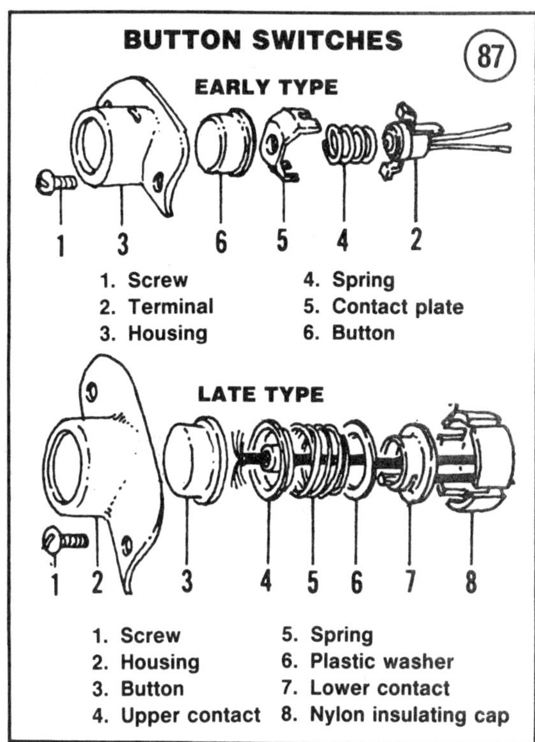

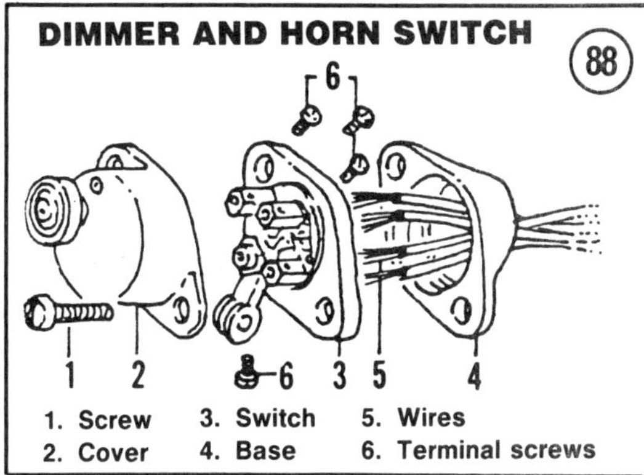

Turn Signal Light Replacement

1. Remove the turn signal lens.
2. Push in on the bulb and remove it.
3. Replace the bulb and install the lens.

SWITCHES

Testing

Switches can be tested for continuity with an ohmmeter (described in Chapter One) at the switch connector plug by operating the switch in each of its operating positions and comparing results with the switch operation. When testing switches, consider the following:

a. First check the main fuse or circuit breaker.
b. Check the battery (if so equipped) as described in Chapter Three and bring the battery to the correct state of charge, if required.
c. When separating 2 connectors, pull on the connector housings and not the wires.
d. After locating a defective circuit, check the connectors to make sure they are clean and properly connected. Check all wires going into a connector housing to make sure each wire is properly positioned and that the wire end is not loose.
e. To properly connect connectors, push them together until they click into place.

Handlebar Switch Replacement (1959-1972)

Refer to **Figure 87** or **Figure 88** for this procedure.

This switch type is used to operate horn, starter and the magneto (on early models). Refer to **Figure 87** or **Figure 88** for this procedure.

7

Early type

1. Remove the switch housing screws and remove the housing.
2. With a screwdriver, carefully remove the switch terminal from the housing.
3. Remove the spring, contact plate and button from the housing.
4. To replace the switch terminal, perform the following:
   a. Cut the terminal wires at the terminal.
   b. Using wire strippers, strip the 2 switch wires as required for resoldering.
   c. Solder the 2 switch wires to the new switch terminal with rosin core solder.
5. Installation is the reverse of these steps.

Late type

1. Remove the switch housing screws and separate the housing.
2. Disassemble the switch in the order shown in **Figure 87** for late switches.
3. To replace the switch wires or contacts, perform the following:
   a. Cut the switch wires at the upper and lower switch contacts.
   b. Remove the wires or contacts as required.
   c. Using wire strippers, strip the 2 switch wires as required for soldering.
   d. Insert the upper switch contact wire through the parts as shown in **Figure 87** for late switches.

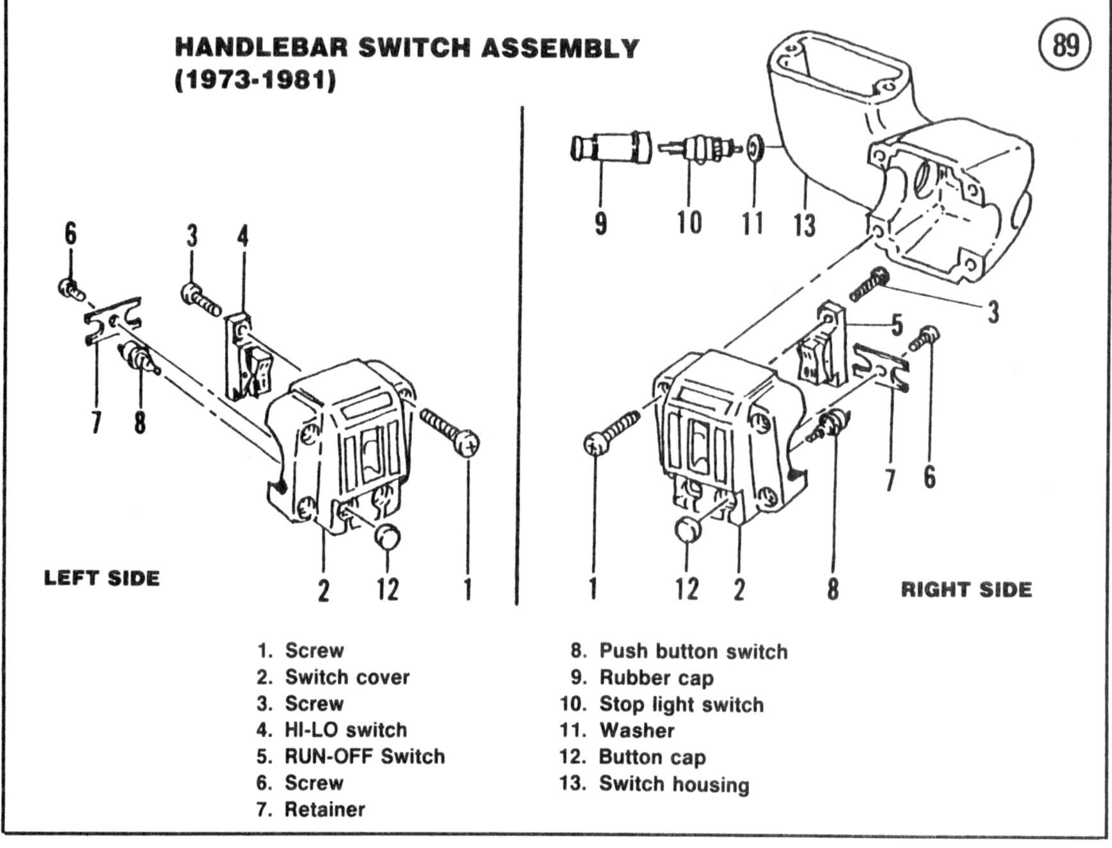

e. Insert the wire through the upper contact. Then fray the end of the wire around the upper end of the contact as shown in **Figure 87**.

f. Solder the wire to the contact with rosin core solder.

g. Insert the lower contact wire up through the nylon insulating cap and next to the lower contact as shown in **Figure 87**.

h. Solder the wire to the lower contact with rosin core solder.

4. Assemble the switch in the order shown in **Figure 87**.

5. Installation is the reverse of these steps.

Handlebar Switch Replacement (1973-On)

The right-hand handlebar switch contains 3 switches: engine start (push button), right turn signal (push button) and RUN-OFF (rocker switch). The left handlebar switch contains 3 switches: horn (push button), left turn signal (push button) and the headlight HI-LO beam (rocker switch). The individual switches (both push and rocker) can be replaced.

Refer to **Figure 89** (1973-1981) or **Figure 90** (1982-on).

1. Remove the screws securing the switch housing to the handlebar. Then carefully separate the switch housing assembly to gain access to the defective switch.

2. Disconnect the switch wire at the electrical connection.

3A. *1972-1981:* Perform the following:

a. To remove a rocker type switch, remove the switch screw and remove the switch.

b. To remove a push button switch, remove the screw and retainer. Then pull the switch out of the housing.

3B. *1982-on:* Replace the defective switch by removing the holding screw. Then pull the switch out of the housing.

4. Installation is the reverse of these steps. Make sure to route the wires to prevent damaging them when tightening the switch housing.

Oil Pressure Switch Removal/Installation

The oil pressure switch is installed in the side of the oil pump. **Figure 91** shows the oil pressure

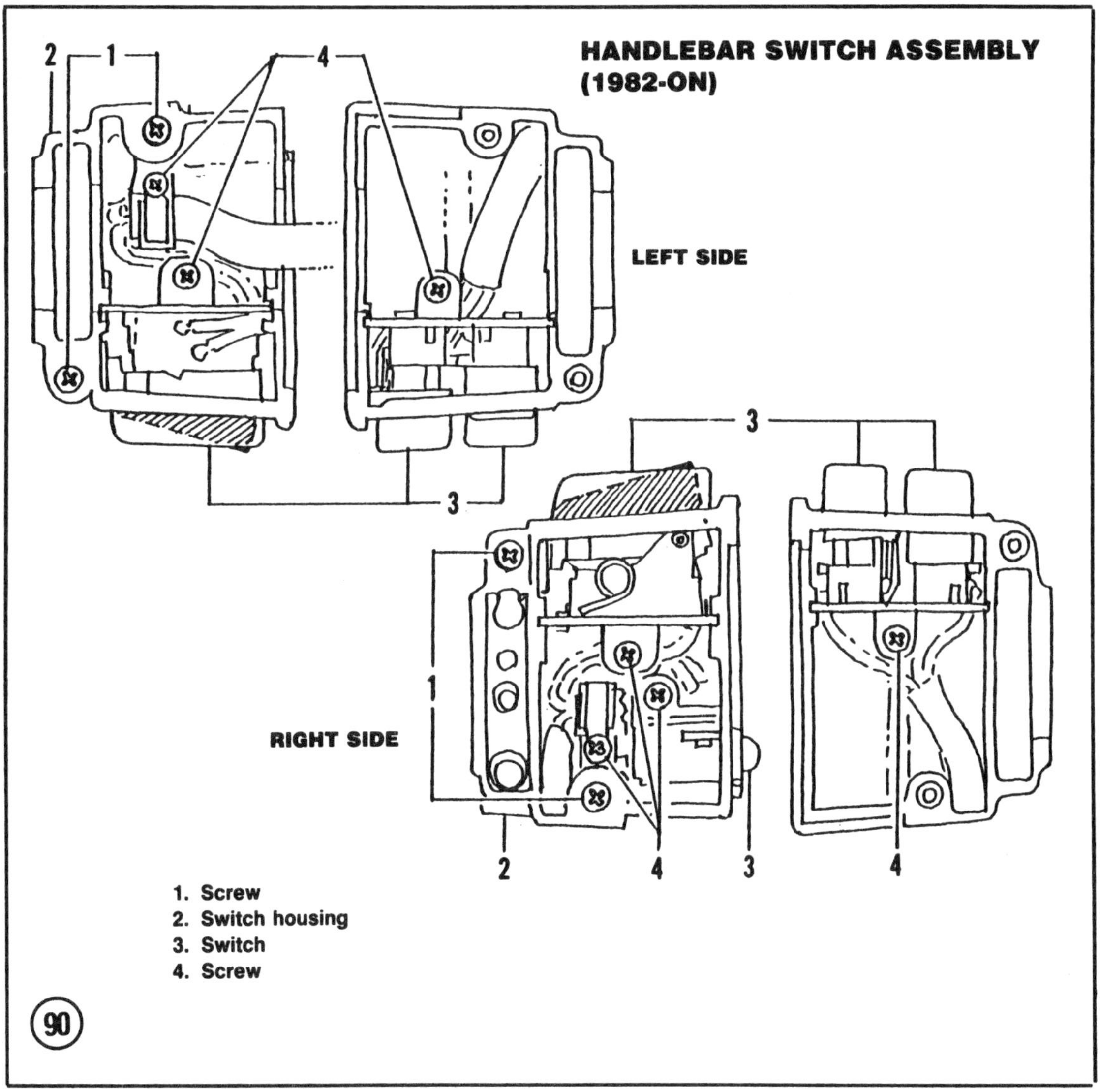

HANDLEBAR SWITCH ASSEMBLY (1982-ON)

LEFT SIDE

RIGHT SIDE

1. Screw
2. Switch housing
3. Switch
4. Screw

(90)

(91)

switch for 1977-1985 models. Switch position for 1976 and earlier models is similar. To remove the oil pressure switch, drain the engine oil as described in Chapter Three. Then disconnect the electrical connector at the switch and remove the switch. Reverse to install.

HORN

The horn is an important safety device and should be kept in working order. If the horn should become damaged, it should be replaced immediately.

Removal/Installation

Refer to **Figure 92** (1959-1964) or **Figure 93** (1965-on).

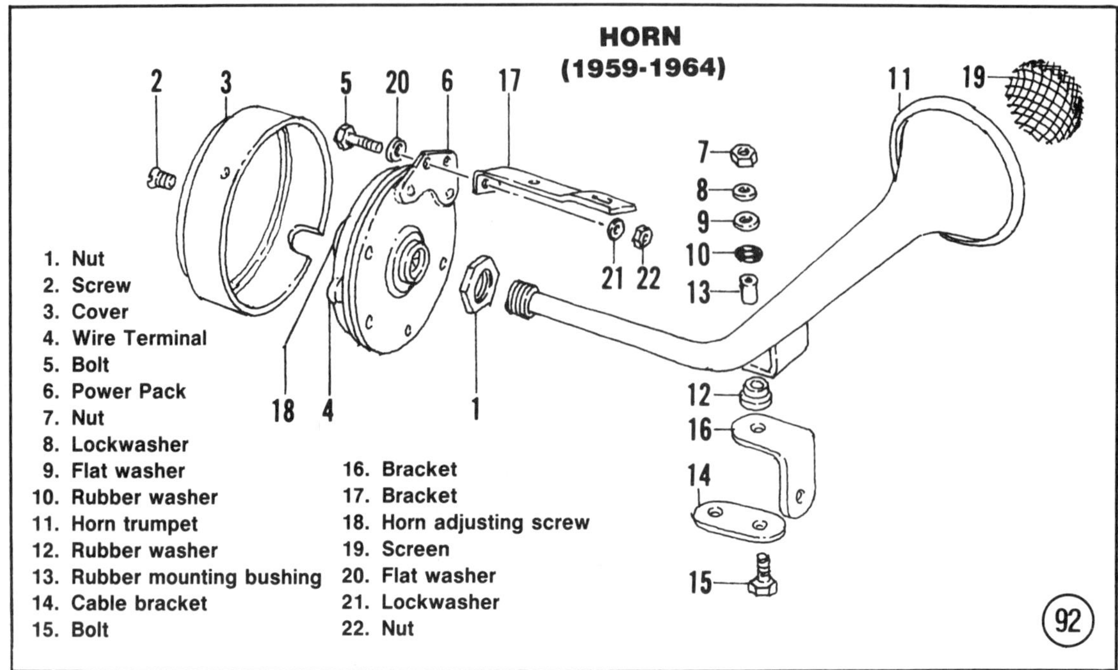

1. Remove all components as necessary to gain access to the horn.
2. Disconnect the horn electrical connector.
3. Remove the horn mounting attachments and remove the horn.
4. Installation is the reverse of these steps.
5. On 1959-1964 models, make sure the horn trumpet does not contact any part of the engine.

Adjustment (1959-1964)

Refer to **Figure 92** for this procedure.

1. If the horn fails to blow properly, check for broken or frayed horn wires. Also check the battery as described in Chapter Three. If these are okay, perform the following.
2. Check the horn power pack and trumpet for misalignment that could cause the power pack diaphragm to compress or squeeze. Correct misalignment by loosening the power pack and trumpet mounting brackets and realigning the units. If the units are still misaligned, check the mounting brackets for bending or damage.
3. Perform the following if the horn was previously diassembled:
   a. Remove the horn as described in this chapter.
   b. Loosen the horn trumpet nut. Then unscrew the horn power pack, counting the number of turns required to remove it. If the power pack is tightened by more than 2-2 1/2 turns, the trumpet stem may obstruct the power pack diaphragm.
   c. Reinstall the power pack by screwing it on the trumphet stem. Do not tighten the power pack by more than 2 turns.
   d. Tighten the horn trumpet nut to lock the power pack.
   e. Reinstall the horn as described in this chapter.
4. If the horn will still not operate correctly, adjust it as follows.
5. Remove the horn cover.
6. Loosen the core screw locknut.
7. With a screwdriver turn the slotted center core screw 1/2 turn counterclockwise.
8. While depressing the horn button, turn the tone adjusting screw (Phillips head) until the horn begins to blow.
9. Turn the slotted center core screw clockwise until the horn rattles. Then turn the screw counterclockwise 1/4 turn.
10. Hold the slotted center core screw in position with a screwdriver and tighten the core screw locknut with a wrench.

Adjustment (1965-On)

The horn on these models cannot be disassembled. If the horn is damaged, it must be replaced. Refer to **Figure 93** for this procedure.

1. If the horn fails to blow properly, check for broken or frayed horn wires. If these are okay perform the following.

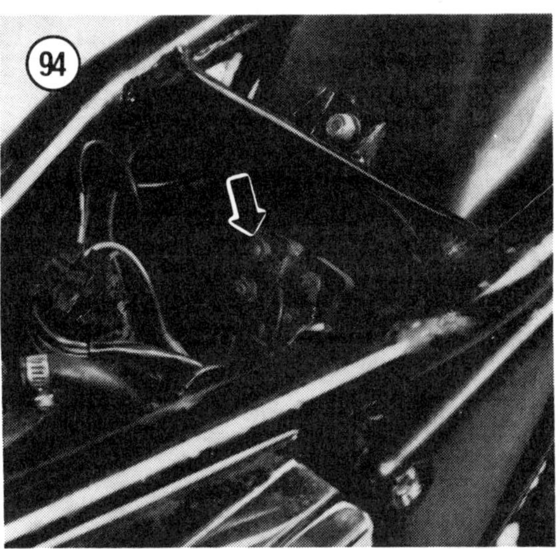

2. While pushing the horn button, turn the contact point adjustment screw clockwise until the horn clicks one time. The adjustment screw is located in the back of the horn.
3. Then turn the adjustment screw counterclockwise while pushing the horn button until the best horn tone is obtained.
4. If the horn fails to operate after performing Steps 1-3, replace the horn.

FUSES AND CIRCUIT BREAKERS

Each model uses either fuses or circuit breakers to protect the electrical circuits. Refer to the wiring diagram for your model at the back of the book for the type of protection used.

Whenever a failure occurs in any part of the electrical system, check the fuse box to see if a fuse has blown. On models equipped with circuit breakers (**Figure 94**), each circuit breaker is self-resetting and will automatically return power to the circuit when the electrical fault is found and corrected.

CAUTION
If the electrical fault on circuit breaker-equipped models is not found and corrected, the breakers will cycle on and off continiously. This will cause the motorcycle to run erratically and eventually the battery will lose its charge.

If a fuse has blown, it will be evident by blackening of the fuse or by a break in the metal link in the fuse.

Usually the trouble can be traced to a short circuit in the wiring connected to the blown fuse or circuit breaker. This may be caused by worn-through insulation or by a wire which has worked loose and shorted to ground. Occasionally, the electrical overload which causes the fuse to blow may occur in a switch or motor. By following the wiring diagrams at the end of the book, the circuits protected by each fuse can be determined.

A blown fuse or tripped circuit breaker should be treated as more than a minor annoyance; it should serve also as a warning that something is wrong in the electrical system. Before replacing a fuse, determine what caused it to blow and then correct the trouble.

WARNING
Never replace a fuse with one of a higher amperage than that of the one originally used. Never use metal foil or other metallic material to bridge fuse terminals. Failure to follow these basic rules could result in heat or fire damage to major parts or loss of the entire vehicle.

Replace a defective fuse by pulling it out of its holder and snapping a new one in place. To replace a circuit breaker (**Figure 94**), disconnect the wires and remove it. Reverse to install.

Table 1 ELECTRICAL SPECIFICATIONS

Ignition coil resistance	
1959-1969	
Primary	5 ohms
Secondary	
6-volt	11,000 ohms
12-volt	18,000 ohms
1970-1979	
Primary	4.7-5.7 ohms
Secondary	16,000-20,000 ohms
1980-on	
Primary	3.3-3.7 ohms
Secondary	16,500-19,500 ohms
Starter brush length (minimum)	
1967-1978	
Prestolite	1/4 in.
Hitachi	7/16 in.
1979-1980	1/4 in.
1981-1985	0.354 in.
Generator brush length (minimum)	1/2 in.

Table 2 VOLTAGE REGULATOR RANGE

Delco-Remy part No.	Voltage regulator setting
1118 388	7.5
11119 187C	7.2-7.5
11119 187D	7.2-7.5
1118 307	7.0 [1]
1118794	7.0 [2]
1118794	7.4 [1]
1118 995	7.0-7.3
1118 989	6.5-6.8

1. Models 125-165 generators.
2. Model 52K generator.
3. Models 58 and 61 generators.

Table 3 CURRENT REGULATOR SPECIFICATIONS

Delco-Remy part No.	Current regulator setting
118 388	18 amperes
1119 187C	13.5-16.5 amperes
1119 187D	13.5-16.5 amperes
1119 614	9.0-11.0 amperes

Table 4 IGNITION TIMING (1980 AND LATER MODELS)

Ignition timing	(Degrees BTDC)
1980-1982	
Start	8
Fast idle	20
2,000 rpm and up	40
1983-on	
Start	10
Fast idle	40
1,800-2,800 rpm and up	55

CHAPTER EIGHT

FRONT SUSPENSION AND STEERING

This chapter discusses service operations on suspension components, steering, wheels and related items. Specifications (**Table 1**) and tightening torques (**Table 2** and **Table 3**) are found at the end of the chapter.

FRONT WHEEL

Removal/Installation

1959-1972

Refer to **Figure 1** for this procedure.

1. Support the bike so that the front wheel clears the ground.
2. Remove the brake clevis pin (5, **Figure 1**) at the brake lever.
3. Remove the front axle nut (2) and lockwasher.
4. Remove the brake shoe anchor, centering bolt (7) and washer.
5. Loosen the front axle pinch bolt (1).
6. Push the axle out with a drift or screwdriver and remove it from the left-hand side.
7. Remove the front wheel and brake assembly.
8. Remove the brake assembly from the wheel.
9. When servicing the wheel assembly, install the washer and nut on the axle to prevent their loss.
10. Inspect the front wheel assembly as described in this chapter.
11. Installation is the reverse of these steps, noting the following:
    a. Inject one ounce of wheel bearing grease into the front hub.

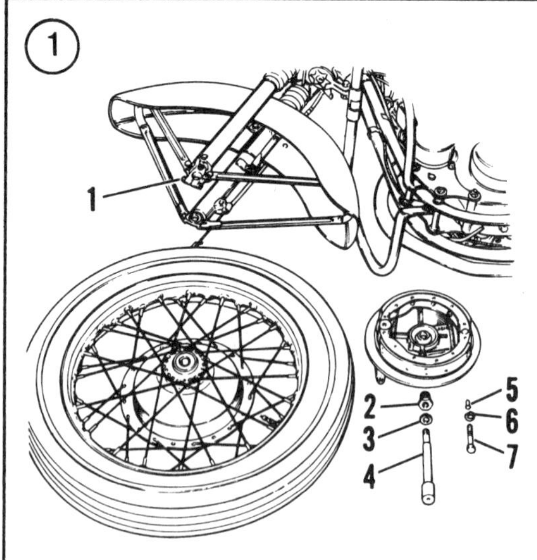

FRONT WHEEL (1959-1972)

1. Front axle pinch bolt
2. Axle nut
3. Axle nut lockwasher
4. Axle
5. Brake clevis pin
6. Lockwasher
7. Brake anchor and centering bolt

2

FRONT WHEEL MOUNTING (1973-1985 TYPICAL)

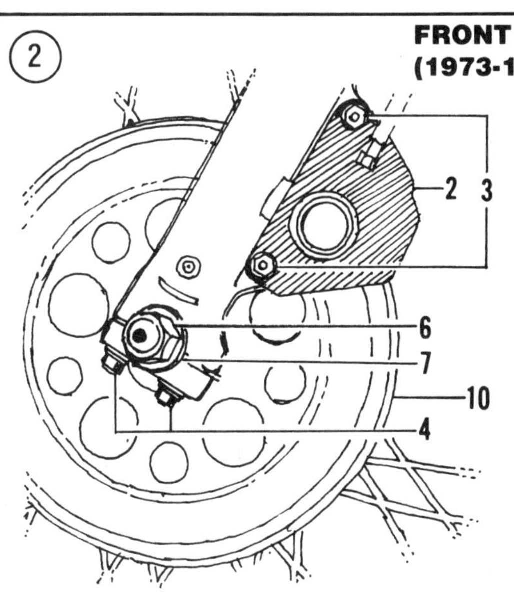

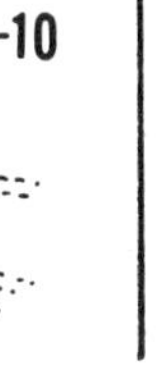

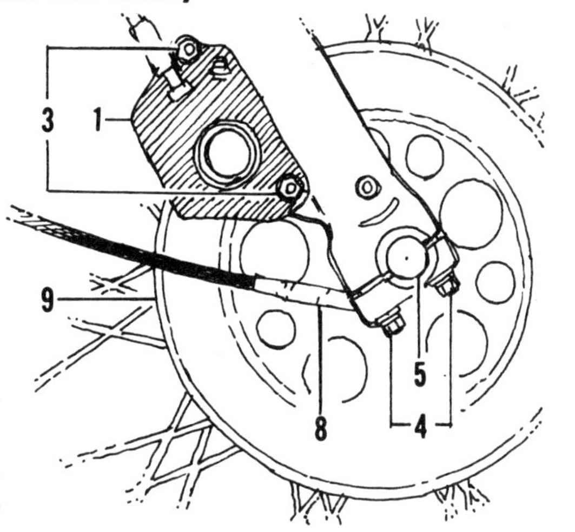

1. Caliper (right-hand side)
2. Caliper (left-hand side)
3. Caliper mounting bolts
4. Nuts
5. Axle
6. Axle nuts
7. Lockwasher and flat washer
8. Speedometer cable
9. Brake disc
10. Brake disc

3

4

b. Tighten the axle nut to specifications in **Table 2.**

c. Adjust the front brake as described in Chapter Three.

1973-on

Refer to **Figure 2** (typical) for this procedure.

1. Suppport the bike so that the front wheel clears the ground.
2. Remove the axle nut (A, **Figure 3**) and lockwasher.
3. Loosen the fork slider cap nuts (B, **Figure 3**) from both sides.
4. Disconnect the speedometer cable (**Figure 4**) at the front wheel.
5. On 1974-on models, remove the brake caliper(s) as described in Chapter Ten.
6. Push the axle out with a punch or drift and remove it from the right-hand side.
7. Pull the wheel forward to disengage the brake disc from the caliper. Then turn the caliper outward to provide clearance for the wheel and remove it.
8. *1979-1985:* Remove the axle spacer from the left-hand side.
9. Remove the speedometer drive from the seal.

CAUTION
Do not set the wheel down on the disc surface, as it may be scratched or warped. Either lean the wheel against a wall or place it on a couple of wood blocks.

NOTE
Insert a piece of wood in the caliper place of the disc. That way, if the brake lever is inadvertently squeezed, the piston will not be forced out of the cylinder. If this does happen, the caliper might have to be disassembled to reseat the piston and the system will have to be bled. By using the wood, bleeding the brake is not necessary after installing the wheel.

10. When servicing the wheel assembly, install the speedometer drive gear, washer and nut on the axle to prevent their loss.
11. Inspect the front wheel assembly as described in this chapter.
12A. *1973-1978:* Installation is the reverse of these steps, noting the following:
   a. Align the notches in the gear case with the speedometer drive dogs.
   b. On 1973 models, *carefully* insert the disc between the pads when installing the wheel.
   c. Tighten the axle nut to specifications in **Table 2**.
   d. Tighten the slider cap nuts to specifications in **Table 2**.
   e. On 1974-1978 models, install the brake caliper as described in Chapter Ten.
12B. *1979-1985:* Installation is the reverse of these steps, noting the following:
   a. Align the notches in the gear case with the speedometer drive dogs.
   b. Tighten the slider cap nut on the axle nut side to 11 ft.-lb. Tighten the axle nut to 50 ft.-lb., then tighten the other slider cap nut to 11 ft.-lb. Make sure gap between the slider cap and fork slider is equal on both sides.
   c. Reinstall the front brake caliper(s) as described in Chapter Ten.

Inspection (All Models)

1. Remove any corrosion on the front axle with a piece of fine emery cloth.
2. Visually check the rims for cracks, fractures, dents or bends. On spoked wheels, the rims can be replaced by a Harley-Davidson dealer if damaged. On cast wheels, the wheel must be replaced if damaged.
3. Measure the axial and radial runout of the wheel with a dial indicator as shown in **Figure 5**. The maximum allowable axial and radial runout is listed in **Table 1**. If the runout exceeds this dimension, check the wheel bearings. Some of this condition can be corrected on spoke wheels as described in this chapter. If the wheel bearings are in good condition on cast wheels and no other cause can be found, the wheel will have to be replaced as it cannot be serviced.

WARNING
Do not try to repair damaged cast wheels as this will result in an unsafe riding condition.

FRONT HUB

Bearing Replacement Service Notes

To remove a ball bearing, insert a soft aluminum or brass drift into the hub. Push the spacer to one side and place the drift on the inner race of the spacer flange. Tap the spacer flange and bearing out of the hub with a hammer working around the perimeter of the spacer flange.

To install a ball bearing, drive it squarely into the hub. Use a socket (**Figure 6**) that matches the

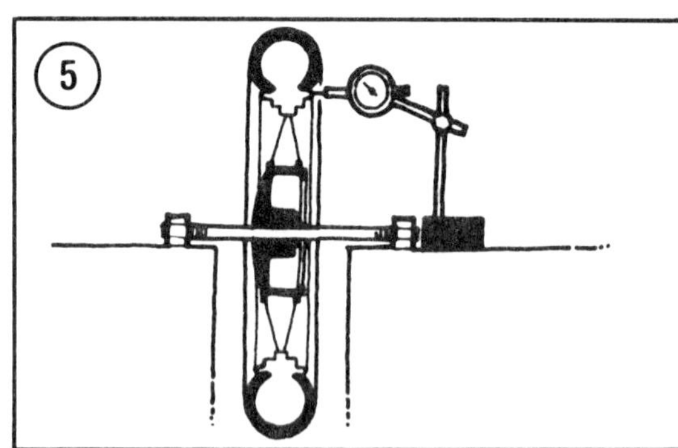

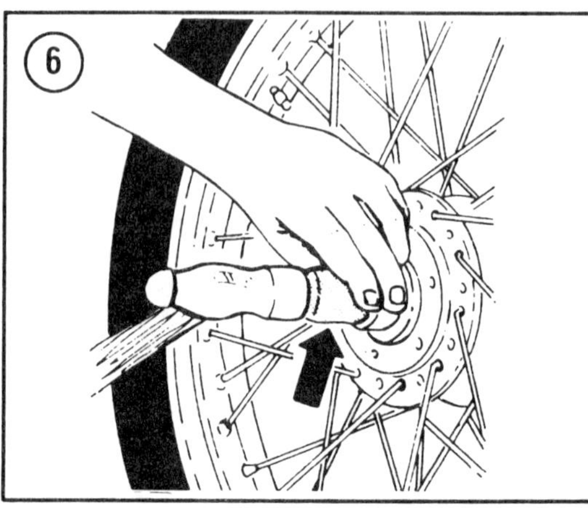

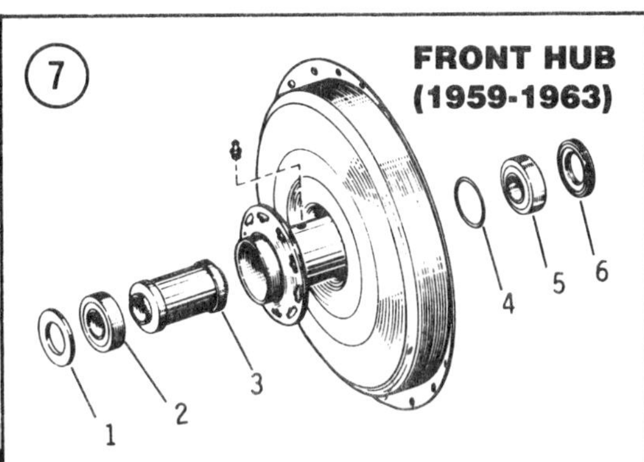

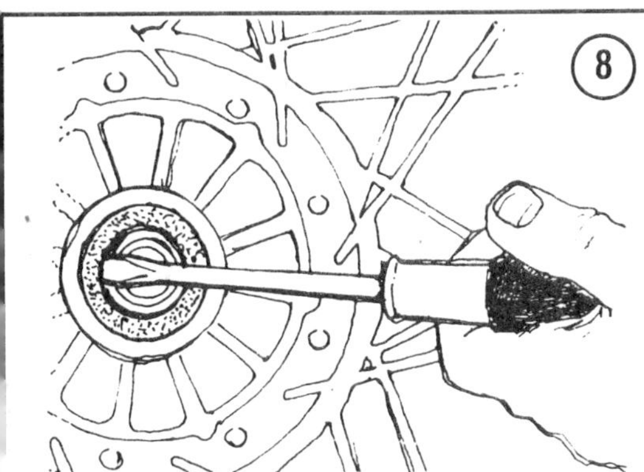

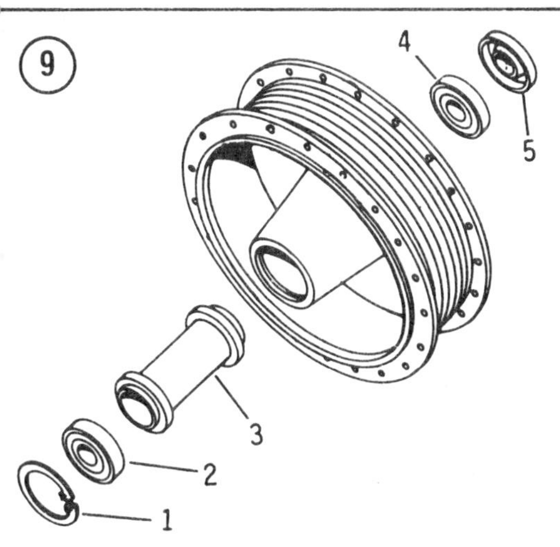

FRONT HUB (1964-1972)

1. Snap ring
2. Ball bearing
3. Bearing spacer
4. Ball bearing
5. Grease seal

outer bearing race diameter. Do not tap on the inner race or the bearing will be damaged. Be sure to tap the bearing until it is seated completely.

Disassembly/Reassembly

1959-1963

Refer to **Figure** 7 for this procedure.

1. Remove the front wheel as described in this chapter.
2. Remove the right-hand bearing locknut (6, **Figure** 7) by turning it out of the hub.

NOTE
The bearing locknut is staked in position. During its removal, the stake is broken.

3. Remove the left-hand grease seal (1) by prying it out of the hub. See **Figure 8**.
4. Drive the right-hand bearing (5) out of the hub.
5. Remove the bearing washer (4) and center spacer (3).
6. Drive the left-hand bearing (2) out of the hub.
7. Inspect the bearings and hub as described in this chapter.
8. Install the bearing washer (4) in the hub. Then install the right-hand bearing (5).
9. Install the right-hand bearing locknut (6). Stake the locknut in 2 places.
10. Install the center spacer (3).
11. Install the left-hand bearing (2) so that it seats against the center spacer (3).
12. Install the oil seal (1) by tapping it into position with a suitable size socket placed on the outside of the seal.

1964-1972

Refer to **Figure 9** for this procedure.

1. Remove the front wheel as described in this chapter.
2. Remove the right-hand bearing snap ring (1, **Figure 9**).
3. Remove the left-hand grease seal (5). See **Figure 8**.
4. Placing a drift on the left-hand bearing outer face (4), drive the bearing into the hub until it seats. This procedure moves the opposite bearing far enough outward so that the bearing spacer (3) can be moved from the bearing.
5. Using a long drift, drive out the right-hand bearing (2).
6. Drive out the left-hand bearing (4) using a suitable size socket on the outer bearing race.
7. Inspect the bearings and hub as described in this chapter.

8

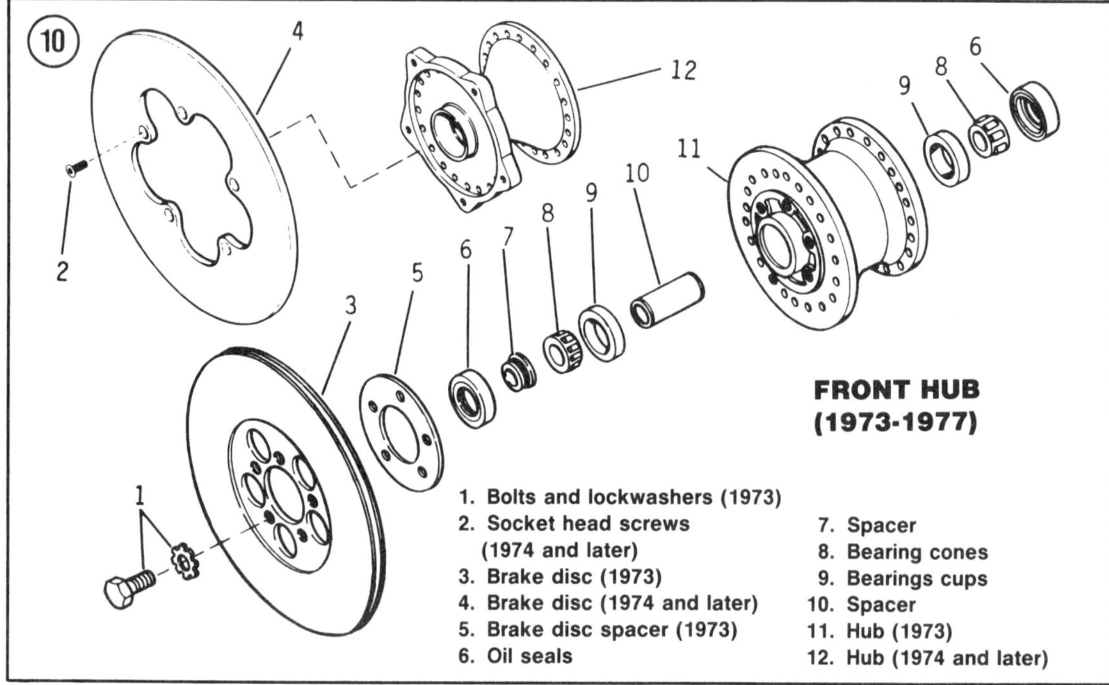

FRONT HUB (1973-1977)

1. Bolts and lockwashers (1973)
2. Socket head screws (1974 and later)
3. Brake disc (1973)
4. Brake disc (1974 and later)
5. Brake disc spacer (1973)
6. Oil seals
7. Spacer
8. Bearing cones
9. Bearings cups
10. Spacer
11. Hub (1973)
12. Hub (1974 and later)

8. Drive the right-hand bearing (2) into the hub until it seats against the shoulder. Note that the sealed side of the bearing faces outward.
9. Install the snap ring (1). Note that the flat side of the snap ring must be installed toward the bearing.
10. Install the center bearing spacer (3).
11. Drive the left-hand bearing (4) in until it seats.
12. Install the oil seal (5) by tapping it into position with a suitable size socket placed on the outside of the seal.

1973-1977

NOTE
The bearing cones and cups on these models are matched pairs. Label all parts so that they may be returned to their original positions.

Refer to **Figure 10** for this procedure.
1. Remove the front wheel as described in this chapter.
2. Remove both oil seals (**Figure 8**).
3. Remove the spacer (7, **Figure 10**) and both bearing cones (8).
4. Using a suitable puller, remove both bearing cups (9).
5. Remove the center spacer (10).
6. Inspect all parts as described in this chapter.
7. Installation is the reverse of these steps, noting the following:
   a. Pack the bearing cones with grease before installation.
   b. Tap the oil seals in until they are flush with the hub.
   c. If the brake disc was removed, refer to Chapter Ten for correct procedures and tightening torques.
   d. After the wheel is installed, the bearing end play should be 0.0025-0.015 in. Longer or shorter spacers (10, **Figure 10**) are available to establish correct end play.

1978-1985

Refer to the following illustration for your model when performing this procedure.
a. **Figure 11** (1978-1983 laced wheels).
b. **Figure 12** (1978-1983 cast wheel).
c. **Figure 13** (1984-1985 cast wheel).

NOTE
The bearing cones and cups on these models are matched pairs. Label all parts so that they may be returned to their original positions.

1. Remove the front wheel as described in this chapter.
2. Remove both oil seals.
3. Remove the left-hand spacer on 1978-1983 models.

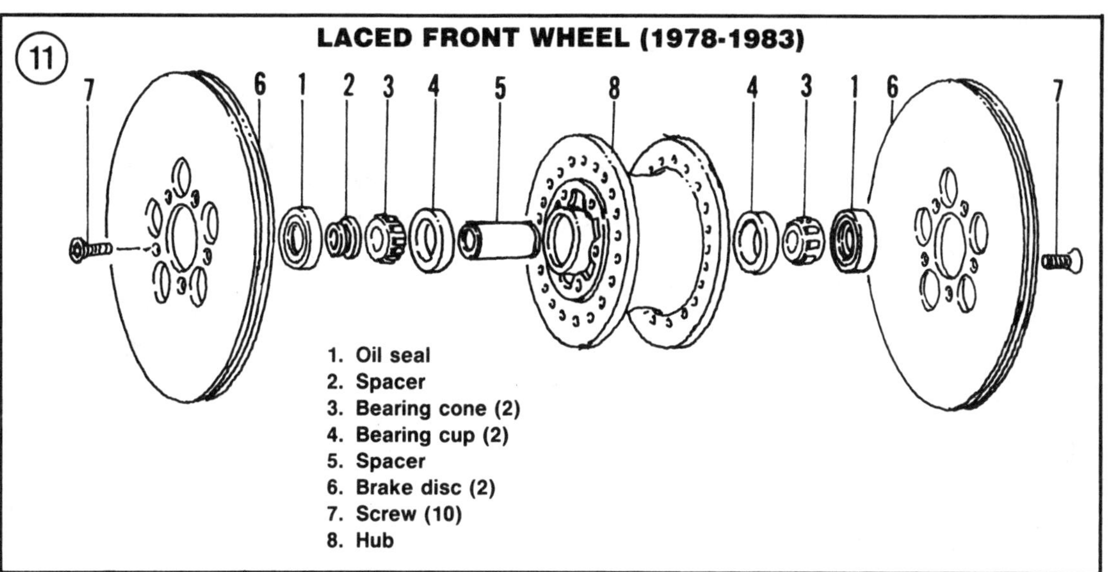
11
LACED FRONT WHEEL (1978-1983)
7
6
1
2
3
4
5
8
4
3
1
6
7
1. Oil seal
2. Spacer
3. Bearing cone (2)
4. Bearing cup (2)
5. Spacer
6. Brake disc (2)
7. Screw (10)
8. Hub

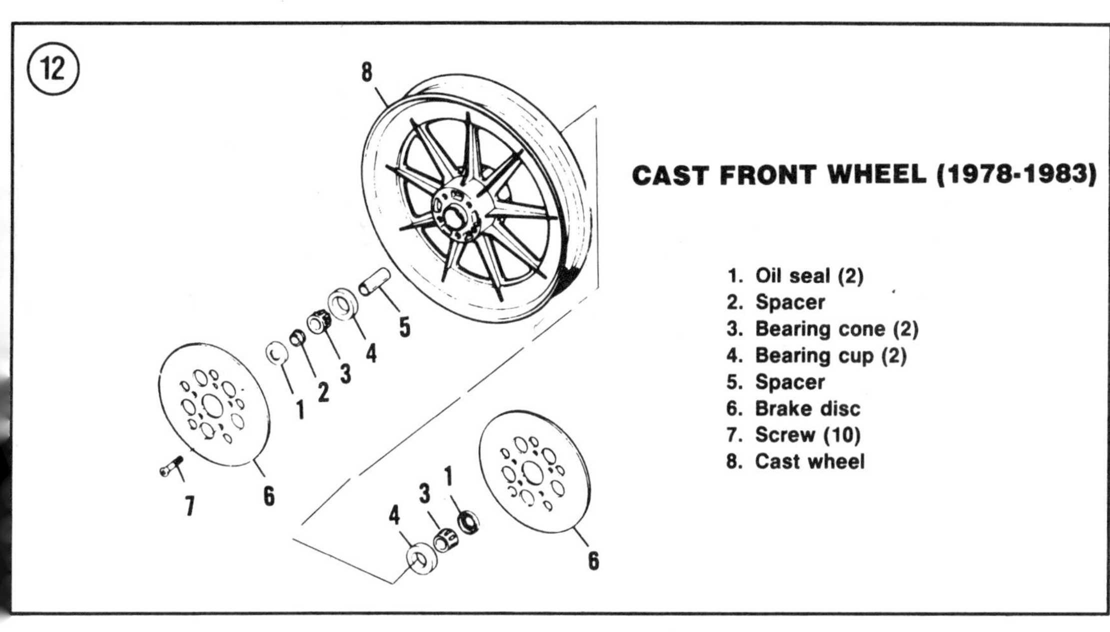
12
CAST FRONT WHEEL (1978-1983)
8
5
4
3
2
1
7
6
4
3
1
6
1. Oil seal (2)
2. Spacer
3. Bearing cone (2)
4. Bearing cup (2)
5. Spacer
6. Brake disc
7. Screw (10)
8. Cast wheel

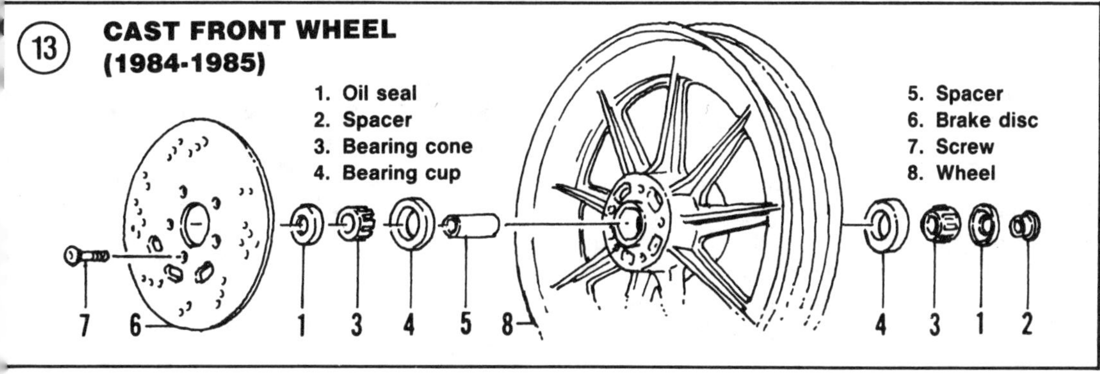
13
CAST FRONT WHEEL
(1984-1985)
1. Oil seal
2. Spacer
3. Bearing cone
4. Bearing cup
5. Spacer
6. Brake disc
7. Screw
8. Wheel
7
6
1
3
4
5
8
4
3
1
2

4. Remove both bearing cones.
5. Using a suitable puller, remove both bearing cups.
6. Remove the center spacer.
7. Inspect all parts as described in this chapter.
8. Installation is the reverse of these steps, noting the following:
   a. Pack the bearing cones with grease before installation.
   b. Tap the oil seals in until they are flush with the hub.
   c. If the brake disc was removed, refer to Chapter Ten for correct procedures and tightening torques.

Inspection

1. Do not clean sealed bearings. If non-sealed bearings are installed, throughly clean them in solvent and dry with compressed air. Do *not* spin bearings with an air hose while drying.
2. Clean the inside and outside of the hub with solvent. Dry with compressed air.

NOTE
Step 3 describes inspection of ball bearings; roller bearings are inspected in Step 4.

3. Turn each bearing by hand (**Figure 14**). Make sure bearings turn smoothly. On non-sealed bearings, check the balls for evidence of wear, pitting or excessive heat (bluish tint). Replace bearings if necessary; always replace as a complete set. When replacing the bearings, be sure to take your old bearings along to ensure a perfect matchup.

NOTE
Fully sealed bearings are available from many good bearing specialty shops. Fully sealed bearings provide better protection from dirt and moisture that may get into the hub.

4. Check the roller bearing cones and cups for wear, pitting or excessive heat (bluish tint). Replace the bearing cones and cups as a complete set.
5. Pack non-sealed bearings thoroughly with wheel bearing grease.
6. Check the axle for wear and straightness.
7. Check the brake hub on 1959-1972 models for any scoring or damage. If damage is apparent, refer to Chapter Ten for further inspection and service.
8. If the hub on spoke wheels is damaged, the hub can be replaced by removing the spokes and having a dealer assemble a new hub. If the hub on cast wheels is damaged, the wheel assembly must be replaced; it cannot be repaired.

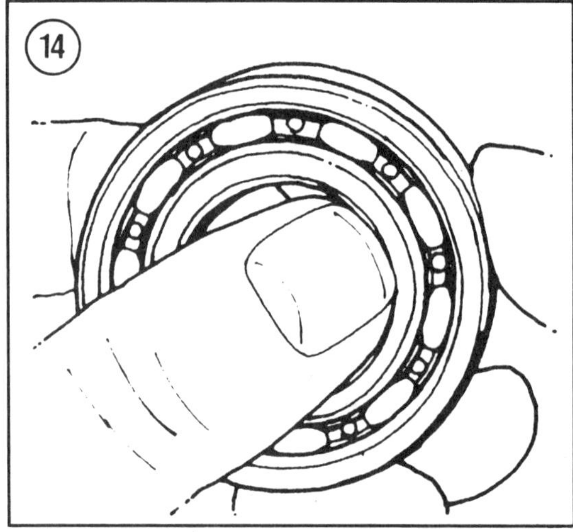

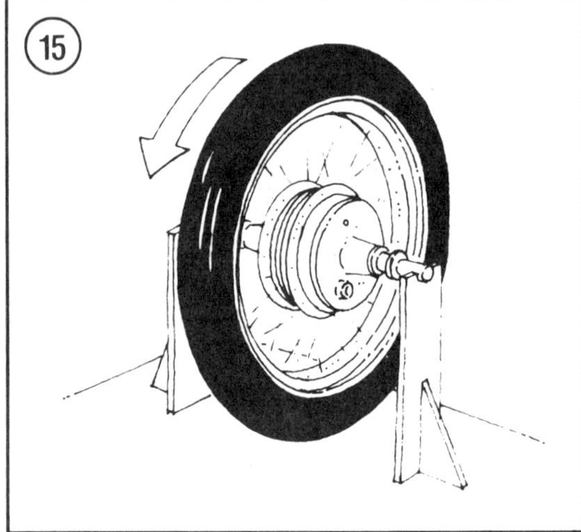

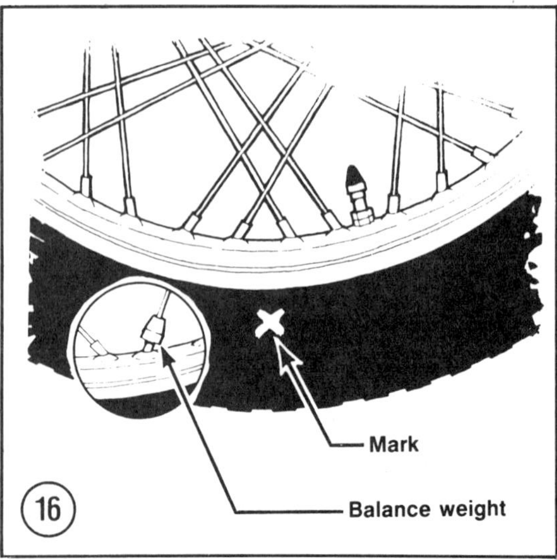

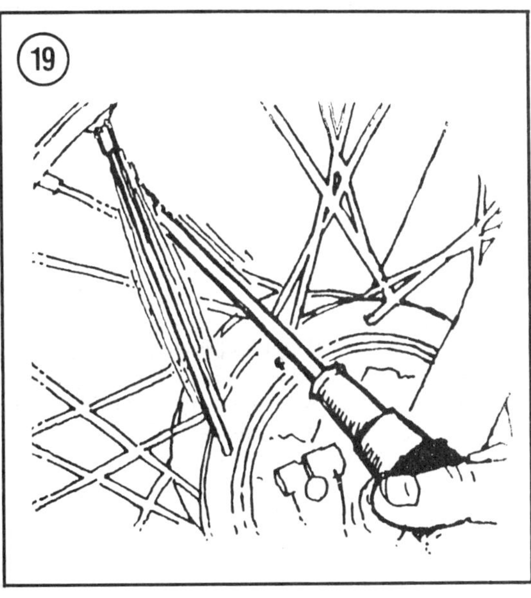

WHEEL BALANCE

An unbalanced wheel results in unsafe riding conditions. Depending on the degree of unbalance and the speed of the bike, the rider may experience anything from a mild vibration to a violent shimmy and loss of control.

NOTE

Be sure to balance the wheel with the brake disc(s) attached as they also affect the balance.

Before attempting to balance the wheels, check to be sure that the wheel bearings are in good condition and properly lubricated. The wheel must rotate freely.

1. Remove the wheel to be balanced.
2. Mount the wheel on a fixture such as the one in **Figure 15** so it can rotate freely.
3. Give the wheel a spin and let it coast to a stop. Mark the tire at the lowest point.
4. Spin the wheel several more times. If the wheel keeps coming to rest at the same point, it is out of balance.
5. Tape a test weight to the upper (or light) side of the wheel (**Figure 16**).
6. Experiment with different weights until the wheel, when spun, comes to rest at a different position each time.
7. Remove the test weight and install the correct size weight.

NOTE

*On spoked wheels, weights are attached to the spokes (**Figure 17**). On cast wheels, weights are attached to the rim (**Figure 18**).*

Spoke Inspection and Replacement

Spokes loosen with use and should be checked periodically. The "tuning fork" method for checking spoke tightness is simple and works well. Tap the center of each spoke with a spoke wrench or the shank of a screwdriver (**Figure 19**) and listen for a tone. A tightened spoke will emit a clear, ringing tone and a loose spoke will sound flat or dull. All the spokes in a correctly tightened wheel will emit tones of similar pitch but not necessarily the same precise tone. The tension of the spokes does not determine wheel balance.

Bent, stripped or broken spokes should be replaced, as soon as they are detected, as they can destroy an expensive hub.

NOTE

If you are riding and one or more spokes should break, tie the broken spoke(s) to an attached spoke with wire

8

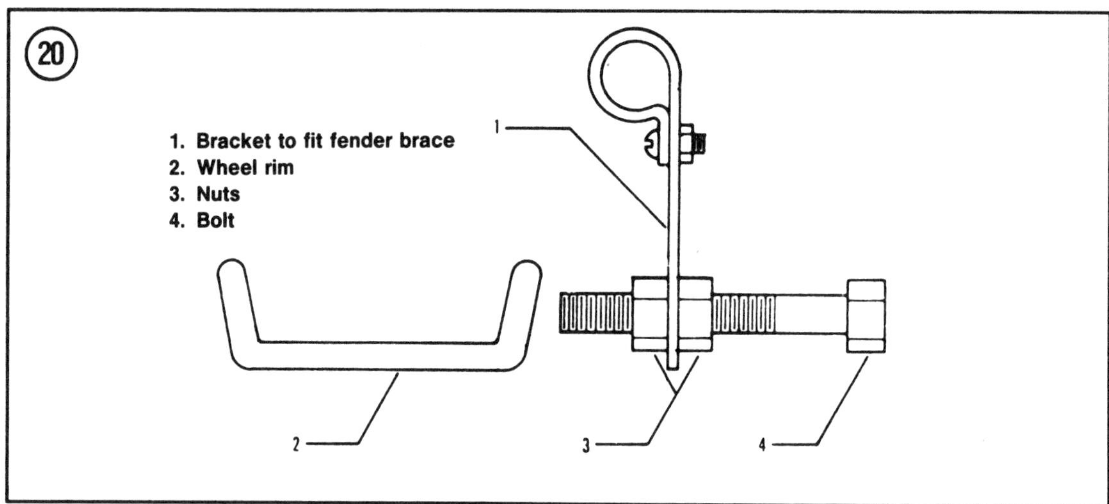

or string until you can ride back home and replace it. This will prevent the spoke from dangling and eventually damaging the fork tubes or the rear sprocket and drive chain.

Unscrew the nipple from the spoke and depress the nipple into the rim far enough to free the end of the spoke; take care not to push the nipple all the way in. Remove the damaged spoke from the hub and use it to match a new spoke of identical length. If necessary, trim the new spoke to match the original and dress the end of the thread with a thread die. Install the new spoke in the hub and screw on the nipple; tighten it until the spoke's tone is similar to the tone of the other spokes in the wheel. Periodically check the new spoke; it will stretch and must be retightened several times before it takes a final set.

Spoke Adjustment

If all spokes appear loose, tighten all on one side of the hub, then tighten all on the other side. One-half to one turn should be sufficient; do not overtighten.

After tightening the spokes, check rim runout to be sure you haven't pulled the rim out of shape.

One way to check rim runout is to mount a dial indicator on the front fork or swing arm, so that it bears against the rim.

If you don't have a dial indicator, improvise one as shown in **Figure 20**. Adjust the position of the bolt until it just clears the rim. Rotate the rim and note whether the clearance increases or decreases. Mark the tire with chalk or light crayon at areas that produce significantly large or small clearances. Clearance must not change by more than 0.08 in.

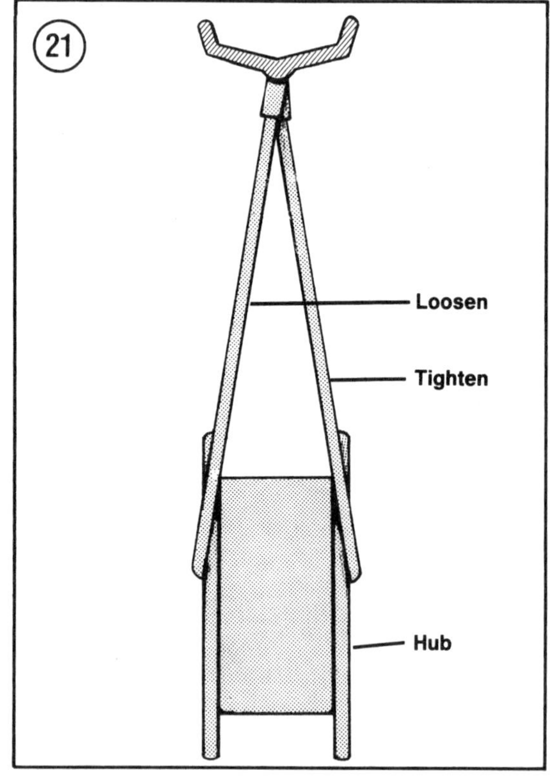

To pull the rim out, tighten spokes which terminate on the same side of the hub and loosen spokes which terminate on the opposite side of the hub (**Figure 21**). In most cases, only a slight amount of adjustment is necessary to true a rim. After adjustment, rotate the rim and make sure another area has not been pulled out of true. Continue adjustment and checking until runout is less than 0.08 in.

Rim Replacement

If the rim should become bent or damaged, it should be replaced. A bent or dented wheel is very dangerous to the handling of the bike.

If the spokes are not bent or damaged, they may be reused. This procedure describes how to replace the rim without removing the spokes.

1. Remove the tire as described in this chapter.
2. Securely fasten the spokes together with wire, string or tape at each point where they cross.
3. Place the replacement rim on top of the old rim and align the nipple holes of both rims. This is to make sure the replacement rim is the correct one. When the rims are aligned correctly, mark one spoke and its corresponding nipple hole on the new rim.
4. Remove the nipples from the spokes using a spoke wrench. If they are coated with dirt or rust, clean them in solvent and allow to dry. Then check the nipples for signs of cracking or other damage. Spoke nipples in this condition can strip when the wheel is later trued. Replace all nipples as necessary.
5. Lift the hub and spokes out of the old rim, making sure not to knock the spokes out of alignment.
6. Position the hub and spokes into the new rim, making sure to align the marks made in Step 3. Then insert the spokes into the rim until they are all in place.
7. Place a drop of oil onto the threaded end of each spoke and install the nipples. Thread the nipples halfway onto the spokes and stop before they make contact with the rim.
8. Lift the wheel and stand it up on the workbench. Check the hub to make sure it is centered in the rim. If not, reposition it by hand.
9. With the hub centered in the rim, thread the nipples until they just seat against the rim. True the wheel as described under *Spoke Adjustment* in this chapter.

Seating Spokes

When spokes loosen or when installing new spokes, the head of the spoke should be checked for proper seating in the hub. If it is not seated correctly, it can loosen further and may cause severe damage to the hub. If one or more spokes require reseating, hit the head of the spoke with a punch. True the wheel as described under *Spoke Adjustment* in this chapter.

TIRE CHANGING

The stock cast wheel is aluminum and the exterior appearance can easily be damaged. Special care must be taken with tire irons when changing a tire to avoid scratches and gouges to the outer rim surface. Insert scraps of leather between the tire iron and the rim to protect the rim from damage.

Stock cast wheels are designed for use with either tubeless or tube-type tires. Tire removal and installation are basically the same for tube and tubeless tires; where differences occur they are noted. Tire repair is different and is covered in separate procedures.

When removing a tubeless tire, take care not to damage the tire beads, inner liner of the tire or the wheel rim flange. Use tire levers or flat-handled tire irons with rounded ends.

Removal

1. Remove the valve core to deflate the tire.
2. Press the entire bead on both sides of the tire into the center of the rim.

NOTE
A bead breaker machine will be required to break the tire bead on 16-inch wheels.

3. Lubricate the beads with soapy water.
4. Insert the tire iron under the bead next to the valve (**Figure 22**). Force the bead on the opposite side of the tire into the center of the rim and pry the bead over the rim with the tire iron.

NOTE
Insert scraps of leather between the tire irons and the rim to protect the rim from damage.

5. Insert a second tire iron next to the first to hold the bead over the rim. Then work around the tire with the first tool prying the bead over the rim (**Figure 23**). On tube-type tires, be careful not to pinch the inner tube with the tools.
6. On tube-type tires, use your thumb and push the valve from its hole in the rim to the inside of

8

the tire. Carefully pull the tube out of the tire and lay it aside.

NOTE
Step 7 is required only if it is necessary to completely remove the tire from the rim, such as for tire replacement or tubeless tire repair.

7. Stand the wheel upright. Insert a tire tool between the second bead and the same side of the rim that the first bead was pried over (**Figure 24**). Force the bead on the opposite side from the tool into the center of the rim. Pry the second bead off the rim, working around the wheel with 2 tire irons as with the first bead.
8. On tubeless tires, inspect the rubber O-ring where the valve stem seats against the inner surface of the wheel. Replace it if it's starting to deteriorate or has lost its resiliency. This is a common location of air loss with tubeless tires.

23

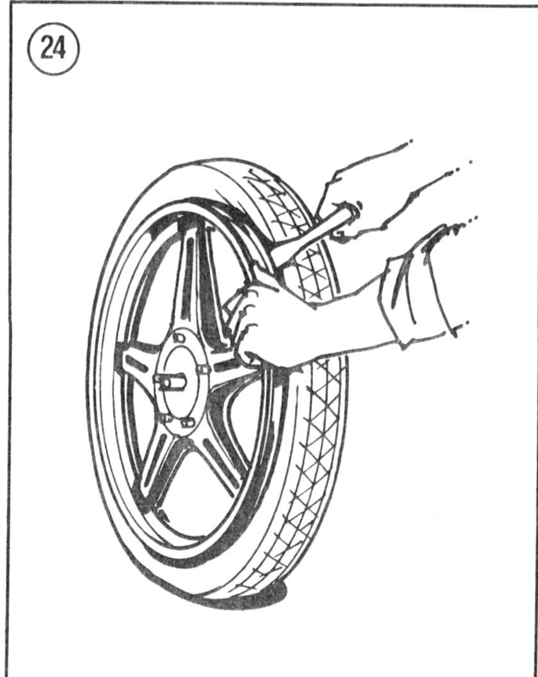
24

Installation

1. Carefully inspect the tire for any damage, especially inside.
2. A new tire may have balancing rubbers inside. These are not patches and should not be disturbed. A colored spot near the bead indicates a lighter point on the tire. This spot should be placed next to the valve stem (**Figure 25**). In addition, most tires have directional arrows labeled on the side of the tire to indicate which direction the tire should rotate. Make sure to install the tire accordingly.
3. On tube-type tires, inflate the tube just enough to round it out. Too much air will make installation difficult. Place the tube inside the tire.
4. Lubricate both beads of the tire with soapy water.
5. Place the backside of the tire into the center of the rim and insert the valve stem through the stem hole in the wheel. The lower bead should go into the center of the rim and the upper bead outside. Work around the tire in both directions (**Figure 26**). Use a tire iron for the last few inches of bead (**Figure 27**).
6. Press the upper bead into the rim opposite the valve. Pry the bead into the rim on both sides of the initial point with a tire tool, working around the rim to the valve (**Figure 28**).
7. On tube-type tires, wiggle the valve to be sure the tube is not trapped under the bead. Set the valve stem squarely in its hole before screwing on the valve nut to hold it against the rim.
8. Check the bead on both sides of the tire for an even fit around the rim.

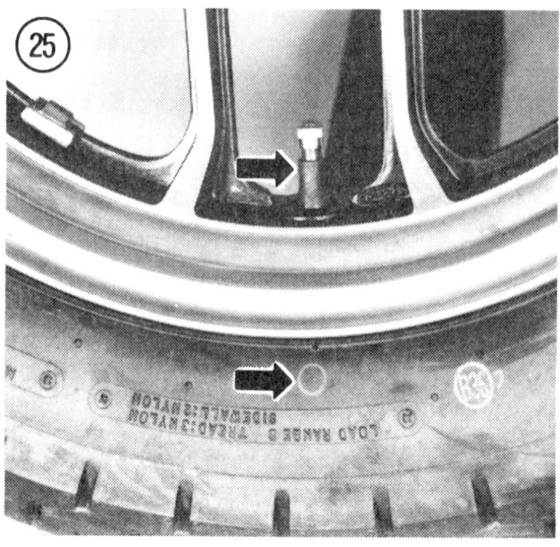
25

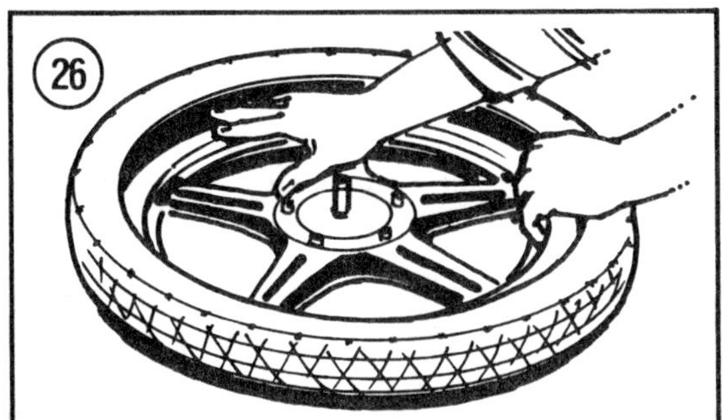

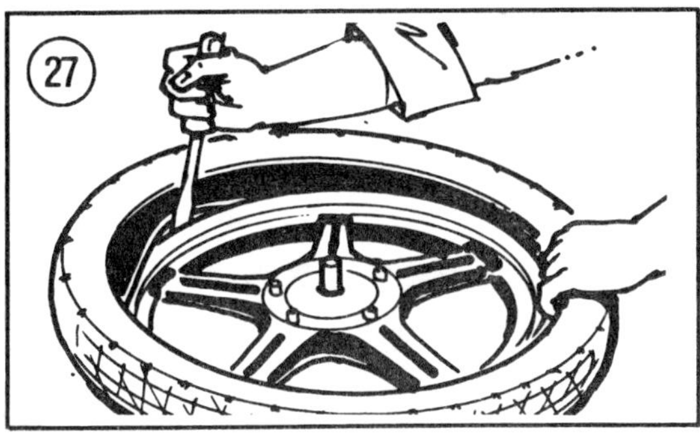

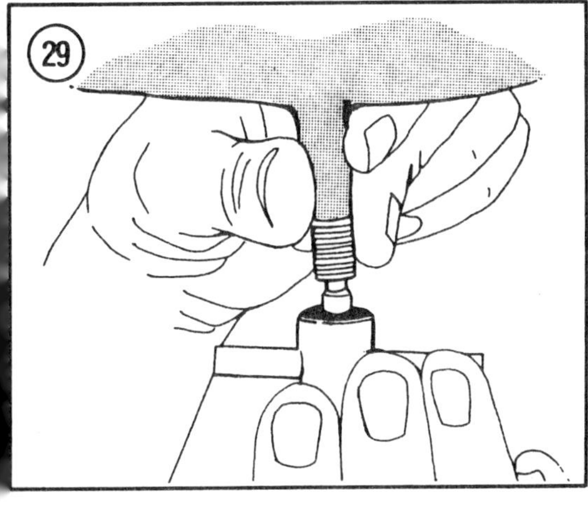

WARNING

During the next steps, never exceed 40 psi inflation pressure as the tire could burst. Never stand directly over the tire while inflating it.

9. On tube-type tires, inflate the tire slowly to seat the beads in the rim. It may be necessary to bounce the tire to complete the seating.
10. On tubeless tires, place an inflatable band around the circumference of the tire. Slowly inflate the band until the tire beads are pressed against the rim. Inflate the tire enough to seat it, deflate the band and remove it.
11. Inflate the tire to the required pressure (Chapter Three). Tighten the valve stem locks and screw on the cover cap.
12. Balance the wheel assembly as described in this chapter.

TIRE REPAIRS (TUBE-TYPE TIRES)

Patching a motorcycle tube is only a temporary fix. A motorcycle tire flexes too much and the patch could rub right off. However, a patched tube should get you far enough to buy a new tube.

8

Tire Repair Kits

The repair kits can be purchased from motorcycle dealers and some auto supply stores. When buying, specify that the kit you want is for motorcycles.

There are 2 types of tire repair kits:

a. Hot patch.
b. Cold patch.

Hot patches are stronger because they actually vulcanize to the tube, becoming part of it. However, they are far too bulky to carry for roadside repairs and the strength is unnecessary for a temporary repair.

Cold patches are not vulcanized to the tube; they are simply glued to it. Though not as strong as hot patches, cold patches are still very durable. Cold patch kits are less bulky than hot and more easily applied under adverse conditions. A cold patch kit contains everything necessary and tucks in easily with your emergency tool kit.

Tube Inspection

1. Remove the inner tube as described under *Tire Changing* in this chapter.
2. Install the valve core into the valve stem (**Figure 29**) and inflate the tube slightly. Do not overinflate.
3. Immerse the tube in water a section at a time. Look carefully for bubbles indicating a hole. Mark

each hole and continue checking until you are certain that all holes are discovered and marked. Also make sure that the valve core is not leaking; tighten it if necessary.

NOTE

If you do not have enough water to immerse sections of the tube, try running your hand over the tube slowly and very close to the surface. If your hand is damp, it works even better. If you suspect a hole anywhere, apply some saliva to the area to verify it.

4. Apply a cold patch using the techniques described by the patch kit manufacturer.
5. Dust the patch area with talcum powder to prevent it from sticking to the tire.
6. Carefully check the inside of the tire casing for small rocks or sand which may have damaged the tube. If the inside of the tire is split, apply a patch to the area to prevent it from pinching and damaging the tube again.
7. Check the inside of the rim.
8. Deflate the tube prior to installation in the tire.

TIRE REPAIRS (TUBELESS TYPE)

Patching a tubeless tire on the road is very difficult. If both beads are still in place against the rim, a can of pressurized tire sealant may inflate the tire and seal the hole. The beads must be against the wheel for this method to work. Another solution is to carry a spare tube that could be temporarily installed and inflated. This will enable you to get to a service station where the tire can be correctly repaired. Be sure that the tube is designed for use with a tubeless tire. The tire industry recommends that tubeless tires be patched from the inside. Therefore, do not patch the tire with an external type plug. If you find an external patch on a tire, it should be patch-reinforced from the inside.

Due to the variations of material supplied with different tubeless tire repair kits, follow the instructions and recommendations supplied with the repair kit.

HANDLEBAR AND THROTTLE CONTROL

Because of the different number of handlebar and cable configurations for the models covered in this manual, this procedure presents a general guideline to handlebar removal and installation. Take Polaroid pictures or make sketches of the handlebar assembly if you are unsure about the routing of the control cables. Bent or damaged handlebars should be replaced immediately.

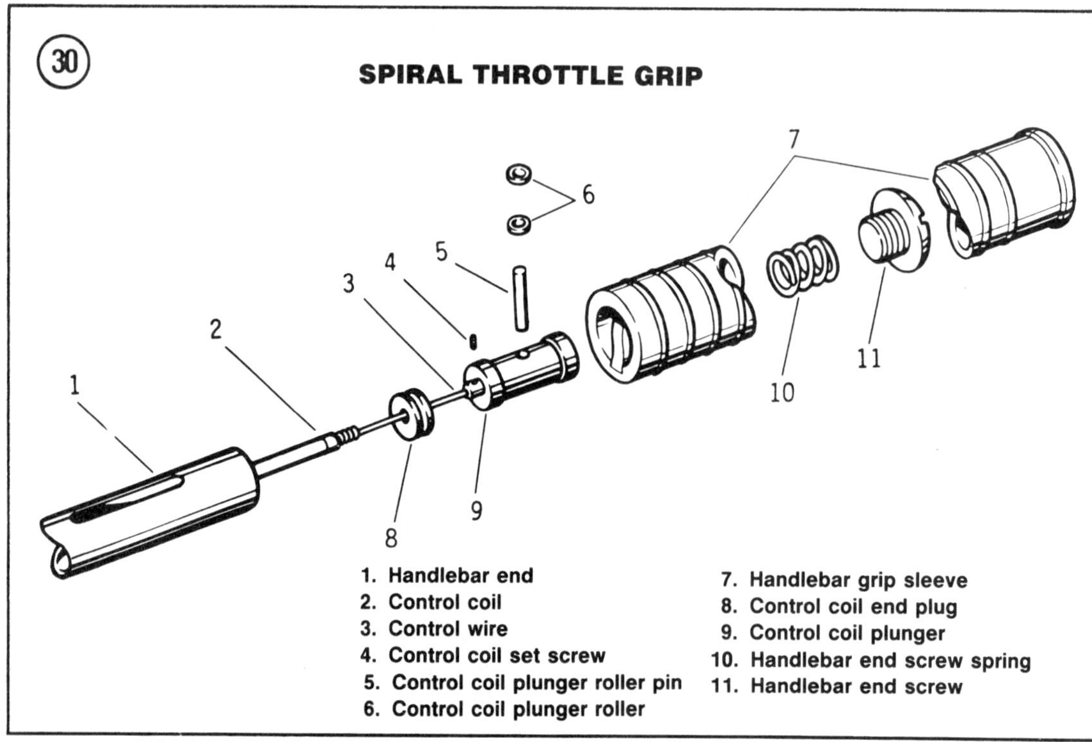

1. Handlebar end
2. Control coil
3. Control wire
4. Control coil set screw
5. Control coil plunger roller pin
6. Control coil plunger roller
7. Handlebar grip sleeve
8. Control coil end plug
9. Control coil plunger
10. Handlebar end screw spring
11. Handlebar end screw

Removal

1. Support the bike on the sidestand.

CAUTION
On models equipped with front disc brakes, cover the fuel tank with a heavy cloth or plastic tarp to protect it from accidental spilling of brake fluid. Wash any spilled brake fluid off any painted or plated surface immediately, as it will destroy the finish. Use soapy water and rinse thoroughly.

2. Remove the mirrors.
3. Remove the throttle control assembly as described in this chapter.
4. On models equipped with disc brake, remove the bolts securing the master cylinder and lay it on the fuel tank. It is not necessary to disconnect the hydraulic brake line.
5. Slacken the clutch cable and disconnect it at the hand lever.
6. Remove the clamps securing the electrical cables to the handlebar.
7. Check the handlebar for any remaining electrical wiring or equipment and either disconnect or remove them.
8. Remove the handlebar clamp bolts and remove the handlebar.
9. Install by reversing these steps.

Throttle Control Assembly

Spiral grip

The spiral grip was used on early models. Refer to **Figure 30** (typical) for this procedure.

1. Disconnect the throttle control wire at the carburetor and circuit breaker.
2. Remove the handlebar end screw (11, **Figure 30**). This screw may be difficult to remove; an impact driver will be helpful.
3. Remove the handlebar grip sleeve (7). Remove the screw end spring (10) from inside the grip.
4. Remove the 2 control coil plunger rollers (6) and the roller pin (5).
5. Pull the control coil plunger (9) and the control wire (3) from the handlebar. If the control wire is broken, pull the other piece from the carburetor or circuit breaker. The control wire is secured in the plunger by the control coil set screw (4).
6. Remove the control coils (2) and the end plug (8).
7. Clean all parts in solvent. Replace any worn or damaged parts.
8. Installation is the reverse of these steps, noting the following:
   a. Make sure that the screw (4) registers in the control coil end plug groove.
   b. Lubricate the control wire with graphite grease or oil as it is inserted into the control coil.
   c. Install both rollers over the roller pin, with the round side of roller facing up as it is positioned on the motorcycle.
   d. The easiest way to install the handlebar end screw (11) is to grasp the grip sleeve assembly (3) and apply slight pressure against the screw as it is started. Make sure to tighten the screw securely.
   e. After completing assembly at handlebar, connect control wire at carburetor and circuit breaker. Be sure that the carburetor lever opens and closes fully as the grip is turned. There should be 1/4 in. between the control clip on carburetor and the throttle control coil when the carburetor lever is fully closed against its stop.
   f. The end of the spark control wire must point directly at the adjuster stud hole on the circuit breaker when the circuit breaker is in its fully advanced position. End of control coil should extend approximately 3/8 in. beyond the clamp.

Drum throttle grip—1980 and earlier

Refer to **Figure 31** (typical) for this procedure.

1. Remove both throttle control coil clamp screws and separate the upper and lower clamps.
2. Disconnect the control wire at the throttle grip. On late 1978-1980 models, the ferrule disconnects from the control wire.
3. If necessary, remove the worn or broken control wire by sliding it through the control adjuster locknut. To replace the control wire on early 1978 and earlier models, unsolder or cut off the control wire ferrule before removing the wire.
4. Lubricate replacement wire with graphite grease and slide it into the control wire casing.
5. If necessary, solder ferrule onto the new wire flush with the wire end.
6. Attach the control wire onto the throttle grip and assemble the throttle assembly.
7. Adjust the throttle assembly as described in Chapter Three.

Drum throttle grip—1981-1985

On 1981-1985 models, a closing throttle cable was added and the throttle grip travel stop screw was eliminated. Refer to **Figure 32**.

1. Remove the throttle clamp screws and the upper clamp (2, **Figure 32**).
2. Slide the cylindrical ferrules out of their throttle grip seats and remove the ferrules from their cable ball ends.
3. Disconnect the lower ends of the cables from the carburetor. Note the routing of the cables, then pull the cable and lower clamp assembly up away from the motorcycle.
4. Loosen the cable elbow locknuts at the lower grip clamp and unscrew the elbows from the clamp.
5. Inspect the throttle spring and replace if necessary. Make sure the friction spring is securely seated on the friction adjuster screw (7).
6. Lubricate the insides of the grip clamps, the end of the handlebar and the cable ends and ferrules lightly with graphite grease.
7. Screw the throttle cable elbows into the lower grip clamp. The "open" cable elbow (9) has a larger thread than the "close" cable (12) and it goes in the left side of the lower clamp. The "close" cable has a spring at its lower end.
8. Slide the throttle grip over handlebar, install the cylindrical ferrules on the cable ends and seat the ferrules in the grip notches.
9. Route the cables through the throttle cable clamp and connect them to the carburetor. The open cable goes through the inside fitting and the close cable (with spring) goes through the outside fitting (**Figure 33**).
10. Install the upper grip clamp and tighten the screws securely. Turn the cable elbows so there is no stress on the cables and tighten the elbow locknuts at the lower grip clamp.
11. Adjust the throttle cables as described in Chapter Three.

STEERING HEAD

Refer to **Figure 34** (1959-1974), **Figure 35** (1975-1978) or **Figure 36** (1979-1985) for this procedure.

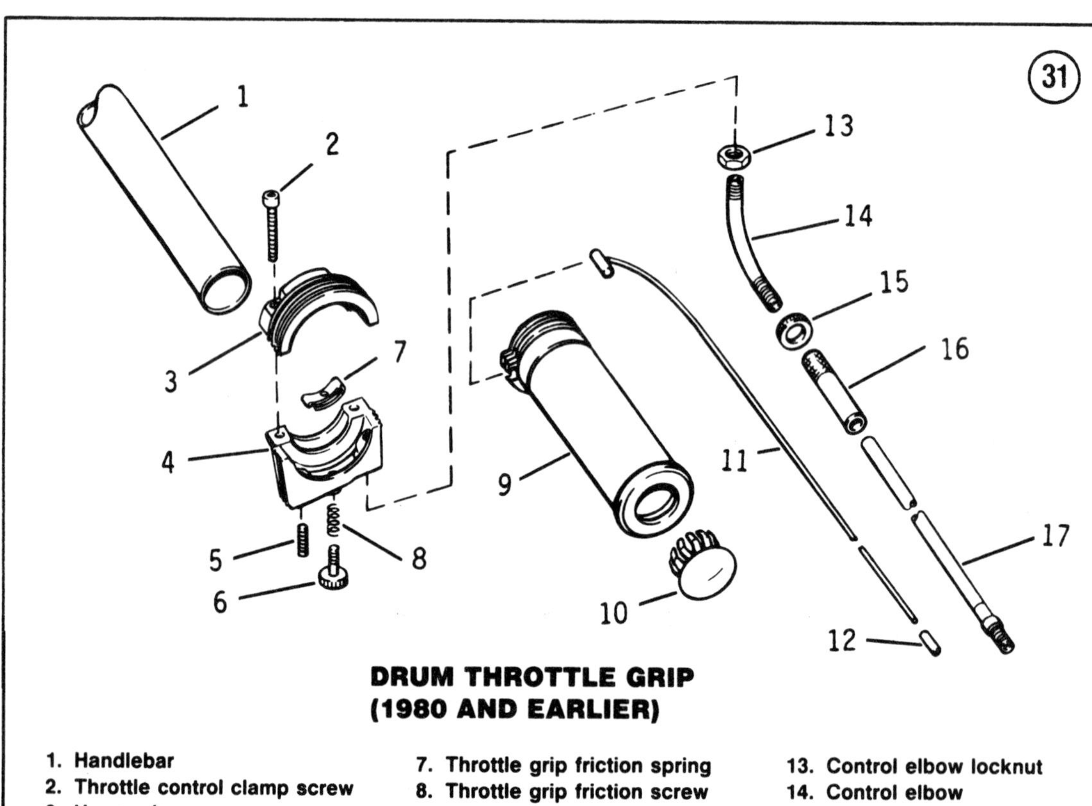

DRUM THROTTLE GRIP (1980 AND EARLIER)

1. Handlebar
2. Throttle control clamp screw
3. Upper clamp
4. Lower clamp
5. Stop screw
6. Throttle grip friction adjusting screw
7. Throttle grip friction spring
8. Throttle grip friction screw spring
9. Throttle grip
10. Throttle grip plug
11. Control wire
12. Control wire ferrule
13. Control elbow locknut
14. Control elbow
15. Control adjuster locknut
16. Control adjuster
17. Control wire casing

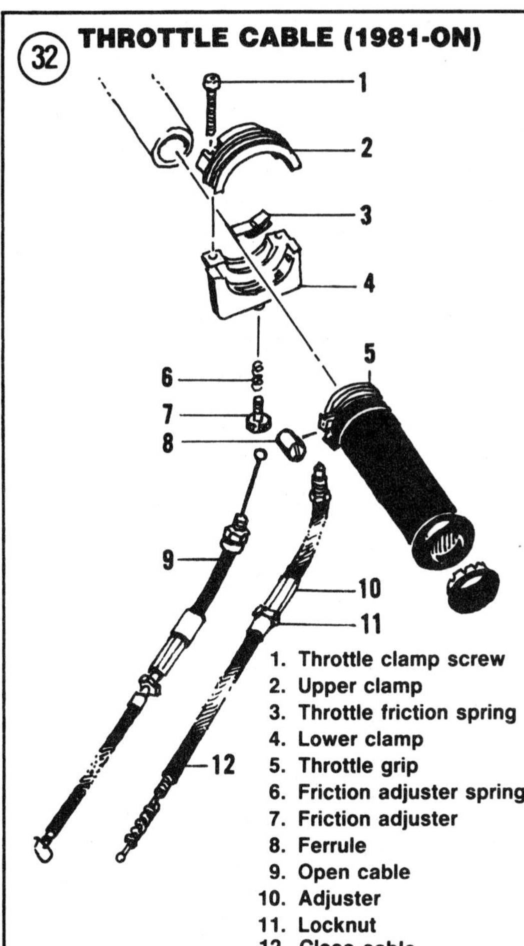

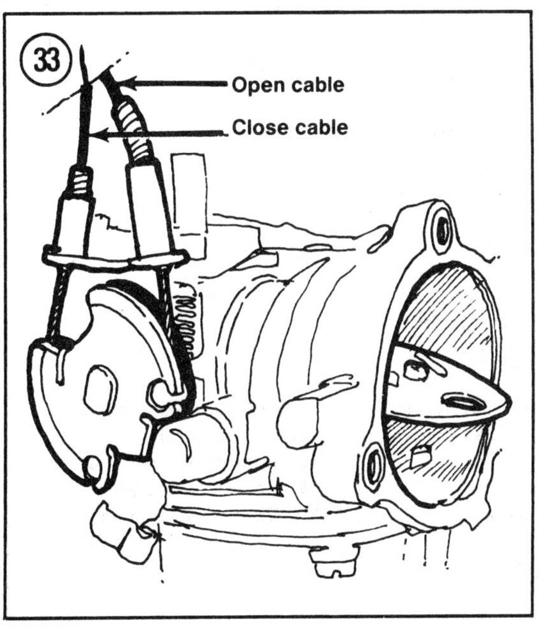

Disassembly

1. Remove the front wheel as described in this chapter.
2. Remove the fuel tank as described in Chapter Six.
3. Disconnect the speedometer and tachometer cables.
4. Remove the front trim panel, if so equipped.
5. Remove the headlight and front turn indicators.
6. Remove the handlebar as described in this chapter.
7. Remove the bolts securing the tachometer/speedometer unit. Lay the components aside.
8. Remove the fork tubes as described in this chapter.
9. Complete removal of the fork stem by performing the applicable procedures.

1959-1974

Refer to **Figure 34**.

1. Remove the upper fork stem end nut (1, **Figure 34**).

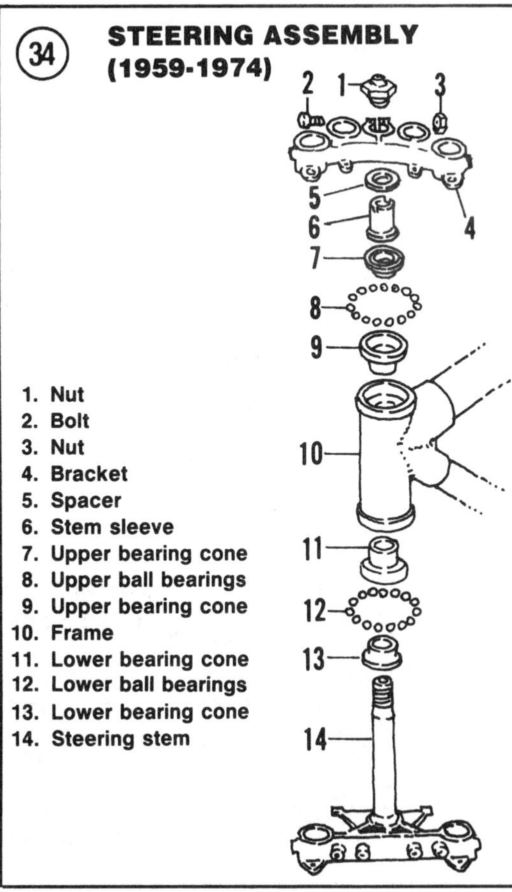

8

STEERING ASSEMBLY (1975-1978)

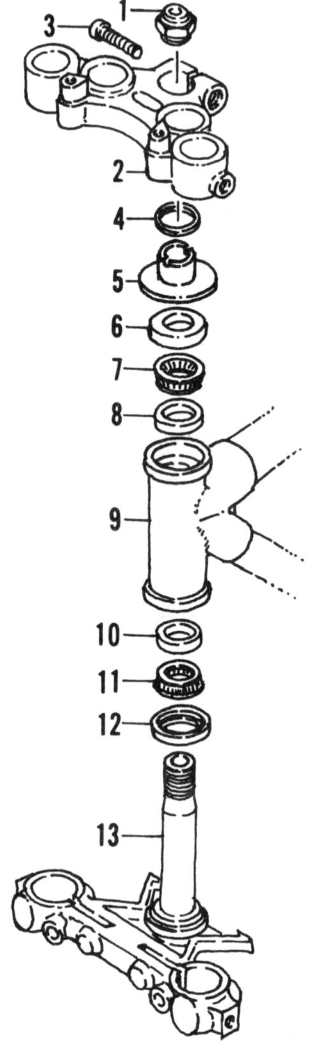

1. Nut
2. Bracket
3. Bolt
4. Spacer
5. Stem sleeve
6. Upper bearing shield
7. Bearing
8. Upper bearing race
9. Frame
10. Lower bearing race
11. Bearing
12. Dust shield
13. Steering stem

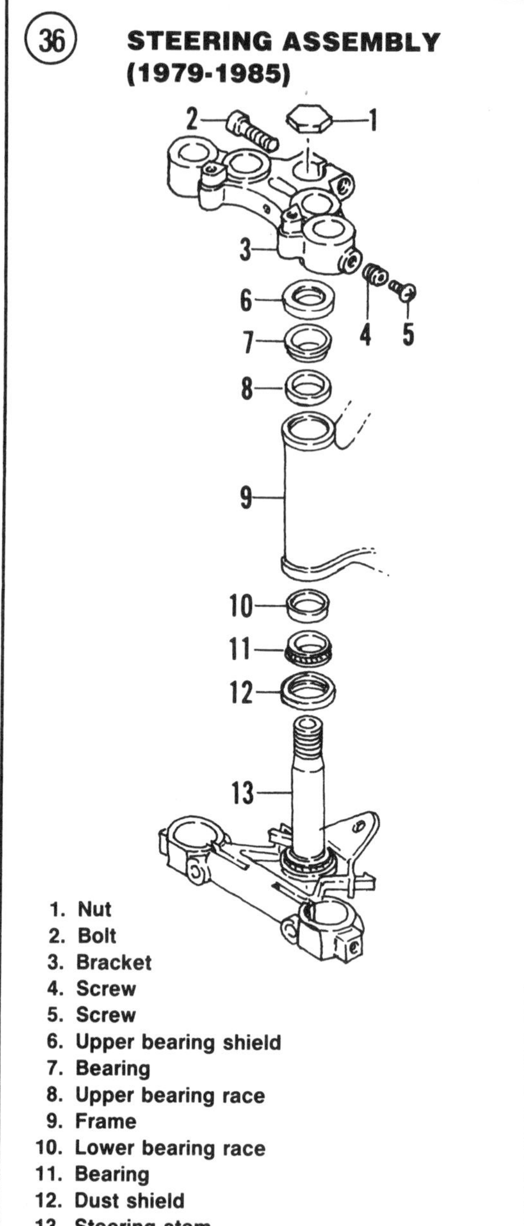

STEERING ASSEMBLY (1979-1985)

1. Nut
2. Bolt
3. Bracket
4. Screw
5. Screw
6. Upper bearing shield
7. Bearing
8. Upper bearing race
9. Frame
10. Lower bearing race
11. Bearing
12. Dust shield
13. Steering stem

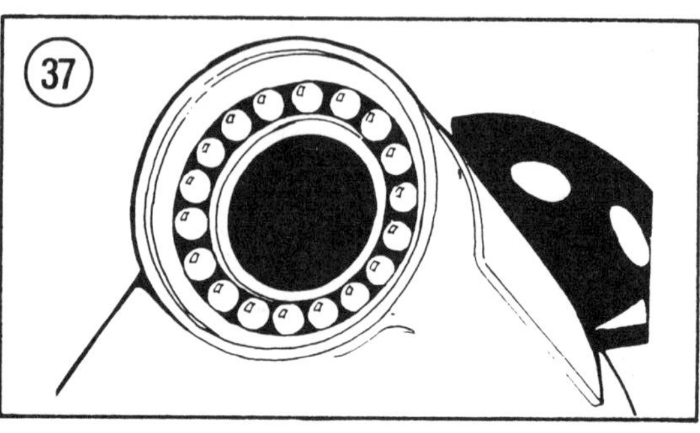

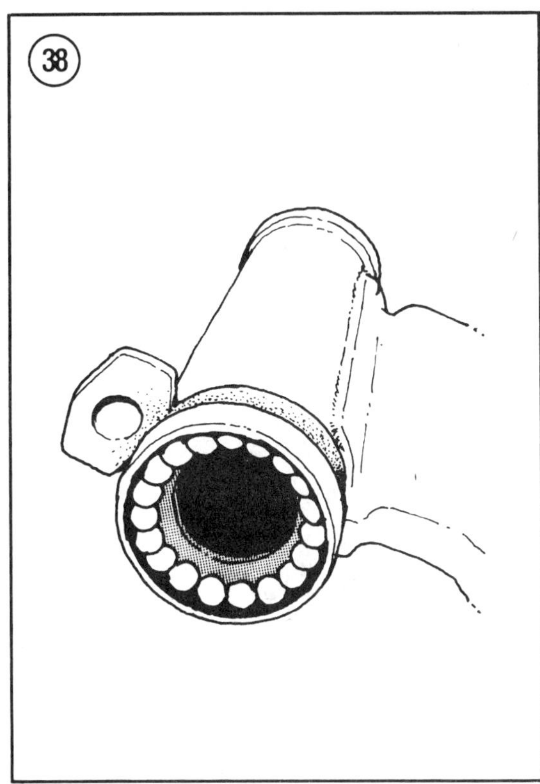

2. Remove the upper fork stem pinch bolt (2) and nut (3).
3. Remove the upper fork bracket (4).
4. Remove the upper bracket spacer (5) and stem sleeve (6).

CAUTION
There is a total of 28 ball bearings used—14 in the top and 14 in the bottom. The bearings should not be intermixed because if worn or damaged, they must be replaced in sets. However, all balls are the same size.

5. Pull the steering stem out of the frame (10). The upper and lower bearings are uncaged ball bearings so be ready to catch them as they fall out.
6. Remove the upper bearing cone (7) from the frame (10) and remove the upper ball bearings (8). See **Figure 37**.
7. Remove the lower ball bearings from the frame (**Figure 38**) or the steering stem.

1975-1978

Refer to **Figure 35** for this procedure.
1. Remove the upper fork stem end nut (1, **Figure 35**).
2. Remove the upper fork stem pinch bolt (3).
3. Remove the upper fork bracket (2).
4. Remove the upper bracket spacer (4) and stem sleeve (5).
5. Remove the upper bearing shield (6).
6. Pull the steering stem (13) out of the frame.
7. Lift the upper roller bearing (7) out of the frame.
8. Remove the lower roller bearing (11) off of the steering stem or frame.
9. Remove the lower dust shield (12) from the steering stem.

1979-1985

Refer to **Figure 36** for this procedure.
1. Remove the upper fork stem end nut (1, **Figure 36**).
2. Remove the upper fork stem pinch bolt (2).
3. Remove the upper fork stem bracket (3).
4. Remove the upper bearing shield (6).
5. Pull the steering stem out of the frame (10).
6. Lift the upper roller bearing (7A) out of the frame.
7. Remove the lower roller bearing (7B) from the steering stem.
8. Remove the lower dust shield (10) from the steering stem.

Inspection

1. Clean the bearing races in the steering head and all ball bearings and bearing cones with solvent.
2. Check for broken welds on the frame around the steering head. If any are found, have them repaired by a competent frame shop or welding service familiar with motorcycle frame repair.
3. Check the balls and bearing cones for pitting, scratches or discoloration indicating wear or corrosion. Replace them in sets if any are bad.
4. Check the upper and lower races in the steering head. See *Bearing Race Replacement* in this chapter if races are pitted, scratched or badly worn.
5. Check steering stem for cracks.

Steering Head Bearing Race Replacement

The headset and steering stem bearing races are pressed into the frame. Because they are easily bent, do not remove them unless they are worn and require replacement. Take old races to the dealer to ensure exact replacement.

To remove a headset race, insert a hardwood stick into the head tube and carefully tap the race out from the inside (**Figure 39**). Tap all around the race so that neither the race nor the head tube is bent. To install a race, fit it into the end of the head tube. Tap it slowly and squarely with a block of wood (**Figure 40**).

Steering Stem Bearing Race Replacement (1959-1974)

To remove the lower bearing race (7B, **Figure 34**), carefully pry it up from the base of the steering stem with a screwdriver. Work around in a circle, prying a little at a time. Remove the bearing assembly.

Tap the race down with a long piece of metal pipe that fits the inner race diameter or use a piece of hardwood. Work in a circle so the race will not be bent. Make sure it is seated squarely and is all the way down.

Assembly

1959-1974

Refer to **Figure 34** for this procedure.

1. Make sure the steering head bearing races are properly seated.

CAUTION
If used balls are being reinstalled, be sure they are placed into their original race—top or bottom.

2. Apply a coat of wheel bearing grease to the upper and lower bearing races.
3. Fit 14 ball bearings around the lower bearing race on the steering stem.
4. Install the steering stem (11, **Figure 34**) with the lower ball bearings in place, into the steering head tube and hold it firmly in place.
5. Fit 14 ball bearings around the upper bearing race in the frame (**Figure 37**).
6. Install the upper bearing race (7A, **Figure 34**).
7. Install the stem sleeve (6, **Figure 34**) and tighten it until all appreciable free play is taken up. Then turn the steering stem from side to side. The bearing action should be smooth and free. If not, the adjustment nut is too tight. Loosen and readjust it.
8. Install the spacer (5, **Figure 34**) and the upper fork bracket (4, **Figure 34**).
9. Slide the fork tubes into the steering stem assembly. Tighten each fork tube cap securely. Then tighten the fork tube pinch bolts to 35 ft.-lb.
10. Install all parts prevously removed.
11. With the front end completely reassembled, turn the handlebar from side to side. There should be no binding or appreciable play. If so, the steem sleeve is too tight.

NOTE
The stem sleeve should be tight enough to remove play, both horizontal and vertical, yet loose enough so that the assembly will turn to both lock positions under its own weight after a light push.

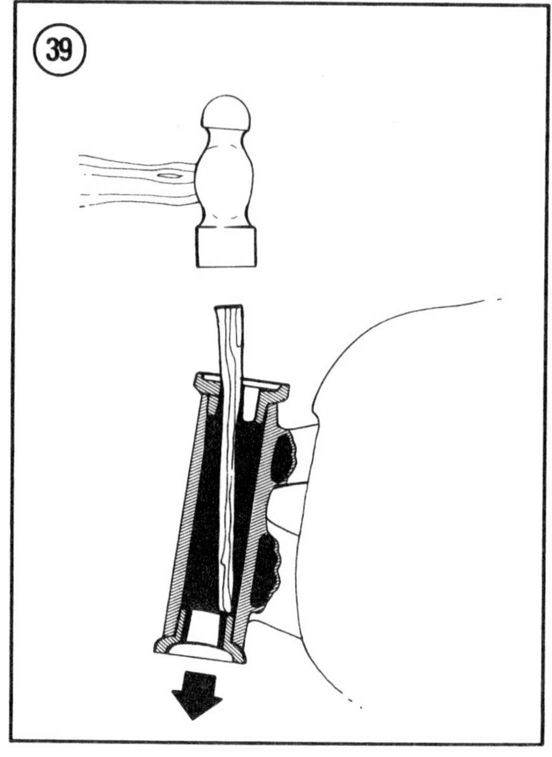

12. Tighten the stem sleeve nut (1, **Figure 34**) and the upper bracket pinch bolt to specifications.

1975-1985

Refer to **Figure 35** or **Figure 36** for this procedure.

1. Make sure the steering stem bearing races are properly seated in the steering head tube.
2. Install the lower dust cover on the steering stem.
3. Install the lower bearing cone on the steering stem.
4. Coat the roller bearings thoroughly with grease. Work the grease into the rollers.
5. Slide the lower roller bearing onto the steering stem.
6. Insert the steering stem into the head tube. Hold it firmly in place.
7. Install the upper roller bearing.
8. Install the upper bearing cover.

9A. *1975-1978:* Perform the following.
   a. Install the stem sleeve (5, **Figure 35**) and tighten it until all appreciable bearing play is taken up and the bearing action is smooth.
   b. Install the spacer (4, **Figure 35**) and the upper fork bracket (2, **Figure 35**).

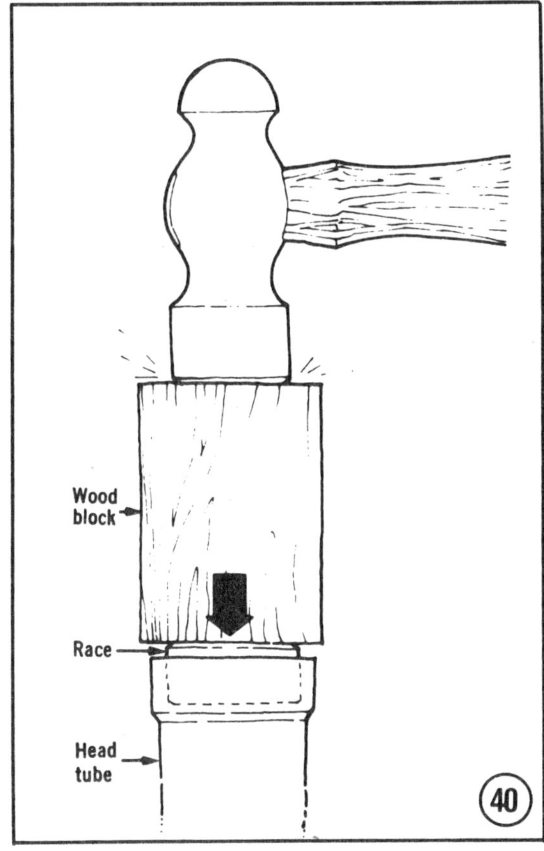

c. Slide the fork tubes into the steering stem assembly. Tighten each fork tube cap securely. Then tighten the fork tube pinch bolts securely.
d. Install all parts prevously removed.
e. With the front end completely reassembled, turn the handlebar from side to side. There should be no binding or appreciable play. If there is binding, the adjusting nut is too tight. If there is play, the nut is too loose.
f. Tighten the end nut (1, **Figure 35**) and the upper bracket pinch bolt (3, **Figure 35**) to specifications in **Table 2**.

9B. *1979-1985:* Perform the following.

a. Install the upper bracket (3, **Figure 36**).
b. Loosely install the fork stem adjusting nut (1, **Figure 36**).
c. Install all parts previously removed.
d. Tighten the adjusting nut (1, **Figure 36**) until the bearing has no free play.

NOTE
The adjusting nut should be tight enough to remove play, both horizontal and vertical, yet loose enough so that the assembly will turn to both lock positions under its own weight after a light push.

10. After the total assembly is completed, check the stem for looseness or binding; readjust if necessary.

Steering Head Adjustment

Adjust the steering head free play as described under *Steering Head Assembly* for your model.

FRONT FORK

The front suspension consists of a spring-controlled, hydraulically dampened telescopic fork.

Before suspecting major trouble, drain the front fork oil and refill with the proper type and quantity; refer to Chapter Three, if you still have trouble, such as poor damping, a tendency to bottom or top out or leakage around the rubber seals, follow the service procedures in this section.

To simplify fork service and to prevent the mixing of parts, the legs should be removed, serviced and installed individually.

8

Removal/Installation

1. Prop the bike so that the front wheel clears the ground.
2. Remove the front wheel as described in this chapter.
3. Remove the brake caliper(s) as described in Chapter Ten. Secure each caliper with a bunji cord to keep tension off the brake hoses.

NOTE
Insert a piece of wood in the caliper(s) in place of the disc. That way, if the brake lever is inadvertently squeezed, the piston will not be forced out of the caliper. If this does happen, the caliper might have to be disassembled to reseat the piston. By using the wood, bleeding the brake is not necessary after installing the wheel.

4. Remove the fork tube cap (**Figure 41**).
5. On models equipped with a lower fork stem cover, loosen the cover screws and raise the cover (**Figure 42**) to gain access to the lower fork stem pinch bolts.
6. On models equipped with rubber fork boots, stretch the boot over the upper boot retainer.
7. Loosen the upper and lower fork tube pinch bolts (**Figure 43**). Then rotate the fork tube (**Figure 44**) and remove it.
8. Reinstall the fork cap.

9. Repeat for the opposite side.
10. Install by reversing these removal steps. Tighten all bolts to specifications (**Table 2** or **Table 3**).

Disassembly/Reassembly (1959-1978)

Refer to **Figure 45** (1959-1969) or **Figure 46** (1970-1978) for this procedure.

1. On 1959-1972 models, disassemble the fork spring retainer from the fork tube using Harley-Davidson tool 94694-52.
2. On 1959-1967 models, there is an additional shock absorber assembly within the spring. Compress the spring and grasp the shock absorber assembly with Vise Grip pliers. Then remove the piston rod retainer.
3. Remove the spring and drain oil from the fork leg.
4. Remove the fork slider lower bolt. On 1968-1978 models it may be necessry to insert a long screwdriver through the fork tube and into the slot in the upper end of the shock absorber to keep it from turning while removing bolt. On 1973-1974 models, a special socket, Harley-Davidson tool 94556-73, and extension are required to keep the shock absorber from turning.
5. Remove the bolt and washer at the bottom of the slider and pull the fork tube out of the slider.
6. If necessary, disassemble the fork shock absorber as described in this chapter.
7. Installation is the reverse of these steps, noting the following.

8A. *1959-1967:* Perform the following:
   a. Insert the shock absorber into the fork tube.
   b. Turn the assembly so that the shock absorber end faces upward.
   c. Install a new gasket on the end screw and dowel pin. Place the fork slider over the tube,

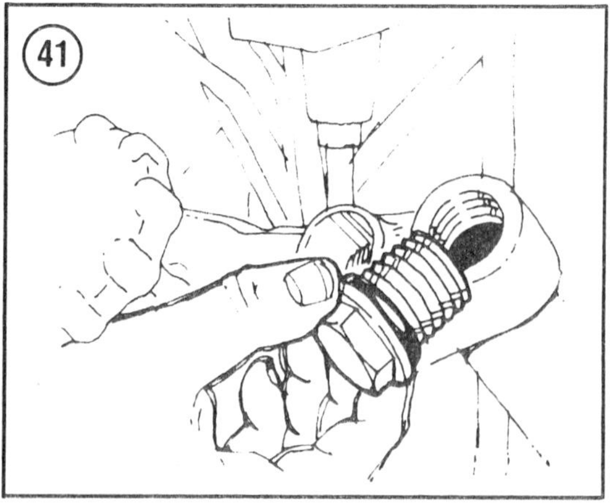

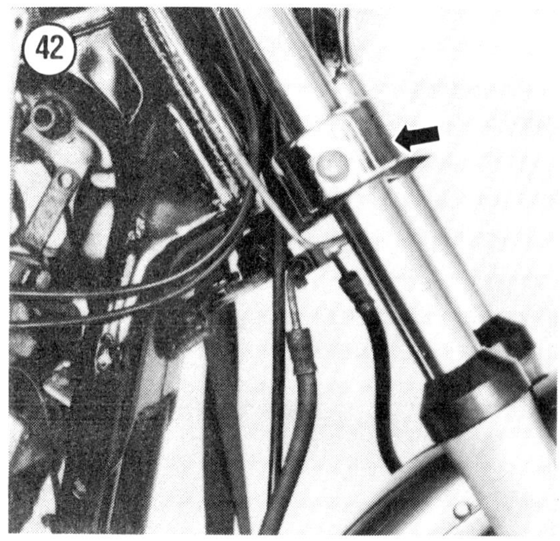

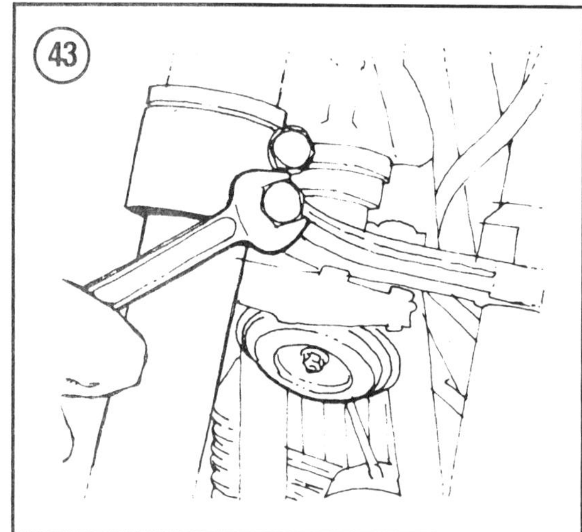

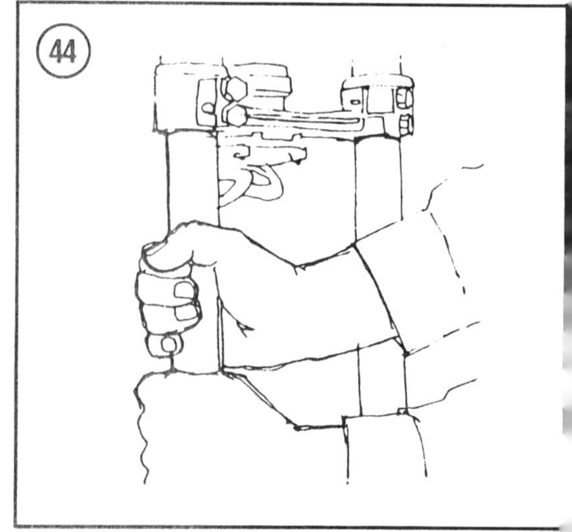

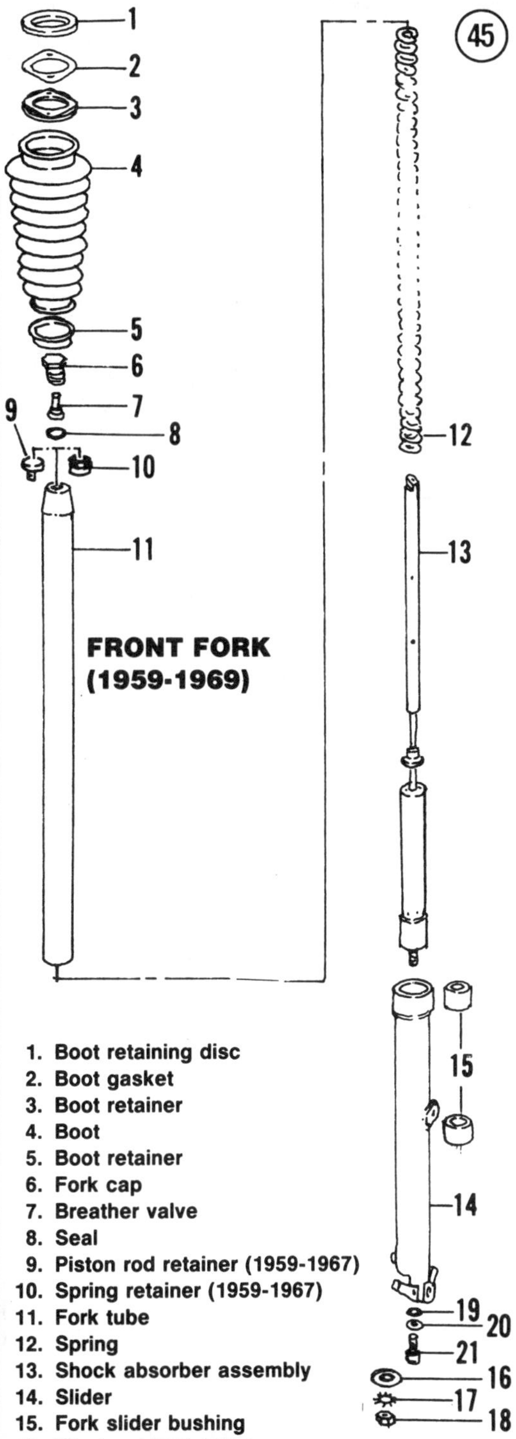

(45)

FRONT FORK (1959-1969)

1. Boot retaining disc
2. Boot gasket
3. Boot retainer
4. Boot
5. Boot retainer
6. Fork cap
7. Breather valve
8. Seal
9. Piston rod retainer (1959-1967)
10. Spring retainer (1959-1967)
11. Fork tube
12. Spring
13. Shock absorber assembly
14. Slider
15. Fork slider bushing
16. Washer (1959-1967)
17. Lockwasher (1959-1969)
18. Nut (1959-1969)
19. O-ring (1968-1969)
20. Washer (1968-1969)
21. Bolt (1968-1969)

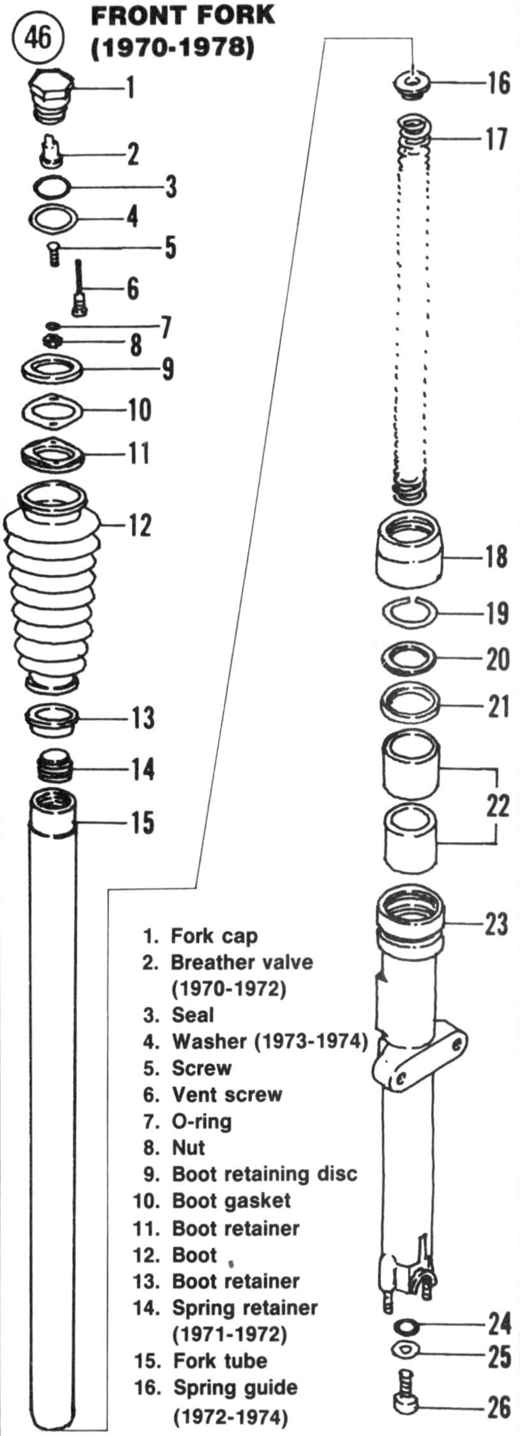

(46) **FRONT FORK (1970-1978)**

1. Fork cap
2. Breather valve (1970-1972)
3. Seal
4. Washer (1973-1974)
5. Screw
6. Vent screw
7. O-ring
8. Nut
9. Boot retaining disc
10. Boot gasket
11. Boot retainer
12. Boot
13. Boot retainer
14. Spring retainer (1971-1972)
15. Fork tube
16. Spring guide (1972-1974)
17. Spring
18. Boot (1971-1974)
19. Retaining ring (1973-1974)
20. Retaining washer (1973-1974)
21. Seal (1971-1974)
22. Fork slider bushing
23. Slider
24. O-ring
25. Washer
26. Allen bolt

then turn it until the dowel pin registers with the pin hole in the slider.

d. Refill fork with correct type and quantity of fork oil. See Chapter Three.

e. Screw a length of 5/16×24 threaded rod into threads on shock absorber rod. Compress spring, then grip flats of shock absorber rod with Vise Grip pliers. Remove threaded rod.

f. Turn piston rod retainer into end of shock absorber rod. Stake retainer threads through small hole on flat side of shock absorber rod near its top.

g. Install piston rod retainer into fork tube. Top of retainer should be 9/16 inch down from top of fork tube after installation.

8B. *1968-1974:* Perform the following:

a. Install the fork slider into the shock absorber.

b. Insert tube end bolt, washer and a new O-ring. Hold slotted end of tube when tightening tube end bolt.

c. Install the spring.

d. Refill fork tube with correct type and amount of fork oil. See Chapter Three.

NOTE
To measure the correct amount of fluid, use a plastic baby bottle. These have measurements in fluid ounces (oz.) and cubic centimeters (cc) on the side.

Shock Absorber Disassembly/Reassembly

1959-1967

Refer to **Figure 47** for this procedure.

1. Remove the piston stop bushing (12, **Figure 47**) from the shock absorber tube using Harley-Davidson tool 94691-52. This bushing is part of the shock absorber stop assembly, which consists of the piston stop collar (10), piston stop spring (11) and the piston stop bushing (12). Each end of the piston stop spring is staked to the ends of the piston stop collar and piston stop bushing.
2. Remove the piston rod nut (2). Then disassemble the shock absorber in the order shown in **Figure 47**.
3. Check all parts for wear or damage as follows:
   a. Check piston rod nut for looseness on piston rod.
   b. Check piston rod guide (13) for wear and looseness on piston rod (14).
   c. Check that recoil valve washer (6) is not jammed in chamfer of piston spacer (5).
   d. Examine piston valve (8) surface for wear and looseness in shock absorber tube.
4. Replace any part that appears worn and damaged in checks performed in Step 3.
5. Installation is the reverse of Step 1 and Step 2, noting the following:
   a. Screw fork piston stop bushing (12) into shock absorber tube (1) until outer bushing surface is flush with end of shock absorber tube.
   b. Stake bushing threads through small hole in upper end of shock absorber tube.

1968-1972

Refer to **Figure 48** for this procedure.

1. Remove the retaining ring (9, **Figure 48**).

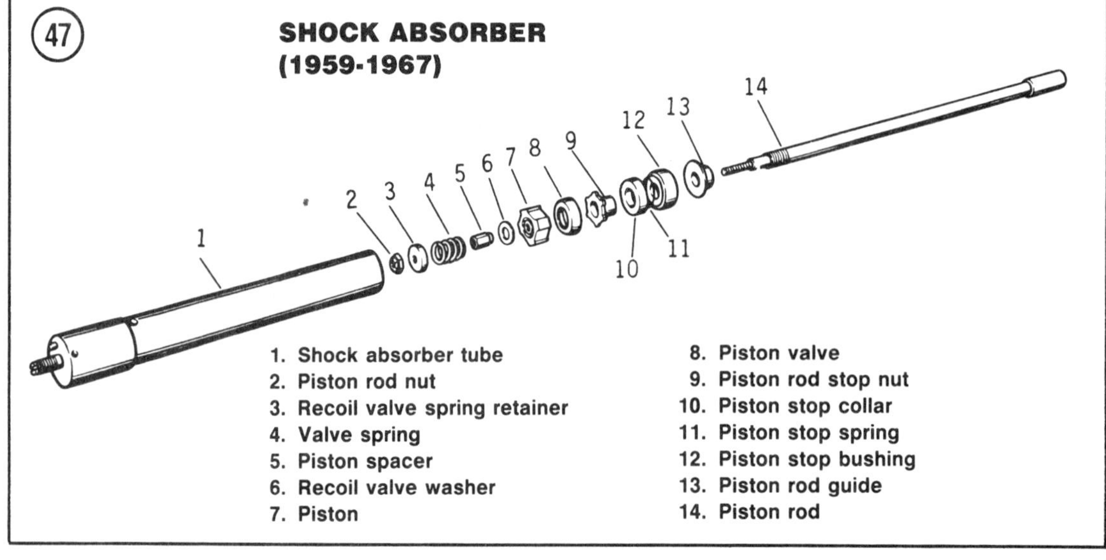

2. Remove the lower valve body (8), valve washer (7) and upper valve body (5). On 1970 models, remove the spring (6).
3. Remove the shock absorber tube (2).
4. Remove the piston retaining ring (4) and piston (3).
5. Check all parts for wear or damage as follows:
   a. Install the piston in the fork tube. Try to move the piston from side to side with your finger. Clearance should not be excessive.
   b. Install the piston on the shock absorber tube. Try to move the piston from side to side. Clearance should not be excessive.
   c. Check the valve washer (7) seating on the upper (5) and lower (8) valve body assemblies.
6. Replace any part that appears worn or damaged when performing the checks in Step 5.
7. Reverse Steps 1-4 to reassemble the shock absorber.

1973-1974

Refer to **Figure 49** for this procedure.

1. Remove the retaining ring (13, **Figure 49**).
2. Remove the following parts in order:
   a. Lower piston (12).
   b. Lower stop (11).

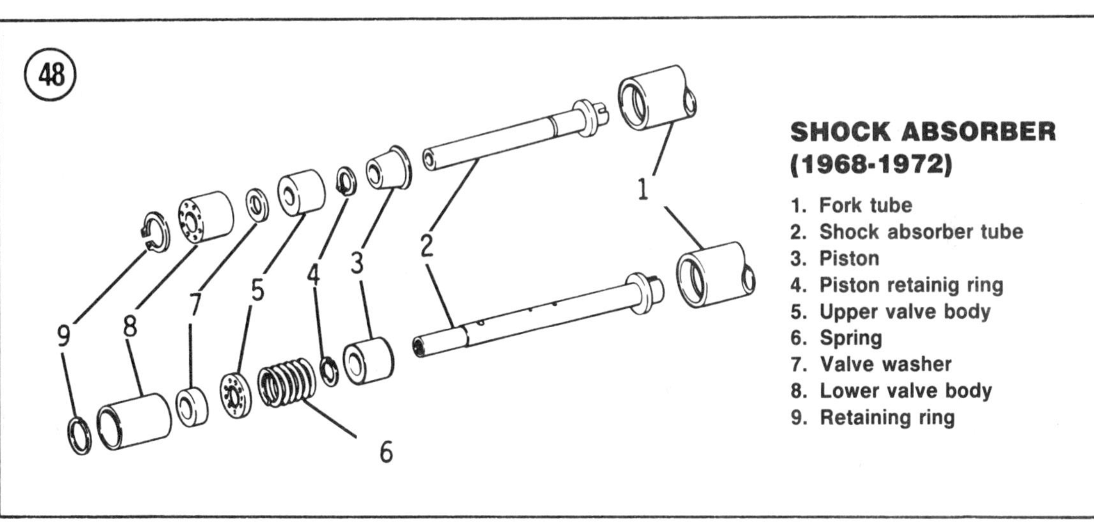

SHOCK ABSORBER (1968-1972)

1. Fork tube
2. Shock absorber tube
3. Piston
4. Piston retainig ring
5. Upper valve body
6. Spring
7. Valve washer
8. Lower valve body
9. Retaining ring

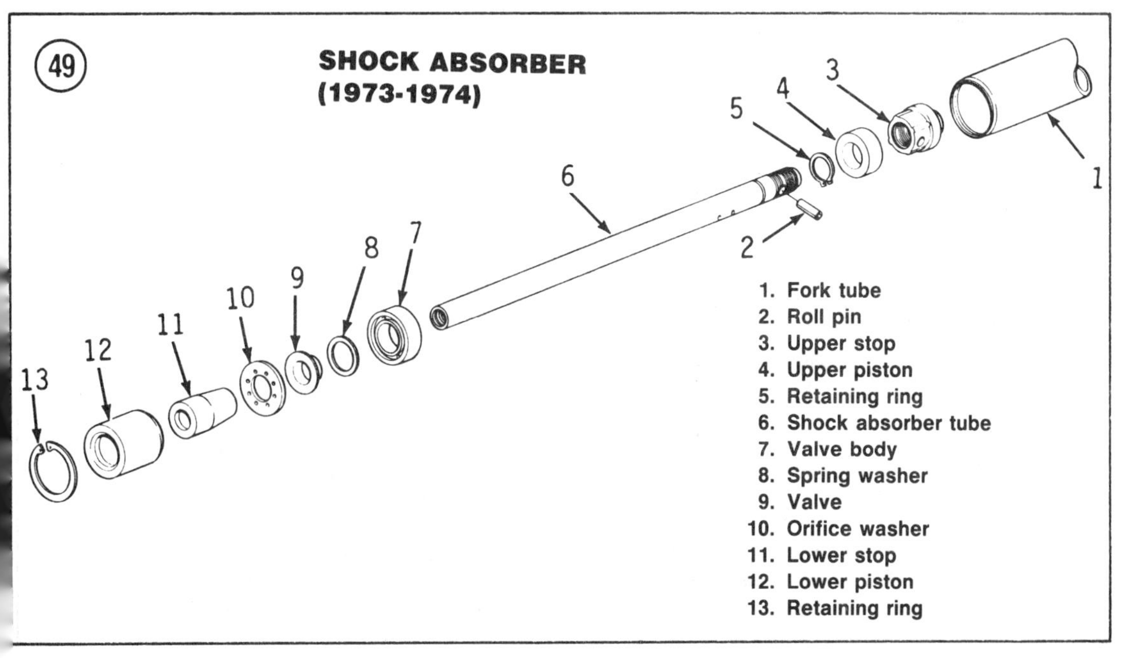

SHOCK ABSORBER (1973-1974)

1. Fork tube
2. Roll pin
3. Upper stop
4. Upper piston
5. Retaining ring
6. Shock absorber tube
7. Valve body
8. Spring washer
9. Valve
10. Orifice washer
11. Lower stop
12. Lower piston
13. Retaining ring

c. Orifice washer (10).
d. Valve (9).
e. Spring washer (8).
f. Valve body (7).
g. Retaining ring (5).
h. Upper piston (4).

3. Remove the roll pin (2) from the tube. Then unscrew the upper stop (3) and remove it.
4. Check each part for wear or damage. Install the lower and upper piston in the fork tube and check for excessive clearance. Check also the piston-to-shock absorber tube clearance. Replace any parts that appears worn or damaged.
5. Reverse Steps 1-3 to assemble the shock absorber. Make sure the retaining rings are seated correctly in the shock absorber tube.

Shock Absorber Disassembly/ Reassembly (1975-on)

1975-1983

Refer to **Figure 50** for this procedure.

1. Remove the tube cap (1, **Figure 50**).
2. Remove the spring (5).
3. Pour the oil out of the fork and discard it. Pump the fork several times by hand to expel most of the remaining oil.
4. Remove the screw (6) and washer (7) at the bottom of the slider and pull the fork tube (2) out of the slider (8).
5. Remove the oil lock (12) from the shock absorber tube (9) and remove the shock absorber from the fork tube.
6. Slide the boot off of the slider.

NOTE
Step 7 and Step 8 are required only if the oil seal is worn and requires replacement.

7. Remove the oil seal lock ring (13).

CAUTION
During the next step, use a dull screwdriver blade to remove the oil seal. Do not damage the outer or inner surface of the slider.

8. Pry the oil seal out of the slider with a screwdriver.
9. Inspect the fork assembly as described in this chapter.
10. Install by reversing these removal steps, noting the following.
11. Lightly grease the outside of the new oil seal. Then install the oil seal by pushing it squarely in the fork tube with a suitable size socket. Secure the oil seal with the lock ring (13).

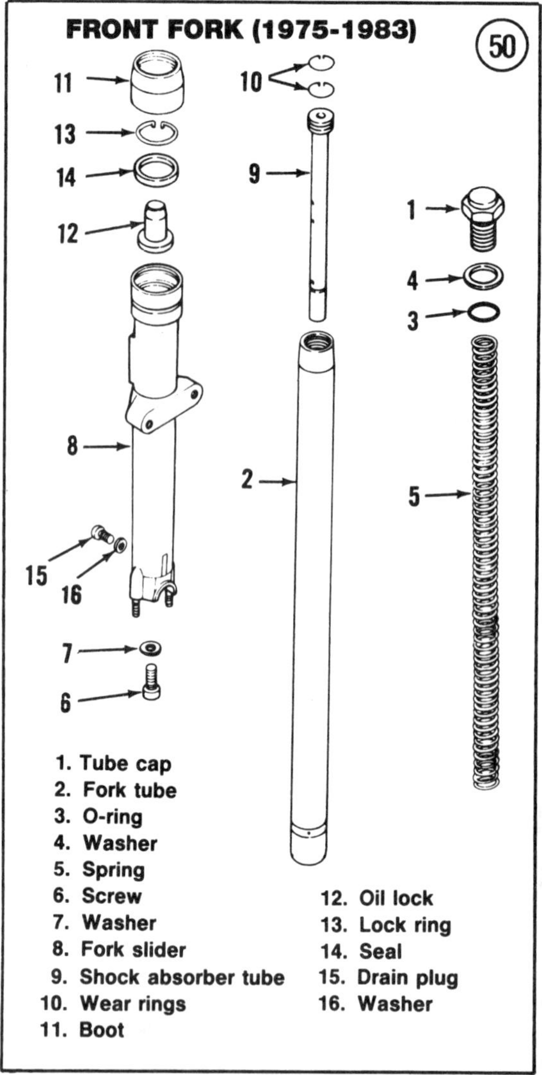

12. To prevent the shock absorber tube from turning when tightening the Allen bolt (6), perform the following:
    a. Install the fork tube (2) and shock absorber tube (9) into the slider.
    b. Temporarily install the spring (5) and fork cap (1) to tension the shock absorber tube.
    c. Install the Allen bolt (6) and washer (7). Tighten the Allen bolt securely.
    d. Remove the fork cap (1) and spring (5).
13. Fill each fork tube with the correct type and amount of fork oil. See Chapter Three.

NOTE
To measure the correct amount of fluid, use a plastic baby bottle. These have measurements in fluid ounces (oz.) and cubic centimeters (cc) on the side.

(51) **FRONT FORK (1984-1985)**

1. Fork tube	11. Shock absorber tube
2. Fork slider	12. Piston ring
3. Cap bolt	13. Oil lock
4. Washer	14. Bolt
5. O-ring	15. Washer
6. Dust seal	16. Bushing
7. Lock ring	17. Bushing
8. Oil seal	18. Rebound spring
9. Spacer seal	19. Drain plug
10. Spring	20. Washer

1984-1985

NOTE
The Harley-Davidson fork seal and bushing tool (HD-34190) is required to reassemble the fork tube.

Refer to **Figure 51** for this procedure.

1. Loosen but do not remove the Allen bolt (14, **Figure 51**).
2. Remove the fork cap bolt (3) and washer (4).
3. Remove the fork spring (10).
4. Pour the oil out of the fork and discard it. Pump the fork several times by hand to expel most of the remaining oil.
5. Remove the dust seal (6).
6. Remove the oil seal lock ring (7).
7. Remove the Allen bolt (14) and washer (15) at the bottom of the slider.
8. The upper bushing (17) is installed in the slider with a slight interference fit. Remove the upper bushing along with the spacer seal (9) and oil seal (8) by pulling up on the fork tube so that the lower bushing (16) hits against the upper bushing (17). Repeat this hammer type action until the fork tube is free.
9. Insert a small diameter rod through the bottom of the fork tube and push the shock absorber tube out of the fork tube.
10. If necessary, slide the lower bushing (16) off of the fork tube.
11. Inspect the fork assembly as described in this chapter.
12. Install the shock absorber tube (11) into the fork tube.
13. Install the spring (10) into the fork tube so that the small end of spring faces downward.
14. Install the rebound spring (18) onto the end of the shock absorber tube (11).
15. Install the fork tube (1) and shock absorber tube (11) into the slider. Temporarily install the spring (10) and fork cap bolt (3) to tension the shock absorber tube and prevent it from turning. Install the Allen bolt (14) and washer (15). Tighten the bolt securely.
16. Slide the lower bushing (16), spacer seal (9) and oil seal (8) down the fork tube. Make sure the dished side of the spacer seal faces downward and that the lettering on the oil seal faces upward.
17. Install the fork seal and bushing tool HD-34190 over the fork tube. Push the bushing (16), spacer seal (9) and oil seal (8) into the slider by lightly ramming the parts with the installation tool.
18. Install the lock ring (7).
19. Install the dust seal (6).
20. Fill each fork tube with the correct type and amount of fork oil. See Chapter Three.

NOTE
To measure the correct amount of fluid, use a plastic baby bottle. These have measurements in fluid ounces (oz.) and cubic centimeters (cc) on the side.

Inspection (All Models)

1. Thoroughly clean all parts in solvent and dry them.
2. Check upper fork tube exterior for scratches and straightness. If bent or scratched, it should be replaced.
3. Check the lower fork tube for dents or exterior damage that may cause the upper fork tube to hang up during riding. Replace if necessary.
4. Check the shock absorber tube for straightness.
5. Check the shock absorber tube piston ring(s) for wear or damage.
6. Check the slider for dents or exterior damage that may cause the fork tube to hang up during riding. Replace if necessary.
7. Inspect the O-ring in the fork cap. Replace if worn or damaged.
8. Any parts that are worn or damaged should be replaced. Simply cleaning and reinstalling unserviceable components will not improve performance of the front suspension.

Table 1 FRONT SUSPENSION SPECIFICATIONS

Front wheel runout	
Lateral (side-to-side)	
Spoked	1/32 in.
Cast	3/64 in.
Radial (up and down)	1/32 in.
Wheel bearing end play	0.004-0.018 in.

Table 2 FRONT SUSPENSION TIGHTENING TORQUES (1969-1978)

	ft.-lb.
Axle nut	50
Fork bracket bolts	20-25
Handlebar bolts	20
Fork slider nuts	11

Table 3 FRONT SUSPENSION TIGHTENING TORQUES (1979-1985)

Item	ft.-lb.
Front axle nut	50
Upper bracket pinch bolts	21-27
Lower bracket pinch bolts	30-35
Handlebar clamp screws	
1979-1983	20
1984-1985	12-15
Fork slider nuts	11

CHAPTER NINE

REAR SUSPENSION

This chapter includes repair and replacement procedures for the rear wheel, drive chain and rear suspension components.

Specifications (**Table 1**) and tightening torques (**Table 2** and **Table 3**) are found at the end of the chapter.

REAR WHEEL

Removal/Installation

1. Support the bike so that the rear wheel clears the ground.
2. Referring to **Figure 1**, loosen the drive chain adjusting locknuts and adjuster bolts.
3. *Drum brake models*: Loosen the rear brake adjusting nut (1, **Figure 2**).
4. Loosen the anchor bolt or nut (4, **Figure 2**), if so equipped.
5. Loosen the rear axle nut (**Figure 1**). Discard the cotter pin; never reuse a cotter pin.
6. Push the wheel as far forward as possible.
7. Remove the drive chain master link (**Figure 3**) and disconnect the drive chain.
8. Remove the axle from the left-hand side (**Figure 4**).
9. Remove the wheel as follows:
   a. *1959-1978:* Remove the axle spacer from the left-hand side. Then slide the wheel out of the brake assembly (**Figure 5**) and remove it.
   b. *1979-1985:* Allow wheel to drop down. Then remove the right-hand axle spacer and remove the rear wheel.

NOTE
On disc brake models, insert a piece of wood in the caliper in place of the disc.

That way, if the rear brake pedal is inadvertently pressed, the piston will not be forced out of the caliper. If this does happen, the caliper might have to be disassembled to reseat the piston and the system will have to be bled. By using the wood, bleeding the brake is not necessary after installing the wheel.

10. If the wheel is going to be off for any length of time, or if it is to be taken to a shop for repair, install the chain adjusters and axle spacers on the axle along with the axle nut to prevent losing any parts.
11. Install by reversing these removal steps, noting the following:
    a. Connect the master link clip so that its open end (**Figure 6**) faces away from the direction of chain travel.
    b. Adjust the drive chain as described in Chapter Three.
    c. Tighten the axle nut to specifications in **Table 2** or **Table 3**.
    d. Adjust the rear brake as described in Chapter Three.
    e. Rotate the wheel several times to make sure it rotates freely and that the brakes work properly.

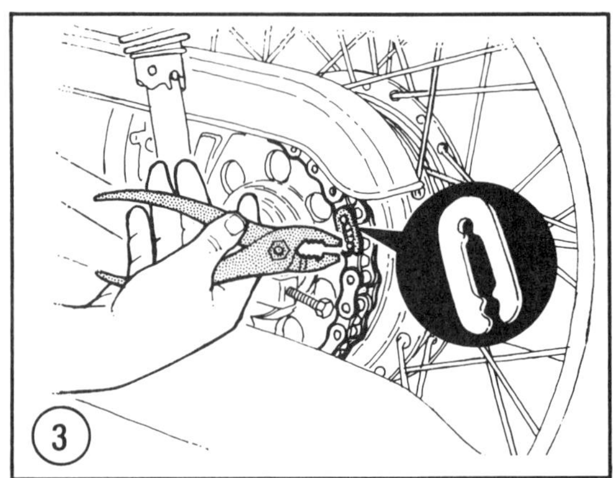

3

4

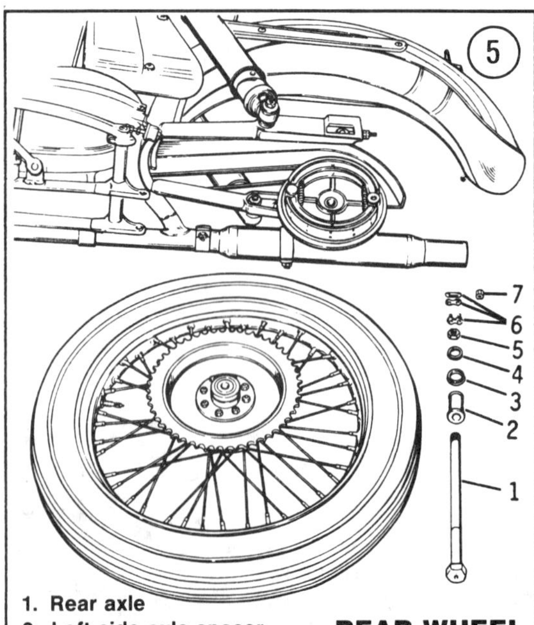

5

1. Rear axle
2. Left side axle spacer
3. Right side centering collar
4. Axle nut lockwasher
5. Axle nut
6. Master link
7. Rear brake adjusting nut

REAR WHEEL

Inspection

Measure the axial and radial runout of the wheel with a dial indicator as shown in **Figure** 7. The maximum allowable axial and radial runout is listed in **Table 1**. If the runout exceeds this dimension, check the wheel bearings. Some of this condition can be corrected on spoke wheels as described in Chapter Eight. If the wheel bearings are in good condition on cast wheels and no other cause can be found, the wheel will have to be replaced as it cannot be serviced.

Inspect the wheel for signs of cracks, fractures, dents or bends.

WARNING
Do not try to repair cast wheels as it will result in an unsafe riding condition.

REAR HUB

Disassembly/Reassembly (1959-1978)

Refer to **Figure 8** or **Figure 9** for this procedure.

1. Remove the rear wheel as described in this chapter.

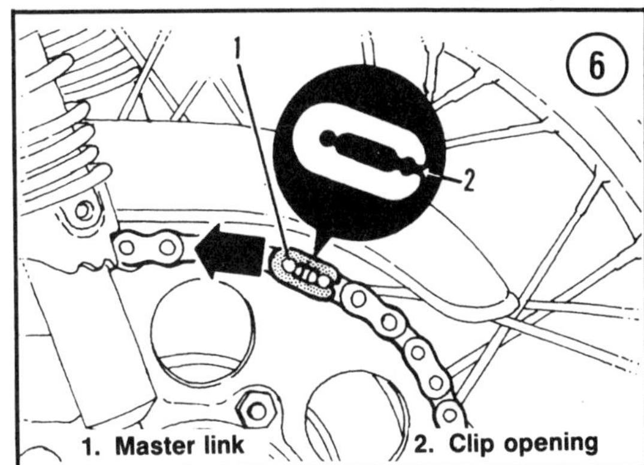

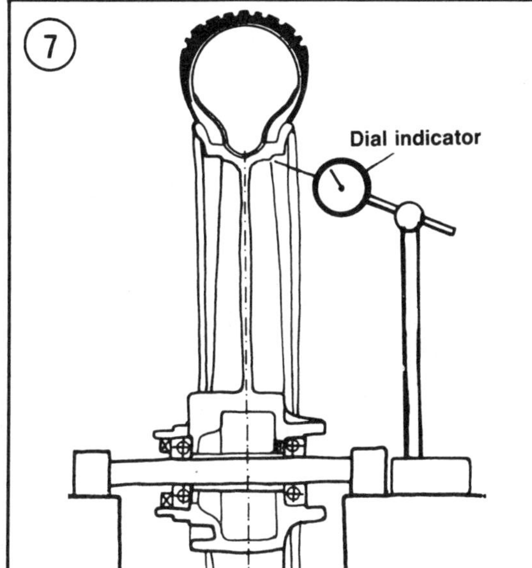

NOTE
The bearing locknut in the next step is staked into position.

2. Remove the bearing locknut.
3. Pry out the left-hand oil seal. See **Figure 10**.
4. Remove the left-hand spacer.
5. To remove a bearing, insert a soft aluminum or brass drift into the hub. Push the spacer to one side and place the drift on the inner race of the spacer flange. Tap the spacer flange and bearing out of the hub with a hammer, working around the perimeter of the spacer flange.
6. Remove the center spacer and the opposite bearing in the same manner.
7. Inspect the hub as described under *Inspection* in this chapter.
8. Assembly is the reverse of these steps, noting the following.
9. On non-sealed bearings, pack the bearings thoroughly with a good quality bearing grease. Work the grease between the balls thoroughly; turn the bearing by hand a couple of times to make sure the grease is distributed evenly inside the bearing.
10. Blow any dirt or foreign matter out of the hub prior to installing the bearings.
11. Install a hub bearing by driving the bearing squarely into place. Use a socket (**Figure 11**) that matches the outer bearing race diameter. Do not tap on the inner race or the bearing will be damaged. Be sure to tap the bearing until it is seated completely.
12. Install the oil seal by tapping it into position lightly with a plastic-tipped hammer.

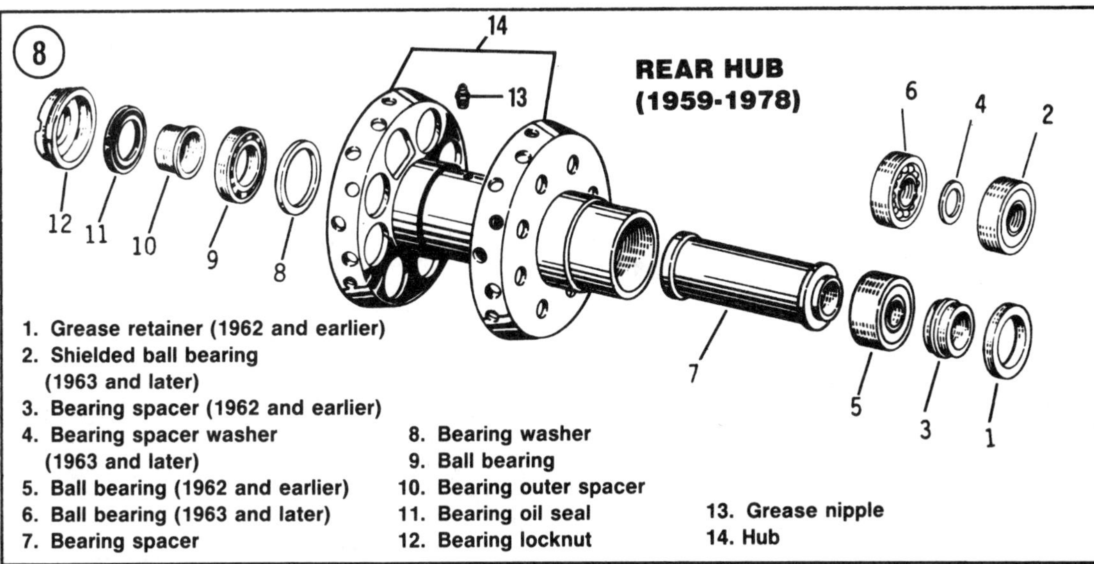

9

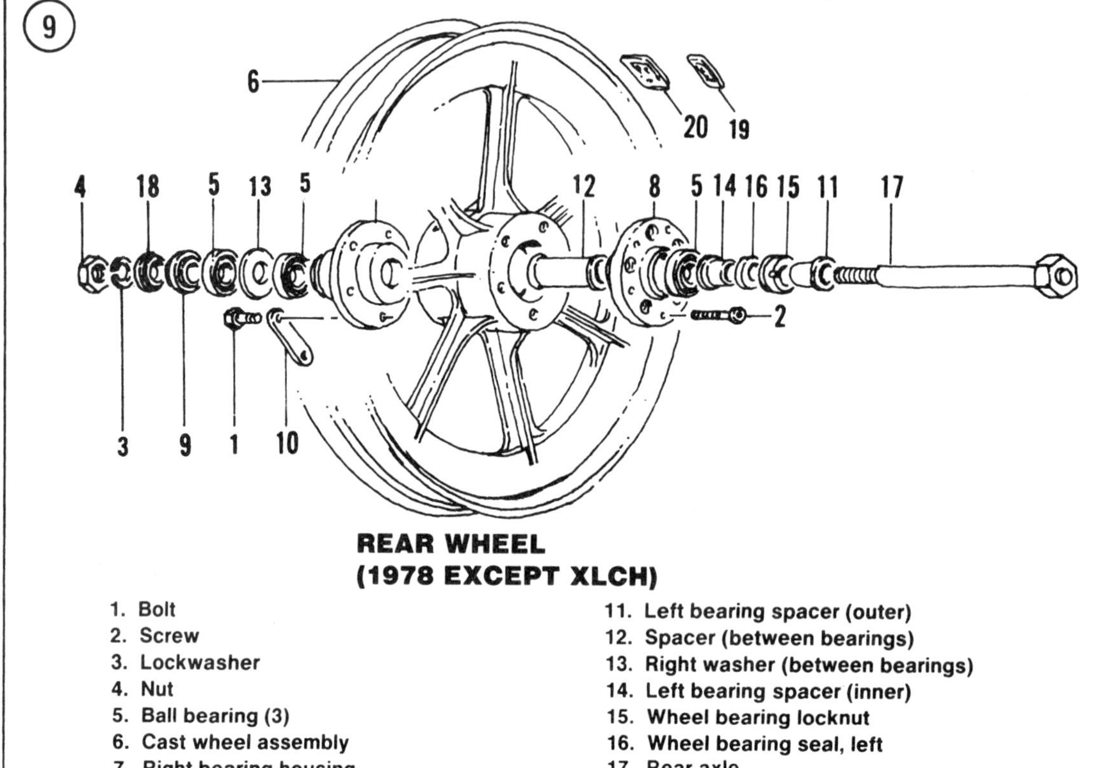

REAR WHEEL (1978 EXCEPT XLCH)

1. Bolt
2. Screw
3. Lockwasher
4. Nut
5. Ball bearing (3)
6. Cast wheel assembly
7. Right bearing housing
8. Left bearing housing
9. Right bearing spacer
10. Right bearing housing lockplate (4)
11. Left bearing spacer (outer)
12. Spacer (between bearings)
13. Right washer (between bearings)
14. Left bearing spacer (inner)
15. Wheel bearing locknut
16. Wheel bearing seal, left
17. Rear axle
18. Axle collar
19. Wheel weight (1/2 ounce)
20. Wheel weight (1 ounce)

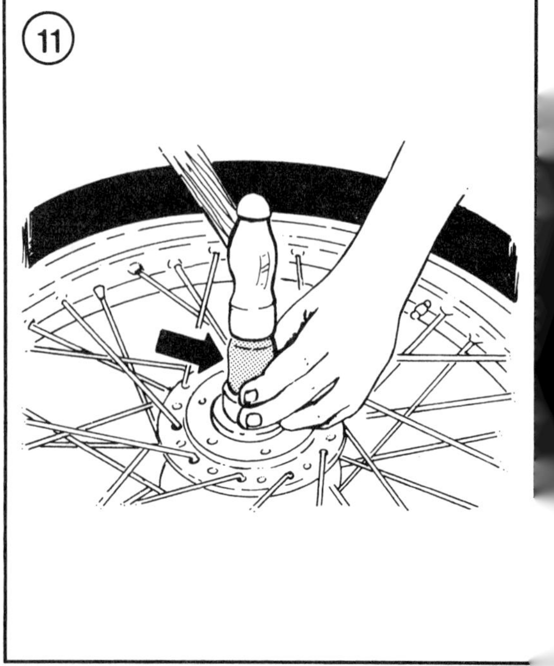

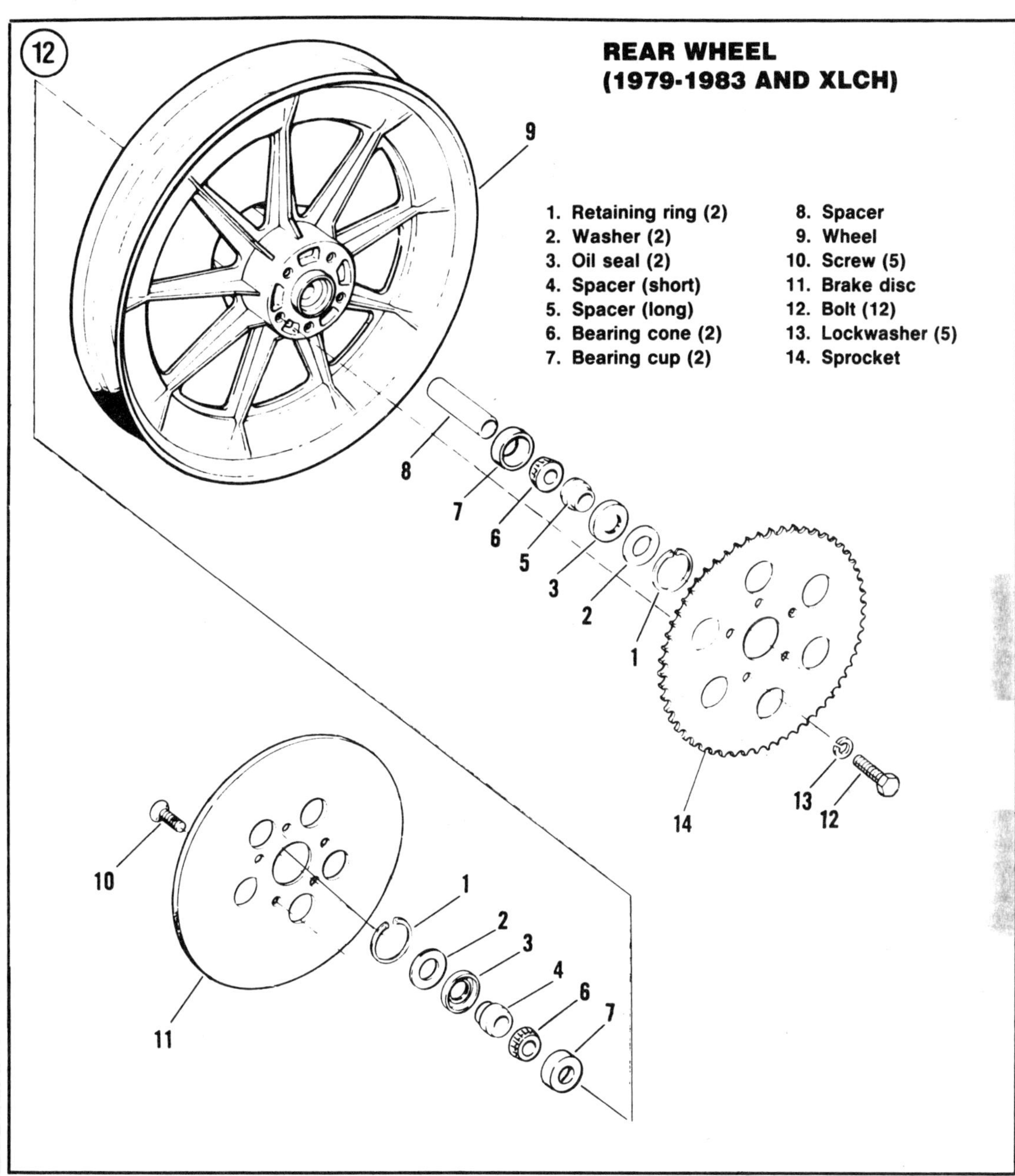

Disassembly/Reassembly (Cast Wheels, 1979-1985)

Refer to **Figure 12** (1979-1983) or **Figure 13** (1984-1985) for this procedure.

1. Remove the rear wheel as described in this chapter.
2. Remove the brake disc as described in Chapter Ten.
3. Remove the driven sprocket as described in this chapter.
4. *1979-1983:* Remove the circlip and washer on both sides of the hub.

NOTE
When removing the spacers in Step 5, note that the spacers are of different lengths. Tag each spacer so that it can be reinstalled in its original position.

5. Remove the left- and right-hand spacers.
6. Pry out the oil seals. See **Figure 10**.

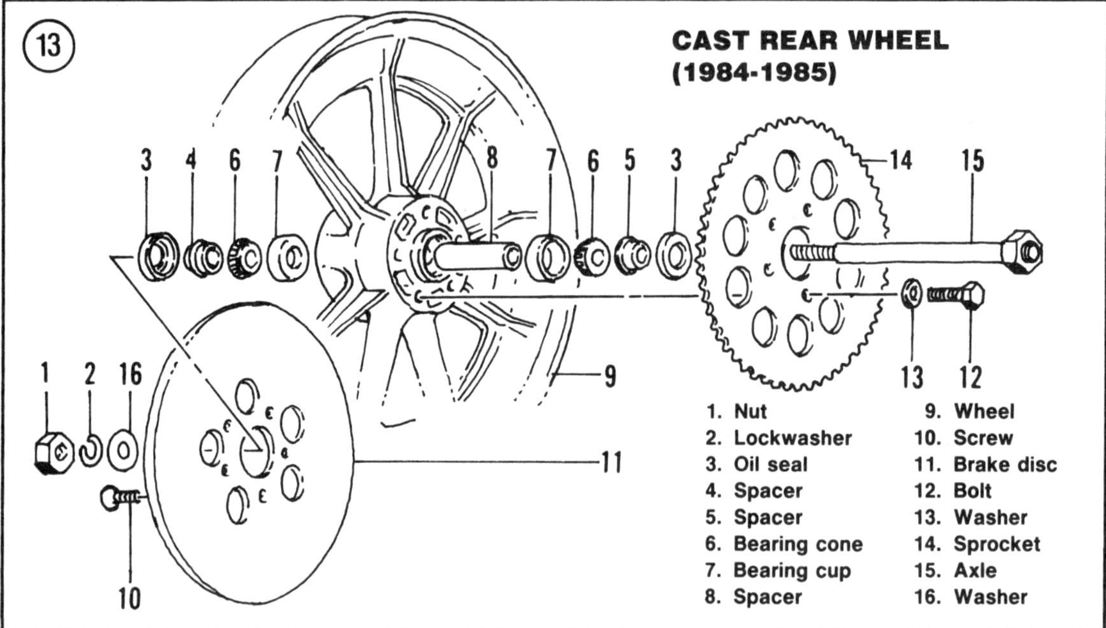

7. Tag the left- and right-hand bearings and remove them.
8. Visually check the bearing cups for cracks, deep scoring and excessive wear. If these conditions are present, remove the bearing cups with a wheel bearing race remover.

NOTE
A press will be required to install new bearing cups.

9. If the bearing cups were removed, remove the center spacer.
10. Inspect the hub as described under *Inspection* in this chapter.
11. Assembly is the reverse of these steps, noting the following.
12. If the bearing cups were removed, have them installed by a Harley-Davidson dealer or machine shop.
13. Lubricate the bearing cups with a high-quality wheel bearing grease.
14. Lubricate the bearing cones. Work the grease between the balls thoroughly; turn the bearing by hand a couple of times to make sure the grease is distributed evenly inside the bearing.
15. Install new oil seals. Install them so that their top surface is 3/16-1/4 in. below the outer surface of the hub. See **Figure 11**.
16. Install the driven sprocket as described in this chapter.
17. Install the rear brake disc as described in Chapter Ten.

Disassembly/Reassembly (Laced Wheels, 1979-1985)

Refer to **Figure 14** (1979-1983) or **Figure 15** (1984-1985) for this procedure.
1. Remove the rear wheel as described in this chapter.
2. Remove the brake disc as described in Chapter Ten.
3. Remove the driven sprocket as described in this chapter.
4. *1979-1983*: Remove the circlip and washer on both sides of the hub.

NOTE
When removing the spacers in Step 5, note that the spacers are of different lengths. Tag each spacer so that it can be reinstalled in its original position.

5. Remove the left- and right-hand spacers.
6. Pry out the oil seals. See **Figure 10**.
7. To remove a bearing, insert a soft aluminum or brass drift into the hub. Push the spacer to one side and place the drift on the inner race of the spacer flange. Tap the spacer flange and bearing out of the hub with a hammer working around the perimeter of the spacer flange.
8. If the bearing cups were removed, remove the center spacer.
9. Inspect the hub as described under *Inspection* in this chapter.

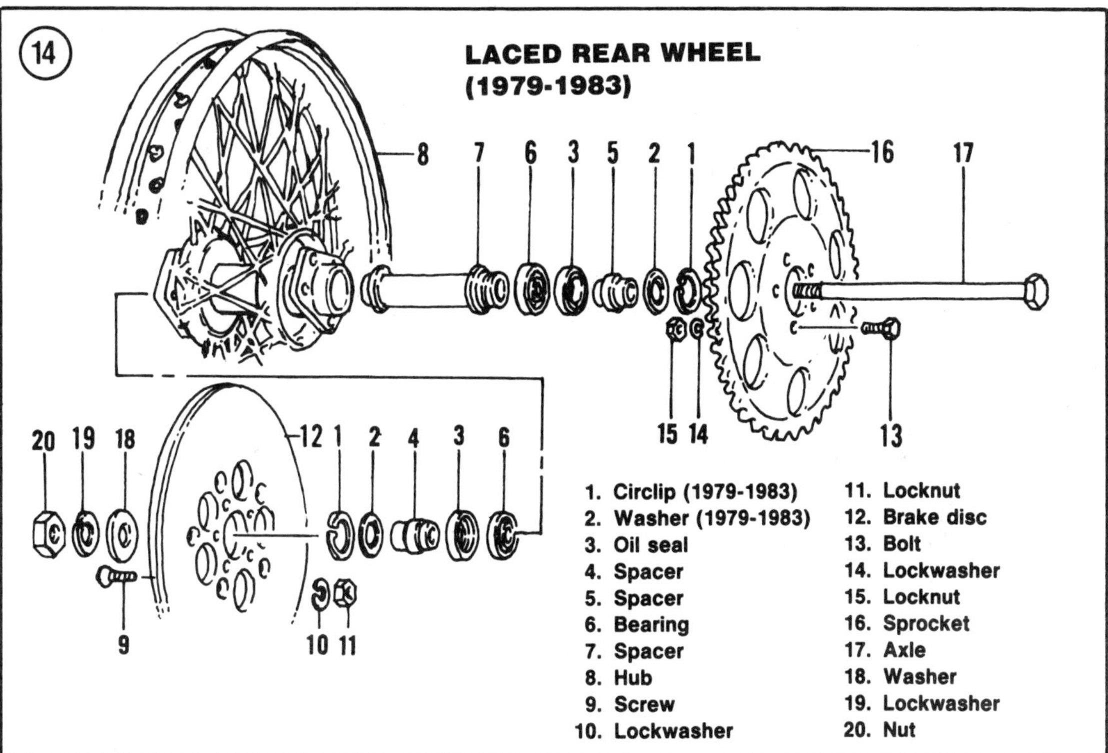

(14)

LACED REAR WHEEL (1979-1983)

1. Circlip (1979-1983)
2. Washer (1979-1983)
3. Oil seal
4. Spacer
5. Spacer
6. Bearing
7. Spacer
8. Hub
9. Screw
10. Lockwasher
11. Locknut
12. Brake disc
13. Bolt
14. Lockwasher
15. Locknut
16. Sprocket
17. Axle
18. Washer
19. Lockwasher
20. Nut

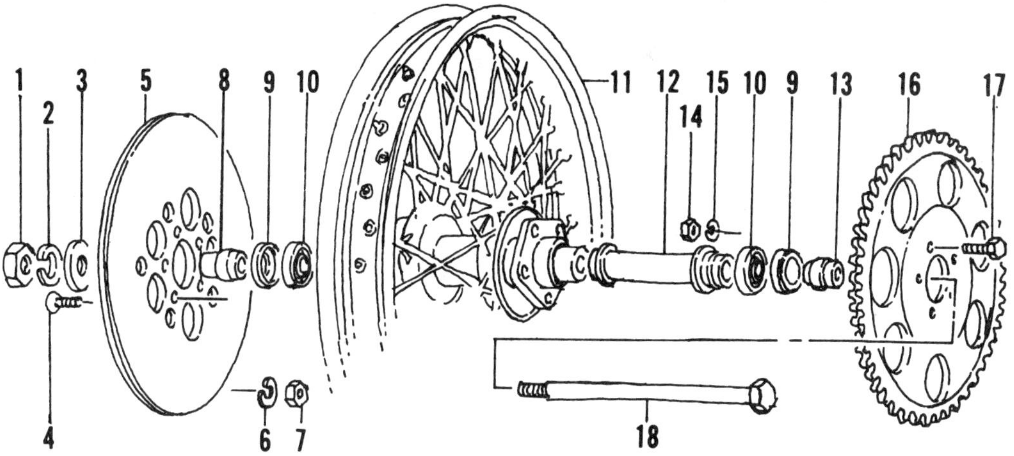

LACED REAR WHEEL (1984-1985)

1. Nut
2. Lockwasher
3. Washer
4. Screw
5. Brake disc
6. Lockwasher
7. Nut
8. Left spacer (short)
9. Oil seal
10. Bearing
11. Wheel assembly
12. Spacer
13. Right spacer (long)
14. Nut
15. Lockwasher
16. Sprocket
17. Bolt
18. Rear axle

(15)

10. Assembly is the reverse of these steps, noting the following.
11. On non-sealed bearings, pack the bearings thoroughly with a good quality bearing grease. Work the grease between the balls thoroughly; turn the bearing by hand a couple of times to make sure the grease is distributed evenly inside the bearing.
12. Blow any dirt or foreign matter out of the hub prior to installing the bearings.
13. Install hub bearings by driving the bearing squarely into place. Use a socket (**Figure 11**) that matches the outer bearing race diameter. Do not tap on the inner race or the bearing will be damaged. Be sure to tap the bearing until it is seated completely.
14. Install new oil seals. Install them so that their top surface is 3/16-1/4 in. below the outer surface of the hub. See **Figure 11**.
15. Install the driven sprocket as described in this chapter.
16. Install the rear brake disc as described in Chapter Ten.

Inspection

WARNING
Do not spin bearings with compressed air while drying them. They may fly apart and cause serious injury.

1. Do not clean sealed bearings. If non-sealed bearings are installed, throughly clean them in solvent and dry with compressed air. Do *not* spin bearings with an air hose while drying.
2. Check bearings as follows:
   a. Turn each bearing by hand. Make sure bearings turn smoothly.
   b. On non-sealed bearings, check the balls for evidence of wear, pitting or excessive heat (bluish tint).
   c. Replace bearings if they do not turn smoothly or if they have noticeable play when turned by hand.
   d. When replacing bearings, be sure to take your old bearings along to ensure a perfect matchup. Always replace bearings in sets of 2, even though only one bearing may appear worn or damaged.
3. Clean the inside and outside of the hub with solvent. Dry with compressed air.
4. Check the axle for wear and straightness. Use V-blocks and a dial indicator as shown in **Figure 16**. If the runout is 0.008 in. or greater, the axle should be replaced.
5. Check the brake hub (**Figure 5**) on 1959-1978 models for any scoring or damage. If damage is apparent, refer to Chapter Ten for further inspection and service.

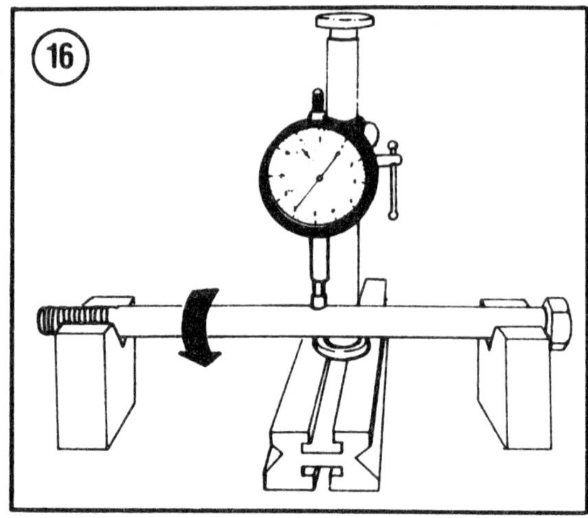

DRIVEN SPROCKET ASSEMBLY

Removal/Installation (1959-1978)

Refer to **Figure 5** for this procedure.
1. Remove the rear wheel as described in this chapter.
2. Remove the rear brake drum as described in Chapter Ten.
3. Place the rear brake drum in a vise.
4. Working from the brake shell side, chisel the heads off of each sprocket-to-brake drum rivet head. Remove the rivets with a drift punch.
5. Separate the rear sprocket from the brake drum.
6. Examine the brake drum as described in Chapter Ten. If the drum is okay, proceed to Step 7.

WARNING
Do not drill new holes more than once.

7. Check the brake drum rivet holes. If the holes are elongated or damaged, new rivet holes will have to be drilled in the brake drum. If new holes have to be drilled, proceed to Step 8. If the holes are okay, proceed to Step 9.
8. Drill new rivet holes in the brake drum as follows:
   a. Purchase a new sprocket, if required.
   b. The sprocket holes will be used as a template to drill the new holes.
   c. Place the sprocket over the brake drum.
   d. Align the sprocket holes midway between the original dowel pins and the old rivet holes.
   e. On all models, use a 9/64 in. drill.

NOTE
It is important to drill the holes as accurately as possible; clamp the

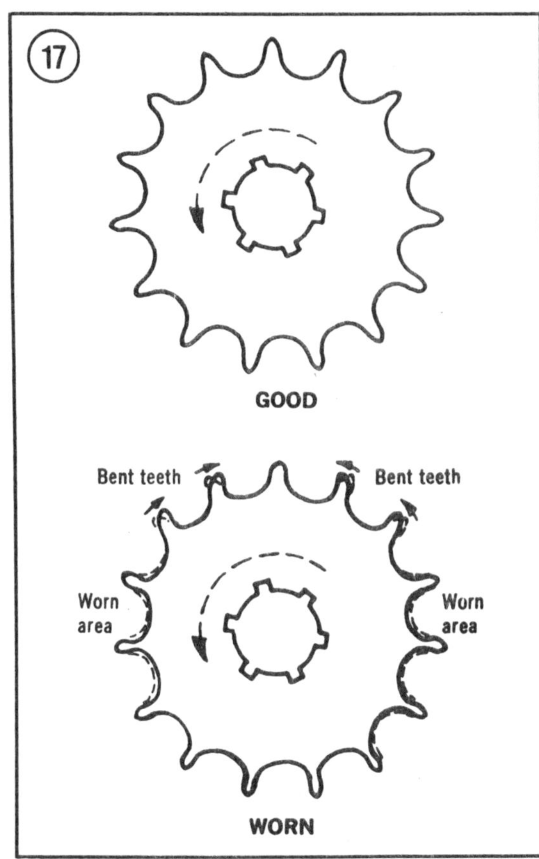

sprocket in place when drilling the holes.

NOTE
All holes are drilled from the brake shell side.

f. Drill the first hole. Then install a new rivet. Do not set rivet heads at this point.
g. Drill the second hole directly opposite the first hole. Install a new rivet as in Step "f".
h. Drill the remaining rivet holes.
i. Remove the 2 rivets and separate the sprocket from the brake drum.
j. Remove all burrs from the new holes.

9. Drill new dowel pin holes as follows:
   a. Assemble the sprocket and brake drum with 2 or 3 new rivets as previously described. Do not secure the rivets.
   b. Using the sprocket as a template, drill the 4 dowel pin holes with a 3/16 in. drill.
   c. Remove the rivets and separate the sprocket from the brake drum.
   d. Remove all burrs from the new holes.

NOTE
The dowel pins and rivets are installed from the brake shell side.

10. Install sprocket over brake hub. Align the new dowel pin holes and install the new dowel pins.
11. Install the new rivets and set them securely.

Removal/Installation (1979-On)

1. Remove the rear wheel as described in this chapter.
2. Remove the bolts and nuts securing the sprocket to the hub and remove the sprocket. See **Figure 9**, **Figure 12**, **Figure 13**, **Figure 14** or **Figure 15**.
3. Remove any sprocket spacer as required.
4. Installation is the reverse of these steps. Tighten the sprocket bolts to specifications in **Table 3**.

Inspection

Inspect the sprocket teeth. If the teeth are visibly worn (**Figure 17**), replace both the drive and driven sprockets and the drive chain. Never replace any one sprocket or chain as a separate item; worn parts will cause rapid wear of the new component. Refer to *Drive Chain Adjustment* in Chapter Three for additional information.

DRIVE CHAIN

Removal/Installation

1. Loosen the rear axle nut, chain adjuster nuts and the anchor bolt as described under *Rear Wheel Removal/Instalation* in this chapter.
2. Push the rear wheel as far forward in the swing arm as possible (**Figure 18**).
3. Turn the rear wheel and locate the drive chain master link on the rear sprocket.
4. Remove the master link spring clip (**Figure 19**) and separate the chain.
5. If installing a new drive chain, connect the new chain to the old chain with the old master link. Pull the new chain through the front sprocket. If the

original chain is to be reinstalled, tie a piece of wire approximately 20 inches long to the drive chain. Pull the chain so that the wire is routed around the front sprocket. Disconnect the wire from the chain so that it can be used to route the chain during installation.

6. Install by reversing these removal steps, noting the following:
   a. Install a new drive chain master link spring clip with the closed end facing in the direction of chain travel (**Figure 20**).
   b. Adjust the drive chain as described in Chapter Three.
   c. Tighten the axle nut to the torque values in **Table** 2 or **Table 3**.
   d. Rotate the wheel several times to make sure it rotates smoothly. Apply the brake several times to make sure it operates correctly.
   e. Adjust the rear brake as described in Chapter Three.

Lubrication

For lubrication of the drive chain, refer to Chapter Three.

WHEEL BALANCING

For complete information refer to *Wheel Balancing* in Chapter Eight.

TIRE CHANGING

Refer to *Tire Changing* in Chapter Eight.

REAR SWING ARM

Removal/Installation (1959-1981)

Refer to **Figure 21** for this procedure.

1. Support the bike so that the rear wheel is off the ground.
2. Remove the mufflers as described in Chapter Six.
3. Remove the rear wheel as described in this chapter.
4. Remove the lower mounting bolts and lockwashers securing the shock absorbers. Do not remove the shock absorber units. Remove the drive chain guard.
5. Disconnect the brake rod from the brake lever.

> NOTE
> *Before removing the swing arm, check its condition by grasping the swing arm on both sides and trying to move it from side to side. If the free play is excessive, replace the swing arm bearings as described under **Rear Swing Arm Bearings Replacement** in this chapter. Harley Davidson does not provide play specifications.*

6. Remove the pivot bolt (12, **Figure 21**) and the bearing lockwasher (13).
7. Pull back on the drive chain and slide the swing arm assembly away from the frame and remove it.
8. Install by reversing these removal steps, noting the following.

> NOTE
> *Be sure to slide the swing arm through the drive chain—the chain **must** be on the inside of the swing arm.*

9. Coat the swing arm pivot shaft thoroughly with bearing grease before installation.
10. Tighten the swing arm pivot shaft as follows:
   a. Loosen the right-hand bearing locknut (8, **Figure 21**).
   b. After swing arm is installed on bike, lift rear end with a spring scale. Note force required to lift swing arm to a horizontal position.

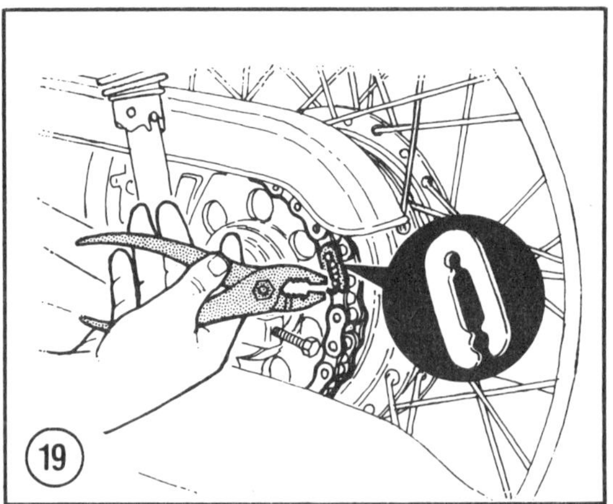

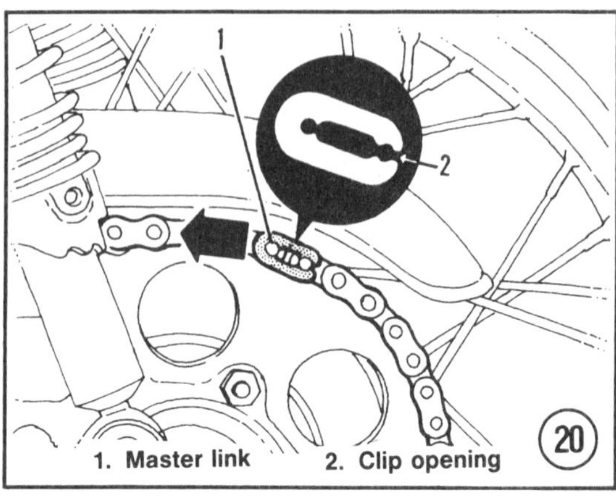

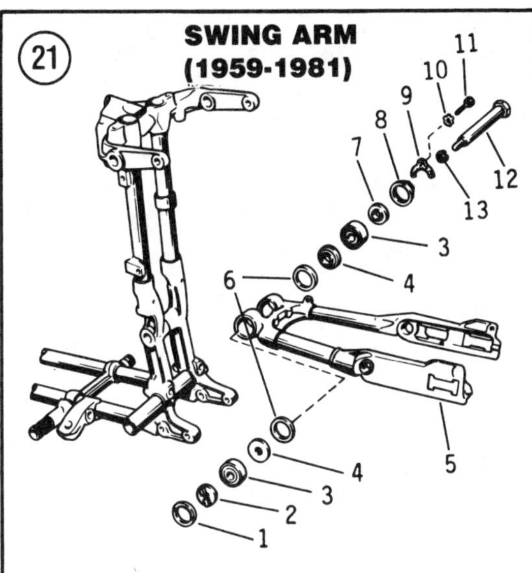

1. Left bearing locknut
2. Pivot bolt nut
3. Bearings
4. Bearing inner spacers
5. Rear fork (swing arm)
6. Bearing shields
7. Outer spacer
8. Right bearing locknut
9. Lockwasher
10. Lockwasher
11. Bearing screw
12. Pivot bolt
13. Bearing lockwasher

c. Tighten the right bearing locknut (8, **Figure 21**) to provide an additional 1-2 pounds drag on the bearing. For example, if 4 pounds is required to lift the swing arm (a), tighten the right bearing locknut until 5-6 pounds force is required.

d. Install the right bearing locknut lockwasher, washer and screw.

Removal/Installation (1982-1985)

Refer to **Figure 22** for this procedure.

1. Remove the rear wheel as described in this chapter.
2. Disconnect all brake hose clamps at the swing arm (A, **Figure 23**).
3. Remove the rear brake caliper from the swing arm as described in Chapter Ten.

NOTE
It is not necessary to disconnect the hydraulic lines. Instead, hang the brake caliper from the frame with wire or bunji cords.

4. Remove the bolts or nuts securing the shock absorbers to the swing arm (B, **Figure 23**) and pull the shock absorbers clear of the mounts.
5. Remove the fasteners securing the rear chain guard and remove the guard. Remove the front chain guard on 1982 models (**Figure 24**).

9

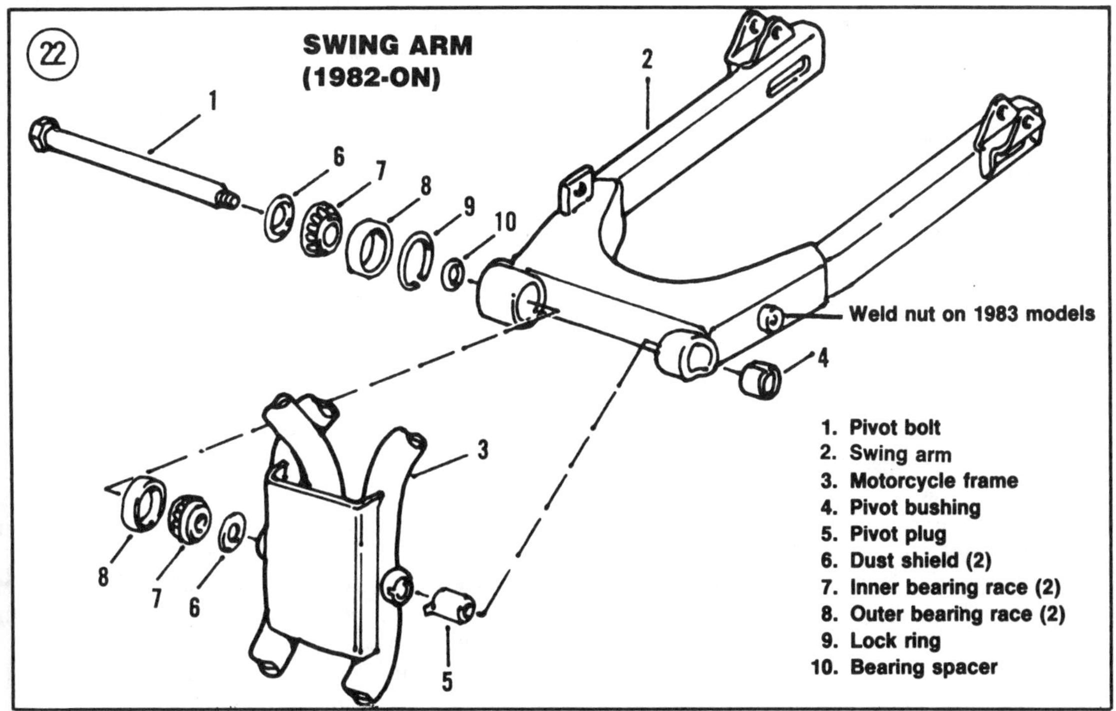

NOTE
Before removing the swing arm, check its condition by grasping the swing arm on both sides and trying to move it from side to side. If the free play is excessive, replace the swing arm bearings as described under (bold)Rear Swing Arm Bearing Replacement(end) in this chapter.

6. Loosen and remove the swing arm pivot bolt (**Figure 25**).
7. Slide the swing arm out of the frame. Make sure the bearings do not drop to the ground.

CAUTION
Keep all bearing components together. If they fall out, reinstall them into their correct assembled position. Wear patterns have developed on these parts and rapid and serious wear may occur if the components are intermixed and not installed as removed.

8. Remove the pivot plug (5, **Figure 22**) from the swing arm.
9. Noting the previous caution, remove the dust shields (6), inner bearing race (7), outer bearing race (8) and bearing spacer (10).
10. Install by reversing these removal steps, noting the following.

NOTE
*Be sure to slide the swing arm through the drive chain—the chain **must** be on the inside of the swing arm.*

11. Coat the swing arm pivot shaft thoroughly with bearing grease before installation.
12. Lubricate the bearings with heavy chassis or wheel bearing grease.
13. Install the bearing spacer (10) between the right-hand side bearings (7).

CAUTION
The bearing spacer must be installed between the bearings as described in Step 13 or the bearings will fail during operation.

14. Install new dust shields (6) with their lip side positioned in toward the inner bearing races.
15. Install the pivot plug (5) into the pivot bushing (4) in the swing arm.
16. Slide the swing arm into position in the frame. Align the ears on the pivot plug with the slots in the frame (3).
17. Install the pivot bolt from the right-hand side. Tighten the bolt to specifications in **Table 3**.

18. Tighten the lower shock absorber bolts or nut securely.
19. Adjust the drive chain and rear brake as described in Chapter Three.

Rear Swing Arm Bearing Replacement

1959-1981

Refer to **Figure 21** for this procedure.

1. Secure the swing arm in a vise with soft jaws.
2. Remove the screws securing the right-hand bearing lockwasher (9, **Figure 21**) and remove it.
3. Remove the right-hand bearing locknut (8) and the outer spacer (7).
4. Using a punch, turn out the left-hand bearing locknut (1). Then remove the the pivot bolt nut (2).
5. Tap the left-hand bearing (3) out with a soft aluminum or brass drift from the opposite end. Place the end of the drift on the bearing spacer. Then remove the spacer (4).
6. Drive out the left-hand bearing shield in the same manner.
7. Repeat Step 5 and Step 6 for the right-hand side.
8. Thoroughly clean out the inside of the swing arm with solvent and dry with compressed air.
9. Install the left-hand bearing shield (6) with a suitable size drift. Drive the shield in until it seats flush in the swing arm. Install the shield so that the shoulder faces in.
10. Install the left-hand bearing spacer (4) so that its shoulder faces in.
11. Coat the left-hand bearing (3) thoroughly with bearing grease.
12. Using a suitable size drift that fits over the outer bearing race, drive the left-hand bearing in until it is flush with the side of the swing arm.
13. Repeat Steps 9-12 for the right-hand side.
14. Install the right-hand outer bearing spacer with its shoulder facing in.
15. Install the right-hand bearing locknut (8) until it is snug, then back it out 1 turn.

16. Install the pivot bolt nut (2) on the left-hand side.
17. Install a new left-hand locknut (1). Tighten with a punch until snug. Stake the locknut in 3 places.

1982-1985

Refer to **Figure 22** for this procedure.

1. Secure the swing arm in a vise with soft jaws.

CAUTION
Tag each component when removed from the swing arm so they can be reinstalled in their original positions. Bearing components must not be intermixed.

2. Remove the following parts from the right-hand side in order:
   a. Inner and outer dust shields (6, **Figure 22**).
   b. Inner and outer bearing race (7 and (8).
   c. Bearings.

CAUTION
Unless replacement is required, do not remove the 2 outer bearing races or the pivot bushing. The complete bearing assembly must be replaced as a unit if any one bearing part is worn or damaged.

NOTE
Steps 3-9 require the use of a hydraulic press. Refer service to a Harley-Davidson dealer or machine shop. Do not attempt to drive the bearing races or pivot bushing out of the swing arm.

3. Press the outer bearing races out of the swing arm.
4. Remove and discard the lock/ring (9).
5. Press the right-hand pivot bushing out of the swing arm.
6. Thoroughly clean out the inside of the swing arm with solvent and dry with compressed air.
7. Install a new lock ring (9).
8. Press 2 new bearing races into position.

WARNING
Never reinstall an outer bearing race that has been removed. During removal it becomes slightly damaged and is no longer true to alignment. If installed, it will create swing arm alignment problems and unsafe riding conditions.

9. Press a new pivot bushing into the swing arm on the left-hand side.
10. Apply bearing grease to all parts.
11. Install the pivot plug into the pivot bushing.
12. Install the bearing and the bearing spacer in the order shown in **Figure 22**.

CAUTION
The bearing spacer must be installed between the inner bearing races during bearing installation or the bearings will fail during operation.

13. Install dust shields over the bearings. The dust shield lip must face in.

SHOCK ABSORBERS

The rear shocks are spring controlled and hydraulically damped. Spring preload can be adjusted on all models.

Spring Preload Adjustment

Refer to Chapter Three for complete details.

Removal/Installation

This procedure is easier if the rear shocks are removed and installed one at a time. The remaining unit will support the rear of the bike and maintain the correct relationship between the top and bottom mounts. If both shock absorbers must be removed at the same time, cut a piece of steel a few inches longer than the shock absorber and drill two holes in the steel the same distance apart as the bolt holes in a shock absorber. Install the steel support after one shock absorber is removed. This will allow the bike to be easily moved around until the shock absorbers are reinstalled or replaced.

1. Place the bike on the centerstand.

2A. *1959-1966:* Referring to **Figure 26**, perform the following:

   a. Loosen the cover clamp (19, **Figure 26**) and remove the top cover (3).
   b. Remove the upper and lower mounting stud nuts (1).
   c. On 1965 models, remove the stud cover (2).
   d. Remove the washers (4 or 5) and the upper and lower bushings (6).
   e. Slip the shock absorber from its mounting studs on the frame.

2B. *1967-1985:* Remove the upper and lower shock absorber bolts or nuts (**Figure 27**) and washers and remove the shock absorber.

3. Install by reversing these removal steps, noting the following:

   a. On 1959-1964 models, install shock absorbers so that letters "A" and "B" stamped on shock face to the rear. On 1965 and later models, shock absorbers may be installed either way.
   b. Torque the upper and lower bolts or nuts securely.

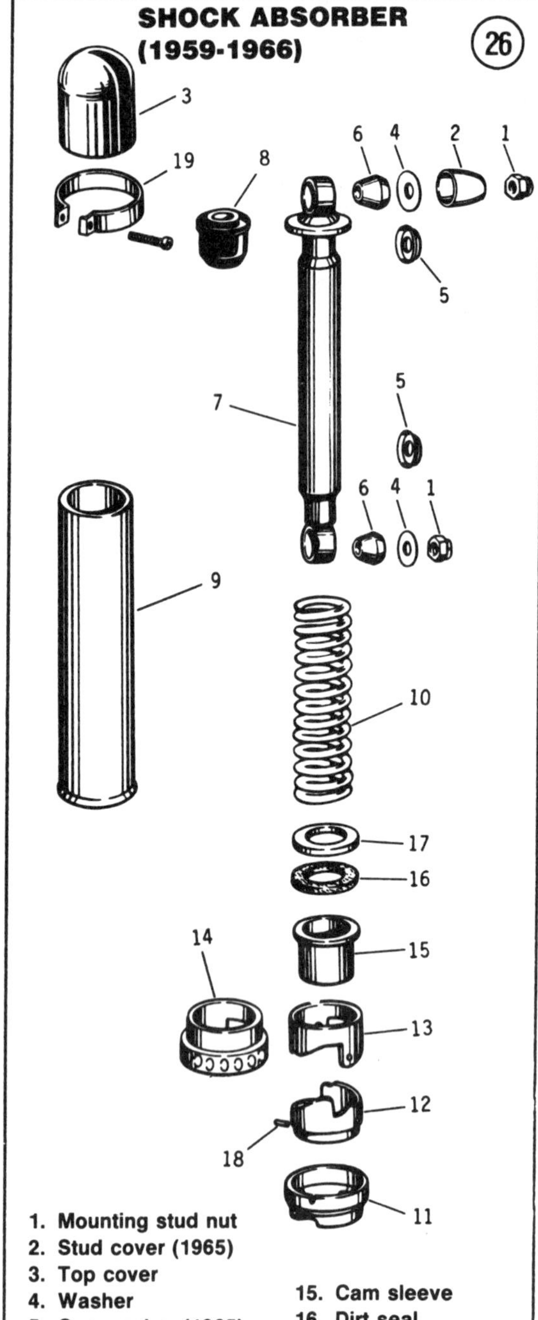

1. Mounting stud nut
2. Stud cover (1965)
3. Top cover
4. Washer
5. Cup washer (1965)
6. Bushing
7. Shock absorber
8. Bumper
9. Cover
10. Spring
11. Cam support
12. Lower cam
13. Spring rotating cam (1964)
14. Rotating cam (1965 and later)
15. Cam sleeve
16. Dirt seal
17. Spacer washer
18. Roll pin
19. Cover clamp

Disassembly/Reassembly

To disassemble the shock absorber, a spring compressor (HD-97010-52A) is required.

WARNING
Do not attempt to remove the shock absorber spring without a spring compressor (HD-97010-52A) or bodily injury may result.

1959-1966

Refer to **Figure 26** for this procedure.

1. Secure the spring compressor in a vise. Then attach the shock absorber to the compressor.
2. Install a spring compressor onto the shock absorber (**Figure 28**).
3. Compress the shock spring (10, **Figure 26**) enough to turn the lower shock eye 90° into the cam support slot (**Figure 28**).
4. Release spring pressure, then remove the shock absorber from the tool.
5. Remove the cam support (11).
6. Tap the lower end of the shock absorber and free the bumper (8) from its retaining flange inside the cover (9).

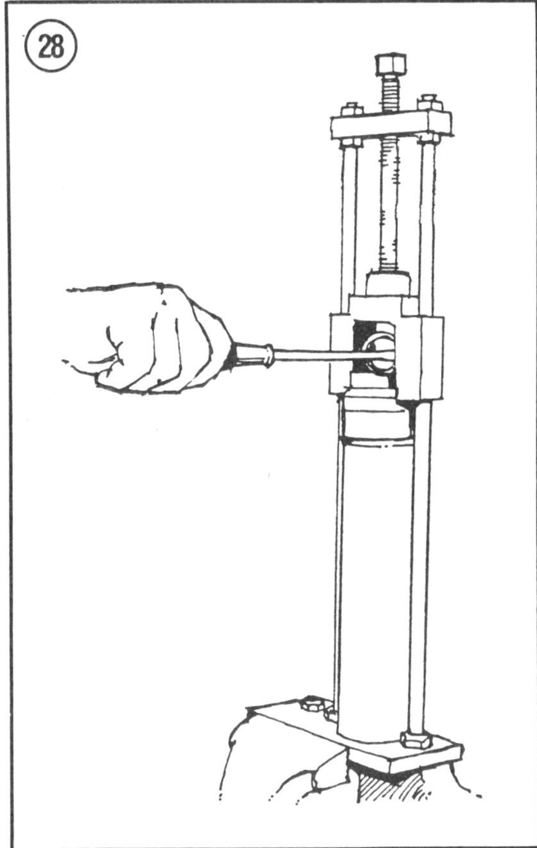

7. Remove the spring and shock absorber from the cover, then remove the following parts:
   a. Lower cam (12).
   b. Spring rotating cam (13 or 14).
   c. Cam sleeve (15).
   d. Dirt seal (16).
   e. Spacer washers (17).
8. Extend the shock absorber and remove the bumper (8).
9. Inspect the shock absorber as described in this chapter.
10. Assembly is the reverse of these steps, noting the following.
11. Lightly grease the cam sleeve and spring rotating cam before reassembly.
12. On 1959-1964 models, the cam support (11) marked "A" is for the left side assembly. On 1965 and later models, either slot may be used.

Disassembly/Assembly (1967-1985)

Refer to **Figure 29** (1967-1978) or **Figure 30** (1979-1985) for this procedure.

1. Remove the shock absorber as described in this chapter.
2. *1967-1978:* Perform the following:
   a. Remove the upper and lower rubber bushings.
   b. Remove the retaining ring (1, **Figure 29**) if so equipped.

WARNING
Do not attempt to disassemble the shock absorbers without using the proper spring compression tool.

3. Using a shock absorber spring compression tool, compress the shock absorber spring and remove the upper spring retainer. **Figure 28** shows the Harley-Davidson spring compressor (HD-97010-52A).
4. Release spring pressure, them remove the shock absorber assembly from tool.
5. Disassemble the shock absorber in the order shown in **Figure 29** or **Figure 30**.
6. Inspect the shock absorber as described in this chapter.
7. Assembly is the reverse of these steps, noting the following.
8. Lightly grease all cam parts before assembly.
9. Make sure cam lobes (8, **Figure 29**) on 1967-1978 models are positioned as shown in **Figure 29**.

Inspection

Inspect all parts for wear or damage. Pay particular attention to the following items.

1. Replace all rubber bushings that show signs of wear, damage or cracking.
2. Check the shock absorber for fluid leakage. Replace the shock body if leaking.

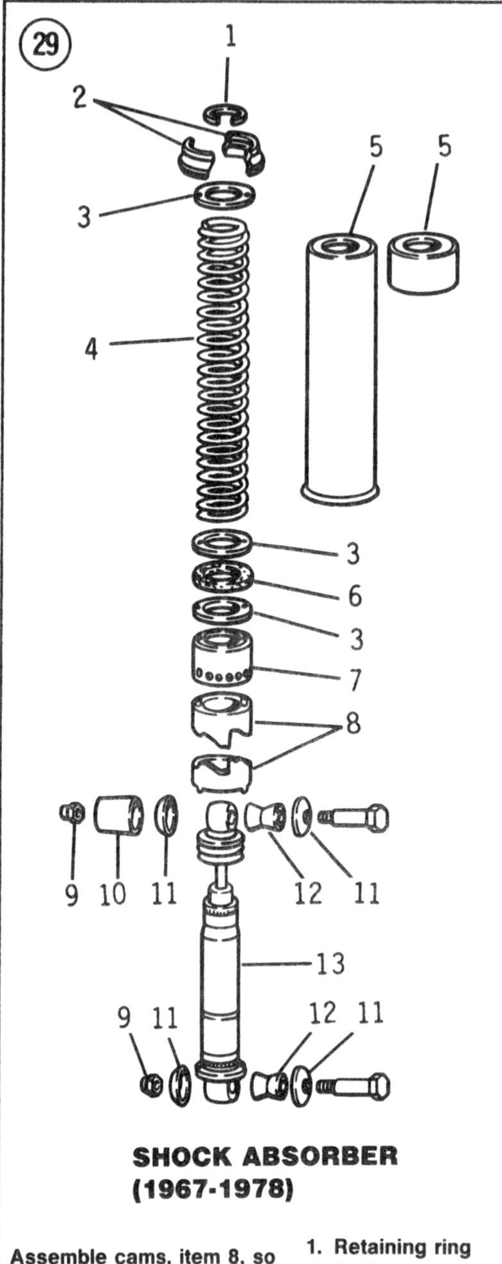

SHOCK ABSORBER (1967-1978)

Assemble cams, item 8, so that high lobes (with notches in tips) are next to each other as shown.

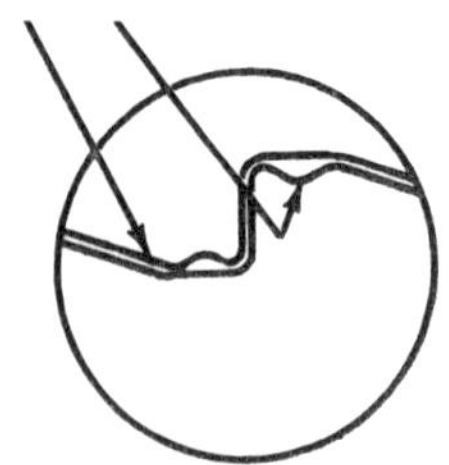

1. Retaining ring
2. Split key
3. Washer
4. Spring
5. Cover
6. Seal washer
7. Adjusting cup
8. Cam
9. Mounting stud nut
10. Stud cover
11. Cup washer
12. Rubber bushing
13. Shock absorber unit

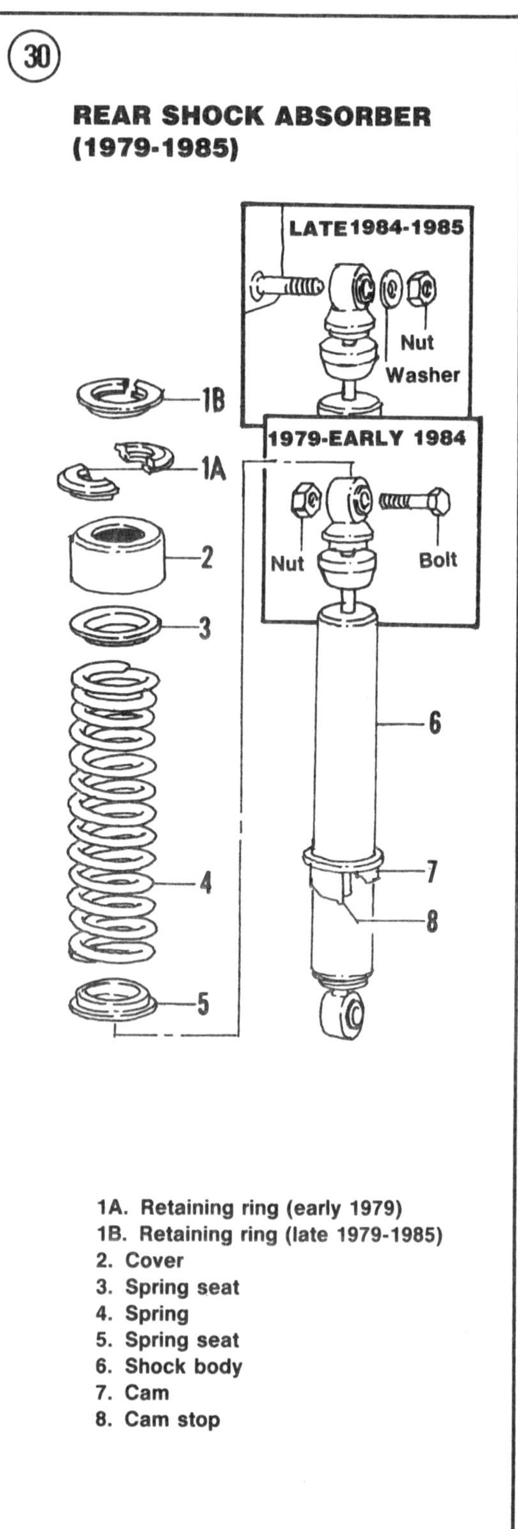

1A. Retaining ring (early 1979)
1B. Retaining ring (late 1979-1985)
2. Cover
3. Spring seat
4. Spring
5. Spring seat
6. Shock body
7. Cam
8. Cam stop

Table 1 REAR SUSPENSION SPECIFICATIONS

Rear wheel runout	
Axial (side-to-side)	
Spoked	1/32 in.
Cast	3/64 in.
Radial (up and down)	1/32 in.
Wheel bearing end play	0.004-0.018 in.

Table 2 REAR SUSPENSION TIGHTENING TORQUES (1959-1978)

	ft.-lb.
Rear axle nut	50
Sprocket mounting bolts	25
Pivot shaft	See text

Table 3 REAR SUSPENSION TIGHTENING TORQUES (1979-1985)

	ft.-lb.
Rear axle nut	60-65
Sprocket mounting bolts	
1979-1983	45-50
1984-1985	
Laced wheels	45-50
Cast wheels	50-55
Pivot shaft	
1979-1981	50
1982-1985	50

CHAPTER TEN

BRAKES

This chapter describes repair and replacement procedures for all brake components. Brake adjustments which are performed on a routine schedule are described in Chapter Three.

Brake specifications are listed in **Table 1**. **Tables 1-3** are at the end of the chapter.

DRUM BRAKES

A typical brake drum system constists of a brake drum, camshaft, pivot post, brake shoes and linings. See **Figure 1**.

FRONT DRUM BRAKES (1959-1972)

Disassembly

Refer to **Figure 2** for this procedure.

1. Remove the front wheel as described in Chapter Eight.
2. Disconnect the brake cable at the backing plate and remove the backing plate assembly.

NOTE
Before performing Step 3, mark the left and right shoes. If the shoes are to be reused, they must be installed in their original positions.

3. Remove the brake shoes (1, **Figure 2**) from the backing plate by pulling up on the center of each shoe as shown in **Figure 3**.

NOTE
Place a clean shop rag on the linings to protect them from oil and grease during removal.

4. Remove the return springs (2) and separate the brake shoes.
5. Loosen the nut (10) on the brake cam shaft (5). Remove the brake lever (9), cam (5) and washer (6).
6. Remove the pivot stud bolt (8) and washer and remove the pivot stud (4).

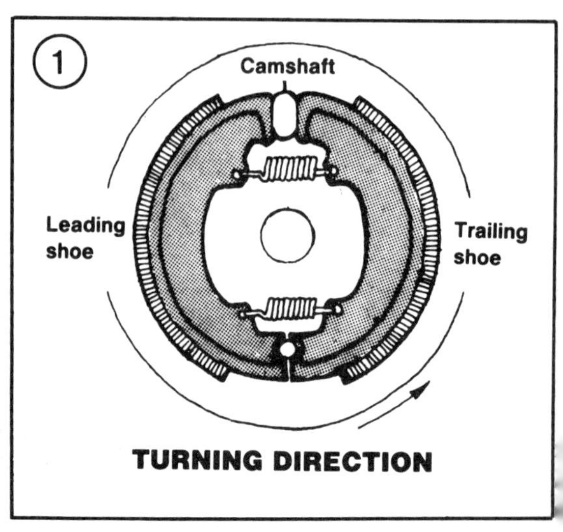

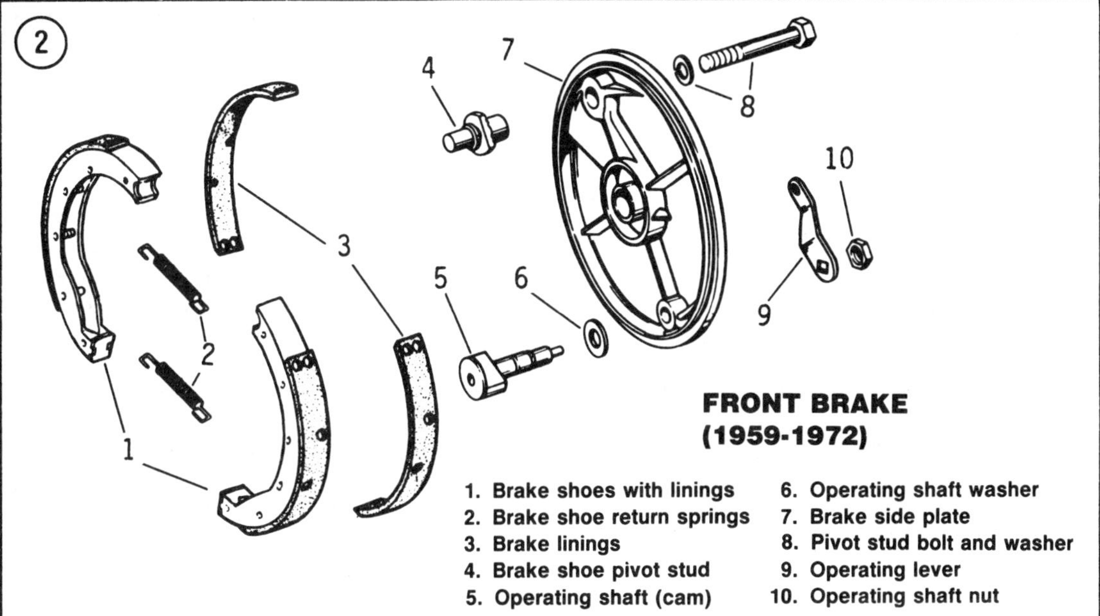

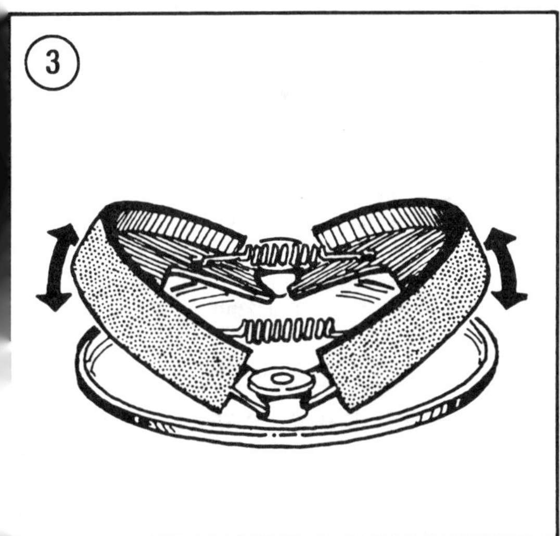

7. Inspect the brake assembly as described under *Inspection*.

Assembly

1. Assemble the brake by reversing the disassembly steps, noting the following.
2. Grease the pivot stud and brake cam posts with a light coat of molybdenum disulfide grease; avoid getting any grease on the brake plate where the linings come in contact with it.
3. Install the brake cam and washer into the backing plate. Install the brake lever and nut. Tighten the nut securely.
4. Install the pivot stud into the backing plate. Install the pivot stud screw and washer. Tighten the screw securely.

NOTE

If the old linings are being reinstalled, they must be installed in their original positions.

5. Hold the brake shoes in V-formation with the return springs attached and snap them in place on the brake backing plate.
6. Install the front wheel as described in Chapter Eight.
7. Adjust the front brakes as described in Chapter Three.

WARNING

Make sure the front brake operates correctly before riding the bike.

Inspection

WARNING

Do not inhale brake dust. It contains asbestos, which can cause lung damage. Don't clean brake parts with compressed air.

1. Thoroughly clean and dry all parts except the linings.
2. Check the contact surface of the drum for cracks, scoring, glaze or roughness. Remove light scoring and glaze with fine emery cloth. Remove all traces of emery when finished. If the brake drum is deeply scored, the brake drum/front hub

assembly (**Figure 4**) should be replaced as described in Chapter Eight.

3. Check the wheel bearing (5, **Figure 4**) in the hub on the brake shoe side. If the bearing's seal is damaged or leaking, grease could contaminate the brake shoes. If necessary, replace the bearing as described in Chapter Nine.

CAUTION
Before installing a brake drum that has been cleaned or sanded, check it for any traces of cuttings or other abrasives left from cleaning. If necessary, clean with lacquer thinner. In addition, do not touch the braking surface with your hands as this would contaminate it, thus reducing brake effectiveness.

CAUTION
Oil and grease on the drum surface should be cleaned with a clean rag soaked in lacquer thinner—do not use any solvent, such as mineral spirits, that may leave an oil residue.

NOTE
Riveted brake linings are used on all models.

4. Inspect the linings for imbedded foreign material. Dirt can be removed with a stiff wire brush. Check for traces of oil or grease; if contaminated, they must be replaced. Brake lining wear depends upon how close the rivet head is to the brake lining surface. Check each rivet-to-lining area for maximum wear. If necessary, the brake linings can be replaced as follows.

NOTE
Always replace brake linings in sets of two.

5. Before replacing brake linings, check the shoe web (**Figure 5**) for cracks or distortion. To check for distortion, lay the web on a flat surface, such as a piece of glass or surface plate. Check how close the web seats along the glass. If the web is twisted at any point, the shoe is bent and must be replaced.
6. Replace riveted brake linings as follows:
   a. Drill out the rivets. Match the drill bit to the rivet head as close as possible to prevent enlarging the rivet hole in the shoe web.

CAUTION
Do not attempt to punch out the rivets as this may distort the shoe web.

   b. With a steel brush, clean the brake lining surface thoroughly.
   c. Rivet the new linings to the brake shoes. It is important to start riveting from one end of the lining and work toward the other end to prevent buckling.
   d. Bevel the ends of both brake shoes with a file (**Figure 6**).

7. Check the fit of the brake cam and pivot stud in the backing plate. If excessive play is detected, replace worn or damaged parts as required.
8. Inspect the brake shoe return springs for wear. If they are stretched, they will not fully retract the brake shoes from the drum, resulting in a

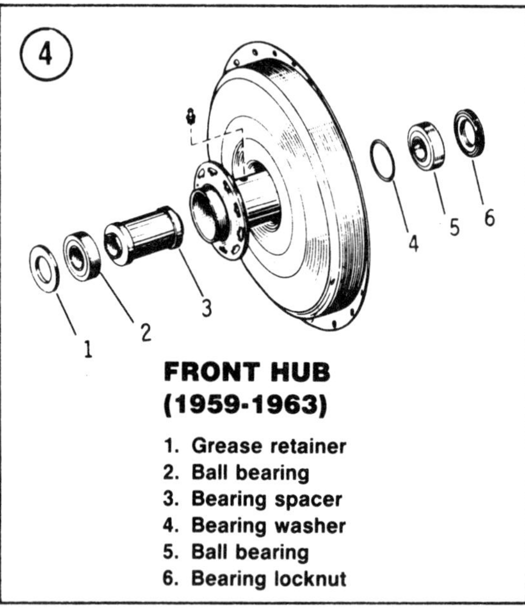

FRONT HUB (1959-1963)

1. Grease retainer
2. Ball bearing
3. Bearing spacer
4. Bearing washer
5. Ball bearing
6. Bearing locknut

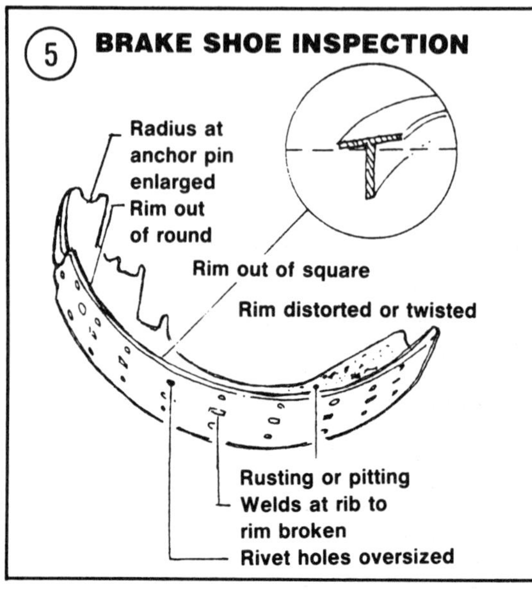

power-robbing drag on the drum and premature wear of the linings. Also check springs for rust. Replace as necessary; always replace as a pair.

REAR DRUM BRAKES (1959-1978)

Disassembly

Refer to **Figure 7** for this procedure.

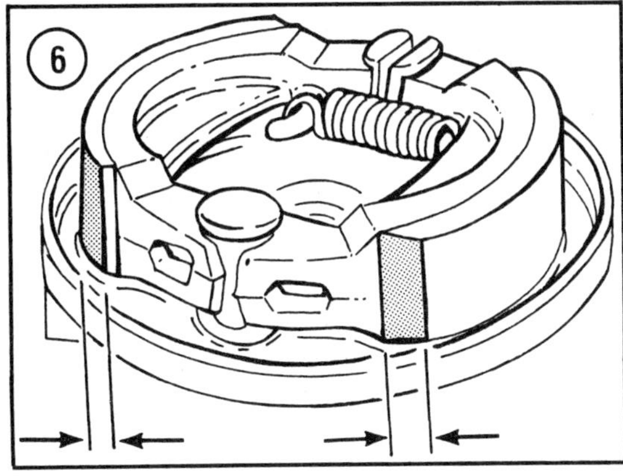

1. Remove the rear wheel as described in Chapter Nine.
2. Pull the rear brake backing plate out of the wheel assembly (16, **Figure 7**).

NOTE
Before performing Step 3, mark the left and right shoes. If the shoes are to be reused, they must be installed in their original positions.

NOTE
Place a clean shop rag on the linings to protect them from oil and grease during removal.

3. Remove the brake shoes from the backing plate by pulling up on the center of each shoe as shown in **Figure 3**.
4. Remove the return springs (21) and separate the brake shoes (23).
5. Remove the nut on the brake cam shaft. Remove the brake lever assembly in the order shown in **Figure 7**. Remove the brake lever (8).

(7)

REAR BRAKE (1959-1978)

1. Brake pedal
2. Brake pedal retaining bolt and nut
3. Spring
4. Brake shaft bushings
5. Clevis pin
6. Clevis pin retaining washer and cotter pin
7. Brake rod
8. Brake lever
9. Brake adjusting nut
10. Cross shaft
11. Cross shaft adjusting screw
12. Pivot stud (1972 and earlier)
13. Anchor bolt (1973 and later)
14. Locating block (1972 and earlier)
15. Spacer (1973 and later)
16. Backing plate
17. Operating shaft washer
18. Pivot stud (1972 and earlier)
19. Pivot stud (1973 and later)
20. Brake cam
21. Brake shoe return springs
22. Brake linings
23. Brake shoes with linings

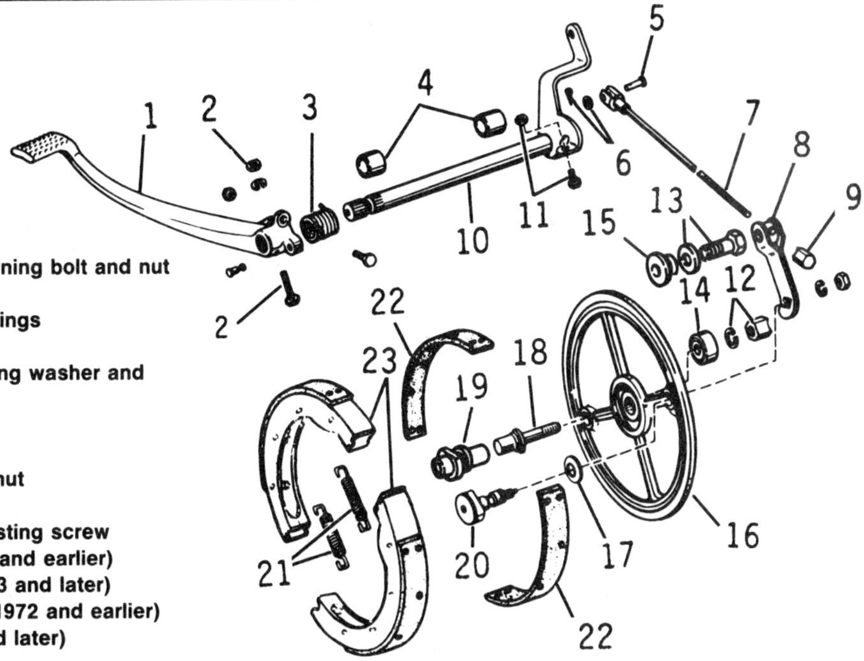

6. Remove the pivot stud screw and washer and remove the pivot stud (18 or 19).
7. If necessary, remove the brake drum from the rear hub assembly.
8. Inspect the brake assembly as described under *Front Drum Brake, Inspection* in this chapter.

Assembly

1. Assemble the brake by reversing the disassembly steps, noting the following.
2. If the brake drum was removed from the rear hub, tighten the attaching bolts and nuts securely on assembly.
3. Grease the brake cam and brake lever posts with a light coat of molybdenum disulfide grease; avoid getting any grease on the brake plate where the linings come in contact with it.
4. Install the brake lever assembly into the backing plate. Install the brake lever and nut. Tighten the nut securely.
5. Install the pivot stud assembly into the backing plate. Install the pivot stud screw and washer. Tighten the screw securely.

NOTE
If the old linings are being reinstalled, they must be installed in their original positions.

6. Hold the brake shoes in V-formation with the return springs attached and snap them in place on the brake backing plate.

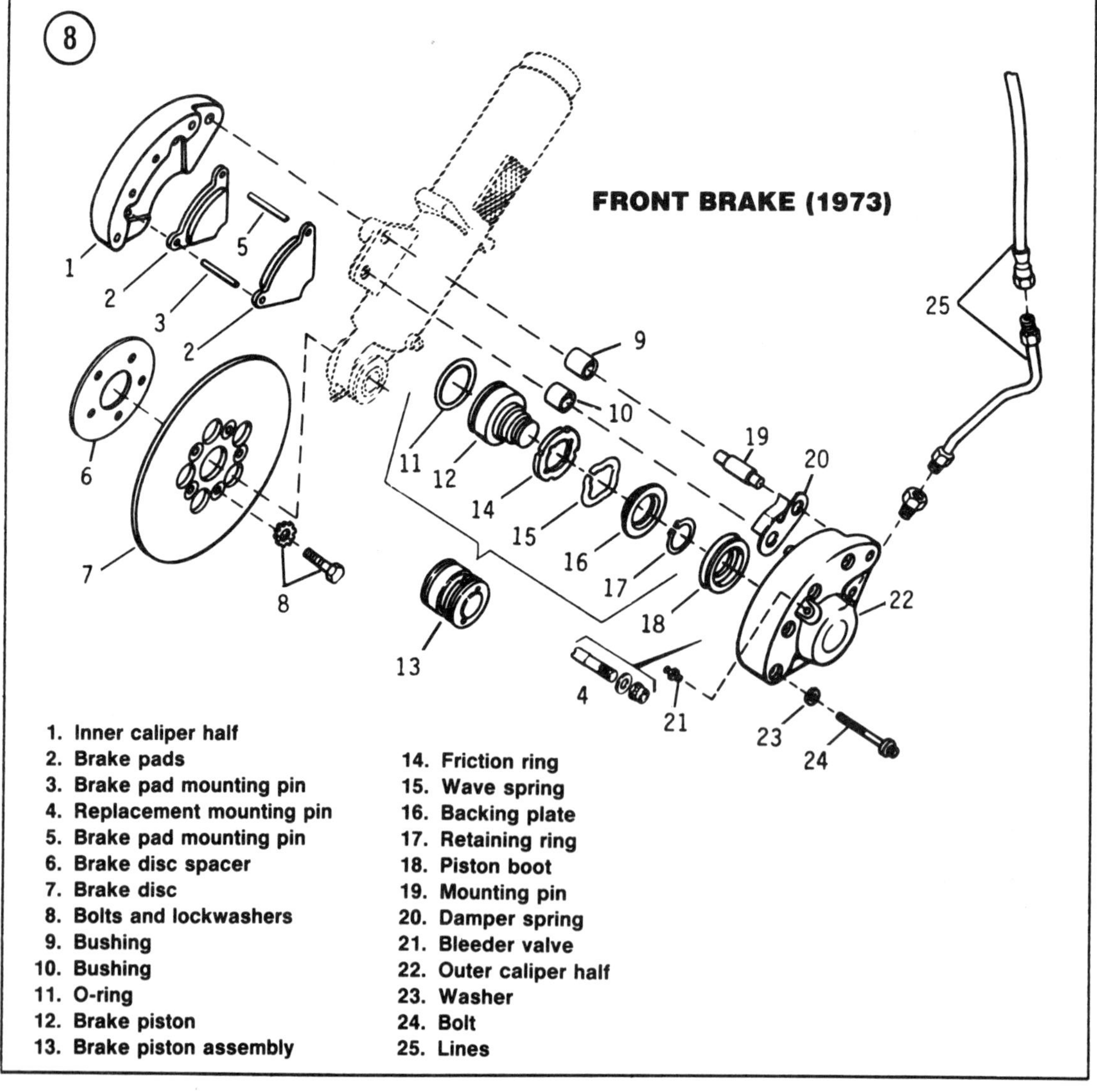

1. Inner caliper half
2. Brake pads
3. Brake pad mounting pin
4. Replacement mounting pin
5. Brake pad mounting pin
6. Brake disc spacer
7. Brake disc
8. Bolts and lockwashers
9. Bushing
10. Bushing
11. O-ring
12. Brake piston
13. Brake piston assembly
14. Friction ring
15. Wave spring
16. Backing plate
17. Retaining ring
18. Piston boot
19. Mounting pin
20. Damper spring
21. Bleeder valve
22. Outer caliper half
23. Washer
24. Bolt
25. Lines

7. Install the rear wheel as described in Chapter Nine.
8. Adjust the rear brakes as described in Chapter Three.

WARNING
Make sure the rear brake operates correctly before riding the bike.

DISC BRAKES

Disc brakes are actuated by hydraulic fluid from the master cylinder. The master cylinder is controlled by the hand or foot lever. As the brake pads wear, the brake fluid level drops in the master cylinder reservoir and automatically adjusts for pad wear. Chapter Three lists brake adjustments.

When working on a hydraulic brake system, it is necessary that the work area and all tools be absolutely clean. Any tiny particles of foreign matter or grit on the caliper assembly or the master cylinder can damage the components.

Also, sharp tools must not be used inside the caliper or on the caliper piston. If there is any doubt about your ability to correctly and safely carry out major service on the brake components, take the job to a Harley-Davidson dealer or brake specialist.

When adding brake fluid use only a type clearly marked DOT 3 (prior to September, 1976 production) or DOT 5 (September, 1976 and later production) and use it from a sealed container. If you are unsure of your bike's production date, take the frame number to a Harley-Davidson dealer. DOT 3 brake fluid will draw moisture which greatly reduces its ability to perform correctly, so it is a good idea to purchase brake fluid in small containers and discard what is not used.

Whenever *any* brake line has been removed from the brake system the system is considered "opened" and must be bled to remove air bubbles. Also, if the brake feels "spongy," this usually means there are air bubbles in the system and it must be bled. For safe brake operation, refer to *Bleeding the System* in this chapter for complete details.

CAUTION
Disc brake components rarely require disassembly, so do not disassemble unless absolutely necessary. Do not use solvents of any kind on the brake system's internal components. Solvents will cause the seals to swell and distort. When disassembling and cleaning brake components (except brake pads) use new brake fluid.

BRAKE PAD REPLACEMENT

Service Notes

1. Brake pads should be replaced only as a complete set.
2. Disconnecting the hydraulic brake hose is not required for brake pad replacement. Disconnect the hose only if caliper removal is required.
3. When new pads are installed in the caliper the master cylinder brake fluid level will rise as the caliper pistons are repositioned. Clean the top of the master cylinder of all dirt and foreign matter. Remove the cap and diaphragm from the master cylinder and slowly push the caliper pistons into the caliper. Constantly check the reservoir to make sure brake fluid does not overflow. Remove fluid, if necessary, prior to it overflowing. The pistons should move freely. If they don't, and there is evidence of them sticking in the cylinder, the caliper should be removed and serviced as described in this chapter.
4. Push the caliper piston in all the way to allow room for the new pads.

WARNING
Harley-Davidson specifies DOT 3 brake fluid for models produced prior to September, 1976 and DOT 5 for later models. Mixing the two types of brake fluids can cause brake failure. If you own a 1976 or 1977 model take your frame number to a Harley-Davidson dealer to find out your bike's production date.

WARNING
After performing any service work to the brakes, do not ride the motorcycle until you are sure the brakes are operating correctly with full hydraulic advantage. If necessary, bleed the brake system as described in this chapter.

Pad Replacement (1973 Front Brake)

Refer to **Figure 8** for this procedure.

1. Remove the caliper housing bolts (24, **Figure 8**) and washers.
2. Pull the outer caliper half (22) away from the brake disc. Hang the caliper with a bunji cord.

CAUTION
Do not let the caliper hang by the brake hose.

3. Remove the damper spring (20).
4. Remove the mounting pin (19) and the inner caliper half (1).

5. Slide the brake pad mounting pins (5) out of the pads. Remove the brake pads (2) from the inner caliper half.
6. Check the brake pads for wear and damage. Measure the brake pad friction material with a caliper. If the lining thickness is 0.062 in. or less, replace both brake pads.
7. Check the brake caliper for brake fluid leaks. If brake fluid has leaked from the caliper, rebuild it as described in this chapter.
8. Inspect the brake disc as described in this chapter.
9. Push the caliper piston in all the way to allow room for the new pads. See *Service Notes* for details.
10. Install the brake mounting pins (5) and the inner brake pad (2) in the inner caliper half (1).
11. Align the inner caliper with the brake disc and the lower fork mounting boss.
12. Align the opposite brake pad (2) with the mounting pins and install it.
13. Install the mounting pin (19) and the damper spring (20) in the order shown in **Figure 8**.
14. Align the outer caliper half (22) with the lower fork mounting boss and brake pads and install it.
15. Apply Harley-Davidson Anti-Seize (part no. 99632-77) to the caliper mounting bolts (24). Install the bolts and washers and tighten securely.
16. Refill the master cylinder reservoir, if necessary, to maintain the correct fluid level. Install the diaphragm and top cap.

Pad Replacement (1974-1977 Front Brake)

Refer to **Figure 9** for this procedure.
1. Remove the 2 caliper housing Allen bolts bolts (6) and washers (25).
2. Pull the outer caliper half (5) away from the brake disc. Hang the outer caliper half with a bunji cord.

CAUTION
Do not let the caliper hang by the brake hose.

3. Remove the inner caliper half (13) with the inner brake pad (14) attached.
4. Remove the pressure plate (21) with the outer brake pad (14) attached.
5. Check the brake pads for looseness and wear. Replace the brake pads if they are worn to the indicator groove on the bottom of the pad. Replace both pads as a set.
6. The brake pads are riveted in place. Replace as follows:
   a. Drill out the rivets (15) with a 9/64 in. drill bit.
   b. Remove the brake pads.
   c. After removing the brake pads, check the inner caliper half for wear or damage. Remove all corrosion from the caliper before installing the new pad.
   d. Check that the pressure plate is flat. If it is bowed, it must be replaced. If the pressure plate is okay, remove all corrosion from its surface before installing new pads.
   e. Install new brake pads using a hollow rivet set.
7. Check the brake caliper for brake fluid leaks. If brake fluid has leaked from the caliper, rebuild it as described in this chapter.
8. Inspect the brake disc as described in this chapter.
9. Push the caliper piston in all the way to allow room for the new pads. See *Service Notes* for details.
10. Make sure that the torque arm bosses are clean and free of all corrosion.

NOTE
The outer brake pad must be attached to the pressure plate when installing the pressure plate in Step 11.

11. Align the pressure plate (21) with the torque arm and install it.
12. Install the outer and inner caliper halves. Install the caliper Allen bolts (6) and washers and tighten to 130 in.-lb.
13. After tightening the caliper bolts, make sure that the caliper moves freely on the torque arm. If not, remove the caliper halves and reinstall.
14. Refill the master cylinder reservoir, if necessary, to maintain the correct fluid level. Install the diaphragm and top cap.

Pad Replacement (1978-1983 Front Brake and 1979-1981 Rear Brake)

Refer to **Figure 10** (front) or **Figure 11** (rear) for this procedure.
1. Remove the 2 caliper housing mounting screws (1, **Figure 10** or **Figure 11**) and washers.
2. Pull the caliper assembly away from the brake disc.
3. Remove the bolt (4) from the rear of the caliper and separate the caliper halves.
4. Hang the outer caliper half with a bunji cord.

CAUTION
Do not allow the outer caliper half to hang by the brake hose.

5. Remove the brake pads and the inner and outer plates.

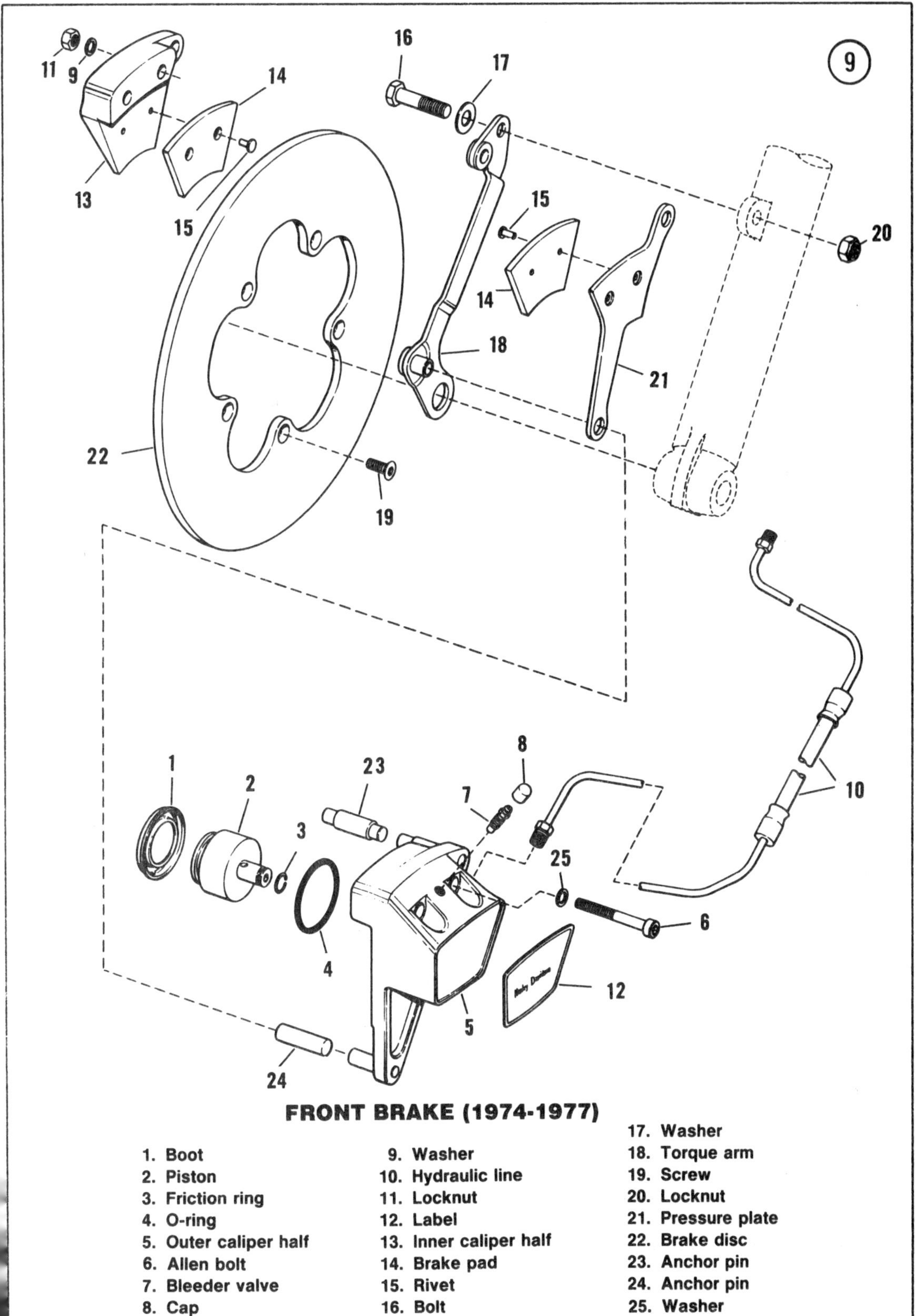

FRONT BRAKE (1974-1977)

1. Boot
2. Piston
3. Friction ring
4. O-ring
5. Outer caliper half
6. Allen bolt
7. Bleeder valve
8. Cap
9. Washer
10. Hydraulic line
11. Locknut
12. Label
13. Inner caliper half
14. Brake pad
15. Rivet
16. Bolt
17. Washer
18. Torque arm
19. Screw
20. Locknut
21. Pressure plate
22. Brake disc
23. Anchor pin
24. Anchor pin
25. Washer

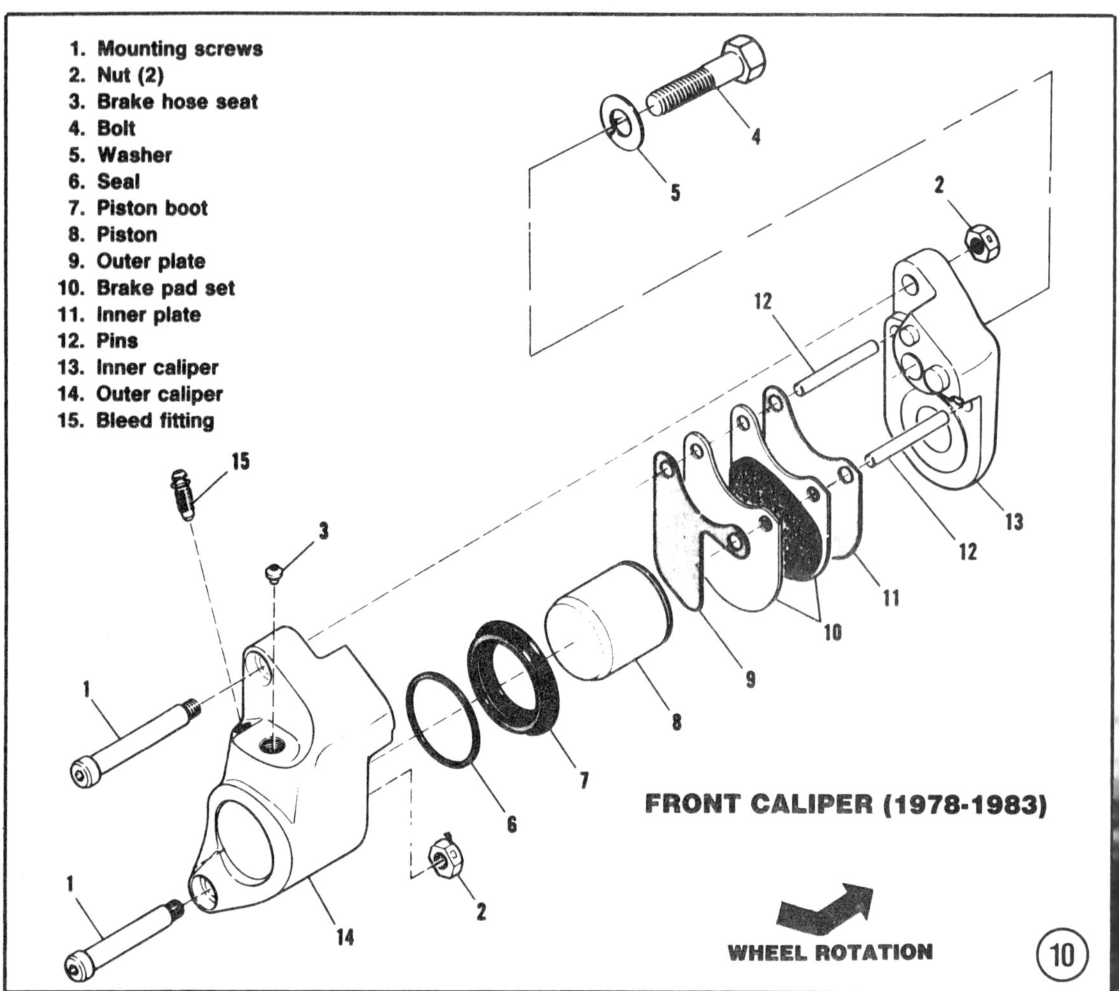

6. Check the brake pads for wear or damage. Replace the brake pads if they are worn to 0.062 in. or less. Replace both pads as a set.
7. Check the inner and outer plates for wear or damage. Replace if necessary.
8. Check the brake caliper for brake fluid leaks. If brake fluid has leaked from the caliper, rebuild it as described in this chapter.
9. Inspect the brake disc as described in this chapter.
10. Push the caliper piston in all the way to allow room for the new pads. See *Service Notes* for details.
11. Install the inner and outer plates and brake pads in the order shown in **Figure 10** or **Figure 11**.

NOTE
*Make sure the outer plate is installed between the caliper piston and the outer brake pad in the direction shown in **Figure 10** or **Figure 11**.*

12. Align the outer caliper with the pins and install it. Install the bolt (4) and washer and tighten to 60-65 ft.-lb.
13. Install the caliper over the brake disc and install the mounting bolts (1) with *new* locknuts. Tighten the bolts to 80-90 in.-lb.
14. Refill the master cylinder reservoir, if necessary, to maintain the correct fluid level. Install the diaphragm and top cap.

Pad Replacement
(1984-1985 Front Brake)

Refer to **Figure 12** for this procedure.
1. Remove the mounting bolt (1, **Figure 12**) and the mounting pin (2).
2. Pull the caliper assembly (16) away from the brake disc.

(11)

REAR CALIPER (1979-1981)

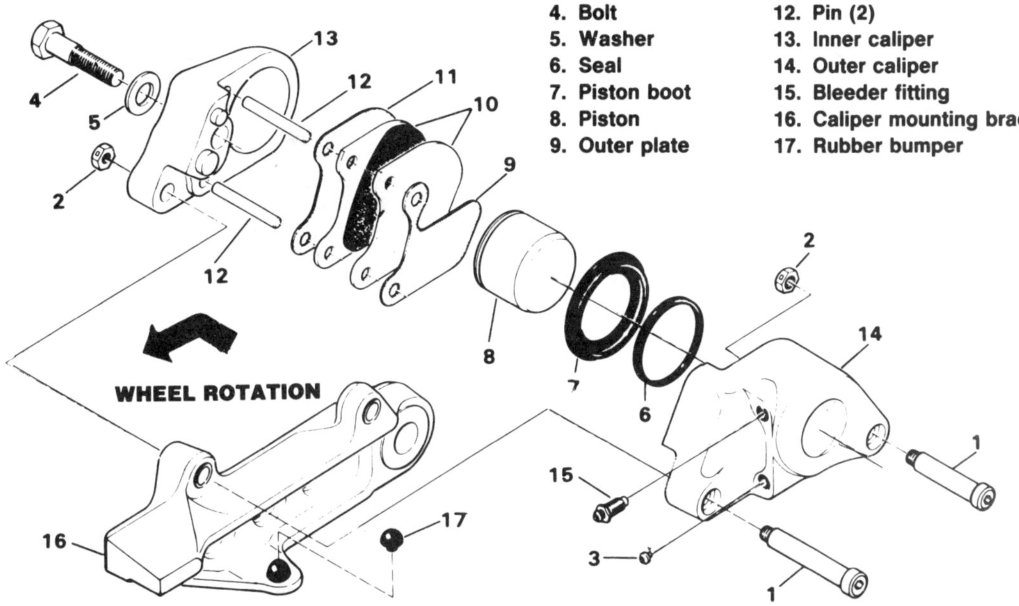

1. Mounting screws
2. Nut (2)
3. Brake hose seat
4. Bolt
5. Washer
6. Seal
7. Piston boot
8. Piston
9. Outer plate
10. Pad set
11. Inner plate
12. Pin (2)
13. Inner caliper
14. Outer caliper
15. Bleeder fitting
16. Caliper mounting bracket
17. Rubber bumper

WHEEL ROTATION

FRONT CALIPER (1984-1985)

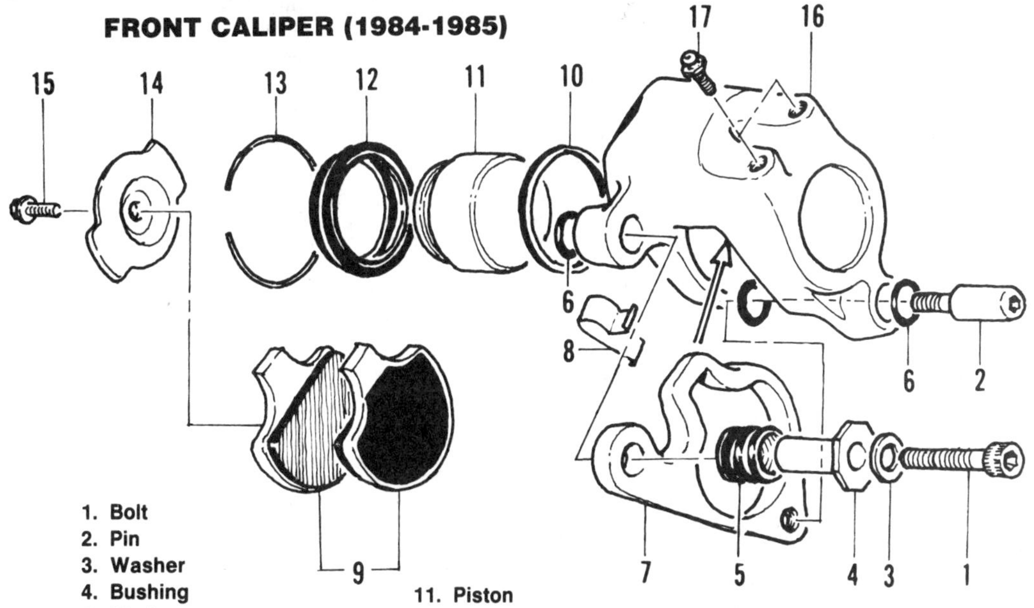

1. Bolt
2. Pin
3. Washer
4. Bushing
5. Pin boot
6. O-ring
7. Pad holder
8. Spring clip
9. Brake pads
10. Piston seal
11. Piston
12. Piston dust boot
13. Retainer wire ring
14. Pad retainer
15. Screw
16. Caliper
17. Bleed screw

(12)

10

3. Hang the caliper with a bunji cord.

CAUTION
Do not allow the caliper to hang by the brake hose.

4. Remove the screw (15) and remove the pad retainer (14) and the inner brake pad (9).
5. Remove the outer pad (9), pad holder (7) and spring clip (8) as an assembly.
6. Push the outer pad free of the spring clip and remove it. See **Figure 13**.
7. Check the brake pads for wear or damage. Replace the brake pads if they are worn to 0.062 in. or less. Replace both pads as a set.
8. Check the brake caliper for brake fluid leaks. If brake fluid has leaked from the caliper, rebuild it as described in this chapter.

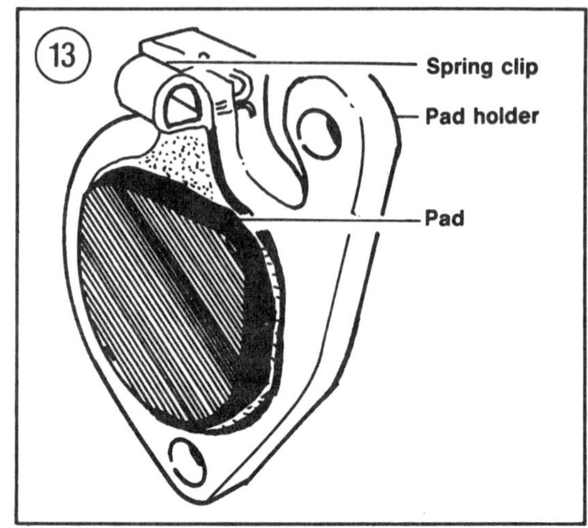

14

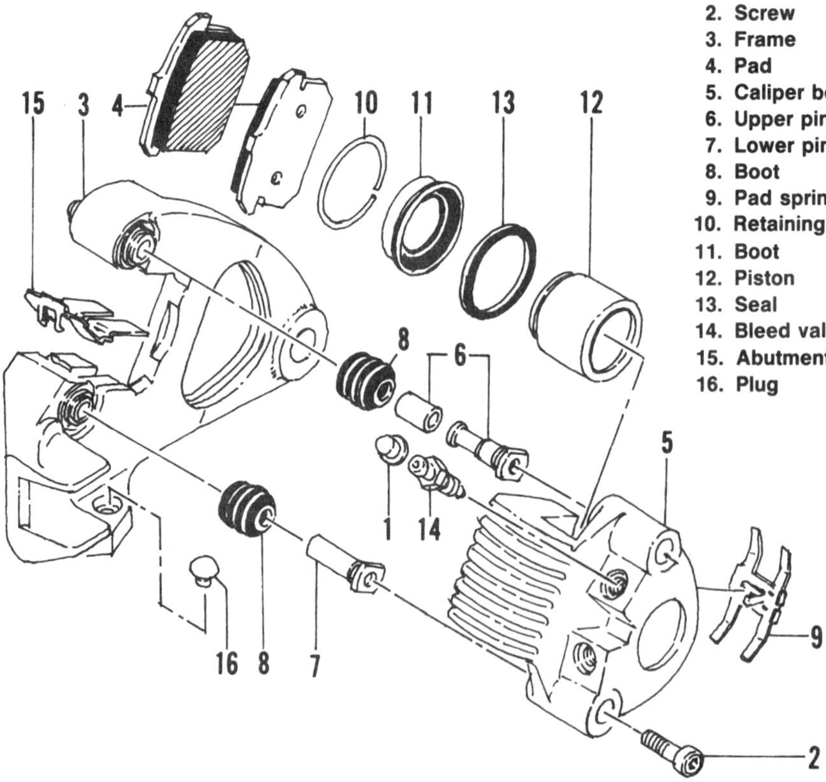

REAR BRAKE CALIPER (1982-1985)

1. Cap
2. Screw
3. Frame
4. Pad
5. Caliper body
6. Upper pin
7. Lower pin
8. Boot
9. Pad spring
10. Retaining wire ring
11. Boot
12. Piston
13. Seal
14. Bleed valve
15. Abutment shims
16. Plug

9. Inspect the brake disc as described in this chapter.
10. Push the caliper piston in all the way to allow room for the new pads. See *Service Notes* for details.
11. Place the pad holder on a workbench with the upper mounting bolt hole positioned at the upper right.
12. Install the spring clip at the top of the pad holder as shown in **Figure 13**.
13. Place the brake pad with the insulator backing on top of the spring clip with the lower end of the pad slightly entering the pad holder opening. With the brake pad insulator backing facing toward the pad holder, push the brake pad down until it is held firmly in the pad holder by the spring clip. See **Figure 13**.
14. Insert the outer brake pad/pad holder assembly into the caliper so that the brake pad insulator backing faces against the piston. See **Figure 12**.

WARNING
The spring clip loop and the brake pad friction material must face away from the piston. Brake failure will occur if the brakes are assembled incorrectly.

15. Install the inner brake pad (without the insulator backing) in the caliper recessed seat.
16. Insert the pad retainer (14, **Figure 12**) within the counterbore inside the caliper. Install the self-tapping screw (15) through the pad retainer and thread into the brake pad. Tighten the screw to 55-70 in.-lb.
17. Coat the mounting pin with Dow Corning Moly 44 grease.
18. Install the caliper over the brake disc and align it with the lower fork tube mounting lugs.
19. Install the bolt (1) and washer (3) through the fork lug, pad holder and into the threaded bushing.
20. Install the pin (2) and O-ring through the caliper, fork lug and into the lower end of the pad holder.
21. Tighten the mounting bolt and pin to 40-45 ft.-lb.
22. Refill the master cylinder reservoir, if necessary, to maintain the correct fluid level. Install the diaphragm and top cap.

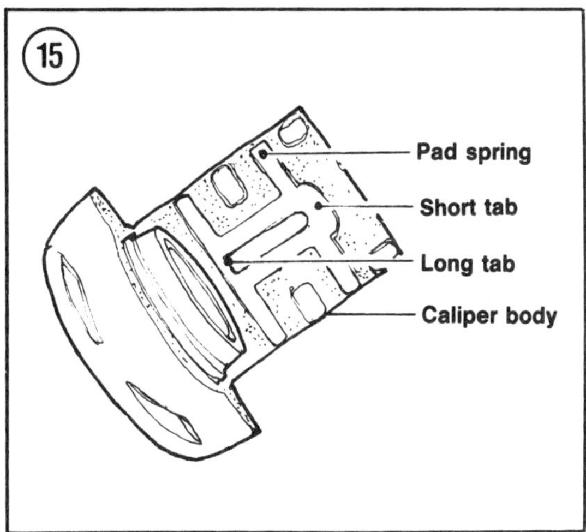

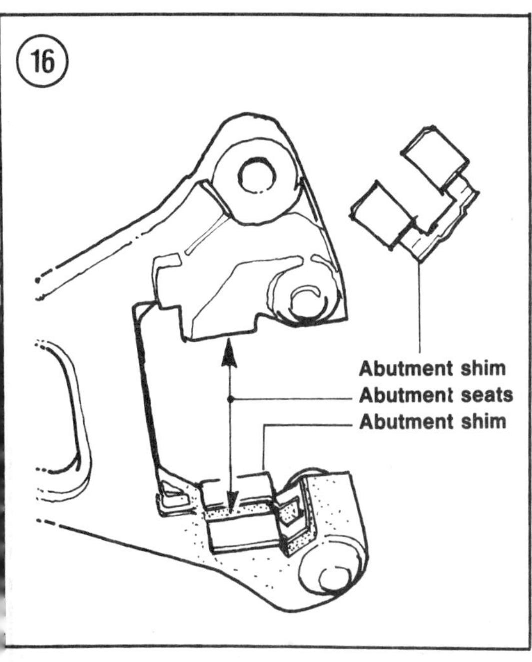

Pad Replacement (1982-1985 Rear Brake)

Refer to **Figure 14** for this procedure.

1. Remove the 2 caliper body screws (2, **Figure 14**).
2. Pull the caliper body (5) away from the mounting frame (3).
3. Support the caliper body with bunji cords.

CAUTION
Do not allow the caliper body to hang by the brake hose.

4. Remove the brake pads (4).
5. Remove the pad spring (9) from inside the caliper. See **Figure 15**.
6. Check the abutment shims (15) in the caliper frame. If it is worn or damaged, replace as follows:
   a. Pry the abutment shim away from the caliper. See **Figure 16**.
   b. Remove all adhesive from the caliper surface where the abutment shim is located.

10

c. Clean the abutment shim surface with rubbing alcohol.
d. Apply silicone sealant to the abutment shim surface on the caliper and install the abutment shim. Hold the shim in position by installing the brake pads in the bracket.
e. Allow the silicone sealant to thoroughly dry before completing brake pad installation.
f. Check that the brake pads slide freely in the bracket.

7. Check the brake pads for wear or damage. Replace the brake pads if they are worn to 0.062 in. or less. Replace both pads as a set.
8. Check the brake caliper for brake fluid leaks. If brake fluid has leaked from the caliper, rebuild it as described in this chapter.
9. Inspect the brake disc as described in this chapter.
10. Push the caliper piston in all the way to allow room for the new pads. See *Service Notes* for details.
11. Refer to **Figure 15**. Install the pad spring into the top of the caliper so that the spring's long tab extends above the piston. Hook the spring's short tab above the ridge on the caliper casting opposite the piston.
12. Install the brake pads (4) on the bracket. Then install the caliper body over the brake pads and onto the bracket. Make sure the upper (6) and lower (7) pins do not move when installing the caliper body.
13. Install the caliper screws and tighten to 11-14 ft.-lb. The upper and lower pins should be aligned as shown in **Figure 17**.
14. Refill the master cylinder reservoir, if necessary, to maintain the correct fluid level. Install the diaphragm and top cap.

BRAKE CALIPER

Removal/Installation

1. Remove the brake pads as described in this chapter.
2. Disconnect the caliper brake line at the caliper (**Figure 18**). Plug the end of the line to prevent brake fluid from dripping onto other motorcycle parts.
3. Remove the caliper(s).
4. Installation is the reverse of these steps.
5. Bleed the brakes as described in this chapter.

Caliper Overhaul (1973 Front Brake)

Refer to **Figure 8** for this procedure.

1. Remove the brake pads as described in this chapter.

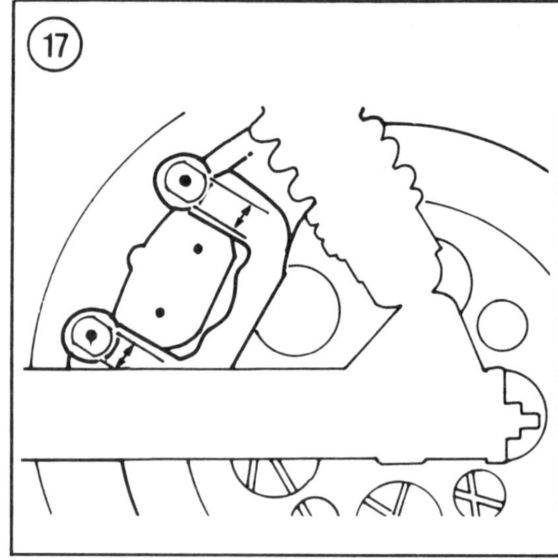

2. Disconnect the caliper brake line. Plug the end of the line to prevent brake fluid from dripping onto the motorcycle.
3. Remove the piston boot (18, **Figure 8**).

WARNING
During the next step, the piston may shoot out like a bullet. Keep your fingers out of the way. Wear shop gloves and apply compressed air gradually.

4. Place a rag or piece of wood in the path of the piston (**Figure 19**). Blow the piston (3) out with compressed air directed through the hydraulic line fitting. Use a service station air hose if you don't have a compressor.
5. Remove the retaining ring (17, **Figure 8**) from the piston bore. Then remove the following parts in order:
b. Wave spring (15).
c. Friction ring (14).
d. O-ring (11).
6. Check the mounting bracket bushings for wear and damage. Replace them if necessary.

NOTE
If the bushings are tight, have a Harley-Davidson dealer or machine shop replace the bushings for you.

7. Inspect the cylinder bore in the outer caliper housing. Replace the outer caliper if wear or damage can be seen. Light dirt or rust may be removed with fine emery paper. Replace the outer caliper if dirt or rust is severe. If serviceable, clean the caliper with rubbing alcohol. After cleaning rinse the bore thoroughly with new brake fluid.

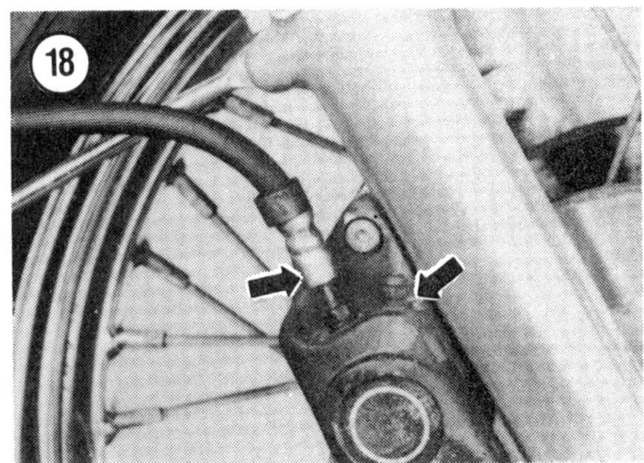

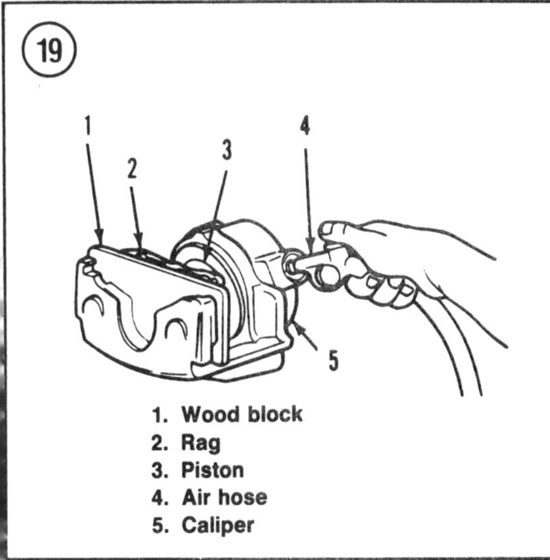

1. Wood block
2. Rag
3. Piston
4. Air hose
5. Caliper

8. Inspect the piston. If the piston can't be cleaned with brake fluid and a rag, replace it.
9. Replace the piston O-ring (11) and friction ring (14) during reassemby.

CAUTION
Never reuse piston seals. Very minor damage or age deterioration can make the seals useless.

10. Coat the following parts with new brake fluid:
   a. Piston (12).
   b. Retaining ring (17).
   c. Backing plate (16).
   d. Wave spring (15).
   e. Friction ring (14).
   f. O-ring (11).
11. Install the piston boot (18) into the caliper bore so that the small hole in the boot faces downward when the caliper is installed on the motorcycle.
12. Install the retaining ring (17). Make sure the ring seats in the caliper groove completely.
13. Install the backing plate (16), wave spring (15) and friction ring (14).
14. Install O-ring (11) on the piston.
15. Align the piston with the caliper bore and install it. Press the piston in all the way.
16. Install the brake pads as described in this chapter.

Overhaul
(1974-1977 Front Brake)

Refer to **Figure 9** for this procedure.
1. Remove the brake pads as described in this chapter.
2. Disconnect the caliper brake line. Plug the end of the line to prevent brake fluid from dripping onto the motorcycle.
3. Remove the rubber boot (1, **Figure 9**).

WARNING
During the next step, the piston may shoot out like a bullet. Keep your fingers out of the way. Wear shop gloves and apply compressed air gradually.

4. Place a rag or piece of wood in the path of the piston (**Figure 19**). Blow the piston out with compressed air directed through the brake line fitting. Use a service station air hose if you don't have a compressor.
5. Remove the friction ring (3, **Figure 9**) from the end of the piston.
6. Remove the O-ring (4) from the piston bore.
7. Check the caliper housing for damage. Replace if necessary.
8. Inspect the cylinder bore in the outer caliper housing. Replace the outer caliper if wear or damage can be seen. Light dirt or rust may be removed with fine emery paper. Replace the outer caliper if dirt or rust is severe. If serviceable, clean the caliper with rubbing alcohol. After cleaning, rinse the bore thoroughly with new brake fluid.
9. Inspect the piston (2). Replace it if necessary.
10. Replace the piston boot (1), piston O-ring (4) and friction ring (3) during reassembly.

CAUTION
Never reuse the piston O-ring. Very minor damage or age deterioration can make the O-ring useless.

11. Coat the following parts with new brake fluid:
   a. Piston (2).
   b. Piston boot (1).
   c. O-ring (4).
   d. Friction ring (3).
12. Install the O-ring (4) in the piston bore groove.
13. Install the friction ring (3) onto the piston.

14. Align the piston with the piston bore and install. Rotate the piston during installation to prevent damaging the friction ring (3).
15. Install the piston boot. Make sure both boot lips mesh with their individual caliper grooves.
16. Align the piston with the caliper bore and install it. Press the piston in all the way.
17. Install the brake pads as described in this chapter.

Caliper Overhaul (All 1978-1985 Front and Rear Brake Calipers)

Refer to the appropriate drawings for your model when performing this procedure.

a. 1978-1983 front brake: **Figure 10**.
b. 1979-1981 rear brake: **Figure 11**.
c. 1984-1985 front brake: **Figure 12**.
d. 1982-1985 rear brake: **Figure 14**.

1. Remove the brake pads as described in this chapter.
2. Disconnect the caliper brake line. Plug the end of the line to prevent brake fluid from dripping onto the motorcycle.
3. If so equipped, remove the retaining wire ring with a small screwdriver. See **Figure 12** or **Figure 14**.
4. Remove the front piston boot, if so equipped.

WARNING
The piston may shoot out like a bullet during the next step. Keep your fingers out of the way. Wear shop gloves and apply compressed air gradually.

5. Place a rag or piece of wood in the path of the piston (**Figure 19**). Blow the piston out with compressed air directed through the hydraulic hole fitting. Use a service station air hose if you don't have a compressor.
6. Remove the piston seal and boot.
7. Check the caliper housing for damage. Replace if necessary.
8. Inspect the cylinder bore in the outer caliper housing. Replace the outer caliper if wear or damage can be seen. Light dirt or rust may be removed with fine emery paper. Replace the outer caliper if dirt or rust is severe. If serviceable, clean the caliper with rubbing alcohol. After cleaning, rinse the bore thoroughly with new brake fluid.
9. Inspect the piston. If the piston can't be cleaned with brake fluid and a rag, replace it.
10. Replace the piston boot and seal during reassembly.

CAUTION
Never reuse the piston seal. Very minor damage or age deterioration can make the seal useless.

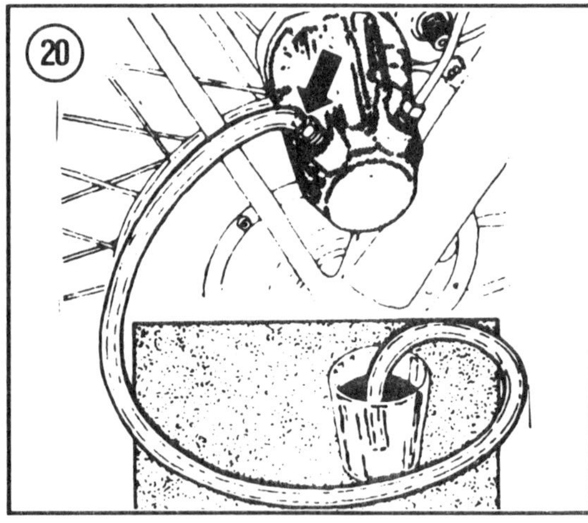

11. Coat the following parts with new brake fluid:
    a. Piston.
    b. Piston boot.
    c. Seal.
12. Install the piston seal.
13. Align the piston with the piston bore and install. Press the piston in all the way.
14. Install the retaining ring.
15. Install the front piston boot, if so equipped.
16. Install the brake pads as described in this chapter.

FRONT MASTER CYLINDER

Draining the Master Cylinder

Before removing the master cylinder, it should first be drained of all brake fluid.

CAUTION
Cover the fuel tank, front fender and instrument cluster with a heavy cloth or plastic tarp to protect them from accidental spilling of brake fluid. Wash any spilled brake fluid off any painted or plated surfaces immediately, as it will destroy the finish. Use soapy water and rinse completely.

1. Open the bleeder screw (**Figure 20**) at the caliper. Then attach one end of a hose to the bleeder screw and insert the opposite end in an empty container. See **Figure 20**.
2. Operate the brake lever to drain the fluid.
3. Close the bleeder screw and disconnect the hose. Discard the brake fluid.

Removal/Installation (1973-1981)

Refer to **Figure 21** for this procedure.

1. Drain the master cylinder as described in this chapter.

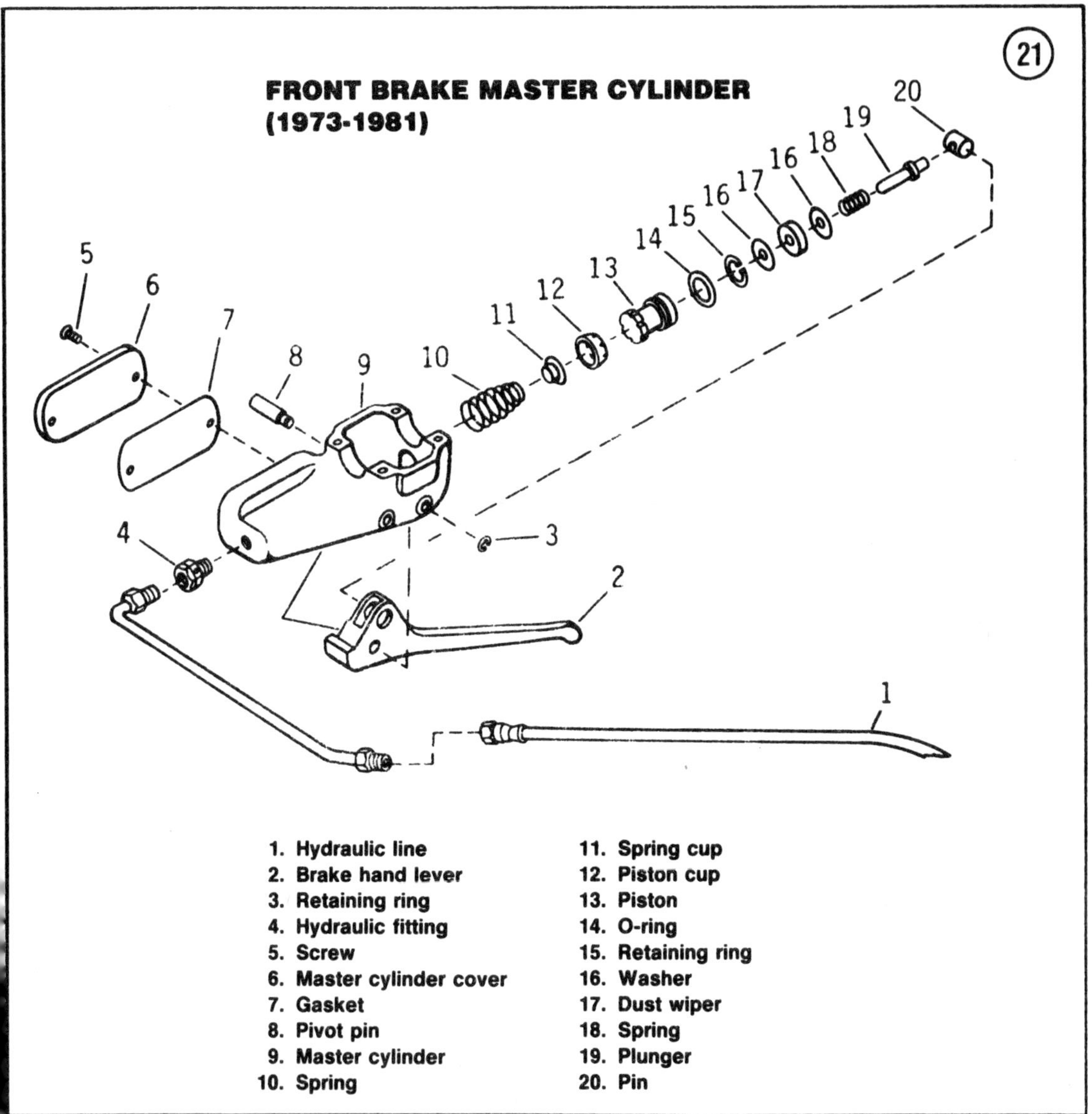

2. Disconnect the hydraulic hose from the master cylinder.
3. Remove the right-hand handlebar switch assembly and disconnect the brake switch wires.
4. Install by reversing these removal steps, noting the following.
5. Install the brake hose onto the master cylinder. Tighten the hose bolt securely.
6. Bleed the brake system as described in this chapter.

Disassembly (1973-1981)

Refer to **Figure 21** for this procedure.

1. Remove the brake lever retaining ring (3, **Figure 21**).
2. Remove the following parts in order:
   a. Pivot pin (8).
   b. Brake lever (2).
   c. Pin (20).
   d. Plunger (19).
   e. Spring (18).
   f. Washers (16).
   g. Dust wiper (17).
3. Remove the internal retaining ring (15). Then remove the following parts in order:
   a. Piston (13) and O-ring (14).
   b. Piston cup (12).
   c. Spring cup (11).
   d. Piston return spring (10).
4. Discard all piston cups.

5. Inspect the master cylinder as described in this chapter.

Assembly (1973-1981)

1. Soak the new cups in fresh brake fluid for at least 15 minutes to make them pliable. Coat the inside of the cylinder with fresh brake fluid prior to assembling the parts.
2. Install a new O-ring (14) on the piston. Then install the piston return spring (10), spring cup (11), piston cup (12) and piston assembly (13) into the cylinder together. Install the spring (10) with the tapered end facing toward the spring cup (11).
3. Compress the piston slightly and install the retaining ring (15). Make sure the retaining ring seats in the groove fully.
4. Install the washers (16), spring (18), dust wiper (17) and plunger (19).
5. Coat the pin (20) with Loctite Anti-Seize and install the pin into the brake lever. Install the brake lever assembly into the master cylinder. Then align the hole in the pin with the plunger. Insert the pin through the lever assembly and master cylinder. Secure the pin with the retaining ring (3).

Removal/Installation (1982-1985)

Refer to **Figure 22** (1982), **Figure 23** (1983) or **Figure 24** (1984-1985).

1. Drain the master cylinder as described in this chapter.
2. Remove the union bolt securing the brake hose to the master cylinder. Remove the brake hose. Tie

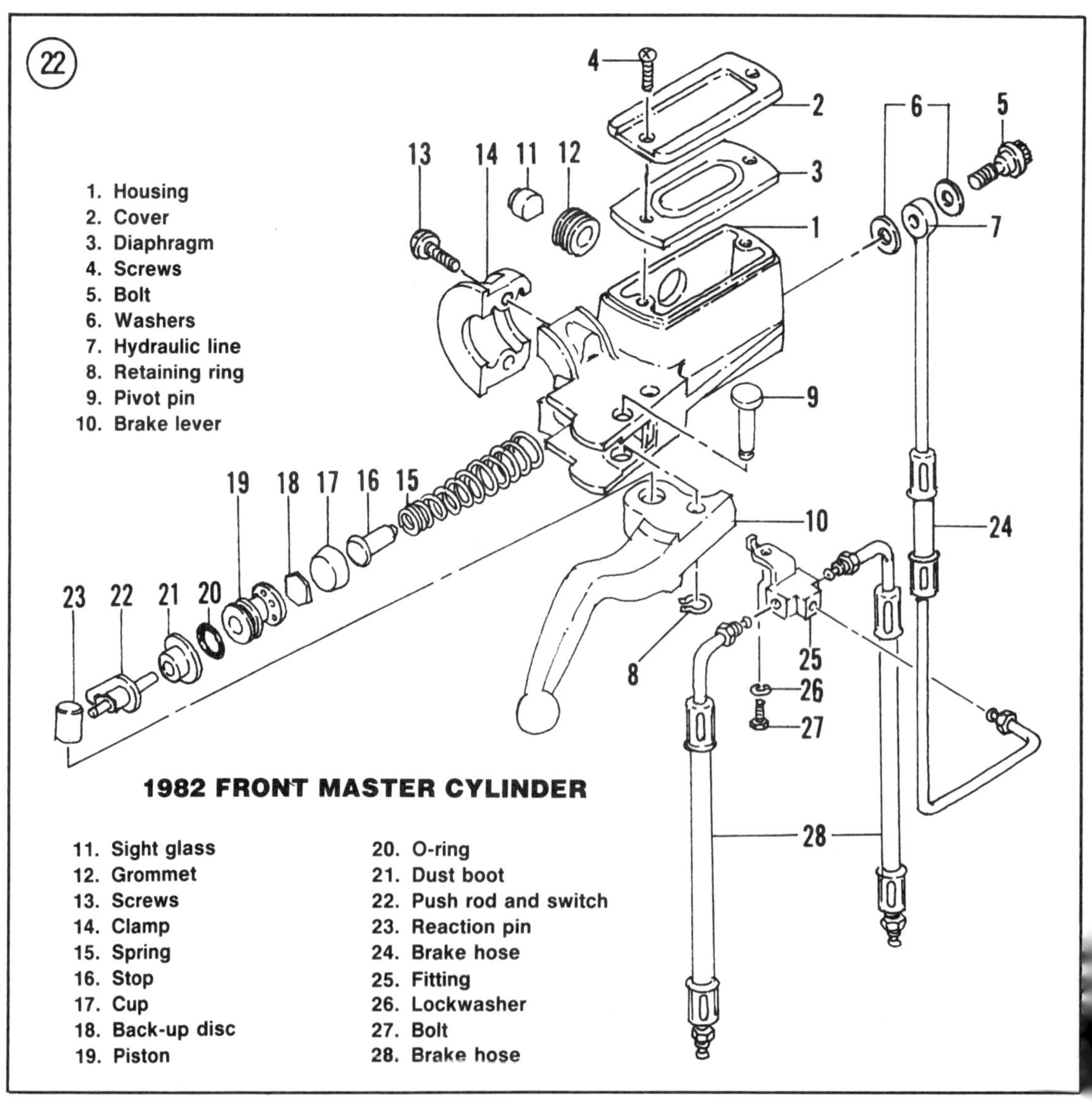

1982 FRONT MASTER CYLINDER

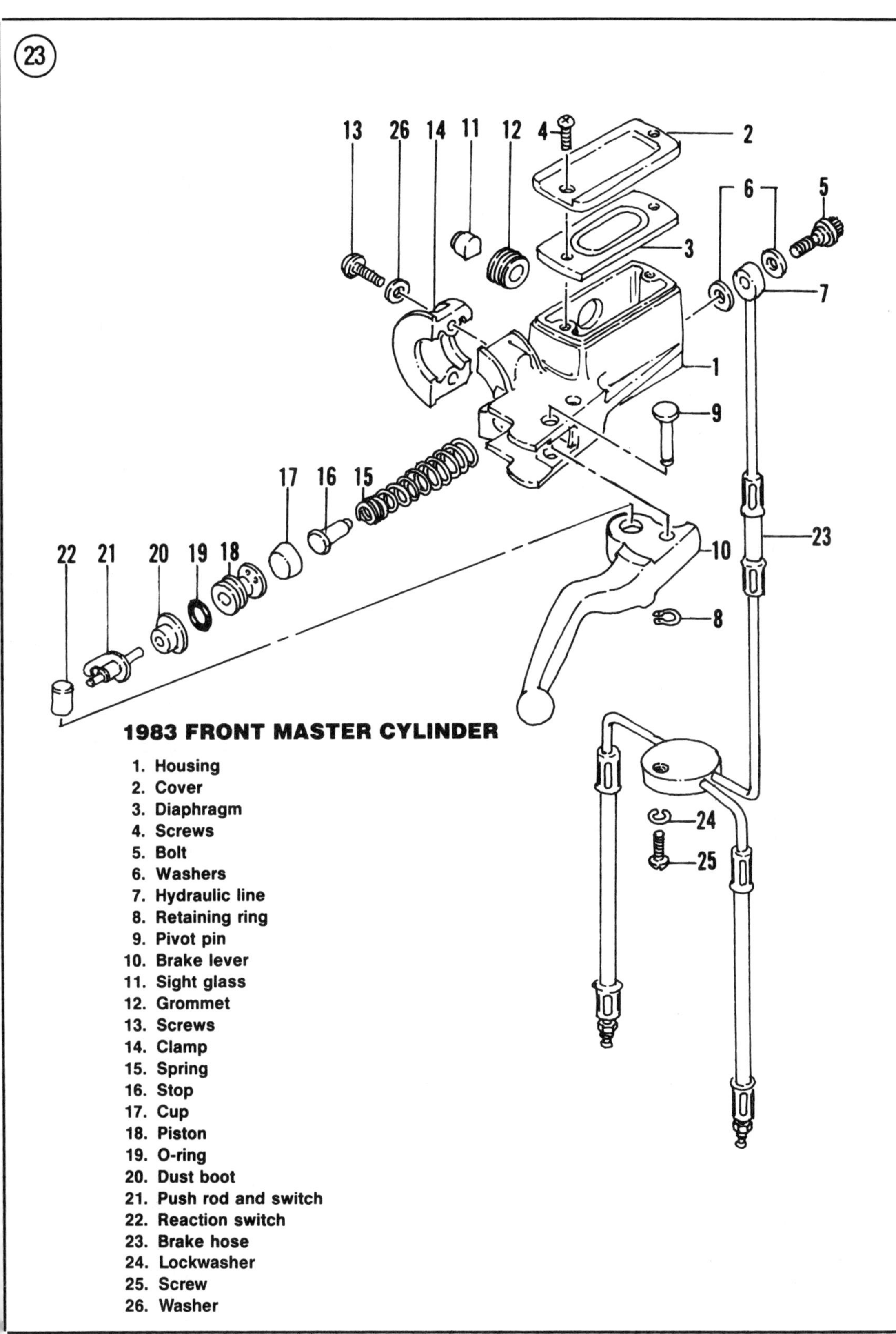

1983 FRONT MASTER CYLINDER

1. Housing
2. Cover
3. Diaphragm
4. Screws
5. Bolt
6. Washers
7. Hydraulic line
8. Retaining ring
9. Pivot pin
10. Brake lever
11. Sight glass
12. Grommet
13. Screws
14. Clamp
15. Spring
16. Stop
17. Cup
18. Piston
19. O-ring
20. Dust boot
21. Push rod and switch
22. Reaction switch
23. Brake hose
24. Lockwasher
25. Screw
26. Washer

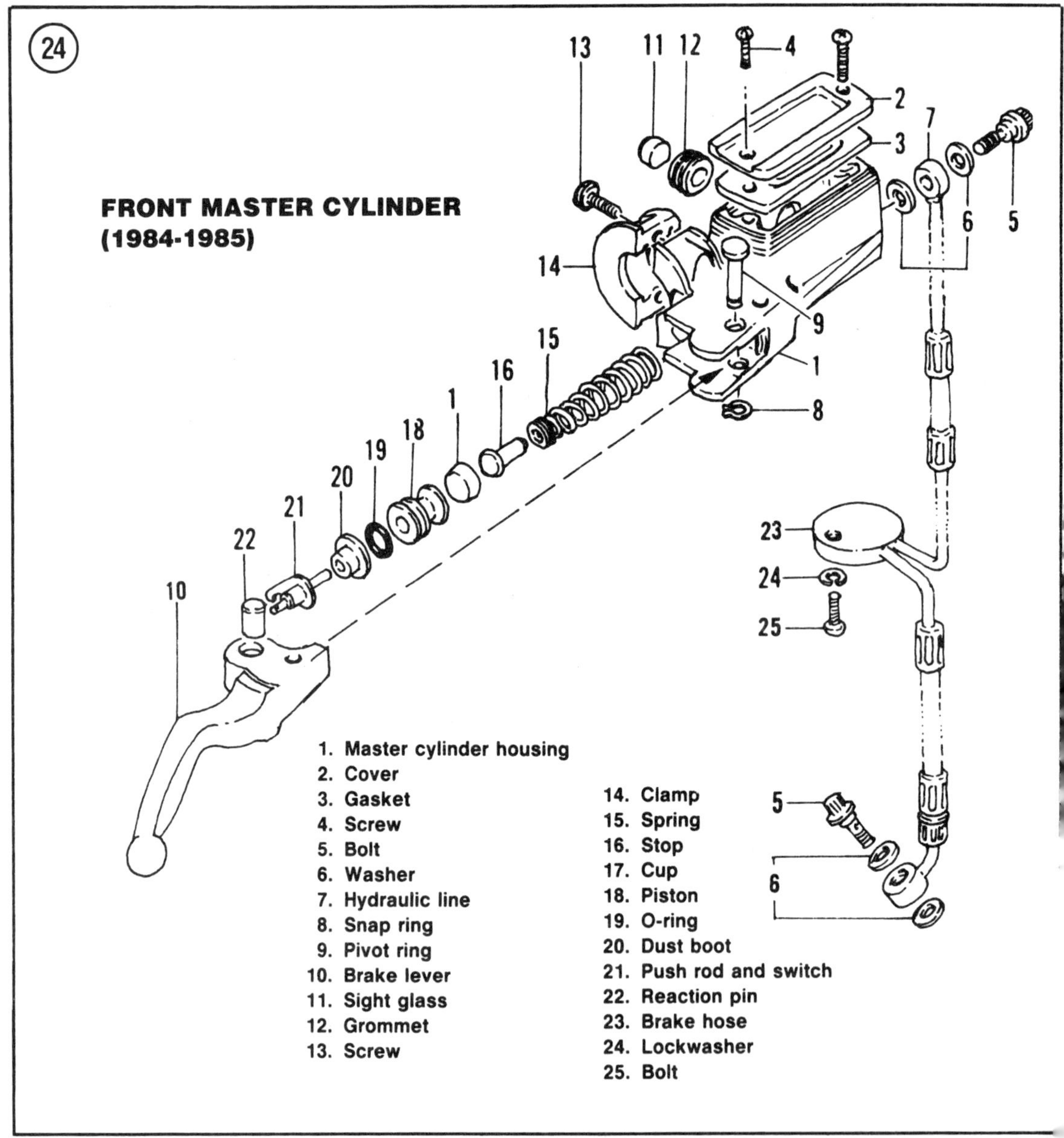

the brake hose up and cover the end to prevent the entry of foreign matter.

3. Remove the clamping bolts and clamp securing the master cylinder to the handlebar and remove the master cylinder.
4. Install by reversing these removal steps, noting the following.
5. Install the brake hose onto the master cylinder. Be sure to place a sealing washer on each side of the fitting and install the union bolt. Tighten the union bolt to specifications in **Table 3**.
6. Bleed the brake system as described in this chapter.

Disassembly (1982-1985)

Refer to **Figure 22** (1982), **Figure 23** (1983) or **Figure 24** (1984-1985).

1. Remove the screws securing the cover and remove the cover and diaphragm.
2. Remove the brake lever circlip and pivot pin. Then remove the following parts in order:
   a. Brake lever.
   b. Reaction pin.
3. Remove the following parts in order:
   a. Push rod.
   b. Dust boot.

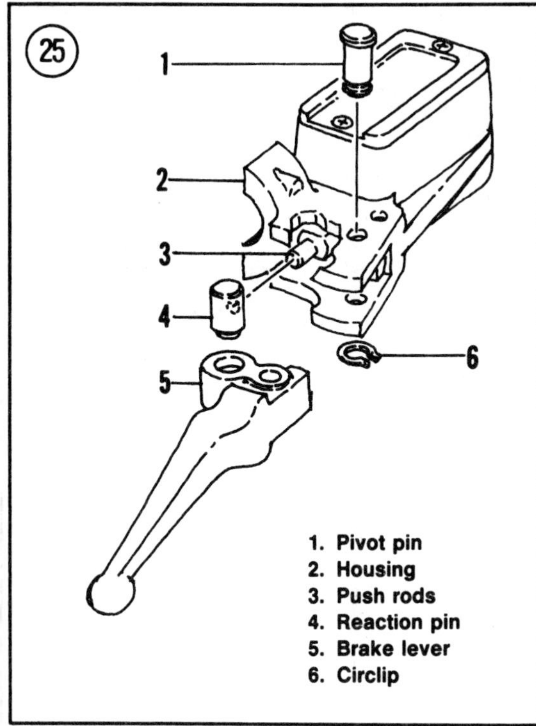

1. Pivot pin
2. Housing
3. Push rods
4. Reaction pin
5. Brake lever
6. Circlip

c. Piston and O-ring.
d. Back up disc (1982 models only). See 18, **Figure 22**.
e. Cup.
f. Stop.
g. Spring.

4. Remove the sight glass and grommet if necessary.
5. Inspect the master cylinder as described in this chapter.

Assembly (1982-1985)

1. Soak the new cups in fresh brake fluid for at least 15 minutes to make them pliable. Coat the inside of the cylinder with fresh brake fluid prior to assembling the parts.
2. Install the grommet (coated with DOT 5 brake fluid) and the sight glass, if removed.
3. Install a new O-ring on the piston. Then install the following parts in order:
   a. Spring.
   b. Stop.
   c. Cup.
   d. Back-up disc (1982 models only). See 18, **Figure 22**.
   e. Piston assembly.
   f. Dust boot.
   g. Push rod.
   h. Switch.

Make sure all parts are installed in their correct order and alignment. See **Figures 22-24**.

4. See **Figure 25**. Coat the reaction pin with Loctite Anti-Seize and install it into the large hole in brake lever.
5. Align the hole in the reaction pin with the installed push rod and install the brake lever assembly. Insert the pivot pin through the master cylinder brake lever. Secure the pivot pin with the circlip.

NOTE
Make sure the push rod fits into the hole in the reaction pin.

6. Check the front brake lever for proper operation.

WARNING
There should be no binding when the hand lever is depressed. If the hand lever does bind, the push rod switch activator is hitting the master cylinder wall. This condition can cause loss of brake. Remove the hand lever and reassemble.

7. Install the master cylinder as described in this chapter.

Inspection

NOTE
Harley-Davidson recommends installing a complete rebuild kit whenever the master cylinder is disassembled.

1. Clean all parts in fresh brake fluid. Inspect the cylinder bore and piston contact surfaces for signs of wear or damage. If either part is less than perfect, replace it.
2. Check the end of the piston for wear caused by the hand lever. Replace the entire piston assembly if any portion of it is worn or damaged.
3. Inspect the pivot hole in the hand lever. If worn, it must be replaced.
4. Make sure the passages in the bottom of the master cylinder are clear. Check the reservoir cap and diaphragm for damage and deterioration. Replace if necessary.
5. Inspect the threads in the master cylinder body where the brake hose screws in. If the threads are damaged or partially stripped, replace the master cylinder body.
6. Check the hand lever pivot lug on the master cylinder body for cracks. Replace the master cylinder body if necessary.

REAR MASTER CYLINDER

Draining the Master Cylinder

Before removing the master cylinder, it should first be drained of all brake fluid.

CAUTION
Cover the swing arm and drive chain with a heavy cloth or plastic tarp to protect them from accidental spilling of brake fluid. Wash any spilled brake fluid off any painted or plated surfaces immediately, as it will destroy the finish. Use soapy water and rinse completely.

1. Open the bleeder screw (**Figure 26**) at the caliper. Then attach one end of a hose to to the bleeder screw and insert the opposite end in an empty container (**Figure 27**).
2. Operate the brake lever to drain the fluid.
3. Close the bleeder screw and disconnect the hose. Discard the brake fluid.

Removal/Installation (1979)

Refer to **Figure 28** for this procedure.
1. Drain the master cylinder as described in this chapter.
2. Disconnect the brake line (9, **Figure 28**) from the master cylinder.
3. Disconnect the brake linkage at the master cylinder.
4. Remove the bolts (12) securing the master cylinder to the sprocket cover and remove the master cylinder (5).
5. Install by reversing these removal steps, noting the following.
6. Install the brake hose onto the master cylinder. Tighten the hose bolt securely.
7. Bleed the brake system as described in this chapter.
8. Adjust rear brake. See Chapter Three.

Disassembly (1979)

Refer to **Figure 28** for this procedure.
1. Pull the rubber boot (13) off the end of the master cylinder.
2. Remove the internal retaining ring (14) from the body. Then remove the following parts in order:
   a. Piston assembly (15).
   b. Wafer (17).
   c. Piston cup (18).
   d. Spring seat (19).
   e. Spring (20).
3. Remove the O-ring (16) from the piston.
4. Discard the piston cups.

5. Inspect the master cylinder as described in thi chapter.

Assembly

1. Soak the new cups in fresh brake fluid for a least 15 minutes to make them pliable. Coat th inside of the cylinder with fresh brake fluid prior t assembling the parts.
2. Install a new O-ring (16) on the piston.
3. Push the spring seat (19) into the spring (20). Then install the assembly into the cylinder bore.
4. Slide the piston cup (18) into the bore and ove the spring seat (19).
5. Position the wafer (17) against the piston cu (18).
6. Install the piston assembly into the bore.
7. Install the retaining ring (14) and slide on th rubber boot (13).
8. Install the master cylinder as described in th chapter.

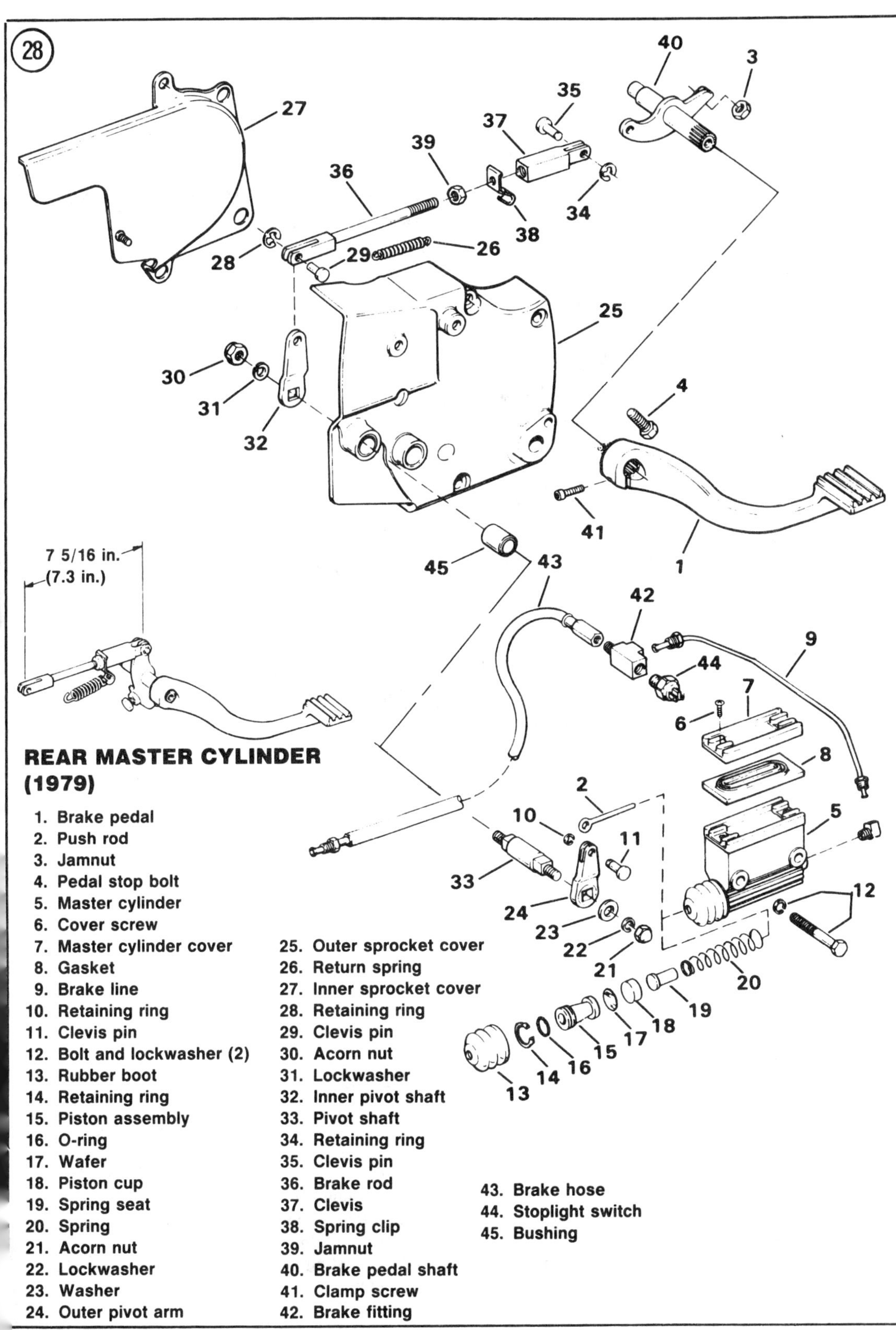

REAR MASTER CYLINDER (1979)

1. Brake pedal
2. Push rod
3. Jamnut
4. Pedal stop bolt
5. Master cylinder
6. Cover screw
7. Master cylinder cover
8. Gasket
9. Brake line
10. Retaining ring
11. Clevis pin
12. Bolt and lockwasher (2)
13. Rubber boot
14. Retaining ring
15. Piston assembly
16. O-ring
17. Wafer
18. Piston cup
19. Spring seat
20. Spring
21. Acorn nut
22. Lockwasher
23. Washer
24. Outer pivot arm
25. Outer sprocket cover
26. Return spring
27. Inner sprocket cover
28. Retaining ring
29. Clevis pin
30. Acorn nut
31. Lockwasher
32. Inner pivot shaft
33. Pivot shaft
34. Retaining ring
35. Clevis pin
36. Brake rod
37. Clevis
38. Spring clip
39. Jamnut
40. Brake pedal shaft
41. Clamp screw
42. Brake fitting
43. Brake hose
44. Stoplight switch
45. Bushing

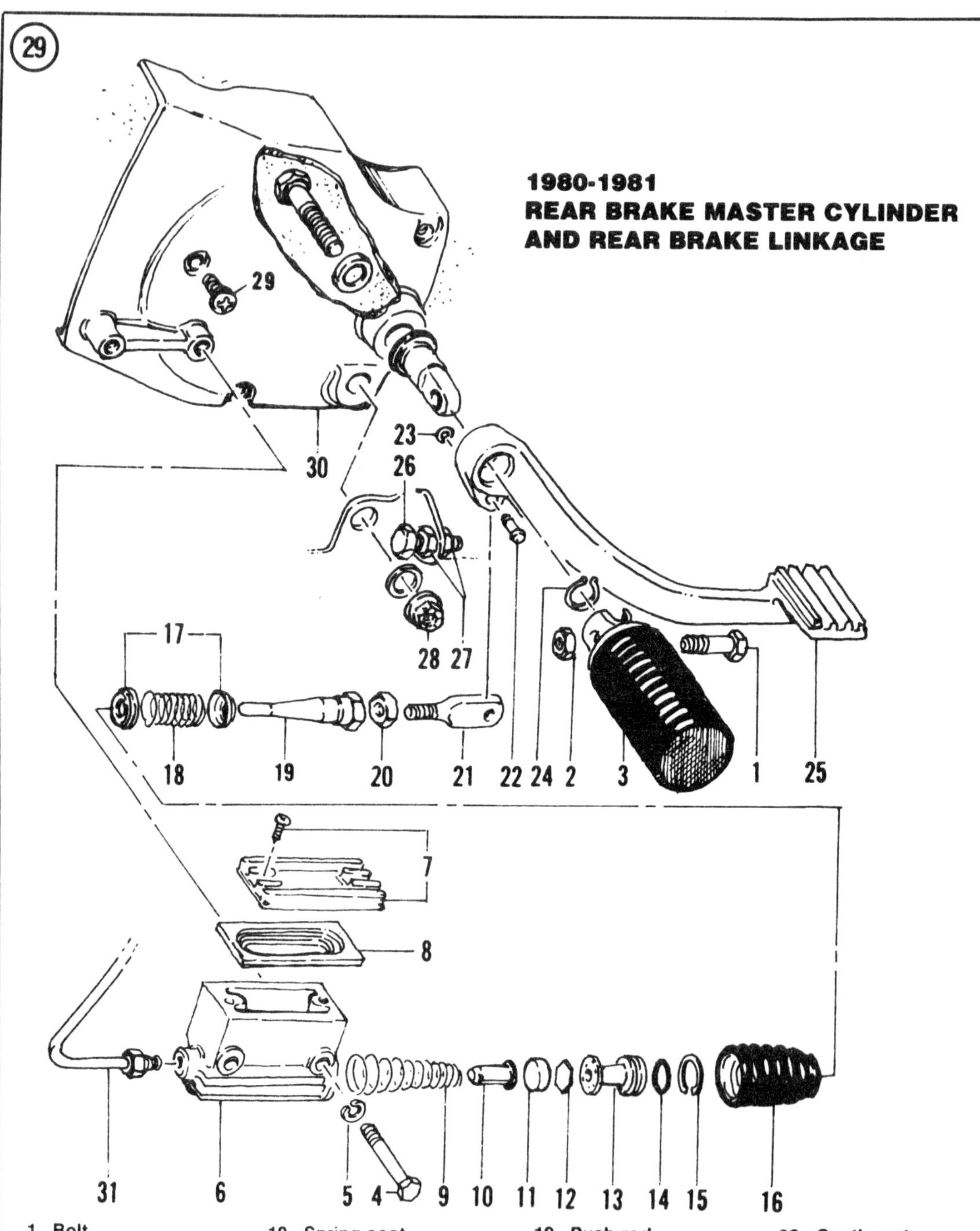
29
1980-1981
REAR BRAKE MASTER CYLINDER
AND REAR BRAKE LINKAGE
29
30
23
26
28 27
17
18
19
20
21
22 24 2
3
1
25
7
8
31
6
5 4
9
10
11
12
13
14
15
16

1. Bolt
2. Nut
3. Footrest assembly
4. Bolt
5. Lockwasher
6. Master cylinder
7. Cover and screws
8. Gasket
9. Spring
10. Spring seat
11. Piston cup
12. Wafer
13. Piston assembly
14. O-ring
15. Retaining ring
16. Boot
17. Cupped washer (2)
18. Spring
19. Push rod
20. Locknut
21. Rod end
22. Pin
23. Retaining ring
24. Retaining ring
25. Brake pedal
26. Adjusting screw
27. Jamnut
28. Castle nut
29. Screw (3)
30. Sprocket cover
31. Brake line

1982-ON REAR MASTER CYLINDER AND LINKAGE

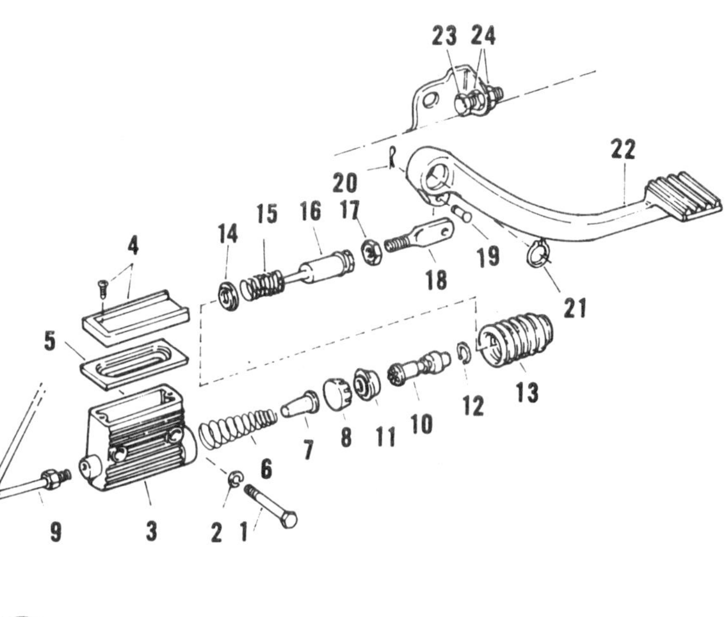

1. Mounting bolt (2)
2. Lockwasher (2)
3. Master cylinder body
4. Reservoir cover and screws
5. Cover gasket
6. Spring
7. Spring seat
8. Piston cup
9. Brake line
10. Piston assembly
11. Seal
12. Retaining clip
13. Boot
14. Cupped washer
15. Spring
16. Pushrod
17. Locknut
18. Rod end
19. Pivot pin
20. Cotter pin
21. Retaining clip
22. Brake pedal
23. Adjusting bolt
24. Locknut

(30)

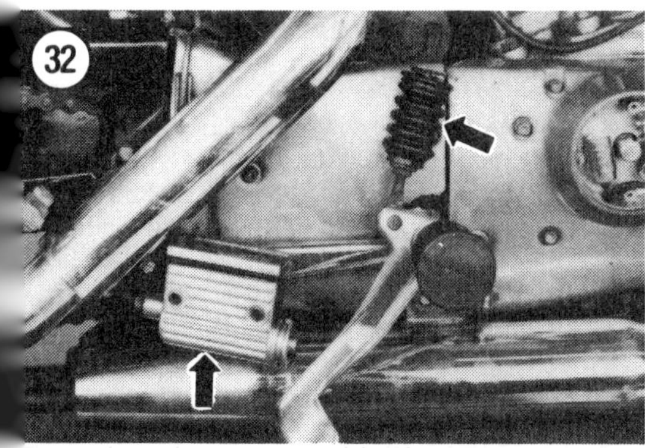

Removal/Installation (1980-1985)

Refer to **Figure 29** (1980-1981) or **Figure 30** (1982-1985).

1. Drain the master cylinder as described in this chapter.
2. Disconnect the hydraulic hose (A, **Figure 31**) from the master cylinder.
3. Remove the bolts (B, **Figure 31**) securing the master cylinder to the sprocket cover.
4. Pull the master cylinder clear of the push rod. See **Figure 32**.
5. Remove the cupped washer(s), spring and rubber boot.
6. Install by reversing these removal steps, noting the following.
7. On 1980-1981 models, install a cupped washer (17, **Figure 29**) on both sides of the spring and install the spring assembly into the rubber boot. On 1982 and later models, only 1 cupped washer is used. See 14, **Figure 30**.
8. Install the boot assembly (**Figure 33**) onto the master cylinder with the boot drain hole facing down.
9. Holding the master cylinder in one hand, guide the push rod through the boot and piston assemblies. Then align the master cylinder body

with the cover mounting holes and install the bolts. Tighten the bolts to 155-190 in.-lb.

10. Install the brake hose (A, **Figure 31**) onto the master cylinder. Tighten the hose bolt securely.
11. Bleed the brake system as described in this chapter.
12. Adjust rear brake. See Chapter Three.

Disassembly (1980-1985)

Refer to **Figure 29** (1980-1981) or **Figure 30** (1982-1985).

1. Remove the master cylinder cover and diaphragm.
2. Remove the retaining ring from the body. Then remove the following parts in order:
   a. Piston assembly.
   b. Wafer (1980-1981 models only). See 12, **Figure 29**.
   c. Piston cup.
   d. Spring seat.
   e. Spring.
3. Remove the O-ring from the piston.
4. Inspect the master cylinder as described in this chapter.

Assembly (1980-1985)

1. Soak the new cups in fresh brake fluid for at least 15 minutes to make them pliable. Coat the inside of the cylinder with fresh brake fluid prior to assembling the parts.
2. Install a new O-ring on the piston.
3. Push the spring seat into the spring. Then install the assembly into the cylinder bore.
4. Slide the piston cup into the bore and over the spring seat.
5. On 1980-1981 models, position the wafer against the piston cup. See 12, **Figure 29**.
6. Install the piston assembly into the bore and install the retaining ring.
7. Install the master cylinder as described in this chapter.

Rear Master Cylinder Inspection (All Models)

NOTE
Harley-Davidson recommends installing a complete rebuild kit whenever the master cylinder is disassembled.

1. Clean all parts in fresh brake fluid. Inspect the cylinder bore and piston contact surfaces for signs of wear or damage. If either part is less than perfect, replace it.

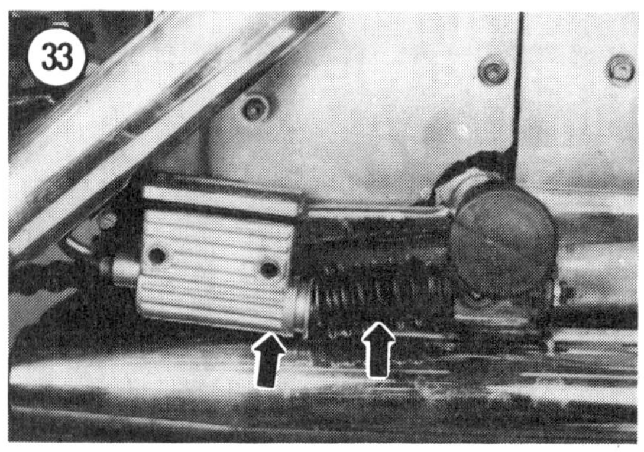

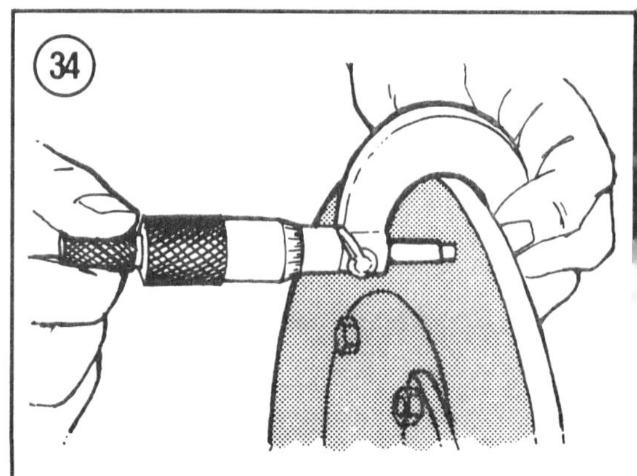

2. Check the end of the piston for wear caused b the pushrod. Replace the entire piston assembly any portion of it is worn or damaged.
3. Make sure the passages in the bottom of th master cylinder are clear. Check the reservoir ca and diaphragm for damage and deterioratio Replace if necessary.
4. Inspect the threads in the master cylinder bod where the brake hose screws in. If the threads ar damaged or partially stripped, replace the mast cylinder body.

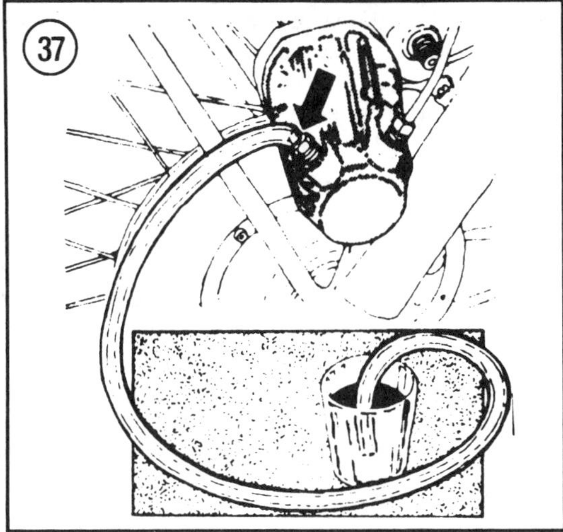

BRAKE DISC (FRONT AND REAR)

Removal/Installation

1. Remove the front or rear wheel as described in Chapter Eight or Chapter Nine.

NOTE
Place a piece of wood in the calipers in place of the disc. This way, if the brake lever is inadvertently squeezed, the piston will not be forced out of the cylinder. If this does happen, the caliper might have to be disassembled to reseat the piston and the system will have to be bled. By using the wood, bleeding the system is not necessary after installing the wheel.

2. Remove the bolts securing the brake disc to the hub and remove the disc. On all 1984-1985 models, a T40 Torx driver is required to remove the brake disc Torx bolts.
3. Installation is the reverse of these steps, noting the following.
4. Make sure all brake disc mating surfaces are clean before reassembly.
5. When installing the brake disc on 1984 and 1985 front wheels, align the notch in the disc with the hole in the hub.
6. Apply Harley-Davidson Stud and Bearing Mount to the brake disc bolts and tighten to specifications in **Table 2** or **Table 3**.

Inspection

It is not necessary to remove the disc from the wheel to inspect it. Small marks on the disc are not important, but scratches deep enough to snag a fingernail reduce braking effectiveness and increase brake pad wear. If these grooves are found, the disc should be replaced.

1. Measure the thickness around the disc at several locations with a vernier caliper or a micrometer (**Figure 34**). Minimum thickness for stock disc units is stamped on the brake disc. Replace the disc if thinner than the minimum factory specification.
2. Clean the disc of any rust or corrosion and wipe clean with lacquer thinner. Never use an oil-based solvent (such as mineral spirits) that may leave an oil residue on the disc.

BLEEDING THE SYSTEM

This procedure is necessary only when the brakes feel spongy, there is a leak in the hydraulic system, a component has been replaced or the brake fluid has been replaced.

1. Flip off the dust cap from the brake bleeder valve.
2. Connect a length of clear tubing to the bleeder valve on the caliper. See **Figure 35** (front) or **Figure 36** (rear). Place the other end of the tube into a clean container. Fill the container with enough fresh brake fluid to keep the end submerged. The tube should be long enough so that a loop can be made higher than the bleeder valve to prevent air from being drawn into the caliper during bleeding (**Figure 37**).

CAUTION
Cover all open surfaces with a heavy cloth or plastic tarp to protect it from the accidental spilling of brake fluid. Wash any spilled brake fluid off of any painted or plated surface immediately, as it will destroy the finish. Use soapy water and rinse completely.

3. Clean the top of the master cylinder of all dirt and foreign matter. Remove the cap and diaphragm. **Figure 37** shows a rear master cylinder cap. Fill the reservoir to about 3/8 in. from the top.

Insert the diaphragm to prevent the entry of dirt and moisture.

WARNING
Harley-Davidson specifies DOT 3 brake fluid for models produced prior to September, 1976 and DOT 5 for later models. Mixing the two types of brake fluids can cause brake failure. If you own a 1976 or 1977 model take your frame number to a Harley-Davidson dealer to find out your bike's production date.

4. Slowly apply the brake lever several times. Hold the lever in the applied position and open the bleeder valve about 1/2 turn. See **Figure 35** or **Figure 36**. Allow the lever to travel to its limit.
5. When this limit is reached, tighten the bleeder screw. As the brake fluid enters the system, the level will drop in the master cylinder reservoir. Maintain the level at about 3/8 in. from the top of the reservoir to prevent air from being drawn into the system.
6. Continue to pump the lever and fill the reservoir until the fluid emerging from the hose is completely free of air bubbles. If you are replacing the fluid, continue until the fluid emerging from the hose is clean.

NOTE
If bleeding is difficult, it may be necessary to allow the fluid to stabilize for a few hours. Repeat the bleeding procedure when the tiny bubbles in the system settle out.

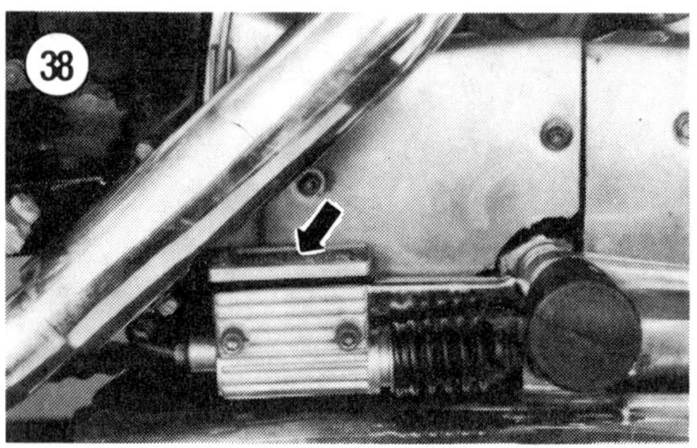
38

7. Hold the lever in the applied position and tighten the bleeder valve. Remove the bleeder tube and install the bleeder valve dust cap.
8. If necessary, add fluid to correct the level in the master cylinder reservoir. It must be above the level line.
9. Install the cap and tighten the screws. See **Figure 38**.
10. Test the feel of the brake lever. It should feel firm and should offer the same resistance each time it's operated. If it feels spongy, it is likely that air is still in the system and it must be bled again. When all air has been bled from the system and the brake fluid level is correct in the reservoir, double-check for leaks and tighten all fittings and connections.

WARNING
Before riding the motorcycle, make certain that the brakes are operating correctly by operating the lever several times. Then make the test ride a slow one at first to make sure the brake is operating correctly.

Table 1 BRAKE SPECIFICATIONS

Brake shoe thickness	see text
Disc pad thickness	see text
Brake disc	
Warpage (maximum)	1/32 in.
Thickness (minimum thickness)	
1973-1977	0.188
1978	see text
1979-1985	
Front	0.180 in.
Rear	0.205 in.

Table 2 BRAKE TIGHENING TORQUES (1973-1978)

	ft.-lb.
Brake caliper bolts	
1973	35
1974-1977	
Torque arm mounting bolt	not specified
Allen head bolts	130 in.-lb.
1978	45-50
Brake disc bolts	35

Table 3 BRAKE TIGHTENING TORQUES (1979-1985)

	ft.-lb.
Brake disc mounting (front)	
1979-1983	
Laced wheels	16-19
Cast wheels	14-16
1984-1985	16-18
Caliper assembly bolt	
1979-1981 rear brake	65
Caliper mounting bolt	
Front	
1979-1983	80-90 in.-lb.
1984-1985	40-45
Rear	155-190 in.-lb.
Front master cylinder	
Union bolts	30-35
Master cylinder screws	70-80 in.-lb.

INDEX

R

S

T

V

W

1959-1964 MODEL H

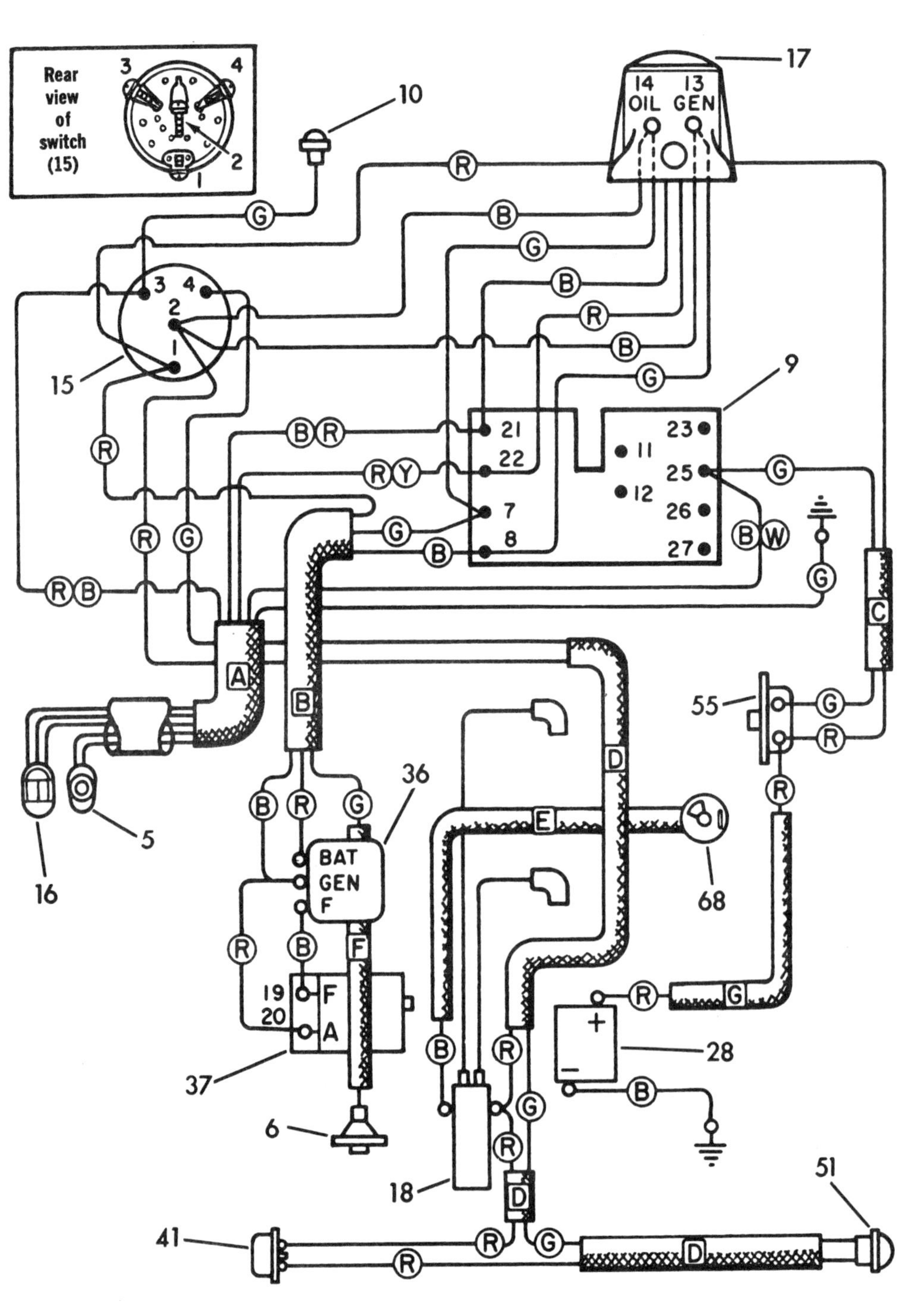

A. Handlebar—red wire with black tracer, black wire with red tracer, red wire with yellow tracer, green wire and black wire with white tracer
B. Conduit (3 wires)—green, red and black
C. Conduit (2 wires)—red and green
D. Conduit (2 wires)—red and green
E. Conduit (1 wire)—black
F. Conduit (1 wire)—green
G. Conduit (1 wire)—red
H. Conduit (2 wires)—black and red
5. Horn switch—green wire and black wire with white tracer
6. Oil signal light switch—green wire
7. Terminal—2 green wires
8. Terminal—black and green wires
9. Terminal plate
10. Speedometer light—green wire
11. Terminal—not used with standard wiring
12. Terminal—not used with standard wiring
13. Generator signal light—green and black wires
14. Oil signal light—green and black wires
15. Ignition—light switch terminal No. 1, 2 red wires; terminal No. 2, red wire and 2 black wires; terminal No. 3, green wire, and red wire with black tracer; and terminal No. 4, green wire
16. Headlight switch—red wire with black tracer, black wire with red tracer, and red wire with yellow tracer
17. Headlight—black and red wires
18. Ignition coil—2 red wires and black wire
19. Generator "F" terminal—black wire
20. Generator "A" terminal—red wire
21. Terminal—black wire and red tracer and black wire
22. Terminal—red wire with yellow tracer and red wire
23. Terminal—not used with standard wiring
25. Terminal—black wire with white tracer and green wire
26. Terminal—not used with standard wiring
27. Terminal—not used with standard wiring
28. Battery—red and black wires
36. Regulator—"B" terminal, red wire; "G" terminal, black and red wires; "F" terminal, black wire
37. Generator
41. Stoplight switch—2 red wires
51. Taillight—green and red wires
55. Horn—green wire and 2 red wires
68. Ignition circuit breaker—black wire

COLOR CODE

B = Black
G = Green
R = Red
BR = Black/Red tracer
BW = Black/White tracer
RB = Red/Black tracer
RY = Red/Yellow tracer

Letters in □ identify cables and conduit housed wires

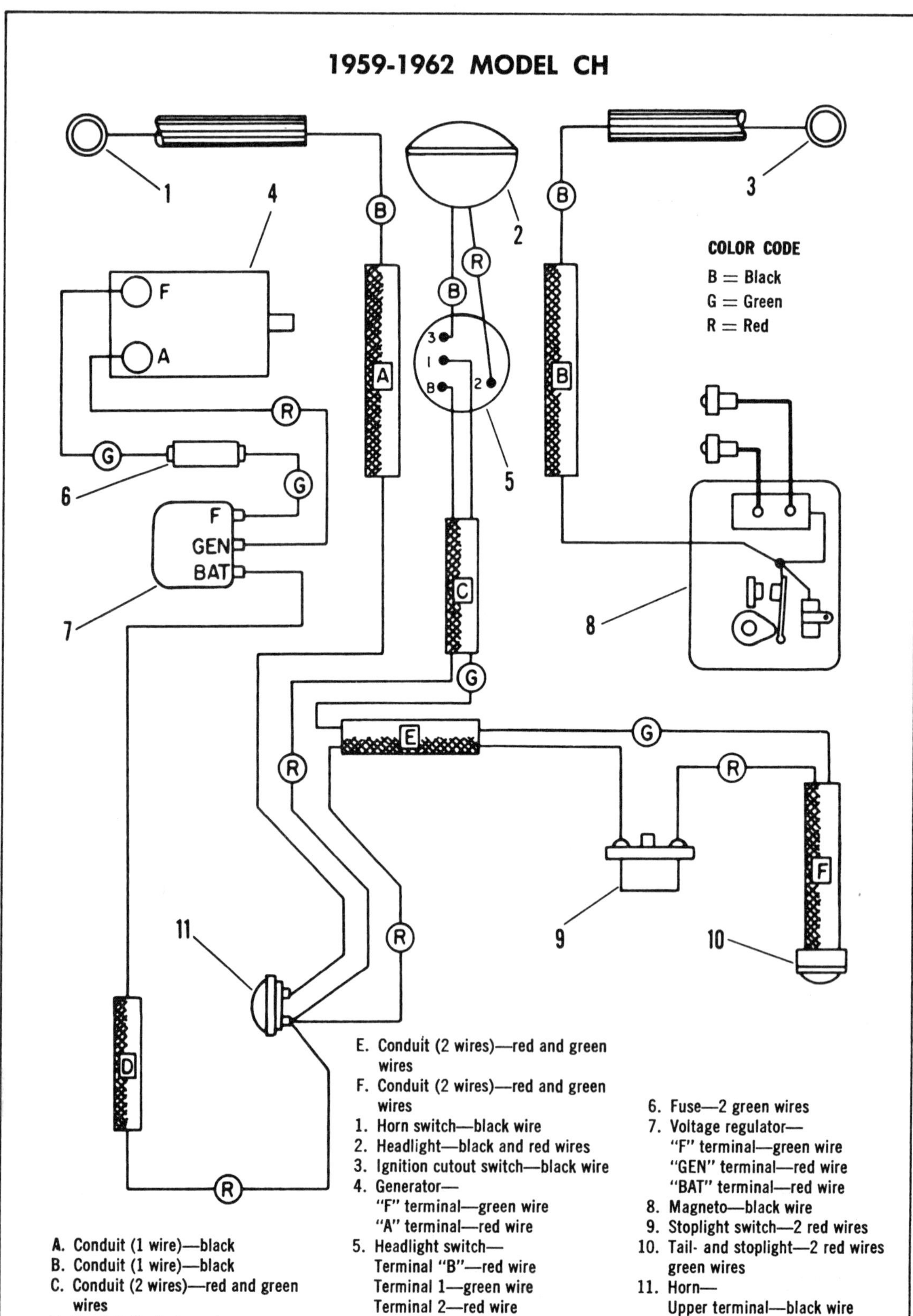
1959-1962 MODEL CH
COLOR CODE
B = Black
G = Green
R = Red
F
A
GEN
BAT
1
2
3
4
5
6
7
8
9
10
11
A
B
C
D
E
F
A. Conduit (1 wire)—black
B. Conduit (1 wire)—black
C. Conduit (2 wires)—red and green wires
D. Conduit (1 wire)—red
E. Conduit (2 wires)—red and green wires
F. Conduit (2 wires)—red and green wires
1. Horn switch—black wire
2. Headlight—black and red wires
3. Ignition cutout switch—black wire
4. Generator—
"F" terminal—green wire
"A" terminal—red wire
5. Headlight switch—
Terminal "B"—red wire
Terminal 1—green wire
Terminal 2—red wire
Terminal 3—black wire
6. Fuse—2 green wires
7. Voltage regulator—
"F" terminal—green wire
"GEN" terminal—red wire
"BAT" terminal—red wire
8. Magneto—black wire
9. Stoplight switch—2 red wires
10. Tail- and stoplight—2 red wires green wires
11. Horn—
Upper terminal—black wire
Lower terminal—3 red wires

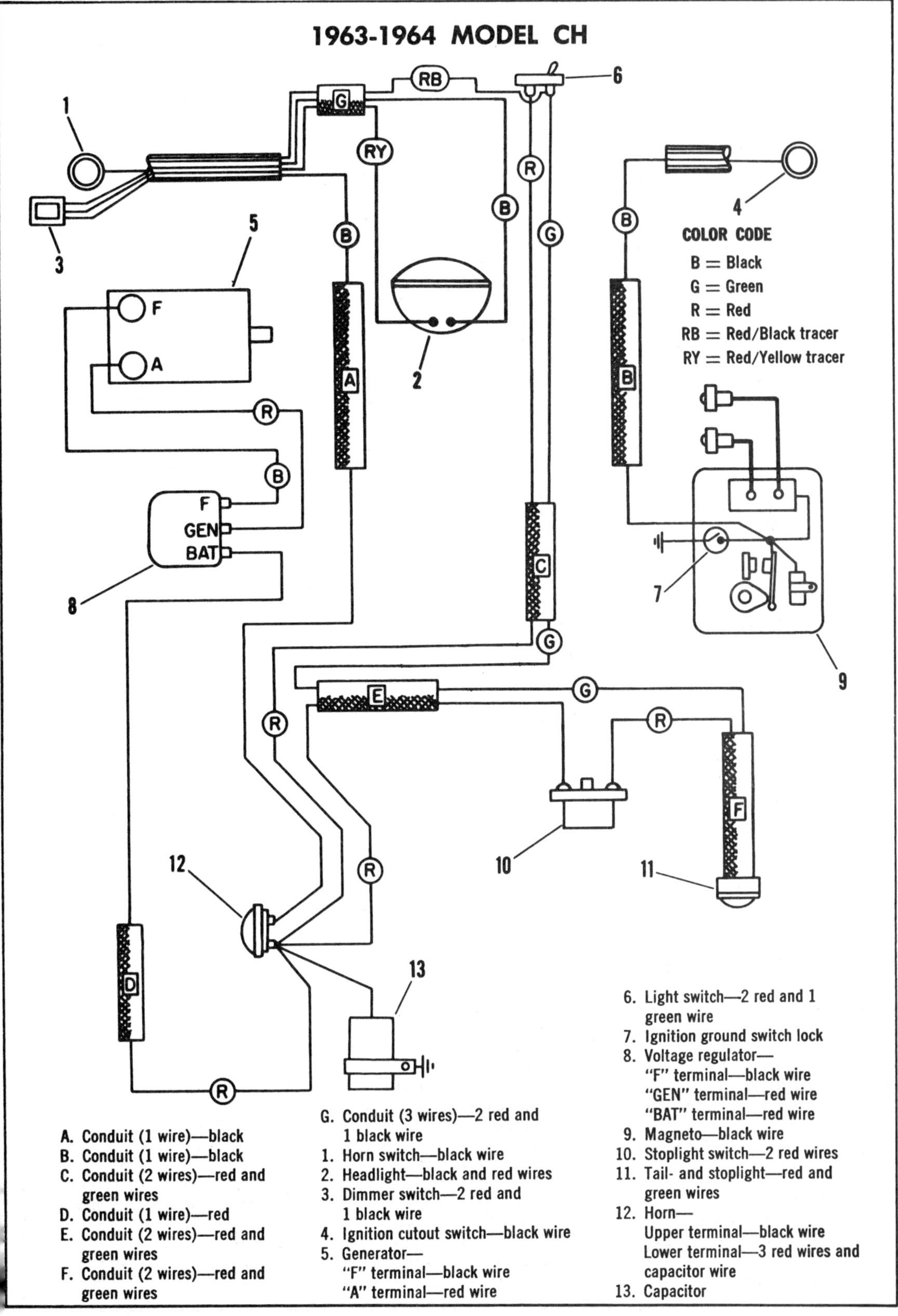
1963-1964 MODEL CH
RB
RY
R
B
G
A
B
C
D
E
F
G
F
A
F
GEN
BAT
1
2
3
4
5
6
7
8
9
10
11
12
13
COLOR CODE
B = Black
G = Green
R = Red
RB = Red/Black tracer
RY = Red/Yellow tracer
A. Conduit (1 wire)—black
B. Conduit (1 wire)—black
C. Conduit (2 wires)—red and green wires
D. Conduit (1 wire)—red
E. Conduit (2 wires)—red and green wires
F. Conduit (2 wires)—red and green wires
G. Conduit (3 wires)—2 red and 1 black wire
1. Horn switch—black wire
2. Headlight—black and red wires
3. Dimmer switch—2 red and 1 black wire
4. Ignition cutout switch—black wire
5. Generator—
"F" terminal—black wire
"A" terminal—red wire
6. Light switch—2 red and 1 green wire
7. Ignition ground switch lock
8. Voltage regulator—
"F" terminal—black wire
"GEN" terminal—red wire
"BAT" terminal—red wire
9. Magneto—black wire
10. Stoplight switch—2 red wires
11. Tail- and stoplight—red and green wires
12. Horn—
Upper terminal—black wire
Lower terminal—3 red wires and capacitor wire
13. Capacitor

1965-1966 MODEL H

COLOR CODE

B = Black
G = Green
R = Red
BR = Black/Red tracer
RB = Red/Black tracer
RY = Red/Yellow tracer

A. Handlebar—red wire with black black tracer, black wire with red tracer, red wire with yellow tracer, 2 black wires
B. Conduit (3 wires)—green, red and black
C. Conduit—green wire
D. Conduit (2 wires)—red and green
E. Conduit (1 wire)—black
F. Conduit (1 wire)—green
G. Conduit (3 wires)—red and 2 green
H. Conduit (2 wires)—black and red
5. Horn switch—2 black wires
6. Oil signal light switch—green wire
7. Terminal—2 green wires
8. Terminal—black, red, and rectifier positive terminal
9. Terminal plate
10. Speedometer light—green wire
11. Terminal—not used with standard wiring
12. Terminal—not used with standard wiring
13. Generator signal light—green and black wires
14. Oil signal light—green and black wires
15. Ignition—light switch—terminal No. 1 red wire, terminal No. 2 red wire and 3 black wires, terminal No. 3 green wire, and red wire with black tracer, and terminal No. 4 green wire
16. Headlight switch—red wire with black tracer, black wire with red tracer, and red wire with yellow tracer
17. Headlight—black and red wires
18. Ignition coil—3 red wires and black wire
19. Generator "F" terminal—green wire
20. Generator "A" terminal—red wire
21. Terminal—black wire with red tracer and black wire
22. Terminal—red wire with yellow tracer and red wire
23. Terminal—not used with standard wiring
25. Terminal—black wire and green wire
26. Terminal—not used with standard wiring
27. Terminal—not used with standard wiring
28. Terminal—green wire and rectifier negative terminal
29. Front battery—
Negative terminal—black wire
Postive terminal—white wire
30. Rear battery—
Positive terminal—red wire
Negative terminal—white wire
31. Generator—see terminals 19-20
32. Regulator—
B+ terminal—2 red wires
DF terminal—green wire
D+ terminal—black wire
Gnd terminal—black wire
G1 terminal—not used with standard wiring
33. Terminal, frame screw—2 black wires
34. Stoplight switch—2 red wires
35. Taillight—red and green wires
36. Horn—green wire
37. Circuit breaker—2 black wires
38. Rectifier—
Positive terminal (painted red) to terminal No. 8
Negative terminal to terminal No. 28

1965 MODEL CH

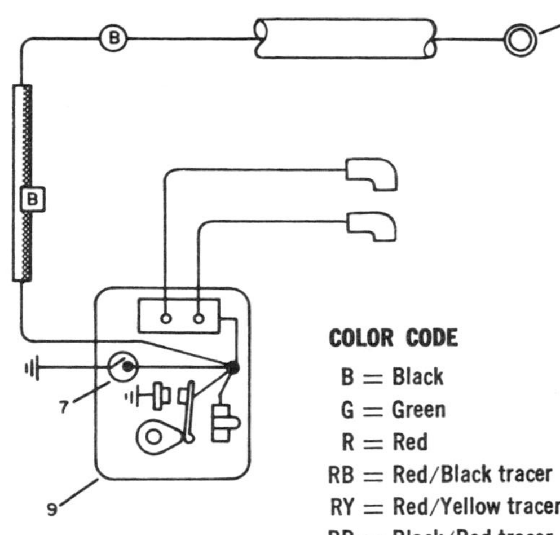

A. Conduit (1 wire)—black
B. Conduit (1 wire)—black
C. Conduit (2 wires)—red and green
D. Conduit (1 wire)—black
E. Conduit (2 wires)—red and green
F. Conduit (2 wires)—red and green
G. Conduit (3 wires)—red wire with black tracer, red wire with yellow tracer, black wire with red tracer
H. Conduit (2 wires)—green and red

1. Horn switch—2 black wires
2. Headlight—black wire with red tracer and red wire with yellow tracer
3. Dimmer switch—red wire with black tracer, red wire with yellow tracer, black wire with red tracer
4. Ignition cutout switch—black wire
5. Generator—
   "F" terminal—green wire
   "A" terminal—red and black wires
6. Light switch—(3 wires)—red, green, and red with black tracer
7. Ignition ground switch lock
8. Voltage regulator—
   "61" terminal—condenser black wire
   DF terminal—green wire
   D+ terminal—red and condenser wire
   D+ terminal—2 red wires
   Gnd terminal—black wire
9. Magneto—black wire
10. Stoplight switch—2 red wires
11. Tail- and stoplight—red and green wires
12. Horn—black wire
13. Capacitor—lead connected to regulator 61 terminal
14. Grounding screw—black wire and condenser ground strap

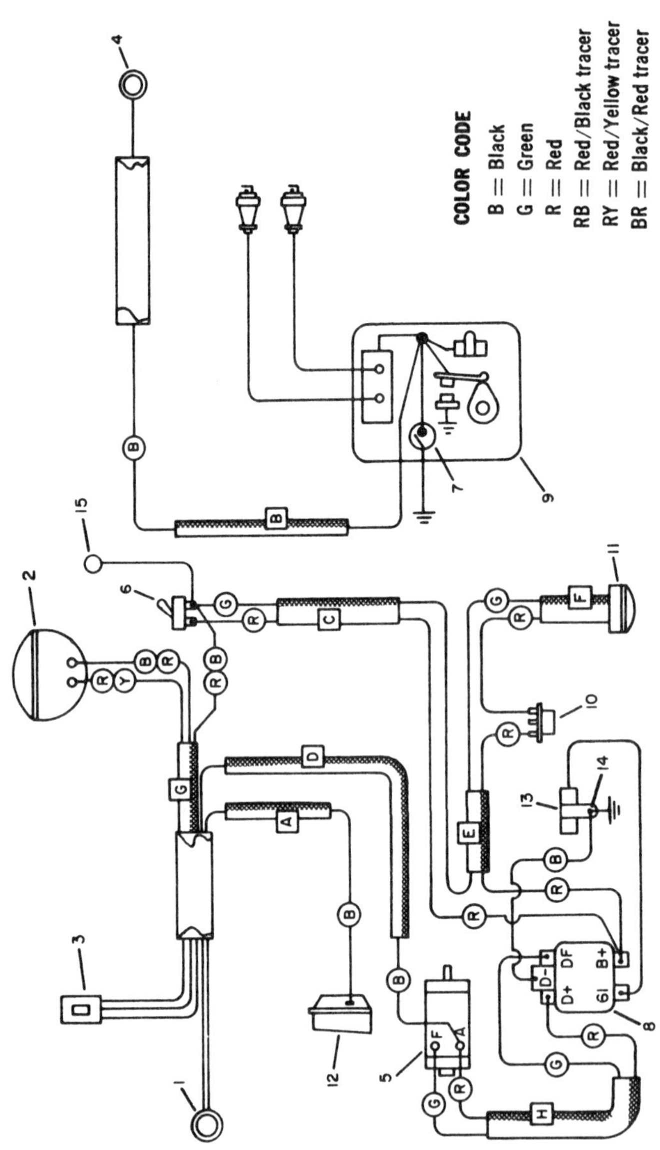

A. Conduit (1 wire)—black
B. Conduit (1 wire)—black
C. Conduit (2 wires)—red and green
D. Conduit (1 wire)—black
E. Conduit (2 wires)—red and green
F. Conduit (2 wires)—red and green
G. Conduit (3 wires)—red wire with black tracer, red wire with yellow tracer, black wire with red tracer
H. Conduit (2 wires)—green and red
1. Horn switch—2 black wires
2. Headlight—black wire with red tracer and red wire with yellow tracer
3. Headlight dimmer switch—red wire with black tracer, red wire with yellow tracer, black wire with red tracer
4. Ignition cutout switch—black wire
5. Generator—
   "F" terminal—green wire
   "A" terminal—black wire
6. Light switch—red, green, and red with black tracer wires
7. Ignition ground switch lock
8. Voltage regulator—
   DF terminal—green wire
   D+ terminal—red wire and condenser wire
   B+ terminal—2 red wires
   "61" terminal—black wire
9. Magneto—black wire
10. Stoplight switch—2 red wires
11. Tail- and stoplight—red and green wires
12. Horn—black wire
13. Capacitor—center black wire connected to regulator "61" terminal
14. Grounding screw—black wire
15. Speedometer light

1967-1969 MODEL CH

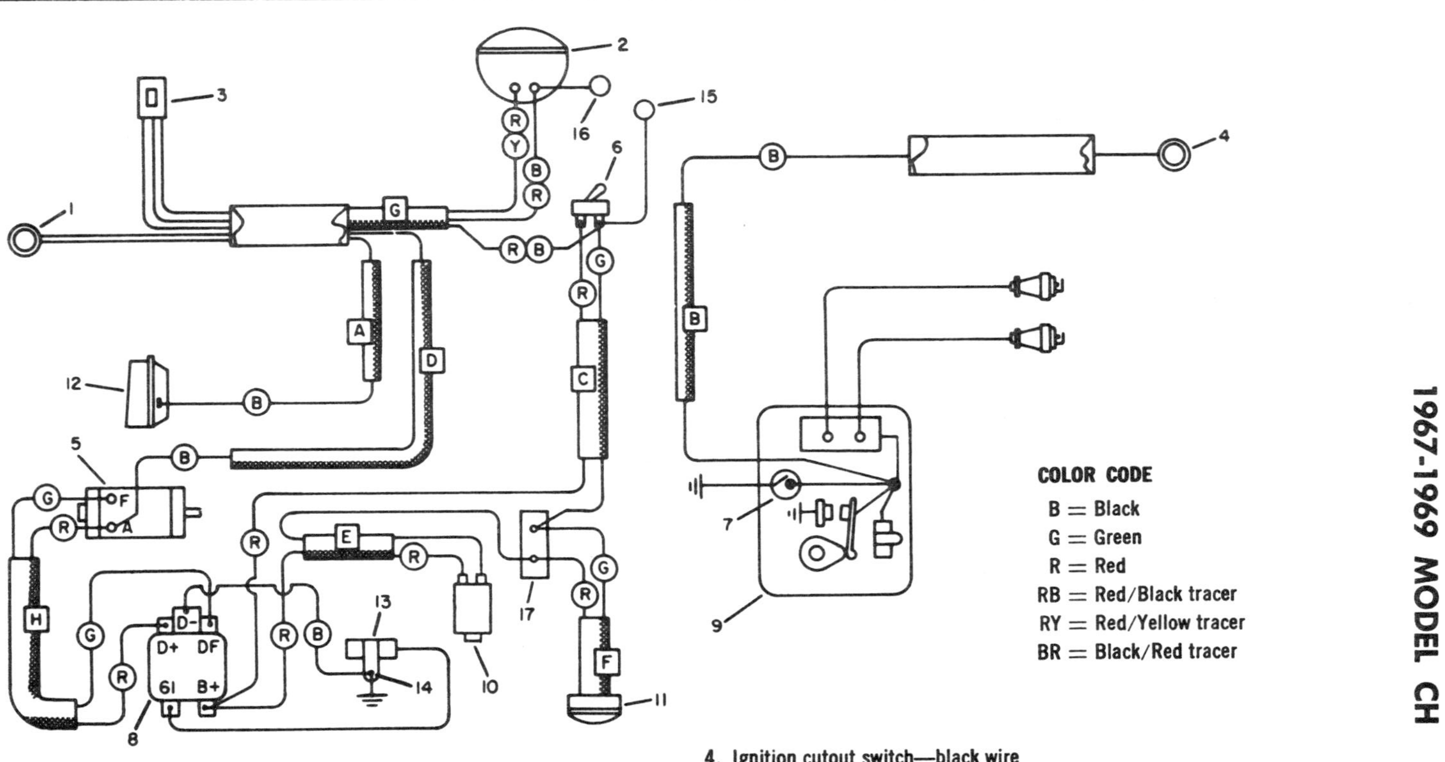

COLOR CODE

B = Black
G = Green
R = Red
RB = Red/Black tracer
RY = Red/Yellow tracer
BR = Black/Red tracer

A. Conduit (1 wire)—black
B. Conduit (1 wire)—black
C. Conduit (2 wires)—red and green
D. Conduit (1 wire)—black
E. Conduit (2 wires)—red
F. Conduit (2 wires)—red and green
G. Conduit (3 wires)—red wire with black tracer, red wire with yellow tracer, black wire with red tracer
H. Conduit (2 wires)—green and red

1. Horn switch—2 black wires
2. Headlight—black wire with red tracer and red wire with yellow tracer
3. Headlight dimmer switch—red wire with black tracer, red wire with yellow tracer, black wire with red tracer
4. Ignition cutout switch—black wire
5. Generator—
   "F" terminal—green wire
   "A" terminal—black wire
6. Light switch—red, green, and red with black tracer wires
7. Ignition ground switch lock
8. Voltage regulator—
   DF terminal—green wire
   D+ terminal—red wire and condenser wire
   B+ terminal—2 red wires
   D— terminal—black wire
9. Magneto—black wire
10. Stoplight switch—2 red wires
11. Tail- and stoplight—red and green wires
12. Horn—black wire
13. Capacitor—black wire connected to regulator D— terminal
14. Grounding screw—black wire
15. Speedometer light
16. High beam indicator light
17. Terminal strip

12

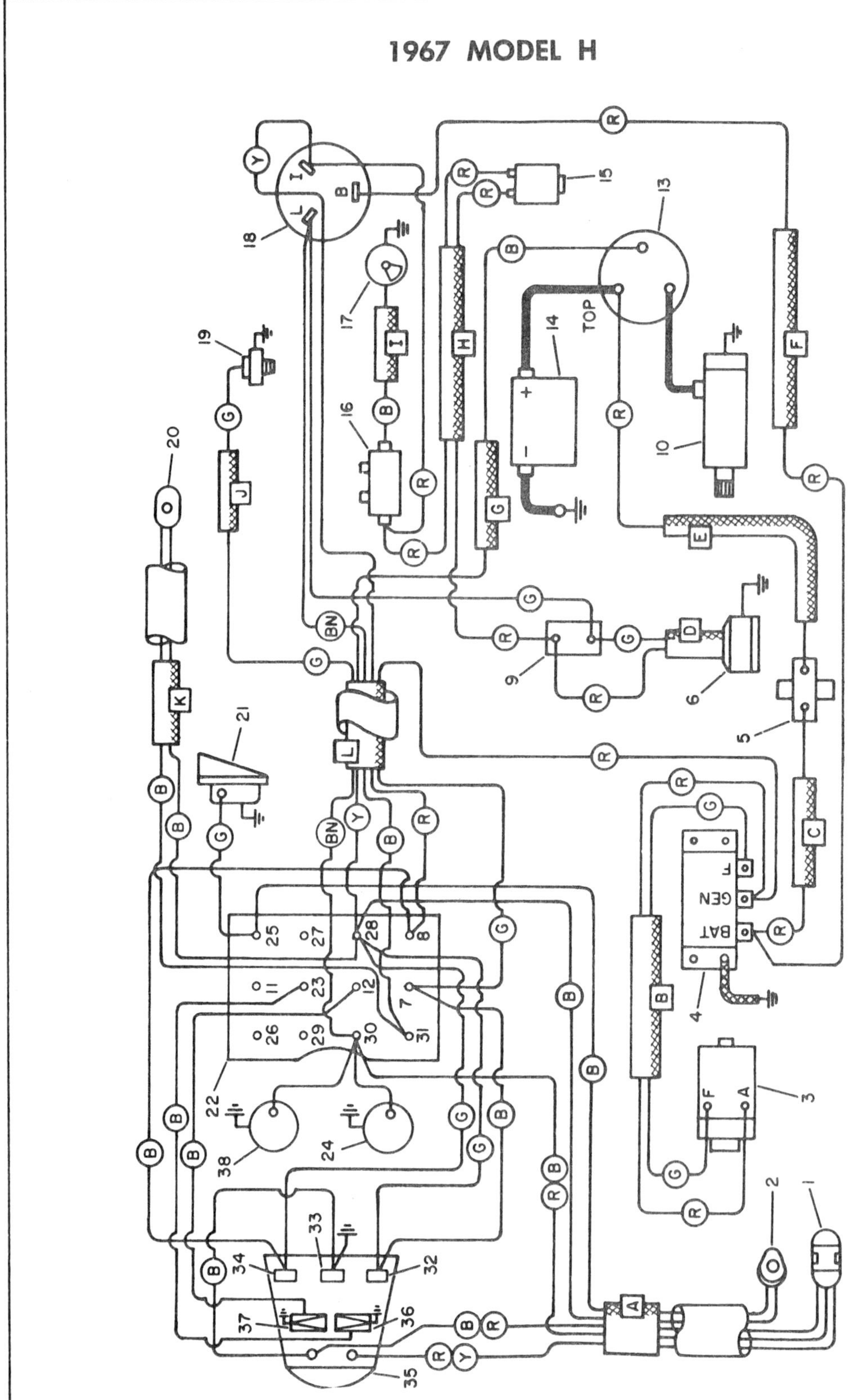
1967 MODEL H

A. Handlebar (5 wires)—red wire with black tracer, black wire with red tracer, red wire with yellow tracer, and 2 black wires
B. Conduit (2 wires)—green and red
C. Conduit (1 wire)—red
D. Conduit (2 wires)—red and green
E. Conduit (1 wire)—red
F. Conduit (1 wire)—red
G. Conduit (1 wire)—black
H. Conduit (2 wires)—red
I. Conduit (1 wire)—black
J. Conduit (1 wire)—green
K. Conduit (2 wires)—black
L. Conduit (5 wires)—brown, yellow black, red and green

1. Headlight dimmer switch
2. Horn switch
3. Generator "F" and "A" terminals
4. Regulator—
   "BAT" terminal
   "GEN" terminal
   "F" terminal
5. Overload circuit breaker
6. Taillight
7. Terminal
8. Terminal
9. Junction terminal board
10. Starter motor
11. Terminal—not used with standard wiring
12. Terminal
13. Starter solenoid
14. Battery
15. Stoplight switch
16. Ignition coil
17. Circuit breaker
18. Ignition—light switch
19. Oil signal light switch
20. Starter button
21. Horn
22. Terminal plate
23. Terminal
24. Speedometer light
25. Terminal
26. Terminal—not used with standard wiring
27. Terminal—not used with standard wiring
28. Terminal
29. Terminal—not used with standard wiring
30. Terminal
31. Terminal
32. Oil signal light
33. High beam indicator light
34. Generator indicator light
35. Headlight
36. Left direction signal pilot light
37. Right direction signal pilot light
38. Tachometer light

Caution: Disconnect ground cable at at battery (—) terminal to prevent accidental starter operation when servicing motorcycle.

COLOR CODE

B = Black
Y = Yellow
BN = Brown
G = Green
R = Red
BR = Black/Red tracer
RB = Red/Black tracer
RY = Red/Yellow tracer

12

1968 AND EARLY 1969 MODEL H

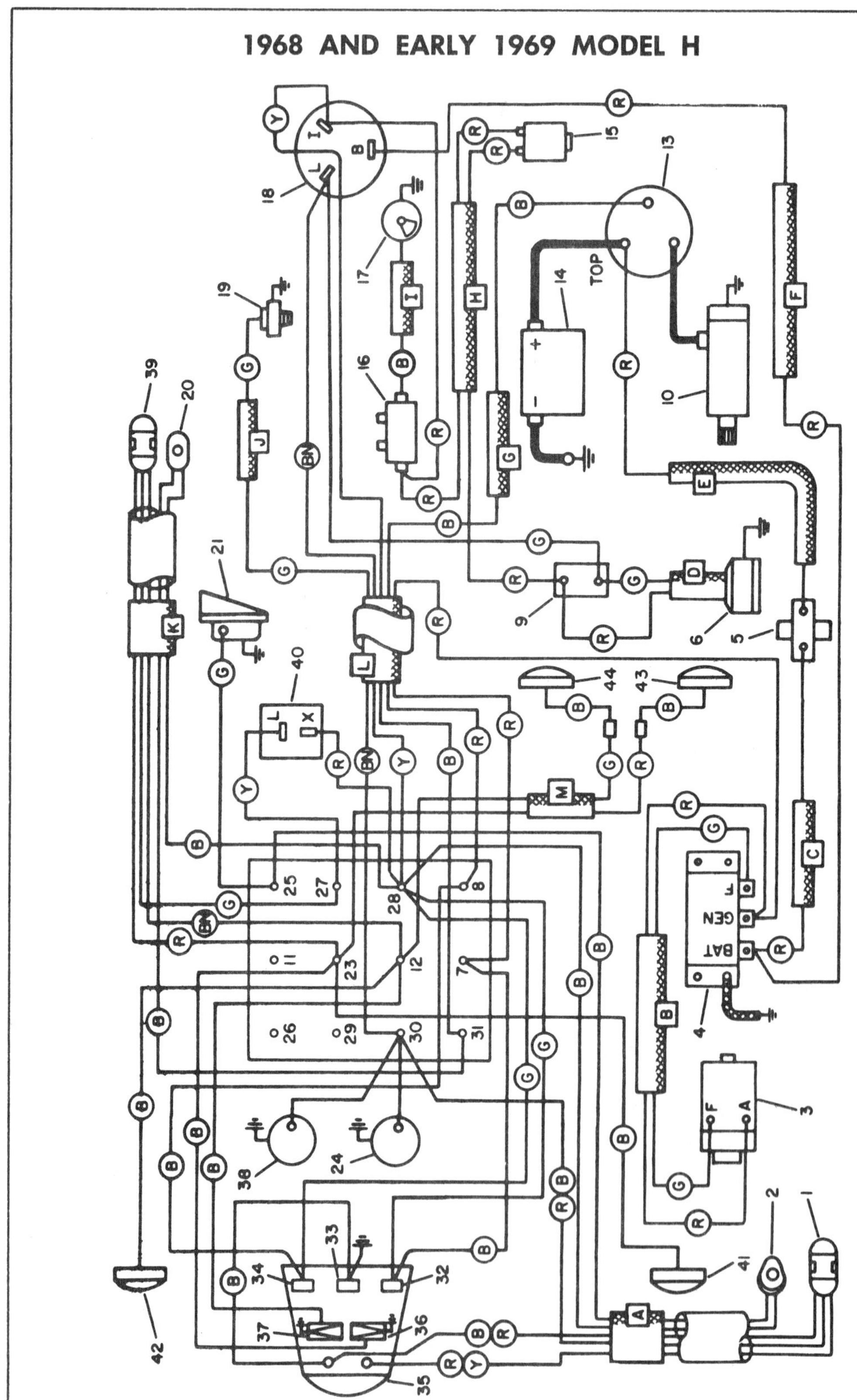

A. Handlebar (5 wires)—red wire with black tracer, black wire with red tracer, red wire with yellow tracer, and 2 black wires
B. Conduit (2 wires)—green and red
C. Conduit (1 wire)—red
D. Conduit (2 wires)—red and green
E. Conduit (1 wire)—red
F. Conduit (1 wire)—red
G. Conduit (1 wire)—black
H. Conduit (2 wires)—red
I. Conduit (1 wire)—black
J. Conduit (1 wire)—green
K. Handlebar (5 wires)—red, brown, green, and 2 black wires
L. Conduit (5 wires)—brown, yellow, black, red, and green
M. Conduit (2 wires)—red and green

1. Headlight dimmer switch
2. Horn switch
3. Generator "F" and "A" terminals
4. Regulator
   "BAT" terminal
   "GEN" terminal
   "F" terminal
5. Overload circuit breaker
6. Taillight
7. Terminal
8. Terminal
9. Junction terminal board
10. Starter motor
11. Terminal—not used with standard wiring
12. Terminal
13. Starter solenoid
14. Battery
15. Stoplight switch
16. Ignition coil
17. Circuit breaker
18. Ignition—light switch
19. Oil signal light switch
20. Starter button
21. Horn
22. Terminal plate
23. Terminal
24. Speedometer light
25. Terminal
26. Terminal—not used with standard wiring
27. Terminal—not used with standard wiring
28. Terminal
29. Terminal—not used with standard wiring
30. Terminal
31. Terminal
32. Oil signal light
33. High beam indicator light
34. Generator indicator light
35. Headlight
36. Left direction signal pilot light
37. Right direction signal pilot light
38. Tachometer light
39. Direction signal switch
40. Direction signal flasher
41. Left front direction light
42. Right front direction light
43. Left rear direction light
44. Right rear direction light

COLOR CODE

B = Black
Y = Yellow
BN = Brown
G = Green
R = Red
BR = Black/Red tracer
RB = Red/Black tracer
RY = Red/Yellow tracer

12

LATE 1969 MODEL H

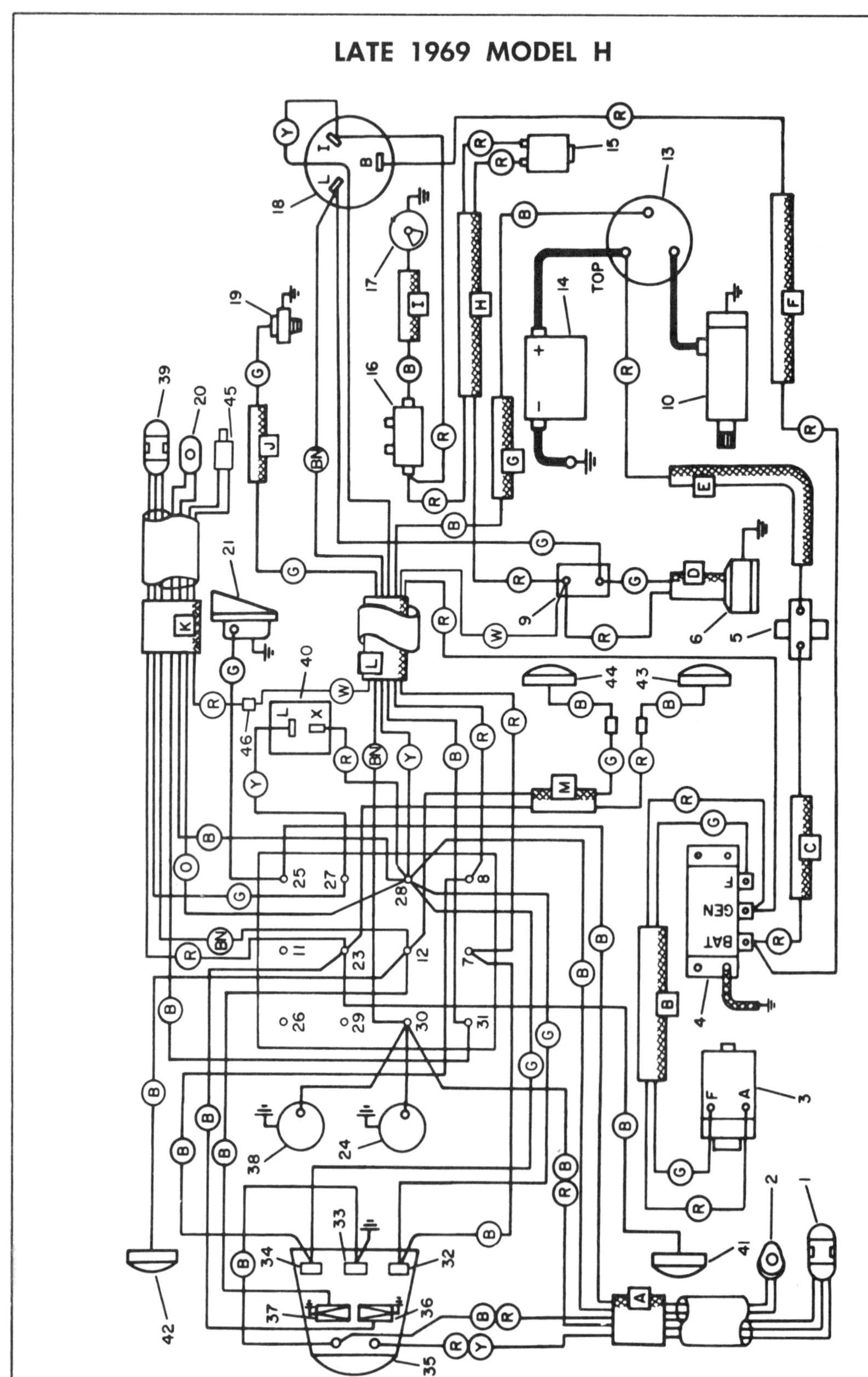

A. Handlebar (5 wires)—red wire with black tracer, black wire with red tracer, red wire with yellow tracer, and 2 black wires
B. Conduit (2 wires)—green and red
C. Conduit (1 wire)—red
D. Conduit (2 wires)—red and green
E. Conduit (1 wire)—red
F. Conduit (1 wire)—red
G. Conduit (1 wire)—black
H. Conduit (2 wires)—red
I. Conduit (1 wire)—black
J. Conduit (1 wire)—green
K. Handlebar (5 wires)—red, brown, green, and 2 black wires
L. Conduit (5 wires)—brown, yellow, black, red, and green
M. Conduit (2 wires)—red and green

1. Headlight dimmer switch
2. Horn switch
3. Generator "F" and "A" terminals
4. Regulator
   "BAT" terminal
   "GEN" terminal
   "F" terminal
5. Overload circuit breaker
6. Taillight
7. Terminal
8. Terminal
9. Junction terminal board
10. Starter motor
11. Terminal—not used with standard wiring
12. Terminal
13. Starter solenoid
14. Battery
15. Stoplight rear switch
16. Ignition coil
17. Circuit breaker
18. Ignition—light switch
19. Oil signal light switch
20. Starter button
21. Horn
22. Terminal plate
23. Terminal
24. Speedometer light
25. Terminal
26. Terminal—not used with standard wiring
27. Terminal—not used with standard wiring
28. Terminal
29. Terminal—not used with standard wiring
30. Terminal
31. Terminal
32. Oil signal light
33. High beam indicator light
34. Generator indicator light
35. Headlight
36. Left direction signal pilot light
37. Right direction signal pilot light
38. Tachometer light
39. Direction signal switch
40. Direction signal flasher
41. Left front direction light
42. Right front direction light
43. Left rear direction light
44. Right rear direction light
45. Stoplight front switch (late 1969)
46. Connector (late 1969)

COLOR CODE

B = Black
Y = Yellow
BN = Brown
G = Green
R = Red
BR = Black/Red tracer
RB = Red/Black tracer
RY = Red/Yellow tracer
O = Orange

LATE 1969 MODEL CH

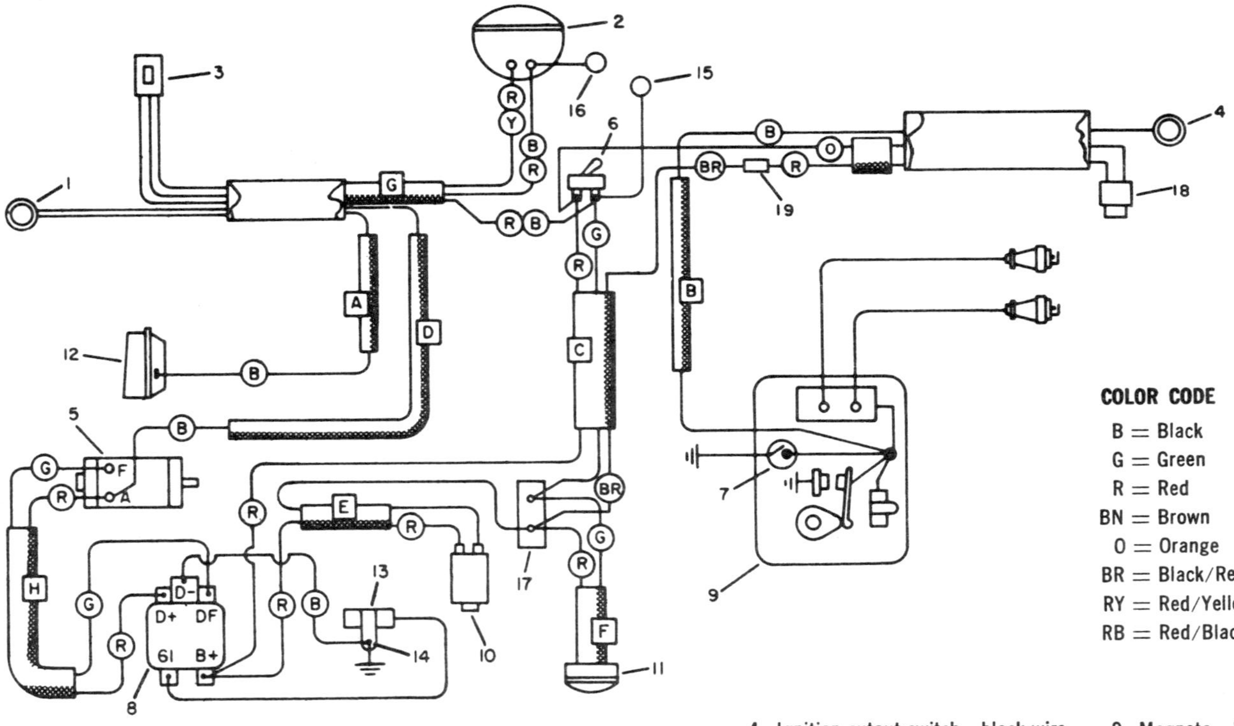

COLOR CODE

B = Black
G = Green
R = Red
BN = Brown
O = Orange
BR = Black/Red tracer
RY = Red/Yellow tracer
RB = Red/Black tracer

A. Conduit (1 wire)—black
B. Conduit (1 wire)—black
C. Conduit (2 wires)—red and green
D. Conduit (1 wire)—black
E. Conduit (2 wires)—red
F. Conduit (2 wires)—red and green
G. Conduit (3 wires)—red wire with black tracer, red wire with yellow tracer, black wire with red tracer
H. Conduit (2 wires)—green and red

1. Horn switch—2 black wires
2. Headlight—black wire with red tracer and red wire with yellow tracer
3. Headlight dimmer switch—red wire with black tracer, red wire with yellow tracer, black wire with red tracer
4. Ignition cutout switch—black wire
5. Generator—
   "F" terminal—green wire
   "A" terminal—black wire
6. Light switch—red, green, and red with black tracer wires
7. Ignition ground switch lock
8. Voltage regulator—
   DF terminal—green wire
   D+ terminal—red wire and condenser wire
   B+ terminal—2 red wires
   D— terminal—black wire
9. Magneto—black wire
10. Stoplight rear switch—2 red wires
11. Tail- and stoplight—red and green wires
12. Horn—black wire
13. Capacitor—black wire connected to regulator D— terminal
14. Grounding screw—black wire
15. Speedometer light
16. High beam indicator light
17. Terminal strip
18. Stoplight front switch (late 1969)
19. Connector (late 1969)

WIRING DIAGRAM KEY — 1970-1972

1. Fork terminal board terminal
2. Fork terminal board terminal
3. Fork terminal board terminal
4. Fork terminal board terminal
5. Fork terminal board terminal
6. Headlight dimmer switch
7. Horn switch
8. Generator "F" and "A" terminals
9. Regulator—
   "BAT" or B terminal
   "GEN" or D
   "F" or DF terminal
10. Overload circuit breaker
11. Taillight
12. Junction terminal board (4 terminals)
13. Starter motor (XLH)
14. Starter solenoid (XLH)
15. Battery
16. Rear stoplight switch
17. Ignition coil
18. Ignition circuit breaker
19. Ignition—light switch
20. Oil signal light switch
21. Starter button (XLH)
22. Horn
23. Speedometer light
24. Oil signal light
25. High beam indicator light
26. Generator indicator light
27. Headlight
28. Tachometer light
29. Directional signal light
30. Directional signal flasher
31. Left front direction light
32. Right front direction light
33. Left rear direction light
34. Right rear direction light
35. Front stoplight switch
36. Crankcase bolt
37. Connector
38. License plate light
39. Starter relay (XLH)

COLOR CODE

B = Black
W = White
O = Orange
R = Red
G = Green
Y = Yellow
V = Violet
BE = Blue
BN = Brown
GY = Gray

1970-1971 MODEL XLH

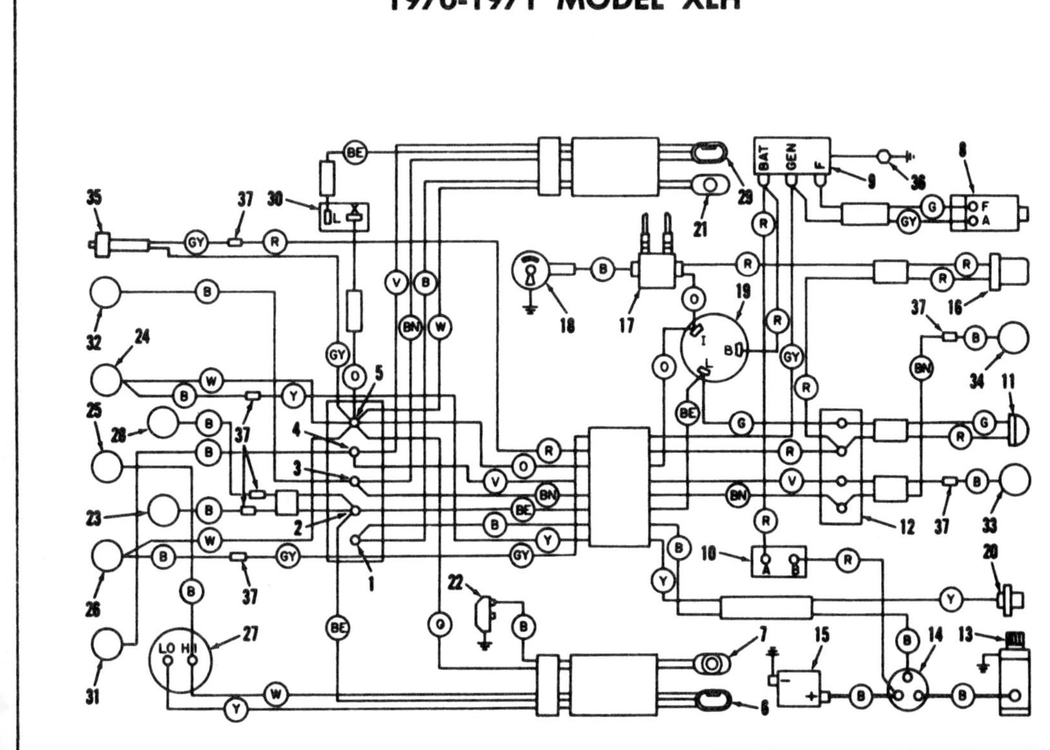

1970-1971 MODEL XLCH

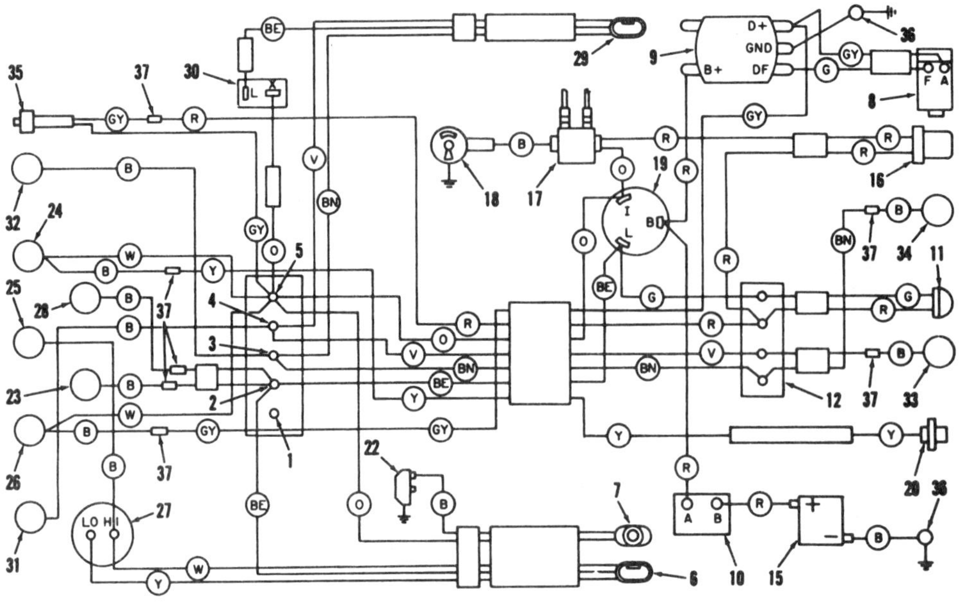

1972 MODEL XLH (STANDARD SEAT)

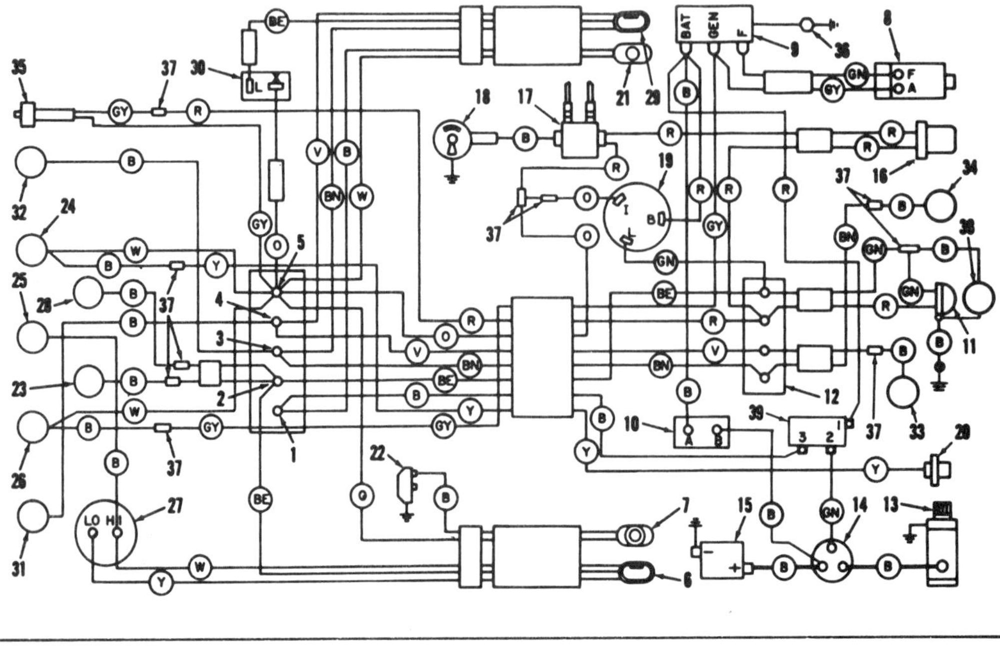

1972 MODEL XLCH (STANDARD SEAT)

1972 MODEL XLH (LOW SEAT)

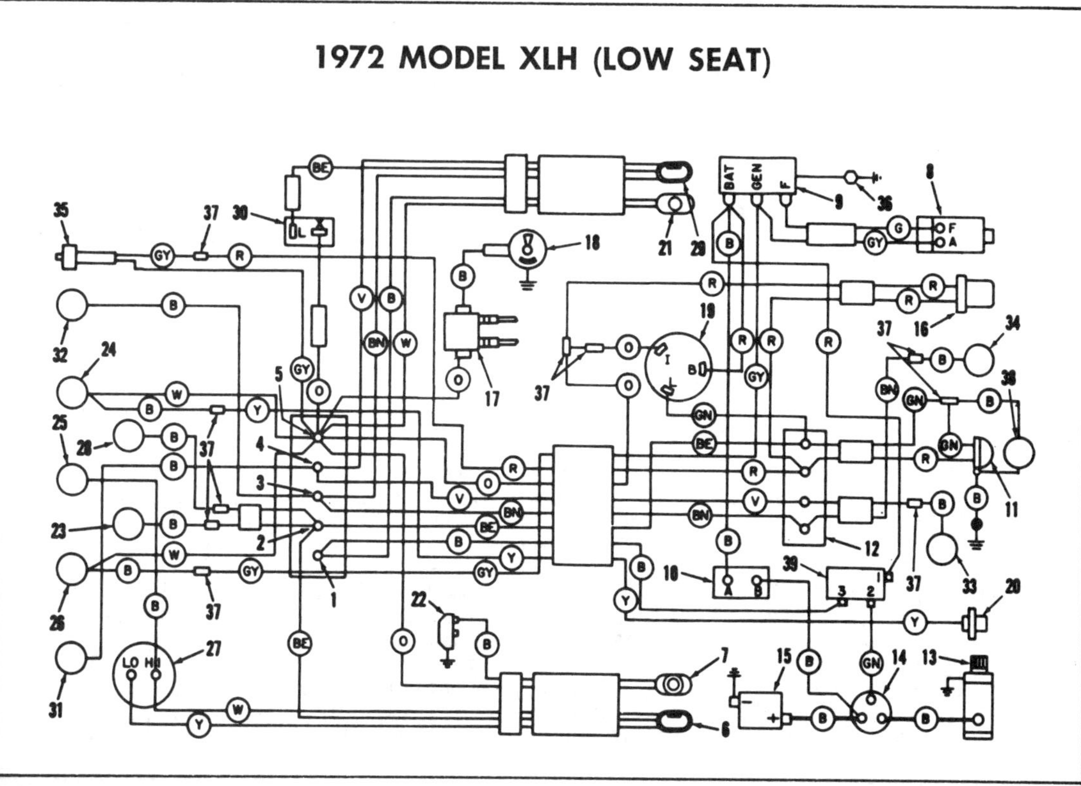

1972 MODEL XLCH (LOW SEAT)

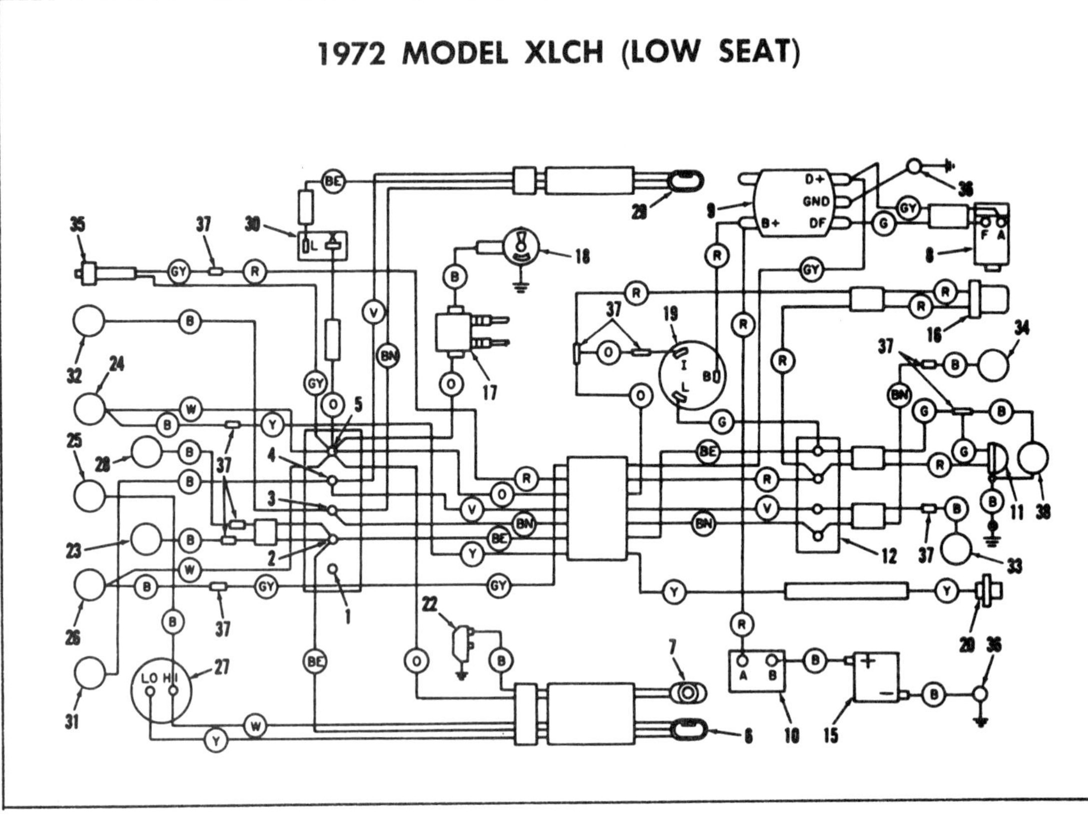

WIRING DIAGRAM KEY — 1973-1974

1. Fork terminal board terminal
2. Fork terminal board terminal
3. Fork terminal board terminal
4. Fork terminal board terminal
5. Fork terminal board terminal
6. Headlight dimmer switch
7. Horn switch
8. Generator "F" and "A" terminals
9. Regulator—
   "BAT" or B+ terminal
   "GEN" or D+
   "F" or DF terminal
10. Taillight
11. Starter motor
12. Starter solenoid
13. Battery
14. Rear stoplight switch
15. Ignition coil
16. Ignition breaker (timer)
17. Ignition—light switch
18. Oil signal light switch
19. Starter button
20. Horn
21. Speedometer light
22. Oil signal light
23. High beam indicator light
24. Generator indicator light
25. Headlight
26. Tachometer light
27. Front stoplight switch
28. Crankcase bolt
29. Starter relay
30. Engine stop switch
31. Rear harness connector
32. Lighting circuit breaker
33. Accessory circuit breaker
34. Ignition circuit breaker
35. Connector
36. Frame bolt
37. Right direction signal switch
38. Left direction signal switch
39. Direction signal flasher
40. Left front direction light
41. Right front direction light
42. Left rear direction light
43. Right rear direction light

COLOR CODE

B = Black
W = White
O = Orange
R = Red
G = Green
Y = Yellow
V = Violet
BE = Blue
BN = Brown
GY = Gray
TN = Tan

1973-1974 MODEL XL

1973-1974 MODEL XLCH

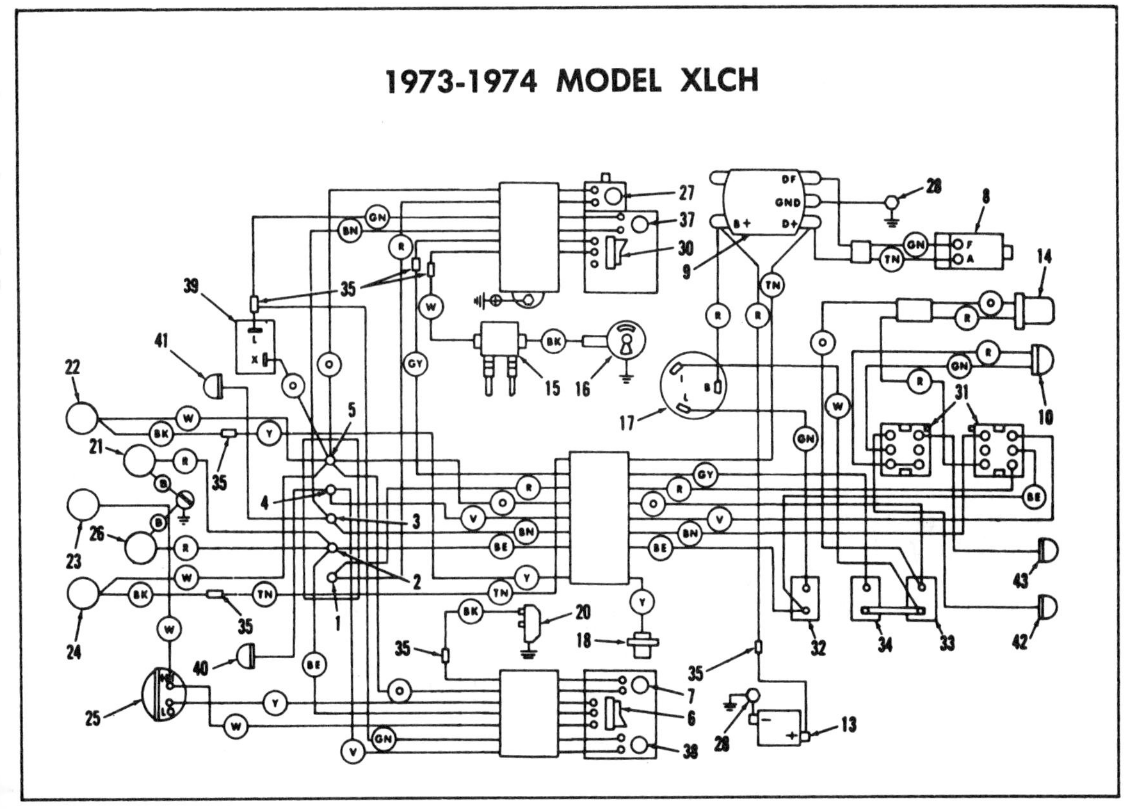

1975-1976 MODEL XL

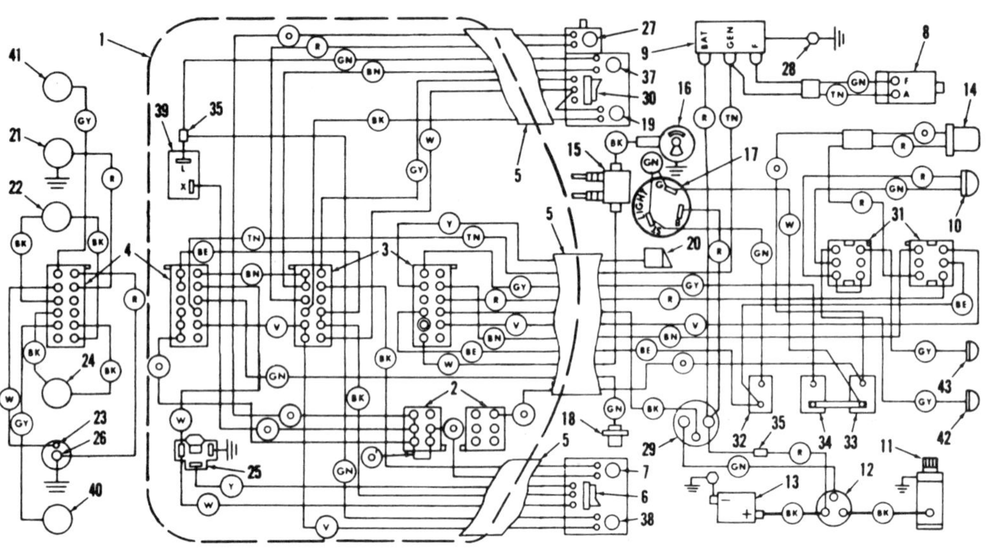

1975-1976 MODEL XLCH

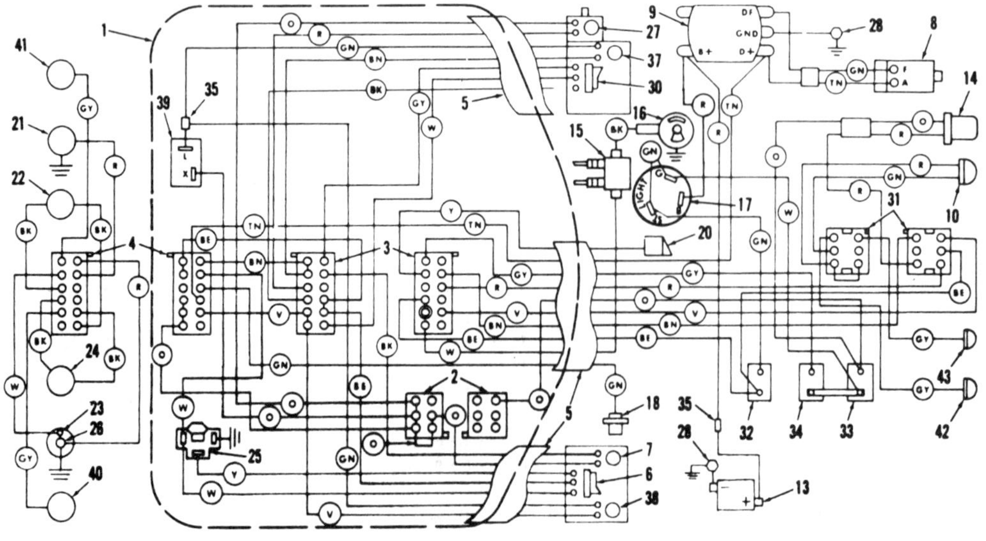

KEY FOR WIRING DIAGRAMS
1975-1976 MODEL XL AND 1975-1976 MODEL XLCH

1. Headlamp housing
2. Socket plug combination
3. Socket plug combination
4. Socket plug combination
5. Wiring harness
6. Headlamp dimmer switch
7. Horn switch
8. Generator "F" and "A" terminals
9. Regulator
   "BAT" or B+ terminal
   "GEN" or D+ terminal
   "F" or DF terminal
10. Tail lamp
11. Starter motor
12. Starter solenoid
13. Battery
14. Rear stoplight switch
15. Ignition coil
16. Ignition breaker (timer)
17. Ignition—light switch
18. Oil signal light switch
19. Starter button
20. Horn
21. Speedometer light
22. Oil signal light
23. High beam indicator light
24. Generator indicator light
25. Headlamp socket
26. Tachometer light
27. Front stoplight switch
28. Crankcase bolt
29. Starter relay
30. Engine stop switch
31. Rear harness connector
32. Lighting circuit breaker
33. Accessory circuit breaker
34. Ignition circuit breaker
35. Connector
37. Right direction signal switch
38. Left direction signal switch
39. Direction signal flasher
40. Left front direction lamp
41. Right front direction lamp
42. Left rear direction lamp
43. Right rear direction lamp

KEY TO COLOR CODE

B = Black
W = White
O = Orange
R = Red
G = Green
Y = Yellow
V = Violet
BE = Blue
BN = Brown
GY = Gray
TN = Tan

1977 MODEL XL

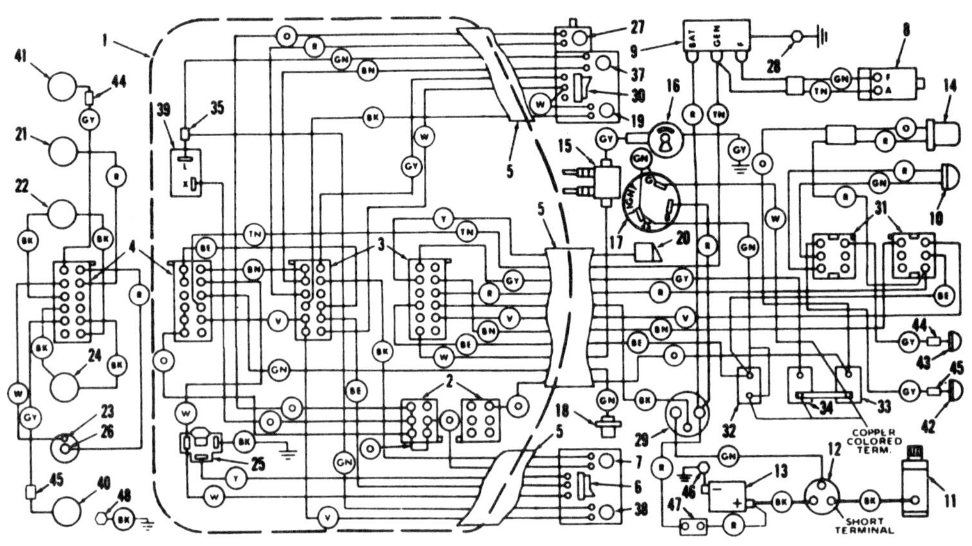

1977 MODEL XLCH

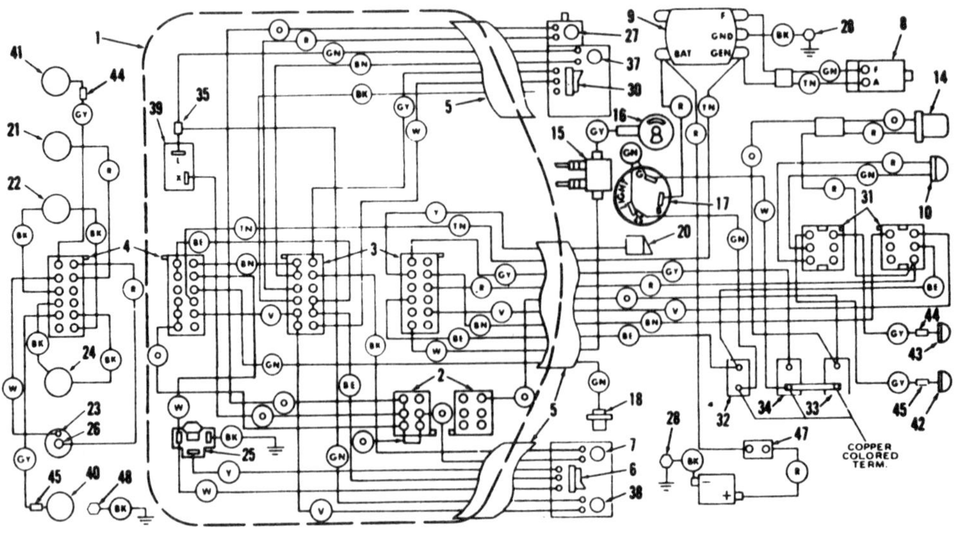

KEY FOR WIRING DIAGRAMS
1977 MODEL XL AND 1977 MODEL XLCH

1. Headlamp housing
2. Socket plug combination
3. Socket plug combination
4. Socket plug combination
5. Wiring harness
6. Headlamp dimmer switch
7. Horn switch
8. Generator "F" and "A" terminals
9. Regulator
   "BAT" or B+ terminal
   "GEN" or D+ terminal
   "F" or DF terminal
   "GND" terminal
10. Tail lamp
11. Starter motor
12. Starter solenoid
13. Battery
14. Rear stoplight switch
15. Ignition coil
16. Ignition breaker (timer)
17. Ignition—light switch
18. Oil signal light switch
19. Starter button
20. Horn
21. Speedometer light
22. Oil signal light
23. High beam indicator light
24. Generator indicator light
25. Headlamp socket
26. Tachometer light
27. Front stoplight switch
28. Crankcase bolt (under battery)
29. Starter relay
30. Engine stop switch
31. Rear harness connector
32. Lighting circuit breaker
33. Accessory circuit breaker
34. Ignition circuit breaker
35. Connector
37. Right direction signal switch
38. Left direction signal switch
39. Direction signal flasher
40. Left front direction lamp
41. Right front direction lamp
42. Left rear direction lamp
43. Right rear direction lamp
44. Tag, brown (R)
45. Tag, violet (L)
46. Bolt to frame
47. Main circuit breaker
48. Handlebar bolt

KEY TO COLOR CODE

B = Black
W = White
O = Orange
R = Red
G = Green
Y = Yellow
V = Violet
BE = Blue
BN = Brown
GY = Gray
TN = Tan

1977-1978 MODEL XLCR

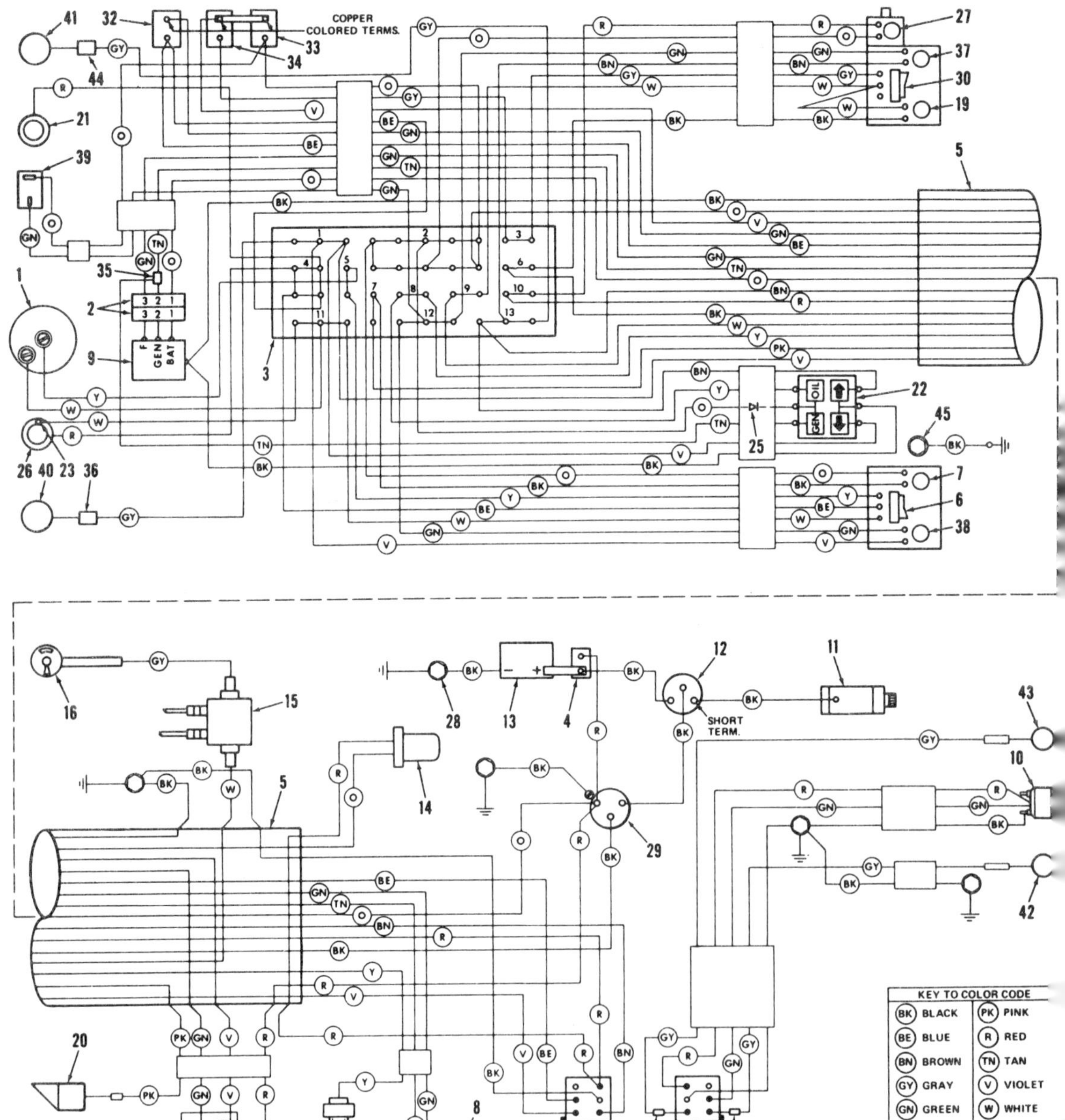

KEY FOR WIRING DIAGRAMS 1977-1978 MODEL XLCR

1. Headlamp housing
2. Socket-plug combination
3. Connector board
4. Main circuit breaker
5. Wiring harness
6. Headlamp dimmer switch
7. Horn switch
8. Generator
9. Regulator
10. Tail lamp
11. Starter motor
12. Starter solenoid
13. Battery
14. Rear stoplight switch
15. Ignition coil
16. Ignition breaker (timer)
17. Ignition—light switch
18. Oil signal light switch
19. Starter button
20. Horn
21. Speedometer light
22. Light cluster
    GEN light
    OIL light
    Left turn signal
    Right turn signal
23. High beam indicator light
24. Not used
25. Diode
26. Tachometer light
27. Front stoplight switch
28. Crankcase bolt
29. Starter relay
30. Engine stop switch
31. Connector
32. Lighting circuit breaker
33. Accessory circuit breaker
34. Ignition circuit breaker
35. Connector
36. Tag, violet
37. Right direction signal switch
38. Left direction signal switch
39. Direction signal flasher
40. Left front direction lamp
41. Right front direction lamp
42. Left rear direction lamp
43. Right rear direction lamp
44. Tag, brown
45. Handlebar bolt

1978 MODEL XLH

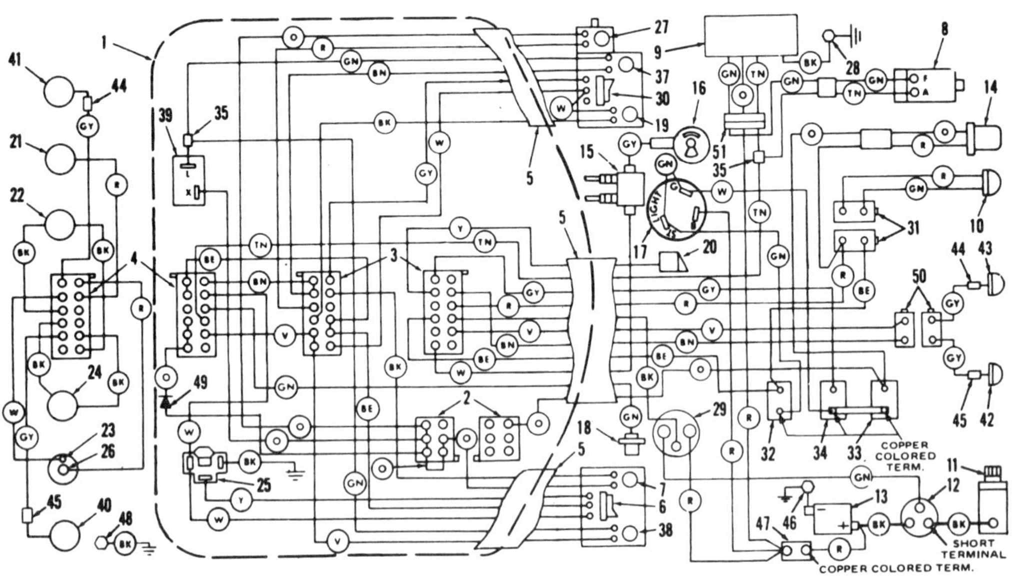

1978 MODEL XLCH

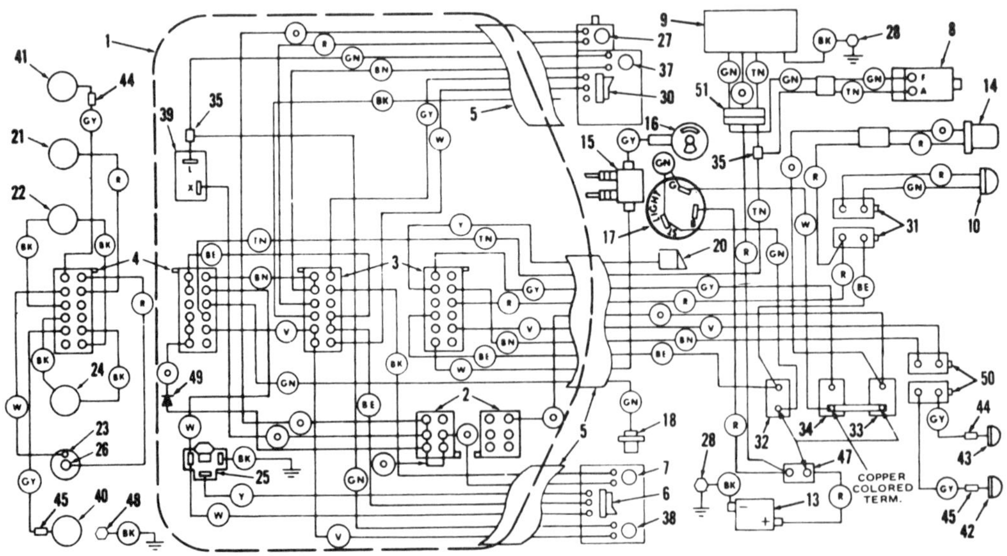

KEY FOR WIRING DIAGRAMS 1978 MODEL XLH AND 1978 MODEL XLCH

1. Headlamp housing
2. Socket plug combination
3. Socket plug combination
4. Socket plug combination
5. Wiring harness
6. Headlamp dimmer switch
7. Horn switch
8. Generator "F" and "A" terminals
9. Regulator
10. Tail lamp
11. Starter motor
12. Starter solenoid
13. Battery
14. Rear stoplight switch
15. Ignition coil
16. Ignition breaker (timer)
17. Ignition—light switch
18. Oil signal light switch
19. Starter button
20. Horn
21. Speedometer light
22. Oil signal light
23. High beam indicator light
24. Generator indicator light
25. Headlamp socket
26. Tachometer light
27. Front stoplight switch
28. Crankcase bolt (under battery)
29. Starter relay
30. Engine stop switch
31. Tail lamp harness connector
32. Lighting circuit breaker
33. Accessory circuit breaker
34. Ignition circuit breaker
35. Connector
37. Right turn signal switch
38. Left turn signal switch
39. Turn signal flasher
40. Left front turn signal lamp
41. Right front turn signal lamp
42. Left rear turn signal lamp
43. Right rear turn signal lamp
44. Tag, brown (R)
45. Tag, violet (L)
46. Bolt to frame
47. Main circuit breaker
48. Handlebar bolt
49. Diode
50. Rear turn signal lamp harness connector
51. Regulator connector

KEY TO COLOR CODE

B = Black
W = White
O = Orange
R = Red
G = Green
Y = Yellow
V = Violet
BE = Blue
BN = Brown
GY = Gray
TN = Tan

1979-1980 MODEL XLH

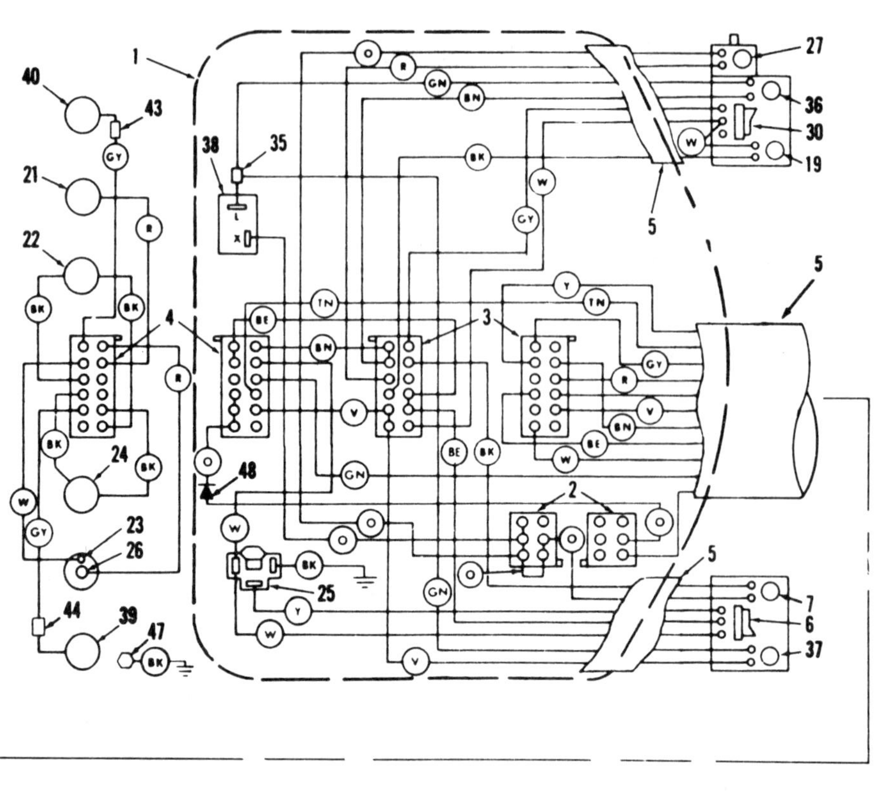

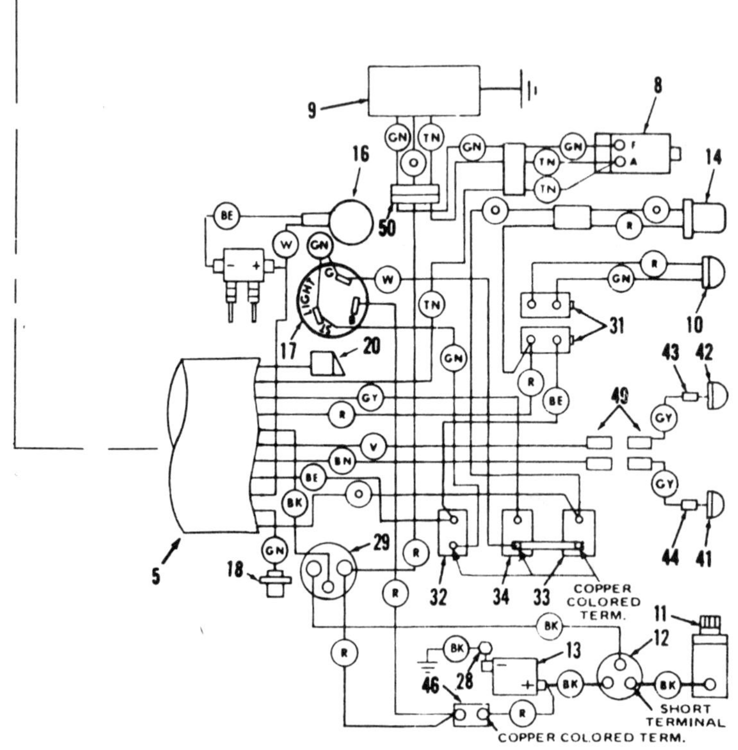

KEY FOR WIRING DIAGRAMS 1979-1980 XLH

1. Headlamp housing
2. Socket plug combination
3. Socket plug combination
4. Socket plug combination
5. Wiring harness
6. Headlamp dimmer switch
7. Horn switch
8. Generator "F" and "A" terminals
9. Regulator
10. Tail lamp
11. Starter motor
12. Starter solenoid
13. Battery
14. Rear stoplight switch
15. Ignition coil
16. Ignition timer
17. Ignition—light switch
18. Oil signal light switch
19. Starter button
20. Horn
21. Speedometer light
22. Oil signal light
23. High beam indicator light
24. Generator indicator light
25. Headlamp socket
26. Tachometer light
27. Front stoplight switch
28. Crankcase bolt (under battery)
29. Starter relay
30. Engine stop switch
31. Tail lamp harness connector
32. Lighting circuit breaker
33. Accessory circuit breaker
34. Ignition circuit breaker
35. Connector
36. Right turn signal switch
37. Left turn signal switch
38. Turn signal flasher
39. Left front turn signal lamp
40. Right front turn signal lamp
41. Left rear turn signal lamp
42. Right rear turn signal lamp
43. Tag, brown (R)
44. Tag, violet (L)
45. Bolt to frame
46. Main circuit breaker
47. Handlebar bolt
48. Diode
49. Rear turn signal lamp harness connector
50. Regulator connector

1979-1980 MODEL XLCH

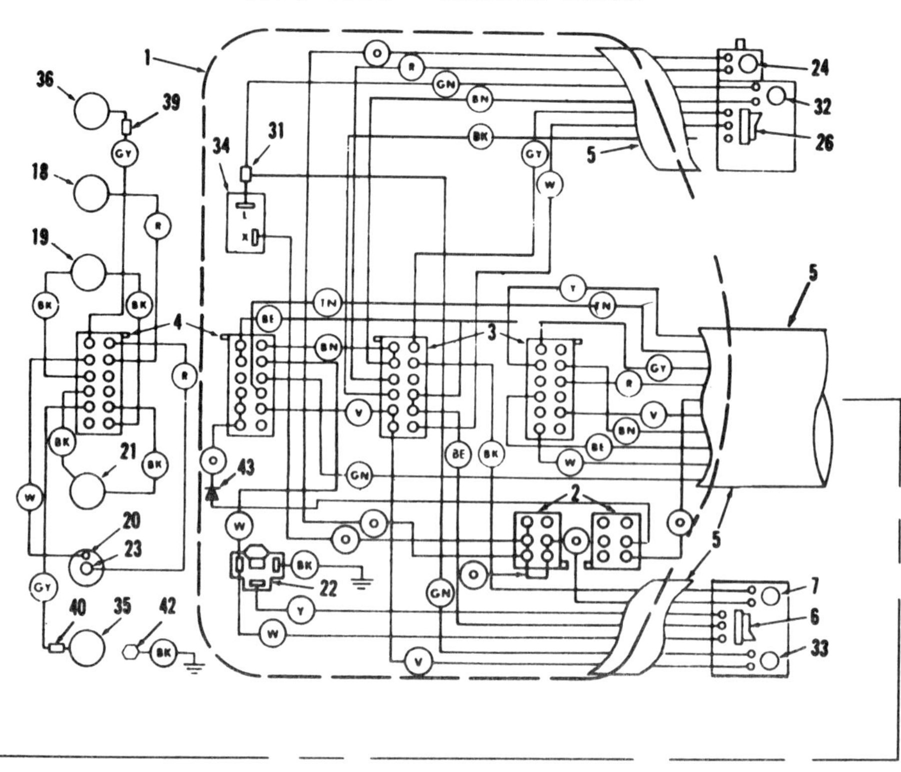

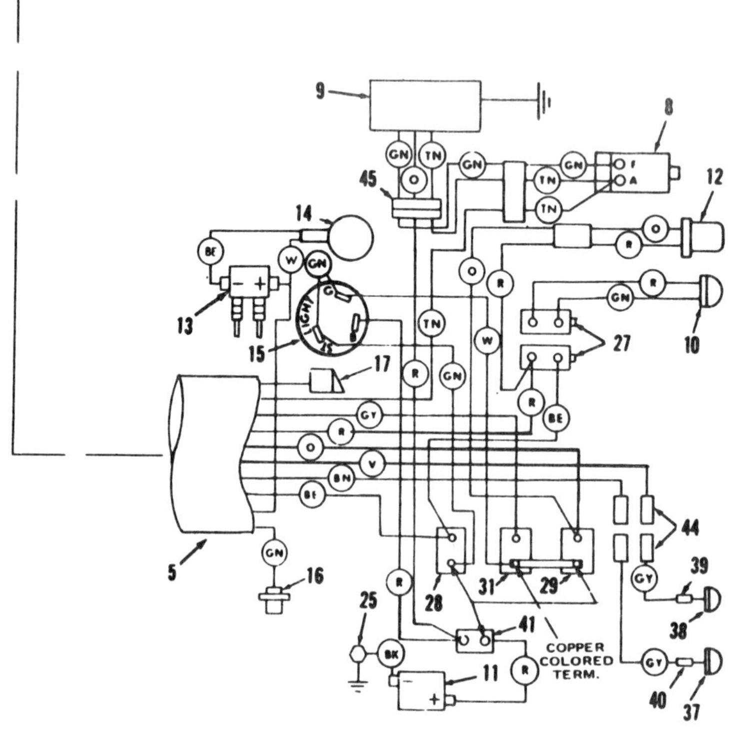

KEY FOR WIRING DIAGRAMS 1979-1980 XLCH

1. Headlamp housing
2. Socket plug combination
3. Socket plug combination
4. Socket plug combination
5. Wiring harness
6. Headlamp dimmer switch
7. Horn switch
8. Generator "F" and "A" terminals
9. Regulator
10. Tail lamp
11. Battery
12. Rear stoplight switch
13. Ignition coil
14. Ignition timer
15. Ignition—light switch
16. Oil signal light switch
17. Horn
18. Speedometer light
19. Oil signal light
20. High beam indicator light
21. Generator indicator light
22. Headlamp socket
23. Tachometer light
24. Front stoplight switch
25. Crankcase bolt (under battery)
26. Engine stop switch
27. Tail lamp harness connector
28. Lighting circuit breaker
29. Accessory circuit breaker
30. Ignition circuit breaker
31. Connector
32. Right turn signal switch
33. Left turn signal switch
34. Turn signal flasher
35. Left front turn signal lamp
36. Right front turn signal lamp
37. Left rear turn signal lamp
38. Right rear turn signal lamp
39. Tag, brown (R)
40. Tag, violet (L)
41. Main circuit breaker
42. Handlebar bolt
43. Diode
44. Rear turn signal lamp harness connector
45. Regulator connector

1980 MODEL XLH/XLS

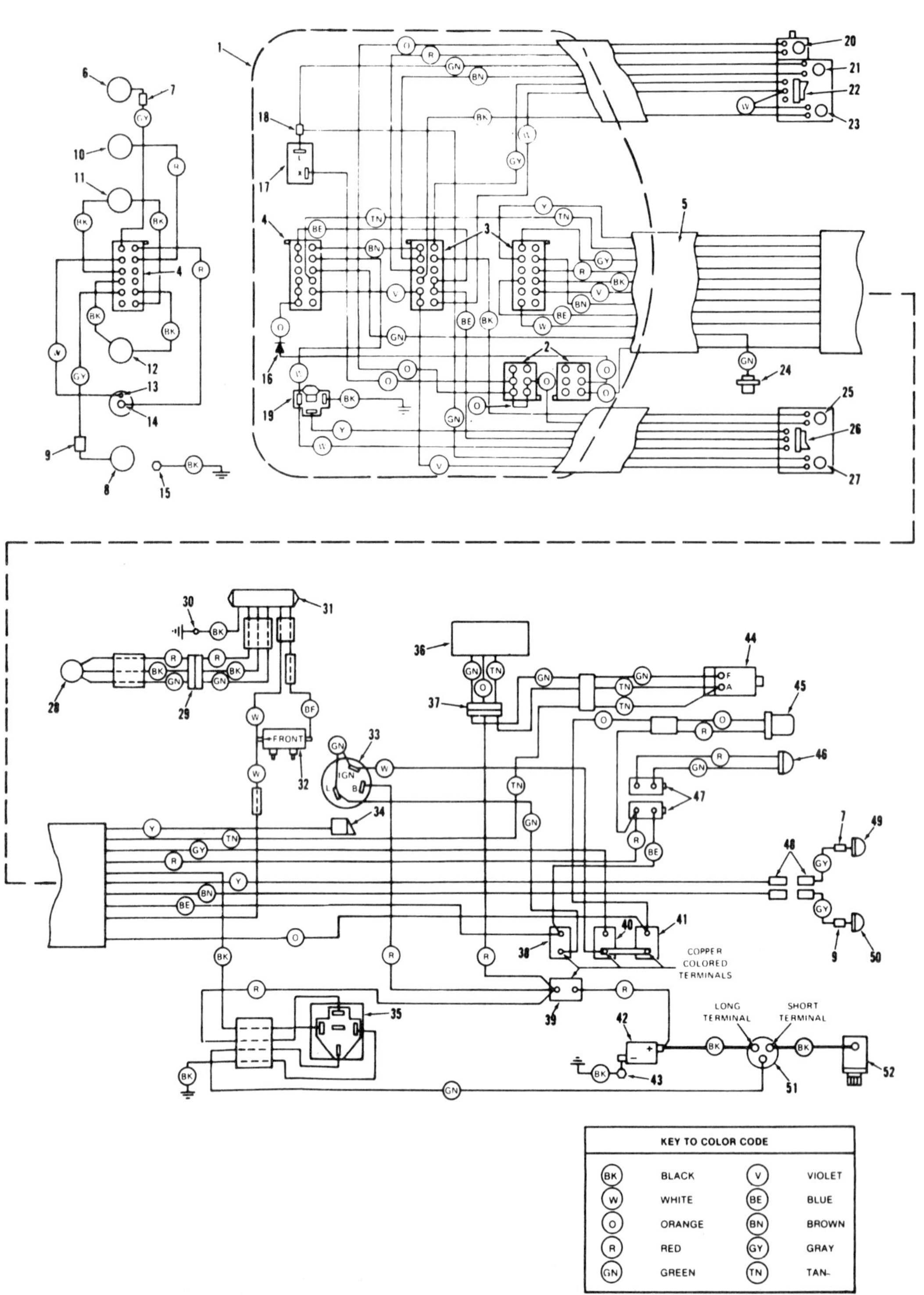

KEY FOR WIRING DIAGRAMS 1980 MODEL XLH/XLS

1. Headlamp housing
2. Socket-plug combination
3. Socket-plug combination
4. Socket-plug combination
5. Main wiring harness
6. Right front turn signal lamp
7. Tag, brown (R)
8. Left front turn signal lamp
9. Tag, violet (L)
10. Speedometer lamp
11. Oil signal lamp
12. Generator indicator lamp
13. High beam indicator lamp
14. Tachometer lamp
15. Handlebar bolt
16. Diode
17. Turn signal flasher
18. Connector
19. Headlamp socket
20. Front stoplight switch
21. Right turn signal switch
22. Engine stop switch
23. Starter switch
24. Oil signal light switch
25. Horn switch
26. Headlamp dimmer switch
27. Left turn signal switch
28. Ignition sensor
29. Ignition sensor connector
30. Screw on oil filter bracket
31. Ignition module
32. Ignition coil
33. Ignition—light switch
34. Horn
35. Starter relay
36. Regulator
37. Regulator connector
38. Lighting circuit breaker (15 amp)
39. Main circuit breaker (30 amp)
40. Ignition circuit breaker (15 amp)
41. Accessory circuit breaker (15 amp)
42. Battery
43. Crankcase bolt (under battery)
44. Generator
45. Rear stoplight switch
46. Tail lamp
47. Tail lamp harness connector
48. Rear turn signal connector
49. Right rear turn signal lamp
50. Left rear turn signal lamp
51. Starter solenoid
52. Starter motor

1981 MODEL XLH/XLS

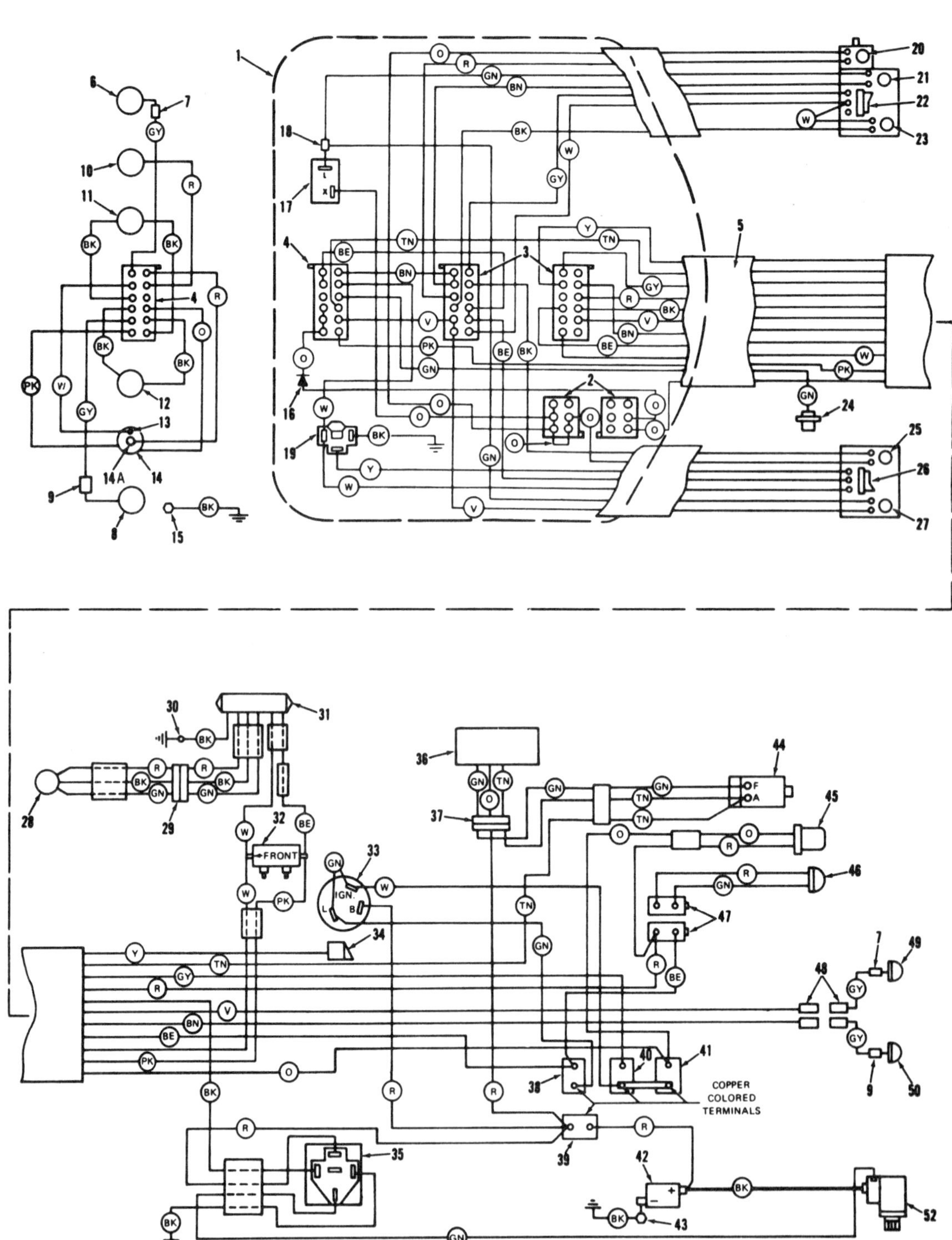

KEY FOR WIRING DIAGRAMS 1981 MODEL XLH/XLS

1. Headlamp housing
2. Socket-plug combination
3. Socket-plug combination
4. Socket-plug combination
5. Main wiring harness
6. Right front turn signal lamp
7. Tag, brown (R)
8. Left front turn signal lamp
9. Tag, violet (L)
10. Speedometer lamp
11. Oil signal lamp
12. Generator indicator lamp
13. High beam indicator lamp
14. Tachometer
14A. Tachometer lamp
15. Handlebar bolt
16. Diode
17. Turn signal flasher
18. Connector
19. Headlamp socket
20. Front stoplight switch
21. Right turn signal switch
22. Engine stop switch
23. Starter switch
24. Oil signal light switch
25. Horn switch
26. Headlamp dimmer switch
27. Left turn signal switch
28. Ignition sensor
29. Ignition sensor connector
30. Screw on oil filter bracket
31. Ignition module
32. Ignition coil
33. Ignition—light switch
34. Horn
35. Starter relay
36. Regulator
37. Regulator connector
38. Lighting circuit breaker (15 amp)
39. Main circuit breaker (30 amp)
40. Ignition circuit breaker (15 amp)
41. Accessory circuit breaker (15 amp)
42. Battery
43. Crankcase bolt (under battery)
44. Generator
45. Rear stoplight switch
46. Tail lamp
47. Tail lamp harness connector
48. Rear turn signal connector
49. Right rear turn signal lamp
50. Left rear turn signal lamp
51. Starter solenoid
52. Starter motor

1982 XLH/XLS

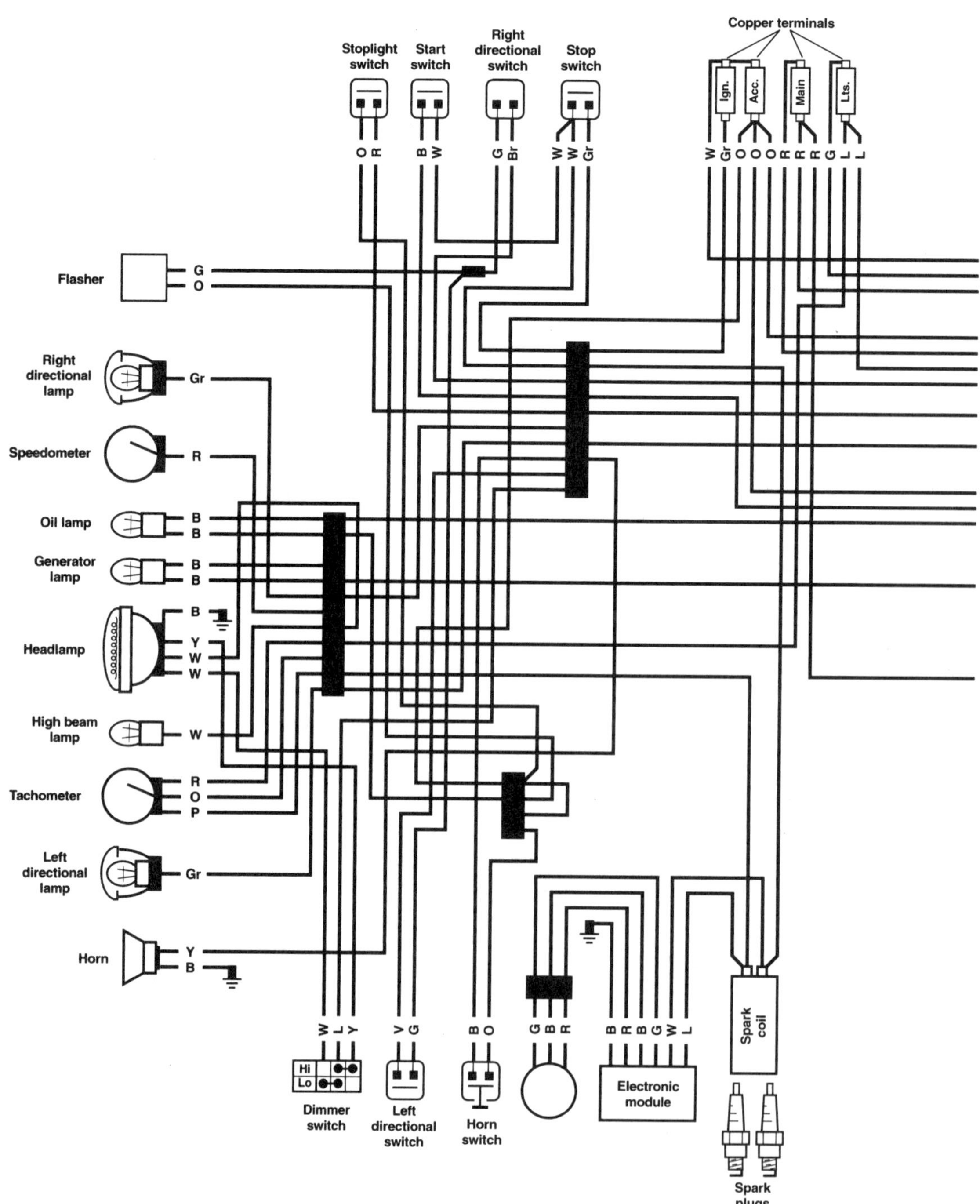
Copper terminals
Stoplight switch
Start switch
Right directional switch
Stop switch
Ign.
Acc.
Main
Lts.
Flasher
Right directional lamp
Speedometer
Oil lamp
Generator lamp
Headlamp
High beam lamp
Tachometer
Left directional lamp
Horn
Hi
Lo
Dimmer switch
Left directional switch
Horn switch
Electronic module
Spark coil
Spark plugs

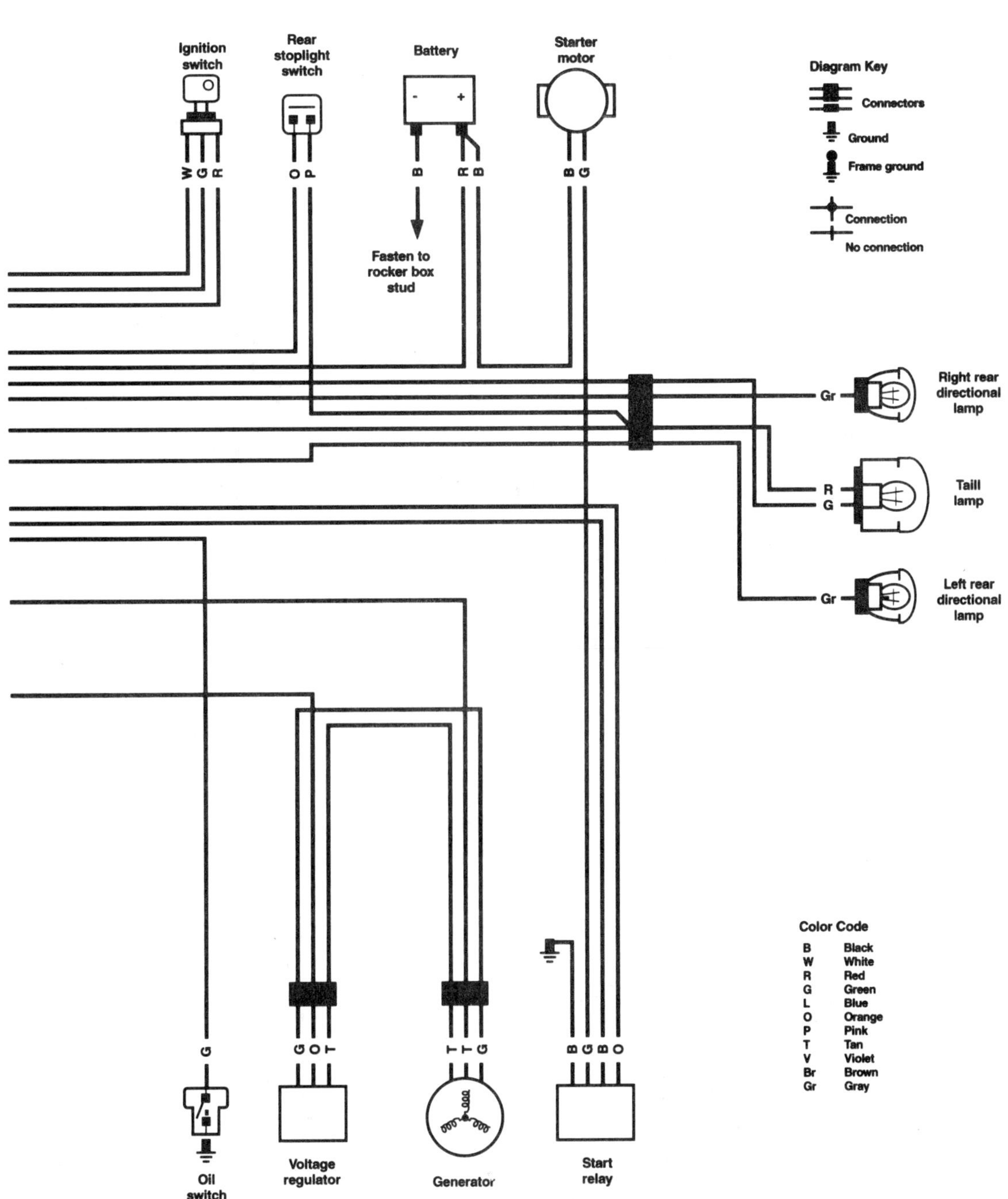
Ignition switch
W G R
Rear stoplight switch
O P
Battery
- +
B
R B
Fasten to rocker box stud
Starter motor
B G
Diagram Key
Connectors
Ground
Frame ground
Connection
No connection
Gr
Right rear directional lamp
R
G
Taill lamp
Gr
Left rear directional lamp
G
Oil switch
G O T
Voltage regulator
T T G
Generator
B G B O
Start relay
Color Code
B Black
W White
R Red
G Green
L Blue
O Orange
P Pink
T Tan
V Violet
Br Brown
Gr Gray

12

1983-EARLY 1984 XLH

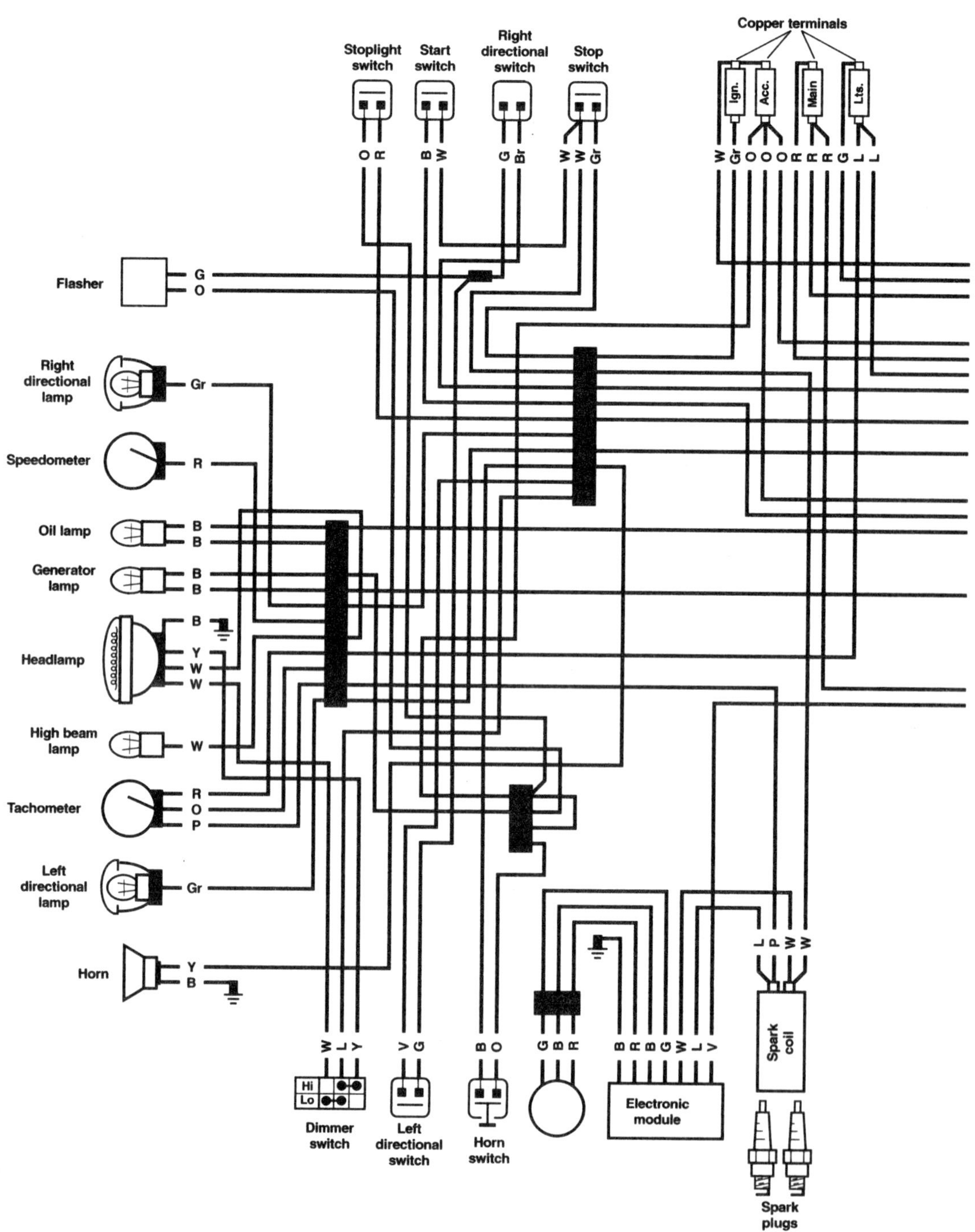

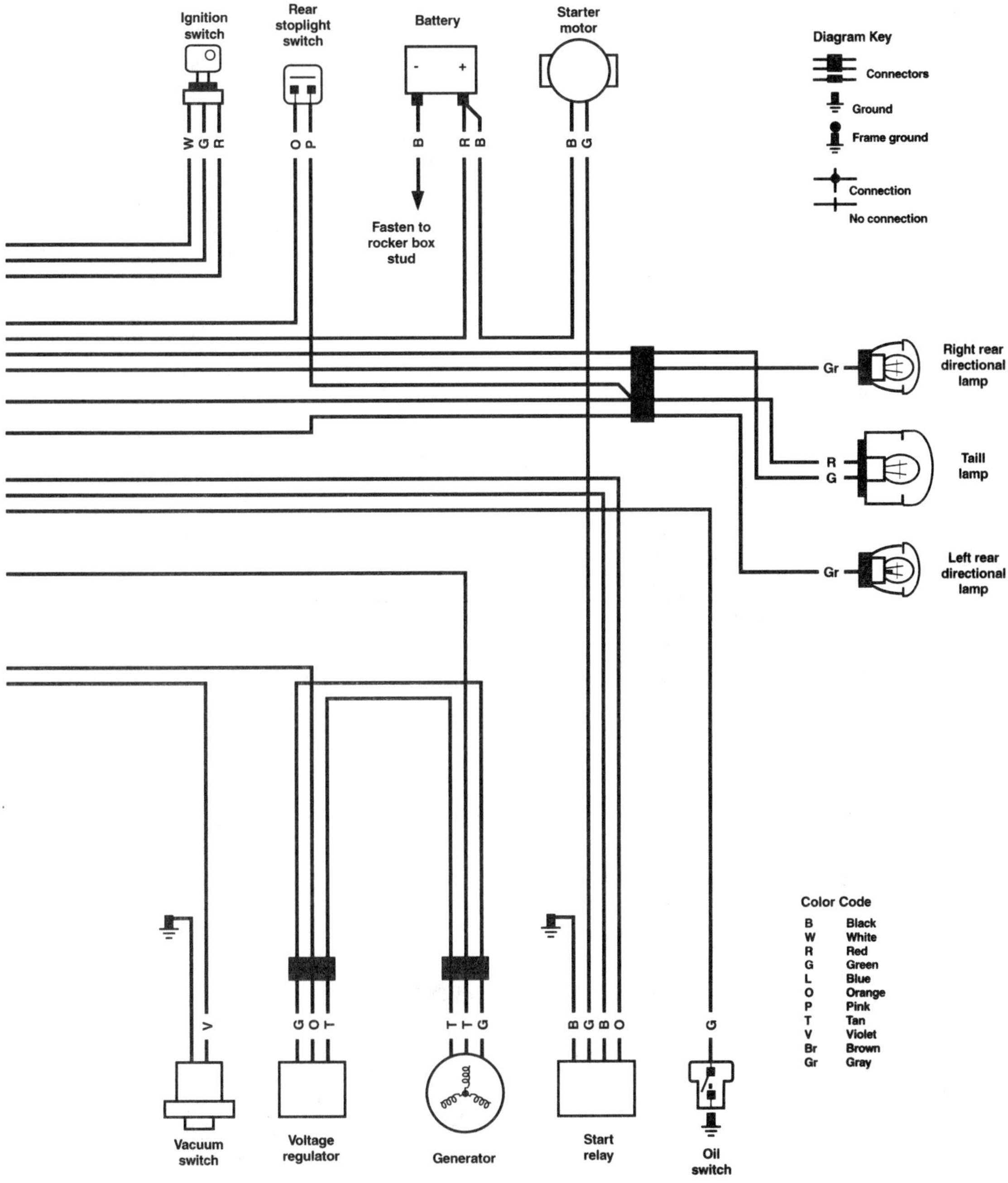

Ignition switch

W G R

Rear stoplight switch

O P

Battery

\- +

B R B

Fasten to rocker box stud

Starter motor

B G

Diagram Key

Connectors

Ground

Frame ground

Connection

No connection

Gr

Right rear directional lamp

R

G

Taill lamp

Gr

Left rear directional lamp

V

Vacuum switch

G O T

Voltage regulator

T T G

Generator

B G B O

Start relay

G

Oil switch

Color Code

B	Black
W	White
R	Red
G	Green
L	Blue
O	Orange
P	Pink
T	Tan
V	Violet
Br	Brown
Gr	Gray

1983 EARLY 1984 XLS

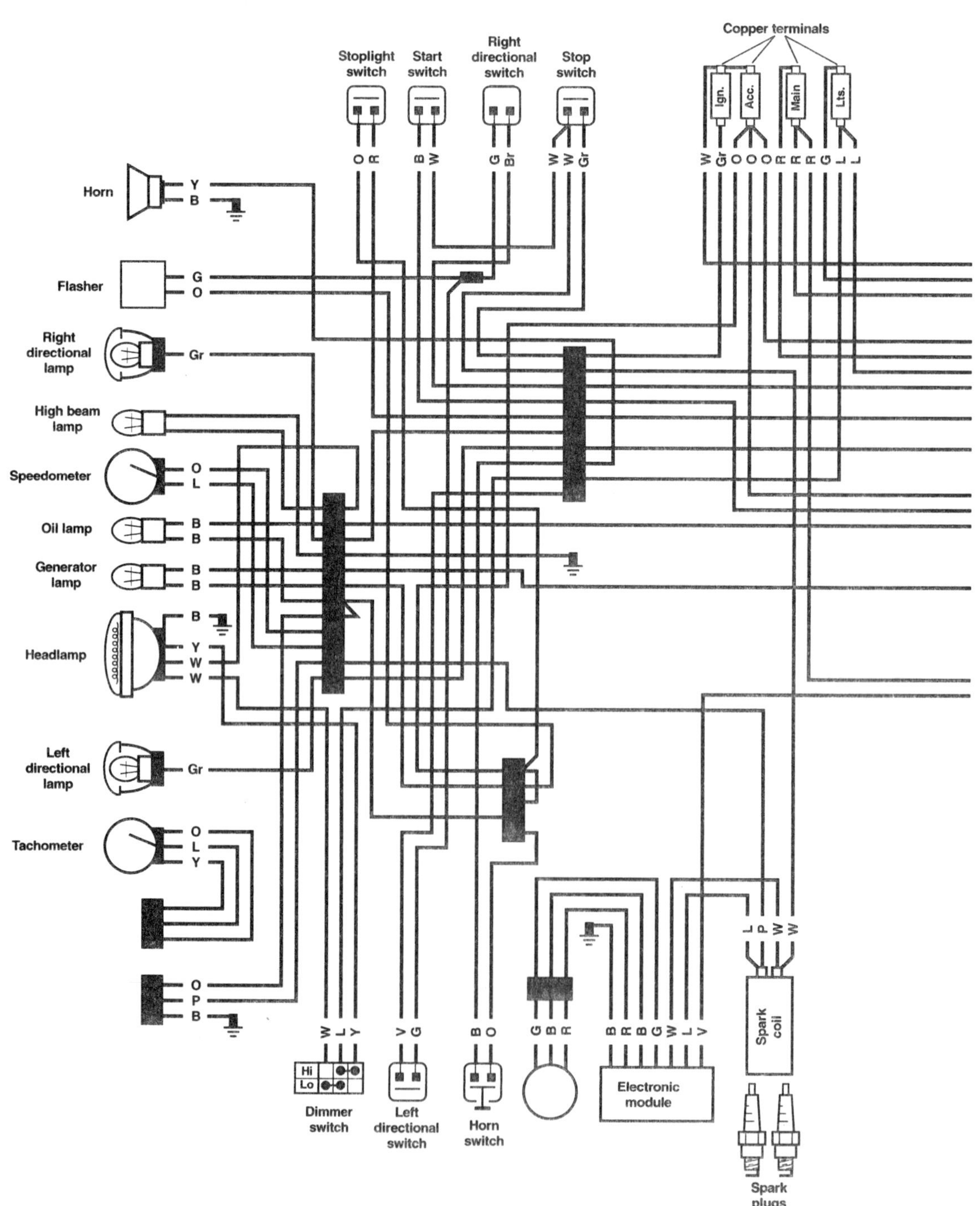

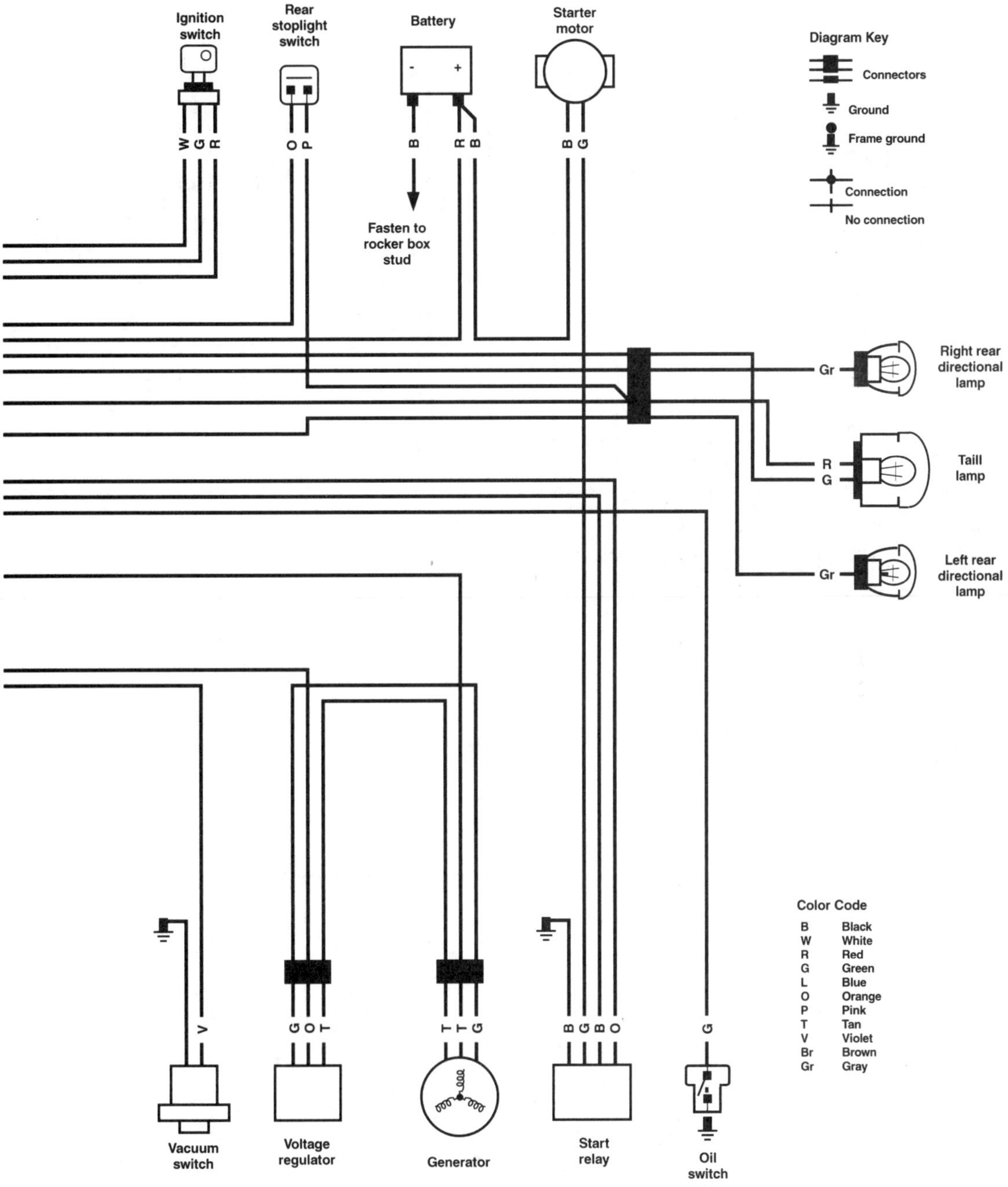

Ignition switch

W G R

Rear stoplight switch

O P

Battery

- +

B R B

Fasten to rocker box stud

Starter motor

B G

Diagram Key

Connectors

Ground

Frame ground

Connection

No connection

Gr

Right rear directional lamp

R

G

Taill lamp

Gr

Left rear directional lamp

12

V

Vacuum switch

G O T

Voltage regulator

T T G

Generator

B G B O

Start relay

G

Oil switch

Color Code

B	Black
W	White
R	Red
G	Green
L	Blue
O	Orange
P	Pink
T	Tan
V	Violet
Br	Brown
Gr	Gray

1983-EARLY 1984 XLX

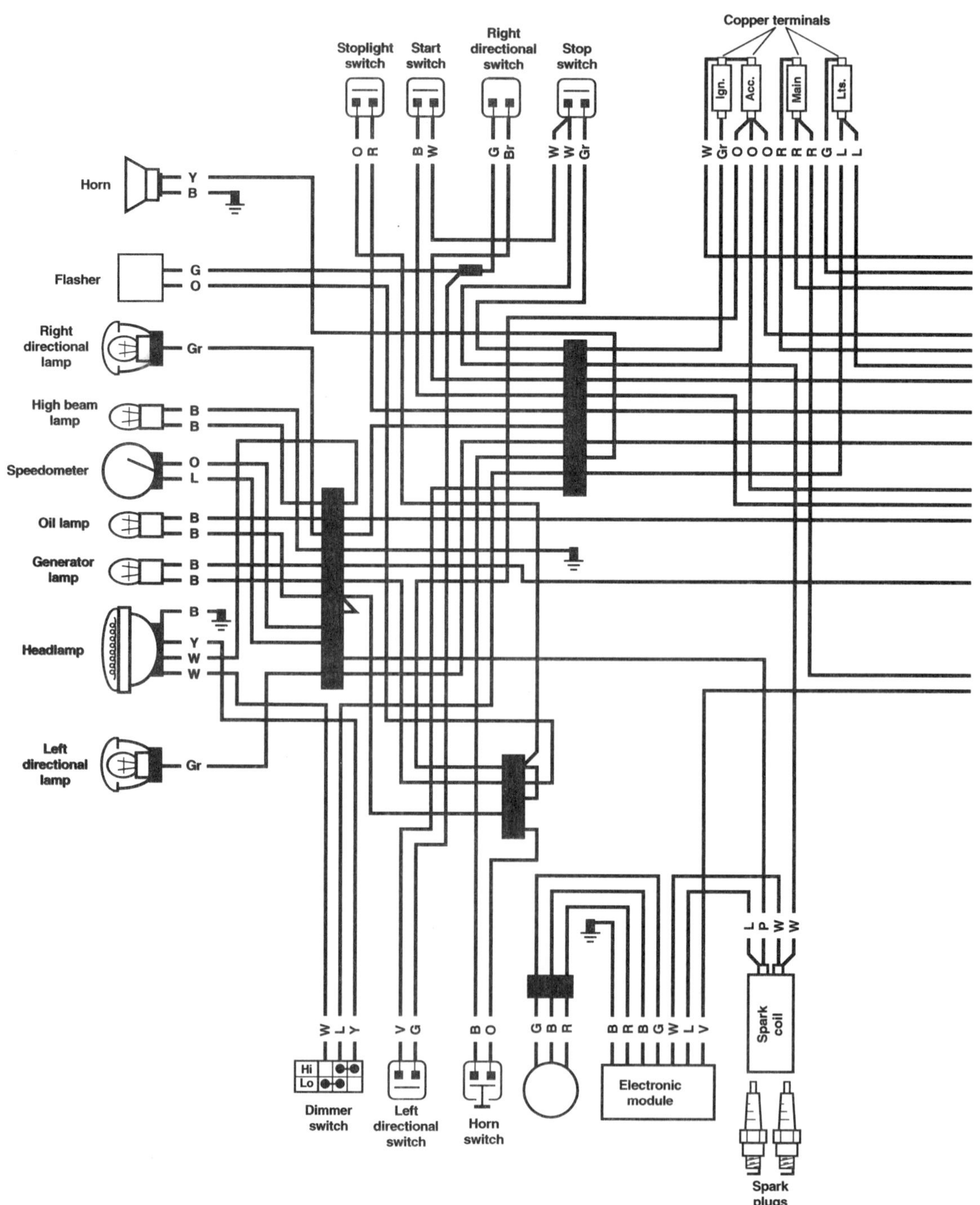

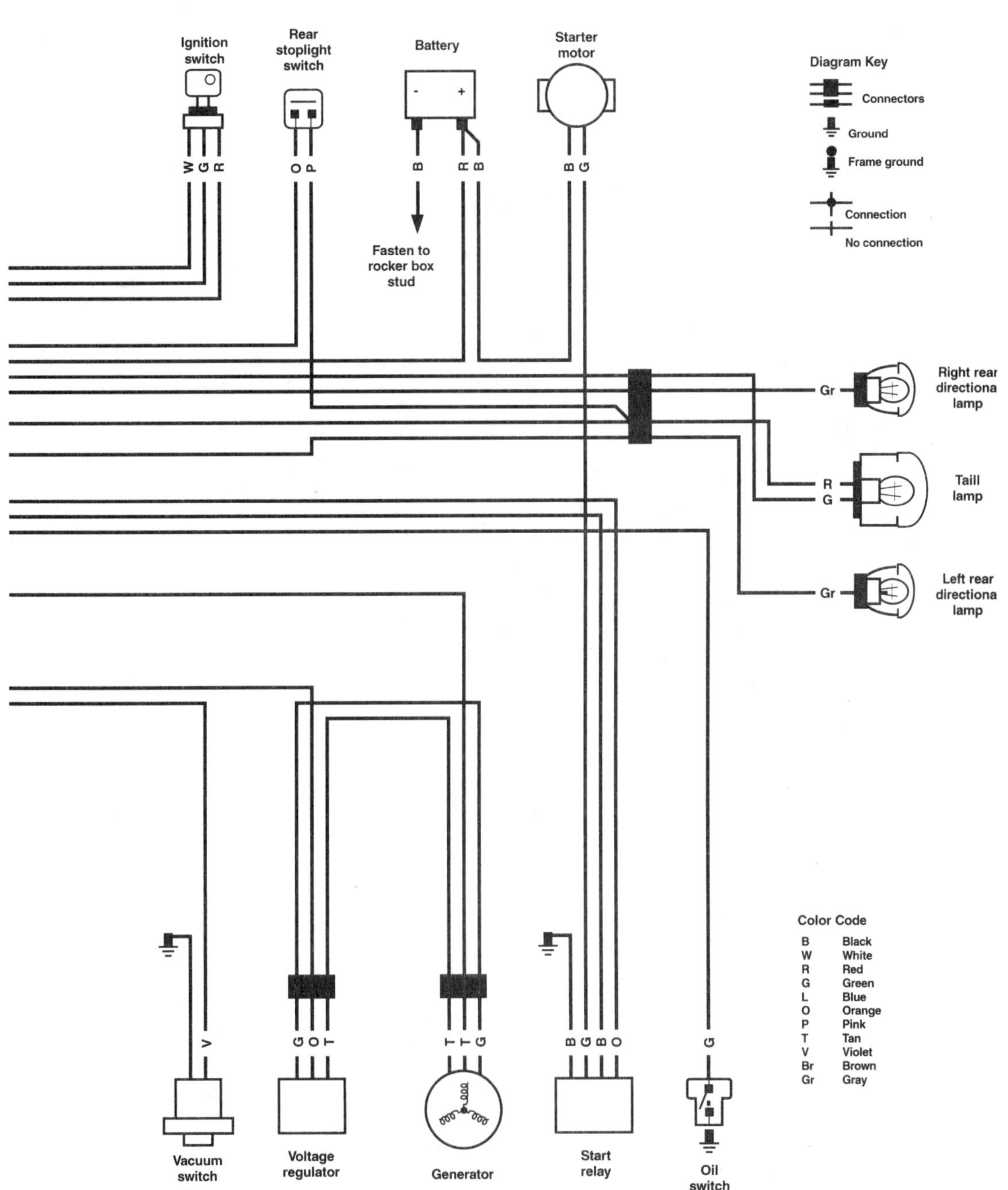
Ignition switch
W G R
Rear stoplight switch
O P
Battery
- +
B
R B
Fasten to rocker box stud
Starter motor
B G
Diagram Key
Connectors
Ground
Frame ground
Connection
No connection
Gr
Right rear directiona lamp
R
G
Taill lamp
Gr
Left rear directiona lamp
V
Vacuum switch
G O T
Voltage regulator
T T G
Generator
B G B O
Start relay
G
Oil switch
Color Code
B Black
W White
R Red
G Green
L Blue
O Orange
P Pink
T Tan
V Violet
Br Brown
Gr Gray

12

LATE 1984-1985 XLH

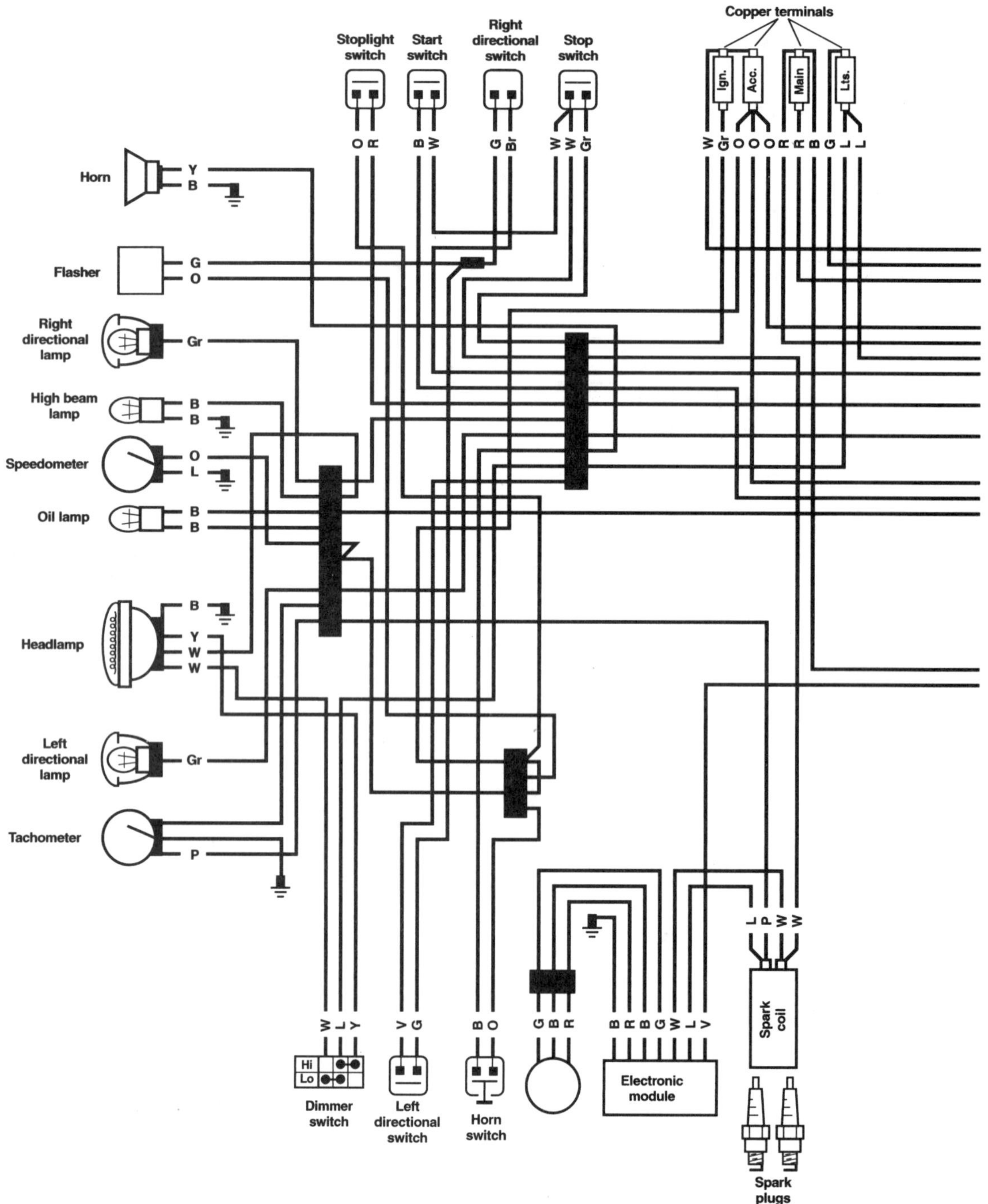

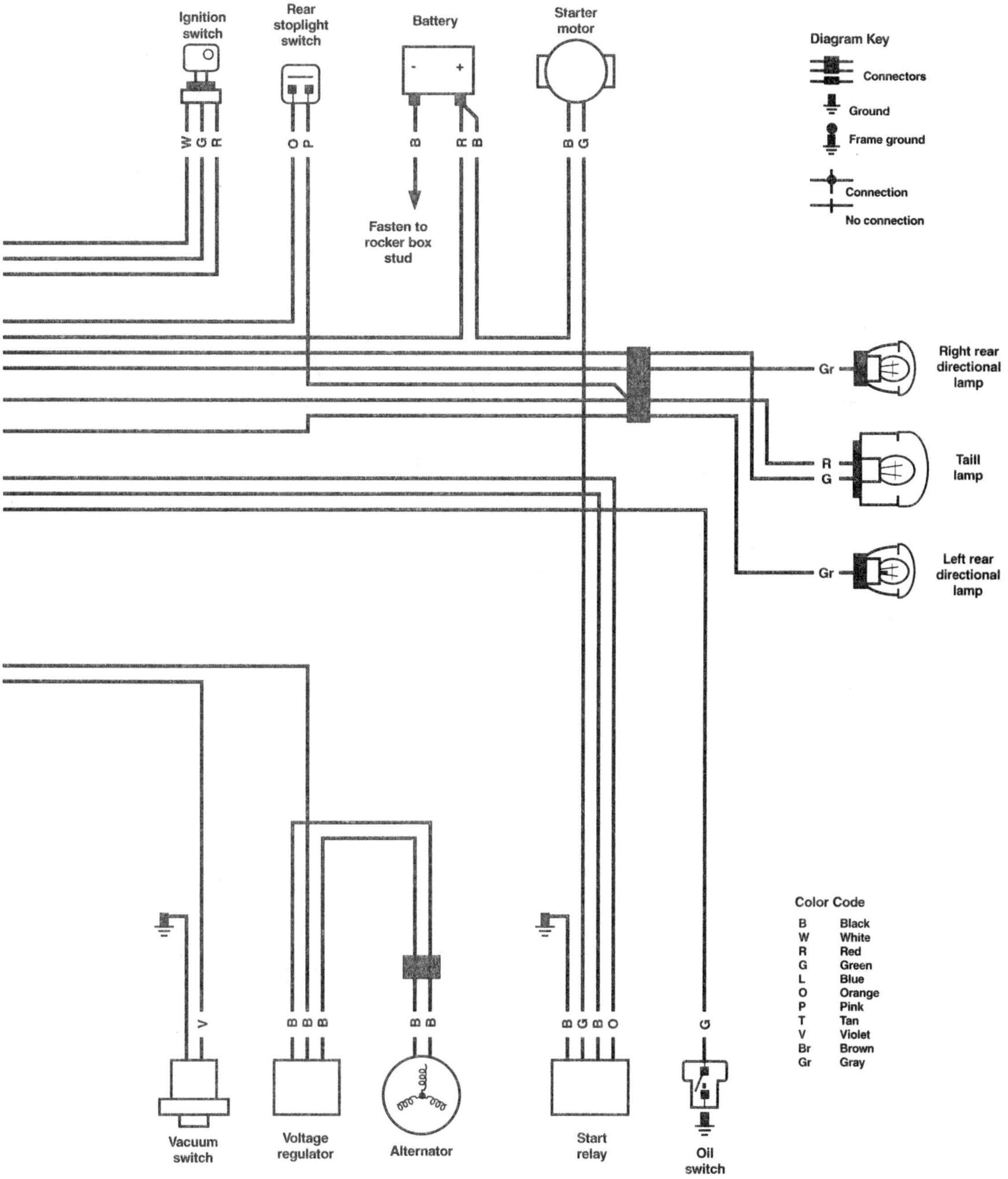

Ignition switch

W G R

Rear stoplight switch

O P

Battery

B R B

Fasten to rocker box stud

Starter motor

B G

Diagram Key

Connectors

Ground

Frame ground

Connection

No connection

Gr Right rear directional lamp

R G Taill lamp

Gr Left rear directional lamp

V Vacuum switch

B B B Voltage regulator

B B Alternator

B G B O Start relay

G Oil switch

Color Code

B	Black
W	White
R	Red
G	Green
L	Blue
O	Orange
P	Pink
T	Tan
V	Violet
Br	Brown
Gr	Gray

LATE 1984-1985 XLS

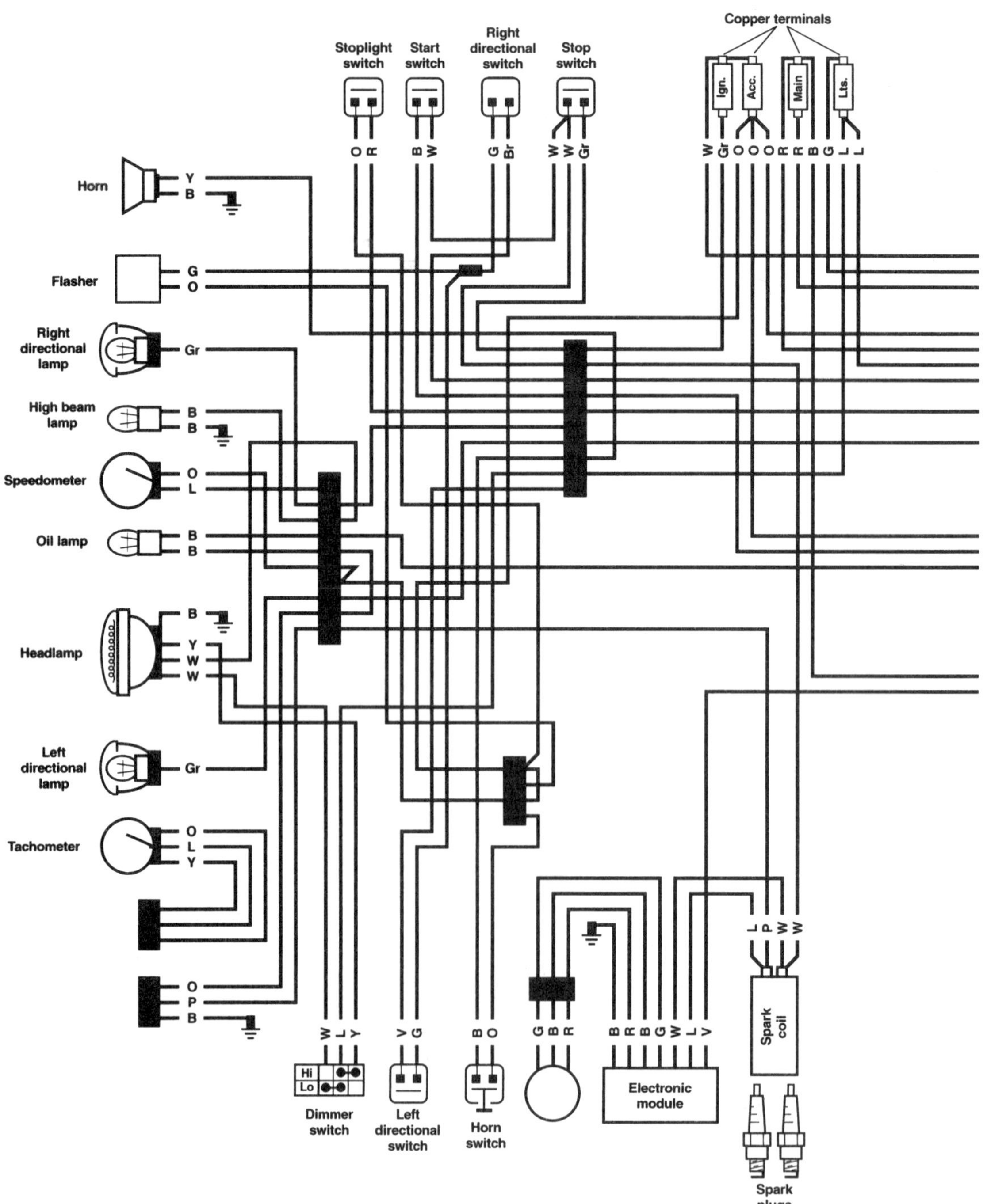

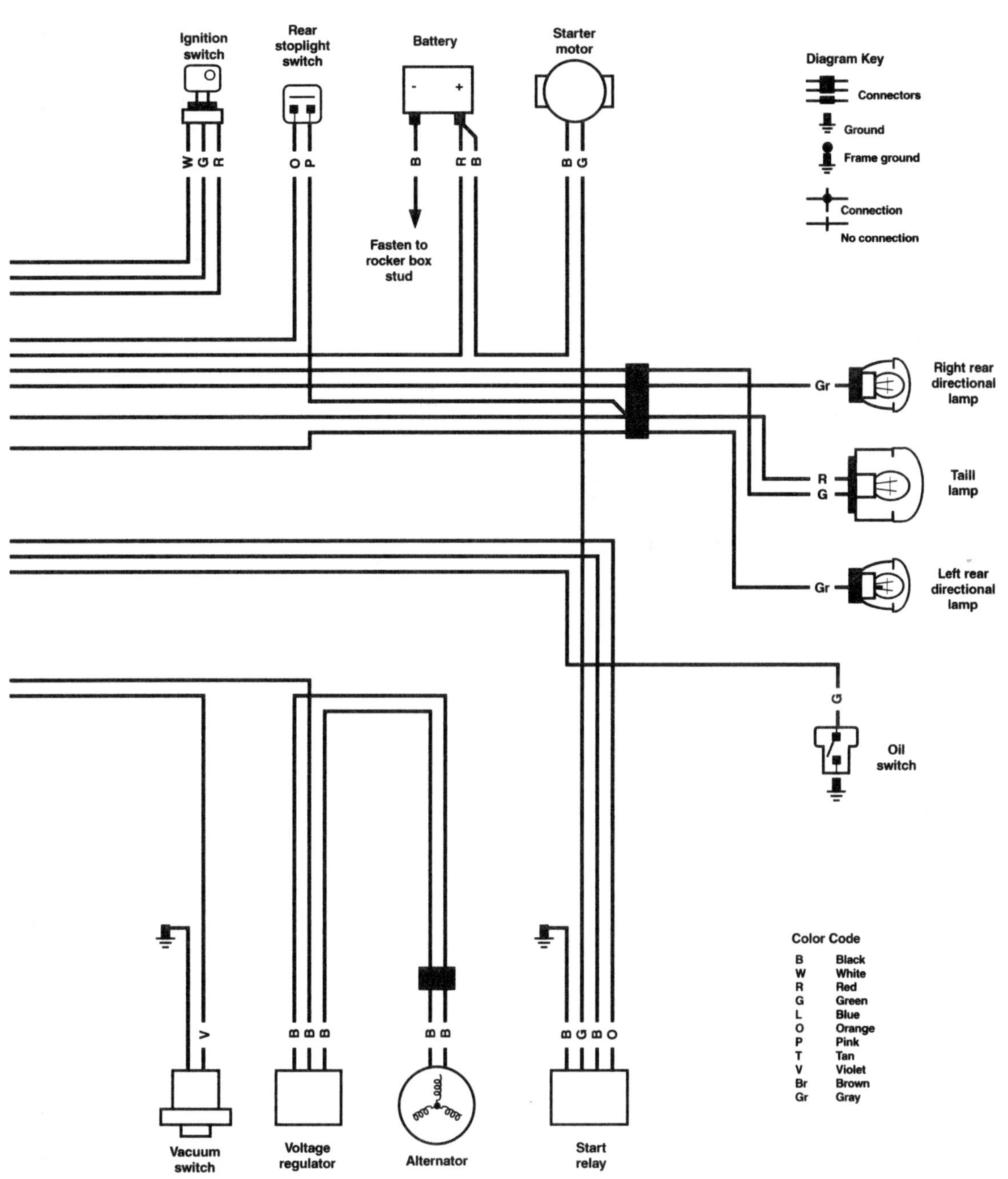
Ignition switch
W G R
Rear stoplight switch
O P
Battery
- +
B
R B
Fasten to rocker box stud
Starter motor
B G
Diagram Key
Connectors
Ground
Frame ground
Connection
No connection
Gr
Right rear directional lamp
R
G
Taill lamp
Gr
Left rear directional lamp
G
Oil switch
V
Vacuum switch
B B B
Voltage regulator
B B
Alternator
B G B O
Start relay
Color Code
B Black
W White
R Red
G Green
L Blue
O Orange
P Pink
T Tan
V Violet
Br Brown
Gr Gray

LATE 1984-1985 XLX

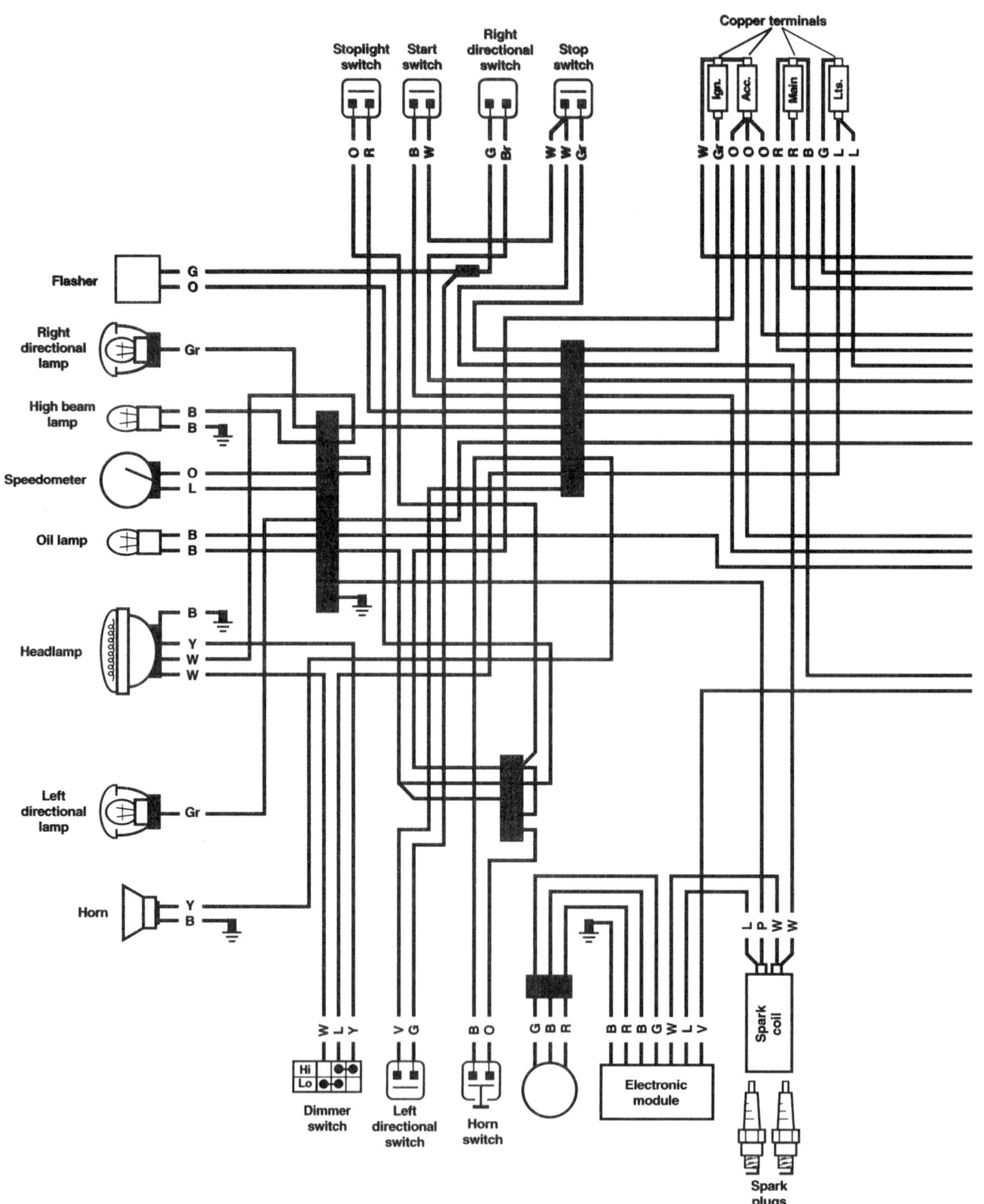

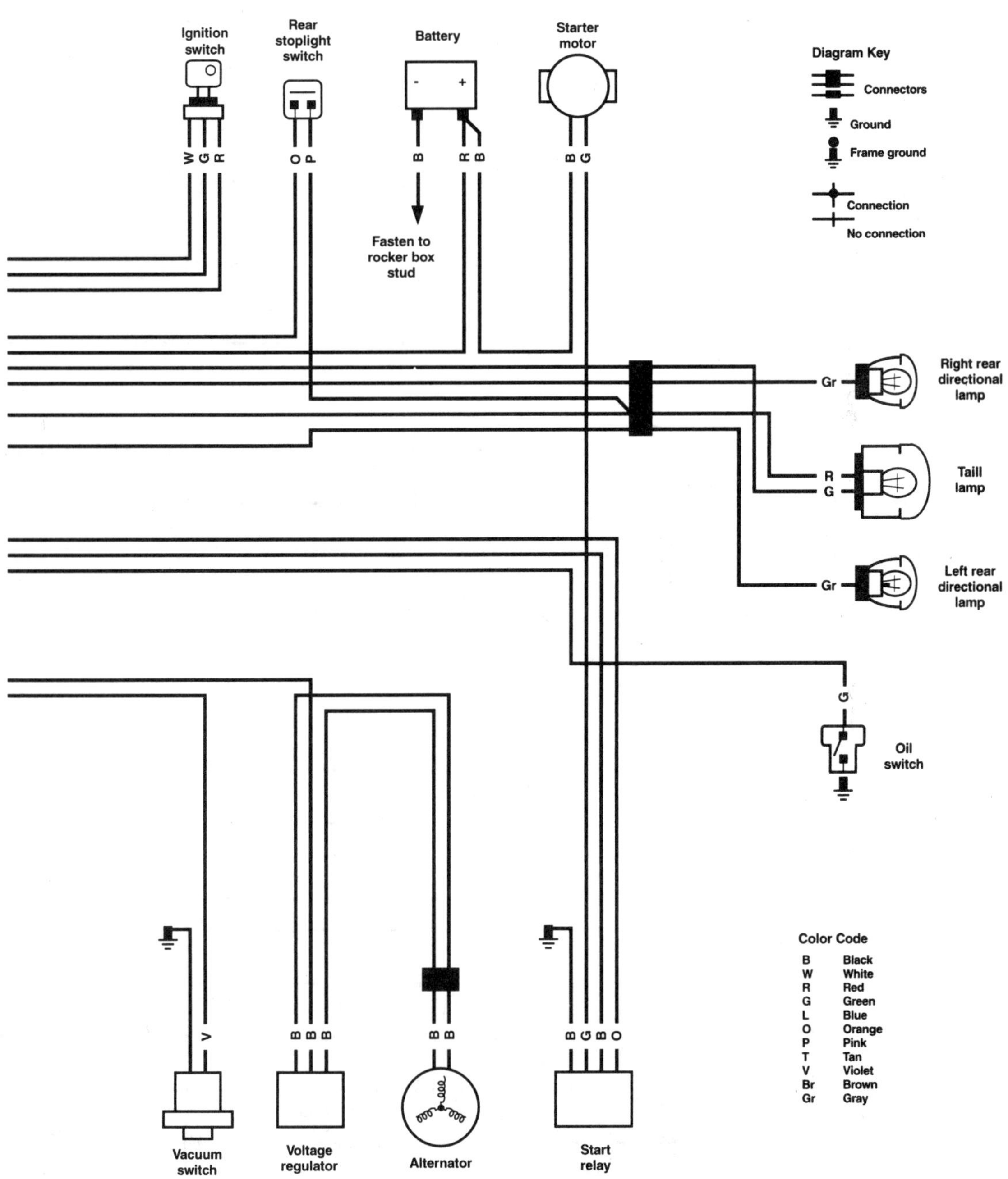
Ignition switch
W G R
Rear stoplight switch
O P
Battery
- +
B
R B
Fasten to rocker box stud
Starter motor
B G
Diagram Key
Connectors
Ground
Frame ground
Connection
No connection
Gr
Right rear directional lamp
R
G
Taill lamp
Gr
Left rear directional lamp
G
Oil switch
V
Vacuum switch
B B B
Voltage regulator
B B
Alternator
B G B O
Start relay
Color Code
B Black
W White
R Red
G Green
L Blue
O Orange
P Pink
T Tan
V Violet
Br Brown
Gr Gray

12

MAINTENANCE LOG

Date	Miles	Type of Service